THE
TOP
100

THE FASTEST-GROWING CAREERS
FOR THE 21ST CENTURY

Fourth Edition

D1384483

THE TOP 100

THE FASTEST-GROWING CAREERS
FOR THE 21ST CENTURY

Fourth Edition

Checkmark Books®
An imprint of Infobase Publishing

The Top 100: The Fastest-Growing Careers for the 21st Century, Fourth Edition

Copyright © 2009 by Infobase Publishing

Checkmark Books
An imprint of Infobase Publishing, Inc.
132 West 31st Street
New York NY 10001

Library of Congress Cataloging-in-Publication Data

The top 100 : the fastest-growing careers for the 21st century. — 4th ed.
    p. cm.
Includes bibliographical references and index.
ISBN-13: 978-0-8160-7729-8 (hc.: alk. paper)
ISBN-10: 0-8160-7729-0 (hc.: alk. paper)
ISBN-13: 978-0-8160-7730-4 (pbk.)
ISBN-10: 0-8160-7730-4 (pbk.)
    1. Occupations—United States—Handbooks, manuals, etc. 2. Vocational guidance—United States—Handbooks, manuals, etc. I. Ferguson Publishing. II. Title: Top one hundred.
  HF5382.T59 2009
  331.7020973—dc22
               2008035415

Text design by Mary Susan Ryan-Flynn
Cover design by Takeshi Takahashi

Printed in the United States of America

VB MSRF 10 9 8 7 6 5 4 3 2 1

This book is printed on acid-free paper.

CONTENTS

INTRODUCTION

The world of work today is a lot different from the one your parents first entered years ago. New technology of all types, especially computer and Internet technology, has become an important part of nearly every industry. Careers have also become more specialized and so has the training and education you will need to get a job and move ahead. Continuing education and training is a fact of life for those wanting to be successful in most occupations these days. In order to stay competitive, you will need to expand and update your skills continuously through after-work reading, on-the-job training, online courses, and formal college and vocational courses.

The Top 100: The Fastest-Growing Careers for the 21st Century, 4th Edition, presents 100 careers that are projected by the U.S. Department of Labor and a variety of other sources as the fastest-growing careers through 2016. Many of these careers, such as Physicians, Elementary School Teachers, and Software Engineers are part of rapidly growing fields such as Health Care Services, Education Services, and Computer Technology. Many other careers—for example, Service Industry careers such as Retail Sales Workers, Cosmetologists, and Food Service Workers—are "fast growing" because of the sheer number of job openings being created.

You'll discover, as you look at the careers profiled in this book, that we discuss far more than 100 careers. Many of the top 100 careers are further broken down into subspecialties. By knowing about these subspecialties, you will also know how to transfer skills or train for positions in entirely different fields.

TRENDS IN THE WORKPLACE

Three trends in the future workplace are important to note: the importance of continuing education, the relationship between years of education and earnings, and the increase in number of technician jobs.

TO STAY AHEAD, PURSUE CONTINUING ED

Advances in technology are moving at a speed few ever thought possible, making training and skills quickly obsolete. Many now realize that they will be left behind and lose the chance for promotion and better jobs if they fail to keep their skills and training as up-to-date as possible. To correct this problem, many workers today supplement their knowledge by attending seminars, completing after-work reading, and participating in on-the-job training. Many workers are returning to college or vocational technical schools to receive advanced training and degrees. According to the Bureau of Labor Statistics (BLS), college graduates enjoy significantly lower unemployment rates (2.2 percent in 2007) than those who have not completed high school (7.1 percent in 2007). This continuing education trend has created another appealing benefit for many workers—better positions and higher pay.

HIT THE BOOKS TO EARN MORE

Job growth is expected for workers from all educational backgrounds, but people with a bachelor's degree or higher typically earn better salaries and enjoy greater chances of promotion and career stability. According to the BLS, those with a bachelor's degree earned average annual salaries of $51,324 in 2007, while those with only a high school diploma earned annual salaries of $31,408. (Note: This statistic can be slightly misleading because there are many fast-growing, well-paying jobs presented in *The Top 100* that do not require completion of an associate degree or higher. Occupations such as Corrections Officers, Cost Estimators, and Electricians require a small amount of postsecondary training or the completion of an apprenticeship.)

TECH-TASTIC!

A technician is defined as a highly specialized worker who works with scientists, physicians, engineers, and a variety of other professionals, as well as with clients and customers. The technician can be further defined as a type of middleperson, between the scientist in the laboratory and the worker on the floor; between the physician and the patient; between the engineer and the factory worker. In short, the technician's realm is

EDUCATION LEVEL AND ANNUAL EARNINGS, 2007	
Doctoral degree:	$77,844
Professional degree:	$74,204
Master's degree:	$60,580
Bachelor's degree:	$51,324
Associate's degree:	$38,480
Some college, no degree:	$35,516
High-school graduate:	$31,408
Less than a high school diploma:	$22,256
Source: U.S. Department of Labor	

U.S. EMPLOYMENT BY MAJOR OCCUPATIONAL GROUP, 2006

Professional and Related:	30 million
Service:	29 million
Office and Administrative Support:	24 million
Sales and Related:	16 million
Management, Business, and Financial:	15 million
Production:	11 million
Transportation and Material Moving:	10 million
Construction and Extraction:	8 million
Installation, Maintenance, and Repair:	6 million
Farming, Fishing, and Forestry:	1 million

Source: U.S. Department of Labor

where the scientific meets the practical application, where theory meets product.

The number and types of technician careers are growing as we increasingly rely on technology to solve problems and help us perform our daily work; in addition, this technology continues to change almost as fast as it is introduced. Skilled technicians design, implement, operate, and repair these highly complex systems and machinery. As you page through *The Top 100: The Fastest-Growing Careers for the 21st Century*, you will see the increasing significance of tech jobs in a variety of fields, but especially in health services. Biomedical Equipment Technicians, Cardiovascular Technologists, Forensic Science Technicians, Medical Laboratory Technicians, and Surveying and Mapping Technicians are but a few of the tech jobs featured in this book.

THE HOTTEST GROWTH FIELDS

Five of the fastest-growing career fields are Health services, community and social services, computers and information services, education, and the service industry.

HEALTH SERVICES

The health services industry is the largest industry in our economy, with approximately 14 million jobs in 2006. More than 30 percent of the jobs in *The Top 100: The Fastest-Growing Careers for the 21st Century* relate to health care services. The BLS reports that health services will grow by 22 percent—or three million jobs—by 2016. Many factors are responsible for this rapid growth. One reason is that the American population is aging; the U.S. Census Bureau predicts that the number of Americans age 65 and older will double in the first half of the 21st century, increasing from approximately 35 million in 2000 to approximately 82 million in 2050. As the median age of the American population rises, more people will need various types of specialized medical care. Another reason for job growth is that increasingly, a variety of high tech equipment will be used to diagnose and treat patients. This new technology will improve the survival rates of seriously ill and injured patients and will require trained specialists of all kinds to operate and repair it. The home health care segment of this field will be exceptionally strong as the population ages—growing by 55 percent through 2016. Another factor that has caused the field to expand is the increasing focus on wellness. Health maintenance organizations (HMOs) are increasingly focusing on preventative care and will need trained professionals to monitor patients and administer tests and preventative treatments.

When considering a career in the health services, you should note that a number of factors may affect employment growth. Continued industry-wide budget cutting, realignment, downsizing, and mergers may affect growth. In terms of the expanding home care sub-field, many predict that Medicare programs will be reduced, forcing Medicare patients to pay for some home care costs themselves. This cutback may reduce demand slightly for professionals in this segment of the industry. HMOs will continue to compete with hospitals, as well as preferred provider organizations, for profits. Most experts predict lucrative opportunities for those employed by HMOs, nursing homes, personal care facilities, and home health agencies. The outlook for hospitals is less positive, but will still offer many employment opportunities. While the overall outlook for health care is good, you will need to study the market carefully to find the best health care concentrations and careers.

COMMUNITY AND SOCIAL SERVICES

A growing and aging population will create strong demand for community and social services professionals. Overall employment in nongovernmental jobs is expected to grow by 59 percent through 2016, according to the U.S. Department of Labor. Strong industry subsectors include individual and family services (expected growth of 73 percent by 2016), vocational rehabilitation services (+22 percent), and community emergency and other relief services (+19 percent). Some of the community and social services careers in this book include Alcohol and Drug Abuse Counselors, Human Services Workers, Rehabilitation Counselors, and Social Workers.

COMPUTERS AND INFORMATION SERVICES

Computers and related technology play an integral role in our society. They are used in almost every field, from the computers Architects use to design buildings, sports stadiums, and skate parks; to those used by Paralegals to research legal information on the Internet; to those used by Medical Record Technicians to keep track of your health records. A grasp of the most basic computer—and Internet—skills is a necessity in almost every field.

Employment for computer and mathematical science professionals will grow by 25 percent through 2016, according to the BLS—or twice as fast as the average for all occupations. Businesses need computer professionals of all types to train their staffs in the latest innovations in technology, to address problems, and to repair and upgrade existing equipment. Furthermore, the cost of computers and related hardware and software has decreased, creating many business opportunities within the home. There is an increased demand for people with data processing, word processing, and desktop publishing skills, as well as people who create the actual systems and software that individuals and businesses use.

Finally, the rapid growth of the Internet—more than 215 million people were online in the United States as of November 2007—has created a wide variety of opportunities—and new jobs—for people with flexible and up-to-date training, such as Computer Support Specialists, Software Designers, and Software Engineers.

It is important to note that employment in the computer industry changes almost as continuously as the evolving technology it is based on. Layoffs, mergers, and downsizing occur all of the time, just like in any other fast-growing industry. The key, as always in the new world of work, is education. Workers who continue to upgrade and expand their skills will prosper in any marketplace. There is also an increasing trend toward hiring those with advanced four-year degrees in computer technology.

EDUCATIONAL SERVICES

The educational services industry is the second largest industry in our economy, with approximately 13.2 million jobs in 2006. Employment in the professional specialty segment of this industry is projected to grow 12.7 percent by 2016. This growth will occur as a result of a marked increase in the school-age population, as well as an increase in the number of people going back to school, namely those looking to change careers and retirees looking to expand their educational horizons. This increased enrollment is expected to create a shortage of more than 1.4 million educational and support professionals by 2016. Other factors that will influence this shortage include the reduction of average class size, teachers leaving the profession for other careers, and the large number of teachers who will reach retirement age in the next decade. Recent reforms to the national educational system—in response to declining test scores and increased global competitiveness—have increased demand for administrative personnel and teachers of all kinds, especially College Professors, Elementary School Teachers, and Preschool Teachers. Factors that may limit growth in this field include budget cuts and school restructuring.

SERVICE INDUSTRY

Service-producing industries are expected to generate about 16 million new jobs from 2006 to 2016, according to the U.S. Department of Labor. The growing U.S. population and the difficulty of automating many job responsibilities in this industry will create strong demand for workers in the service industry. Many ser-

---

EMPLOYMENT GROWTH BY EDUCATION AND TRAINING
(Projected 2006–2016)

First professional degree	14.0%
Doctoral degree	21.6%
Master's degree	18.9%
Work experience plus bachelor's or higher degree	9.1%
Bachelor's degree	16.5%
Associate's degree	18.7%
Postsecondary vocational training	13.6%
Work experience in a related occupation	9.0%
Long-term on-the-job training	6.2%
Moderate-term on-the-job training	7.4%
Short-term on-the-job training	8.8%

Source: U.S. Department of Labor

vice occupations are resistant to offshoring, a work-place trend in which companies move jobs overseas to countries that pay their workers lower wages than are paid to workers in the United States. Some of the service-oriented careers covered in this book include Cosmetologists, Customer Service Representatives, Food Service Workers, Home Health Care Aides, Nail Technicians, and Retail Sales Workers.

HOW TO USE THIS BOOK

The following paragraphs describe the major headings used throughout *The Top 100: The Fastest-Growing Careers for the 21st Century.*

With each article is a sidebar featuring information on recommended School Subjects, Personal Skills, the Minimum Education Level necessary to work in the field, Certification or Licensing requirements, and Work Conditions.

The **Overview** section of a chapter is a brief intro-ductory description of the duties and responsibilities of someone in this career. Oftentimes, a career may have a variety of job titles. When that is the case, alternate career titles are presented in this section. If available, this section also lists the number of workers currently employed in this field.

The **Job** section describes an average day for a worker in this field, including primary and secondary duties; the types of tools, machinery, or equipment used to perform this job; and other types of work-ers interacted with on a daily basis. Growing subfields or subspecialties of this career are also discussed in detail.

The **Requirements** section describes the formal educational requirements—from high school diploma to advanced college degree—that are necessary to become employed in the field. This section provides information on how students can receive training if a college degree is not required, via on-the-job training, apprenticeships, the armed forces, or other activities. Explained here are certification, licensing, and con-tinuing-education requirements. Finally, the Require-ments section recommends personal qualities that will be helpful to someone working in this field.

In the **Exploring** section, you will find a variety of suggestions for exploring the field—such as periodicals to read, Web sites to visit, summer jobs and programs to check out, volunteer opportunities, associations and clubs to join, and hobbies to explore—before you invest time and money in education and training.

The **Employers** section lists major employers of workers in the field.

The **Starting Out** section offers tips on how to land your first job, be it through newspaper ads, the Inter-net, college career services offices, or personal con-tacts, This section explains how the average person finds employment in this field.

The **Advancement** section describes the possible career path and the tools or experience you might need—advanced training or outside education—to move up in the career.

The **Earnings** section lists salary ranges for begin-ning, mid-range, and experienced workers in this field. Average starting salaries by educational achievement are also listed, when available. Fringe benefits, such as paid vacation and sick days, health insurance, pen-sions, and profit sharing plans, are covered.

In the **Work Environment** section, you will see what a typical day on the job is like. Is indoor or out-door work required? Are safety measures and equip-ment such as protective clothing necessary? Is the job in a quiet office or on a noisy assembly line? What are the standard hours of work? Are overtime and weekend work often required? Is travel frequent? If so, to where, and for how long? This is a good place to gauge your true interest in the field.

The **Outlook** section predicts the potential long-term employment outlook for the field: which areas are growing because of technology and which are in decline. Most of this information is obtained from the Bureau of Labor Statistics. Job growth terms fol-low those used in the *Occupational Outlook Hand-book*: growth much faster than the average means an increase of 21 percent or more; growth faster than the average means an increase of 14 to 20 percent; growth about as fast as the average means an increase of 7 to 13 percent.

In the last section, **For More Information**, you'll find the names, street addresses, phone numbers, email, and Web addresses of a variety of associations, government agencies, or unions that can provide fur-ther information regarding educational requirements, accreditation and certification, and other general career information.

IN CONCLUSION

We hope this book will expand your knowledge and help you to make informed career choices. But this is only the beginning of your career discovery. If you find a career that catches your interest, find out more. Contact the associations listed at the end of each article. Ask your friends and family if they know someone in this field you can talk to: an expert, a teacher, or someone who is, at least, very experienced in the field. Or, ask your school counselor to arrange a presentation or interview with a worker in this field. Maybe you can take a tour of a job site to see people actually doing the work you're interested in. You'll be surprised at the response you receive. People like to talk about their work, and by listening to someone describe his or her career, likes and dislikes, and career hopes and dreams, you'll find out more about yourself and your future. Only then will you be able to decide if the career is really for you.

No one can be interested in every one of these careers. Browse through these titles, however, and we guarantee that you'll find at least a few careers that match your talents and interests. You may even discover a career that you never knew existed. It's important to note that what is hot today may be only lukewarm tomorrow. That is why your career education must never stop. To survive in this challenging new world of work you will constantly need to analyze the changing marketplace and continue to expand and improve upon your training and skills. That is the only way to guarantee that you will find and keep a good job.

The Editors

☐ ACCOUNTANTS AND AUDITORS

OVERVIEW

Accountants compile, analyze, verify, and prepare financial records, including profit and loss statements, balance sheets, cost studies, and tax reports. Accountants may specialize in areas such as auditing, tax work, cost accounting, budgeting and control, or systems and procedures. Accountants also may specialize in a particular business or field; for example, *agricultural accountants* specialize in drawing up and analyzing financial statements for farmers and for farm equipment companies. *Auditors* examine and verify financial records to ensure that they are accurate, complete, and in compliance with federal laws. There are approximately 1.3 million accountants and auditors employed in the United States.

THE JOB

Accountants' duties depend on the size and nature of the company in which they are employed. The major fields of employment are public, private, and government accounting.

Public accountants work independently on a fee basis or as members of an accounting firm, and they perform a variety of tasks for businesses or individuals. These may include auditing accounts and records, preparing and certifying financial statements, conducting financial investigations and furnishing testimony in legal matters, and assisting in formulating budget policies and procedures.

Private accountants, sometimes called *industrial* or *management accountants,* handle financial records of the firms at which they are employed.

Government accountants work on the financial records of government agencies or, when necessary, they audit the records of private companies. In the federal government, many accountants are employed as *bank examiners, Internal Revenue Service agents and investigators,* as well as in regular accounting positions.

Within these fields, accountants can specialize in a variety of areas.

General accountants supervise, install, and devise general accounting, budget, and cost systems. They maintain records, balance books, and prepare and analyze statements on all financial aspects of business. Administrative officers use this information to make sound business decisions.

SCHOOL SUBJECTS
Business, Economics

PERSONAL SKILLS
Following Instructions, Leadership/Management

MINIMUM EDUCATION LEVEL
Bachelor's Degree

CERTIFICATION OR LICENSING
Recommended

WORK ENVIRONMENT
Primarily Indoors, One Location with Some Travel

Budget accountants review expenditures of departments within a firm to make sure expenses allotted are not exceeded. They also aid in drafting budgets and may devise and install budget control systems.

Cost accountants determine unit costs of products or services by analyzing records and depreciation data. They classify and record all operating costs so that management can control expenditures.

Property accountants keep records of equipment, buildings, and other property owned or leased by a company. They prepare mortgage schedules and payments as well as appreciation or depreciation statements, which are used for income tax purposes.

Environmental accountants help utilities, manufacturers, and chemical companies set up preventive systems to ensure environmental compliance and provide assistance in the event that legal issues arise.

Systems accountants design and set up special accounting systems for organizations whose needs cannot be handled by standardized procedures. This may involve installing automated or computerized accounting processes and includes instructing personnel in the new methods.

Forensic accountants and auditors use accounting principles and theories to support or oppose claims being made in litigation.

Tax accountants prepare federal, state, or local tax returns of an individual, business, or corporation according to prescribed rates, laws, and regulations. They also may conduct research on the effects of taxes on firm operations and recommend changes to reduce taxes. This is one of the most intricate fields of accounting, and many accountants therefore specialize in one particular phase such as corporate, individual income, or property tax.

Assurance accountants help improve the quality of information for clients in assurance services areas such as electronic commerce, risk assessment, and elder care. This information may be financial or non-financial in nature.

Auditors ensure that financial records are accurate, complete, and in compliance with federal laws. To do so they review items in original entry books, including purchase orders, tax returns, billing statements, and other important documents. Auditors may also prepare financial statements for clients and suggest ways to improve productivity and profits. *Internal auditors* conduct the same kind of examination and evaluation for one particular company. Because they are salaried employees of that company, their financial audits then must be certified by a qualified independent auditor. Internal auditors also review procedures and controls, appraise the efficiency and effectiveness of operations, and make sure their companies comply with corporate policies and government regulations.

Tax auditors review financial records and other information provided by taxpayers to determine the appropriate tax liability. State and federal tax auditors usually work in government offices, but they may perform a field audit in a taxpayer's home or office.

Revenue agents are employed by the federal government to examine selected income tax returns and, when necessary, conduct field audits and investigations to verify the information reported and adjust the tax liability accordingly.

Chief bank examiners enforce good banking practices throughout a state. They schedule bank examinations to ensure that financial institutions comply with state laws and, in certain cases, they take steps to protect a bank's solvency and the interests of its depositors and shareholders.

REQUIREMENTS
High School

If you are interested in an accounting career, you must be very proficient in arithmetic and basic algebra. Familiarity with computers and their applications is equally important. Course work in English and communications will also be beneficial.

Postsecondary Training

Postsecondary training in accounting may be obtained in a wide variety of institutions such as private business schools, junior colleges, universities, and correspondence schools. A bachelor's degree with a major in accounting, or a related field such as economics, is highly recommended by professional associations for those entering the field and is required by all states before taking the licensing exam. It is possible, however, to become a successful accountant by completing a program at any of the above-mentioned institutions. A four-year college curriculum usually includes about two years of liberal arts courses, a year of general business subjects, and a year of specific accounting work. Better positions, particularly in public accounting, require a bachelor's degree with a major in accounting. Large public accounting firms often prefer people with a master's degree in accounting. For beginning positions in accounting, the federal government requires four years of college (including 24 semester hours in accounting or auditing) or an equivalent combination of education and experience.

Certification or Licensing

Certified public accountants (CPAs) must pass a qualifying examination and hold a certificate issued by the state in which they wish to practice. In most states, a college degree is required for admission to the CPA examinations; a few states allow candidates to substitute years of public accounting experience for the college degree requirement. Currently 42 states and the District of Columbia require CPA candidates to have 150 hours of education, which is an additional 30 hours beyond the standard bachelor's degree. Five additional states plan to enact the 150-hour requirement in the future. These criteria can be met by combining an undergraduate accounting program with graduate study or participating in an integrated five-year professional accounting program. You can obtain information from a state board of accountancy or check out the Web site of the American Institute of Certified Public Accountants (AICPA) to read about new regulations and review last year's exam.

The Uniform CPA Examination administered by the AICPA is used by all states. Nearly all states require at least two years of public accounting experience or its equivalent before a CPA certificate can be earned.

The AICPA offers additional credentialing programs (involving a test and additional requirements) for members with valid CPA certificates. These designations include accredited in business valuation, certified information technology professional, and personal financial specialist. These credentials indicate that a CPA has developed skills in non-traditional areas in which accountants are starting to play larger roles.

Some accountants seek out other credentials. Those who have earned a bachelor's degree, pass a four-part examination, agree to meet continuing education requirements, and have at least two years of experience in management accounting may become a certified management accountant through the Institute of Management Accounting.

The Accreditation Council for Accountancy and Taxation confers the following three designations: accredited business accountant or accredited business advisor, accredited tax preparer, and accredited tax advisor.

To become a certified internal auditor, college graduates with two years of experience in internal auditing must pass a four-part examination given by the Institute of Internal Auditors (IIA). The IIA also offers the following specialty certifications: certified financial services auditor and certified government auditing professional. Visit the IIA's Web site for more information.

The designation certified information systems auditor is conferred by the Information Systems Audit and Control Association to candidates who pass an examination and who have five years of experience auditing electronic data processing systems.

Other organizations, such as the Bank Administration Institute, confer specialized auditing designations.

Other Requirements

To be a successful accountant you will need strong mathematical, analytical, and problem-solving skills. You need to be able to think logically and to interpret facts and figures accurately. Effective oral and written communication are also essential in working with both clients and management.

Other important skills are attentiveness to detail, patience, and industriousness. Business acumen and the ability to generate clientele are crucial to service-oriented businesses, as are honesty, dedication, and a respect for the work of others.

EXPLORING

If you think a career as an accountant or auditor might be for you, try working in a retail business, either part time or during the summer. Working at the cash register or even pricing products as a stockperson is good introductory experience. You should also consider working as a treasurer for a student organization requiring financial planning and money management. It may be possible to gain some experience by volunteering with local groups such as churches and small businesses. You should also stay abreast of news in the field by reading trade magazines and checking out the industry Web

sites of the AICPA and other accounting associations. The AICPA has numerous free educational publications available.

EMPLOYERS

More than 1.3 million people are employed as accountants and auditors. Accountants and auditors work throughout private industry and government. About 21 percent work for accounting, tax preparation, bookkeeping, and payroll services firms. Approximately 10 percent are self-employed. A large percentage of all accountants and auditors are certified.

STARTING OUT

Junior public accountants usually start in jobs with routine duties such as counting cash, verifying calculations, and other detailed numerical work. In private accounting, beginners are likely to start as cost accountants and junior internal auditors. They may also enter in clerical positions as cost clerks, ledger clerks, and timekeepers or as trainees in technical or junior executive positions. In the federal government, most beginners are hired as trainees at the GS-5 level after passing the civil service exam.

Some state CPA societies arrange internships for accounting majors, and some offer scholarships and loan programs.

You might also visit the Landing a Job section (http://www.aicpa.org/YoungCPANetwork/Planning_Developing.htm) of the AICPA's Web site. It has detailed information on accounting careers, hiring trends, job search strategies, resumes and cover letters, and job interviews. The section also has a list of internship opportunities for students.

ADVANCEMENT

Talented accountants and auditors can advance quickly. Junior public accountants usually advance to senior positions within several years and to managerial positions soon after. Those successful in dealing with top-level management may eventually become supervisors, managers, and partners in larger firms or go into independent practice. However, only 2 to 3 percent of new hires advance to audit manager, tax manager, or partner.

Private accountants in firms may become audit managers, tax managers, cost accounting managers, or controllers, depending on their specialty. Some become controllers, treasurers, or corporation presidents. Others on the finance side may rise to become managers of financial planning and analysis or treasurers.

Federal government trainees are usually promoted within a year or two. Advancement to controller and to higher administrative positions is ultimately possible.

Although advancement may be rapid for skilled accountants, especially in public accounting, those with inadequate academic or professional training are often assigned to routine jobs and find it difficult to obtain promotions. All accountants find it necessary to continue their study of accounting and related areas in their spare time. Even those who have already obtained college degrees, gained experience, and earned a CPA certificate may spend many hours studying to keep up with new industry developments. Thousands of practicing accountants enroll in formal courses offered by universities and professional associations to specialize in certain areas of accounting, broaden or update their professional skills, and become eligible for advancement and promotion.

EARNINGS

Beginning salaries for accountants with a bachelor's degree averaged $46,718 a year in 2006; those with a master's degree averaged $49,277 a year, according to the National Association of Colleges and Employers. General accountants and internal auditors with up to one year of experience earned between $31,500 and $48,250, according to a 2007 survey by Robert Half International. Some experienced auditors may earn between $60,000 and $208,000, depending on such factors as their education level, the size of the firm, and the firm's location.

According to the U.S. Department of Labor, accountants and auditors had median annual earnings of $54,630 in 2006. The lowest paid 10 percent earned less than $34,470, and the highest paid 10 percent earned more than $94,050. In the federal government, the average starting salary for junior accountants and auditors was $28,862 in 2007. Some entry-level positions paid slightly more if the candidate had an advanced degree or superior academic performance. Accountants working for the federal government in supervisory and management positions had average salaries of $78,665 a year in 2007; auditors averaged $83,322. Although government accountants and auditors make less than those in other areas, they do receive more benefits.

WORK ENVIRONMENT

Accounting is known as a desk job, and a 40-hour (or longer) workweek can be expected in public and private accounting. Although computer work is replacing paperwork, the job can be routine and monotonous, and

concentration and attention to detail are critical. Public accountants experience considerable pressure during the tax period, which runs from November to April, and they may have to work long hours. There is potential for stress aside from tax season, as accountants can be responsible for managing multimillion-dollar finances with no margin for error. Self-employed accountants and those working for a small firm can expect to work longer hours; 40 percent work more than 50 hours per week, compared to 20 percent of public and private accountants.

In smaller firms, most of the public accountant's work is performed in the client's office. A considerable amount of travel is often necessary to service a wide variety of businesses. In a larger firm, however, an accountant may have very little client contact, spending more time interacting with the accounting team.

OUTLOOK

Employment of accountants and auditors is expected to grow faster than the average for all occupations through 2016, according to the U.S. Department of Labor. This is due to business growth, changing tax and finance laws, and increased scrutiny of financial practices across all businesses. There have been several notable scandals in the accounting industry in recent years, and this accounts for much of the increased scrutiny and changing legislation in this industry.

As firms specialize their services, accountants will need to follow suit. Firms will seek out accountants with experience in marketing and proficiency in computer systems to build management consulting practices. As trade increases, so will the demand for CPAs with international specialties and foreign language skills. CPAs with an engineering degree would be well equipped to specialize in environmental accounting. Other accounting specialties that will enjoy good prospects include assurance and forensic accounting.

The number of CPAs dropped off a bit after most states embraced the 150-hour standard for CPA education. However, numbers are once again starting to rise as students realize the many opportunities this industry holds, especially in the wake of recent accounting scandals. CPAs with valid licenses should experience favorable job prospects for the foreseeable future. Pursuing advanced degrees and certifications will also greatly increase one's chances of finding employment.

Accounting jobs are more secure than most during economic downswings. Despite fluctuations in the nation's economy, there will always be a need to manage financial information, especially as the number, size, and complexity of business transactions increases. However, competition for jobs will remain, certification requirements will become more rigorous, and accountants and auditors with the highest degrees will be the most competitive.

FOR MORE INFORMATION

For information on accreditation and testing, contact

Accreditation Council for Accountancy and Taxation
1010 North Fairfax Street
Alexandria, VA 22314-1574
Tel: 888-289-7763
Email: info@acatcredentials.org
http://www.acatcredentials.org

For information on the Uniform CPA Examination and student membership, contact

American Institute of Certified Public Accountants
1211 Avenue of the Americas
New York, NY 10036-8775
Tel: 212-596-6200
http://www.aicpa.org

For information on accredited programs in accounting, contact

Association to Advance Collegiate Schools of Business
777 South Harbour Island Boulevard, Suite 750
Tampa, FL 33602-5730
Tel: 813-769-6500
http://www.aacsb.edu

For information on certification for bank auditors, contact

Bank Administration Institute
One North Franklin, Suite 1000
Chicago, IL 60606-3421
Email: info@bai.org
http://www.bai.org

For more information on women in accounting, contact

Educational Foundation for Women in Accounting
PO Box 1925
Southeastern, PA 19399-1925
Tel: 610-407-9229
Email: info@efwa.org
http://www.efwa.org

For information on certification, contact

Information Systems Audit and Control Association and Foundation
3701 Algonquin Road, Suite 1010
Rolling Meadows, IL 60008-3124
Tel: 847-253-1545

Email: certification@isaca.org
http://www.isaca.org

For information on internal auditing and certification, contact

Institute of Internal Auditors
247 Maitland Avenue
Altamonte Springs, FL 32701-4201
Tel: 407-937-1100
Email: iia@theiia.org
http://www.theiia.org

For information about management accounting and the CMA designation, as well as student membership, contact

Institute of Management Accountants
10 Paragon Drive
Montvale, NJ 07645-1718
Tel: 800-638-4427
Email: ima@imanet.org
http://www.imanet.org

OVERVIEW

Actuaries use statistical formulas and techniques to calculate the probability of events such as death, disability, sickness, unemployment, retirement, and property loss. Actuaries develop formulas to predict how much money an insurance company will pay in claims, which determines the overall cost of insuring a group, business, or individual. Increase in risk raises potential cost to the company, which, in turn, raises its rates. Actuaries analyze risk to estimate the number and amount of claims an insurance company will have to pay. They assess the cost of running the business and incorporate the results into the design and evaluation of programs.

Casualty actuaries specialize in property and liability insurance, *life actuaries* in health and life insurance. In recent years, there has been an increase in the number of actuaries—called *pension actuaries*—who deal only with pension plans. The total number of actuaries employed in the United States is approximately 18,000.

THE JOB

Should smokers pay more for their health insurance? Should younger drivers pay higher car insurance

SCHOOL SUBJECTS

Business, Mathematics

PERSONAL SKILLS

Following Instructions, Leadership/Management

MINIMUM EDUCATION LEVEL

Bachelor's Degree

CERTIFICATION OR LICENSING

Required

WORK ENVIRONMENT

Primarily Indoors, One Location with Some Travel

premiums? Actuaries answer questions like these to ensure that insurance and pension organizations can pay their claims and maintain a profitable business.

Using their knowledge of mathematics, probability, statistics, and principles of finance and business, actuaries determine premium rates and the various benefits of insurance plans. To accomplish this task, they first assemble and analyze statistics on birth, death, marriage, parenthood, employment, and other pertinent facts and figures. Based on this information, they are able to develop mathematical models of rates of death, accident, sickness, disability, or retirement and then construct tables regarding the probability of such things as property loss from fire, theft, accident, or natural disaster. After calculating all probabilities and the resulting costs to the company, the actuaries can determine the premium rates to allow insurance companies to cover predicted losses, turn a profit, and remain competitive with other businesses.

For example, based on analyses, actuaries are able to determine how many of each 1,000 people 21 years of age are expected to survive to age 65. They can calculate how many of them are expected to die this year or how many are expected to live until age 85. The probability that an insured person may die during the period before reaching 65 is a risk to the company. The actuaries must figure a price for the premium that will cover all claims and expenses as they occur and still earn a profit for the company assuming the risk. In the same way, actuaries calculate premium rates and determine policy provisions for every type of insurance coverage.

Employment opportunities span across the variety of different types of insurance companies, including life,

health, accident, automobile, fire, or workers' compensation organizations. Most actuaries specialize either as casualty actuaries, dealing with property and liability insurance, or as life actuaries, working with life and health insurance. In addition, actuaries may concentrate on pension plan programs sponsored and administered by various levels of government, private business, or fraternal or benevolent associations.

Actuaries work in many departments in insurance companies, including underwriting, group insurance, investment, pension, sales, and service. In addition to their own company's business, they analyze characteristics of the insurance business as a whole. They study general economic and social trends as well as legislative, health, and other developments, all of which may affect insurance practices. With this broad knowledge, some actuaries reach executive positions, where they can influence and help determine company policy and develop new lines of business. *Actuary executives* may communicate with government officials, company executives, policyholders, or the public to explain complex technical matters. They may testify before public agencies regarding proposed legislation that has a bearing on the insurance business, for example, or they may explain proposed changes in premium rates or contract provisions.

Actuaries may also work with a consulting firm, providing advice to clients including insurance companies, corporations, hospitals, labor unions, and government agencies. They develop employee benefits, calculating future benefits and employer contributions, and set up pension and welfare plans. *Consulting actuaries* also advise health care and financial services firms, and they may work with small insurance companies lacking an actuarial department.

Since the government regulates the insurance industry and administers laws on pensions, it also requires the services of actuaries to determine whether companies are complying with the law. A small number of actuaries are employed by the federal government and deal with Social Security, Medicare, disability and life insurance, and pension plans for veterans, members of the armed forces, and federal employees. Those in state governments may supervise and regulate insurance companies, oversee the operations of state retirement or pension systems, and manage problems related to unemployment insurance and workers' compensation.

REQUIREMENTS
High School

If you are interested in this field, you should pursue a traditional college preparatory curriculum including mathematical and computer science classes and also take advantage of advanced courses such as calculus. Introductory business, economics, accounting, and finance courses are important, as is English to develop your oral and written skills.

Postsecondary Training

A bachelor's degree with a major in actuarial science, mathematics, or statistics is highly recommended for entry into the industry. Courses in elementary and advanced algebra, differential and integral calculus, descriptive and analytical statistics, principles of mathematical statistics, probability, and numerical analysis are all important. Computer science is also a vital part of actuarial training. Employers are increasingly hiring graduates with majors in economics, business, and engineering who have a strong math background. College students should broaden their education to include business, economics, and finance as well as English and communications. Because actuarial work revolves around social and political issues, course work in the humanities and social sciences will also prove useful.

Certification or Licensing

Full professional status in an actuarial specialty is based on completing a series of 10 examinations. Success is based on both formal and on-the-job training. Actuaries can become Associate members of the Society of Actuaries after successfully completing seven of the 10 examinations for the life and health insurance, finance, and pension fields. Similarly, they can reach Associate status in the Casualty Actuarial Society after successfully completing seven out of 10 exams in the property and liability field. Most actuaries achieve Associateship in three to five years. Actuaries who successfully complete the entire series of exams for either organization are granted full membership and become fellows.

The American Society of Pension Professionals and Actuaries also offers several different designations (both actuarial and nonactuarial) to individuals who pass the required examinations in the pension field and have the appropriate work experience.

Consulting pension actuaries who service private pension plans must be enrolled and licensed by the Joint Board for the Enrollment of Actuaries (http://www.irs.gov/taxpros/actuaries), a U.S. government agency. Only these actuaries can work with pension plans set up under the Employee Retirement Income Security Act. To be accepted, applicants must meet certain professional and educational requirements stipulated by the Joint Board.

Completion of the entire series of exams may take from five to 10 years. Because the first exams offered by these various boards and societies cover core material (such as calculus, linear algebra, probability and statistics, risk theory, and actuarial math), students generally wait to commit to a specialty until they have taken the initial tests. Students pursuing a career as an actuary should complete the first two or three preliminary examinations while still in college, since these tests cover subjects usually taught in school; the more advanced examinations cover aspects of the profession itself.

Employers prefer to hire individuals who have already passed the first two exams. Once employed, companies generally give employees time during the workday to study. They may also pay exam fees, provide study materials, and award raises upon an employee's successful completion of an exam.

Other Requirements

An aptitude in mathematics, statistics, and computer science is a must to become a successful actuary, as are sound analytical and problem-solving skills. Solid oral and written communication skills are also required in order to be able to explain and interpret complex work to the client, as is skill with programming languages such as Visual Basic.

Prospective actuaries should also have an inquisitive mind with an interest in historical, social, and political issues and trends. You should have a general feel for the business world and be able to assimilate a wide range of complex information in order to see the "big picture" when planning policies. Actuaries like to solve problems; they are strategists who enjoy and generally excel at games such as chess. Actuaries need to be motivated and self-disciplined to concentrate on detailed work, especially under stress, and to undertake the rigorous study for licensing examinations.

EXPLORING

If you think you are interested in the actuarial field, try pursuing extracurricular opportunities that allow you to practice strategic thinking and problem-solving skills; these may include chess, math, or investment clubs at your school. Other activities that foster leadership and management, such as student council positions, will also be beneficial. Any kind of business or research-oriented summer or part-time experience will be valuable, especially with an accounting or law firm.

There are more than 45 local actuarial clubs and regional affiliates throughout the United States that offer opportunities for informal discussion and networking. Talk with people in the field to better understand the nature of the work, and use the association's resources to learn more about the field. The Society of Actuaries offers free educational publications.

College undergraduates can take advantage of summer internships and employment in insurance companies and consulting firms. Students will have the chance to rotate among jobs to learn various actuarial operations and different phases of insurance work.

EMPLOYERS

There are approximately 18,000 actuaries employed in the United States, and about 50 percent work in the insurance industry. Approximately 21 percent of actuaries work for professional, scientific and technical consulting services. Other actuaries work for financial services firms including commercial banks, investment banks, and retirement funds. Others are employed by actuarial consulting services and in academia. Some actuaries are self-employed.

STARTING OUT

The best way to enter this field is by taking the necessary beginning examinations while still in college. Once students have graduated and passed these exams, they are in a very good position to apply for entry-level jobs in the field and can command higher starting salaries. Some college students organize interviews and find jobs through their college career service office, while others interview with firms recruiting on campus. Many firms offer summer and year-round actuarial training programs or internships that may result in a full-time job.

Beginning actuaries may prepare calculations for actuarial tables or work with policy settlements or funds. With experience, they may prepare correspondence, reports, and research. Beginners who have already passed the preliminary exams often start with more responsibility and higher pay.

ADVANCEMENT

Advancement within the profession to assistant, associate, or chief actuary greatly depends on the individual's on-the-job performance, competence on the actuarial examinations, and leadership capabilities.

Some actuaries qualify for administrative positions in underwriting, accounting, or investment because of their broad business knowledge and specific insurance experience. Because their judgment is so valuable, actuaries may advance to administrative or executive positions, such as head of a department, vice president or president of a company, manager of an insurance rating bureau,

partner in a consulting firm, or, possibly, state insurance commissioner. Actuaries with management skills and a strong business background may move into other areas such as marketing, advertising, and planning.

EARNINGS

Starting salaries for actuaries with bachelor's degrees in actuarial science averaged $53,754 in 2007, according to a survey conducted by the National Association of Colleges and Employers. New college graduates who have not passed any actuarial examinations earn slightly less. Insurance companies and consulting firms offer merit increases or bonuses to those who pass examinations.

The U.S. Department of Labor reports that actuaries earned a median annual salary of $82,800 in 2006. Ten percent earned less than $46,470, while the top 25 percent earned more than $114,570. Actuaries working for insurance companies receive paid vacations, health and life insurance, pension plans, and other fringe benefits.

WORK ENVIRONMENT

Actuaries spend much of their 40-hour workweek behind a desk poring over facts and figures, although some travel to various units of the organization or to other businesses. This is especially true of the consulting actuary, who will most likely work longer hours and travel more. Consulting actuaries tend to have more diverse work and more personal interaction in working with a variety of clients. Though the work can be stressful and demands intense concentration and attention to detail, actuaries find their jobs to be rewarding and satisfying and feel that they make a direct and positive impact on people's lives.

OUTLOOK

The U.S. Department of Labor predicts that employment for actuaries will grow much faster than the average for all occupations through 2016. Growth of the insurance industry—traditionally the leading employer of actuaries—is expected to continue at a stable pace, with many new fields such as annuities and terrorism-related property-risk analysis, compensating for the shrinking life insurance industry. The field's stringent entrance requirements and competition for entry-level jobs will also continue to restrict the number of candidates for jobs.

The insurance industry continues to evolve, and actuaries will be in demand to establish rates in several new areas of coverage, including prepaid legal, dental, and kidnapping insurance. In many cases, actuarial data that have been supplied by rating bureaus are now being developed in new actuarial departments created in companies affected by states' new competitive rating laws. Other new areas of insurance coverage that will involve actuaries include product and pollution liability insurance as well as greater workers' compensation and medical malpractice coverage. Insurers will call on actuaries to help them respond to new state and federal regulations while cutting costs, especially in the areas of pension reform and no-fault automobile insurance. In the future, actuaries will also be employed by non-insurance businesses or will work in business- and investment-related fields. Some are already working in banking and finance.

Actuaries will be needed to assess the financial impact of current issues such as AIDS, terrorism, and the changing health care system. As demographics change, people live and work longer, and as medicine advances, actuaries will need to reexamine the probabilities of death, sickness, and retirement.

Casualty actuaries will find more work as companies find themselves held responsible for product liability. In the wake of recent environmental disasters, there will also be a growing need to evaluate environmental risk.

As business goes global, it presents a whole new set of risks and problems as economies develop and new markets emerge. As private enterprise expands in the former Soviet Union, how does a company determine the risk of opening, say, a department store in Moscow?

Actuaries are no longer just mathematical experts. With their unique combination of analytical and business skills, their role is expanding as they become broad-based business professionals solving social as well as financial problems.

FOR MORE INFORMATION
For general information about actuary careers, contact
American Academy of Actuaries
1100 17th Street, NW, Seventh Floor
Washington, DC 20036-4601
Tel: 202-223-8196
http://www.actuary.org

For information about continuing education and professional designations, contact
American Society of Pension Professionals and Actuaries
4245 North Fairfax Drive, Suite 750
Arlington, VA 22203-1648
Tel: 703-516-9300
Email: asppa@asppa.org
http://www.aspa.org

The Be An Actuary section of the CAS's Web site offers comprehensive information on the career of actuary.
Casualty Actuarial Society (CAS)
4350 North Fairfax Drive, Suite 250
Arlington, VA 22203-1695
Tel: 703-276-3100
Email: office@casact.or
http://www.casact.org
http://www.beanactuary.org

For information about continuing education and professional designations, contact
Society of Actuaries
475 North Martingale Road, Suite 600
Schaumburg, IL 60173-2252
Tel: 847-706-3500
http://www.soa.org

AEROBICS INSTRUCTORS AND FITNESS TRAINERS

OVERVIEW
Aerobics instructors choreograph and teach aerobics classes of varying types. Classes are geared toward people with general good health as well as to specialized populations, including the elderly and those with specific health problems that affect their ability to exercise. Many people enjoy participating in the lively exercise routines set to music.

Depending on where they are employed, *fitness trainers* help devise health conditioning programs for clients, from professional athletes to average individuals looking for guidance. Fitness trainers motivate clients to follow prescribed exercise programs and monitor their progress. When injuries occur, either during training or sporting events, fitness trainers determine the extent of the injury and administer first aid for minor problems such as blisters, bruises, and scrapes. Following more serious injury, trainers may work with a physical therapist to help the athlete perform rehabilitative exercises.

There are approximately 235,000 aerobics instructors and fitness trainers employed in the United States.

THE JOB
Three general levels of aerobics classes are recognized today: low impact, moderate, and high intensity. A

SCHOOL SUBJECTS

Health, Physical Education, Theater/Dance

PERSONAL SKILLS

Helping/Teaching, Leadership/Management

MINIMUM EDUCATION LEVEL

High School Diploma

CERTIFICATION OR LICENSING

Required for Certain Positions

WORK ENVIRONMENT

Primarily Indoors, Primarily One Location

typical class starts with warm-up exercises (slow stretching movements to loosen up muscles), followed by 35 to 40 minutes of nonstop activity to raise the heart rate, then ends with a cool-down period of stretching and slower movements. Instructors teach class members to monitor their heart rates and listen to their bodies for signs of personal progress.

Aerobics instructors prepare activities prior to their classes. They choose exercises to work different muscles and accompany these movements to music during each phase of the program. Generally, instructors use upbeat music for the more intense exercise portion and more soothing music for the cool-down period. Instructors demonstrate each step of a sequence until the class can follow along. Additional sequences are added continuously as the class progresses, making up a longer routine that is set to music. Most classes are structured so that new participants can start any given class. The instructor either faces the rest of the room or faces a mirror in order to observe class progress and ensure that participants do exercises correctly. Many aerobics instructors also lead toning and shaping classes. In these classes, the emphasis is not on aerobic activity but on working particular areas of the body. An instructor begins the class with a brief aerobic period followed by stretching and weight-bearing exercises that loosen and work major muscle groups.

In a health club, fitness trainers evaluate their clients' fitness level with physical examinations and fitness tests. Using various pieces of testing equipment, they determine such things as percentage of body fat and optimal heart and pulse rates. Clients fill out questionnaires about their medical background, general fitness level, and fitness goals. Fitness trainers use this information to design a customized workout plan using weights and other exercise options such as swimming and running to help clients meet these goals. Trainers also advise clients on weight control, diet, and general health. Some fitness trainers also work at the client's home or office. This convenient way of staying physically fit meets the needs of many busy, active adults today.

To start a client's exercise program, the trainer often demonstrates the proper use of weight-lifting equipment to reduce the chance of injury, especially if the client is a beginner. As the client uses the equipment, the trainer observes and corrects any problems before injury occurs. Preventing injury is extremely important, according to American Council Exercise certified personal trainer (CPT) Nicole Gutter. "It is a good idea to carry your own liability insurance. The bottom line is, know what you're doing because there is a huge risk of injury or even death for high-risk people," she says. "You should be insured in case anything beyond your control does happen."

Fitness trainers also use exercise tape to wrap weak or injured hands, feet, or other parts of the body. The heavy-duty tape helps strengthen and position the joint to prevent further injury or strain. Fitness trainers also help athletes with therapy or rehabilitation, using special braces or other equipment to support or protect the injured part until it heals. Trainers ensure that the athlete does not overuse a weak joint or muscle, risking further damage.

REQUIREMENTS
High School

Aerobics instructors and fitness trainers should have a high school diploma. If you are interested in a fitness career, take courses in physical education, biology, and anatomy. In addition, be involved in sports, weight lifting, or dance activities to stay fit and learn to appreciate the value of exercise.

Postsecondary Training

Although it isn't always necessary, a college degree will make you more marketable in the fitness field. Typically, aerobics instructors do not need a college education to qualify for jobs; however, some employers may be more interested in candidates with a balance of ability and education.

Fitness trainers are usually required to have a bachelor's degree from an accredited athletic training program or a related program in physical education or health.

These programs often require extensive internships that can range from 500 to 1,800 hours of hands-on experience. Essential college-level courses include anatomy, biomechanics, chemistry, first aid, health, kinesiology, nutrition, physics, physiology, psychology, and safety.

Tony Hinsberger, owner of Summit Fitness Personal Training, highly recommends getting a college degree in physiology, kinesiology, exercise science, or athletic training. "As an owner of a small personal training firm, I hire trainers," he says. "If I had to make a choice between equally experienced and qualified candidates, I would pick the one with a degree."

Certification or Licensing

Most serious fitness trainers and aerobics instructors become certified. Certification is not required in most states, but most clients and fitness companies expect these professionals to have credentials to prove their worth.

As a current employer of fitness professionals, Hinsberger recommends certification. "I only hire certified trainers," he says. "Most facilities require certification and there are many, many certifying agencies. Certification is also required by most liability insurance plans."

Certifying agencies include the following: Aerobics and Fitness Association of America, IDEA Health and Fitness Association, American Fitness Professionals and Associates, American College of Sports Medicine, American Council on Exercise, and National Academy of Sports Medicine. Aerobics instructors should also be certified in cardiopulmonary resuscitation (CPR) before finding a job.

The National Athletic Trainers' Association and the American Athletic Trainers Association certify fitness trainers who have graduated from accredited college programs or have completed the necessary internship following a degree in a related field. Fitness trainers who seek certification generally also need Red Cross certification in CPR or as an emergency medical technician.

Whichever career path they follow, aerobics instructors and fitness trainers are expected to keep up to date with their fields, becoming thoroughly familiar with the latest knowledge and safety practices. They must take continuing education courses and participate in seminars to keep their certification current.

Other Requirements

Aerobics instructors and fitness trainers are expected to be physically fit, but are not expected to be specimens of human perfection. For example, members of an aerobics class geared to overweight people might feel more comfortable with a heavier instructor; a class geared toward the elderly may benefit from an older instructor.

EXPLORING

A visit to a health club, park district, or YMCA aerobics class is a good way to observe the work of fitness trainers and aerobics instructors. Part-time or summer jobs are sometimes available for high school students in these facilities. It may also be possible to volunteer in a senior citizen center where aerobics classes are offered.

"To explore this [career] path, I recommend working part-time in a gym or fitness facility," Tony Hinsberger suggests. "Some clubs have an orientation position. People in this job take new members on a tour of the facility and show new members how to use the equipment safely. It typically doesn't require a degree, only on-site training."

If possible, enroll in an aerobics class or train with a fitness trainer to experience firsthand what their jobs entail and to see what makes a good instructor. Brett Vicknair, owner of an in-home personal training company, agrees: "I would encourage someone wanting to pursue a career as a personal trainer to get involved with working out first, maybe at a local fitness center, and take advantage of any help that is usually offered when someone first becomes a member."

Aerobics instructor workshops are taught to help prospective instructors gain experience. These are usually offered in adult education courses at such places as the YMCA. Unpaid apprenticeships are also a good way for future instructors to obtain supervised experience before teaching classes on their own. The facility may allow prospective aerobics instructors to take their training class for free if there is a possibility that they will work there in the future.

Opportunities for student fitness trainers are available in schools with fitness trainers on staff. This is an excellent way for students to observe and assist a professional fitness trainer on an ongoing basis.

EMPLOYERS

Approximately 235,000 fitness workers are employed in the United States. Most aerobics instructors work for fitness centers and gymnasiums. Most employers are for-profit businesses, but some are community-based, such as the YMCA or a family center. Other job possibilities can be found in corporate fitness centers, colleges, retirement centers, and resorts.

Some fitness trainers work in more than one facility. Others are self-employed and take clients on an appointment basis, working either in personal homes or in a public gym. Some fitness trainers will work with high-profile athletes on a one-on-one basis to meet specific fitness requirements.

"Trainers work in gyms or fitness centers, in private personal fitness centers where members are seen on an appointment basis only, and in country clubs, just to name some of the opportunities," Brett Vicknair says.

Most medium to large cities have one or more gyms or fitness centers; however, smaller towns may not have any such facilities. However, there may be limited openings at retirement homes, schools, and community centers in these small towns.

STARTING OUT

Students should use their schools' career services offices for information on available jobs. Often, facilities that provide training or internships will hire or provide job leads to individuals who have completed programs. Students can also find jobs through classified ads and by applying to health and fitness clubs, YMCAs, YWCAs, Jewish community centers, local schools, park districts, church groups, and other fitness organizations. Because exercise is understood to be a preventive measure for many health and medical problems, insurance companies often reward businesses that offer fitness facilities to their employees with lower insurance rates. As a result, students should consider nearby companies for prospective fitness instructor and trainer positions.

ADVANCEMENT

Experienced aerobics instructors can become instructor trainers, providing tips and insight on how to lead a class and what routines work well.

A bachelor's degree in either sports physiology or exercise physiology is especially beneficial for those who want to advance to the position of health club director or to teach corporate wellness programs.

Fitness trainers working at schools can advance from assistant positions to head athletic director, which may involve relocating to another school. Fitness trainers can advance to instruct new fitness trainers in college. They also can work in sports medicine facilities, usually in rehabilitation work. In health clubs, fitness trainers can advance to become health club directors or work in administration. Often, fitness trainers who build up a reputation and a clientele go into business for themselves as personal trainers.

EARNINGS

Aerobics instructors are usually paid by the class and generally start out at about $10 per class. Experienced aerobics instructors can earn up to $50 or $60 per class. The U.S. Department of Labor reports that fitness workers such as aerobics instructors had median annual earnings of $25,910 in 2006. The lowest paid 10 percent earned less than $14,880, and the highest paid 10 percent earned more than $56,750 per year.

Although a sports season lasts only about six months, athletes train year-round to remain in shape and require trainers to guide them. Many personal trainers are paid on a client-by-client basis. Contracts are drawn up and the payment is agreed upon before the training starts. Some trainers get paid more or less depending on the results.

A compensation survey by health and fitness organization IDEA reports that many employers offer health insurance and paid sick and vacation time to full-time employees. They also may provide discounts on products sold in the club (such as shoes, clothes, and equipment) and free memberships to use the facility.

WORK ENVIRONMENT

Most weight training and aerobics classes are held indoors. Depending on the popularity of the class and/or instructor, aerobics classes can get crowded and hectic at times. Instructors need to keep a level head and keep a positive, outgoing personality in order to motivate people and keep them together. It is important that aerobics instructors make the class enjoyable yet challenging so that members will return class after class. They also need to be unaffected by complaints of class members, some of whom may find the routines too hard, too easy, or who may not like the music selections. Instructors need to realize that these complaints are not personal attacks.

Fitness trainers need to be able to work on a one-on-one basis with amateur and professional athletes and nonathletes. They may work with individuals who are in pain after an injury and must be able to coax them to use muscles they would probably rather not. Trainers must possess patience, especially for beginners or those who are not athletically inclined, and offer encouragement to help them along.

Most trainers find it rewarding to help others achieve fitness goals. "To truly be a great personal fitness trainer, first you must enjoy helping and being around people. I love being able to motivate and give my clients the knowledge to help them meet their fitness goals," Brett Vicknair says.

OUTLOOK

Because of the country's ever-expanding interest in health and fitness, the U.S. Department of Labor predicts that the job outlook for aerobics instructors should remain very strong through 2016, with much faster than average growth. As the population ages, more opportunities will arise to work with the elderly in retirement homes. Large companies and corporations are also interested in keeping insurance costs down by hiring aerobics instructors to hold classes for their employees. The struggle with obesity in the U.S. will also have an effect on the popularity and demand for aerobics instructors. As communities, schools, and individuals attempt to shed the pounds, the need for fitness instructors and motivators will continue.

Fitness trainers are also in strong demand, especially at the high school level. Currently, some states require high schools to have a fitness trainer on staff. According to Brett Vicknair, home fitness trainers will remain in high demand. The convenience of being able to work out with a personal trainer before work, at lunch, early Saturday morning, or late Friday night make the use of a personal trainer a flexible option. With the hectic lifestyle of most people today, that aspect alone should keep personal training positions on the rise.

FOR MORE INFORMATION

For information on various certifications, contact the following organizations:

Aerobics and Fitness Association of America
15250 Ventura Boulevard, Suite 200
Sherman Oaks, CA 91403 -3215
Tel: 877-968-7263
Email: contactAFAA@afaa.com
http://www.afaa.com

For free information and materials about sports medicine topics, contact

American College of Sports Medicine
PO Box 1440
Indianapolis, IN 46206-1440
Tel: 317-637-9200
http://www.acsm.org

For more information about certification and careers in fitness, contact the ACE.

American Council on Exercise (ACE)
4851 Paramount Drive
San Diego, CA 92123
Tel: 888-825-3636
http://www.acefitness.org

For information on home study and various fitness certifications, contact

American Fitness Professionals and Associates
PO Box 214
Ship Bottom, NJ 08008-0234

Tel: 800-494-7782
Email: afpa@afpafitness.com
http://www.afpafitness.com

For fitness facts and articles and information on certification, visit IDEA's Web site.

IDEA: The Health and Fitness Association
10455 Pacific Center Court
San Diego, CA 92121-4339
Tel: 800-999-4332
http://www.ideafit.com

For information on certification, contact

National Academy of Sports Medicine
26632 Agoura Road
Calabasas, CA 91302-1954
Tel: 800-460-6276
http://www.nasm.org

ALCOHOL AND DRUG ABUSE COUNSELORS

OVERVIEW

Alcohol and drug abuse counselors (sometimes called *substance abuse counselors*) work with people who abuse or are addicted to drugs or alcohol. Through individual and group counseling sessions, they help their clients understand and change their destructive substance abuse behaviors. There are about 83,000 substance-abuse counselors in the United States.

THE JOB

The main goal of alcohol and drug abuse counselors is to help patients stop their destructive behaviors. Counselors may also work with the families of clients to give them support and guidance in dealing with the problem.

Counselors begin by trying to learn about a patient's general background and history of drug or alcohol use. They may review patient records, including police reports, employment records, medical records, or reports from other counselors.

Counselors also interview the patient to determine the nature and extent of substance abuse. During an interview, the counselor asks questions about what

SCHOOL SUBJECTS
Health, Psychology, Sociology

PERSONAL SKILLS
Communication/Ideas, Helping/Teaching

MINIMUM EDUCATION LEVEL
Associate's Degree

CERTIFICATION OR LICENSING
Required by Certain States

WORK ENVIRONMENT
Primarily Indoors, Primarily One Location

types of substances the patient uses, how often, and for how long. The counselor may also ask patients about previous attempts to stop using the substance and about how the problem has affected their lives in various respects.

Using the information they obtain from the patient and their knowledge of substance abuse patterns, counselors formulate a program for treatment and rehabilitation. A substantial part of the rehabilitation process involves individual, group, or family counseling sessions. During individual sessions, counselors do a great deal of listening, perhaps asking appropriate questions to guide patients to insights about themselves. In group therapy sessions, counselors supervise groups of several patients, helping move their discussion in positive ways. In counseling sessions, counselors also teach patients methods of overcoming their dependencies. For example, they might help a patient develop a series of goals for behavioral change.

Counselors monitor and assess the progress of their patients. In most cases, counselors deal with several different patients in various stages of recovery—some may need help breaking the pattern of substance abuse; some may already have stopped using, but still need support; others may be recovered users who have suffered a relapse. Counselors maintain ongoing relationships with patients to help them adapt to the different recovery stages.

Working with families is another aspect of many alcohol and drug abuse counselors' jobs. They may ask a patient's family for insight into the patient's behavior. They may also teach the patient's family members how to deal with and support the patient through the recovery process.

Counselors may work with other health professionals and social agencies, including physicians, psychiatrists, psychologists, employment services, and court systems. In some cases, the counselor, with the patient's permission, may serve as a spokesperson for the patient, working with corrections officers, social workers, or employers. In other cases, a patient's needs might exceed the counselor's abilities; when this is the case, the counselor refers the patient to an appropriate medical expert, agency, or social program.

There is a substantial amount of paperwork involved in counseling alcohol and drug abusers. Detailed records must be kept on patients in order to follow their progress. For example, a report must be written after each counseling session. Counselors who work in residential treatment settings are required to participate in regular staff meetings to develop treatment plans and review patient progress. They may also meet periodically with family members or social service agency representatives to discuss patient progress and needs.

In some cases, alcohol and drug abuse counselors specialize in working with certain groups of people. Some work only with children or teenagers; others work with businesses to counsel employees who may have problems related to drugs and alcohol. In still other cases, counselors specialize in treating people who are addicted to specific drugs, such as cocaine, heroin, or alcohol. Counselors may need special training in order to work with specific groups.

REQUIREMENTS
High School

High school students who are considering a career in alcohol and drug abuse counseling should choose a curriculum that meets the requirements of the college or university they hope to attend. Typically, four years of English, history, mathematics, a foreign language, and social sciences are necessary. In addition, psychology, sociology, physiology, biology, and anatomy provide a good academic background for potential counselors.

The educational requirements for alcohol and drug abuse counselors vary greatly by state and employer. A high school education may be the minimum requirement for employers who provide on-the-job training, which ranges from six weeks to two years. These jobs, however, are becoming increasingly rare as more states are leaning toward stricter requirements for counselors.

Postsecondary Training

Some employers require an associate's degree in alcohol and drug technology. Most substance abuse counselors, however, have a bachelor's degree in counseling, psychology, health sociology, or social work. Many two- and four-year colleges now offer specific courses for students training to be substance abuse counselors.

Many counselors have a master's degree in counseling with a specialization in substance abuse counseling. Accredited graduate programs in substance abuse counseling are composed of a supervised internship as well as regular class work.

Certification or Licensing

Certification in this field, which is mandatory in some states, is available through state accreditation boards. Currently, 48 states and the District of Columbia have credentialing laws for alcohol and drug abuse counselors. These laws typically require that counselors have a minimum of a master's degree and two to three years of postacademic supervised counseling experience. Candidates must also have passed a written test.

Additionally, the NAADAC, the Association for Addiction Professionals, offers several professional designations including national certified addiction counselor, master addiction counselor, tobacco addiction specialist credential, certificate in spiritual caregiving to help addicted persons and families, and adolescent specialist endorsement.

The National Board for Certified Counselors also offers the master addiction counselor designation to counselors who hold the national certified counselor designation and meet educational and professional experience requirements.

Other Requirements

In order to be successful in this job, you should enjoy working with people. You must have compassion, good communication and listening skills, and a desire to help others. You should also be emotionally stable and able to deal with the frustrations and failures that are often a part of the job.

EXPLORING

Students interested in this career can find a great deal of information on substance abuse and substance abuse counseling at any local library. In addition, by contacting a local hospital, mental health clinic, or treatment center, it might be possible to talk with a counselor about the details of his or her job.

Volunteer work or a part-time job at a residential facility such as a hospital or treatment center is another good way of gaining experience and exploring an aptitude for counseling work. Finally, the professional and government organizations listed at the end of this article can provide information on alcohol and drug abuse counseling.

EMPLOYERS

Approximately 83,000 substance-abuse counselors are employed in the United States. Counselors are hired by hospitals, private and public treatment centers, government agencies, prisons, public school systems, colleges and universities, health maintenance organizations (HMOs), crisis centers, and mental health centers. More and more frequently, large companies are hiring alcohol and drug abuse counselors as well, to deal with employee substance abuse problems.

STARTING OUT

Counselors who have completed a two- or four-year college degree might start a job search by checking with the career services office of their college or university. Those who plan to look for a position without first attending college might want to start by getting an entry-level or volunteer position in a treatment center or related agency. In this way, they can obtain practical experience and also make connections that might lead to full-time employment as a counselor.

Job seekers should also watch the classified advertisements in local newspapers. Job openings for counselors are often listed under "Alcohol and Drug Counselor," "Substance Abuse Counselor," or "Mental Health Counselor." Finally, one might consider applying directly to the personnel department of various facilities and agencies that treat alcohol and drug abusers.

ADVANCEMENT

Counselors in this field often advance initially by taking on more responsibilities and earning a higher wage. They may also better themselves by taking a similar position in a more prestigious facility, such as an upscale private treatment center.

As they obtain more experience and perhaps more education, counselors sometimes move into supervisory or administrative positions. They might become directors of substance abuse programs in mental health facilities or executive directors of agencies or clinics.

Career options are more diverse for those counselors who continue their education. They may move into research, consulting, or teaching at the college level.

EARNINGS

Salaries of alcohol and drug abuse counselors depend on education level, amount of experience, and place of employment. Generally, the more education and experience a counselor has, the higher his or her earnings will be. Counselors who work in private treatment centers also tend to earn more than their public sector counterparts.

Alcohol and drug abuse counselors earned a median annual salary of $34,040 in 2006, according to the U.S. Department of Labor. The lowest 10 percent earned less than $22,600. The highest 10 percent earned $52,340 or more. Directors of treatment programs or centers could earn considerably more that the national median salary. Almost all treatment centers provide employee benefits to their full-time counselors. Benefits usually include paid vacations and sick days, insurance, and pension plans.

WORK ENVIRONMENT

The hours that an alcohol and drug abuse counselor works depends upon where he or she is employed. Many residential treatment facilities and mental health centers—and all crisis centers—have counselors on duty during evening and weekend hours. Other employers, such as government agencies and universities, are likely to have more conventional working hours.

Work settings for counselors also vary by employer. Counselors may work in private offices, in the rooms or homes of patients, in classrooms, or in meeting rooms. In some cases, they conduct support group sessions in churches, community centers, or schools. For the most part, however, counselors work at the same work site or sites on a daily basis.

The bulk of a counselor's day is spent dealing with various people—patients, families, social workers, and health care professionals. There may be very little time during a workday for quiet reflection or organization.

Working with alcohol and drug abusers can be an emotionally draining experience. Overcoming addiction is a very hard battle, and patients respond to it in various ways. They may be resentful, angry, discouraged, or profoundly depressed. They may talk candidly with their counselors about tragic and upsetting events in their lives. Counselors spend much of their time listening to and dealing with very strong, usually negative, emotions.

This work can also be discouraging, due to a high failure rate. Many alcoholics and drug addicts do not respond to treatment and return immediately to their addictions. Even after months and sometimes years of recovery, many substance abusers suffer relapses. The counselor must learn to cope with the frustration of having his or her patients fail, perhaps repeatedly.

There is a very positive side to drug and alcohol abuse counseling, however. When it is successful, counselors have the satisfaction of knowing that they had a positive effect on someone's life. They have the reward of seeing some patients return to happy family lives and productive careers.

OUTLOOK

Employment of alcohol and drug abuse counselors is projected to grow much faster than the average for all occupations through 2016, according to the U.S. Department of Labor. There are nearly 18 million alcoholics in the United States and an equal, if not greater, number of drug abusers. Because no successful method to significantly reduce drug and alcohol abuse has emerged, these numbers are not likely to decrease. Overall population growth will also lead to a need for more substance abuse counselors. Finally, many states are shifting away from criminalizing drug use, seeing it as a mental-health problem that should be treated through the medical system, not the criminal-justice system.

Another reason for the expected growth in counselors' jobs is that an increasing number of employers are offering employee assistance programs that provide counseling services for mental health and alcohol and drug abuse.

Finally, many job openings will arise as a result of job turnover. Because of the stress levels and the emotional demands involved in this career, there is a high burnout rate. As alcohol and drug abuse counselors leave the field, new counselors are needed to replace them.

FOR MORE INFORMATION

For more information on substance abuse and counseling careers, contact

American Counseling Association
5999 Stevenson Avenue
Alexandria, VA 22304-3300
Tel: 800-347-6647
http://www.counseling.org

For information on certification, contact
National Board for Certified Counselors
3 Terrace Way

Greensboro, NC 27403-3660
Tel: 336-547-0607
Email: nbcc@nbcc.org
http://www.nbcc.org

NAADAC, The Association for Addiction Professionals
1001 North Fairfax Street, Suite 201
Alexandria, VA 22314-1797
Tel: 800-548-0497
Email: naadac@naadac.org
http://www.naadac.org

For more information on alcohol and substance abuse, contact the following organizations:
National Institute on Alcohol Abuse and Alcoholism
National Institutes of Health
5635 Fishers Lane, MSC 9304
Bethesda, MD 20892-9304
http://www.niaaa.nih.gov

National Institute on Drug Abuse
National Institutes of Health
6001 Executive Boulevard, Room 5213
Bethesda, MD 20892-9561
Tel: 301-443-1124
Email: information@nida.nih.gov
http://www.nida.nih.gov

National Clearinghouse for Alcohol and Drug Information
http://ncadi.samhsa.gov

ARCHITECTS

OVERVIEW

Architects plan, design, and observe construction of facilities used for human occupancy and of other structures. They consult with clients, plan layouts of buildings, prepare drawings of proposed buildings, write specifications, and prepare scale and full-sized drawings. Architects also may help clients to obtain bids, select a contractor, and negotiate the construction contract, and they also visit construction sites to ensure that the work is being completed according to specification. There are approximately 132,000 architects working in the United States.

SCHOOL SUBJECTS
Art, Mathematics

PERSONAL SKILLS
Artistic, Communication/Ideas

MINIMUM EDUCATION LEVEL
Bachelor's Degree

CERTIFICATION OR LICENSING
Required

WORK ENVIRONMENT
Primarily Indoors, Primarily One Location

THE JOB

The architect normally has two responsibilities: to design a building that will satisfy the client and to protect the public's health, safety, and welfare. This second responsibility requires architects to be licensed by the state in which they work. Meeting the first responsibility involves many steps. The job begins with learning what the client wants. The architect takes many factors into consideration, including local and state building and design regulations, climate, soil on which the building is to be constructed, zoning laws, fire regulations, and the client's financial limitations.

The architect then prepares a set of plans that, upon the client's approval, will be developed into final design and construction documents. The final design shows the exact dimensions of every portion of the building, including the location and size of columns and beams, electrical outlets and fixtures, plumbing, heating and air-conditioning facilities, windows, and doors. The architect works closely with consulting engineers on the specifics of the plumbing, heating, air conditioning, and electrical work to be done.

The architect then assists the client in getting bids from general contractors, one of whom will be selected to construct the building to the specifications. The architect helps the client through the completion of the construction and occupancy phases, making certain the correct materials are used and that the drawings and specifications are faithfully followed.

Throughout the process the architect works closely with a design or project team. This team is usually made up of the following: *designers,* who specialize in design development; a *structural designer,* who designs the frame of the building in accordance with the work of the architect; the *project manager* or *job superintendent,* who sees that the full detail drawings are completed to the satisfaction of the architect; and the *specification writer* and *estimator,* who prepare a project manual that describes in more detail the materials to be used in the building, their quality and method of installation, and all details related to the construction of the building.

The architect's job is very complex. He or she is expected to know construction methods, engineering principles and practices, and materials. Architects also must be up to date on new design and construction techniques and procedures. Although architects once spent most of their time designing buildings for the wealthy, they are now more often involved in the design of housing developments, individual dwellings, supermarkets, industrial plants, office buildings, shopping centers, airport terminals, schools, banks, museums, churches and religious structures of other faiths, and dozens of other types of buildings.

Architects may specialize in any one of a number of fields, including building appraisal, city planning, teaching, architectural journalism, furniture design, lighting design, or government service. Regardless of the area of specialization, the architect's major task is that of understanding the client's needs and then reconciling them into a meaningful whole.

REQUIREMENTS
High School

To prepare for this career while in high school, take a college preparatory program that includes courses in English, mathematics, physics, art (especially freehand drawing), social studies, history, and foreign languages. Courses in business and computer science also will be useful.

Postsecondary Training

Because most state architecture registration boards require a professional degree, high school students are advised, early in their senior year, to apply for admission to a professional program that is accredited by the National Architectural Accrediting Board. Competition to enter these programs is high. Grades, class rank, and aptitude and achievement scores count heavily in determining who will be accepted.

Most schools of architecture offer degrees through either a five-year bachelor's program or a three- or four-year master's program. The majority of architec-

ture students seek out the bachelor's degree in architecture, going from high school directly into a five-year program. Though this is the fastest route, you should be certain that you want to study architecture. Because the programs are so specialized, it is difficult to transfer to another field of study if you change your mind. The master's degree option allows for more flexibility but takes longer to complete. In this case, students first earn a liberal arts degree then continue their training by completing a master's program in architecture.

A typical college architecture program includes courses in architectural history and theory, the technical and legal aspects of building design, science, and liberal arts.

Certification or Licensing

All states and the District of Columbia require that individuals be licensed before contracting to provide architectural services in that particular state. Though many work in the field without licensure, only licensed architects are required to take legal responsibility for all work. Using a licensed architect for a project is, therefore, less risky than using an unlicensed one. Architects who are licensed usually take on projects with larger responsibilities and have greater chances to advance to managerial or executive positions.

The requirements for registration include graduation from an accredited school of architecture and three years of practical experience (called an internship) with a licensed architect. After these requirements are met, individuals can take the rigorous Architect Registration Examination. Some states require architects to maintain their licensing through continued education. These individuals may complete a certain number of credits every year or two through seminars, workshops, university classes, self-study courses, or other sources.

In addition to becoming licensed, a growing number of architects choose to obtain certification by the National Council of Architectural Registration Boards. If an architect plans to work in more than one state, obtaining this certification can make it easier to become licensed in different states.

Other Requirements

If you are interested in architecture, you should be intelligent, observant, responsible, and self-disciplined. You should have a concern for detail and accuracy, be able to communicate effectively both orally and in writing, and be able to accept criticism constructively. Although great artistic ability is not necessary, you should be able to visualize spatial relationships and have the capacity to solve technical problems. Mathematical ability is also important. In addition, you should possess organizational skills and leadership qualities and be able to work well with others.

EXPLORING

Most architects will welcome the opportunity to talk with young people interested in entering architecture. You may be able to visit their offices to gain a firsthand knowledge of the type of work done by architects. You can also visit a design studio of a school of architecture or work for an architect or building contractor during summer vacations. Also, many architecture schools offer summer programs for high school students. Books and magazines on architecture also can give you a broad understanding of the nature of the work and the values of the profession.

EMPLOYERS

Of the 132,000 architects working in the United States, most are employed by architectural or engineering firms or other firms related to the construction industry. About one in five architects, however, are self-employed—the ultimate dream of many people in the profession. A few develop graphic design, interior design, or product specialties. Still others put their training to work in the theater, film, or television fields, or in museums, display firms, and architectural product and materials manufacturing companies. A small number are employed in government agencies such as the Departments of Defense, Interior, and Housing and Urban Development and the General Services Administration.

STARTING OUT

Students entering architecture following graduation start as interns in an architectural office. As interns, they assist in preparing architectural construction documents. They also handle related details, such as administering contracts, coordinating the work of other professionals on the project, researching building codes and construction materials, and writing specifications. As an alternative to working for an architectural firm, some architecture graduates go into allied fields such as construction, engineering, interior design, landscape architecture, or real estate development.

ADVANCEMENT

Interns and architects alike are given progressively more complex jobs. Architects may advance to supervisory or managerial positions. Some architects become partners in established firms, while others take steps to establish their own practice.

EARNINGS

Architects earned a median annual salary of $64,150 in 2006, according to the U.S. Department of Labor. The lowest paid 10 percent earned less than $39,420 annually, while the highest paid 10 percent earned $104,970 or more.

Well-established architects who are partners in an architectural firm or who have their own businesses generally earn much more than salaried employees. Most employers offer such fringe benefits as health insurance, sick and vacation pay, and retirement plans.

WORK ENVIRONMENT

Architects normally work a 40-hour week. There may be a number of times when they will have to work overtime, especially when under pressure to complete an assignment. Self-employed architects work less regular hours and often meet with clients in their homes or offices during the evening. Architects usually work in comfortable offices, but they may spend a considerable amount of time outside the office visiting clients or viewing the progress of a particular job in the field. Their routines usually vary considerably.

OUTLOOK

Employment in the field is expected to grow faster than the average for all occupations through 2016, according to the U.S. Department of Labor. The number of architects needed will depend on the volume of construction. The construction industry is extremely sensitive to fluctuations in the overall economy, and a bad economic climate could result in layoffs. In the next decade, employment is expected to be best in nonresidential construction. On the positive side, employment of architects is not likely to be affected by the growing use of computer technologies. Rather than replacing architects, computers are being used to enhance the architect's work.

Demographic trends will also play a strong role in fueling employment growth for architects. As a larger percentage of Americans reach the age of 65 and older, architects will be needed to design new healthcare facilities, nursing homes, and retirement communities. Aging educational facilities will also require the construction of new, larger, and more energy efficient structures. Architects with knowledge of sustainable design techniques should have excellent employment opportunities.

Competition for employment will continue to be strong, particularly in prestigious architectural firms.

Openings will not be newly created positions but will become available as the workload increases and established architects transfer to other occupations or leave the field.

FOR MORE INFORMATION

For information on education, scholarships, and student membership opportunities, contact

American Institute of Architects
1735 New York Avenue, NW
Washington, DC 20006-5292
Tel: 800-AIA-3837
Email: infocentral@aia.org
http://www.aia.org

For information on education and student membership opportunities, contact

American Institute of Architecture Students
1735 New York Avenue, NW
Washington, DC 20006-5292
Tel: 202-626-7472
Email: mailbox@aias.org
http://www.aiasnatl.org

For information on schools of architecture, contact

Association of Collegiate Schools of Architecture
1735 New York Avenue, NW
Washington, DC 20006-5292
Tel: 202-783-6500
http://www.acsa-arch.org

For information on careers in architecture, visit

ARCHcareers.org
http://www.archcareers.org

ASSESSORS AND APPRAISERS

OVERVIEW

Assessors and appraisers collect and interpret data to make judgments about the value, quality, and use of property. Assessors are government officials who evaluate property for the express purpose of determining how much the real estate owner should pay the city or county government in property taxes. Appraisers evaluate the market value of property to help people make decisions about purchases, sales, investments, mortgages, or loans.

Rural districts or small towns may have only a few assessors, while large cities or urban counties may have several hundred. Appraisers are especially in demand in large cities but also work in smaller communities. There are approximately 101,000 real estate assessors and appraisers employed in the United States.

THE JOB

Property is divided into two distinct types: real property and personal property. Real property is land and the structures built upon the land, while personal property includes all other types of possessions. Appraisers determine the value, quality, and use of real property and personal property based on selective research into market areas, the application of analytical techniques, and professional judgment derived from experience. In evaluating real property, they analyze the supply and demand for different types of property, such as residential dwellings, office buildings, shopping centers, industrial sites, and farms, to estimate their values. Appraisers analyze construction, condition, and functional design. They review public records of sales, leases, previous assessments, and other transactions pertaining to land and buildings to determine the market values, rents, and construction costs of similar properties. Appraisers collect information about neighborhoods, such as availability of gas, electricity, power lines, and transportation. They also may interview people familiar with the property, and they consider the cost of making improvements on the property.

Appraisers also must consider such factors as location and changes that might influence the future value of the property. A residence worth $300,000 in the suburbs may be worth only a fraction of that in the inner city or in a remote rural area. But that same suburban residence may depreciate in value if an airport will be built nearby. After conducting a thorough investigation, appraisers usually prepare a written report that documents their findings and conclusions.

Assessors perform the same duties as appraisers and then compute the amount of tax to be levied on property, using applicable tax tables. The primary responsibility of the assessor is to prepare an annual assessment roll, which lists all properties in a district and their assessed values.

To prepare the assessment roll, assessors and their staffs first must locate and identify all taxable property in the district. To do so, they prepare and maintain complete and accurate maps that show the size, shape, location, and legal description of each parcel of land. Next, they collect information about other features, such as zoning, soil characteristics, and availability of water, electricity, sewers, gas, and telephones. They describe each building and how land and buildings are used. This information is put in a parcel record.

Assessors also analyze relationships between property characteristics and sales prices, rents, and construction costs to produce valuation models or formulas. They use these formulas to estimate the value of every property as of the legally required assessment date. For example, assessors try to estimate the value of adding a bedroom to a residence or adding an acre to a farm, or how much competition from a new shopping center detracts from the value of a downtown department store. Finally, assessors prepare and certify an assessment roll listing all properties, owners, and assessed values and notify owners of the assessed value of their properties. Because taxpayers have the right to contest their assessments, assessors must be prepared to defend their estimates and methods.

Most appraisers deal with land and buildings, but some evaluate other items of value. Specialized appraisers evaluate antiques, gems and jewelry, machinery, equipment, aircraft, boats, oil and gas reserves, and businesses. These appraisers obtain special training in their areas of expertise but generally perform the same functions as real property appraisers.

Personal property assessors help the government levy taxes by preparing lists of personal property owned by businesses and, in a few areas, householders. In addition to listing the number of items, these assessors also estimate the value of taxable items.

REQUIREMENTS
High School

If you are interested in the fields of assessing or appraising, there are a number of courses you can take in high school to help prepare you for this work. Take plenty of math classes, since you will need to be comfortable working with numbers and making calculations. Accounting classes will also be helpful for the same reasons. English courses will help you develop your researching and writing skills as well as verbal skills. Take computer classes in order to become accustomed to using this tool. Courses in civics or government may also be beneficial.

Postsecondary Training

Appraisers and assessors need a broad range of knowledge in such areas as equity and mortgage finance, architectural function, demographic statistics, and business trends. In addition, they must be competent writers and able to communicate effectively with people. In the past,

SCHOOL SUBJECTS

Computer Science, English, Mathematics

PERSONAL SKILLS

Communication/Ideas, Mechanical/Manipulative

MINIMUM EDUCATION LEVEL

Some Postsecondary Training

CERTIFICATION OR LICENSING

Recommended (Certification), Required for Certain Positions (Licensing)

WORK ENVIRONMENT

Primarily Indoors, Primarily Multiple Locations

some people have been able to enter these fields with only a high school education and learn specialized skills on the job. Today, however, most appraisers and assessors have at least some college education. A number work in appropriate businesses, such as auction houses, while they earn their degrees. Some with several years of college experience are able to find employment and receive on-the-job training. Those wanting to receive professional designations and to have the best job opportunities, however, should complete a college degree.

A few colleges and universities, such as Lindenwood University (http://www.lindenwood.edu) in St. Charles, Missouri, now offer degrees in valuation sciences that will prepare you for this career. If you are unable to attend such a specialized program, though, there are numerous classes you can take at any college to prepare for this career. A liberal arts degree provides a solid background, as do courses in finance, statistics, mathematics, public administration and business administration, real estate and urban land economics, engineering, architecture, and computer science. Appraisers choosing to specialize in a particular area should have a solid background in that field.

Courses in assessment and appraisal are offered by professional associations such as the American Society of Appraisers (ASA), the Appraisal Institute (AI), and the International Association of Assessing Officers.

Certification or Licensing

A number of professional organizations, such as the ASA and the AI, offer certification or designations in the field.

It is highly recommended that you attain professional designation in order to enhance your standing in the field and demonstrate to consumers your level of expertise. To receive a designation, you will typically need to pass a written exam, demonstrate ethical behavior, and have completed a certain amount of education. To maintain your designation, you will also need to fulfill continuing education requirements.

Because all appraisals used for federally regulated real estate transactions must be conducted by licensed appraisers, most appraisers now obtain a state license. In addition, some states—known as "mandatory states"—require real estate appraisers to be licensed even if the appraisers do not deal with federally regulated transactions. You will need to check with your state's regulatory agency to learn more about the exact requirements for your state. In addition to a license, some states may require assessors who are government employees to pass civil service tests or other examinations before they can start work.

Other Requirements

Good appraisers are skilled investigators and must be proficient at gathering data. They must be familiar with sources of information on such diverse topics as public records, construction materials, building trends, economic trends, and governmental regulations affecting use of property. They should know how to read survey drawings and blueprints and be able to identify features of building construction.

EXPLORING

One simple way you can practice the methods used by appraisers is to write a detailed analysis of something you are considering investing in, such as a car, a computer, or even which college to attend. Your analysis should include both the benefits and the shortcomings of the investment as well as your final recommendation. Is the car overpriced? Does one particular school offer a better value for you? By doing this, you will begin to get a feel for the researching and writing done by an appraiser. Another way to explore this career is to look for part-time or summer work with an appraisal firm. Some firms also have jobs as appraiser assistants or trainees. Working at county assessors' or treasurers' offices, financial institutions, or real estate companies also might provide experience. If you are interested in working with real estate, you may want to learn the particulars of building construction by finding summer work with a construction company.

EMPLOYERS

Assessors are public servants who are either elected or appointed to office. The United States is divided into assessment districts, with population size affecting the number of assessors in a given area. Appraisers are employed by private businesses, such as accounting firms, real estate companies, and financial institutions, and by larger assessors' offices. Appraisers also work at auction houses, art galleries, and antique shops; some also work in government offices or for U.S. Customs and Border Protection. Assessors' offices might employ administrators, property appraisers, mappers, systems analysts, computer technicians, public relations specialists, word processors, and clerical workers. In small offices, one or two people might handle most tasks; in large offices, some with hundreds of employees, specialists are more common. Approximately 101,000 real estate assessors and appraisers are employed in the United States.

STARTING OUT

After you have acquired the necessary technical and mathematical knowledge in the classroom, you should apply to area appraisal firms, local county assessors, real estate brokers, or large accounting firms. Because assessing jobs are often civil service positions, they may be listed with government employment agencies. If you have graduated from a degree program in valuation sciences, your school's career services office should also be able to provide you with assistance in finding that first job.

ADVANCEMENT

Appraising is a dynamic field, affected yearly by new legislation and technology. To distinguish themselves in the business, top appraisers continue their education and pursue certification through the various national appraising organizations, such as the Appraisal Institute, the American Society of Appraisers, and the International Association of Assessing Officers. Certified appraisers are entrusted with the most prestigious projects and can command the highest fees. In addition to working on more and more prestigious projects, some appraisers advance by opening their own appraisal firms. Others may advance by moving to larger firms or agency offices, where they are more able to specialize.

EARNINGS

Income for assessors is influenced by their location and employer; their salaries generally increase as the population of their jurisdiction increases. For example, those working in large counties, such as Los Angeles County, may make up to $100,000 annually. Appraisers employed in the private sector tend to earn higher incomes than those in the public sector.

According to a recent survey by *Appraisal Today,* the average annual income of all appraisers is $58,132. Salaries range from $12,500 to $225,000.

The average fee for appraisal of a standard residential property is about $300, but fees can range from $75 for a re-inspection of new construction or repairs to $600 for inspection of a small residential income property.

According to the U.S. Department of Labor, real estate appraisers and assessors earned a median salary of $44,460 in 2006. The lowest paid 10 percent earned $24,000 or less per year on average, while the highest paid earned $86,140 or more.

Earnings at any level are enhanced by higher education and professional designations. Fringe benefits for both public and private employees usually include paid vacations and health insurance.

WORK ENVIRONMENT

Appraisers and assessors have a variety of working conditions, from the comfortable offices where they write and edit appraisal reports to outdoor construction sites, which they visit in both the heat of summer and the bitter cold of winter. Many appraisers spend mornings at their desks and afternoons in the field. Experienced appraisers may need to travel out of state.

Appraisers and assessors who work for a government agency or financial institution usually work 40-hour weeks, with overtime when necessary. Independent appraisers often can set their own schedules.

Appraisal is a very people-oriented occupation. Appraisers must be unfailingly cordial, and they have to deal calmly and tactfully with people who challenge their decisions (and are usually angry). Appraising can be a high-stress occupation because a considerable amount of money and important personal decisions ride on appraisers' calculations.

OUTLOOK

The U.S. Department of Labor estimates that employment of assessors and appraisers will grow faster than the average for all occupations through 2016 due to increases in real estate sales. In general, assessors work in a fairly secure field. As long as governments levy property taxes, assessors will be needed to provide them with information. The real estate industry, how-

ever, is influenced dramatically by the overall health of the economy, so appraisers in real estate can expect to benefit during periods of growth and experience slowdowns during recessions and depressions. Appraisers will also be hired to assist with probate cases, foreclosures, litigation claims, divorce settlements, and business valuations.

FOR MORE INFORMATION

For information on education and professional designations, contact

American Society of Appraisers
555 Herndon Parkway, Suite 125
Herndon, VA 20170-5250
Tel: 703-478-2228
Email: asainfo@appraisers.org
http://www.appraisers.org

Visit this organization's Web site for a listing of state real estate appraiser regulatory boards.

The Appraisal Foundation
1155 15th Street, NW, Suite 1111
Washington, DC 20005-2706
Tel: 202-347-7722
Email: info@appraisalfoundation.org
http://www.appraisalfoundation.org

For information on professional designations, education, careers, and scholarships, contact

Appraisal Institute
550 West Van Buren Street, Suite 1000
Chicago, IL 60607-3805
Tel: 312-335-4100
http://www.appraisalinstitute.org

For information on professional designations, education, and publications, contact

International Association of Assessing Officers
314 West 10th Street
Kansas City, MO 64105-1616
Tel: 816-701-8100
http://www.iaao.org

For information on education and appraisal careers, contact

National Association of Independent Fee Appraisers
401 North Michigan Avenue, Suite 2200
Chicago, IL 60611-4245
Tel: 312-321-6830
Email: info@naifa.com
http://www.naifa.com

For information on jewelry appraising, contact
National Association of Jewelry Appraisers
PO Box 18
Rego Park, NY 11374-0018
http://www.najaappraisers.com

AUTOMOBILE SERVICE TECHNICIANS

OVERVIEW

Automobile service technicians maintain and repair cars, vans, small trucks, and other vehicles. Using both hand tools and specialized diagnostic test equipment, they pinpoint problems and make the necessary repairs or adjustments. In addition to performing complex and difficult repairs, technicians perform a number of routine maintenance procedures, such as oil changes, tire rotation, and battery replacement. Technicians interact frequently with customers to explain repair procedures and discuss maintenance needs. Approximately 773,000 automotive service technicians work in the United States.

THE JOB

Many automobile service technicians feel that the most exciting part of their work is troubleshooting—locating the source of a problem and successfully fixing it. Diagnosing mechanical, electrical, and computer-related troubles requires a broad knowledge of how cars work, the ability to make accurate observations, and the patience to logically determine what went wrong. Technicians agree that it frequently is more difficult to find the problem than it is to fix it. With experience, knowing where to look for problems becomes second nature.

Generally, there are two types of automobile service technicians: *generalists* and *specialists*. Generalists work under a broad umbrella of repair and service duties. They have proficiency in several kinds of light repairs and maintenance of many different types of automobiles. Their work, for the most part, is routine and basic. Specialists concentrate in one or two areas and learn to master them for many different car makes and models. Today, in light of the sophisticated technology common in new cars, there is an increasing demand for specialists. Automotive systems are not as easy or as standard as they used to be, and they now require many hours of experience to master. To gain a broad knowledge in auto maintenance and repair, specialists usually begin as generalists.

When a car does not operate properly, the owner brings it to a service technician and describes the problem. At a dealership or larger shop, the customer may talk with a *repair service estimator,* who writes down the customer's description of the problem and relays it to the service technician. The technician may test-drive the car or use diagnostic equipment, such as motor analyzers, spark plug testers, or compression gauges, to determine the problem. If a customer explains that the car's automatic transmission does not shift gears at the right times, the technician must know how the functioning of the transmission depends on the engine vacuum, the throttle pressure, and—more common in newer cars—the onboard computer. Each factor must be thoroughly checked. With each test, clues help the technician pinpoint the cause of the malfunction. After successfully diagnosing the problem, the technician makes the necessary adjustments or repairs. If a part is too badly damaged or worn to be repaired, he or she replaces it after first consulting the car owner, explaining the problem, and estimating the cost.

Normal use of an automobile inevitably causes wear and deterioration of parts. Generalist automobile technicians handle many of the routine maintenance tasks to help keep a car in optimal operating condition. They change oil, lubricate parts, and adjust or replace components of any of the car's systems that might cause a malfunction, including belts, hoses, spark plugs, brakes, filters, and transmission and coolant fluids.

SCHOOL SUBJECTS
Business, Technical/Shop

PERSONAL SKILLS
Mechanical/Manipulative, Technical/Scientific

MINIMUM EDUCATION LEVEL
High School Diploma

CERTIFICATION OR LICENSING
Recommended

WORK ENVIRONMENT
Primarily Indoors, Primarily One Location

Technicians who specialize in the service of specific parts usually work in large shops with multiple departments, car diagnostic centers, franchised auto service shops, or small independent shops that concentrate on a particular type of repair work.

Tune-up technicians evaluate and correct engine performance and fuel economy. They use diagnostic equipment and other computerized devices to locate malfunctions in fuel, ignition, and emissions-control systems. They adjust ignition timing and valves and may replace spark plugs, points, triggering assemblies in electronic ignitions, and other components to ensure maximum engine efficiency.

Electrical-systems technicians have been in healthy demand in recent years. They service and repair the complex electrical and computer circuitry common in today's automobile. They use both sophisticated diagnostic equipment and simpler devices such as ammeters, ohmmeters, and voltmeters to locate system malfunctions. As well as possessing excellent electrical skills, electrical-systems technicians require basic mechanical aptitude to get at electrical and computer circuitry located throughout the automobile.

Front-end technicians are concerned with suspension and steering systems. They inspect, repair, and replace front-end parts such as springs, shock absorbers, and linkage parts such as tie rods and ball joints. They also align and balance wheels.

Brake repairers work on drum and disk braking systems, parking brakes, and their hydraulic systems. They inspect, adjust, remove, repair, and reinstall such items as brake shoes, disk pads, drums, rotors, wheel and master cylinders, and hydraulic fluid lines. Some specialize in both brake and front-end work.

Transmission technicians adjust, repair, and maintain gear trains, couplings, hydraulic pumps, valve bodies, clutch assemblies, and other parts of automatic transmission systems. Transmissions have become complex and highly sophisticated mechanisms in newer model automobiles. Technicians require special training to learn how they function.

Automobile-radiator mechanics clean radiators using caustic solutions. They locate and solder leaks and install new radiator cores. In addition, some radiator mechanics repair car heaters and air conditioners and solder leaks in gas tanks.

Alternative fuel technicians are relatively new additions to the field. This specialty has evolved with the nation's efforts to reduce its dependence on foreign oil by exploring alternative fuels, such as ethanol, biobutanol, and electricity.

As more automobiles rely on a variety of electronic components, technicians have become more proficient in the basics of electronics, even if they are not electronics specialists. Electronic controls and instruments are located in nearly all the systems of today's cars. Many previously mechanical functions in automobiles are being replaced by electronics, significantly altering the way repairs are performed. Diagnosing and correcting problems with electronic components often involves the use of specialty tools and computers.

Automobile service technicians use an array of tools in their everyday work, ranging from simple hand tools to computerized diagnostic equipment. Technicians supply their own hand tools at an investment of $6,000 to $25,000 or more, depending on their specialty. It is usually the employer's responsibility to furnish the larger power tools, engine analyzers, and other test equipment.

To maintain and increase their skills and to keep up with new technology, automobile technicians must regularly read service and repair manuals, shop bulletins, and other publications. They must also be willing to take part in training programs given by manufacturers or at vocational schools. Those who have voluntary certification must periodically retake exams to keep their credentials.

REQUIREMENTS
High School

In today's competitive job market, aspiring automobile service technicians need a high school diploma to land a job that offers growth possibilities, a good salary, and challenges. There is a big demand in the automotive service industry to fill entry-level positions with well-trained, highly skilled persons. Technology demands more from the technician than it did 10 years ago.

In high school, you should take automotive and shop classes, mathematics, English, and computer classes. Adjustments and repairs to many car components require the technician to make numerous computations, for which good mathematical skills are essential. Good reading skills are also valuable, as a technician must do a lot of reading to stay competitive in today's job market. English classes will prepare you to handle the many volumes of repair manuals and trade journals you will need to remain informed. Computer skills are also vital, as computers are now common in most repair shops. They keep track of customers' histories and parts and often detail repair procedures. Use of computers in repair shops will only increase in the future.

Postsecondary Training

Employers today prefer to hire only those who have completed some kind of formal training program in automobile mechanics—usually a minimum of two years. A wide variety of such programs are offered at community colleges, vocational schools, independent organizations, and manufacturers. Many community colleges and vocational schools around the country offer accredited postsecondary education. These programs are accredited by the National Automotive Technicians Education Foundation and the Accrediting Commission of Career Schools and Colleges of Technology. Postsecondary training programs prepare students through a blend of classroom instruction and hands-on practical experience. They range in length from six months to two years or more, depending on the type of program. Shorter programs usually involve intensive study. Longer programs typically alternate classroom courses with periods of work experience. Some two-year programs include courses on applied mathematics, reading and writing skills, and business practices and lead to an associate's degree.

Some programs are conducted in association with automobile manufacturers. Students combine work experience with hands-on classroom study of up-to-date equipment and new cars provided by manufacturers. In other programs, students alternate time in the classroom with internships in dealerships or service departments. These students may take up to four years to finish their training, but they become familiar with the latest technology and also earn a modest salary.

Certification or Licensing

Automobile service technicians may be certified by the ASE in one of the following eight areas—automatic transmission/transaxle, brakes, electrical/electronic systems, engine performance, engine repair, heating and air conditioning, manual drive train and axles, and suspension and steering. Those who become certified in all eight areas are known as master mechanics. Although certification is voluntary, it is a widely recognized standard of achievement for automobile technicians and is highly valued by many employers. Certification also provides the means and opportunity to advance. To maintain their certification, technicians must retake the examination for their specialties every five years. Many employers only hire ASE-accredited technicians and base salaries on the level of the technicians' accreditation.

Other Requirements

To be a successful automobile service technician, you must be patient and thorough in your work; a shoddy repair job may put the driver's life at risk. You must have excellent troubleshooting skills and be able to logically deduce the cause of system malfunctions.

EXPLORING

Many community centers offer general auto maintenance and mechanics workshops where you can practice working on real cars and learn from instructors. Trade magazines are excellent sources for learning what's new in the industry and can be found at most public libraries or large bookstores. Many public television stations broadcast automobile maintenance and repair programs that can be of help to beginners to see how various types of cars differ.

Working on cars as a hobby provides valuable first-hand experience in the work of a technician. An after-school or weekend part-time job in a repair shop or dealership can give you a feel for the general atmosphere and kinds of problems technicians face on the job. Oil and tire changes, battery and belt replacement, and even pumping gas may be some of the things you will be asked to do on the job; this work will give you valuable experience before you move on to more complex repairs. Experience with vehicle repair work in the armed forces is another way to pursue your interest in this field.

EMPLOYERS

Approximately 773,000 automotive service technicians are employed in the United States. Because the automotive industry is so vast, automobile service technicians have many choices concerning type of shop and geographic location. Automobile repairs are needed all over the country, in large cities as well as rural areas.

The majority of automobile service technicians work for automotive dealers and independent automotive repair shops and gasoline service stations. The field offers a variety of other employment options as well. The U.S. Department of Labor estimates that nearly 17 percent of automobile service technicians are self-employed. Other employers include franchises such as PepBoys and Midas that offer routine repairs and maintenance, and automotive service departments of automotive and home supply stores. Some automobile service technicians maintain fleets for taxicab and automobile leasing companies or for government agencies with large automobile fleets.

Technicians with experience and/or ASE certification certainly have more career choices. Some master mechanics may go on to teach at technical and vocational schools or at community colleges. Others put in many years working for someone else and go into business for themselves after they have gained the experience to handle many types of repairs and oversee other technicians.

STARTING OUT

The best way to start out in this field is to attend one of the many postsecondary training programs available throughout the country. Trade and technical schools usually provide job placement assistance for their graduates. Schools often have contacts with local employers who need to hire well-trained people. Frequently, employers post job openings at nearby trade schools with accredited programs. Job openings are frequently listed on the Internet through regional and national automotive associations or career networks.

A decreasing number of technicians learn the trade on the job as apprentices. Their training consists of working for several years under the guidance of experienced mechanics. Fewer employers today are willing to hire apprentices due to the time and money it takes to train them. Those who do learn their skills on the job will inevitably require some formal training if they wish to advance and stay in step with the changing industry.

Intern programs sponsored by car manufacturers or independent organizations provide students with excellent opportunities to actually work with prospective employers. Internships can provide students with valuable contacts who will be able to recommend future employers once they have completed their training. Many students may even be hired by the shop at which they interned.

ADVANCEMENT

With today's complex automobile components requiring hundreds of hours of study and practice to master, more repair shops prefer to hire specialists. Generalist automobile technicians advance as they gain experience and become specialists. Other technicians advance to diesel repair, where the pay may be higher. Those with good communications and planning skills may advance to shop foreman or service manager at large repair shops or to sales workers at dealerships. Master mechanics with good business skills often go into business for themselves and open their own shops.

EARNINGS

Salary ranges of automobile service technicians vary depending on the level of experience, type of shop the technician works in, and geographic location. Generally, technicians who work in small-town, family-owned gas stations earn less than those who work at dealerships and franchises in metropolitan areas.

According to the U.S. Department of Labor, automobile service technicians had median annual salaries of $33,780 ($16.24 an hour) in 2006. The lowest paid 10 percent made less than $19,070 ($9.17 an hour), and the highest paid 10 percent made more than $56,620 ($27.22 an hour). Since most technicians are paid on an hourly basis and frequently work overtime, their salaries can vary significantly. In many repair shops and dealerships, technicians can earn higher incomes by working on commission. Master technicians who work on commission can earn more than $100,000 annually. Employers often guarantee a minimum level of pay in addition to commissions.

Benefit packages vary from business to business. Most technicians receive health insurance and paid vacation days. Additional benefits may include dental, life, and disability insurance and a pension plan. Employers usually pay for a technician's work clothes and may pay a percentage on hand tools purchased. An increasing number of employers pay for all or most of an employee's certification training, if he or she passes the test. A technician's salary can increase through yearly bonuses or profit sharing if the business does well.

WORK ENVIRONMENT

Depending on the size of the shop and whether it's an independent or franchised repair shop, dealership, or private business, automobile technicians work with anywhere from two to 20 other technicians. Most shops are well lighted and well ventilated. They can frequently be noisy with running cars and power tools. Minor hand and back injuries are the most common problems of technicians. When reaching in hard-to-get-at places or loosening tight bolts, technicians often bruise, cut, or burn their hands. With caution and experience most technicians learn to avoid hand injuries. Working for long periods of time in cramped or bent positions often results in a stiff back or neck. Technicians also lift many heavy objects that can cause injury if not handled carefully; however, this is becoming less of a problem with new cars, as automakers design smaller and lighter parts to improve fuel economy. Some technicians may experience allergic reactions to solvents and oils used in cleaning, maintenance, and repair. Shops must comply with strict safety procedures set by the Occupational Safety and Health Administration and Environmental Protection Agency to help employees avoid accidents and injuries.

The U.S. Department of Labor reports that most technicians work a standard 40-hour week, but 30 percent of all technicians work more than 40 hours a week. Some technicians make emergency repairs to stranded automobiles on the roadside during odd hours.

OUTLOOK

With an estimated 221 million vehicles in operation today, automobile service technicians should feel confident that a good percentage will require servicing and repair. Skilled and highly trained technicians will be in particular demand. Less-skilled workers will face tough competition. The U.S. Department of Labor predicts that this field will grow faster than the average for all occupations through 2016. According to the ASE, even if school enrollments were at maximum capacity, the demand for automobile service technicians still would exceed the supply in the immediate future. As a result, many shops are beginning to recruit employees while they are still in vocational or even high school.

Another concern for the industry is the automobile industry's trend toward developing the "maintenance-free" car. Manufacturers are producing high-end cars that require no servicing for their first 100,000 miles. In addition, many new cars are equipped with on-board diagnostics that detect both wear and failure for many of the car's components, eliminating the need for technicians to perform extensive diagnostic tests. Also, parts that are replaced before they completely wear out prevent further damage from occurring to connected parts that are affected by a malfunction or breakdown. Although this will reduce troubleshooting time and the number of overall repairs, the components that need repair will be more costly and require a more experienced (and hence, more expensive) technician.

Most new jobs for technicians will be at independent service dealers, specialty shops, and franchised new car dealers. Because of the increase of specialty shops, fewer gasoline service stations will hire technicians, and many will eliminate repair services completely. Other opportunities will be available at companies or institutions with private fleets (e.g., cab, delivery, and rental companies, and government agencies and police departments).

FOR MORE INFORMATION

For information on accredited training programs, contact
Accrediting Commission of Career Schools and Colleges of Technology
2101 Wilson Boulevard, Suite 302
Arlington, VA 22201-3062
Tel: 703-247-4212
Email: info@accsct.org
http://www.accsct.org

For more information on the automotive service industry, contact
Automotive Aftermarket Industry Association
7101 Wisconsin Avenue, Suite 1300
Bethesda, MD 20814-3415
Tel: 301-654-6664
Email: aaia@aftermarket.org
http://www.aftermarket.org

For industry information and job listings, contact
Automotive Service Association
PO Box 929
Bedford, TX 76095-0929
Tel: 800-272-7467
Email: asainfo@asashop.org
http://www.asashop.org

For information and statistics on automotive dealers, contact
National Automobile Dealers Association
8400 Westpark Drive
McLean, VA 22102-5116
Tel: 800-252-6232
Email: nadainfo@nada.org
http://www.nada.org

For information on certified educational programs, careers, and certification, contact
National Automotive Technicians Education Foundation
101 Blue Seal Drive, Suite 101
Leesburg, VA 20175-5646
Tel: 703-669-6650
http://www.natef.org

For information on certification, contact
National Institute for Automotive Service Excellence
101 Blue Seal Drive, SE, Suite 101
Leesburg, VA 20175-5646
Tel: 703-669-6600
http://www.asecert.org

BIOCHEMISTS

OVERVIEW

Biochemists explore the tiny world of the cell, study how illnesses develop, and search for ways to improve life on earth. Through studying the chemical makeup of living organisms, biochemists strive to understand the dynamics of life, from the secrets of cell-to-cell communication to the chemical changes in our brains that give us memories. Biochemists examine the chemical combinations and reactions involved in such functions as growth, metabolism, reproduction, and heredity. They also study the effect of environment on living tissue. If cancer is to be cured, the earth's pollution cleaned up, or the aging process slowed, it will be biochemists and molecular biologists who will lead the way.

The science of biophysics is the study of biological systems and biological occurrences using the principles of physics and chemistry, along with mathematical methods. Scientists working in this field are referred to as *biophysicists*. There are approximately 20,000 biochemists and biophysicists employed in the United States.

THE JOB

Depending on their education level and area of specialty, biochemists can do many types of work for a variety of employers. For instance, a biochemist could do basic research for a federal government agency or for individual states with laboratories that employ skilled persons to analyze food, drug, air, water, waste, or animal tissue samples. A biochemist might work for a drug company as part of a basic research team searching for the cause of diseases or conduct applied research to develop drugs to cure disease. A biochemist might work in a biotechnology company focusing on the environment, energy, human health care, agriculture, or animal health. There, he or she might do research or quality control, or work on manufacturing/production or information systems. Another possibility is for the biochemist to specialize in an additional area, such as law, business, or journalism, and use his or her biochemistry or molecular biology background for a career that combines science with regulatory affairs, management, writing, or teaching.

Ph.D. scientists who enter the highest levels of academic life combine teaching and research. In addition to teaching in university classrooms and laboratories, they also do basic research designed to increase biochemistry and molecular biology knowledge. As Ph.D. scientists, these professionals could also work for an industry or government laboratory doing basic research or research and development (R&D). The problems studied, research styles, and type of organization vary widely across different laboratories. The Ph.D. scientist may lead a research group or be part of a small team of Ph.D. researchers. Other Ph.D. scientists might opt for administrative positions. In government, for example, these scientists might lead programs concerned with the safety of new devices, food, drugs, or pesticides and

SCHOOL SUBJECTS
Biology, Chemistry

PERSONAL SKILLS
Mechanical/Manipulative, Technical/Scientific

MINIMUM EDUCATION LEVEL
Bachelor's Degree

CERTIFICATION OR LICENSING
Required in Certain Positions

WORK ENVIRONMENT
Primarily Indoors, Primarily One Location

other chemicals. Or they might influence which projects will get federal funding.

Generally, biochemists employed in the United States work in one of three major fields: medicine, nutrition, or agriculture. In medicine, biochemists mass-produce life-saving chemicals usually found only in minuscule amounts in the body. Some of these chemicals have helped diabetics and heart attack victims for years. Biochemists employed in the field of medicine might work to identify chemical changes in organs or cells that signal the development of such diseases as cancer, diabetes, or schizophrenia. Or they may look for chemical explanations for why certain people develop muscular dystrophy or become obese. While studying chemical makeup and changes in these situations, biochemists may work to discover a treatment for or a way to prevent a disease. For instance, biochemists discovering how certain diseases such as AIDS and cancer escape detection by the immune system are also devising ways to enhance immunity to fight these diseases. Biochemists are also finding out the chemical basis of fertility and how to improve the success of in vitro fertilization to help couples have children or to preserve endangered species.

Biochemists in the pharmaceutical industry design, develop, and evaluate drugs, antibiotics, diagnostic kits, and other medical devices. They may search out ways to produce antibiotics, hormones, enzymes, or other drug components, or they may do quality control on the way in which drugs and dosages are made and determined.

In the field of nutrition, biochemists examine the effects of food on the body. For example, they might study the relationship between diet and diabetes.

Biochemists doing this study could look at the nutrition content of certain foods eaten by people with diabetes and study how these foods affect the functioning of the pancreas and other organs. Biochemists in the nutrition field also look at vitamin and mineral deficiencies and how they affect the human body. They examine these deficiencies in relation to body performance, and they may study anything from how the liver is affected by a lack of vitamin B to the effects of poor nutrition on the ability to learn.

Biochemists involved in agriculture undertake studies to discover more efficient methods of crop cultivation, storage, and pest control. For example, they might create genetically engineered crops that are more resistant to frost, drought, spoilage, disease, and pests. They might focus on helping to create fruit trees that produce more fruit by studying the biochemical composition of the plant and determining how to alter or select for this desirable trait. Biochemists may study the chemical composition of insects to determine better and more efficient methods of controlling the pest population and the damage they do to crops. Or they could work on programming bacteria to clean up the environment by "eating" toxic chemicals.

About seven out of 10 biochemists are engaged in basic research, often for a university medical school or nonprofit organization, such as a foundation or research institute. The remaining 30 percent do applied research, using the discoveries of basic research to solve practical problems or develop products. For example, a biochemist working in basic research may make a discovery about how a living organism forms hormones. This discovery will lead to a scientist doing applied research, making hormones in the laboratory, and eventually to mass production. Discoveries made in DNA research have led to techniques for identifying criminals from a single strand of hair or a tiny blood stain left at the scene of a crime. The distinction between basic and applied research is one of degree, however; biochemists often engage in both types of work.

Biochemistry requires skillful use of a wide range of sophisticated analytical equipment and application of newly discovered techniques requiring special instruments or new chemical reagents. Sometimes, biochemists themselves must invent and test new instruments if existing methods and equipment do not meet their needs. Biochemists must also be patient, methodical, and careful in their laboratory procedures.

The work of biophysicists varies according to their industry, though most falls within the following categories: molecular structures—studying the functions of cells, tissues, and organisms and their structural makeup and behavior; biophysical techniques—researching various methods for gaining information about biological systems, such as lasers, heat, or other analytical methods; or biophysical mechanisms—researching and developing detailed models to help visualize and explain biological processes.

Biophysicists can find employment in many different environments including private or government funded laboratories, pharmaceutical companies, universities, and medical centers. Pharmaceutical companies, such as Gilead or Abbott Laboratories, may hire biophysicists as part of a team to conduct research and models on how different strains of bacteria affect healthy cells in animals. Such work is necessary and vital to help design and produce antibacterial vaccines and drugs effective in combating human illnesses ranging from uterine tract infections to influenza. Other biophysicists in governmental laboratories and agencies, for example the Centers for Disease Control and Prevention, may conduct research, collect data, and make observations regarding the molecular basis of diseases as compared to healthy cells. Such experiments give us more information on how to diagnose and treat diseases and conditions such as Alzheimer's, HIV/AIDS, or autism.

Biophysicists use different tools and methods to conduct their research including computers for data collection and analysis, highly specialized X rays, centrifuges, and electromagnetic radiation.

REQUIREMENTS

Although they usually specialize in one of many areas in the field, biochemists and biophysicists should also be familiar with several scientific disciplines, including chemistry, physics, mathematics, and computer science. High school classes can provide the foundation for getting this knowledge, while four years of college expands it, and postgraduate work directs students to explore specific areas more deeply. The following describes possible strategies at each level and includes a community college option.

High School

If you have an interest in biochemistry or biophysics as a high school student, you should take at least one year each of biology, chemistry, physics, algebra, geometry, and trigonometry. Introductory calculus is also a good idea. Because scientists must clearly and accurately communicate their results verbally and in writing, English courses that emphasize writing skills are strongly recommended. Many colleges and universities also require several years of a foreign language, a useful skill today, as scientists frequently exchange information with researchers from other countries.

Postsecondary Training

Some biochemistry programs have their own special requirements for admission, so you should do a little research and take any special courses you need for the college that interests you. Also, check the catalogs of colleges and universities to see if they offer a program in biochemistry or related sciences. Some schools award a bachelor's degree in biochemistry, and nearly all colleges and universities offer a major in biology or chemistry.

To best prepare yourself for a career in biochemistry or molecular biology, you should start by earning a bachelor's degree in either of these two areas. Even if your college does not offer a specific program in biochemistry or molecular biology, you can get comparable training by doing one of two things: (1) working toward a bachelor's degree in chemistry and taking courses in biology, molecular genetics, and biochemistry, including a biochemistry laboratory class, or (2) earning a bachelor's degree in biology, but taking more chemistry, mathematics, and physics courses than the biology major may require, and also choosing a biochemistry course that has lab work with it.

It really doesn't matter if you earn a bachelor of science or a bachelor of arts degree; some schools offer both. It is more important to choose your courses thoughtfully and to get advice in your freshman year from a faculty member who knows about the fields of biochemistry and molecular biology.

Only a few colleges offer degree programs in biophysics. Most students prepare for the field by earning a degree in physics, chemistry, or mathematics with supplementary courses in biology. Students who plan to pursue an advanced education typically earn degrees in the physical sciences or mathematics. According to the Biophysics Society, an ideal educational program would include classes in biology (introductory biology, cell biology, molecular biology, and genetics), physics (mechanics, electricity and magnetism, optics, and atomic and molecular physics), chemistry (general chemistry, organic chemistry, and physical chemistry), and mathematics (calculus, differential equations, linear algebra, numerical analysis and statistics, and computer programming). Students should also take courses in the humanities and social sciences to ensure that they achieve a well-rounded education.

Many careers in biochemistry and biophysics, especially those that involve teaching at a college or directing scientific research at a university, a government laboratory, or a commercial company, require at least a master's degree and preferably a doctorate or Ph.D. degree. Because biochemistry and biophysics are so broad-based, you can enter their graduate programs from such diverse fields as physics, psychology, nutrition, microbiology, or engineering. Graduate schools prefer students with laboratory or research experience.

However you get there, a graduate education program is intense. A master's degree requires about a year of course work and often a research project as well. For a Ph.D. degree, full-time course work can last up to two years, followed by one or more special test exams. But the most important part of Ph.D. training is the requirement for all students to conduct an extensive research project leading to significant new scientific findings. Most students work under a faculty member's direction. This training is vital, as it will help you develop the skills to frame scientific questions and discover ways to answer them. It will also teach you important laboratory skills useful in tackling other biochemical and biophysical problems. Most students complete a Ph.D. program in four or five years.

The Biophysical Society offers a list of graduate programs in biophysics at its Web site, http://www.biophysics.org.

Certification or Licensing

Biochemists who wish to work in a hospital may need certification by a national certifying board such as the American Board of Clinical Chemistry.

Other Requirements

A scientist never stops learning, even when formal education has ended. This is particularly true for biochemists and biophysicists because constant breakthroughs and technology advances make for a constantly changing work environment. That is why most Ph.D.'s go for more research experience (postdoctoral research) before they enter the workplace. As a "postdoc," you would not take course work, earn a degree, or teach; you would likely work full-time on a high-level research project in the laboratory of an established scientist. Typically, this postdoctoral period lasts two to three years, during which time you would get a salary or be supported by a fellowship. Though not essential for many industry research jobs, postdoctoral research is generally expected of those wishing to become professors. Also, because biochemistry, biophysics, and medicine are such allies, some Ph.D. recipients also earn their medical degrees, or M.D.'s, as a physician does. This is to get the broadest possible base for a career in medical research.

EXPLORING

The analytical, specialized nature of biochemistry and biophysics makes it unlikely that you will gain much exposure to these disciplines before college. Many high school chemistry, physics, and biology courses, however, allow students to work with laboratory tools and techniques that will give them a valuable background before college. In some cases, high school students can take advantage of opportunities to train as laboratory technicians by taking courses at a community college. You might also want to contact local colleges, universities, or laboratories to set up interviews with biochemists and biophysicists to learn as much as you can about these fields. In addition, reading science and medical magazines will help you to stay current with recent breakthroughs in the biochemistry and biophysics fields.

Students who are interested in learning more about biophysics should visit the Biophysical Society's Web site, http://www.biophysics.org/careers, which offers career information, profiles of workers in the field, a discussion of current research topics, and other resources.

EMPLOYERS

There are approximately 20,000 biochemists and biophysicists employed in the United States. Government agencies at the federal, state, and local levels employ nearly four out of every 10 biological scientists. Some major governmental employers of biochemists and biophysicists include the National Institutes of Health, the Departments of Agriculture and Defense, the National Aeronautics and Space Administration, and national laboratories. At such agencies these scientists may do basic research and analyze food, drug, air, water, waste, or animal tissue samples. Biochemists and biophysicists also work for university medical schools or nonprofit organizations, such as a foundation or research institute, doing basic research. Drug companies employ biochemists and biophysicists to search for the causes of diseases or develop drugs to cure them. Biochemists and biophysicists work in quality control, research, manufacturing/production, or information systems at biotechnology companies that concentrate on the environment, energy, human health care, agriculture, or animal health. Universities hire biochemists and biophysicists to teach in combination with doing research.

STARTING OUT

A bachelor's degree in biochemistry, molecular biology, or biophysics can help you get into medical, dental, veterinary, law, or business school. It can also be a stepping-stone to a career in many different but related fields: biotechnology, toxicology, biomedical engineering, clinical chemistry, plant pathology, animal science, or other fields. Biochemists and biophysicists fresh from a college undergraduate program can take advantage of opportunities to get valuable on-the-job experience in a biochemistry or biophysics laboratory. The National Science Foundation and the National Institutes of Health, both federal government agencies, sponsor research programs for undergraduates. Groups who can particularly benefit from these programs include women, Hispanic Americans, African Americans, Native Americans, Native Alaskans, and students with disabilities. Your college or university may also offer senior research projects that provide hands-on experience.

Another way to improve your chances of getting a job is to spend an additional year at a university with training programs for specialized laboratory techniques. Researchers and companies like these "certificate programs" because they teach valuable skills related to cell culture, genetic engineering, recombinant DNA technology, biotechnology, in vitro cell biology, protein engineering, or DNA sequencing and synthesis. In some universities, you can work toward a bachelor's degree and a certificate at the same time.

Biochemists and biophysicists with bachelor's degrees usually begin work in industry or government as research assistants doing testing and analysis. In the drug industry, for example, you might analyze the ingredients of a product to verify and maintain its quality. Biochemists and biophysicists with master's degrees may enter the field in management, marketing, or sales positions, whereas those with doctorates usually go into basic or applied research. Many Ph.D. graduates work at colleges and universities where the emphasis is on teaching.

ADVANCEMENT

The more education you have, the greater your reward potential. Biochemists and biophysicists with a graduate degree have more opportunities for advancement than those with only an undergraduate degree. It is not uncommon for students to go back to graduate school after working for a while in a job that required a lesser degree. Some graduate students become research or teaching assistants in colleges and universities, qualifying for professorships when they receive their advanced degrees. Having a doctorate allows you to design research initiatives and direct others in carrying out experiments. Experienced biochemists and biophysicists with doctorates can move up to high-level administrative positions and supervise entire research programs. Other highly qualified biochemists and biophysicists who prefer to devote themselves to research often become leaders in a particular aspect of their profession.

EARNINGS

According to a report by the National Association of Colleges and Employers, beginning salaries in 2007 for graduates with bachelor's degrees in biological and life sciences averaged $34,953 per year.

The U.S. Department of Labor reports that biochemists and biophysicists had average annual incomes of $76,320 in 2006. Salaries ranged from less than $40,820 to more than $129,510 per year.

Colleges and universities also employ many biochemists as professors and researchers. The U.S. Department of Labor reports that in 2006 postsecondary chemistry teachers had median salaries of $61,220; biological science teachers, $69,210; and physics professors, $68,170.

Biochemists and biophysicists who work for universities, the government, or industry all tend to receive good benefits packages, such as health and life insurance, pension plans, and paid vacation and sick leave. Those employed as university faculty operate on the academic calendar, which means that they can get summer and winter breaks from teaching classes.

WORK ENVIRONMENT

Biochemists and biophysicists generally work in clean, quiet, and well-lighted laboratories where physical labor is minimal. They must, however, take the proper precautions in handling chemicals and organic substances that could be dangerous or cause illness. They may work with plants and animals; their tissues, cells, and products; and with yeast and bacteria.

Biochemists and biophysicists in industry generally work a 40-hour week, although they, like their counterparts in research, often put in many extra hours. They must be ready to spend a considerable amount of time keeping up with current literature, for example. Many biochemists and biophysicists occasionally travel to attend meetings or conferences. Those in research write papers for presentation at meetings or for publication in scientific journals.

Individuals interested in biochemistry or biophysics must have the patience to work for long periods of time on a project without necessarily getting the desired results. Both disciplines are often a team affair, requiring an ability to work well and cooperate with others. Successful biochemists and biophysicists are continually learning and increasing their skills.

OUTLOOK

Employment for biological scientists, including biochemists and biophysicists, is expected to grow faster than the average for all occupations through 2016, according to the U.S. Department of Labor. Competition will be strong for basic research positions, and candidates with more education and the experience it brings will be more likely to find the positions they want. Employment is available in health-related fields, where the emphasis is on finding cures for such diseases as cancer, muscular dystrophy, HIV/AIDS, and Alzheimer's. Additional jobs will be created to produce genetically engineered drugs and other products in the new and rapidly expanding field of genetic engineering. In this area, the outlook is best for biochemists and biophysicists with advanced degrees who can conduct genetic and cellular research. A caveat exists, however. Employment growth may slow somewhat as the number of new biotechnology firms slows and existing firms merge. Biochemists and biophysicists with bachelor's degrees who have difficulty entering their chosen career field may find openings as technicians or technologists or may choose to transfer their skills to other biological science fields.

FOR MORE INFORMATION

For a copy of Partnerships in Health Care, *a brochure discussing clinical laboratory careers, and other information, contact*

American Association for Clinical Chemistry
1850 K Street, NW, Suite 625
Washington, DC 20006-2213
Tel: 800-892-1400
Email: info@aacc.org
http://www.aacc.org

For general information about chemistry careers and approved education programs, contact

American Chemical Society
1155 16th Street, NW
Washington, DC 20036-4801
Tel: 800-227-5558
Email: service@acs.org
http://www.chemistry.org

For information on careers in the biological sciences, contact

American Institute of Biological Sciences
1444 I Street, NW, Suite 200
Washington, DC 20005
Tel: 202-628-1500
Email: admin@aibs.org
http://www.aibs.org

For information on educational programs, contact
**American Society for Biochemistry and
    Molecular Biology**
Education Information
9650 Rockville Pike
Bethesda, MD 20814-3996
Tel: 301-530-7145
Email: asbmb@asbmb.faseb.org
http://www.asbmb.org

For career resources, contact
American Society for Investigative Pathology
9650 Rockville Pike
Bethesda, MD 20814-3993
Tel: 301-634-7130
Email: asip@asip.org
http://www.asip.org

*For information on biophysics and graduate programs in
the field, contact*
Biophysical Society
9650 Rockville Pike
Bethesda, MD 20814-3999
Tel: 301-634-7133
http://www.biophysics.org

BIOMEDICAL ENGINEERS

OVERVIEW

Biomedical engineers are highly trained scientists who use engineering and life science principles to research biological aspects of animal and human life. They develop new theories, and they modify, test, and prove existing theories on life systems. They design health care instruments and devices or apply engineering principles to the study of human systems. There are approximately 14,000 biomedical engineers employed in the United States.

THE JOB

Using engineering principles to solve medical and health-related problems, the biomedical engineer works closely with life scientists, members of the medical profession, and chemists. Most of the work revolves around the laboratory. There are three interrelated work areas: research, design, and teaching.

Biomedical research is multifaceted and broad in scope. It calls upon engineers to apply their knowledge of mechanical, chemical, and electrical engineering as well as anatomy and physiology in the study of living systems. Using computers, biomedical engineers use their knowledge of graphic and related technologies to develop mathematical models that simulate physiological systems.

In biomedical engineering design, medical instruments and devices are developed. Engineers work on artificial organs, ultrasonic imagery devices, cardiac pacemakers, and surgical lasers, for example. They design and build systems that will update hospital, laboratory, and clinical procedures. They also train health care personnel in the proper use of this new equipment.

Biomedical engineering is taught on the university level. Teachers conduct classes, advise students, serve on academic committees, and supervise or conduct research.

Within biomedical engineering, an individual may concentrate on a particular specialty area. Some of the well-established specialties are *bioinstrumentation, biomechanics, biomaterials, systems physiology, clinical engineering*, and *rehabilitation engineering*. These specialty areas frequently depend on one another.

Biomechanics is mechanics applied to biological or medical problems. Examples include the artificial heart, the artificial kidney, and the artificial hip. *Biomaterials* is the study of the optimal materials with which to construct such devices, *bioinstrumentation* is the science of measuring physiological functions. *Systems physiology* uses engineering strategies, techniques, and tools to gain a comprehensive and integrated understanding of living organisms ranging from bacteria to humans. Biomedical engineers in this specialty examine such things as the biochemistry of metabolism and the control of limb movements.

Rehabilitation engineering is a new and growing specialty area of biomedical engineering. Its goal is to expand the capabilities and improve the quality of life for individuals with physical impairments. Rehabilitation engineers often work directly with the disabled person and modify equipment for individual use.

REQUIREMENTS
High School

You can best prepare for a career as a biomedical engineer by taking courses in biology, chemistry, physics, mathematics, drafting, and computers. Communication and problem-solving skills are necessary, so classes in

English, writing, and logic are important. Participating in science clubs and competing in science fairs will give you the opportunity to design and invent systems and products.

Postsecondary Training

Most biomedical engineers have an undergraduate degree in biomedical engineering or a related field and a Ph.D. in some facet of biomedical engineering. Undergraduate study is roughly divided into halves. The first two years are devoted to theoretical subjects, such as abstract physics and differential equations in addition to the core curriculum most undergraduates take. The third and fourth years include more applied science. Worldwide, there are more than 80 colleges and universities that offer programs in biomedical engineering.

During graduate programs, students work on research or product development projects headed by faculty.

Certification or Licensing

Engineers whose work may affect the life, health, or safety of the public must be registered according to regulations in all 50 states and the District of Columbia. Applicants for registration must have received a degree from an American Board for Engineering and Technology–accredited engineering program and have four years of experience. They must also pass a written examination administered by the state in which they wish to work.

Other Requirements

You should have a strong commitment to learning if you plan on becoming a biomedical engineer. You should be scientifically inclined and be able to apply that knowledge in problem solving. Becoming a biomedical engineer requires long years of schooling because a biomedical engineer needs to be an expert in the fields of engineering and biology. Also, biomedical engineers have to be familiar with chemical, material, and electrical engineering as well as physiology and computers.

EXPLORING

Undergraduate courses offer a great deal of exposure to the field. Working in a hospital where biomedical engineers are employed can also provide you with insight into the field, as can interviews with practicing or retired bio-

---

SCHOOL SUBJECTS
Biology, Chemistry

PERSONAL SKILLS
Helping/Teaching, Technical/ Scientific

MINIMUM EDUCATION LEVEL
Bachelor's Degree

CERTIFICATION OR LICENSING
Voluntary

WORK ENVIRONMENT
Primarily Indoors, Primarily One Location

---

medical engineers. You can also read *Planning a Career in Biomedical Engineering*, which can be found at the Biomedical Engineering Society's Web site, http://www.bmes.org/careers.asp.

EMPLOYERS

There are approximately 14,000 biomedical engineers working in the United States. About 20 percent are employed in scientific research and development and 20 percent work in medical equipment and supplies manufacturing. In addition, many biomedical engineers are employed in hospitals and medical institutions, and in research and educational facilities. Employment opportunities also exist in government regulatory agencies.

STARTING OUT

A variety of routes may be taken to gain employment as a biomedical engineer. Recent graduates may use college placement services, or they may apply directly to employers, often to personnel offices in hospitals and industry. A job may be secured by answering an advertisement in the employment section of a newspaper. Information on job openings is also available at the local office of the U.S. Employment Service or by visiting http://www.usajobs.opm.gov.

ADVANCEMENT

Advancement opportunities are tied directly to educational and research background. In a nonteaching capacity, a biomedical engineer with an advanced degree can rise to a supervisory position. In teaching, a doctorate is usually necessary to become a full professor. By demonstrating excellence in research, teaching, and departmental committee involvement, one can move from instructor to assistant professor and then to full professor, department chair, or even dean.

Qualifying for and receiving research grant funding can also be a means of advancing one's career in both the nonteaching and teaching sectors.

EARNINGS

The amount a biomedical engineer earns is dependent upon education, experience, and type of employer. According to the U.S. Department of Labor, biomedical engineers had a median yearly income of $73,930 in 2006. At the low end of the pay scale, 10 percent earned less than $44,930 per year, and at the high end, 10 percent earned more than $116,330 annually.

According to a 2007 survey by the National Association of Colleges and Employers, the average beginning salary for biomedical engineers with bachelor's degrees was $51,356, while those with master's degrees started at $59,240.

Biomedical engineers can expect benefits from employers, including health insurance, paid vacation and sick days, and retirement plans.

WORK ENVIRONMENT

Biomedical engineers who teach in a university will have much student contact in the classroom, the laboratory, and the office. They also will be expected to serve on relevant committees while continuing their teaching, research, and writing responsibilities. As competition for teaching positions increases, the requirement that professors publish papers will increase. Professors usually are responsible for obtaining government or private research grants to support their work.

Those who work in industry and government have much contact with other professionals, including chemists, medical scientists, and doctors. They often work as part of a team, testing and developing new products. All biomedical engineers who do lab work are in clean, well-lighted environments, using sophisticated equipment.

OUTLOOK

It is expected that there will be a greater need for skilled biomedical engineers in the future. Prospects look particularly good in the health care industry, which will continue to grow rapidly, primarily because people are living longer and require better medical devices and equipment. The U.S. Department of Labor pre-

dicts that employment for biomedical engineers will increase much faster than the average for all occupations through 2016. New jobs will become available in biomedical research in prosthetics, pharmaceutical manufacturing and related industries, artificial internal organs, computer applications, and instrumentation and other medical systems. In addition, a demand will exist for professors to train the biomedical engineers needed to fill these positions.

Because of the increased demand for biomedical engineers, the number of degrees granted in the field has increased significantly. Graduates with a bachelor's degree will face stiff competition for entry-level jobs. Thus, people entering this field are strongly encouraged to pursue a graduate degree to increase their job prospects.

FOR MORE INFORMATION

For information on medical and biological engineering, contact

American Institute of Medical and Biological Engineering
1901 Pennsylvania Avenue, NW, Suite 401
Washington, DC 20006-3405
Tel: 202-496-9660
Email: info@aimbe.org
http://www.aimbe.org

For more information on careers in biomedical engineering, contact

American Society for Engineering Education
1818 N Street, NW, Suite 600
Washington, DC 20036-2479
Tel: 202-331-3500
http://www.asee.org

For information on careers, student chapters, and to read the brochure Planning a Career in Biomedical Engineering, *contact*

Biomedical Engineering Society
8401 Corporate Drive, Suite 140
Landover, MD 20785-2224
Tel: 301-459-1999
Email: info@bmes.org
http://www.bmes.org

For information on high school programs that provide opportunities to learn about engineering technology, contact JETS.

Junior Engineering Technical Society (JETS)
1420 King Street, Suite 405
Alexandria, VA 22314-2794

Tel: 703-548-5387
Email: info@jets.org
http://www.jets.org

For Canadian career information, contact
Canadian Medical and Biological Engineering Society
PO Box 51023
Orleans, ON K1E 3W4 Canada
Tel: 613-837-8649
Email: cmbes@magma.ca
http://www.cmbes.ca

Visit the following Web site for more information on educational programs, job listings, grants, and links to other biomedical engineering sites:
The Biomedical Engineering Network
http://www.bmenet.org

SCHOOL SUBJECTS
Biology, Technical/Shop

PERSONAL SKILLS
Mechanical/Manipulative, Technical/Scientific

MINIMUM EDUCATION LEVEL
Associate's Degree

CERTIFICATION OR LICENSING
Recommended

WORK ENVIRONMENT
Primarily Indoors, Primarily One Location

BIOMEDICAL EQUIPMENT TECHNICIANS

OVERVIEW

Biomedical equipment technicians handle the complex medical equipment and instruments found in hospitals, clinics, and research facilities. This equipment is used for medical therapy and diagnosis and includes heart-lung machines, artificial kidney machines, patient monitors, chemical analyzers, and other electrical, electronic, mechanical, or pneumatic devices.

Technicians' main duties are to inspect, maintain, repair, and install this equipment. They disassemble equipment to locate malfunctioning components, repair or replace defective parts, and reassemble the equipment, adjusting and calibrating it to ensure that it operates according to manufacturers' specifications. Other duties of biomedical equipment technicians include modifying equipment according to the directions of medical or supervisory personnel, arranging with equipment manufacturers for necessary equipment repair, and safety-testing equipment to ensure that patients, equipment operators, and other staff members are safe from electrical or mechanical hazards. Biomedical equipment technicians work with hand tools, power tools, measuring devices, and manufacturers' manuals.

Technicians may work for equipment manufacturers as salespeople or as service technicians, or for a health care facility specializing in the repair or maintenance of specific equipment, such as that used in radiology, nuclear medicine, or patient monitoring. In the United States, approximately 38,000 people work as biomedical equipment technicians.

THE JOB

Biomedical equipment technicians are an important link between technology and medicine. They repair, calibrate, maintain, and operate biomedical equipment working under the supervision of researchers, biomedical engineers, physicians, surgeons, and other professional health care providers.

Biomedical equipment technicians may work with thousands of different kinds of equipment. Some of the most frequently encountered are the following: patient monitors; heart-lung machines; kidney machines; blood-gas analyzers; spectrophotometers; X-ray units; radiation monitors; defibrillators; anesthesia apparatus; pacemakers; blood pressure transducers; spirometers; sterilizers; diathermy equipment; patient-care computers; ultrasound machines; and diagnostic scanning machines, such as the CT (computed tomography) scan machine, PET (positron emission tomography) scanner, and MRI (magnetic resonance imaging) machines.

Repairing faulty instruments is one of the chief functions of biomedical equipment technicians. They investigate equipment problems, determine the extent of malfunctions, make repairs on instruments that have had minor breakdowns, and expedite the repair of instruments with major breakdowns, for instance, by writing an analysis of the problem for the factory. In doing this work, technicians rely on manufacturers' diagrams, maintenance manuals, and standard and specialized test instruments, such as oscilloscopes and pressure gauges.

Installing equipment is another important function of biomedical equipment technicians. They inspect and test new equipment to make sure it complies with performance and safety standards as described in the manufacturer's manuals and diagrams, and as noted on the purchase order. Technicians may also check on proper installation of the equipment, or, in some cases, install it themselves. To ensure safe operations, technicians need a thorough knowledge of the regulations related to the proper grounding of equipment, and they need to actively carry out all steps and procedures to ensure safety.

Maintenance is the third major area of responsibility for biomedical equipment technicians. In doing this work, technicians try to catch problems before they become more serious. To this end, they take apart and reassemble devices, test circuits, clean and oil moving parts, and replace worn parts. They also keep complete records of all machine repairs, maintenance checks, and expenses.

In all three of these areas, a large part of technicians' work consists of consulting with physicians, administrators, engineers, and other related professionals. For example, they may be called upon to assist hospital administrators as they make decisions about the repair, replacement, or purchase of new equipment. They consult with medical and research staffs to determine that equipment is functioning safely and properly. They also consult with medical and engineering staffs when called upon to modify or develop equipment. In all of these activities, they use their knowledge of electronics, medical terminology, human anatomy and physiology, chemistry, and physics.

In addition, biomedical equipment technicians are involved in a range of other related duties. Some biomedical equipment technicians maintain inventories of all instruments in the hospital, their condition, location, and operators. They reorder parts and components, assist in providing people with emergency instruments, restore unsafe or defective instruments to working order, and check for safety regulation compliance.

Other biomedical equipment technicians help physicians, surgeons, nurses, and researchers conduct procedures and experiments. In addition, they must be able to explain to staff members how to operate these machines,

the conditions under which a certain apparatus may or may not be used, how to solve small operating problems, and how to monitor and maintain equipment.

In many hospitals, technicians are assigned to a particular service, such as pediatrics, surgery, or renal medicine. These technicians become specialists in certain types of equipment. However, unlike electrocardiograph technicians or dialysis technicians, who specialize in one kind of equipment, most biomedical equipment technicians must be thoroughly familiar with a large variety of instruments. They might be called upon to prepare an artificial kidney or to work with a blood-gas analyzer. Biomedical equipment technicians also maintain pulmonary function machines. These machines are used in clinics for ambulatory patients, hospital laboratories, departments of medicine for diagnosis and treatment, and rehabilitation of cardiopulmonary patients.

While most biomedical equipment technicians are trained in electronics technology, there is also a need for technicians trained in plastics to work on the development of artificial organs and for people trained in glass blowing to help make the precision parts for specialized equipment.

Many biomedical equipment technicians work for medical instrument manufacturers. These technicians consult and assist in the construction of new machinery, helping to make decisions concerning materials and construction methods to be used in the manufacture of the equipment.

REQUIREMENTS
High School

There are a number of classes you can take in high school to help you prepare for this work. Science classes, such as chemistry, biology, and physics, will give you the science background you will need for working in a medical environment. Take shop classes that deal with electronics, drafting, or blueprint reading. These classes will give you experience working with your hands, following printed directions, using electricity, and working with machinery. Mathematics classes will help you become comfortable working with numbers and formulas. Don't neglect your English studies. English classes will help you develop your communication skills, which will be important to have when you deal with a variety of different people in your professional life.

Postsecondary Training

To become qualified for this work, you will need to complete postsecondary education that leads either to an associate's degree from a two-year institution or a bachelor's degree from a four-year college or university. Most biomedical equipment technicians choose to receive an associate's degree. Biomedical equipment technology is a relatively new program in some schools and may also be referred to as *medical electronics technology* or *biomedical engineering technology*. No matter what the name of the program, however, you should expect to receive instruction in such areas as anatomy, physiology, electrical and electronic fundamentals, chemistry, physics, and biomedical equipment construction and design. In addition, you will study safety methods in health care facilities and medical equipment troubleshooting, as it will be your job to be the problem solver. You should also expect to continue taking communication or English classes since communications skills will be essential to your work. In addition to the classroom work, many programs often provide you with practical experience in repairing and servicing equipment in a clinical or laboratory setting under the supervision of an experienced equipment technician. In this way, you learn about electrical components and circuits, the design and construction of common pieces of machinery, and computer technology as it applies to biomedical equipment.

By studying various pieces of equipment, you learn a problem-solving technique that applies not only to the equipment studied, but also to equipment you have not yet seen, and even to equipment that has not yet been invented. Part of this problem-solving technique includes learning how and where to locate sources of information.

Some biomedical equipment technicians receive their training in the armed forces. During the course of an enlistment period of four years or less, military personnel can receive training that prepares them for entry-level or sometimes advanced-level positions in the civilian workforce.

A handful of schools that offer training in biomedical equipment technology are accredited by the Technology Accreditation Commission for the Accreditation Board for Engineering and Technology (http://www.abet.org).

Certification or Licensing

The Board of Examiners for Biomedical Equipment Technicians, which is affiliated with the Association for the Advancement of Medical Instrumentation (AAMI), maintains certification programs for biomedical equipment technicians. The following categories are available: biomedical equipment technician, radiology equipment specialist, and clinical laboratory equipment specialist. Contact the AAMI for more information. Although certification is not required for employment, it is highly recommended. Technicians with certification have demonstrated that they have attained an overall knowledge of the field and are dedicated to their profession. Many employers prefer to hire technicians who are certified.

Other Requirements

Biomedical equipment technicians need mechanical ability and should enjoy working with tools. Because this job demands quick decision-making and prompt repairs, technicians should work well under pressure. You should also be extremely precise and accurate in your work, have good communications skills, and enjoy helping others—an essential quality for anyone working in the health care industry.

EXPLORING

You will have difficulty gaining any direct experience in biomedical equipment technology until you are in a training program or working professionally. Your first hands-on opportunities generally come in the clinical and laboratory phases of your education. You can, however, visit school and community libraries to seek out books written about careers in medical technology. You can also join a hobby club devoted to chemistry, biology, radio equipment, or electronics.

Perhaps the best way to learn more about this job is to set up, with the help of teachers or guidance counselors, a visit to a local health care facility or to arrange for a biomedical technician to speak to interested students, either on site or at a career exploration seminar hosted by the school. You may be able to ask the technician about his or her educational background, what a day on the job is like, and what new technologies are on the horizon. Try to visit a school offering a program in biomedical equipment technology and discuss your career plans with an admissions counselor there. The counselor may also be able to provide you with helpful insights about the career and your preparation for it.

Finally, because this work involves the health care field, consider getting a part-time job or volunteering at a local hospital. Naturally, you won't be asked to work with the biomedical equipment, but you will have the opportunity to see professionals on the job and experience being in the medical environment. Even if your duty is only to escort patients to their tests, you may gain a greater understanding of this work.

EMPLOYERS

Approximately 38,000 biomedical equipment technicians are employed in the United States. Many schools place students in part-time hospital positions to help them gain practical experience. Students are often able to return to these hospitals for full-time employment after graduation. Other places of employment include research institutes and biomedical equipment manufacturers. Government hospitals and the military also employ biomedical equipment technicians.

STARTING OUT

Most schools offering programs in biomedical equipment technology work closely with local hospitals and industries, and school career services officers are usually informed about openings when they become available. In some cases, recruiters may visit a school periodically to conduct interviews. Also, many schools place students in part-time hospital jobs to help them gain practical experience. Students are often able to return to these hospitals for full-time employment after graduation.

Another effective method of finding employment is to write directly to hospitals, research institutes, or biomedical equipment manufacturers. Other good sources of leads for job openings include state employment offices and newspaper want ads.

ADVANCEMENT

With experience, biomedical equipment technicians can expect to work with less supervision, and in some cases they may find themselves supervising less-experienced technicians. They may advance to positions in which they serve as instructors, assist in research, or have administrative duties. Although many supervisory positions are open to biomedical equipment technicians, some positions are not available without additional education. In large metropolitan hospitals, for instance, the minimum educational requirement for biomedical engineers, who do much of the supervising of biomedical equipment technicians, is a bachelor's degree; many engineers have a master's degree as well.

EARNINGS

Salaries for biomedical equipment technicians vary in different institutions and localities and according to the experience, training, certification, and type of work done by the technician. According to the U.S. Department of Labor, the median annual salary for medical equipment repairers was $40,580 in 2006. The top 10 percent of workers in this profession made $66,160 or more a year, while the lowest 10 percent made $23,700 or less per year. In general, biomedical equipment technicians who work for manufacturers have higher earnings than those who work for hospitals. Naturally, those in supervisory or senior positions also command higher salaries. Benefits, such as health insurance and vacation days, vary with the employer.

WORK ENVIRONMENT

Working conditions for biomedical equipment technicians vary according to employer and type of work done. Hospital employees generally work a 40-hour week; their schedules sometimes include weekends and holidays, and some technicians may be on call for emergencies. Technicians who are employed by equipment manufacturers may have to travel extensively to install or service equipment.

The physical surroundings in which biomedical equipment technicians work may vary from day to day. Technicians may work in a lab or treatment room with patients or consult with engineers, administrators, and other staff members. Other days, technicians may spend most of their time at a workbench repairing equipment.

OUTLOOK

Because of the expanding healthcare field and increasing use of electronic medical devices and other sophisticated biomedical equipment, there is a steady demand for skilled and trained biomedical equipment technicians. The U.S. Department of Labor predicts that employment for these workers will grow much faster than the average for all occupations through 2016.

In hospitals the need for more biomedical equipment technicians exists not only because of the increasing use of biomedical equipment but also because hospital administrators realize that these technicians can help hold down costs. Biomedical equipment technicians do this through their preventive maintenance checks and by taking over some routine activities of engineers and administrators, thus releasing those professionals for activities that only they can perform. Through the coming decades, cost containment will remain a high priority for hospital administrators, and as long as biomedical equipment technicians can contribute to that effort, the demand for them should remain strong.

For the many biomedical equipment technicians who work for companies that build, sell, lease, or service biomedical equipment, job opportunities should also continue to grow.

The federal government employs biomedical equipment technicians in its hospitals, research institutes, and the military. Employment in these areas will depend largely on levels of government spending. In the research area, spending levels may vary; however, in health care delivery, spending should remain high for the near future.

FOR MORE INFORMATION

For information on student memberships, biomedical technology programs, and certification, contact

Association for the Advancement of
Medical Instrumentation
1110 North Glebe Road, Suite 220
Arlington, VA 22201-4795
Tel: 800-332-2264
Email: certifications@aami.org
http://www.aami.org

For industry information, contact

American Society for Healthcare Engineering
One North Franklin, 28th Floor
Chicago, IL 60606-4425
Email: ashe@aha.org
http://www.ashe.org

Medical Equipment and Technology Association
http://www.mymeta.org

BOOKKEEPING AND ACCOUNTING CLERKS

OVERVIEW

Bookkeeping and accounting clerks record financial transactions for government, business, and other organizations. They compute, classify, record, and verify numerical data in order to develop and maintain accurate financial records. There are approximately 2.1 million bookkeeping, accounting, and auditing clerks employed in the United States.

THE JOB

Bookkeeping workers keep systematic records and current accounts of financial transactions for businesses, institutions, industries, charities, and other organizations. The bookkeeping records of a firm or business are a vital part of its operational procedures because these

---

SCHOOL SUBJECTS
Business, Computer Science, Mathematics

PERSONAL SKILLS
Following Instructions, Technical/Scientific

MINIMUM EDUCATION LEVEL
High School Diploma

CERTIFICATION OR LICENSING
Voluntary

WORK ENVIRONMENT
Primarily Indoors, Primarily One Location

---

records reflect the assets and the liabilities, as well as the profits and losses, of the operation.

Bookkeepers record these business transactions daily in spreadsheets on computer databases, and accounting clerks often input the information. The practice of posting accounting records directly onto ledger sheets, in journals, or on other types of written accounting forms is decreasing as computerized record keeping becomes more widespread. In small businesses, bookkeepers sort and record all the sales slips, bills, check stubs, inventory lists, and requisition lists. They compile figures for cash receipts, accounts payable and receivable, and profits and losses.

Accounting clerks handle the clerical accounting work; they enter and verify transaction data and compute and record various charges. They may also monitor loans and accounts payable and receivable. More advanced clerks may reconcile billing vouchers, while senior workers review invoices and statements.

Accountants set up bookkeeping systems and use bookkeepers' balance sheets to prepare periodic summary statements of financial transactions. Management relies heavily on these bookkeeping records to interpret the organization's overall performance and uses them to make important business decisions. The records are also necessary to file income tax reports and prepare quarterly reports for stockholders.

Bookkeeping and accounting clerks work in retail and wholesale businesses, manufacturing firms, hospitals, schools, charities, and other types of institutional agencies. Many clerks are classified as financial institution bookkeeping and accounting clerks, insurance firm bookkeeping and accounting clerks, hotel bookkeeping and accounting clerks, and railroad bookkeeping and accounting clerks.

General bookkeepers and *general-ledger bookkeepers* are usually employed in smaller business operations. They may perform all the analysis, maintain the financial records, and complete any other tasks that are involved in keeping a full set of bookkeeping records. These employees may have other general office duties, such as mailing statements, answering telephone calls, and filing materials. *Audit clerks* verify figures and may be responsible for sending them on to an audit clerk supervisor.

In large companies, an accountant may supervise a department of bookkeepers who perform more specialized work. *Billing and rate clerks* and *fixed capital clerks* may post items in accounts payable or receivable ledgers, make out bills and invoices, or verify the company's rates for certain products and services. *Account information clerks* prepare reports, compile payroll lists and deductions, write company checks, and compute federal tax reports or personnel profit shares. Large companies may employ workers to organize, record, and compute many other types of financial information.

In large business organizations, bookkeepers and accountants may be classified by grades, such as Bookkeeper I or II. The job classification determines their responsibilities.

REQUIREMENTS
High School

In order to be a bookkeeper, you will need at least a high school diploma. It will be helpful to have a background in business mathematics, business writing, typing, and computer training. Pay particular attention to developing sound English and communication skills along with mathematical abilities.

Postsecondary Training

Some employers prefer people who have completed a junior college curriculum or those who have attended a post–high school business training program. In many instances, employers offer on-the-job training for various types of entry-level positions. In some areas, work-study programs are available in which schools, in cooperation with businesses, offer part-time, practical on-the-job training combined with academic study. These programs often help students find immediate employment in similar work after graduation. Local business schools may also offer evening courses.

Certification or Licensing

The American Institute of Professional Bookkeepers offers voluntary certification to bookkeepers who have at least two years of full-time experience (or the part-time or freelance equivalent), pass an examination, and sign a code of ethics. Bookkeepers who complete this requirement may use the designation certified bookkeeper.

Other Requirements

Bookkeepers need strong mathematical skills and organizational abilities, and they have to be able to concentrate on detailed work. The work is quite sedentary and often tedious, and you should not mind long hours behind a desk. You should be methodical, accurate, and orderly and enjoy working on detailed tasks. Employers look for honest, discreet, and trustworthy individuals when placing their business in someone else's hands.

Once you are employed as a bookkeeping and accounting clerk, some places of business may require you to have union membership. Larger unions include the Office and Professional Employees International Union; the International Union of Electronic, Electrical, Salaried, Machine, and Furniture Workers-Communications Workers of America; and the American Federation of State, County, and Municipal Employees. Also, depending on the business, clerks may be represented by the same union as other manufacturing employees.

EXPLORING

You can gain experience in bookkeeping by participating in work-study programs or by obtaining part-time or summer work in beginning bookkeeping jobs or related office work. Any retail experience dealing with cash management, pricing, or customer service is also valuable.

You can also volunteer to manage the books for extracurricular student groups. Managing income or cash flow for a club or acting as treasurer for student government are excellent ways to gain experience in maintaining financial records.

Other options are visiting local small businesses to observe their work and talking to representatives of schools that offer business training courses.

EMPLOYERS

Of the approximately 2.1 million bookkeeping, auditing, and accounting clerks, many work for personnel supplying companies; that is, those companies that provide part-time or temporary office workers. Approximately 24 percent of bookkeeping and accounting clerks work part time, according to the U.S. Department of Labor.

Many others are employed by government agencies and organizations that provide educational, health, business, and social services.

STARTING OUT

You may find jobs or establish contacts with businesses that are interested in interviewing graduates through your guidance or career services offices. A work-study program or internship may result in a full-time job offer. Business schools and junior colleges generally provide assistance to their graduates in locating employment.

You may locate job opportunities by applying directly to firms or responding to ads in newspaper classified sections. State employment agencies and private employment bureaus can also assist in the job search process.

ADVANCEMENT

Bookkeeping workers generally begin their employment by performing routine tasks, such as the simple recording of transactions. Beginners may start as entry-level clerks, cashiers, bookkeeping machine operators, office assistants, or typists. With experience, they may advance to more complex assignments that include computer training in databases and spreadsheets and assume a greater responsibility for the work as a whole.

With experience and education, clerks become department heads or office managers. Further advancement to positions such as office or division manager, department head, accountant, or auditor is possible with a college degree and years of experience. There is a high turnover rate in this field, which increases the promotion opportunities for employees with ability and initiative.

EARNINGS

According to the U.S. Department of Labor, bookkeepers and accounting clerks earned a median income of $30,560 a year in 2006. Earnings are also influenced by such factors as the size of the city where they work and the size and type of business for which they are employed. Clerks just starting out earn approximately $19,760 or less. Those with one or two years of college generally earn higher starting wages. Top-paying jobs averaged $46,020 or more a year.

Employees usually receive six to eight paid holidays yearly and one week of paid vacation after six to 12 months of service. Paid vacations may increase to four weeks or more, depending on length of service and place of employment. Fringe benefits may include health and life insurance, sick leave, and retirement plans.

WORK ENVIRONMENT

The majority of office workers, including bookkeeping workers, usually work a 40-hour week, although some employees may work a 35- to 37-hour week. Bookkeeping and accounting clerks usually work in typical office settings. They are more likely to have a cubicle than an office. While the work pace is steady, it can also be routine and repetitive, especially in large companies where the employee is often assigned only one or two specialized job duties.

Attention to numerical details can be physically demanding, and the work can produce eyestrain and nervousness. While bookkeepers usually work with other people and sometimes under close supervision, they can expect to spend most of their day behind a desk; this may seem confining to people who need more variety and stimulation in their work. In addition, the constant attention to detail and the need for accuracy can place considerable responsibility on the worker and cause much stress.

OUTLOOK

A growing number of financial transactions and the implementation of the Sarbanes-Oxley Act of 2002, which requires more accurate reporting of financial data for public companies, has created steady employment growth for bookkeeping and accounting clerks. Employment of bookkeeping and accounting clerks is expected to grow about as fast as the average for all occupations through 2016, according to the U.S. Department of Labor.

There will be numerous replacement job openings, since the turnover rate in this occupation is high. Offices are centralizing their operations, setting up one center to manage all accounting needs in a single location. As more companies trim back their workforces, opportunities for temporary work should continue to grow.

The automation of office functions will continue to improve overall worker productivity, which may limit job growth in some settings. Excellent computer skills and professional certification will be vital to securing a job.

FOR MORE INFORMATION

For information on certification and career opportunities, contact

American Institute of Professional Bookkeepers
6001 Montrose Road, Suite 500
Rockville, MD 20852-4873

Tel: 800-622-0121
Email: info@aipb.org
http://www.aipb.org

For information on accredited educational programs, contact
Association to Advance Collegiate Schools of Business
777 South Harbour Island Boulevard, Suite 750
Tampa, FL 33602-5730
Tel: 813-769-6500
http://www.aacsb.edu

For more information on women in accounting, contact
Educational Foundation for Women in Accounting
PO Box 1925
Southeastern, PA 19399-1925
Tel: 610-407-9229
Email: info@efwa.org
http://www.efwa.org

BROADCAST ENGINEERS

OVERVIEW

Broadcast engineers, also referred to as *broadcast technicians,* or *broadcast operators,* operate and maintain the electronic equipment used to record and transmit the audio for radio signals and the audio and visual images for television signals to the public. They may work in a broadcasting station or assist in broadcasting directly from an outside site as a *field technician.* Approximately 38,000 broadcast engineers work in the United States.

THE JOB

Broadcast engineers are responsible for the transmission of radio and television programming, including live and recorded broadcasts. Broadcasts are usually transmitted directly from the station; however, engineers are capable of transmitting signals on location from specially designed, mobile equipment. The specific tasks of the broadcast engineer depend on the size of the television or radio station. In small stations, engineers have a wide variety of responsibilities. Larger stations are able to hire a greater number of engineers and specifically delegate responsibilities to each engineer.

In both small and large stations, however, engineers are responsible for the operation, installation, and repair of the equipment.

The *chief engineer* in both radio and television is the head of the entire technical operation and must orchestrate the activities of all the technicians to ensure smooth programming. He or she is also responsible for the budget and must keep abreast of new broadcast communications technology.

Larger stations also have an *assistant chief engineer* who manages the daily activities of the technical crew, controls the maintenance of the electronic equipment, and ensures the performance standards of the station.

Maintenance technicians are directly responsible for the installation, adjustment, and repair of the electronic equipment.

The move toward digital recording, editing, and broadcasting has changed the field of broadcast engineering. Broadcast professionals now use computer software and related technology—instead of electronic equipment—to record and edit programming. This programming is stored on computer hard drives and other computer data storage systems.

The introduction of robotic cameras, six-foot-tall cameras that stand on two legs, created a need for a new kind of technician called a *video-robo technician.* Video-robo technicians operate the cameras from a control room computer, using joysticks and a video panel to tilt and focus each camera. With the help of new technology, one person can now effectively perform the work of two or three camera operators. Engineers may work with producers, directors, and reporters to put together recorded material from various sources. These include computer networks, mobile camera units, and studio productions. Depending on their employer, engineers may be involved in any number of activities related to editing recorded material into a complete program.

REQUIREMENTS
High School

Take as many classes as you can in mathematics, science, computers, and shop, especially electronics. Speech classes will help you hone your abilities to effectively communicate ideas to others.

Postsecondary Training

Positions that are more advanced require a bachelor's degree in broadcast communications or a related field. To become a chief engineer, you should aim for a bachelor's degree in electronics or electrical engineering. Because field technicians also act as announcers on occasion, speech courses and experience as an announcer in a school radio station can be helpful. Seeking education beyond a bachelor's degree will further the possibilities for advancement, although it is not required.

Certification or Licensing

The Federal Communications Commission licenses and permits are no longer required of broadcast engineers. However, certification from the Society of Broadcast Engineers (SBE) is desirable, and certified engineers consistently earn higher salaries than uncertified engineers. The SBE offers an education scholarship and accepts student members; members receive a newsletter and have access to its job line.

Other Requirements

Broadcast engineers must have both an aptitude for working with highly technical electronic equipment and computer software and hardware and minute attention to detail to be successful in the field. You should enjoy both the technical and artistic aspects of working in the radio or television industry. You should also be able to communicate with a wide range of people with various levels of technical expertise.

EXPLORING

Reading association publications is an excellent way to learn more about broadcast engineering. Many of the associations listed at the end of this article offer newsletters and other publications to members—some even post back issues or selected articles on their Web sites. You might also consider reading *Broadcast Engineering* (http://www.broadcastengineering.com), a trade publication for broadcast engineers and technicians.

Experience is necessary to begin a career as a broadcast engineer, and volunteering at a local broadcasting station is an excellent way to gain experience. Many schools have clubs for persons interested in broadcasting. Such clubs sponsor trips to broadcasting facilities, schedule lectures, and provide a place where students can meet others with similar interests. Local television station technicians are usually willing to share their experiences with interested young people. They can be a helpful source of informal career guidance. Visits or tours can be arranged by school officials. Tours will

SCHOOL SUBJECTS
Computer Science, Mathematics

PERSONAL SKILLS
Mechanical/Manipulative, Technical/Scientific

MINIMUM EDUCATION LEVEL
Some Postsecondary Training

CERTIFICATION OR LICENSING
Recommended

WORK ENVIRONMENT
Primarily Indoors, Primarily Multiple Locations

allow you to see engineers involved in their work. Most colleges and universities also have radio and television stations where students can gain experience with broadcasting equipment.

Exposure to broadcasting technology also may be obtained through building and operating an amateur, or ham, radio and experimenting with electronic kits. Dexterity and an understanding of home-operated broadcasting equipment will aid in promoting success in education and work experience within the field of broadcasting.

EMPLOYERS

According to the *CIA World Factbook*, there were 13,750 radio stations and 2,218 television stations in the United States in 2006. These stations might be independently operated or owned and operated by a network. Smaller stations in smaller cities are good starting places, but it is at the larger networks and stations in major cities where the higher salaries are found. Some broadcast engineers work outside of the radio and television industries, producing, for example, corporate employee training and sales programs. Approximately 38,000 broadcast technicians are employed in the United States.

STARTING OUT

In many towns and cities there are public-access cable television stations and public radio stations where high school students interested in broadcasting and broadcast technology can obtain an internship. An entry-level technician should be flexible about job location; most begin their careers at small stations and with experience may advance to larger-market stations.

ADVANCEMENT

Entry-level engineers deal exclusively with the operation and maintenance of their assigned equipment; in contrast, a more advanced broadcast engineer directs the activities of entry-level engineers and makes judgments on the quality, strength, and subject of the material being broadcast.

After several years of experience, a broadcast engineer may advance to *assistant chief engineer*. In this capacity, he or she may direct the daily activities of all of the broadcasting engineers in the station as well as the field engineers broadcasting on location. Advancement to chief engineer usually requires at least a college degree in engineering and many years of experience. A firm grasp of management skills, budget planning, and a thorough knowledge of all aspects of broadcast technology are necessary to become the chief engineer of a radio or television station.

EARNINGS

Larger stations usually pay higher wages than smaller stations, and television stations tend to pay more than radio stations. Also, commercial stations generally pay more than public broadcasting stations. The median annual earnings for broadcast technicians were $30,690 in 2006, according to the U.S. Department of Labor. The department also reported that the lowest paid 10 percent earned less than $15,680 and the highest paid 10 percent earned more than $64,860 during that same period. Technicians employed in radio and television broadcasting had mean annual salaries of $32,890 in 2006. Experience, job location, and educational background are all factors that influence a person's pay.

WORK ENVIRONMENT

Most engineers work in broadcasting stations that are modern and comfortable. The hours can vary; because most broadcasting stations operate 24 hours a day, seven days a week, there are engineers who must work at night, on weekends, and on holidays. Transmitter technicians usually work behind the scenes with little public contact. They work closely with their equipment and as members of a small crew of experts whose closely coordinated efforts produce smooth-running programs. Constant attention to detail and having to make split-second decisions can cause tension. Since broadcasts also occur outside of the broadcasting station on location sites, field technicians may work anywhere and in all kinds of weather.

OUTLOOK

According to the U.S. Department of Labor, the overall employment of broadcast and sound engineering technicians is expected to grow faster than the average for all occupations through 2016. There will be strong competition for jobs in metropolitan areas. In addition, the Department of Labor predicts that a slow growth in the number of new radio and television stations may mean few new job opportunities in the field. Technicians trained in the installation of transmitters should have better work prospects as television stations switch from their old analog transmitters to digital transmitters. Job openings will also result from the need to replace existing engineers who often leave the industry for other jobs in electronics.

Some engineers may find work outside of broadcasting. As the new technology becomes more accessible, new industries are discovering the usefulness of visual communications. More and more corporations are creating in-house communications departments to produce their own corporate and industrial programming. This type of programming effectively explains company policies ranging from public safety (aimed at their customers) to first aid (aimed at their employees). Also, high-quality programming can introduce a company to potential clients in the best light.

In addition to industrial work, broadcast engineers are in great demand today for the production of commercials, animation, and computer graphics. The field is changing rapidly with the introduction of new and cheaper computer systems and desktop software packages. Maintenance workers will always be in demand, even with the new technology. Someone will always have to be on hand to fix broken equipment and to keep new equipment in good working order.

FOR MORE INFORMATION

Visit the BEA's Web site for useful information about broadcast education and the broadcasting industry.

Broadcast Education Association (BEA)
1771 N Street, NW
Washington, DC 20036-2891
Tel: 888-380-7222
Email: beainfo@beaweb.org
http://www.beaweb.org

For information on union membership, contact

National Association of Broadcast Employees and Technicians/Communications Workers of America
http://nabetcwa.org

For broadcast education, support, and scholarship information, contact

National Association of Broadcasters
1771 N Street, NW
Washington, DC 20036-2891
Tel: 202-429-5300
Email: nab@nab.org
http://www.nab.org

For information on student membership, scholarships, and farm broadcasting, contact

National Association of Farm Broadcasting
PO Box 500
Platte City, MO 64079-0500
Tel: 816-431-4032
Email: nafboffice@aol.com
http://nafb.com

For information on careers in the cable industry, visit the NCTA's Web site.

National Cable and Telecommunications Association (NCTA)
25 Massachusetts Avenue, NW, Suite 100
Washington, DC 20001-1413
Tel: 202-222-2300
http://www.ncta.com

For scholarship and internship information, contact

Radio-Television News Directors Association and Foundation
1600 K Street, NW, Suite 700
Washington, DC 20006-2838
Tel: 202-659-6510
Email: rtnda@rtnda.org
http://www.rtnda.org

For information on membership, scholarships, and certification, contact

Society of Broadcast Engineers
9102 North Meridian Street, Suite 150
Indianapolis, IN 46260-1896
Tel: 317-846-9000
Email: mclappe@sbe.org
http://www.sbe.org

Visit the society's Web site for information on scholarships, membership for college students, and links to useful resources.

Society of Motion Picture and Television Engineers
3 Barker Avenue
White Plains, NY 10601-1509
Tel: 914-761-1100
http://www.smpte.org

☐ CARDIOVASCULAR TECHNOLOGISTS

OVERVIEW

Cardiovascular technologists assist physicians in diagnosing and treating heart and blood vessel ailments. Depending on their specialties, they operate electrocardiograph machines, perform Holter monitor and stress testing, and assist in cardiac catheterization procedures and ultrasound testing. These tasks help the physicians diagnose heart disease and monitor progress during treatment. Cardiovascular technologists hold approximately 45,000 jobs in the United States.

THE JOB

Technologists who assist physicians in the diagnosis and treatment of heart disease are known as cardiovascular technologists. (Cardio means heart; vascular refers to the blood vessel/circulatory system.) Increasingly, hospitals are centralizing cardiovascular services under one full cardiovascular "service line" overseen by the same administrator. In addition to cardiovascular technologists, the cardiovascular team at a hospital may include *radiology (X-ray) technologists*, *nuclear medicine technologists*, *nurses*, *physician assistants*, *respiratory technicians*, and *respiratory therapists*. Cardiovascular technologists contribute by performing one or more of a wide range of procedures in cardiovascular medicine, including invasive (enters a body cavity or interrupts normal body functions), noninvasive, peripheral vascular, or echocardiography (ultrasound) procedures. In most facilities, technologists use equipment that is among the most advanced in the medical field; drug therapies also may be used as part of the diagnostic imaging procedures or in addition to them. Technologists' services may be required when the patient's condition is first being explored, before surgery, during surgery (cardiology technologists

SCHOOL SUBJECTS

Biology, Health

PERSONAL SKILLS

Communication/Ideas, Technical/Scientific

MINIMUM EDUCATION LEVEL

Some Postsecondary Training

CERTIFICATION OR LICENSING

Voluntary

WORK ENVIRONMENT

Primarily Indoors, Primarily One Location

primarily), or during rehabilitation of the patient. Some of the work is performed on an outpatient basis.

Depending on their specific areas of skill, some cardiovascular technologists are employed in nonhospital health care facilities. For example, they may work for clinics, mobile medical services, or private doctors' offices. Much of their equipment can go just about anywhere.

Some of the specific duties of cardiovascular technologists are described in the following paragraphs. Exact titles of these technologists often vary from medical facility to medical facility because there is no standardized naming system. *Electrocardiograph technologists*, or *EKG technologists*, use an electrocardiograph machine to detect the electronic impulses that come from a patient's heart. The EKG machine records these signals on a paper graph called an electrocardiogram. The electronic impulses recorded by the EKG machine can tell the physician about the action of the heart during and between the individual heartbeats. This in turn reveals important information about the condition of the heart, including irregular heartbeats or the presence of blocked arteries, which the physician can use to diagnose heart disease, monitor progress during treatment, or check the patient's condition after recovery.

To use an EKG machine, the technologist attaches electrodes (small, disklike devices about the size of a silver dollar) to the patient's chest. Wires attached to the electrodes lead to the EKG machine. Twelve or more leads may be attached. To get a better reading from the electrodes, the technologist may first apply an adhesive gel to the patient's skin that helps to conduct the electrical impulses. The technologist then operates controls on the EKG machine or (more commonly) enters commands for the machine into a computer. The electrodes pick up the electronic signals from the heart and transmit them to the EKG machine. The machine registers and makes a printout of the signals, with a stylus (pen) recording their pattern on a long roll of graph paper.

During the test, the technologist may move the electrodes in order to get readings of electrical activity in different parts of the heart muscle. Since EKG equipment can be sensitive to electrical impulses from other sources, such as other parts of the patient's body or equipment in the room where the EKG test is being done, the technologist must watch for false readings.

After the test, the EKG technologist takes the electrocardiogram off the machine, edits it or makes notes on it, and sends it to the physician (usually a cardiologist, or heart specialist). Physicians may have computer assistance to help them use and interpret the electrocardiogram; special software is available to assist them with their diagnoses.

EKG technologists do not have to repair EKG machines, but they do have to keep an eye on them and know when they are malfunctioning so they can call someone for repairs. They also may keep the machines stocked with paper. Of all the cardiovascular technical positions, EKG technologist positions are the most numerous.

Holter monitoring and stress testing may be performed by *Holter monitor technologists* or *stress test technologists*, respectively, or they may be additional duties of some *EKG technologists*. In Holter monitoring, electrodes are fastened to the patient's chest, and a small, portable monitor is strapped to the patient's body, often at the waist. The small monitor contains a tape that records the action of the heart during activity—as the patient moves, sits, stands, and sleeps. The patient is required to wear the Holter monitor for 24 to 48 hours while he or she goes about normal daily activities. When the patient returns to the hospital, the technologist removes the tape from the monitor and puts it in a scanner to produce audio and visual representations of heart activity. (Hearing how the heart sounds during activity helps physicians diagnose a possible heart condition.) The technologist reviews and analyzes the information revealed in the tape. Finally, the technologist may print out the parts of the tape that show abnormal heart patterns or make a full tape for the physician.

Stress tests record the heart's performance during physical activity. In one type of stress test, the technologist connects the patient to the EKG machine, attaching electrodes to the patient's arms, legs, and chest, and obtains a reading of the patient's resting heart activity and blood pressure. Then, the patient is asked to walk on a treadmill for a designated period of time while the technologist and the physician monitor the heart. The treadmill speed is increased so that the technologist and physician can see what happens when the heart is put under higher levels of exertion.

Cardiology technologists specialize in providing support for cardiac catheterization (tubing) procedures. These procedures are classified as invasive because they require the physician and attending technologists to enter a body cavity or interrupt normal body functions. In one cardiac catheterization procedure—an angiogram—a catheter (tube) is inserted into the heart (usually by way of a blood vessel in the leg) in order to see the condition of the heart blood vessels, whether there is a blockage. In another procedure, known as angioplasty, a catheter with a balloon at the end is inserted into an artery to widen it. According to the American Heart Association's 2008 Heart and Stroke Statistical Update, 1,271,000 angioplasties (known officially as percutaneous coronary interventions) were done in the United States in 2005. Cardiology technologists also perform a variety of other procedures, such as electrophysiology tests, which locate areas of heart tissue that cause arrhythmias.

Unlike some of the other cardiovascular technologists, cardiology technologists actually assist in surgical procedures. They may help secure the patient to the table, set up a camera or other imaging device under the instructions of the physician (to produce images that assist the physician in guiding the catheter through the cardiovascular system), enter information about the surgical procedure (as it is taking place) into a computer, and provide other support. After the procedure, the technologist may process the angiographic film for use by the physician. Cardiology technologists may also assist during open-heart surgery by preparing and monitoring the patient and placing or monitoring pacemakers.

Vascular technologists and *echocardiographers* are specialists in noninvasive cardiovascular procedures and use ultrasound equipment to obtain and record information about the condition of the heart. Ultrasound equipment is used to send out sound waves to the area of the body being studied; when the sound waves hit the part being studied, they send echoes to the ultrasound machine. The echoes are "read" by the machine, which creates an image on a monitor, permitting the technologist to get an instant "image" of the part of the body and its condition. Vascular technologists are specialists in the use of ultrasound equipment to study blood flow and circulation problems. Echocardiographers are specialists in the use of ultrasound equipment to evaluate the heart and its structures, such as the valves.

Cardiac monitor technicians are similar to and sometimes perform some of the same duties as EKG technologists. Usually working in the intensive care unit or cardio-care unit of the hospital, cardiac monitor technicians keep watch over the patient, monitoring screens to detect any sign that a patient's heart is not beating as it should. Cardiac monitor technicians begin their shift by reviewing the patient's records to familiarize themselves with what the patient's normal heart rhythms should be, what the current pattern is, and what types of problems have been observed. Throughout the shift, cardiac monitor technicians watch for heart rhythm irregularities that need prompt medical attention. Should there be any, they notify a nurse or doctor immediately so that appropriate care can be given.

In addition to these positions, other cardiovascular technologists specialize in a particular aspect of health care. For example, cardiopulmonary technologists specialize in procedures for diagnosing problems with the heart and lungs. They may conduct electrocardiograph, phonocardiograph (sound recordings of the heart's valves and of the blood passing through them), echocardiograph, stress testing, and respiratory test procedures.

Cardiopulmonary technologists also may assist on cardiac catheterization procedures, measuring and recording information about the patient's cardiovascular and pulmonary systems during the procedure and alerting the cardiac catheterization team to any problems.

REQUIREMENTS
High School

At a minimum, cardiovascular technologists need a high school diploma or equivalent to enter the field. Although no specific high school classes will directly prepare you to be a technologist, learning how to learn and getting a good grounding in basic high school subjects are important to all technologist positions.

During high school, you should take English, health, biology, and typing. You also might consider courses in social sciences to help you understand the social and psychological needs of patients.

Postsecondary Training

In the past, many EKG operators were trained on the job by an EKG supervisor. This still may be true for some EKG technician positions. Increasingly, however, EKG technologists get postsecondary schooling before they are hired. Holter monitoring and stress testing may be part of your EKG schooling, or they may be learned through additional training. Ultrasound and cardiology technologists tend to have the most postsecondary schooling (up to a four-year bachelor's degree) and have the most extensive academic/experience requirements for credentialing purposes.

You can enter these positions without having had previous health care experience. However, some previous exposure to the business side of health care or even training in related areas is helpful. With academic training or professional experience in nursing, radiology science, or respiratory science, for example, you may be able to move into cardiology technology.

As a rule of thumb, medical employers value postsecondary schooling that gives you actual hands-on experience with patients in addition to classroom training. At many of the schools that train cardiovascular technologists, you work with patients in a variety of health care settings and train on more than one brand of equipment.

Some employers still have a physician or EKG department manager train EKG technicians on the job. Training generally lasts from one to six months. Trainees learn how to operate the EKG machine, how to produce and edit the electrocardiogram, and other related tasks.

Some vocational, technical, and junior colleges have one- or two-year training programs in EKG technology, Holter monitoring, stress testing, or all three; otherwise, EKG technologists may obtain training in Holter and stress procedures after they've already started working, either on the job or through an additional six months or more of schooling. Formal academic programs give technologists more preparation in the subject than is available with most on-the-job training and allow them to earn a certificate (one-year programs) or associate's degree (two-year programs). The American Medical Association (AMA)'s *Health Professions Career and Education Directory* has listings of accredited EKG programs.

Ultrasound technologists usually need a high school diploma or equivalent plus one, two, or four years of postsecondary schooling in a trade school, technical school, or community college. Vascular technologists also may be trained on the job. Again, a list of accredited programs can be found in the AMA's *Health Professions Career and Education Directory*; also, a list of training opportunities in sonography is available at the Society of Diagnostic Medical Sonography's Web site, http://www.sdms.org/career/selection.asp.

Cardiology technologists tend to have the highest academic requirements of all; for example, a four-year bachelor's degree, a two-year associate's degree, or an advanced certificate of completion from a hospital, trade, or technical cardiovascular program. A two-year program at a junior or community college might include one year of core classes (e.g., mathematics, biology, chemistry, and anatomy) and one year of specialized classes in cardiology procedures.

Cardiac monitor technicians need a high school diploma or equivalent, with additional educational requirements similar to those of EKG technicians.

Certification or Licensing

Right now, certification or licensing for cardiovascular technologists is voluntary, but the move to state licensing is expected in the near future. Many credentialing bodies for cardiovascular and pulmonary positions exist, including American Registry of Diagnostic Medical Sonographers (ARDMS), Cardiovascular Credentialing International, and others, and there are more than a dozen possible credentials for cardiovascular technologists. For example, sonographers can take an exam from ARDMS to receive credentialing in sonography. Their credentials may be as registered diagnostic medical sonographer, registered diagnostic cardiac sonographer, or registered vascular technologist. Credentialing requirements for cardiology technologists or ultrasound technologists may include a test plus formal academic and on-the-job requirements. Professional experience or academic training in a related field, such as nursing, radiology science, and respiratory science, may be acceptable as part of these formal academic and professional requirements. As with continuing education, certification is a sign of interest and dedication to the field and is generally favorably regarded by potential employers.

Cardiology is a cutting-edge area of medicine, with constant advancements, and medical equipment relating to the heart is continually updated. Therefore, keeping up with new developments is vital. In addition, technologists who add to their qualifications through taking part in continuing education tend to earn more money and have more employment opportunities. Major professional societies encourage and provide the opportunities for professionals to continue their education.

Other Requirements

Technicians must be able to put patients at ease about the procedure they are to undergo. Therefore, you should be pleasant, patient, alert, and able to understand and sympathize with the feelings of others. When explaining a procedure to patients, cardiovascular technicians should be able to do so in a calm, reassuring, and confident manner.

EXPLORING

Prospective cardiovascular technologists will find it difficult to gain any direct experience on a part-time basis in electrocardiography. The first experience with the work generally comes during on-the-job training sessions. You may, however, be able to gain some exposure to patient-care activities in general by signing up for volunteer work at a local hospital. In addition, you can arrange to visit a hospital, clinic, or physician's office where electrocardiographs are taken. In this way, you may be able to watch a technician at work or at least talk to a technician about what the work is like.

EMPLOYERS

There are approximately 45,000 cardiovascular technologists employed in the United States. Most work in hospitals (75 percent), but employment can be found in physicians' offices, diagnostic imaging centers, clinics, rehab centers, or anyplace electrocardiographs are taken.

STARTING OUT

Because most cardiovascular technologists receive their initial training on their first job, great care should be taken in finding this first employer. Pay close attention not only to the pay and working conditions, but also to the kind of on-the-job training that is provided for each prospective position. High school vocational counselors may be able to tell you which hospitals have good reputations for EKG training programs. Applying directly to hospitals is a common way of entering the field. Information also can be gained by reading the classified ads in the newspaper and from talking with friends and relatives who work in hospitals.

For students who graduate from one- to two-year training programs, finding a first job should be easier. First, employers are always eager to hire people who are already trained. Second, these graduates can be less concerned about the training programs offered by their employers. Third, they should find that their teachers and guidance counselors can be excellent sources of information about job possibilities in the area. If the training program includes practical experience, graduates may find that the hospital in which they trained or worked before graduation would be willing to hire them after graduation.

ADVANCEMENT

Opportunities for advancement are best for cardiovascular technologists who learn to do or assist with more complex procedures, such as stress testing, Holter monitoring, echocardiography, and cardiac catheterization. With proper training and experience, these technicians may eventually become cardiovascular technologists, echocardiography technologists, cardiopulmonary technicians, cardiology technologists, or other specialty technicians or technologists.

In addition to these kinds of specialty positions, experienced technicians may also be able to advance to various supervisory and training posts.

EARNINGS

The median salary for cardiovascular technologists was $40,420 in 2006, according to the U.S. Department of Labor. The lowest paid 10 percent earned less than $23,670, and the highest paid 10 percent earned more than $67,410 annually. Earnings can vary by size and type of employer. For example, technologists working in doctors' offices had a mean annual income $46,380, while those in hospitals had a mean salary of $43,000. Those with formal training earn more than those who trained on the job, and those who are able to perform more sophisticated tests, such as Holter monitoring and stress testing, are paid more than those who perform only the basic electrocardiograph tests.

Technologists working in hospitals receive the same fringe benefits as other hospital workers, including medical insurance, paid vacations, and sick leave. In some cases, benefits also include educational assistance, retirement plans, and uniform allowances.

WORK ENVIRONMENT

Cardiovascular technologists usually work in clean, quiet, well-lighted surroundings. They generally work five-day, 40-hour weeks, although technicians working in small hospitals may be on 24-hour call for emergencies, and all technicians in hospitals, large or small, can expect to do occasional evening or weekend work. With the growing emphasis in health care on cost containment, more jobs are likely to develop in outpatient settings, so in the future it is likely that cardiovascular technologists will work more often in clinics, health maintenance organizations, and other nonhospital locations.

Cardiovascular technologists generally work with patients who are ill or who have reason to fear they might be ill. With this in mind, there are opportunities for the technicians to do these people some good, but there is also a chance of causing some unintentional harm as well: A well-conducted test can reduce anxieties or make a physician's job easier; a misplaced electrode or an error in recordkeeping could cause an incorrect diagnosis.

Technicians need to be able to cope with these responsibilities and consistently conduct their work in the best interests of their patients.

Part of the technician's job includes putting patients at ease about the procedure they are to undergo. Toward that end, technicians should be pleasant, patient, alert, and able to understand and sympathize with the feelings of others. In explaining the nature of the procedure to patients, cardiovascular technicians should be able to do so in a calm, reassuring, and confident manner.

Inevitably, some patients will try to get information about their medical situation from the technician. In such cases, technicians need to be both tactful and firm in explaining that they are only taking the electrocardiogram; the interpretation is for the physician to make.

Another large part of a technician's job involves getting along well with other members of the hospital staff. This task is sometimes made more difficult by the fact that in most hospitals there is a formal, often rigid, status structure, and cardiovascular technologists may find themselves in a relatively low position in that structure. In emergency situations or at other moments of frustration, cardiovascular technologists may find themselves dealt with brusquely or angrily. Technicians should not take outbursts or rude treatment personally, but instead should respond with stability and maturity.

OUTLOOK

The overall employment of cardiovascular technologists and technicians should grow much faster than the average for all occupations through 2016, according to the U.S. Department of Labor. Growth will be primarily due to the increasing numbers of older people who have a higher incidence of heart problems. Specialties that will be in particularly high demand include vascular technologists, echocardiographers, and electrophysiologists. The labor department, however, projects employment for EKG technicians to decline during this same period as hospitals train other health care personnel to perform basic EKG procedures. EKG technicians who have received training in Holter monitoring and stress testing will have better employment prospects.

FOR MORE INFORMATION

For information on careers, contact
Alliance of Cardiovascular Professionals
PO Box 2007
Midlothian, VA 23112-9007
Tel: 804-632-0078
http://www.acp-online.org

For information on the medical field, including listings of accredited medical programs, contact
American Medical Association
515 North State Street
Chicago, IL 60610-5453
Tel: 800-621-8335
http://www.ama-assn.org

For information on certification or licensing, contact
American Registry of Diagnostic Medical Sonographers
51 Monroe Street
Plaza East One
Rockville, MD 20850-2400
Tel: 800-541-9754
http://www.ardms.org

For information on credentials, contact
Cardiovascular Credentialing International
1500 Sunday Drive, Suite 102
Raleigh, NC 27607-5151
Tel: 800-326-0268
http://cci-online.org

CAREER AND EMPLOYMENT COUNSELORS AND TECHNICIANS

OVERVIEW

Career and employment counselors, who are also known as *vocational counselors*, provide advice to individuals or groups about occupations, careers, career decision making, career planning, and other career development-related questions or conflicts. *Career guidance technicians* collect pertinent information to support both the counselor and applicant during the job search. Approximately 260,000 educational, vocational, and school counselors are employed in the United States.

THE JOB

Certified career counselors help people make decisions and plan life and career directions. They tailor strategies and techniques to the specific needs of the person seeking help. Counselors conduct individual and group counseling sessions to help identify life and career goals.

They administer and interpret tests and inventories to assess abilities and interests and identify career options. They may use career planning and occupational information to help individuals better understand the work world. They assist in developing individualized career plans, teach job-hunting strategies and skills, and help develop resumes. Sometimes this involves resolving personal conflicts on the job. They also provide support for people experiencing job stress, job loss, and career transition.

Vocational-rehabilitation counselors work with disabled individuals to help the counselees understand what skills they have to offer to an employer. A good counselor knows the working world and how to obtain detailed information about specific jobs. To assist with career decisions, counselors must know about the availability of jobs, the probable future of certain jobs, the education or training necessary to enter them, the kinds of salary or other benefits that certain jobs offer, the conditions that certain jobs impose on employees (night work, travel, work outdoors), and the satisfaction that certain jobs provide their employees. Professional career counselors work in both private and public settings and are certified by the National Board for Certified Counselors (NBCC).

College career planning counselors and *college placement counselors* work exclusively with the students of their universities or colleges. They may specialize in some specific area appropriate to the students and graduates of the school, such as law and education, as well as in part-time and summer work, internships, and field placements. In a liberal arts college, the students may need more assistance in identifying an appropriate career. To do this, the counselor administers interest and aptitude tests and interviews students to determine their career goals.

The counselor may work with currently enrolled students who are seeking internships and other work programs while still at school. Alumni who wish to make a career change also seek the services of the career counseling and placement office at their former schools.

College placement counselors also gather complete job information from prospective employers and make the information available to interested students and alumni. Just as counselors try to find applicants for particular job listings, they also must seek out jobs for specific applicants. To do this, they will call potential employers to encourage them to consider a qualified individual.

College and career planning and placement counselors are responsible for the arrangements and details of on-campus interviews by large corporations. They also

SCHOOL SUBJECTS
Business, Psychology, Sociology

PERSONAL SKILLS
Communication/Ideas, Helping/Teaching

MINIMUM EDUCATION LEVEL
High School Diploma

CERTIFICATION OR LICENSING
Required by Certain States

WORK ENVIRONMENT
Primarily Indoors, Primarily One Location

maintain an up-to-date library of vocational guidance material and recruitment literature.

Counselors also give assistance in preparing the actual job search by helping the applicant to write resumes and letters of application, as well as by practicing interview skills through role-playing and other techniques. They also provide information on business procedures and personnel requirements in the applicant's chosen field. University-based counselors will set up online accounts on career Web sites for students, giving them access to information regarding potential employers.

Some career planning and placement counselors work with secondary school authorities, advising them on the needs of local industries and specific preparation requirements for both employment and further education. In two-year colleges the counselor may participate in the planning of course content, and in some smaller schools the counselor may be required to teach as well.

The principal duty of *career guidance technicians* is to help order, catalog, and file materials relating to job opportunities, careers, technical schools, scholarships, careers in the armed forces, and other programs. Guidance technicians also help students and teachers find materials relating to a student's interests and aptitudes. These various materials may be in the form of books, pamphlets, magazine articles, microfiche, videos, computer software, or other media.

Often, career guidance technicians help students take and score self-administered tests that determine their aptitude and interest in different careers or job-related activities. If the career guidance center has audiovisual equipment, such as VCRs, DVD players, or film or slide projectors, career guidance technicians are usually responsible for the equipment.

REQUIREMENTS
High School

In order to work in the career and employment counseling field, you must have at least a high school diploma. For most jobs in the field, however, higher education is required. In high school, in addition to studying a core curriculum, with courses in English, history, mathematics, and biology, you should take courses in psychology and sociology. You will also find it helpful to take business and computer science classes.

Postsecondary Training

In some states, the minimum educational requirement in career and vocational counseling is a graduate degree in counseling or a related field from a regionally accredited higher education institution, and a completed supervised counseling experience, which includes career counseling. A growing number of institutions offer post-master's degrees with training in career development and career counseling. Such programs are highly recommended if you wish to specialize in vocational and career counseling. These programs are frequently called advanced graduate specialist programs or certificates of advanced study programs.

For a career as a college career planning and placement counselor, the minimum educational requirement is commonly a master's degree in guidance and counseling, education, college student personnel work, behavioral science, or a related field. Graduate work includes courses in vocational and aptitude testing, counseling techniques, personnel management and occupational research, industrial relations, and group dynamics and organizational behavior.

As in any profession, there is usually an initial period of training for newly hired counselors and counselor trainees. Some of the skills you will need as an employment counselor, such as testing-procedures skills and interviewing skills, can be acquired only through on-the-job training.

When hiring a career guidance technician, most employers look for applicants who have completed two years of training beyond high school, usually at a junior, community, or technical college. These two-year programs, which usually lead to an associate's degree, may combine classroom instruction with practical or sometimes even on-the-job experience.

Certification or Licensing

The NBCC offers the national certified counselor (NCC) designation as well as the national certified school counselor (NCSC) designation. In order to apply for the NCC, you must have earned a master's degree with a major study in counseling and you must pass the National Counselor Examination. NCCs are certified for a period of five years. In order to be recertified, they must complete 100 contact clock hours of continuing education or pass the examination again. In order to receive the NCSC credential, you must complete the above requirements, plus gain field experience in school counseling as a graduate student and then complete three years of post-graduate supervised school counseling. Many states require some type of credentialing or certification for counselors, and all states require those who work in school settings to be certified.

Other Requirements

In order to succeed as a career counselor, you must have a good background in education, training, employment trends, the current labor market, and career resources. You should be able to provide your clients with information about job tasks, functions, salaries, requirements, and the future outlook of broad occupational fields.

Knowledge of testing techniques and measures of aptitude, achievement, interests, values, and personality is required. The ability to evaluate job performance and individual effectiveness is helpful. You must also have management and administrative skills.

EXPLORING

Summer work in an employment agency is a good way to explore the field of employment counseling. Interviewing the director of a public or private agency might give you a better understanding of what the work involves and the qualifications such an organization requires of its counselors.

If you enjoy working with others, you will find helpful experiences working in the dean's or counselor's office. Many schools offer opportunities in peer tutoring, both in academics and in career guidance-related duties. (If your school does not have such a program in place, consider putting together a proposal to institute one. Your guidance counselor should be able to help you with this.) Your own experience in seeking summer and part-time work is also valuable in learning what job seekers must confront in business or industry. You could write a feature story for your school newspaper on your and others' experiences in the working world.

If you are interested in becoming a career counselor, you should seek out professional career counselors and discuss the field with them. Most people are happy to talk about what they do.

While in high school, consider working part time or as a volunteer in a library. Such work can provide you with some of the basic skills for learning about information resources, cataloging, and filing. In addition, assisting schools or clubs with any media presentations, such as video or slide shows, will help you become familiar with the equipment used by counselors. You may also find it helpful to read publications relating to this field, such as *The National Certified Counselor* newsletter (http://www. nbcc.org/users/productseekers.htm).

EMPLOYERS

There are approximately 260,000 educational, vocational, and school counselors employed in the United States. Career and employment counselors work in guidance offices of high schools, colleges, and universities. They are also employed by state, federal, and other bureaus of employment, and by social service agencies.

STARTING OUT

Journals specializing in information for career counselors frequently have job listings or information on job hotlines and services. School career services offices also are a good source of information, both because of their standard practice of listing job openings from participating firms and because schools are a likely source of jobs for you as a career counselor. Placement officers will be aware of which schools are looking for applicants.

To enter the field of college career planning and placement, you might consider working for your alma mater as an assistant in the college or university career services office. Other occupational areas that provide an excellent background for college placement work include teaching, business, public relations, previous placement training, positions in employment agencies, and experience in psychological counseling.

Career guidance technicians should receive some form of career placement from schools offering training in that area. Newspapers may list entry-level jobs. One of the best methods, however, is to contact libraries and education centers directly to inquire about their needs for assistance in developing or staffing their career guidance centers.

ADVANCEMENT

Employment counselors in federal or state employment services or in other vocational counseling agencies are usually considered trainees for the first six months of their employment. During this time, they learn the specific skills that will be expected of them during their careers with these agencies. The first year of a new counselor's employment is probationary.

Positions of further responsibility include supervisory or administrative work, which may be attained by counselors after several years of experience on the job. Advancement to administrative positions often means giving up the actual counseling work, which is not an advantage to those who enjoy working with people in need of counseling.

Opportunity for advancement for college counselors—to assistant and associate placement director, director of student personnel services, or similar administrative positions—depends largely on the type of college or university and the size of the staff. In general, a doctorate is preferred and may be necessary for advancement.

With additional education, career guidance technicians can advance to become career and employment counselors.

EARNINGS

Salaries vary greatly within the career and vocational counseling field. The U.S. Department of Labor (DOL) places career counselors within the category of educational, vocational, and school counselors. The median yearly earnings for this group were $47,530 in 2006, according to the DOL. The lowest paid 10 percent of these workers earned $27,240 or less per year, and the highest paid 10 percent made $75,920 or more annually. The department further broke down salaries by type of employer: those working for elementary and secondary schools had mean annual incomes of $55,560 in 2006; for junior colleges, $53,650; for colleges and universities, $44,730; for individual and family services, $35,020; and for vocational rehabilitation services, $34,320. Annual earnings of career counselors vary greatly among educational institutions, with larger institutions offering the highest salaries. Counselors in business or industry tend to earn higher salaries.

In private practice, the salary range is even wider. Some practitioners earn as little as $20,000 per year, and others, such as elite "headhunters" who recruit corporate executives and other high-salaried positions, earn in excess of $100,000 per year.

Salaries for career guidance technicians vary according to education and experience and the geographic location of the job. In general, career guidance technicians who are graduates of two-year post high school training programs can expect to receive starting salaries averaging $20,000 to $25,000 a year.

Benefits depend on the employer, but they usually include paid holidays and vacation time, retirement plans, and, for those at some educational institutions, reduced tuition.

WORK ENVIRONMENT

Employment counselors usually work about 40 hours a week, but some agencies are more flexible. Counseling is done in offices designed to be free from noise and distractions, to allow confidential discussions with clients.

College career planning and placement counselors also normally work a 40-hour week, although irregular hours and overtime are frequently required during the peak recruiting period. They generally work on a 12-month basis.

Career guidance technicians work in very pleasant surroundings, usually in the career guidance office of a college or vocational school. They will interact with a great number of students, some of whom are eagerly looking for work, and others who are more tense and anxious. The technician must remain unruffled in order to ease any tension and provide a quiet atmosphere.

OUTLOOK

Employment in the field of employment counseling is expected to grow about as fast as the average for all occupations through 2016, according to the U.S. Department of Labor. One reason for this steady growth is increased school enrollments, even at the college level, which means more students needing the services of career counselors. Another reason is that there are more counselor jobs than graduates of counseling programs. Opportunities should also be available in government agencies as many states institute welfare-to-work programs or simply cut welfare benefits. And finally, in this age of outsourcing and lack of employment security, "downsized" workers, those re-entering the workforce, and those looking for second careers all create a need for the skills of career and employment counselors.

FOR MORE INFORMATION

For a variety of career resources for career seekers and career counseling professionals, contact the following organizations:

American Counseling Association
5999 Stevenson Avenue
Alexandria, VA 22304-3300
Tel: 800-347-6647
http://www.counseling.org

Career Planning & Adult Development Network
543 Vista Mar Avenue
Pacifica, CA 94044-1951
Tel: 650-359-6911
Email: admin@careernetwork.org
http://www.careernetwork.org

For resume and interview tips, general career information, and advice from experts, visit the NACE's Web site:

National Association of Colleges and Employers (NACE)
62 Highland Avenue
Bethlehem, PA 18017-9085
Tel: 800-544-5272
http://www.naceweb.org

For information on certification, contact
National Board for Certified Counselors
3 Terrace Way
Greensboro, NC 27403-3660
Tel: 336-547-0607
Email: nbcc@nbcc.org
http://www.nbcc.org

For more information on career counselors, contact
National Career Development Association
305 North Beech Circle
Broken Arrow, OK 74012-2293
Tel: 918-663-7060
http://ncda.org

CARPENTERS

OVERVIEW

Carpenters cut, shape, level, and fasten together pieces of wood and other construction materials, such as wallboard, plywood, and insulation. Many carpenters construct, remodel, or repair houses and other kinds of buildings. Other carpenters work at construction sites where roads, bridges, docks, boats, mining tunnels, and wooden vats are built. They may specialize in building the rough framing of a structure, and thus be considered *rough carpenters,* or they may specialize in the finishing details of a structure, such as the trim around doors and windows, and be *finish carpenters.* Approximately 1.5 million carpenters work in the United States.

THE JOB

Carpenters remain the largest group of workers in the U.S. building trades today. The vast majority of them work for contractors involved in building, repairing, and remodeling buildings and other structures. Manufacturing firms, schools, stores, and government bodies employ most other carpenters.

Carpenters do two basic kinds of work: rough carpentry and finish carpentry. Rough carpenters construct and install temporary structures and supports and wooden structures used in industrial settings, as well as parts of buildings that are usually covered up when the rooms are finished. Among the structures built by such carpenters are scaffolds for other workers to stand on, chutes used as channels for wet concrete, forms for concrete foundations, and timber structures that support machinery. In buildings, they may put up the frame and install rafters, joists, subflooring, wall sheathing, prefabricated wall panels and windows, and many other components.

Finish carpenters install hardwood flooring, staircases, shelves, cabinets, trim on windows and doors, and other woodwork and hardware that make the building look complete, inside and outside. Finish carpentry requires especially careful, precise workmanship, since the result must have a good appearance in addition to being sturdy. Many carpenters who are employed by building contractors do both rough and finish work on buildings.

Although they do many different tasks in different settings, carpenters generally follow the same basic steps. First, they review blueprints or plans (or they obtain instructions from a supervisor) to determine the dimensions of the structure to be built and the types of materials to be used. Sometimes local building codes mandate how a structure should be built, so carpenters need to know about such regulations.

Using rulers, framing squares, chalk lines, and other measuring and marking equipment, carpenters lay out how the work will be done. Using hand and power tools, they cut and shape the wood, plywood, fiberglass, plastic, or other materials. Then they nail, screw, glue, or staple the pieces together. Finally, they use levels, plumb bobs, rulers, and squares to check their work, and they make any necessary adjustments. Sometimes carpenters work with prefabricated units for components such as wall panels or stairs. Installing these is, in many ways, a much less complicated task, because much less layout, cutting, and assembly work is needed.

Carpenters who work outside of the building construction field may do a variety of installation and maintenance jobs, such as repairing furniture and installing ceiling tiles or exterior siding on buildings. Other carpenters specialize in building, repairing, or modifying

ships, wooden boats, wooden railroad trestles, timber framing in mine shafts, woodwork inside railcars, storage tanks and vats, or stage sets in theaters.

SCHOOL SUBJECTS
Mathematics, Technical/Shop

PERSONAL SKILLS
Following Instructions, Mechanical/Manipulative

MINIMUM EDUCATION LEVEL
Apprenticeship

CERTIFICATION OR LICENSING
Voluntary

WORK ENVIRONMENT
Primarily Indoors, Primarily Multiple Locations

REQUIREMENTS
High School

A high school education is not mandatory for a good job as a carpenter, but most contractors and developers prefer applicants with a diploma or a GED. A good high school background for prospective carpenters would include carpentry and woodworking courses as well as other shop classes; applied mathematics; mechanical drawing; and blueprint reading.

Postsecondary Training

As an aspiring carpenter, you can acquire the skills of your trade in various ways, through formal training programs and through informal on-the-job training. Of the different ways to learn, an apprenticeship is considered the best, as it provides a more thorough and complete foundation for a career as a carpenter than do other kinds of training. However, the limited number of available apprenticeships means that not all carpenters can learn the trade this way.

You can pick up skills informally on the job while you work as a carpenter's helper—and many carpenters enter the field this way. You will begin with little or no training and gradually learn as you work under the supervision of experienced carpenters. The skills that you will develop as a helper will depend on the jobs that your employers contract to do. Working for a small contracting company, a beginner may learn about relatively few kinds of carpentry tasks. On the other hand, a large contracting company may offer a wider variety of learning opportunities. Becoming a skilled carpenter by this method can take much longer than an apprenticeship, and the completeness of the training varies. While some individuals are waiting for an apprenticeship to become available they may work as helpers to gain experience in the field.

Some people first learn about carpentry while serving in the military. Others learn skills in vocational educational programs offered in trade schools and through correspondence courses. Vocational programs can be very good, especially as a supplement to other practical training. But without additional hands-on instruction, vocational school graduates may not be adequately prepared to get many jobs in the field because some programs do not provide sufficient opportunity for students to practice and perfect their carpentry skills.

Apprenticeships, which will provide you with the most comprehensive training available, usually last four years. They are administered by employer groups and by local chapters of labor unions that organize carpenters. Applicants must meet the specific requirements of local apprenticeship committees. Typically, you must be at least 17 years old, have a high school diploma, and be able to show that you have some aptitude for carpentry.

Apprenticeships combine on-the-job work experience with classroom instruction in a planned, systematic program. Initially, you will work at such simple tasks as building concrete forms, doing rough framing, and nailing subflooring. Toward the end of your training, you may work on finishing trimwork, fitting hardware, hanging doors, and building stairs. In the course of this experience, you will become familiar with the tools, materials, techniques, and equipment of the trade, and you will learn how to do layout, framing, finishing, and other basic carpentry jobs.

The work experience segment of an apprenticeship is supplemented by about 144 hours of classroom instruction per year. Some of this instruction concerns the correct use and maintenance of tools, safety practices, first aid, building code requirements, and the properties of different construction materials. Other subjects you will study include the principles of layout, blueprint reading, shop mathematics, and sketching. Both on the job and in the classroom, you will learn how to work effectively with members of other skilled building trades.

Certification or Licensing

The United Brotherhood of Carpenters and Joiners of America (UBCJA), the national union for the indus-

try, offers certification courses in a variety of specialty skills. These courses teach the ins and outs of advanced skills—like scaffold construction—that help to ensure worker safety, while at the same time giving workers ways to enhance their abilities and so qualify for better jobs. Some job sites require all workers to undergo training in safety techniques and guidelines specified by the Occupational Safety and Health Administration. Workers who have not passed these courses are considered ineligible for jobs at these sites.

Other Requirements

In general, as a carpenter, you will need to have manual dexterity, good hand-eye coordination, and a good sense of balance. You will need to be in good physical condition, as the work involves a great deal of physical activity. Stamina is much more important than physical strength. On the job, you may have to climb, stoop, kneel, crouch, and reach as well as deal with the challenges of weather.

EXPLORING

Beyond classes such as woodshop or mechanical drawing, there are a number of real-world ways to begin exploring a career in carpentry and the construction trades. Contact trade organizations like the National Association of Home Builders or the Associated General Contractors of America; both sponsor student chapters around the country. Consider volunteering for an organization like Habitat for Humanity; Its Youth Programs accept volunteers between the ages of five and 25, and their group building projects provide hands-on experience. If your school has a drama department, look into it—building sets can be a fun way to learn simple carpentry skills. In addition, your local home improvement store is likely to sponsor classes that teach a variety of skills useful around the house; some of these will focus on carpentry.

A less direct method to find out about carpentry is via television and the Internet. PBS and some cable stations show how-to programs—such as *This Old House* and *New Yankee Workshop*—that feature the work of carpenters. Both shows also offer companion Web sites that can be found at http://www.thisoldhouse.com/toh and http://www.newyankee.com, respectively.

EMPLOYERS

Carpenters account for a large group of workers in the building trades, holding approximately 1.5 million jobs. About 32 percent of carpenters work for general-building contractors, and 23 percent work for specialty contractors. About 32 percent are self-employed.

Some carpenters work for manufacturing firms, government agencies, retail and wholesale establishments, or schools. Others work in the shipbuilding, aircraft, or railroad industries. Still others work in the arts, for theaters and movie and television production companies as set builders, or for museums or art galleries, building exhibits.

STARTING OUT

Information about available apprenticeships can be obtained by contacting the local office of the state employment service, area contractors that hire carpenters, or the local offices of the United Brotherhood of Carpenters, which cooperates in sponsoring apprenticeship programs. Helper jobs that can be filled by beginners without special training in carpentry may be advertised in newspaper classified ads or with the state employment service. You also might consider contacting potential employers directly.

ADVANCEMENT

Once an applicant has completed and met all the requirements of apprenticeship training, he or she will be considered a journeyman carpenter. With sufficient experience, journeymen may be promoted to positions responsible for supervising the work of other carpenters. If a carpenter's background includes exposure to a broad range of construction activities, he or she may eventually advance to a position as a general construction supervisor. A carpenter who is skillful at mathematical computations and has a good knowledge of the construction business, may become an estimator. An experienced carpenter might one day go into business for himself or herself, doing repair or construction work as an independent contractor.

EARNINGS

According to the U.S. Department of Labor, carpenters had median hourly earnings of $17.57 in 2006. Someone making this wage and working full-time for the year would have an income of approximately $36,550. The lowest paid 10 percent of carpenters earned less than $10.87 per hour (or approximately $22,610 per year), and the highest paid 10 percent made more than $30.45 hourly (approximately $63,330 annually). It is important to note, however, that these annual salaries are for full-time work. Many carpenters, like others in the building trades, have periods of unemployment during the year, and their incomes may not match these.

Starting pay for apprentices can range from $5 per hour to $17 per hour. The wage is increased periodically so that by the fourth year of training apprentice pay is 80 percent of the journeyman carpenter's rate.

Fringe benefits, such as health insurance, pension funds, and paid vacations, are available to most workers in this field and vary with local union contracts. In general, benefits are more likely to be offered on jobs staffed by union workers.

WORK ENVIRONMENT

Carpenters may work either indoors or outdoors. If they do rough carpentry, they will probably do most of their work outdoors. Carpenters may have to work on high scaffolding, or in a basement making cement forms. A construction site can be noisy, dusty, hot, cold, or muddy. Carpenters can expect to be physically active throughout the day, constantly standing, stooping, climbing, and reaching. Some of the possible hazards of the job include being hit by falling objects, falling off scaffolding or a ladder, straining muscles, and getting cuts and scrapes on fingers and hands. Carpenters who follow recommended safety practices and procedures minimize these hazards.

Work in the construction industry involves changing from one job location to another, and from time to time being laid off because of poor weather, shortages of materials, or simply lack of jobs. Carpenters must be able to arrange their finances so that they can make it through sometimes long periods of unemployment.

Though it is not required, many carpenters are members of a union such as the UBCJA. Among many other services, such as the certification courses mentioned previously, the union works with employers, seeking to ensure that members receive equitable pay and work in safe conditions.

OUTLOOK

Although the U.S. Department of Labor predicts employment growth for carpenters to increase about as fast as the average for all occupations through 2016, job opportunities for carpenters are expected to be very strong. This is because replacement carpenters are needed for the large number of experienced carpenters who leave the field every year for work that is less strenuous. Replacement workers are also needed for the fair amount of workers just starting out in the field who decide to move on to more comfortable occupations. And, of course, replacements are needed for those who retire. Home-building and construction of hotels, restaurants, and other businesses, as well as roads and bridges; home modifications for the growing elderly population; two-income couples' desire for larger homes; and the growing population of all ages should contribute to the demand for carpenters.

Factors that will hold down employment growth in the field include the use of more prefabricated building parts and improved tools that make construction easier and faster. In addition, a weak economy has a major impact on the building industry, causing companies and individuals to put off expensive building projects until better times. Carpenters with good all-around skills, such as those who have completed apprenticeships, will have the best job opportunities even in difficult times.

FOR MORE INFORMATION

For information on activities and student chapters, contact

Associated General Contractors of America
2300 Wilson Boulevard, Suite 400
Arlington, VA 22201-5426
Tel: 703-548-3118
Email: info@agc.org
http://www.agc.org

Habitat for Humanity is an internationally recognized nonprofit organization dedicated to the elimination of poverty housing. For information on programs and local chapters found all over the United States, contact

Habitat for Humanity International
121 Habitat Street
Americus, GA 31709-3498
Tel: 229-924-6935, ext. 2551
Email: publicinfo@hfhi.org
http://www.habitat.org

For information on apprenticeships, training programs, and general information about trends in the industry, contact

Home Builders Institute
1201 15th Street, NW, Sixth Floor
Washington, DC 20005-2842
Tel: 800-795-7955
Email: postmaster@hbi.org
http://www.hbi.org

For information about careers in the construction trades and student chapters, contact

National Association of Home Builders
1201 15th Street, NW
Washington, DC 20005-2842
Tel: 800-368-5242
http://www.nahb.com

For information on union membership and apprenticeships, contact

United Brotherhood of Carpenters and Joiners of America
Carpenters Training Fund
6801 Placid Street
Las Vegas, NV 89119-4205
http://www.carpenters.org

CHIROPRACTORS

OVERVIEW

Chiropractors, or *doctors of chiropractic,* are health care professionals who emphasize health maintenance and disease prevention through proper nutrition, exercise, posture, stress management, and care of the spine and the nervous system. Approximately 53,000 chiropractors practice in the United States. Most work in solo practice; other work settings include group practices, health care clinics, and teaching institutions.

Because of its emphasis on health maintenance, the whole person, and natural healing, chiropractic is considered an alternative health care approach. At the same time, chiropractic has more of the advantages enjoyed by the medical profession than does any other alternative health care field: Chiropractic has licensure requirements, accredited training institutions, a growing scientific research base, and insurance reimbursement.

THE JOB

Chiropractors are trained primary health care providers, much like medical physicians. Chiropractors focus on the maintenance of health and disease prevention. In addition to symptoms, they consider each patient's nutrition, work, stress levels, exercise habits, posture, and so on. Chiropractors treat people of all ages—from children to senior citizens. They see both women and men. Doctors of chiropractic most frequently treat conditions such as backache, disk problems, sciatica, and whiplash. They also care for people with headaches, respiratory disorders, allergies, digestive disturbances, elevated blood pressure, and many other common ailments. Some specialize in areas such as sports medicine or nutrition. Chiropractors do not use drugs or surgery. If they determine that drugs or surgery are needed, they refer the individual to another professional who can meet those needs.

Doctors of chiropractic look for causes of disorders of the spine. They consider the spine and the nervous system to be vitally important to the health of the individual. Chiropractic teaches that problems in the spinal column (backbone) affect the nervous system and the body's natural defense mechanisms and are the underlying causes of many diseases. Chiropractors use a special procedure called a "spinal adjustment" to try to restore the spine to its natural healthy state. They believe this will also have an effect on the individual's total health and well-being.

On the initial visit, doctors of chiropractic meet with the patient and take a complete medical history before beginning treatment. They ask questions about all aspects of the person's life to help determine the nature of the illness. Events in the individual's past that may seem unrelated or unimportant may be significant to the chiropractor.

After the consultation and the case history, chiropractors perform a careful physical examination, sometimes including laboratory tests. When necessary, they use X rays to help locate the source of patients' difficulties. Doctors of chiropractic study the X rays for more than just bone fractures or signs of disease. X rays are the only means of seeing the outline of the spinal column. Chiropractors are trained to observe whether the structural alignment of the spinal column is normal or abnormal.

Once they have made a diagnosis, chiropractic physicians use a variety of natural approaches to help restore the individual to health. The spinal adjustment is the treatment for which chiropractic is most known. During this procedure, patients usually lie on a specially designed adjusting table. Chiropractic physicians generally use their hands to manipulate the spine. They apply pressure and use specialized techniques of manipulation that are designed to help the affected areas of the spine. Doctors of chiropractic must know many sophisticated techniques of manipulation, and they spend countless hours learning to properly administer spinal adjustments. Chiropractic treatments must often be repeated over the course of several visits. The number of treatments needed varies greatly.

In addition to the spinal adjustment, chiropractic physicians may use "physiologic therapeutics" to relieve symptoms. These are drugless natural therapies, such as light, water, electrical stimulation, massage, heat, ultrasound, and biofeedback. Chiropractors also make suggestions about diet, rest, exercise, and support of the afflicted body part. They may recommend routines for the patient to do at home to maintain and improve the results of the manipulation.

SCHOOL SUBJECTS
Biology, Chemistry

PERSONAL SKILLS
Mechanical/Manipulative, Technical/Scientific

MINIMUM EDUCATION LEVEL
Medical Degree

CERTIFICATION OR LICENSING
Required

WORK ENVIRONMENT
Primarily Indoors, Primarily One Location

Chiropractors pay special attention to lifestyle factors, such as nutrition and exercise. They believe the body has an innate ability to remain healthy if it has the proper ingredients. Doctors of chiropractic propose that the essential ingredients include clean air, water, proper nutrition, rest, and a properly functioning nervous system. Their goal is to maintain the health and well being of the whole person. In this respect they have been practicing for many years what has recently become known as "health maintenance."

Chiropractors who are in private practice and some who work as group practitioners also have responsibility for running their businesses. They must promote their practices and develop their patient base. They are responsible for keeping records on their patients and for general bookkeeping. Sometimes they hire and train employees. In larger practices or clinics, chiropractic assistants or office managers usually perform these duties.

REQUIREMENTS
High School

To become a doctor of chiropractic (DC), you will have to study a minimum of six to seven years after high school. Preparing for this profession is just as demanding as preparing to be a medical doctor, and the types of courses you will need are also similar. Science classes, such as biology, chemistry, physics, and psychology, will prepare you for medical courses in college. English, speech, drama, and debate can sharpen the communication skills that are essential for this profession. Math, business, and computer classes can help you get ready to run a private practice.

Postsecondary Training

Most chiropractic colleges require at least two years of undergraduate study before you can enroll. Some require a bachelor's degree. Currently, 16 chiropractic programs and two chiropractic institutions in the United States and Canada are accredited by the Council on Chiropractic Education (CCE). Find out which chiropractic colleges interest you and learn about their requirements. Selecting chiropractic schools well in advance will allow you to structure your undergraduate study to meet the requirements of the schools of your choice. Some chiropractic colleges provide opportunities for prechiropractic study and bachelor's degree programs. In general, you need course work in biology, communications, English, chemistry, physics, psychology, and social sciences or humanities. Contact the national professional associations listed at the end of this article for information about schools and their requirements.

Upon completing the required undergraduate work and enrolling in a chiropractic college, you can expect to take an array of science and medical courses, such as anatomy, pathology, and microbiology. During the first two years of most chiropractic programs you will spend a majority of your time in the classroom or the laboratory. The last two years generally focus on courses in spinal adjustments. During this time, potential chiropractors also train in outpatient clinics affiliated with the college. Upon successful completion of the six- or seven-year professional degree program, you will receive the DC degree.

Certification or Licensing

All 50 states and the District of Columbia require that chiropractors pass a state board examination to obtain a license to practice. Educational requirements and types of practice for which a chiropractor may be licensed vary from state to state. Most state boards recognize academic training only in chiropractic colleges accredited by the CCE. Most states will accept all or part of the National Board of Chiropractic Examiners' test given to fourth-year chiropractic students in place of a state exam. Most states require that chiropractors take continuing education courses each year to keep their licenses.

Other Requirements

Perhaps the most important personal requirement for any health care professional is the desire to help people and to promote wholeness and health. To be a successful chiropractor, you need good listening skills, empathy, and understanding. As a doctor of chiropractic, you will also need a good business sense and the ability to work independently. Especially sharp observational skills are essential in order for you to recognize physical abnormalities. Good hand dexterity is necessary to perform the spinal adjustments and other manipulations. However, you do not need unusual strength.

EXPLORING

If you are interested in becoming a chiropractor, there are many ways to start preparing right now. Join all the science clubs you can, design projects, and participate in science fairs. To develop interviewing and communication skills, you might join the school newspaper staff and ask for interview assignments. Learn to play chess, take up fencing, or study art history to increase your powers of observation. Take up an instrument, such as the piano, guitar, or violin, to improve your manual dexterity. Learning to give massages is another way to increase manual dexterity and learn the human body. Be sure to stay in shape and maintain your own health, and learn all you can about homeopathy, yoga, the Alexander technique, Rolfing, and other systems of mind/body wholeness.

Contact the chiropractic professional associations and ask about their student programs. Check the Internet for bulletin boards or forums related to chiropractic and other areas of health care. Volunteer at a hospital or nursing home to gain experience working with those in need of medical care.

If there is a doctor of chiropractic or a clinic in your area, ask to visit and talk to a chiropractor. Make an appointment for a chiropractic examination so you can experience what it is like. You may even find a part-time or summer job in a chiropractic office.

EMPLOYERS

There are approximately 53,000 chiropractors employed in the United States. A newly licensed doctor of chiropractic might find a salaried position in a chiropractic clinic or with an experienced chiropractor. Other salaried positions can be found in traditional hospitals, in hospitals that specialize in chiropractic treatment, or in alternative health care centers and clinics. More than 50 percent of the doctors of chiropractic in the United States are in private practice. Most maintain offices in a professional building with other specialists or at their own clinics.

Chiropractors practice throughout the United States. Jobs in clinics, hospitals, and alternative health care centers may be easier to find in larger cities that have the population to support them. However, most doctors of chiropractic choose to work in small communities. Chiropractors tend to remain near chiropractic institutions, and this has resulted in higher concentrations of chiropractic practices in those geographical areas.

STARTING OUT

Career services offices of chiropractic colleges have information about job openings, and they may be able to help with job placement. As a newly licensed chiropractor, you might begin working in a clinic or in an established practice with another chiropractor on a salary or income-sharing basis. This would give you a chance to start practicing without the major financial investment of equipping an office. It is sometimes possible to purchase the practice of a chiropractor who is retiring or moving. This is usually easier than starting a new solo practice because the purchased practice will already have patients. However, some newly licensed practitioners do go straight into private practice.

National chiropractic associations and professional publications may also list job openings. Attend an association meeting to get to know professionals in the field. Networking is an important way to learn about job openings.

ADVANCEMENT

As with many other professions, advancement in chiropractic usually means building a larger practice. A chiropractor who starts out as a salaried employee in a large practice may eventually become a partner in the practice. Chiropractors also advance their careers by building their clientele and setting up their own group practices. They sometimes buy the practices of retiring practitioners to add to their own practices.

Another avenue for advancement is specialization. Chiropractors specialize in areas such as neurology, sports medicine, or diagnostic imaging (X ray). As the demand for chiropractors is growing, more are advancing their careers through teaching at chiropractic institutions or conducting research. A few doctors of chiropractic become executives with state or national organizations.

EARNINGS

Self-employed chiropractors usually earn more than salaried chiropractors, such as those working as an associate with another chiropractor or doctor. Chiropractors running their own office, however, must pay such expenses as equipment costs, staff salaries, and health insurance.

According to the U.S. Department of Labor, the median annual income for chiropractors working on a salary basis was $65,220 in 2006. The lowest 10 percent earned $32,670 that same year, while the top 25 percent earned more than $96,500 per year. According to a survey conducted by *Chiropractic Economics* magazine, the mean income for chiropractors was $104,363 in 2005.

Self-employed chiropractors must provide for their own benefits. Chiropractors who are salaried employees, such as those working on the staff of another doctor or those working for health clinics, usually receive benefits including health insurance and retirement plans.

WORK ENVIRONMENT

Chiropractic physicians work in clean, quiet, comfortable offices. Most solo practitioners and group practices have an office suite. The suite generally has a reception area. In clinics, several professionals may share this area. The suite also contains examining rooms and treatment rooms. In a clinic where several professionals work, there are sometimes separate offices for the individual professionals. Most chiropractors have chiropractic assistants and a secretary or office manager. Those who are in private practice or partnerships need to have good business skills and self-discipline to be successful.

Doctors of chiropractic who work in clinics, hospitals, universities, or professional associations need to work well in a group environment. They will frequently work under supervision or in a team with other professionals. Chiropractors may have offices of their own, or they may share offices with team members, depending on their work and the facility. In these organizations, the physical work environment varies, but it will generally be clean and comfortable. Because they are larger, these settings may be noisier than the smaller practices.

Most chiropractors work about 40 hours per week, although many put in longer hours. Larger organizations may determine the hours of work, but chiropractors in private practice can set their own. Evening and weekend hours are often scheduled to accommodate patients' needs.

OUTLOOK

Employment for doctors of chiropractic is expected to grow faster than the average for all occupations through 2016, according to the U.S. Department of Labor. Many areas have a shortage of chiropractors. Public interest in alternative health care is growing. Many health-conscious individuals are attracted to chiropractic because it is natural, drugless, and surgery-free. Because of their holistic, personal approach to health care, chiropractors are increasingly seen as primary physicians, especially in rural areas. The average life span is increasing, and so are the numbers of older people in this country. The elderly frequently have more structural and mechanical difficulties, and the growth of this segment of the population will increase the demand for doctors of chiropractic.

More insurance policies and health maintenance organizations (HMOs) now cover chiropractic services, but this still varies according to the insurer. As a result of these developments in HMO and insurance coverage, chiropractors receive more referrals for treatment of injuries that result from accidents.

While the demand for chiropractic is increasing, college enrollments are also growing. New chiropractors may find increasing competition in geographic areas where other practitioners are already located. Because of the high cost of equipment such as X-ray and other diagnostic tools, group practices with other chiropractors or related health care professionals are likely to provide more opportunity for employment or for purchasing a share of a practice.

FOR MORE INFORMATION

For general information and a career kit, contact

American Chiropractic Association
1701 Clarendon Boulevard
Arlington, VA 22209-2799
Tel: 703-276-8800
http://www.amerchiro.org

For information on educational requirements and accredited colleges, contact

Council on Chiropractic Education
8049 North 85th Way
Scottsdale, AZ 85258-4321
Tel: 480-443-8877
Email: cce@cce-usa.org
http://www.cce-usa.org

For information on student membership and member chiropractors in your area, contact

International Chiropractors Association
1110 North Glebe Road, Suite 650
Arlington, VA 22201-4795
Tel: 800-423-4690
http://www.chiropractic.org

For information on licensure, contact

National Board of Chiropractic Examiners
901 54th Avenue
Greeley, CO 80634-4405
Tel: 970-356-9100
Email: nbce@nbce.org
http://www.nbce.org

CIVIL ENGINEERS

OVERVIEW

Civil engineers are involved in the design and construction of the physical structures that make up our surroundings, such as roads, bridges, buildings, and harbors. Civil engineering involves theoretical knowledge applied to the practical planning of the layout of our cities, towns, and other communities. It is concerned with modifying the natural environment and building new environments to better the lifestyles of the general public. Civil engineers are also known as *structural engineers*. There are approximately 256,000 civil engineers in the United States.

THE JOB

Civil engineers use their knowledge of materials science, engineering theory, economics, and demographics to devise, construct, and maintain our physical surroundings. They apply their understanding of other branches of science—such as hydraulics, geology, and physics—to design the optimal blueprint for the project.

Feasibility studies are conducted by *surveying and mapping engineers* to determine the best sites and approaches for construction. They extensively investigate the chosen sites to verify that the ground and other surroundings are amenable to the proposed project. These engineers use sophisticated equipment, such as satellites and other electronic instruments, to measure the area and conduct underground probes for bedrock and groundwater. They determine the optimal places where explosives should be blasted in order to cut through rock.

Many civil engineers work strictly as consultants on projects, advising their clients. These consultants usually specialize in one area of the industry, such as water systems, transportation systems, or housing structures. Clients include individuals, corporations, and the government. Consultants will devise an overall design for the proposed project, perhaps a nuclear power plant commissioned by an electric company. They will estimate the cost of constructing the plant, supervise the feasibility studies and site investigations, and advise the client on whom to hire for the actual labor involved. Consultants are also responsible for such details as accuracy of drawings and quantities of materials to order.

Other civil engineers work mainly as contractors and are responsible for the actual building of the structure; they are known as *construction engineers.* They interpret the consultants' designs and follow through with the best methods for getting the work done, usually working directly at the construction site. Contractors are responsible for scheduling the work, buying the materials, maintaining surveys of the progress of the work, and choosing the machines and other equipment used for construction. During construction, these civil engineers must supervise the labor and make sure the work is completed correctly and efficiently. After the project is finished, they must set up a maintenance schedule and periodically check the structure for a certain length of time. Later, the task of ongoing maintenance and repair is often transferred to local engineers.

Civil engineers may be known by their area of specialization. *Transportation engineers,* for example, are concerned mainly with the construction of highways and mass transit systems, such as subways and commuter rail lines. When devising plans for subways, engineers are responsible for considering the tunneling that is involved. *Pipeline engineers* are specialized civil engineers who are involved with the movement of water, oil, and gas through miles of pipeline.

REQUIREMENTS
High School

Because a bachelor's degree is considered essential in the field, high school students interested in civil engineering must follow a college prep curriculum. Students should focus on mathematics (algebra, trigonometry, geometry, and calculus), the sciences (physics and chemistry), computer science, and English and the humanities (history, economics, and sociology). Students should also aim for honors-level courses.

Postsecondary Training

In addition to completing the core engineering curriculum (including mathematics, science, drafting, and computer applications), students can choose their specialty from the following types of courses: structural analysis; materials design and specification; geology; hydraulics; surveying and design graphics; soil mechanics; and oceanography. Bachelor's degrees can be achieved through a number of programs: a four- or five-year accredited college or university; two years in a community college engineering program plus two or three years in a college or university; or five or six years in a co-op program (attending classes for part of the

SCHOOL SUBJECTS
Mathematics, Physics

PERSONAL SKILLS
Leadership/Management, Technical/Scientific

MINIMUM EDUCATION LEVEL
Bachelor's Degree

CERTIFICATION OR LICENSING
Recommended

WORK ENVIRONMENT
Primarily Indoors, Primarily Multiple Locations

year and working in an engineering-related job for the rest of the year). About 30 percent of civil engineering students go on to receive a master's degree.

Certification or Licensing

Most civil engineers go on to study and qualify for a professional engineer (P.E.) license. It is required before one can work on projects affecting property, health, or life. Because many engineering jobs are found in government specialties, most engineers take the necessary steps to obtain the license. Requirements are different for each state—they involve educational, practical, and teaching experience. Applicants must take an examination on a specified date.

Other Requirements

Basic personal characteristics often found in civil engineers are an avid curiosity; a passion for mathematics and science; an aptitude for problem solving, both alone and with a team; and an ability to visualize multidimensional, spatial relationships.

EXPLORING

High school students can become involved in civil engineering by attending a summer camp or study program in the field. For example, the Worcester Polytechnic Institute in Massachusetts has a summer program for high school students who have completed their junior year and will be entering their senior year in the fall. Studies and events focus on science and math and include specialties for those interested in civil engineering. Visit http://www.admissions.wpi.edu/Frontiers for more information.

Additionally, the Web site of the American Society of Civil Engineers (http://www.asce.org) offers a wealth of information about careers in the field.

After high school, another way to learn about civil engineering duties is to work on a construction crew that is involved in the actual building of a project designed and supervised by engineers. Such hands-on experience would provide an opportunity to work near many types of civil workers. Try to work on highway crews or even in housing construction.

EMPLOYERS

Nearly half of all civil engineers work for companies involved in architectural and engineering consulting services. Others work for government agencies at the local, state, or federal level. A small percentage are self-employed, running their own consulting businesses. Approximately 256,000 civil engineers work in the United States.

STARTING OUT

To establish a career as a civil engineer, one must first receive a bachelor's degree in engineering or another appropriate scientific field. College career services offices are often the best sources of employment for beginning engineers. Entry-level jobs usually involve routine work, often as a member of a supervised team. After a year or more (depending on job performance and qualifications), one becomes a junior engineer, then an assistant to perhaps one or more supervising engineers. Establishment as a professional engineer comes after passing the P.E. exam.

ADVANCEMENT

Professional engineers with many years' experience often join with partners to establish their own firms in design, consulting, or contracting. Some leave long-held positions to be assigned as top executives in industries such as manufacturing and business consulting. Also, there are those who return to academia to teach high school or college students. For all of these potential opportunities, it is necessary to keep abreast of engineering advancements and trends by reading industry journals and taking courses.

EARNINGS

Civil engineers are among the lowest paid in the engineering field; however, their salaries are high when compared to those of many other occupations. The median annual earnings for civil engineers were $68,600 in 2006, according to the U.S. Department of Labor. The lowest paid 10 percent made less than $44,810 per year, and, at the other end of the pay scale, 10 percent earned more than $104,420 annually. Civil engineers working for the federal government had a mean salary of $77,970 in 2006. According to a 2007 survey by the National Association of Colleges and Employers, starting salaries by degree level averaged as follows: bachelor's, $48,509; master's, $48,280; and doctorate, $62,275. As with all occupations, salaries are higher for those with more experience. Top civil engineers earn as much as $120,000 a year.

Benefits typically include such extras as health insurance, retirement plans, and paid vacation days.

WORK ENVIRONMENT

Many civil engineers work regular 40-hour weeks, often in or near major industrial and commercial areas. Sometimes they are assigned to work in remote areas and foreign countries. Because of the diversity of civil engineering positions, working conditions vary widely. Offices, labs, factories, and actual sites are typical environments for engineers.

A typical work cycle involving various types of civil engineers involves three stages: planning, constructing, and maintaining. Those involved with development of a campus compound, for example, would first need to work in their offices developing plans for a survey. Surveying and mapping engineers would have to visit the proposed site to take measurements and perhaps shoot aerial photographs. The measurements and photos would have to be converted into drawings and blueprints. Geotechnical engineers would dig wells at the site and take core samples from the ground. If toxic waste or unexpected water is found at the site, the contractor determines what should be done.

Actual construction then begins. Very often, a field trailer on the site becomes the engineers' makeshift offices. The campus might take several years to build—it is not uncommon for engineers to be involved in long-term projects. If contractors anticipate that deadlines will not be met, they often put in weeks of 10- to 15-hour days on the job.

After construction is complete, engineers spend less and less time at the site. Some may be assigned to stay on-site to keep daily surveys of how the structure is holding up and to solve problems when they arise. Eventually, the project engineers finish the job and move on to another long-term assignment.

OUTLOOK

Employment for civil engineers is expected to grow faster than the average for all occupations through 2016, according to the U.S. Department of Labor. Employment will come from the need to maintain and repair public works, such as highways, bridges, and water systems. In addition, as the population grows, so does the need for more transportation and pollution control systems, which creates jobs for those who construct these systems. Firms providing management consulting and computer services may also be sources of jobs for civil engineers. However, employment is affected by several factors, including decisions made by the government to spend further on renewing and adding to the country's basic infrastructure and the health of the economy in general.

FOR MORE INFORMATION

For information on training and scholarships, and to read Career Paths in Civil Engineering, *visit the society's Web site.*

American Society of Civil Engineers
1801 Alexander Bell Drive
Reston, VA 20191-4400
Tel: 800-548-2723
http://www.asce.org

For information on careers and colleges and universities with ITE student chapters, contact

Institute of Transportation Engineers (ITE)
1099 14th Street, NW, Suite 300 West
Washington, DC 20005-3438
Tel: 202-289-0222
Email: ite_staff@ite.org
http://www.ite.org

JETS offers high school students the opportunity to try engineering through a number of programs and competitions. To find out more about these opportunities or for general career information, contact

Junior Engineering Technical Society (JETS)
1420 King Street, Suite 405
Alexandria, VA 22314-2794
Tel: 703-548-5387
Email: info@jets.org
http://www.jets.org

CLERGY

OVERVIEW

Clergy are religious and spiritual leaders, as well as teachers and interpreters of their faith. They prepare and lead religious services, officiate special ceremonies such as

---

SCHOOL SUBJECTS
Religion, Speech

PERSONAL SKILLS
Communication/Ideas, Helping/Teaching

MINIMUM EDUCATION LEVEL
Some Postsecondary Training

CERTIFICATION OR LICENSING
None Available

WORK ENVIRONMENT
Primarily Indoors, Primarily One Location With Some Travel

---

marriage, baptism, and funerals, deliver sermons, read from sacred texts such as the Bible, Talmud, or Koran, and head religious education programs for their spiritual communities. Clergy members also visit the sick and poor, and offer spiritual and moral counsel to those that seek help. They are responsible for the administrative staff, as well as upkeep and management, of their church, temple, or mosque.

THE JOB

Protestant ministers are the spiritual leaders of Protestant congregations. They interpret the tenets and doctrines of their faith and instruct people who seek conversion. Like other clergy, they lead their congregations in worship, supervise religious educational programs and Bible study, and teach confirmation and adult education courses. They may also play a role in preparing church newsletters and Sunday bulletins. They may answer telephone calls, written requests, or questions, or even counsel walk-in visitors requiring spiritual advice or practical aid such as food or shelter.

Some Protestant denominations or congregations within a denomination have a traditional order of service. Others require that the minister adapt the service to the specific needs of the congregation. Most Protestant services include Bible readings, hymn singing, prayers, and a sermon prepared and delivered by the minister.

Protestant clergy also administer specific church rites, such as baptism, holy communion, and confirmation. They conduct weddings and funerals. Ministers advise couples concerning the vows and responsibilities of marriage. They may also act as marriage counselors for couples who are having marital difficulties. They visit the sick, comfort the bereaved, and participate in the administration of their parish or congregation.

Ministers may share duties with an associate or with an assistant minister as well as other church staff. Some ministers teach in seminaries and other schools. Others write for publications and give speeches within the Protestant community and to those in the community at large. A growing number of ministers are employed only part-time and may serve more than one congregation or have a secular part-time job.

Roman Catholic priests are the spiritual leaders of Roman Catholic congregations. Like other clergy, they conduct services, give sermons, called homilies, and help and counsel those in need. Priests administer the sacraments, such as baptism and communion. Priests usually begin the day with meditation and mass. They counsel those who are troubled and often visit the sick. Many priests involve themselves in the work of various church committees, civic and charitable organizations, and community projects. Some priests have become involved in concerns such as human rights and other nonliturgical issues. Others may teach in a variety of educational settings.

There are two categories of priests—diocesan and religious. All priests have the same powers bestowed on them through ordination by a bishop, but their way of life, the type of work they do, and the authority to whom they report depends on whether they are members of a religious order or working in a diocese. *Diocesan,* or *secular, priests* generally work in parishes to which they are assigned by their bishop. *Religious priests,* such as Dominicans, Jesuits, or Franciscans, work as members of a religious community, teaching, doing missionary work, or engaging in other specialized activities as assigned by their superiors. Both categories of priests teach and hold administrative positions in Catholic seminaries and educational institutions.

Roman Catholic clergy do not choose their work assignments; this is done in collaboration with their religious superiors. Work assignments, however, are always made with the interests and abilities of the individual priest in mind. Every effort is made to place a priest in the type of ministry requested. Priests may serve in a wide range of ministries, from counseling full-time and working in social services to being chaplains in the armed forces, prisons, or hospitals.

Rabbis serve congregations affiliated with four movements of American Judaism: Orthodox, Conservative, Reform, and Reconstructionist. Regardless of their affiliation, all rabbis have similar responsibilities. They conduct religious services, officiate at weddings and funerals, help the needy, supervise religious educational programs, and teach confirmation and adult education courses. They also counsel members of their congregation and visit the sick.

Rabbis are the teachers of their community. They help congregants and other interested individuals apply religious teachings to their lives. Within Judaism the rabbi has an elevated status in spiritual matters, but most Jewish synagogues and temples have a relatively democratic form of decision making in which all members participate. Rabbis of large congregations spend much of their time working with their staffs and various committees. They often receive assistance from an associate or assistant rabbi.

The Jewish traditions differ somewhat in their view of God and of history. These differences also extend to such variations in worship as the wearing of head coverings, the amount of Hebrew used during prayer, the use of music, the level of congregational participation, and the status of women. Whatever their particular point of view, all Jewish congregations—Orthodox, Conservative, Reform, or Reconstructionist—preserve the substance of Jewish worship in a manner consistent with their beliefs.

In the Buddhist religion, clergy are referred to as *monks* and *priests*. Monks spend most of their time in meditation and prayer. Priests head temple ceremonies. Monks and priests give religious instruction and pastoral services for laypersons.

In the Hindu religion, *gurus* conduct ceremonies held in temples, and give religious instruction. *Monks* serve as pastors, and live in monasteries. *Sadhus,* or *sannyasis,* are wandering holy men that travel to spread the Hindu faith.

In the religion of Islam there is no ordained ministry or priesthood, although there are *religious teachers,* called *ulama,* or *mullahs,* and religious orders consisting of *sufis* (*mystics*) called *dervishes*.

REQUIREMENTS
High School

In high school, prospective Protestant ministers should study history and religion, plus English and speech to improve their teaching and oration skills. Music and fine arts classes will help strengthen their understanding and appreciation of the liturgy. Knowledge of a foreign language may help ministers better serve the needs of their congregations.

Some high schools offer preparation for the Roman Catholic priesthood that is similar to that of a college preparatory high school. High school seminary studies focus on English, speech, literature, and social studies. Latin may or may not be required; the study of other foreign languages, such as Spanish, is encouraged. Other recommended high school courses include typing, debating, and music.

Many aspiring rabbis informally begin their training early in life in Jewish grade schools and high schools. Aspiring rabbis should take all religious and Hebrew language courses available to them. It is also important to study English and communications to become an effective leader. Business and mathematics courses are a good foundation for administrative work as the leader of a congregation.

Postsecondary Training

While some denominations require little more than a high school education or Bible study, the majority of Protestant groups require a bachelor's degree plus several years of specialized theological training. An undergraduate degree in the liberal arts is the typical college program for prospective clergy, although entrants come from a range of academic backgrounds. Course work should include English, foreign languages, philosophy, the natural sciences, psychology, history, social sciences, and comparative religions, as well as fine arts and music. In general, the major Protestant denominations have their own schools of theological training, but many of these schools admit students of other denominations. There are also several interdenominational colleges and theological schools that give training for the ministry. This may be augmented by training in the denomination in which the student will be ordained. More than 250 Protestant schools in the United States and Canada are accredited by the Association of Theological Schools in the United States and Canada. Accredited schools require a bachelor's degree, or its equivalent, for admission. After three years of study and an internship, students earn a Master of Divinity degree.

Eight years of post-high school study are usually required to become an ordained Roman Catholic priest. Candidates for the priesthood often choose to enter at the college level or begin their studies in theological seminaries after college graduation. The liberal arts program offered by seminary colleges stresses philosophy, religion, the behavioral sciences, history, the natural sciences, and mathematics. Some priestly formation programs may insist on seminarians majoring in philosophy. The additional four years of preparation for ordination are given over entirely to the study of theology, including studies in moral (ethics) and pastoral and dogmatic

(doctrine) theology. Other areas of study include church history, scripture, homiletics (the art of preaching), liturgy (worship), and canon (church) law. In the third year of advanced training, candidates undertake fieldwork in parishes and the wider community. Because the work expected of secular and religious priests differs, they are trained in different major seminaries offering slightly varied programs. Postgraduate work in theology and other fields is available and encouraged for priests, who may study in American Catholic universities, ecclesiastical universities in Rome, or other places around the world. Continuing education for ordained priests in the last several years has stressed sociology, psychology, and the natural sciences.

Completion of a course of study in a seminary is a prerequisite for ordination as a rabbi. Entrance requirements, curriculum, and length of the seminary program vary depending on the particular branch of Judaism. Prospective rabbis normally need to complete a bachelor's degree before entering the seminary. Degrees in Jewish studies, philosophy, and even English and history can fulfill seminary entrance requirements. It is advisable to study Hebrew at the undergraduate level if at all possible. Seminarians without a solid background in Jewish studies and the Hebrew language may have to take remedial courses. While seminary studies differ between the four movements of Judaism, there are many similarities between them. Most seminary programs lead to the Master of Arts in Hebrew Letters degree and ordination as a rabbi. Most programs last about five years, and many of them include a period of study in Jerusalem. It is becoming more common for seminarians to complete internships—usually as assistants to experienced rabbis in the area—as part of their educational requirements.

Other Requirements

Protestant ministers must meet the requirements of their individual denominations. Both men and women can become ordained ministers in most denominations today.

In the Roman Catholic Church, only men are called to the priesthood. A vow of celibacy is required, along with vows of poverty and obedience. Some orders take a special fourth vow, often related to the charism of their community; for example, a vow of stability to stay in one place or a vow of silence.

Jewish Orthodox seminaries accept only men, but all other denominations accept men and women into the rabbinate.

Beyond formal ordination requirements, all clergy must possess a religious vocation—a strong feeling that

God is calling them to the service of others through religious ministry. Clergy also need to be outgoing and friendly and have a strong desire to help others. They need to be able to get along with people from a wide variety of backgrounds. They need patience, sympathy, and open-mindedness to be able to listen to the problems of others, while maintaining a discreet and sincere respect. They need leadership abilities, including self-confidence, decisiveness, and the ability to supervise others. Clergy must set a high moral and ethical standard for the members of their church, temple, or mosque.

EXPLORING

People interested in becoming a religious leader should talk with the leaders of their own church, temple, or mosque to get a clear idea of the rewards and responsibilities of this profession. Choosing a religious career entails much thought. There are numerous opportunities to investigate this life. If a religious career sounds appealing, volunteer at a church or other religious institution to get better acquainted with the type of job responsibilities involved in the work. Essentially, however, there is no single experience that can adequately prepare a person for the demands of a religious career. Formal religious training will offer you the best opportunity to explore the many facets of the ministry.

EMPLOYERS

Protestant ministers are usually employed by the congregations they serve. Most, but not all, congregations play a decisive role in selecting someone to serve as their pastor. Other ministers may choose to work in seminaries, hospitals, or other church-run institutions. Other employment opportunities for clergy include social service work, such as counseling, youth work, family relations guidance, and teaching. Ministers may also find opportunities as chaplains in the armed forces, hospitals, mental health centers, prisons, and social agencies such as the YMCA. There are approximately 400,000 Protestant ministers employed in the United States.

While some Roman Catholic priests serve in dioceses and others serve in religious orders, all priests ultimately serve the church. Most priests can count on a pretty conventional life in the settings they have chosen: the hustle and bustle of an urban mission, the steady work of a suburban parish or school, the serenity of a monastery. Still, it is important to be ready and willing to serve wherever the church needs you. Priests know that by following the church's call to wherever they are needed, they are accomplishing God's will. There are approximately 45,000 Roman Catholic priests.

Most rabbis are employed by their congregations. Others work for schools, colleges, seminaries, and publications. Some serve as chaplains in hospitals or in the various branches of the armed forces. There are approximately 1,800 Reform; 1,175 Conservative; 1,100 Orthodox; and 250 Reconstructionist rabbis.

STARTING OUT

Protestant ministry students should consult with their minister or contact the appropriate theological seminary to learn how to best meet entrance requirements. Some denominations do not require seminary training to become ordained. Smaller denominations may train part-time leaders, who eventually may seek ordination. Seminary graduates who cannot find ready employment may become directors of homes for the aged or mentally handicapped, or of orphanages. Others may find employment in the social services, as missionaries, or in church-sponsored summer camps. Some ministers may take an unpaid position with a financially disadvantaged church in order to gain valuable experience.

Newly ordained diocesan priests generally begin their ministry as associate pastors, while new priests of religious orders are assigned duties for which they are specially trained, such as missionary work. Both diocesan and religious priests work under the supervision of more experienced colleagues until they are deemed ready for more responsibility.

Only ordained rabbis can lead congregations in the Jewish faith. Many newly ordained rabbis find jobs through the seminary from which they graduated or through professional rabbinical organizations within their particular Jewish movement. With the growing popularity of internships for seminaries, it is possible that these will lead to permanent positions after ordination. Rabbis generally begin their careers as leaders of small congregations, assistants to experienced rabbis, directors of Hillel foundations on college campuses, or chaplains in the armed forces.

ADVANCEMENT

Newly ordained ministers generally begin their careers as pastors of small congregations or as assistant pastors (curates) in larger congregations. From there, advancement depends on individual interests, abilities, and available positions.

Newly ordained diocesan priests generally begin their ministry as associate pastors, while new priests of religious orders are assigned duties for which they are specially trained, such as missionary work. Priests may also become teachers in seminaries and other educational institutions, or chaplains in the armed forces. The pulpits of large, well-established churches are usually filled by priests of considerable experience. A small number of priests become bishops, archbishops, and cardinals. Only cardinals can be elevated to the position of Pope.

Newly ordained rabbis generally begin their careers as leaders of small congregations, assistants to experienced rabbis, directors of Hillel foundations on college campuses, teachers in seminaries and other educational institutions, or chaplains in the armed forces. With experience, they may acquire their own or larger congregations or choose to remain in their original position. The pulpits of large, well-established synagogues and temples are usually filled by rabbis of considerable experience. They may also choose to open new synagogues in growing communities that require more religious facilities. Others may discover that their talents and abilities are most useful in teaching, fundraising, or leadership positions within their particular denomination.

EARNINGS

It should be noted that becoming a member of the clergy is not only a career, but a life choice as well. All clergy enter this profession to spread and teach their faith--reward comes in the form of being able to help others.

Salaries for all clergy ranged from less than $20,730 to $69,720 or more annually in 2006, according to the U.S. Department of Labor.

Salaries vary substantially for Protestant clergy depending on the individual's experience, as well as the size of the congregation, its denominational branch, location, and financial status. The average income of Protestant ministers is $40,000 per year, according to "How Much Should We Pay the Pastor: A Fresh Look at Clergy Salaries in the 21st Century," a survey conducted by Duke University's Divinity School. Ministers employed in larger, wealthier denominations earn more than $60,000. Some ministers of smaller congregations may add to their earnings by working at part-time secular jobs.

Roman Catholic religious priests take a vow of poverty and are supported by their religious order. Any salary that they may receive for writing or other activities is usually returned to their religious order. Diocesan priests receive small salaries calculated to cover their basic needs. These salaries vary according to the size of the parish, as well as its location and financial status. Priests who teach or do specialized work usually receive a small stipend, often

referred to as "contributed service," that is equal to that paid to lay persons in similar positions. Priests who serve in the Armed Forces receive the same amount of pay as other officers of equal rank. The Internal Revenue Service recognizes the vow of poverty and does not require priests to pay federal income tax.

Salaries for rabbis vary according to the size, denominational branch, location, and financial status of the congregation. According to limited information, the earnings of rabbis range from $50,000 to $100,000. Smaller congregations pay less, usually between $30,000 and $50,000 a year. Some congregations may allow their rabbi to teach at local universities or other settings to earn additional income.

Additional benefits for ministers, priests, rabbis, and other members of the clergy usually include a housing stipend, which includes utilities, a monthly transportation allowance, health insurance and retirement fund. Some receive travel stipends for research and rest. Protestant ministers may receive grants for the education of their children. Clergy often are given a monetary gift when they officiate at weddings, funerals, and other ceremonies of life. This is sometimes donated to the church or a charity by clergy. Rabbis often receive gifts for officiating at bar mitzvahs.

WORK ENVIRONMENT

Clergy spend long hours working under a variety of conditions. There is no such thing as a standard work week. They are on call at any hour of the day or night, sometimes, in the case of ministers and rabbis, interfering with their own family life. They visit the sick, comfort and counsel families in times of crisis, and help raise funds for the church. Much time is also spent reading, studying, writing, attending and chairing meetings, and talking to people. They also must prepare sermons and keep up with religious and secular events. Clergy may also have many administrative responsibilities working with staff and various committees. They also participate in community and interfaith events.

Despite the long hours and sometimes stressful and demanding work conditions, most clergy enjoy their work and find helping and administering to their congregation a satisfying occupation. The public in general and congregations in particular expect clergy members to set high examples of moral and ethical conduct. There is the added pressure of being "on call" 24 hours a day, and the need to often comfort people in difficult situations.

Protestant ministers may be reassigned to a new pastorate by a central governing body. Religious priests are responsible to the superior of their order, the bishop in the diocese that they work, as well as the Supreme Pontiff of the Catholic Church, the Pope. Rabbis are generally independent in their positions, responsible only to the board of directors of their congregation rather than to any formal hierarchy.

OUTLOOK

Membership growth in Protestant churches—such as the Baptist, Lutheran, Methodist, and Presbyterian denominations—has been stagnant in the past few years. Aging membership has caused church budgets and membership to shrink, lessening the demand for full-time ministers. There has been a significant increase in membership in evangelical churches. Overall, the increased cost of church operations is expected to limit the demand for ministers. The closing or combining of smaller parishes, and the reduced availability of funds, has lessened the need for full-time ministers. And, although the number of ministry graduates is also declining, ministers should expect competition for some parish jobs, especially the more desirable, urban ones.

Demand for ministers will vary depending on affiliation, with nondenominational churches needing the most ministers. Graduates of theological schools have the best prospects for employment, as do ministers willing to work in rural churches with smaller congregations, salary, and benefits. They may also have to minister to two or more smaller congregations to earn a sufficient salary. Employment opportunities may depend on ministers retiring, passing away, or leaving the profession.

Employment opportunities for priests through 2016 are favorable. The Roman Catholic Church is currently facing a severe shortage of priests. The Catholic population in the United States, currently 72 million, continues to steadily grow, while the number of students entering the seminary decreases and more priests reach retirement age. The needs of newly established parishes and Catholic institutions are far greater than the number of ordained priests.

As a result of the continuing shortage of priests, more than 10,000 deacons have been ordained to preach, baptize, perform Holy Communion, and other sacraments. Saying mass and hearing confessions are the only duties that deacons may not perform. Lay people, called *Eucharistic Ministers,* give Holy Communion and assist priests and deacons in other ways. As a result, future priests may become less involved in teaching and administrative functions to devote themselves to other duties. There has also been limited debate regarding short-term commitments to the priestly life, as well as women in the priesthood, as a way of attracting more interest in the vocation.

Job opportunities for rabbis are good for all four major branches of Judaism. Orthodox rabbis should have good job prospects as older rabbis retire and smaller communities become large enough to hire their own rabbi. Conservative and Reform rabbis should also have excellent employment opportunities, especially because of retirement and new Jewish communities. Reconstructionist rabbis should find very good opportunities because this branch of Judaism is growing rapidly.

FOR MORE INFORMATION
Christianity

Besides your own pastor, you can consult the headquarters of your denomination for information about becoming a Protestant minister. Through the Web sites listed below, you can gather information and link to affiliated seminaries:

The Episcopal Church, USA
815 Second Avenue
New York, NY 10017-4503
Tel: 800-334-7626
http://www.episcopalchurch.org

Evangelical Lutheran Church in America
8765 West Higgins Road
Chicago, IL 60631-4101
Tel: 800-638-3522
Email: info@elca.org
http://www.elca.org

Lutheran Church—Missouri Synod
1333 South Kirkwood Road
St. Louis, MO 63122-7295
Tel: 888-843-5267
http://www.lcms.org

Presbyterian Church (USA)
100 Witherspoon Street
Louisville, KY 40202-1396
Tel: 888-728-7228
http://www.pcusa.org

Southern Baptist Convention
901 Commerce
Nashville, TN 37203-3620
Tel: 615-244-2355
http://www.sbc.net

United Methodist Church
Board of Higher Education and Ministry
810 12th Avenue South

Nashville, TN 37203-4704
Tel: 800-251-8140
http://www.umc.org

For information on accredited training programs,
contact

Association of Theological Schools in the United States and Canada
10 Summit Park Drive
Pittsburgh, PA 15275-1110
Tel: 412-788-6505
Email: ats@ats.edu
http://www.ats.edu

The NRVC can provide information about all kinds
of Roman Catholic vocations; it also publishes Vision,
a vocation discernment guide available in print and
online.

National Religious Vocation Conference (NVRC)
5401 South Cornell Avenue, Suite 207
Chicago, IL 60615-5664
Tel: 773-363-5454
Email: nrvc@nrvc.net
http://www.nrvc.net

For information on conventions, publications, seminars,
and recent news, contact

National Federation of Priests' Councils
333 North Michigan Avenue, Suite 1205
Chicago, IL 60601-4002
Tel: 888-271-6372
Email: nfpc@nfpc.org
http://www.nfpc.org

Judaism

The following organizations serve ordained rabbis, but can
be of some help to those considering the ministry

Central Conference of American Rabbis (Reform)
355 Lexington Avenue
New York, NY 10017-6603
Tel: 212-972-3636
Email: info@ccarnet.org
http://ccarnet.org

Jewish Reconstructionist Federation (Reconstructionism)
Beit Devora
101 Greenwood Avenue
Jenkintown, PA 19046-2627
Tel: 215-885-5601
Email: info@jrf.org
http://www.jrf.org

The Rabbinical Assembly (Conservative)
3080 Broadway
New York, NY 10027-4650
Tel: 212-280-6000
Email: info@rabbinicalassembly.org
http://www.rabbinicalassembly.org

Rabbinical Council of America (Orthodox)
305 Seventh Avenue
New York, NY 10001-6008
Tel: 212-807-9000
Email: office@rabbis.org
http://rabbis.org

The following educational institution has four campuses;
Cincinnati, New York, Los Angeles, and Jerusalem. Visit its
Web site to learn about the different schools and the train-
ing required to become a rabbi.

Hebrew Union College-Jewish Institute of Religion (Reform)
http://www.huc.edu

For information on other training programs, contact
Jewish Theological Seminary of America (Conservative)
3080 Broadway
New York, NY 10027-4650
Tel: 212-678-8000
http://www.jtsa.edu

Reconstructionist Rabbinical College
1299 Church Road
Wyncote, PA 19095-6143
Tel: 215-576-0800
Email: info@rrc.edu
http://www.rrc.edu

Buddhism

For more information on Buddhism, visit
Buddha Dharma Education Association
http://www.buddhanet.net

Hinduism

For more information on Hinduism, visit
A Study of Hindu Religion
http://www.us-hindus.com

Islam

For more information on the Islamic faith, visit
Islam 101
http://www.islam101.com

☐ COLLEGE PROFESSORS

OVERVIEW

College professors instruct undergraduate and graduate students in specific subjects at colleges and universities. They lecture classes, lead small seminar groups, and create and grade examinations. They also may conduct research, write for publication, and aid in administration. Approximately 1.7 million postsecondary teachers are employed in the United States.

THE JOB

College and university faculty members teach at junior colleges or at four-year colleges and universities. At four-year institutions, most faculty members are *assistant professors, associate professors,* or *full professors.* These three types of professorships differ in regards to status, job responsibilities, and salary. Assistant professors are new faculty members who are working to get tenure (status as a permanent professor); they seek to advance to associate and then to full professorships.

College professors perform three main functions: teaching, advising, and research. Their most important responsibility is to teach students. Their role within a college department will determine the level of courses they teach and the number of courses per semester. Most professors work with students at all levels, from college

freshmen to graduate students. They may head several classes a semester or only a few a year. Some of their classes will have large enrollment, while graduate seminars may consist of only 12 or fewer students. Though college professors may spend fewer than 10 hours a week in the actual classroom, they spend many hours preparing lectures and lesson plans, grading papers and exams, and preparing grade reports. They also schedule office hours during the week to be available to students outside of the lecture hall, and they meet with students individually throughout the semester. In the classroom, professors lecture, lead discussions, administer exams, and assign textbook reading and other research. In some courses, they rely heavily on laboratories to transmit course material.

Another important responsibility is advising students. Not all faculty members serve as advisers, but those who do must set aside large blocks of time to guide students through the program. College professors who serve as advisers may have any number of students assigned to them, from fewer than 10 to more than 100, depending on the administrative policies of the college. Their responsibility may involve looking over a planned program of studies to make sure the students meet requirements for graduation, or it may involve working intensively with each student on many aspects of college life.

The third responsibility of college and university faculty members is research and publication. Faculty members who are heavily involved in research programs sometimes are assigned a smaller teaching load. College professors publish their research findings in various scholarly journals. They also write books based on their research or on their own knowledge and experience in the field. Most textbooks are written by college and university teachers. In arts-based programs, such as master's of fine arts programs in painting, writing, and theater, professors practice their craft and exhibit their art work in various ways. For example, a painter or photographer will have gallery showings, while a poet will publish in literary journals.

Publishing a significant amount of work has been the traditional standard by which assistant professors prove themselves worthy of becoming permanent, tenured faculty. Typically, pressure to publish is greatest for assistant professors. Pressure to publish increases again if an associate professor wishes to be considered for a promotion to full professorship.

In recent years, some liberal arts colleges have recognized that the pressure to publish is taking faculty away from their primary duties to the students, and these institutions have begun to place a decreasing emphasis on

SCHOOL SUBJECTS
English, History, Speech

PERSONAL SKILLS
Communications/Ideas, Helping/Teaching

MINIMUM EDUCATION LEVEL
Master's Degree

CERTIFICATION OR LICENSING
None Available

WORK ENVIRONMENT
Primarily Indoors, Primarily One Location

publishing and more on performance in the classroom. Professors in junior colleges face less pressure to publish than those in four-year institutions.

Some faculty members eventually rise to the position of *department chair,* where they govern the affairs of an entire department, such as English, history, mathematics, or biological sciences. Department chairs, faculty, and other professional staff members are aided in their myriad duties by *graduate assistants,* who may help develop teaching materials, conduct research, give examinations, teach lower-level courses, and carry out other activities.

Some college professors may also conduct classes in an extension program. In such a program, they teach evening and weekend courses for the benefit of people who otherwise would not be able to take advantage of the institution's resources. They may travel away from the campus and meet with a group of students at another location. They may work full time for the extension division or may divide their time between on-campus and off-campus teaching.

Distance learning programs, an increasingly popular option for students, give professors the opportunity to use today's technologies to remain in one place while teaching students who are at a variety of locations simultaneously. The professor's duties, like those when teaching correspondence courses conducted by mail, include grading work that students send in at periodic intervals and advising students of their progress. Computers, the Internet, email, and video conferencing, however, are some of the technology tools that allow professors and students to communicate in "real time" in a virtual classroom setting. Meetings may be scheduled during the same time as traditional classes or during evenings and weekends. Professors who do this work are sometimes known as *extension work, correspondence,* or *distance learning instructors.* They may teach online courses in addition to other classes or may have distance learning as their major teaching responsibility.

The *junior college instructor* has many of the same kinds of responsibilities as does the teacher in a four-year college or university. Because junior colleges offer only a two-year program, they teach only undergraduates.

REQUIREMENTS
High School

Your high school's college preparatory program likely includes courses in English, science, foreign language, history, math, and government. In addition, you should take courses in speech to get a sense of what it will be like to lecture to a group of students. Your school's debate team can also help you develop public speaking skills, along with research skills.

Postsecondary Training

At least one advanced degree in your field of study is required to be a professor in a college or university. The master's degree is considered the minimum standard, and graduate work beyond the master's is usually desirable. If you hope to advance in academic rank above instructor, most institutions require a doctorate.

In the last year of your undergraduate program, you'll apply to graduate programs in your area of study. Standards for admission to a graduate program can be high and the competition heavy, depending on the school. Once accepted into a program, your responsibilities will be similar to those of your professors—in addition to attending seminars, you'll research, prepare articles for publication, and teach some undergraduate courses.

You may find employment in a junior college with only a master's degree. Advancement in responsibility and in salary, however, is more likely to come if you have earned a doctorate.

Other Requirements

You should enjoy reading, writing, and researching. Not only will you spend many years studying in school, but your whole career will be based on communicating your thoughts and ideas. People skills are important because you'll be dealing directly with students, administrators, and other faculty members on a daily basis. You should feel comfortable in a role of authority and possess self-confidence.

EXPLORING

Your high school teachers use many of the same skills as college professors, so talk to your teachers about their careers and their college experiences. You can develop your own teaching experience by volunteering at a community center, working at a day care center, or working at a summer camp. Also, spend some time on a college campus to get a sense of the environment. Write to colleges for their admissions brochures and course catalogs (or check them out online); read about the faculty members and the courses they teach. Before visiting college campuses, make arrangements to speak to professors who teach courses that interest you. These professors may allow you to sit in on their classes and observe. Also, make appointments with college advisers and with people in the admissions and recruitment offices. If your grades are good enough, you might be able to serve as a teaching assistant during your undergraduate years, which can give you experience leading discussions and grading papers.

EMPLOYERS

Employment opportunities vary based on area of study and education. Most universities have many different departments that hire faculty. With a doctorate, a number of publications, and a record of good teaching, professors should find opportunities in universities all across the country. There are more than 3,800 colleges and universities in the United States. Professors teach in undergraduate and graduate programs. The teaching jobs at doctoral institutions are usually better paying and more prestigious. The most sought-after positions are those that offer tenure. Teachers that have only a master's degree will be limited to opportunities with junior colleges, community colleges, and some small private institutions. There are approximately 1.7 million postsecondary teachers employed in the United States.

STARTING OUT

You should start the process of finding a teaching position while you are in graduate school. The process includes developing a curriculum vitae (a detailed, academic resume), writing for publication, assisting with research, attending conferences, and gaining teaching experience and recommendations. Many students begin applying for teaching positions while finishing their graduate program. For most positions at four-year institutions, you must travel to large conferences where interviews can be arranged with representatives from the universities to which you have applied.

Because of the competition for tenure-track positions, you may have to work for a few years in temporary positions, visiting various schools as an adjunct professor. Some professional associations maintain lists of teaching opportunities in their areas. They may also make lists of applicants available to college administrators looking to fill an available position.

ADVANCEMENT

The normal pattern of advancement is from instructor to assistant professor, to associate professor, to full professor. All four academic ranks are concerned primarily with teaching and research. College faculty members who have an interest in and a talent for administration may be advanced to chair of a department or to dean of their college. A few become college or university presidents or other types of administrators.

The instructor is usually an inexperienced college teacher. He or she may hold a doctorate or may have completed all the Ph.D. requirements except for the dissertation. Most colleges look upon the rank of instructor as the period during which the college is trying out the teacher. Instructors usually are advanced to the position of assistant professors within three to four years. Assistant professors are given up to about six years to prove themselves worthy of tenure, and if they do so, they become associate professors. Some professors choose to remain at the associate level. Others strive to become full professors and receive greater status, salary, and responsibilities.

Most colleges have clearly defined promotion policies from rank to rank for faculty members, and many have written statements about the number of years in which instructors and assistant professors may remain in grade. Administrators in many colleges hope to encourage younger faculty members to increase their skills and competencies and thus to qualify for the more responsible positions of associate professor and full professor.

EARNINGS

Full professors working in disciplines such as law, architecture, business and related fields, health professions, computer and information sciences, and engineering have the highest salaries. Lower-paying disciplines include theology, recreation and fitness studies, English, liberal arts/humanities, and visual and performing arts.

Earnings vary by the departments professors work in, by the size of the school, by the type of school (public, private, women's only, for example), and by the level of position the professor holds. In its 2006–07 salary survey, the American Association of University Professors reported the average yearly income for all full-time faculty was $73,207. It also reports that professors earned the following average salaries by rank: full professors, $98,974; associate professors, $69,911; assistant professors, $58,662; instructors, $42,609; and lecturers, $48,289.

According to the U.S. Department of Labor, in 2006, the median salary for all postsecondary instructors was $63,930, with 10 percent earning $120,580 or more and 10 percent earning $33,590 or less. Those with the highest earnings tend to be senior tenured faculty; those with the lowest, graduate assistants. Professors working on the West Coast and the East Coast and those working at doctorate-granting institutions also tend to have the highest salaries. Many professors try to increase their earnings by completing research, publishing in their field, or teaching additional courses.

Benefits for full-time faculty typically include health insurance and retirement funds and, in some cases, stipends for travel related to research, housing allowances, and tuition waivers for dependents.

WORK ENVIRONMENT

A college or university is usually a pleasant place in which to work. Campuses bustle with all types of activities and events, stimulating ideas, and a young, energetic population. Much prestige comes with success as a professor and scholar; professors have the respect of students, colleagues, and others in their community.

Depending on the size of the department, college professors may have their own office, or they may have to share an office with one or more colleagues. Their department may provide them with a computer, Internet access, and research assistants. College professors are also able to do much of their office work at home. They can arrange their schedule around class hours, academic meetings, and the established office hours when they meet with students. Most college teachers work more than 40 hours each week. Although college professors may teach only two or three classes a semester, they spend many hours preparing for lectures, examining student work, and conducting research.

OUTLOOK

The U.S. Department of Labor predicts much faster than average employment growth for college and university professors through 2016. College enrollment is projected to grow due to an increased number of 18- to 24-year-olds, an increased number of adults returning to college, and an increased number of foreign-born students. Additionally, opportunities for college teachers will be good in areas such as engineering, business, computer science, and health science, which offer strong career prospects in the world of work. Retirement of current faculty members will also provide job openings. However, competition for full-time, tenure-track positions at four-year schools will be very strong.

A number of factors threaten to change the way colleges and universities hire faculty. Some university leaders are developing more business-based methods of running their schools, focusing on profits and budgets. This can affect college professors in a number of ways. One of the biggest effects is in the replacement of tenure-track faculty positions with part-time instructors. These part-time instructors include adjunct faculty, visiting professors, and graduate students. Organizations such as the AAUP and the American Federation of Teachers are working to prevent the loss of these full-time jobs, as well as to help part-time instructors receive better pay and benefits. Other issues involve the development of long-distance education departments in many schools. Though these correspondence courses have become very popular in recent years, many professionals believe that students in long-distance education programs receive only a second-rate education. A related concern is about the proliferation of computers in the classroom. Some courses consist only of instruction by computer software and the Internet. The effects of these alternative methods on the teaching profession will be offset somewhat by the expected increases in college enrollment in coming years.

FOR MORE INFORMATION

To read about the issues affecting college professors, contact the following organizations:

American Association of University Professors
1012 14th Street, NW, Suite 500
Washington, DC 20005-3406
Tel: 202-737-5900
Email: aaup@aaup.org
http://www.aaup.org

American Federation of Teachers
555 New Jersey Avenue, NW
Washington, DC 20001-2029
Tel: 202-879-4400
Email: online@aft.org
http://www.aft.org

❑ COMPUTER NETWORK ADMINISTRATORS

OVERVIEW

Computer network administrators, or *network specialists,* design, install, and support an organization's local area network (LAN), wide area network (WAN), network segment, or Internet or intranet system. They maintain network hardware and software, analyze problems, and monitor the network to ensure availability to system users. Administrators also might plan, coordinate, and implement network security measures, including firewalls. Approximately 309,000 computer network and systems administrators work in the United States.

SCHOOL SUBJECTS

Computer Science, Mathematics

PERSONAL SKILLS

Helping/Teaching, Leadership/Management, Technical/Scientific

MINIMUM EDUCATION LEVEL

Bachelor's Degree

CERTIFICATION OR LICENSING

Recommended

WORK ENVIRONMENT

Primarily Indoors, Primarily One Location

THE JOB

Businesses use computer networks for several reasons. One important reason is that networks make it easy for many employees to share hardware and software as well as printers, fax machines, and modems. For example, it would be very expensive to buy individual copies of word-processing programs for each employee in a company. By investing in a network version of the software that all employees can access, companies can often save a lot of money. Also, businesses that rely on databases for daily operations use networks to allow authorized personnel quick and easy access to the most updated version of the database.

Networks vary greatly in size; even just two computers connected together are considered a network. They can also be extremely large and complex, involving hundreds of computer terminals in various geographical locations around the world. A good example of a large network is the Internet, which is a system that allows people from every corner of the globe to access millions of pieces of information about any subject under the sun. Besides varying in size, networks are all at least slightly different in terms of configuration, or what the network is designed to do; businesses customize networks to meet their specific needs. All networks, regardless of size or configuration, experience problems. For example, communications with certain equipment can break down, users might need extra training or forget their passwords, back-up files may be lost, or new software might need to be installed and configured. Whatever the crisis, computer network administrators must know the network system well enough to diagnose and fix the problem.

Computer network administrators or specialists may hold one or several networking responsibilities. The specific job duties assigned to one person depend on the nature and scope of the employer. For example, in a medium-size company that uses computers only minimally, a computer network specialist might be expected to do everything associated with the office computer system. In larger companies with more sophisticated computing systems, computer network administrators are likely to hold more narrow and better-defined responsibilities. The following descriptions highlight the different kinds of computer network administrators.

In the narrowest sense, computer network administrators are responsible for adding and deleting files to the network server, a centralized computer. Among other things, the server stores the software applications used by network users on a daily basis. Administrators update files from the database, electronic mail, and word-processing applications. They are also responsible for making sure that printing jobs run properly. This task entails telling the server where the printer is and establishing a printing queue, or line, designating which print jobs have priority.

Another duty of some network administrators is setting up user access. Since businesses store confidential information on the server, users typically have access to only a limited number of applications. Network administrators tell the computer who can use which programs and when they can use them. They create a series of passwords to secure the system against internal and external spying. They also troubleshoot problems and questions encountered by staff members.

In companies with large computer systems, *network security specialists* concentrate solely on system security. They set up and monitor user access and update security files as needed. For example, it is very important in universities that only certain administrative personnel have the ability to change student grades on the database. Network security specialists must protect the system from unauthorized grade changes. Network security specialists grant new passwords to users who forget them, record all nonauthorized entries, report unauthorized users to appropriate management, and change any files that have been tampered with. They also maintain security files with information about each employee.

Network control operators are in charge of all network communications, most of which operate over telephone lines or fiber optic cables. When users encounter communications problems, they call the network control operator. A typical communications problem is when a user cannot send or receive files from other computers. Since users seldom have a high level of technical expertise on the network, the network control operator knows how to ask appropriate questions in user-friendly language to determine the source of the problem. If it is not a user error, the network control operator checks the accuracy of computer files, verifies that modems are functioning properly, and runs noise tests on the communications lines using special equipment. As with all network specialists, if the problem proves to be too difficult for the network control operator to resolve, he or she seeks help directly from the manufacturer or warranty company.

Network control operators also keep detailed records of the number of communications transactions made, the number and nature of network errors, and the methods used to resolve them. These records help them address problems as they arise in the future.

Network systems administrators that specialize in Internet technology are essential to its success. One of their responsibilities is to prepare servers for use and link them together so others can place things on them. Under the supervision of the *Webmaster,* the systems administrator might set aside areas on a server for particular types of information, such as documents, graphics, or audio. At sites that are set up to handle secure credit card transactions, administrators are responsible for setting up the secure server that handles this job. They also monitor site traffic and take the necessary steps to ensure uninterrupted operation. In some cases, the solution is to provide additional space on the server. In others, the only solution might be to increase bandwidth by upgrading the telephone line linking the site to the Internet.

REQUIREMENTS
High School

In high school, take as many courses as possible in computer science, mathematics, and science, which provide a solid foundation in computer basics and analytical-thinking skills. You should also practice your verbal and written communications skills in English and speech classes. Business courses are valuable in that they can give you an understanding of how important business decisions, especially those concerning investment in computer equipment, are made.

Postsecondary Training

Most network jobs require at least a bachelor's degree in computer science, information systems, or computer engineering. More specialized positions require an advanced degree. Workers with a college education are more likely to deal with the theoretical aspects of computer networking and are more likely to be promoted

to management positions. Opportunities in computer design, systems analysis, and computer programming, for example, are open only to college graduates. If you are interested in this field, you should also pursue postsecondary training in network administration or network engineering.

"I believe that you cannot have enough education and that it should be an ongoing thing," says Nancy Nelson, a network administrator at Baxter Healthcare Corporation in Deerfield, Ill. "You can learn a lot on your own, but I think you miss out on a lot if you don't get the formal education. Most companies don't even look at a resume that doesn't have a degree. Keeping up with technology can be very rewarding."

Certification or Licensing

Besides the technical/vocational schools that offer courses related to computer networking, several major companies offer professionally taught courses and nationally recognized certification; chief among them are Novell and Microsoft. The certified network professional program supports and complements the aforementioned vendor product certifications. Offered by the Network Professional Association, the program covers fundamental knowledge in client operating systems, microcomputer hardware platforms, network operating system fundamentals, protocols, and topologies. Commercial postsecondary training programs are flexible. You can complete courses at your own pace, but you must take all parts of the certification test within one year. You may attend classes at any one of many educational sites around the country or you can study on your own. Many students find certification exams difficult.

Other Requirements

Continuing education for any computer profession is crucial to success. Many companies will require you to keep up to date on new technological advances by attending classes, workshops, and seminars throughout the year. Also, many companies and professional associations update network specialists through newsletters, other periodicals, and online bulletin boards.

Computer work is complex, detailed, and often very frustrating. In order to succeed in this field, you must be well organized and patient. You should enjoy challenges and problem solving, and you should be a logical thinker. You must also be able to communicate complex ideas in simple terms, as well as be able to work well under pressure and deadlines. As a network specialist, you should be naturally curious about the computing field; you must always be willing to learn more about new and different technologies.

EXPLORING

"One of the greatest learning experiences in this field is just unpacking a new computer, setting it up, and getting connected to the Internet, continually asking yourself how and why as you go," says Dan Creedon, a network administrator at Nesbitt Burns Securities in Chicago.

If you are interested in computer networking you should join computer clubs at school and community centers and surf the Internet or other online services. Ask your school administration about the possibility of working with the school system's network specialists for a day or longer. Parents' or friends' employers might also be a good place to find this type of opportunity.

If seeking part-time jobs, apply for those that include computer work. Though you will not find networking positions, any experience on computers will increase your general computing knowledge. In addition, once employed, you can actively seek exposure to the other computer functions in the business.

You might also try volunteering at local-area charities that use computer networks in their office. Because many charities have small budgets, they may offer more opportunities to gain experience with some of the simpler networking tasks. In addition, experiment by creating networks with your own computer, those of your friends, and any printers, modems, and faxes that you have access to.

Basically, you should play around on computers as much as possible. Read and learn from any resource you can, such as magazines, newsletters, and online bulletin boards.

EMPLOYERS

Approximately 309,000 computer network and systems administrators are employed in the United States. Any company or organization that uses computer networks in its business employs network administrators. These include insurance companies, banks, financial institutions, health care organizations, federal and state governments, universities, and other corporations that rely on networking. Also, since smaller companies are moving to client-server models, more opportunities at almost any kind of business are becoming available.

STARTING OUT

There are several ways to obtain a position as a computer network specialist. If you are a student in a technical school or university, take advantage of your campus career services office. Check regularly for internship postings, job listings, and notices of on-campus recruitment. Career services offices are also valuable resources for resume tips and interviewing techniques. Internships and summer jobs with corporations are always beneficial and provide experience that will give you the edge over your competition. General computer job fairs are also held throughout the year in larger cities.

There are many online career sites listed on the World Wide Web that post job openings, salary surveys, and current employment trends. The Web also has online publications that deal specifically with computer jobs. You can also obtain information from computer organizations, such as the IEEE Computer Society and the Network Professional Association (see contact information at the end of this article).

When a job opportunity arises, you should send a cover letter and resume to the company promptly. Follow up your mailing with a phone call about one week later. If interested, the company recruiter will call you to ask questions and possibly arrange an interview. The commercial sponsors of network certification, such as Novell and Microsoft, also publish newsletters that list current job openings in the field. The same information is distributed through online bulletin boards and on the Internet as well. Otherwise, you can scan the classified ads in local newspapers and computer magazines or work with an employment agency to find such a position.

Individuals already employed but wishing to move into computer networking should investigate the possibility of tuition reimbursement from their employer for network certification. Many large companies have this type of program, which allows employees to train in a field that would benefit company operations. After successfully completing classes or certification, individuals are better qualified for related job openings in their own company and more likely to be hired into them.

ADVANCEMENT

"I would say that as much as a person is willing to learn is really the amount of advancement opportunities that are open to them," notes Dan Creedon. Among the professional options available are promotion to network manager or movement into network engineering. *Network engineers* design, test, and evaluate network systems, such as LAN, WAN, Internet, wireless, and other data communications systems. They also perform modeling, analysis, and planning. Network engineers might also research related products and make hardware and software recommendations.

Network specialists also have the option of going into a different area of computing. They can become computer programmers, systems analysts, software engineers, or multimedia professionals. All of these promotions require additional education and solid computer experience.

EARNINGS

Factors such as the size and type of employer, the administrator's experience, and specific job duties influence the earnings of network administrators. According to the U.S. Department of Labor, the median yearly income for computer network and systems administrators was $62,130 in 2006. The lowest paid 10 percent made less than $38,610 per year, and the highest paid 10 percent earned more than $97,080 annually that same year.

Most computer network administrators are employed by companies that offer the full range of benefits, including health insurance, paid vacation, and sick leave. In addition, many companies have tuition reimbursement programs for employees seeking to pursue education or professional certification.

WORK ENVIRONMENT

Computer network administrators work indoors in a comfortable office environment. Their work is generally fast paced and can be frustrating at times. Some tasks, however, are routine and might get a little boring after a while. But many times, network specialists are required to work under a lot of pressure. If the network goes down, for example, the company is losing money, and it is the network specialist's job to get it up and running as fast as possible. The specialist must be able to remember complicated relationships and many details accurately and quickly. Specialists are also called on to deal effectively with the many complaints from network users.

When working on the installation of a new system, many network specialists are required to work overtime until it is fully operational. This usually includes long and frequent meetings. During initial operations of the system, some network specialists may be on call during other shifts for when problems arise, or they may have to train network users during off hours.

One other potential source of frustration is communications with other employees. Network specialists deal every day with people who usually don't understand the system as well as they do. Network administrators must be able to communicate at different levels of understanding.

OUTLOOK

The U.S. Department of Labor projects that employment for computer network and systems administrators will grow much faster than the average for all occupations through 2016. Network administrators are in high demand, particularly those with experience with the Internet, electronic commerce, and mobile technologies. "Technology is constantly changing," Nancy Nelson says. "It is hard to tell where it will lead in the future. I think that the Internet and all of its pieces will be the place to focus on." As more and more companies and organizations discover the economic and convenience advantages linked to using computer networks at all levels of operations, the demand for well-trained network specialists will increase. Job opportunities should be best for those with certification and up-to-date training.

FOR MORE INFORMATION

For information on internships, student membership, and the student magazine Crossroads, *contact*

Association for Computing Machinery
1515 Broadway
New York, NY 10036-8901
Tel: 800-342-6626
Email: sigs@acm.org
http://www.acm.org

For information on career opportunities for women in computing, contact

Association for Women in Computing
41 Sutter Street, Suite 1006
San Francisco, CA 94104-5414
Tel: 415-905-4663
Email: info@awc-hq.org
http://www.awc-hq.org

For information on scholarships, student membership, and to read Careers in Computer Science and Computer Engineering, *visit the IEEE's Web site:*

IEEE Computer Society
1828 L Street NW, Suite 1202
Washington, DC 20036-5104
Tel: 202-371-0101
Email: membership@computer.org
http://www.computer.org

For information on certification, contact

Network Professional Association
1401 Hermes Lane
San Diego, CA 92154-2721
Tel: 888-NPA-NPA0
http://www.npanet.org

For information on systems administration, contact

SAGE

c/o USENIX, the Advanced Computing Systems
　Association

2560 9th Street, Suite 215

Berkeley, CA 94710-2565

Tel: 510-528-8649

Email: office@sage.org

http://www.sage.org

☐ COMPUTER SUPPORT SPECIALISTS

OVERVIEW

Computer support specialists investigate and resolve problems in computer functioning. They listen to customer complaints, walk customers through possible solutions, and write technical reports based on their work. Computer support specialists have different duties depending on whom they assist and what they fix. Regardless of specialty, all computer support specialists must be very knowledgeable about the products with which they work and be able to communicate effectively with users from different technical backgrounds. They must be patient and professional with frustrated users and be able to perform well under stress. Computer support is similar to

SCHOOL SUBJECTS
Computer Science, English, Mathematics

PERSONAL SKILLS
Helping/Teaching, Technical/Scientific

MINIMUM EDUCATION LEVEL
Some Postsecondary Training

CERTIFICATION OR LICENSING
Recommended

WORK ENVIRONMENT
Primarily Indoors, Primarily One Location

solving mysteries, so support specialists should enjoy the challenge of problem solving and have strong analytical skills. There are approximately 552,000 computer support specialists employed in the United States.

THE JOB

It is relatively rare today to find a business that does not rely on computers for at least something. Some use them heavily and in many areas: daily operations, such as employee time clocks; monthly projects, such as payroll and sales accounting; and major reengineering of fundamental business procedures, such as form automation in government agencies, insurance companies, and banks. As more companies become increasingly reliant on computers, it becomes increasingly critical that they function properly all the time. Any computer downtime can be extremely expensive, in terms of work left undone and sales not made, for example. When employees experience problems with their computer system, they call computer support for help. Computer support specialists investigate and resolve problems in computer functioning.

Computer support can generally be broken up into at least three distinct areas, although these distinctions vary greatly with the nature, size, and scope of the company. The three most prevalent areas are user support, technical support, and microcomputer support. Most computer support specialists perform some combination of the tasks explained below.

The jobs of computer support specialists vary according to whom they assist and what they fix. Some specialists help private users exclusively; others are on call to a major corporate buyer. Some work with computer hardware and software, while others help with printer, modem, and fax problems. *User support specialists*, also known as *help desk specialists*, work directly with users themselves, who call when they experience problems. The support specialist listens carefully to the user's explanation of the precise nature of the problem and the commands entered that seem to have caused it. Some companies have developed complex software that allows the support specialist to enter a description of the problem and wait for the computer to provide suggestions about what the user should do.

The initial goal is to isolate the source of the problem. If user error is the culprit, the user support specialist explains procedures related to the program in question, whether it is a graphics, database, word processing, or printing program. If the problem seems to lie in the hardware or software, the specialist asks the user to enter certain commands in order to see if the computer makes the appropriate response. If it does not, the support specialist is closer to isolating the cause. The support specialist consults supervisors, programmers, and others in order to outline the cause and possible solutions.

Some *technical support specialists* who work for computer companies are mainly involved with solving problems whose cause has been determined to lie in the computer system's operating system, hardware, or software. They make exhaustive use of resources, such as colleagues or books, and try to solve the problem through a variety of methods, including program modifications and the replacement of certain hardware or software.

Technical support specialists employed in the information systems departments of large corporations do this kind of troubleshooting as well. They also oversee the daily operations of the various computer systems in the company. Sometimes they compare the system's work capacity to the actual daily workload in order to determine if upgrades are needed. In addition, they might help out other computer professionals in the company with modifying commercial software for their company's particular needs.

Microcomputer support specialists are responsible for preparing computers for delivery to a client, including installing the operating system and desired software. After the unit is installed at the customer's location, the support specialists might help train users on appropriate procedures and answer any questions they have. They help diagnose problems that occur, transferring major concerns to other support specialists.

All computer support work must be well documented. Support specialists write detailed technical reports on every problem they work on. They try to tie together different problems on the same software, so programmers can make adjustments that address all of the issues. Record keeping is crucial because designers, programmers, and engineers use technical support reports to revise current products and improve future ones. Some support specialists help write training manuals. They are often required to read trade magazines and company newsletters in order to keep up to date on their products and the field in general.

REQUIREMENTS
High School

A high school diploma is a minimum requirement for computer support specialists. Any technical courses you can take, such as computer science, schematic drawing, or electronics, can help you develop the logical and analytical thinking skills necessary to be successful in this field. Courses in math and science are also valuable for this reason. Since computer support specialists have to deal with both computer programmers on the one hand

and computer users who may not know anything about computers on the other, you should take English and speech classes to improve your verbal and written communications skills.

Postsecondary Training

Computer support is a field as old as computer technology itself, so it might seem odd that postsecondary programs in this field are not more common or standardized. The reason behind this situation is relatively simple: Formal education curricula cannot keep up with the changes, nor can they provide specific training on individual products. Some large corporations might consider educational background, both as a way to weed out applicants and to insure a certain level of proficiency. Most major computer companies, however, look for energetic individuals who demonstrate a willingness and ability to learn new things quickly and who have general computer knowledge. These employers count on training new support specialists themselves.

Individuals interested in pursuing a job in this field should first determine what area of computer support appeals to them the most and then honestly assess their level of experience and knowledge. Large corporations often prefer to hire people with an associate's degree and some experience. They may also be impressed with commercial certification in a computer field, such as networking. However, if they are hiring from within the company, they will probably weigh experience more heavily than education when making a final decision.

Employed individuals looking for a career change may want to commit themselves to a program of self-study in order to be qualified for computer support positions. Many computer professionals learn a lot of what they know by playing around on computers, reading trade magazines, and talking with colleagues. Self-taught individuals should learn how to effectively demonstrate their knowledge and proficiency on the job or during an interview. Besides self-training, employed individuals should investigate tuition reimbursement programs offered by their company.

High school students with no experience should seriously consider earning an associate's degree in a computer-related technology. The degree shows the prospective employer that the applicant has attained a certain level of proficiency with computers and has the intellectual ability to learn technical processes, a promising sign for success on the job.

There are many computer technology programs that lead to an associate's degree. A specialization in personal computer support and administration is certainly applicable to work in computer support. Most computer professionals eventually need to go back to school to earn a bachelor's degree in order to keep themselves competitive in the job market and prepare themselves for promotion to other computer fields.

Certification or Licensing

Though certification is not an industry requirement, it is highly recommended. According to HDI (formerly the Help Desk Institute), most individuals wishing to qualify to work in a support/help desk environment will need to obtain certification within a month of being on the job. A number of organizations offer several different types of certification. CompTIA: The Computing Technology Industry Association, for example, offers the "A+" certification for entry-level computer service technicians. HDI has training courses and offers a number of certifications for those working in support and help desk positions.

To become certified, you will need to pass a written test and in some cases may need a certain amount of work experience. Although going through the certification process is voluntary, becoming certified will most likely be to your advantage. It will show your commitment to the profession as well as demonstrate your level of expertise. In addition, certification may qualify you for certain jobs and lead to new employment opportunities.

Other Requirements

To be a successful computer support specialist, you should be patient, enjoy challenges of problem solving, and think logically. You should work well under stress and demonstrate effective communication skills. Working in a field that changes rapidly, you should be naturally curious and enthusiastic about learning new technologies as they are developed.

EXPLORING

If you are interested in becoming a computer support specialist, you should try to organize a career day with an employed computer support specialist. Local computer repair shops that offer computer support service might be a good place to contact. Otherwise, you should contact major corporations, computer companies, and even the central office of your school system.

If you are interested in any computer field, you should start working and playing on computers as much as possible; many working computer professionals became computer hobbyists at a very young age. You can surf the Internet, read computer magazines, and join school or community computer clubs.

You might also attend a computer technology course at a local technical/vocational school. This would give you hands-on exposure to typical computer support training. In addition, if you experience problems with your own hardware or software, you should call computer support, paying careful attention to how the support specialist handles the call and asking as many questions as the specialist has time to answer.

EMPLOYERS

Computer support specialists work for computer hardware and software companies, as well as in the information systems departments of large corporations and government agencies. There are approximately 552,000 computer support specialists employed in the United States.

STARTING OUT

Most computer support positions are considered entry-level. They are found mainly in computer companies and large corporations. Individuals interested in obtaining a job in this field should scan the classified ads for openings in local businesses and may want to work with an employment agency for help finding out about opportunities. Since many job openings are publicized by word of mouth, it is also very important to speak with as many working computer professionals as possible. They tend to be aware of job openings before anyone else and may be able to offer a recommendation to the hiring committee.

If students of computer technology are seeking a position in computer support, they should work closely with their school's career services office. Many employers inform career services offices at nearby schools of openings before ads are run in the newspaper. In addition, career services office staffs are generally very helpful with resume writing assistance and interviewing techniques.

If an employee wants to make a career change into computer support, he or she should contact the human resources department of the company or speak directly with appropriate management. In companies that are expanding their computing systems, it is often helpful for management to know that current employees would be interested in growing in a computer-related direction. They may even be willing to finance additional education.

ADVANCEMENT

Computer support specialists who demonstrate leadership skills and a strong aptitude for the work may be promoted to supervisory positions within computer support departments. Supervisors are responsible for the more complicated problems that arise, as well as for some administrative duties such as scheduling, interviewing, and job assignments.

Further promotion requires additional education. Some computer support specialists may become commercially certified in computer networking so that they can install, maintain, and repair computer networks. Others may prefer to pursue a bachelor's degree in computer science, either full time or part time. The range of careers available to college graduates varies widely. *Software engineers* analyze industrial, business, and scientific problems and develop software programs to handle them effectively. *Quality assurance engineers* design automated quality assurance tests for new software applications. *Internet quality assurance* specialists work specifically with testing and developing companies' Web sites. *Computer systems/ programmer analysts* study the broad computing picture for a company or a group of companies in order to determine the best way to organize the computer systems.

There are limited opportunities for computer support specialists to be promoted into managerial positions. Doing so would require additional education in business but would probably also depend on the individual's advanced computer knowledge.

EARNINGS

Computer support specialist jobs are plentiful in areas where clusters of computer companies are located, such as northern California and Seattle, Washington. Median annual earnings for computer support specialists were $41,470 in 2006, according to the U.S. Department of Labor. The highest 10 percent earned more than $68,540, while the lowest 10 percent earned less than $25,290. Those who have more education, responsibility, and expertise have the potential to earn much more.

Computer support specialists earned the following mean annual salaries by industry in 2006, according to the U.S. Department of Labor: software publishers; $51,180; computer systems design and related services, $46,020; colleges and universities, $41,450; and elementary and secondary schools, $39,810.

Most computer support specialists work for companies that offer a full range of benefits, including health insurance, paid vacation, and sick leave. Smaller service or start-up companies may hire support specialists on a contractual basis.

WORK ENVIRONMENT

Computer support specialists work in comfortable business environments. They generally work regular, 40-hour weeks. For certain products, however, they may be asked to work evenings or weekends or at least be on call during those times in case of emergencies. If they work for service companies, they may be required to travel to clients' sites and log overtime hours.

Computer support work can be stressful, since specialists often deal with frustrated users who may be difficult to work with. Communication problems with people who are less technically qualified may also be a source of frustration. Patience and understanding are essential for handling these problems.

Computer support specialists are expected to work quickly and efficiently and be able to perform under pressure. The ability to do this requires thorough technical expertise and keen analytical ability.

OUTLOOK

The U.S. Department of Labor predicts that employment for computer support specialists will grow about as fast as the average for all occupations through 2016. Due to the considerable size of this field, there should continue to be many job openings for computer support specialists. Each time a new computer product is released on the market or another system is installed, there will be problems, whether from user error or technical difficulty. Therefore, there will always be a need for computer support specialists to solve the problems. Since technology changes so rapidly, it is very important for these professionals to keep up to date on advances. They should read trade magazines, surf the Internet, and talk with colleagues in order to know what is happening in the field.

Since some companies stop offering computer support on old products or applications after a designated time, the key is to be flexible with your understanding of technology. This is important for another reason as well. While the industry as a whole will require more computer support specialists in the future, it may be the case that certain computer companies go out of business. It can be a volatile industry for start-ups or young companies dedicated to the development of one product. Computer support specialists interested in working for computer companies should therefore consider living in areas in which many such companies are clustered. In this way, it will be easier to find another job if necessary.

FOR MORE INFORMATION

For information on internships, scholarships, student membership, and the student magazine Crossroads, *contact*
Association for Computing Machinery
2 Penn Plaza, Suite 701
New York, NY 10121-0701

Tel: 800-342-6626
Email: acmhelp@acm.org
http://www.acm.org

To learn more about membership and career training seminars, contact

Association of Computer Support Specialists
333 Mamaroneck Avenue, #129
White Plains, NY 10605-1440
http://www.acss.org

For information on certification, contact

CompTIA: The Computing Technology Industry Association
1815 South Meyers Road, Suite 300
Oakbrook Terrace, IL 60181-5228
Tel: 630-678-8300
http://www.comptia.org

For more information on this organization's training courses and certification, contact

HDI
102 South Tejon, Suite 1200
Colorado Springs, CO 80903-2231
Tel: 800-248-5667
Email: support@thinkhdi.com
http://www.thinkhdi.com

For information on scholarships, student membership, and to read Careers in Computer Science and Computer Engineering, *visit the IEEE's Web site:*

IEEE Computer Society
1828 L Street, NW, Suite 1202
Washington, DC 20036-5104
Tel: 202-371-0101
http://www.computer.org

❑ COMPUTER SYSTEMS PROGRAMMER-ANALYSTS

OVERVIEW

Computer systems programmer-analysts analyze the computing needs of a business and then design a new system or upgrade an old system to meet those needs.

The position can be split between two people, the *systems programmer* and the *systems analyst,* but it is frequently held by just one person, who oversees the work from beginning to end. There are about 504,000 computer systems programmer-analysts employed in the United States.

THE JOB

Businesses invest hundreds of thousands of dollars in computer systems to make their operations more efficient and thus more profitable. As older systems become obsolete, businesses are also faced with the task of replacing them or upgrading them with new technology. Computer systems programmer-analysts plan and develop new computer systems or upgrade existing systems to meet changing business needs. They also install, modify, and maintain functioning computer systems. The process of choosing and implementing a computer system is similar for programmer analysts who work for very different employers. However, specific decisions in terms of hardware and software differ depending on the industry.

The first stage of the process involves meeting with management and users in order to discuss the problem at hand. For example, a company's accounting system might be slow, unreliable, and generally outdated. During many hours of meetings, systems programmer-analysts and management discuss various options, including commercial software, hardware upgrades, and customizing possibilities that may solve the problems. At the end of the discussions, which may last as long as several weeks or months, the programmer analyst defines the specific system goals as agreed upon by participants.

Next, systems programmer-analysts engage in highly analytic and logical activities. They use tools such as structural analysis, data modeling, mathematics, and cost accounting to determine which computers, including hardware and software and peripherals, will be required to meet the goals of the project. They must consider the trade-offs between extra efficiency and speed and increased costs. Weighing the pros and cons of each additional system feature is an important factor in system planning. Whatever preliminary decisions are made must be supported by mathematical and financial evidence.

As the final stage of the planning process, systems programmer-analysts prepare reports and formal presentations to be delivered to management. Reports must be written in clear, concise language that business professionals, who are not necessarily technical experts, can understand thoroughly. Formal presentations in front of groups of various sizes are often required as part of the system proposal.

If the system or the system upgrades are approved, equipment is purchased and installed. Then, the programmer analysts get down to the real technical work so that all the different computers and peripherals function well together. They prepare specifications, diagrams, and other programming structures and, often using computer-aided systems engineering technology, they write the new or upgraded programming code. If they work solely as systems analysts, it is at this point that they hand over all of their information to the systems programmer so that he or she can begin to write the programming code.

Systems design and programming involves defining the files and records to be accessed by the system, outlining the processing steps, and suggesting formats for output that meet the needs of the company. User-friendliness of the front-end applications is extremely important for user productivity. Therefore, programmer-analysts must be able to envision how nontechnical system users view their on-screen work. Systems programmer-analysts might also specify security programs that allow only authorized personnel access to certain files or groups of files.

As the programs are written, programmer-analysts set up test runs of various parts of the system, making sure each step of the way that major goals are reached. Once the system is up and running, problems, or "bugs," begin to pop up. Programmer-analysts are responsible for fixing these last-minute problems. They must isolate the problem and review the hundreds of lines of programming commands to determine where the mistake is located. Then they must enter the correct command or code and recheck the program.

Depending on the employer, some systems programmer-analysts might be involved with computer networking. Network communication programs tell two or more computers or peripherals how to work with each other. When a system is composed of equipment from various manufacturers, networking is essential for smooth system functioning. For example, shared printers have to know how to order print jobs as they come in from various terminals. Some programmer-analysts write the code that establishes printing queues. Others might be involved in user training, since they know the software applications well. They might also customize commercial software programs to meet the needs of their company.

Many programmer-analysts become specialized in an area of business, science, or engineering. They seek education and further on-the-job training in these areas

SCHOOL SUBJECTS
Computer Science, Mathematics

PERSONAL SKILLS
Mechanical/Manipulative, Technical/Scientific

MINIMUM EDUCATION LEVEL
Bachelor's Degree

CERTIFICATION OR LICENSING
Voluntary

WORK ENVIRONMENT
Primarily Indoors, Primarily One Location

to develop expertise. They may therefore attend special seminars, workshops, and classes designed for their needs. This extra knowledge allows them to develop a deeper understanding of the computing problems specific to the business or industry.

REQUIREMENTS
High School

Take a college preparatory program with advanced classes in math, science, and computer science to prepare you for this work. This will provide a foundation of basic concepts and encourage the development of analytic and logical thinking skills. Since programmer-analysts do a lot of proposal writing that may or may not be technical in nature, English classes are valuable as well. Speech classes will help prepare you for making formal presentations to management and clients.

Postsecondary Training

A bachelor's degree in computer science, information science, or management information systems is a minimum requirement for systems programmer-analysts. Course work in preparation for this field includes math, computer programming, science, and logic. Several years of related work experience, including knowledge of programming languages, are often necessary as well. For some very high-level positions, an advanced degree in a specific computer subfield may be required. As a result of the rapid growth of electronic commerce, some firms are also seeking analysts with a master's degree in business administration, with a concentration in information systems. Also, depending on the employer, proficiency in business, science, or engineering may be necessary.

Certification or Licensing

Some programmer-analysts pursue certification through the Institute for Certification of Computing Professionals. In particular, they take classes and exams to become certified computing professionals. Others pursue the information systems analyst designation, which requires applicants to complete a four-year undergraduate information systems degree program and pass an examination. Certification is voluntary and is an added credential for job hunters. Certification demonstrates to employers that applicants have achieved a recognized level of knowledge and experience in principles and practices related to systems.

Other Requirements

Successful systems programmer-analysts demonstrate strong analytic skills and enjoy the challenges of problem solving. They are able to understand problems that exist on many levels, from technical to practical to business oriented. They can visualize complicated and abstract relationships between computer hardware and software and are good at matching needs to equipment.

Systems programmer-analysts have to be flexible as well. They routinely deal with many different kinds of people, from management to data entry clerks. Therefore, they must be knowledgeable in a lot of functional areas of the company. They should be able to talk to management about cost-effective solutions, to programmers about detailed coding, and to clerks about user-friendliness of the applications.

As is true for all computer professionals, systems programmer-analysts must be able to learn about new technology quickly. They should be naturally curious about keeping up on cutting-edge developments, which can be time consuming. Furthermore, they are often so busy at their jobs that staying in the know is done largely on their own time.

EXPLORING

You have several options to learn more about what it is like to be a computer systems programmer-analyst. You can spend a day with a working professional in this field in order to experience a typical day firsthand. Career

days of this type can usually be arranged through school guidance counselors or the public relations manager of local corporations.

Strategy games, such as chess, played with friends or school clubs are a good way to put your analytic thinking skills to use while having fun. When choosing a game, the key is to make sure it relies on qualities similar to those used by programmer analysts.

Lastly, you should become a computer hobbyist and learn everything you can about computers by working and playing with them on a daily basis. Surfing the Internet regularly, as well as reading trade magazines, will also be helpful. You might also want to try hooking up a mini-system at home or school, configuring terminals, printers, modems, and other peripherals into a coherent system. This activity requires a fair amount of knowledge and should be supervised by a professional.

EMPLOYERS

Approximately 504,000 computer systems-programmer analysts are employed in the United States. Computer systems programmer/analysts work for all types of firms and organizations that do their work on computers. Such companies may include manufacturing companies, data processing service firms, hardware and software companies, banks, insurance companies, credit companies, publishing houses, government agencies, financial institutions, Internet service providers, and colleges and universities. Many programmer-analysts are employed by businesses as consultants on a temporary or contractual basis.

STARTING OUT

Since systems programmer-analysts typically have at least some experience in a computer-related job, most are hired into these jobs from lower-level positions within the same company. For example, programmers, software engineering technicians, and network and database administrators all gain valuable computing experience that can be put to good use at a systems job. Alternatively, individuals who acquire expertise in systems programming and analysis while in other jobs may want to work with a headhunter to find the right systems positions for them. Also, trade magazines, newspapers, and employment agencies regularly feature job openings in this field.

Students in four-year degree programs should work closely with their schools' career services offices. Companies regularly work through such offices in order to find the most qualified graduates. Since it may be difficult to find a job as a programmer-analyst to begin with, it is important for students to consider their long-term potential within a certain company. The chance for promotion into a systems job can make lower-level jobs more appealing, at least in the short run.

For those individuals already employed in a computer-related job but wanting to get into systems programming and analysis, additional formal education is a good idea. Some employers have educational reimbursement policies that allow employees to take courses inexpensively. If the employee's training could directly benefit the business, companies are more willing to pay for the expense.

ADVANCEMENT

Systems programmer-analysts already occupy a relatively high-level technical job. Promotion, therefore, usually occurs in one of two directions. First, programmer-analysts can be put in charge of increasingly larger and more complex systems. Instead of concentrating on a company's local system, for example, an analyst can oversee all company systems and networks. This kind of technically based promotion can also put systems programmer/analysts into other areas of computing. With the proper experience and additional training, they can get into database or network management and design, software engineering, or even quality assurance.

The other direction in which programmer-analysts can go is managerial. Depending on the position sought, formal education (either a bachelor's degree in business or a master's in business administration) may be required. As more administrative duties are added, more technical ones are taken away. Therefore, programmer-analysts who enjoy the technical aspect of their work more than anything else may not want to pursue this advancement track. Excellent computing managers have both a solid background in various forms of computing and a good grasp of what it takes to run a department. Also, having the vision to see how technology will change in the short and long terms, and how those changes will affect the industry concerned, is a quality of a good manager.

EARNINGS

According to the U.S. Department of Labor, the median annual salary for computer systems analysts was $69,760 in 2006. At the low end of the pay range, 10 percent of systems analysts earned less than $42,780. The top 10 percent earned $106,820 or more. Salaries are slightly higher in geographic areas where many computer companies are clustered, such as Silicon Valley in Calif. and Seattle, Wash.

In 2007, starting salaries for those with bachelor's degrees in computer science averaged $53,396, according to the National Association of Colleges and Employers. Those with bachelor's degrees in information sciences and systems averaged $50,852. Those in senior positions can earn much higher salaries. *Computerworld* reports that senior systems analysts earned a national average of $83,390 in 2006. Most programmer analysts receive health insurance, paid vacation, and sick leave. Some employers offer tuition reimbursement programs and in-house computer training workshops.

WORK ENVIRONMENT

Computer systems programmer-analysts work in comfortable office environments. If they work as consultants, they may travel frequently. Otherwise, travel is limited to trade shows, seminars, and visitations to vendors for demonstrations. They might also visit other businesses to observe their systems in action.

Programmer-analysts usually work 40-hour weeks and enjoy the regular holiday schedule of days off. However, as deadlines for system installation, upgrades, and spot-checking approach, they are often required to work overtime. Extra compensation for overtime hours may come in the form of time-and-a-half pay or compensatory time off, depending on the precise nature of the employee's duties, company policy, and state law. If the employer operates off-shifts, programmer-analysts may be on-call to address any problems that might arise at any time of the day or night. This is relatively rare in the service sector but more common in manufacturing, heavy industry, and data processing firms.

Computer systems programming and analysis is very detailed work. The smallest error can cause major system disruptions, which can be a great source of frustration. Systems programmer-analysts must be prepared to deal with this frustration and be able to work well under pressure.

OUTLOOK

Employment for computer systems programmer-analysts will grow much faster than the average for all occupations through 2016. Increases are mainly a product of the growing number of businesses that rely extensively on computers, electronic commerce, and Internet technologies. When businesses automate, their daily operations depend on the capacity of their computer systems to perform at desired levels. The continuous development of new technologies means that businesses must also update their old systems to remain competitive in the marketplace. Additionally, the need for businesses to network their information adds to the demand for qualified programmer analysts. Businesses will rely increasingly on systems programmer-analysts to make the right purchasing decisions and to keep systems running smoothly.

Many computer manufacturers are beginning to expand the range of services they offer to business clients. In the years to come, they may hire many systems programmer-analysts to work as consultants on a per-project basis with a potential client. These workers would perform essentially the same duties, with the addition of extensive follow-up maintenance. They would analyze business needs and suggest proper systems to answer them. In addition, more and more independent consulting firms are hiring systems programmer-analysts to perform the same tasks.

Analysts with advanced degrees in computer science or computer engineering will be in great demand. Individuals with master's degrees in business administration with emphasis in information systems will also be highly desirable.

FOR MORE INFORMATION

For more information about systems programmer-analyst positions, contact

Association of Information Technology Professionals
401 North Michigan Avenue, Suite 2400
Chicago, IL 60611-4267
Tel: 800-224-9371
http://www.aitp.org

For information on becoming an independent consultant, contact

Independent Computer Consultants Association
11131 South Towne Square, Suite F
St. Louis, MO 63123-7817
Tel: 314-892-1675
Email: info@icca.org
http://www.icca.org

For information on certification, contact

Institute for Certification of Computing Professionals
2350 East Devon Avenue, Suite 115
Des Plaines, IL 60018-4610
Tel: 800-843-8227
Email: office@iccp.org
http://www.iccp.org

CONSTRUCTION INSPECTORS

OVERVIEW

Construction inspectors work for federal, state, and local governments. Their job is to examine the construction, alteration, or repair of highways, streets, sewer and water systems, dams, bridges, buildings, and other structures to ensure that they comply with building codes and ordinances, zoning regulations, and contract specifications. Approximately 110,000 construction and building inspectors work in the United States.

THE JOB

This occupation is made up of four broad categories of specialization: building, electrical, mechanical, and public works.

Building inspectors examine the structural quality of buildings. They check the plans before construction, visit the work site a number of times during construction, and make a final inspection when the project is completed. Some building inspectors specialize in areas such as structural steel or reinforced concrete buildings.

Electrical inspectors visit work sites to inspect the installation of electrical systems and equipment. They check wiring, lighting, generators, and sound and security systems. They may also inspect the wiring for elevators, heating and air-conditioning systems, kitchen appliances, and other electrical installations.

Mechanical inspectors inspect plumbing systems and the mechanical components of heating and air-conditioning equipment and kitchen appliances. They also examine gas tanks, piping, and gas-fired appliances. Some mechanical inspectors specialize in elevators, plumbing, or boilers.

Elevator inspectors inspect both the mechanical and the electrical features of lifting and conveying devices, such as elevators, escalators, and moving sidewalks. They also test their speed, load allowances, brakes, and safety devices.

Plumbing inspectors inspect plumbing installations, water supply systems, drainage and sewer systems, water heater installations, fire sprinkler systems, and air and gas piping systems; they also examine building sites for soil type to determine water table level, seepage rate, and similar conditions.

Heating and refrigeration inspectors examine heating, ventilating, air-conditioning, and refrigeration installations in new buildings and approve alteration plans for those elements in existing buildings.

Public works inspectors make sure that government construction of water and sewer systems, highways, streets, bridges, and dams conforms to contract specifications. They visit work sites to inspect excavations, mixing and pouring of concrete, and asphalt paving. They also keep records of the amount of work performed and the materials used so that proper payment can be made. These inspectors may specialize in highways, reinforced concrete, or ditches.

Construction inspectors use measuring devices and other test equipment, take photographs, keep a daily log of their work, and write reports. If any detail of a project does not comply with the various codes, ordinances, or specifications, or if construction is being done without proper permits, the inspectors have the authority to issue a stop-work order.

REQUIREMENTS
High School

People interested in becoming construction inspectors must be high school graduates who have taken courses in drafting, algebra, geometry, and English. Additional shop courses will undoubtedly prove helpful as well.

Postsecondary Training

Employers prefer graduates of an apprenticeship program, community or junior college, or people with at least two years toward an engineering or architectural degree. Required courses include construction technology, blueprint reading, technical math, English, and building inspection. Only 28 percent of construction and building inspectors had a bachelor's degree or higher in 2006, according to the U.S. Department of Labor.

Most construction inspectors have several years' experience either as a construction contractor or supervisor, or as a craft or trade worker such as a carpenter, electrician, plumber, or pipefitter. This experience demonstrates a knowledge of construction materials and practices, which is necessary in inspections. Construction inspectors receive most of their training on the job.

Certification or Licensing

Some states require certification for employment. Inspectors can earn a certificate by passing examinations on construction techniques, materials, and code requirements. The exams are offered by the International Code

SCHOOL SUBJECTS
Mathematics, Technical/Shop

PERSONAL SKILLS
Leadership/Management, Technical/Scientific

MINIMUM EDUCATION LEVEL
High School Diploma

CERTIFICATION OR LICENSING
Required by Certain States

WORK ENVIRONMENT
Indoors and Outdoors, Primarily Multiple Locations

Council. The Association of Construction Inspectors, the International Association of Electrical Inspectors, and the National Association of Home Inspectors also offer certification designations. Contact these organizations for more information.

Other Requirements

A construction inspector should have experience in construction, have a good driving record, be in good physical shape, have good communication skills, be able to pay attention to details, and have a strong personality. Although there are no standard requirements to enter this occupation, an inspector should be a responsible individual with in-depth knowledge of the construction trades. Inexperience can lead to mistakes that can cost someone a staggering amount of money or even cause a person's death.

The trade is not considered hazardous, but most inspectors wear hard hats as a precaution. Inspectors might need to climb ladders and walk across rooftops or perhaps trudge up numerous flights of stairs at building projects where elevators are not yet installed. Or they might occasionally find themselves squirming through the dirty, narrow, spider-infested crawl space under a house to check a foundation or crawling across the joists in a cramped, dusty, unfinished attic, inhaling insulation fibers and pesticides.

After the inspection a construction inspector needs to explain his or her findings clearly in reports and should expect to spend many hours answering questions in person, by telephone, and in letters. Because they often deliver bad news, they also need the emotional strength to stand firm on their reports, even when someone calls them a liar or threatens to sue.

On the other hand, an inspector knows that their work is to protect people. For example, they help ensure that a couple's new house will not be apt to burn down from an electrical short, and they might point out less dangerous problems, such as a malfunctioning septic tank or a leaking roof, that could require expensive repairs.

EXPLORING

Field trips to construction sites and interviews with contractors or building trade officials are good ways to gain practical information about what it is like to work in the industry and how best to prepare for it. Summer jobs at a construction site provide an overview of the work involved in a building project. Students may also seek part-time jobs with a general contracting company, with a specialized contractor (such as a plumbing or electrical contractor), or as a carpenter's helper. Jobs in certain supply houses will help students become familiar with construction materials.

EMPLOYERS

Approximately 110,000 construction and building inspectors are employed in the United States. Approximately 41 percent work for local governments, such as municipal or county building departments. Another 26 percent work for architecture or engineering firms. Inspectors employed at the federal level work for such agencies as the Department of Defense and the Departments of Housing and Urban Development, Agriculture, and the Interior.

STARTING OUT

People without postsecondary education usually enter the construction industry as a trainee or apprentice. Graduates of technical schools or colleges of construction and engineering can expect to start work as an engineering aide, drafter, estimator, or assistant engineer. Jobs may be found through school career services offices, employment agencies, and unions or by applying directly to contracting company personnel offices. Application may also be made directly to the employment offices of the federal, state, or local governments.

ADVANCEMENT

The federal, state, and large city governments provide formal training programs for their construction inspectors to keep them abreast of new building code developments and to broaden their knowledge of construction

materials, practices, and inspection techniques. Inspectors for small agencies can upgrade their skills by attending state-conducted training programs or taking college or correspondence courses. An engineering degree is usually required to become a supervisory inspector.

EARNINGS

The U.S. Department of Labor reports the median annual income for construction and building inspectors was $46,570 in 2006. The lowest paid 10 percent of these workers had annual earnings of less than $29,210; the highest paid 10 percent made more than $72,590, also in 2006. Earnings vary based on the inspector's experience, the type of employer, and the location of the work. Salaries are slightly higher in the North and West than in the South and are considerably higher in large metropolitan areas. Building inspectors earn slightly more than other inspectors.

Full-time construction and building inspectors usually receive paid vacations and holidays, sick leave, hospitalization and insurance benefits, and pension programs.

WORK ENVIRONMENT

Construction inspectors work both indoors and outdoors, dividing their time between their offices and the work sites. Inspection sites are dirty and cluttered with tools, machinery, and debris. Although the work is not considered hazardous, inspectors must climb ladders and stairs and crawl under buildings.

The hours are usually regular, but when there is an accident at a site, the inspector has to remain on the job until reports have been completed. The work is steady year-round, rather than seasonal, as are some other construction occupations. In slow construction periods, the inspectors are kept busy examining the renovation of older buildings.

OUTLOOK

As the concern for public safety and an emphasis on green and sustainable design continue to increase, the demand for inspectors should grow faster than the average for all occupations through 2016 even if construction activity does not increase. The level of new construction fluctuates with the economy, but maintenance and renovation continue during the downswings, so inspectors are rarely laid off. Applicants who have a college education, are already certified inspectors, or who have experience as carpenters, electricians, or plumbers will have the best opportunities. Construction and building inspectors tend to be older, more experienced workers who have worked in other construction occupations for many years.

FOR MORE INFORMATION

For additional information on a career as a construction inspector, contact the following organizations:

American Construction Inspectors Association
530 South Lake Avenue, #431
Pasadena, CA 91101-3515
Tel: 888-867-2242
Email: office@acia.com
http://www.acia.com

American Society of Home Inspectors
932 Lee Street, Suite 101
Des Plaines, IL 60016-6546
Tel: 800-743-2744
http://www.ashi.com

Association of Construction Inspectors
21640 North 19th Avenue, Suite C-2
Phoenix, AZ 85027-2720
Tel: 623-580-4646
Email: info@aci-assoc.org
http://www.aci-assoc.org

International Association of Electrical Inspectors
901 Waterfall Way, Suite 602
Richardson, TX 75080-7702
Tel: 972-235-1455
http://www.iaei.org

International Code Council
500 New Jersey Avenue, NW, 6th Floor
Washington, DC 20001-2070
Tel: 888-422-7233
http://www.iccsafe.org

National Association of Elevator Safety Authorities International
6957 Littlerock Road, SW, Suite A
Tumwater, WA 98512-7246
Tel: 360-292-4968
Email: info@naesai.org
http://www.naesai.org

National Association of Home Inspectors
4248 Park Glen Road
Minneapolis, MN 55416-4758
Tel: 800-448-3942
http://www.nahi.org

CORRECTIONS OFFICERS

OVERVIEW

Corrections officers guard people who have been arrested and are awaiting trial or who have been tried, convicted, and sentenced to serve time in a penal institution. They search prisoners and their cells for weapons, drugs, and other contraband; inspect windows, doors, locks, and gates for signs of tampering; observe the conduct and behavior of inmates to prevent disturbances or escapes; and make verbal or written reports to superior officers. Corrections officers assign work to inmates and supervise their activities. They guard prisoners who are being transported between jails, courthouses, mental institutions, or other destinations, and supervise prisoners receiving visitors. When necessary, these workers use weapons or force to maintain discipline and order. There are approximately 500,000 corrections officers employed in the United States.

THE JOB

To prevent disturbances or escapes, corrections officers carefully observe the conduct and behavior of the inmates at all times. They watch for forbidden activities and infractions of the rules, as well as for poor attitudes or unsatisfactory adjustment to prison life on the part of the inmates. They try to settle disputes before violence

---

SCHOOL SUBJECTS
Government, Physical Education, Psychology

PERSONAL SKILLS
Communication/Ideas, Helping/Teaching

MINIMUM EDUCATION LEVEL
High School Diploma

CERTIFICATION OR LICENSING
Required by Certain States

WORK ENVIRONMENT
Primarily Indoors, Primarily One Location

can erupt. They may search the prisoners or their living quarters for weapons or drugs and inspect locks, bars on windows and doors, and gates for any evidence of tampering. The inmates are under guard constantly while eating, sleeping, exercising, bathing, and working. They are counted periodically to be sure all are present. Some officers are stationed on towers and at gates to prevent escapes. All rule violations and anything out of the ordinary are reported to a superior officer such as a chief jailer. In case of a major disturbance, corrections officers may use weapons or force to restore order.

Corrections officers give work assignments to prisoners, supervise them as they carry out their duties, and instruct them in unfamiliar tasks. Corrections officers are responsible for the physical needs of the prisoners, such as providing or obtaining meals and medical aid. They assure the health and safety of the inmates by checking the cells for unsanitary conditions and fire hazards.

These workers may escort inmates from their cells to the prison's visiting room, medical office, or chapel. Certain officers, called *patrol conductors,* guard prisoners who are being transported between courthouses, prisons, mental institutions, or other destinations, either by van, car, or public transportation. Officers at a penal institution may also screen visitors at the entrance and accompany them to other areas within the facility. From time to time, they may inspect mail addressed to prisoners, checking for contraband, help investigate crimes committed within the prison, or aid in the search for escapees.

Some police officers specialize in guarding juvenile offenders being held at a police station house or detention room pending a hearing, transfer to a correctional institution, or return to their parents. They often investigate the backgrounds of first offenders to check for a criminal history or to make a recommendation to the magistrate regarding disposition of the case. Lost or runaway children are also placed in the care of these officers until their parents or guardians can be located.

Immigration guards guard aliens held by the immigration service awaiting investigation, deportation, or release. *Gate tenders* check the identification of all persons entering and leaving the penal institution.

In most correctional institutions, psychologists and social workers are employed to counsel inmates with mental and emotional problems. It is an important part of a corrections officer's job, however, to supplement this with informal counseling. Officers may help inmates adjust to prison life, prepare for return to civilian life, and avoid committing crimes in the future. On a more immediate level, they may arrange for an inmate to visit the library, help inmates get in touch with their families,

suggest where to look for a job after release from prison, or discuss personal problems. In some institutions, corrections officers may lead more formal group counseling sessions. As they fulfill more rehabilitative roles, corrections officers are increasingly required to possess a college-level education in psychology, criminology, or related areas of study.

Corrections officers keep a daily record of their activities and make regular reports, either verbal or written, to their supervisors. These reports concern the behavior of the inmates and the quality and quantity of work they do, as well as any disturbances, rule violations, and unusual occurrences that may have taken place.

Head corrections officers supervise and coordinate other corrections officers. They perform roll call and assign duties to the officers; direct the activities of groups of inmates; arrange the release and transfer of prisoners in accordance with the instructions on a court order; maintain security and investigate disturbances among the inmates; maintain prison records and prepare reports; and review and evaluate the performance of their subordinates.

In small communities, corrections officers (who are sometimes called *jailers*) may also act as deputy sheriffs or police officers when they are not occupied with guard duties.

REQUIREMENTS
High School

To work as a corrections officer, candidates generally must meet the minimum age requirement—usually 18 or 21—and have a high school diploma or its equivalent. Individuals without a high school education may be considered for employment if they have qualifying work experience, such as probation and parole experience.

Postsecondary Training

Many states and correctional facilities prefer or require officers to have postsecondary training in psychology, criminology, or related areas of study. Some states require applicants to have one or two years of previous experience in corrections or related police work. Military experience or related work experience is also required by some state governments. On the federal level, applicants should have at least two years of college or two years of work or military experience.

Training for corrections officers ranges from the special academy instruction provided by the federal government in some states to the informal, on-the-job training furnished by most states and local governments. The

Federal Bureau of Prisons operates a training center in Glynco, Georgia, where new hires generally undergo a three-week program of basic corrections education. Training academies have programs that last from four to eight weeks and instruct trainees on institutional policies, regulations, and procedures; the behavior and custody of inmates; security measures; and report writing. Training in self-defense, the use of firearms and other weapons, and emergency medical techniques is often provided. On-the-job trainees spend two to six months or more under the supervision of an experienced officer. During that period of time, they receive in-house training while gaining actual experience. Periodically, corrections officers may be given additional training as new ideas and procedures in criminal justice are developed.

Certification or Licensing

Numerous certification programs are available to corrections officers; these are optional in most states. Common certifications include self-defense, weapons use, urine analysis, shield and gun, shotgun/handgun, CPR, and cell extraction. Many officers also take advantage of additional training that is offered at their facility, such as suicide prevention, AIDS awareness, use of four-point restraints, and emergency preparedness. At most prisons, there is annual mandatory in-service training that focuses on policies and procedures. The American Correctional Association and the American Jail Association offer certification programs to corrections officers and corrections managers.

Corrections officers who work for the federal government and most state governments are covered by civil service systems or merit boards and may be required to pass a competitive exam for employment. Many states require random or comprehensive drug testing of their officers, either during hiring procedures or while employed at the facility.

Other Requirements

There is no denying that handling the inherent stress of this line of work takes a unique person. In a maximum-security facility, the environment is often noisy, crowded, poorly ventilated, and even dangerous. Corrections officers need the physical and emotional strength to handle the stress involved in working with criminals, some of whom may be violent. A corrections officer has to stay alert and aware of prisoners' actions and attitudes. This constant vigilance can be harder on some people. Work in a minimum-security prison is usually more comfortable, cleaner, and less stressful.

Officers need to use persuasion rather than brute force to get inmates to follow the rules. Certain inmates take a disproportionate amount of time and attention because they are either violent, mentally ill, or victims of abuse by other inmates. Officers have to carry out routine duties while being alert for the unpredictable outbursts. Sound judgment and the ability to think and act quickly are important qualities for corrections officers. With experience and training, corrections officers are usually able to handle volatile situations without resorting to physical force.

The ability to communicate clearly verbally and in writing is extremely important. Corrections officers have to write a number of reports, documenting routine procedures as well as any violations by the inmates. A correction officer's eight-hour shift can easily extend to 10 hours because of the reports that must be written.

An effective corrections officer is not easily intimidated or influenced by the inmates. There is a misconception, however, that corrections officers need to be "tough guys" (or "tough girls"). While it's true that a person needs some physical strength to perform the job, corrections officers also need to be able to use their head to anticipate and defuse any potentially dangerous situations between inmates or between guards and inmates.

Most correctional institutions require candidates to be at least 18 years old (sometimes 21 years old), have a high school diploma, and be a U.S. citizen with no criminal record. There are also health and physical strength requirements, and many states have minimum height, vision, and hearing standards. Other common requirements are a driver's license and a job record that shows that they've been dependable.

EXPLORING

Because of age requirements and the nature of the work, there are no opportunities for high school students to gain actual experience while still in school. Where the minimum age requirement is 21, prospective corrections officers may prepare for employment by taking college courses in criminal justice or police science. Enrollment in a two- or four-year college degree program in a related field is encouraged. Military service may also offer experience and training in corrections. Social work is another way to gain experience. You may also look into obtaining a civilian job as a clerk or other worker for the police department or other protective service organization. Related part-time, volunteer, or summer work may also be available in psychiatric hospitals and other institutions providing physical and emotional counseling and services. Many online services also have forums for corrections officers and other public safety employees, and these may provide opportunities to read about and communicate with people active in this career.

EMPLOYERS

Most corrections officers work for the government at the local, state, and federal levels in penal institutions and in jobs connected with the penal system. Of the approximately 500,000 corrections officers employed in the United States, roughly 60 percent work in state-run correctional facilities such as prisons, prison camps, and reformatories. Most of the rest are employed at city and county jails or other institutions. Roughly 18,000 work for the federal government and approximately 16,000 are employed by private corrections contractors.

STARTING OUT

To apply for a job as a corrections officer, contact federal or state civil service commissions, state departments of correction, or local correctional facilities and ask for information about entrance requirements, training, and job opportunities. Private contractors and other companies are also a growing source of employment opportunities. Many officers enter this field from social work areas and parole and probation positions.

ADVANCEMENT

Many officers take college courses in law enforcement or criminal justice to increase their chances of promotion. In some states, officers must serve two years in each position before they can be considered for a promotion.

With additional education and training, experienced officers can also be promoted to supervisory or administrative positions such as head corrections officer, assistant warden, or prison director. Officers who want to continue to work directly with offenders can move into various other positions. For example, *probation and parole officers* monitor and counsel offenders, process their release from prison, and evaluate their progress in becoming productive members of society. *Recreation leaders* organize and instruct offenders in sports, games, and arts and crafts.

EARNINGS

Wages for corrections officers vary considerably depending on their employers and their level of experience. According to the U.S. Department of Labor, the 2006 mean annual earnings for corrections officers employed by the federal government were $48,000; for those employed by state governments, $38,960; and for those employed by local governments, $37,330. The U.S. Department of Labor reports that overall the lowest paid 10 percent of corrections officers earned less than $23,600 per year in 2006, and the highest paid 10 percent earned more than $58,580. Median earnings for corrections officers were $35,760.

The U.S. Department of Labor reports higher earnings for supervisors/managers, with a median yearly income of $52,580 in 2006. The lowest paid 10 percent earned less than $33,270, and the highest paid 10 percent earned more than $81,230.

Overtime, night shift, weekend, and holiday pay differentials are generally available at most institutions. Fringe benefits may include health, disability, and life insurance; uniforms or a cash allowance to buy their own uniforms; and sometimes meals and housing. Officers who work for the federal government and for most state governments are covered by civil service systems or merit boards. Some corrections officers also receive retirement and pension plans, and retirement is often possible after 20 to 25 years of service.

WORK ENVIRONMENT

Because prison security must be maintained around the clock, work schedules for corrections officers may include nights, weekends, and holidays. The workweek, however, generally consists of five days, eight hours per day, except during emergencies, when many officers work overtime.

Corrections officers may work indoors or outdoors, depending on their duties. Conditions can vary even within an institution: Some areas are well lighted, ventilated, and temperature-controlled, while others are overcrowded, hot, and noisy. Officers who work outdoors, of course, are subject to all kinds of weather. Correctional institutions occasionally present unpredictable or even hazardous situations. If violence erupts among the inmates, corrections officers may be in danger of injury or death. Although this risk is higher than for most other occupations, corrections work is usually routine.

Corrections officers need physical and emotional strength to cope with the stress inherent in dealing with criminals, many of whom may be dangerous or incapable of change. A corrections officer has to remain alert and aware of the surroundings, prisoners' movements and attitudes, and any potential for danger or violence. Such continual, heightened levels of alertness often create psychological stress for some workers. Most institutions have stress-reduction programs or seminars for their employees, but if not, insurance usually covers some form of therapy for work-related stress.

OUTLOOK

Employment in this field is expected to grow faster than the average for all occupations through 2016, according to the U.S. Department of Labor. There should be thousands of job openings annually for qualified workers. The ongoing prosecution of illegal drugs, new tough-on-crime legislation, and increasing mandatory sentencing policies will create a need for more prison beds and more corrections officers. The extremely crowded conditions in today's correctional institutions have created a need for more corrections officers to guard the inmates more closely and relieve the tensions. A greater number of officers will also be required as a result of the expansion or new construction of facilities. As prison sentences become longer through mandatory minimum sentences set by state law, the number of prisons needed will increase. In addition, many job openings will occur from a characteristically high turnover rate, as well as from the need to fill vacancies caused by the death or retirement of older workers. Traditionally, correction agencies have difficulty attracting qualified employees due to job location and salary considerations.

Some states are reconsidering their mandatory sentencing guidelines because of budgetary constraints, court decisions, and doubts about their effectiveness, according to the U.S. Department of Labor. This may limit employment growth for corrections officer in some states.

Because security must be maintained at correctional facilities at all times, corrections officers can depend on steady employment. They are not usually affected by poor economic conditions or changes in government spending. Corrections officers are rarely laid off, even when budgets need to be trimmed. Instead, because of high turnover, staffs can be cut simply by not replacing those officers who leave.

Most jobs will be found in relatively large institutions located near metropolitan areas, although opportunities for corrections officers exist in jails and other smaller facilities throughout the country. The increasing use of private companies and privately run prisons may limit the growth of jobs in this field as these companies are more likely to keep a close eye on the bottom line. Use of new technologies, such as surveillance equipment, automatic gates, and other devices, may also allow institutions to employ fewer officers.

FOR MORE INFORMATION

For information on certification, training, conferences, and membership, contact

American Correctional Association
206 North Washington Street, Suite 200
Alexandria, VA 22314-2528
Tel: 703-224-0000
http://www.aca.org

American Jail Association
1135 Professional Court
Hagerstown, MD 21740-5853
Tel: 301-790-3930
http://www.aja.org

American Probation and Parole Association
2760 Research Park Drive
Lexington, KY 40511-8410
Tel: 859-244-8203
Email: appa@csg.org
http://www.appa-net.org

For information on entrance requirements, training, and career opportunities for corrections officers at the federal level, contact

Federal Bureau of Prisons
320 First Street, NW
Washington, DC 20534-0002
Tel: 202-307-3198
http://www.bop.gov

For information about the corrections industry, visit

The Corrections Connection
http://www.corrections.com

COSMETOLOGISTS

OVERVIEW

Cosmetologists practice hair-care skills (including washing, cutting, coloring, perming, and applying various conditioning treatments), esthetics (performing skin care treatments), and nail care (grooming of hands and feet). Barbers are not cosmetologists; they undergo separate training and licensing procedures. There are approximately 677,000 cosmetologists, barbers, hairdressers, and hairstylists employed in the United States.

THE JOB

Cosmetology uses hair as a medium to sculpt, perm, color, or design to create a fashion attitude. Cosmetologists, also known as hair stylists, perform all of these tasks as well as provide other services, such as deep

SCHOOL SUBJECTS
Art, Business, Speech

PERSONAL SKILLS
Artistic, Mechanical/Manipulative

MINIMUM EDUCATION LEVEL
Some Postsecondary Training

CERTIFICATION OR LICENSING
Required by All States

WORK ENVIRONMENT
Primarily Indoors, Primarily One Location

conditioning treatments, special-occasion hair designs, and a variety of hair-addition techniques.

A licensed hair stylist can perform the hair services noted above and also is trained and licensed to do the basics of esthetics and nail technology. To specialize in esthetics or nail technology, additional courses are taken in each of these disciplines—or someone can study just esthetics or just nail technology and get a license in either or both of these areas.

Cosmetology schools teach some aspects of human physiology and anatomy, including the bone structure of the head and some elementary facts about the nervous system, in addition to hair skills. Some schools have now added psychology-related courses, dealing with people skills and communications.

Hair stylists may be employed in shops that have as few as one or two employees, or as many as 20 or more. They may work in privately owned salons or in a salon that is part of a large or small chain of beauty shops. They may work in hotels, department stores, hospitals, nursing homes, resort areas, or on cruise ships. In recent years, a number of hair professionals—especially in big cities—have gone to work in larger facilities, sometimes known as spas or institutes, which offer a variety of health and beauty services. One such business, for example, offers complete hair design/treatment/color services; manicures and pedicures; makeup; bridal services; spa services including different kinds of facials (thermal mask, anti-aging, acne treatment), body treatments (exfoliating sea salt glow, herbal body wrap), scalp treatments, hydrotherapy water treatments, massage therapy, eyebrow/eyelash tweezing and tinting,

and hair-removal treatments for all parts of the body; a fashion boutique; and even a wellness center staffed with board-certified physicians.

Those who operate their own shops must also take care of the details of business operations. Bills must be paid, orders placed, invoices and supplies checked, equipment serviced, and records and books kept. The selection, hiring, and termination of other workers are also the owner's responsibility. Like other responsible business people, shop and salon owners are likely to be asked to participate in civic and community projects and activities.

Some stylists work for cosmetic/hair product companies. Sean Woodyard, for instance, in addition to being employed as a stylist at a big-city salon, teaches hair coloring for a major national cosmetics/hair care company. When the company introduces a new product or sells an existing product to a new salon, the company hires hair professionals as "freelance educators" to teach the stylists at the salon how to use the product. Woodyard has traveled all over the country during the past six years, while still keeping his full-time job, teaching color techniques at salons, and also participating in demonstrations for the company at trade shows. "I've taught all levels of classes," he says, "from a very basic color demonstration to a very complex color correction class. I've also been responsible for training other educators. I have really enjoyed traveling to other locales and having the opportunity to see other salons and other parts of the beauty and fashion industry."

At industry shows, what he does has varied. Woodyard is representing the company, "whether I'm standing behind a booth selling products or working on stage, demonstrating the product, or assisting a guest artist backstage, doing preparatory work. This has given me a real hands-on education, and I've been able to work with some of the top hair stylists in the country."

Woodyard has been working, as he says, "behind the chair" for 14 years. His first job after graduating from cosmetology school was at a small barbershop in his hometown. From there, he moved on to a larger salon and then on to work in a big city. "Work behind the chair led me to want to do color," he said. "This really interested me. I guess wanting to know more about it myself is the reason why I researched it and became so involved with color. As I learned more about hair coloring, I became competent and more confident." The challenge, he said, is to learn the "laws of color"— how to choose a shade to get a specific result on a client's hair. He is now considered a color expert and is the head of the chemical department at his salon. "I've always been involved some way in outside education," Woodyard notes. "I've never been in a job where I have just worked 40 hours behind the chair. I've always been involved in some kind of training. I like to share what I know."

Cosmetologists must know how to market themselves to build their business. Whether they are self-employed or work for a salon or company, they are in business for themselves. It is the cosmetologist's skills and personality that will attract or fail to attract clients to that particular cosmetologist's chair. A marketing strategy Woodyard uses is to give several of his business cards to each of his clients. When one of his clients recommends him to a prospective new client, he gives both the old and new client a discount on a hair service.

Karol Thousand is the managing director of corporate school operations for a large cosmetology school that has four campuses in metropolitan areas in two states. She began as a stylist employed by salons and then owned her own shop for seven years. Her business was in an area that was destroyed by a tornado. It was then that she looked at different opportunities to decide the direction of her career. "I looked at the business end of the profession," she said, "and I took some additional business courses and was then introduced to the school aspect of the profession. I have a passion for the beauty business, and as I explored various training programs, I thought to myself, 'Hey, this is something I'd like to do!'"

She managed a cosmetology school in Wisconsin before moving to Chicago for her current position. "This is an empowering and satisfying profession," she says. "Not only do you make someone look better, but 99 percent of the time, they will feel better about themselves. In cosmetology, you can have the opportunity several times a day to help change the total look and perspective of an individual."

Cosmetologists serving the public must have pleasant, friendly, yet professional attitudes, as well as skill, ability, and an interest in their craft. These qualities are necessary in building a following of steady customers. The nature of their work requires cosmetologists to be aware of the psychological aspects of dealing with all types of personalities. Sometimes this can require diplomacy skills and a high degree of tolerance in dealing with different clients.

"To me," Sean Woodyard admits, "doing hair is just as much about self-gratification as it is about pleasing the client. It makes me feel good to make somebody else look good and feel good. It's also, of course, a great artistic and creative outlet."

REQUIREMENTS
High School

High school students interested in the cosmetology field can help build a good foundation for postsecondary training by taking subjects in the areas of art, science (especially a basic chemistry course), health, business, and communication arts. Psychology and speech courses could also be helpful.

Postsecondary Training

To become a licensed cosmetologist, you must have completed an undergraduate course of a certain amount of classroom credit hours. The required amount varies from state to state—anywhere from 1,050 to 2,200 hours. The program takes from 10 to 24 months to complete, again depending on the state. Evening courses are also frequently offered, and these take two to four months longer to complete. Applicants must also pass a written test, and some states also give an oral test, before they receive a license. Most states will allow a cosmetologist to work as an apprentice until the license is received, which normally just involves a matter of weeks.

A 1,500-hour undergraduate course at a cosmetology school in Illinois is typical of schools around the country. The program consists of theoretical and practical instruction divided into individual units of learning. Students are taught through the media of theory, audiovisual presentation, lectures, demonstrations, practical hands-on experiences, and written and practical testing. All schools have what they call clinic areas or floors, where people can have their hair done (or avail themselves of esthetics or nail services) by students at a discounted price, compared to what they would pay in a regular shop or salon.

One course, Scientific Approach to Hair Sculpture, teaches students how to sculpt straight and curly hair, ethnic and Caucasian, using shears, texturizing tools and techniques, razors, and electric clippers. Teaching tools include mannequins, slip-ons, hair wefts, rectangles, and profiles. People skills segments are part of each course. Among other courses are Scientific Approach to Perm Design, Systematic Approach to Color, and Systematic Approach to Beauty Care. Three different salon prep courses focus on retailing, business survival skills, and practical applications for contemporary design. The program concludes with final testing, as well as extensive reviews and preparations for state board testing through a mock state board written practical examination.

Karol Thousand notes that, at her school and others throughout the country, "Twenty-five years ago, the courses focused mainly on technical skills. This is still the core focus, but now we teach more interpersonal skills. Our People Skills program helps students understand the individual, the different personality types—to better comprehend how they fit in and how to relate to their clients. We also teach sales and marketing skills—how to sell themselves and their services and products, as well as good business management skills."

Some states offer student internship programs. One such program that was recently initiated in Illinois aims to send better-prepared students/junior stylists into the workforce upon completion of their training from a licensed school. This program allows students to enter into a work-study program for 10 percent of their training in either cosmetology, esthetics, or nail technology. The state requires a student to complete at least 750 hours of training prior to making application for the program.

The program allows a student to experience firsthand the expectations of a salon, to perform salon services to be evaluated by their supervisor, and to experience different types of salon settings. The participating salons have the opportunity to pre-qualify potential employees before they graduate and work with the school regarding the skill levels of the student interns. This will also enhance job placement programs already in place in the school. The state requires that each participating salon be licensed and registered with the appropriate state department and file proof of registration with the school, along with the name and license number of their cosmetologist who is assigned to supervise students, before signing a contract or agreement.

Certification or Licensing

At the completion of the proper amount of credit hours, students must pass a formal examination before they can be licensed. The exam takes just a few hours. Some states also require a practical (hands-on) test and oral exams. Most, however, just require written tests. State board examinations are given at regular intervals. After about a month, test scores are available. Those who have passed then send in a licensure application and a specified fee to the appropriate state department. It takes about four to six weeks for a license to be issued.

Temporary permits are issued in most states, allowing students who have passed the test and applied for a license to practice their profession while they wait to receive the actual license. Judy Vargas, manager of the professional regulation section of the Illinois Department of Financial and Professional Regulation, warns students not to practice without a temporary permit or a license. "This is the biggest violation we see," she said, "and there are penalties of up to $1,000 per violation."

Graduate courses on advanced techniques and new methods and styles are also available at many cosmetology schools. Many states require licensed cosmetologists to take a specified number of credit hours, called continuing education units, or CEUs. Illinois, for instance, requires each licensed cosmetologist to complete 10 to 14 CEUs each year. Licenses must be renewed in all states, generally every year or every two years.

In the majority of states, the minimum age for an individual to obtain a cosmetology license is 16. Because standards and requirements vary from state to state, students are urged to contact the licensing board of the state in which they plan to be employed.

Other Requirements

Hairstyles change from season to season. As a cosmetologist, you will need to keep up with current fashion trends and often be learning new procedures to create new looks. You should be able to visualize different styles and make suggestions to your clients about what is best for them. And even if you don't specialize in coloring hair, you should have a good sense of color. One of your most important responsibilities will be to make your clients feel comfortable around you and happy with their looks. To do this, you will need to develop both your talking and listening skills.

EXPLORING

Talk to friends or parents of friends who are working in the industry, or just go to a local salon or cosmetology school and ask questions about the profession. Go to the library and get books on careers in the beauty/hair care industry. Search the Internet for related Web sites. Individuals with an interest in the field might seek after-school or summer employment as a general shop helper in a barbershop or a salon. Some schools may permit potential students to visit and observe classes.

EMPLOYERS

Approximately 677,000 cosmetologists, barbers, hairdressers, and hairstylists are employed in the United States. The most common employers of hair stylists are, of course, beauty salons. However, hair stylists also find work at department stores, hospitals, nursing homes, spas, resorts, cruise ships, and cosmetics companies. The demand for services in the cosmetology field—hair styling in particular—far exceeds the supply; additionally, the number of salons increases by 2 percent each year. Considering that most cosmetology schools have placement services to assist graduates, finding employment usually is not difficult for most cosmetologists. As with most jobs in the cosmetology field, opportunities will be concentrated in highly populated areas; however, there will be jobs available for hair stylists virtually everywhere. Many hair stylists/cosmetologists aspire ultimately to be self-employed. This can be a rewarding avenue if one has plenty of experience and good business sense (not to mention start-up capital or financial backing); it also requires long hours and a great deal of hard work.

STARTING OUT

To be a licensed cosmetologist/hair stylist, you must graduate from an accredited school and pass a state test. Once that is accomplished, you can apply for jobs that are advertised in the newspapers or over the Internet, or apply at an employment agency specializing in these professions. Most schools have career services offices to help their graduates find jobs. Some salons have training programs from which they hire new employees.

Scholarships or grants that can help you pay for your schooling are available. One such program is the Access to Cosmetology Education (ACE) Grant. It is sponsored by the American Association of Cosmetology Schools (AACS) and the Cosmetology Advancement Foundation. Interested students can find out about ACE Grants and obtain applications at participating schools, salons, and distributors or through these institutions. The criteria for receiving an ACE Grant include approval from an AACS member school, recommendations from two salons, and a high school diploma or GED.

ADVANCEMENT

Individuals in the beauty/hair care industry most frequently begin by working at a shop or salon. Many aspire to be self-employed and own their own shop. There are many factors to consider when contemplating going into business on one's own. Usually it is essential to obtain experience and financial capital before seeking to own a shop. The cost of equipping even a one-chair shop can be very high. Owning a large shop or a chain of shops is an aspiration for the very ambitious.

Some pursue advanced educational training in one aspect of beauty culture, such as hair styling or coloring. Others who are more interested in the business aspects can take courses in business management skills and move into shop or salon management, or work for a corporation related to the industry. Manufacturers and distributors frequently have exciting positions available for those with exceptional talent and creativity. Cosmetologists work on the stage as platform artists, or take some additional education courses and teach at a school of cosmetology.

Some schools publish their own texts and other printed materials for students. They want people who have cosmetology knowledge and experience as well as writing skills to write and edit these materials. An artistic director for the publishing venue of one large school has a cosmetology degree in addition to degrees in art. Other cosmetologists might design hairstyles for fashion magazines, industry publications, fashion shows, television presentations, or movies. They might get involved in the regulation of the business, such as working for a state licensing board. There are many and varied career possibilities cosmetologists can explore in the beauty/hair care industry.

EARNINGS

Cosmetologists can make an excellent living in the beauty/hair care industry, but as in most careers, they don't receive very high pay when just starting out. Though their raise in salary may start slowly, the curve quickly escalates. The U.S. Department of Labor reports cosmetologists and hairstylists had a median annual income (including tips) of $21,320 in 2006. The lowest paid 10 percent, which generally included those beginning in the profession, made less than $13,880. The highest paid 10 percent earned more than $39,070. Again, both those salaries include tips. On the extreme upward end of the pay scale, some fashion stylists in New York or Hollywood charge $300 per haircut. Their annual salary can go into six figures. Salaries in larger cities are greater than those in smaller towns; but then the cost of living is higher in the big cities, too.

Most shops and salons give a new employee a guaranteed income instead of commission. If the employee goes over the guaranteed amount, then he or she earns a commission. Usually, this guarantee will extend for the first three months of employment, so that the new stylist can focus on building up business before going on straight commission.

In addition, most salon owners grant incentives for product sales; and, of course, there are always tips. However, true professionals never depend on their tips. If a stylist receives a tip, it is a nice surprise for a job well done, but it is good business practice not to expect these bonuses. All tips must be recorded and reported to the Internal Revenue Service.

The benefits a cosmetologist receives, such as health insurance and retirement plans, depend on the place of employment. A small independent salon cannot afford to supply a hefty benefit package, but a large shop or salon or a member of a chain can be more generous. However, some of the professional associations and organizations offer benefit packages at reasonable rates.

WORK ENVIRONMENT

Those employed in the cosmetology industry usually work a five- or six-day week, which averages approximately 40 hours. Weekends and days preceding holidays may be especially busy. Cosmetologists are on their feet a lot and are usually working in a small space. Strict sanitation codes must be observed in all shops and salons, and they are comfortably heated, ventilated, and well lighted.

Hazards of the trade include nicks and cuts from scissors and razors, minor burns when care is not used in handling hot towels or instruments, and occasional skin irritations arising from constant use of grooming aids that contain chemicals. Some of the chemicals used in hair dyes or permanent solutions can be very abrasive; plastic gloves are required for handling and contact. Pregnant women are advised to avoid contact with many of the chemicals present in hair products.

Conditions vary depending on what environment the stylist is working in. Those employed in department store salons will have more of a guaranteed client flow, with more walk-ins from people who are shopping. A freestanding shop or salon might have a more predictable pace, with more scheduled appointments and fewer walk-ins. In a department store salon, for example, stylists have to abide by the rules and regulations of the store. In a private salon, stylists are more like entrepreneurs or freelancers, but they have much more flexibility as to when they come and go and what type of business they want to do.

Stylist Sean Woodyard says, "I've always enjoyed the atmosphere of a salon. There's constant action and something different happening every day. A salon attracts artistic, creative people and the profession allows me to be part of the fashion industry."

Some may find it difficult to work constantly in such close, personal contact with the public at large, especially when they strive to satisfy customers who are difficult to please or disagreeable. The work demands an even temperament, pleasant disposition, and patience.

OUTLOOK

The future looks good for cosmetology. According to the U.S. Department of Labor, employment should grow about as fast as the average for all occupations through 2016. Our growing population, the availability of disposable income, and changes in hair fashion that are practically seasonal all contribute to the demand for cosmetologists. In addition, turnover in this career is fairly high as cosmetologists move up into management positions, change careers, or leave the field for other reasons. This will create a large number of annual job openings for cosmetologists. Competition for jobs at higher paying, prestigious salons, however, is strong.

FOR MORE INFORMATION

For information on cosmetology careers, schools, and the ACE Grant, contact
American Association of Cosmetology Schools
15825 North 71st Street, Suite 100
Scottsdale, AZ 85254-1521
Tel: 800-831-1086
http://www.beautyschools.org

For information on membership, contact
Cosmetologists of America
PO Box 1083
Newport, RI 02840-0999
Tel: 401-662-2181
http://www.cosmetologistsofamerica.com

For information on accredited cosmetology programs, contact
National Accrediting Commission of Cosmetology Arts and Sciences
4401 Ford Avenue, Suite 1300
Alexandria, VA 22302-1432
Tel: 703-600-7600
http://www.naccas.org

For information on scholarships, contact
National Cosmetology Association
401 North Michigan Avenue, 19th Floor
Chicago, IL 60611-4274
Tel: 312-527-6765
http://www.salonprofessionals.org

For information on careers in the beauty industry, visit
Careers in Beauty
http://www.beautyschools.org/associations/7485/careersinbeauty.cfm

COST ESTIMATORS

OVERVIEW

Cost estimators use standard estimating techniques to calculate the cost of a construction or manufacturing project. They help contractors, owners, and project planners determine how much a project or product will cost to decide if it is economically viable. There are approximately 221,000 cost estimators employed in the United States.

Cost estimators collect and analyze information on various factors influencing costs, such as the labor, materials, and machinery needed for a particular project. Cost estimating became a profession as production techniques became more complex. Weighing the many costs involved in a construction or manufacturing project soon required specialized knowledge beyond the skills and training of the average builder or contractor. Today, cost estimators work in many industries but are predominantly employed in construction and manufacturing.

THE JOB

In the construction industry, the nature of the work is largely determined by the type and size of the project being estimated. For a large building project, for example, the estimator reviews architectural drawings and other bidding documents before any construction begins. The estimator then visits the potential construction site to collect information that may affect the way the structure is built, such as the site's access to transportation, water, electricity, and other needed resources. While out in the field, the estimator also analyzes the topography of the land, taking note of its general characteristics, such as drainage areas and the location of trees and other vegetation. After compiling thorough research, the estimator writes a quantity survey, or takeoff. This is an itemized report of the quantity of materials and labor a firm will need for the proposed project.

Large projects often require several estimators, all specialists in a given area. For example, one estimator may assess the electrical costs of a project, while another concentrates on the transportation or insurance costs. In this case, it is the responsibility of a *chief estimator* to combine the reports and submit one development proposal.

In manufacturing, estimators work with engineers to review blueprints and other designs. They develop

---

SCHOOL SUBJECTS
Business, Economics, Mathematics

PERSONAL SKILLS
Leadership/Management, Technical/Scientific

MINIMUM EDUCATION LEVEL
Some Postsecondary Training

CERTIFICATION OR LICENSING
Recommended

WORK ENVIRONMENT
Indoors and Outdoors, Primarily Multiple Locations

---

a list of the materials and labor needed for production. Aiming to control costs but maintain quality, estimators must weigh the option of producing parts in-house or purchasing them from other vendors. After this research, they write a report on the overall costs of manufacturing, taking into consideration influences such as improved employee learning curves, material waste, overhead, and the need to correct problems as manufacturing goes along.

To write their reports, estimators must know current prices for labor and materials and other factors that influence costs. They obtain this data through commercial price books, catalogs, and the Internet or by calling vendors directly to obtain quotes.

Estimators should also be able to compute and understand accounting and mathematical formulas in order to make their cost reports. Computer programs are frequently used to do the routine calculations, producing more accurate results and leaving the estimator with more time to analyze data.

REQUIREMENTS

High School

To prepare for a job in cost estimating, you should take courses in accounting, business, economics, and mathematics. Because a large part of this job involves comparing calculations, it is essential that you are comfortable and confident with your math skills. English courses with a heavy concentration in writing are also recommended to develop your communication skills. Cost estimators must be able to write clear and accurate reports of their analyses. Finally, drafting and shop courses are also useful since estimators must be able to review and understand blueprints and other design plans.

Postsecondary Training

Though not required for the job, most employers of cost estimators in both construction and manufacturing prefer applicants with formal education. In construction, cost estimators generally have associate's or bachelor's degrees in construction management, construction science, or building science. Those employed with manufacturers often have degrees in physical science, business, mathematics, operations research, statistics, engineering, economics, finance, or accounting.

Many colleges and universities offer courses in cost estimating as part of the curriculum for an associate's, bachelor's, or master's degree. These courses cover subjects such as cost estimating, cost control, project planning and management, and computer applications. The Association for the Advancement of Cost Engineering International offers a list of education programs related to cost engineering. Check out the association's Web site, http://www.aacei.org, for more information.

Certification or Licensing

Although it is not required, many cost estimators find it helpful to become certified to improve their standing within the professional community. Obtaining certification proves that the estimator has obtained adequate job training and education. Information on certification procedures is available from organizations such as the American Society of Professional Estimators, the Association for the Advancement of Cost Engineering International, and the Society of Cost Estimating and Analysis.

Other Requirements

To be a cost estimator, you should have sharp mathematical and analytical skills. Cost estimators must work well with others, and be confident and assertive when presenting findings to engineers, business owners, and design professionals. To work as a cost estimator in the construction industry, you will likely need some experience before you start, which can be gained through an internship or cooperative education program.

EXPLORING

Practical work experience is necessary to become a cost estimator. Consider taking a part-time position with a construction crew or manufacturing firm during your summer vacations. Because of more favorable working conditions, construction companies are the busiest during the summer months and may be looking for additional assistance. Join any business or manufacturing clubs that your school may offer.

Another way to discover more about career opportunities is simply by talking to a professional cost estimator. Ask your school counselor to help arrange an interview with an estimator to ask questions about his or her job demands, work environment, and personal opinion of the job.

EMPLOYERS

Approximately 221,000 cost estimators are employed in the United States: 62 percent by the construction industry and 15 percent by manufacturing companies. Other employers include engineering and architecture firms, business services, the government, and a wide range of other industries.

Estimators are employed throughout the country, but the largest concentrations are found in cities or rapidly growing suburban areas. More job opportunities exist in or near large commercial or government centers.

STARTING OUT

Cost estimators often start out working in the industry as laborers, such as construction workers. After gaining experience and taking the necessary training courses, a worker may move into the more specialized role of estimator. Another possible route into cost estimating is through a formal training program, either through a professional organization that sponsors educational programs or through technical schools, community colleges, or universities. School career services counselors can be good sources of employment leads for recent graduates. Applying directly to manufacturers, construction firms, and government agencies is another way to find your first job.

Whether employed in construction or manufacturing, most cost estimators are provided with intensive on-the-job training. Generally, new hires work with experienced estimators to become familiar with the work involved. They develop skills in blueprint reading and learn construction specifications before accompanying estimators to the construction site. In time, new hires learn how to determine quantities and specifications from project designs and report appropriate material and labor costs.

ADVANCEMENT

Promotions for cost estimators are dependent on skill and experience. Advancement usually comes in the form of more responsibility and higher wages. A skilled cost estimator at a large construction company may become a chief estimator. Some experienced cost estimators go into consulting work, offering their services to government, construction, and manufacturing firms.

EARNINGS

Salaries vary according to the size of the construction or manufacturing firm and the experience and education of the worker. According to the U.S. Department of Labor, the median annual salary for cost estimators was $52,940 in 2006. The lowest 10 percent earned less than $31,600 and the highest 10 percent earned more than $88,310. By industry, the mean annual earnings were as follows: nonresidential building construction, $64,550; residential building construction, $56,280; building foundation, structure, and exterior contractors, $56,170; and building finishing contractors, $55,640. Starting salaries for graduates of engineering or construction management programs were higher than those with degrees in other fields. A salary survey by the National Association of Colleges and Employers reports that candidates with degrees in construction science/management were offered average starting salaries of $46,930 a year in 2007.

Benefits for full-time workers include vacation and sick time, health, and sometimes dental, insurance, and pension or 401(k) plans.

WORK ENVIRONMENT

Much of the cost estimator's work takes place in a typical office setting with access to accounting records and other information. However, estimators must also visit construction sites or manufacturing facilities to inspect production procedures. These sites may be dirty, noisy, and potentially hazardous if the cost estimator is not equipped with proper protective gear such as a hard hat or earplugs. During a site visit, cost estimators consult with engineers, work supervisors, and other professionals involved in the production or manufacturing process.

Estimators usually work a 40-hour week, although longer hours may be required if a project faces a deadline. For construction estimators, overtime hours almost always occur in the summer when most projects are in full force.

OUTLOOK

Employment for cost estimators is expected to increase faster than the average for all occupations through 2016, according to the U.S. Department of Labor. As in most industries, highly trained college graduates and those with the most experience will have the best job prospects.

Many jobs will arise from the need to replace workers leaving the industry, either to retire or change jobs. In addition, growth within the residential and commercial construction industry is a large cause for much of the employment demand for estimators. The fastest-growing areas in construction are in special trade and government projects, including the building and repairing of highways, streets, bridges, subway systems, airports, water and sewage systems, and electric power plants and transmission lines. Additionally, opportunities will be good in residential and school construction, as well as in the construction of nursing and extended care facilities. Cost estimators with degrees in construction management, construction science, or building science will have the best employment prospects. In manufacturing, employment is predicted to remain stable, though growth is not expected to be as strong as in construction. Estimators will be in demand because employers will continue to need their services to control operating costs. Estimators with degrees in engineering, statistics, accounting, mathematics, business administration, or economics will have the best employment prospects in this field.

FOR MORE INFORMATION

For information on certification and educational programs, contact

American Society of Professional Estimators
2525 Perimeter Place Drive, Suite 103
Nashville, TN 37214-3674
Tel: 888-EST-MATE
Email: SBO@aspenational.org
http://www.aspenational.org

For information on certification, educational programs, and scholarships, contact

Association for the Advancement of Cost Engineering International
209 Prairie Avenue, Suite 100
Morgantown, WV 26501-5934
Tel: 800-858-2678
Email: info@aacei.org
http://www.aacei.org

For information on certification, job listings, and a glossary of cost-estimating terms, visit the SCEA's Web site:

Society of Cost Estimating and Analysis (SCEA)

527 Maple Avenue East, Suite 301

Vienna, VA 22180-4753

Tel: 703-938-5090

Email: scea@sceaonline.net

http://www.sceaonline.net

COURT REPORTERS

OVERVIEW

Court reporters record every word at hearings, trials, depositions, and other legal proceedings by using a stenotype machine to take shorthand notes. Most court reporters transcribe the notes of the proceedings by using computer-aided transcription systems that print out regular, legible copies of the proceedings. The court reporter must also edit and proofread the final transcript and create the official transcript of the trial or other legal proceeding. Approximately 19,000 court reporters work in the United States.

THE JOB

Court reporters are best known as the men or women sitting in the courtroom silently typing to record what is said by everyone involved. While that is true, it is only part of the court reporter's job. Much more work is done after the court reporter leaves the trial or hearing.

In the courtroom, court reporters use symbols or shorthand forms of complete words to record what is said as quickly as it is spoken on a stenotype machine that looks like a miniature typewriter. The stenotype machine has 24 keys on its keyboard. Each key prints a single symbol. Unlike a typewriter, however, the court reporter using a stenotype machine can press more than one key at a time to print different combinations of symbols. Each symbol or combination represents a different sound, word, or phrase. As testimony is given, the reporter strikes one or more keys to create a phonetic representation of the testimony on a strip of paper, as well as on a computer hard drive inside the stenotype machine. The court reporter later uses a computer to translate and transcribe the testimony into legible, full-page documents or stores them for reference. Remember, people in court may speak at a rate of between 250 and 300 words a minute, and court reporters must record this testimony word for word and quickly.

Accurate recording of a trial is vital because the court reporter's record becomes the official transcript for the entire proceeding. In our legal system, court transcripts can be used after the trial for many important purposes. If a legal case is appealed, for example, the court reporter's transcript becomes the foundation for any further legal action. The appellate judge refers to the court reporter's transcript to see what happened in the trial and how the evidence was presented.

Because of the importance of accuracy, a court reporter who misses a word or phrase must interrupt the proceedings to have the words repeated. The court reporter may be asked by the judge to read aloud a portion of recorded testimony during the trial to refresh everyone's memory. Court reporters must pay close attention to all the proceedings and be able to hear and understand everything. Sometimes it may be difficult to understand a particular witness or attorney due to poor diction, a strong accent, or a soft speaking voice. Nevertheless, the court reporter cannot be shy about stopping the trial and asking for clarification.

Court reporters must be adept at recording testimony on a wide range of legal issues, from medical malpractice to income tax evasion. In some cases, court reporters may record testimony at a murder trial or a child-custody case. Witnessing tense situations and following complicated arguments are unavoidable parts of the job. The court reporter must be able to remain detached from the drama that unfolds in court while faithfully recording all that is said.

SCHOOL SUBJECTS

English, Foreign Language, Government

PERSONAL SKILLS

Communication/Ideas, Following Instructions

MINIMUM EDUCATION LEVEL

Some Postsecondary Training

CERTIFICATION OR LICENSING

Required by Certain States

WORK ENVIRONMENT

Primarily Indoors, Primarily Multiple Locations

After the trial or hearing, the court reporter has more work to do. Using a CAT program, the stenotype notes are translated to English. The majority of these translated notes are accurate. This rough translation is then edited either by the court reporter or by a *scopist*—an assistant to the court reporter who edits and cleans up the notes. If a stenotype note did not match a word in the court reporter's CAT dictionary during translation, it shows up still in stenotype form. The court reporter must manually change these entries into words and update the dictionary used in translating. If there are any meanings of words or spellings of names that are unfamiliar to the court reporter, research must be done to verify that the correct term or spelling is used. The court reporter then proofreads the transcript to check for any errors in meaning, such as the word *here* instead of the word *hear*. If necessary or requested by the lawyer or judge, special indexes and concordances are compiled using computer programs. The last step the court reporter must take is printing and binding the transcript to make it an organized and usable document for the lawyers and judge.

In some states, the court reporter is responsible for swearing in the witnesses and documenting items of evidence.

In addition to the traditional method of court reporting discussed above, a number of other methods of reporting have emerged in recent years. In real-time court reporting, the court reporter types the court proceedings on a stenotype machine, which is connected to a computer. The symbols that the court reporter types on the stenotype machine are converted to words that can be read by those involved in the case. This process is known as Communications Access Real-time Translation (CART). In addition to its use in court, CART is used in meetings, educational settings, and for closed captioning for the hearing-impaired on television.

In electronic reporting, the court reporter uses audio equipment to record court proceedings. The court reporter is responsible for overseeing the recording process, taking notes to identify speakers and clarify other issues, and ensuring the quality of the recording. Court reporters who specialize in this method are often asked to create a written transcript of the recorded proceeding.

In voice writing, a court reporter wears a hand-held mask (known as a voice silencer) that is equipped with a microphone, and repeats the testimony of all parties involved in the trial. Some reporters translate the voice recording in real time using computer speech recognition technology. Others wait till after the proceedings to create the translation using voice recognition technology or by doing the translation manually.

REQUIREMENTS
High School

To be a court reporter, you need to have a high school diploma or its equivalent. Take as many high-level classes in English as you can and get a firm handle on grammar and spelling. Take typing classes and computer classes to give you a foundation in using computers and a head start in keyboarding skills. Classes in government and business will be helpful as well. Training in Latin can also be a great benefit because it will help you understand the many medical and legal terms that arise during court proceedings. Knowledge of foreign languages can also be helpful because as a court reporter, you will often transcribe the testimony of non-English speakers with the aid of court-appointed translators.

Postsecondary Training

Court reporters are required to complete a specialized training program in shorthand reporting. These programs usually last between two and four years and include instruction on how to enter at least 225 words a minute on a stenotype machine. Other topics include computer operations, transcription methods, English grammar, and the principles of law. For court cases involving medical issues, students must also take courses on human anatomy and physiology. Basic medical and legal terms are also explained.

About 130 postsecondary schools and colleges have two- and four-year programs in court reporting; approximately 70 of these programs are approved by the National Court Reporters Association (NCRA). Many business colleges offer these programs. As a court reporting student in these programs, you must master machine shorthand, or stenotyping, and real-time reporting. The NCRA states that to graduate from one of these programs, you must be able to type at least 225 words per minute and pass tests that gauge your written knowledge and speed.

Certification or Licensing

The NCRA offers several levels of certification for its members. To receive the registered professional reporter certification, you must pass tests that are administered twice a year at more than 100 sites in the United States and overseas. The registered merit reporter certification means you have passed an exam with speeds up to 260 words per minute. The registered diplomate reporter certification is obtained by passing a knowledge exam. This certification shows that the court reporter has gained valuable professional knowledge and experience through years of reporting. The certified realtime reporter certification is given to reporters who have obtained the specialized skill of converting the spoken word into written word within seconds. Several other specialized certifications are available for the court reporter.

The American Association of Electronic Reporters and Transcribers offers the following voluntary certifications: certified electronic court reporter, certified electronic court transcriber, and certified electronic court reporter and transcriber. The National Verbatim Reporters Association offers the following voluntary certifications: certified verbatim reporter, certificate of merit, and real-time verbatim reporter. Contact these organizations for information on requirements for each certification.

Some states require reporters to be notary publics or to be licensed through a state certification exam. Currently, more than 40 states grant licenses in either shorthand reporting or court reporting, although not all of these states require a license to work as a court reporter. Licenses are granted after the court reporter passes state examinations and fulfills any prerequisites (usually an approved shorthand reporting program).

Other Requirements

Because part of a court reporter's work is done within the confines of a courtroom, being able to work under pressure is a must. Court reporters need to be able to meet deadlines with accuracy and attention to detail. As stated previously, a court reporter must be highly skilled at the stenotype machine. A minimum of 225 words per minute is expected from a beginning court reporter.

Court reporters must be familiar with a wide range of medical and legal terms and must be assertive enough to ask for clarification if a term or phrase goes by without the reporter understanding it. Court reporters must be as unbiased as possible and accurately record what is said, not what they believe to be true. Patience and perfectionism are vital characteristics, as is the ability to work closely with judges and other court officials.

EXPLORING

Can you see yourself as a court reporter someday? As with any career, you have much to consider. To get an idea of what a court reporter does—at least the work they do in public—attend some trials at your local courts. Instead of focusing on the main players—witnesses, lawyers, judges—keep an eye on the court reporter. If you can, watch several reporters in different courtrooms under different judges to get a perspective on what the average court reporter does. Try to arrange a one-on-one meeting with a court reporter so you can ask the questions you really want answers for. Maybe you can convince one of your teachers to arrange a field trip to a local court.

EMPLOYERS

Approximately 19,000 court reporters are employed in the United States. Many court reporters are employed by city, county, state, or federal courts. Others work for themselves as freelancers or as employees of freelance reporting agencies. These freelance reporters are hired by attorneys to record the pretrial statements, or depositions, of experts and other witnesses. When people want transcripts of other important discussions, freelance reporters may be called on to record what is said at business meetings, large conventions, or similar events.

Most court reporters work in middle- to large-size cities, although they are needed anywhere a court of law is in session. In smaller cities, a court reporter may only work part time.

A new application of court-reporting skills and technology is in the field of television captioning. Using specialized computer-aided transcription systems, reporters can produce captions for live television events, including sporting events and national and local news, for the benefit of hearing-impaired viewers.

STARTING OUT

After completing the required training, court reporters usually work for a freelance reporting company that provides court reporters for business meetings and courtroom proceedings on a temporary basis. Qualified reporters can also contact these freelance reporting companies on their own. Occasionally a court reporter will be hired directly out of school as a courtroom official, but ordinarily only those with several years of experience are hired for full-time judiciary work. A would-be court reporter may start out working as a medical transcriptionist or other specific transcriptionist to get the necessary experience.

Career services counselors at community colleges can be helpful in finding that first job. Also, try looking in the Yellow Pages of the phone books in the areas that you are interested in working. Do not forget, the Internet is often rich with job boards and employment information for all careers, including court reporting.

ADVANCEMENT

Skilled court reporters may be promoted to a larger court system or to an otherwise more demanding position, with an accompanying increase in pay and prestige. Those working for a freelance company may be hired permanently by a city, county, state, or federal court. Those with experience working in a government position may choose to become a freelance court reporter and thereby have greater job flexibility and perhaps earn more money. Those with the necessary training, experience, and business skills may decide to open their own freelance reporting company.

According to a study funded by the National Court Reporters Foundation, court reporters advance by assuming more responsibility and greater skill levels; that gives the court reporter credibility in the eyes of the professionals in the legal system. Those advanced responsibilities include real-time reporting, coding and cross-referencing the official record, assisting others in finding specific information quickly, and helping the judge and legal counsel with procedural matters.

Court reporters can also follow alternative career paths as captioning experts, legal and medical transcriptionists, and cyber-conference moderators.

EARNINGS

Earnings vary according to the skill, speed, and experience of the court reporter, as well as geographic location. Those who are employed by large court systems generally earn more than their counterparts in smaller communities. The median annual income for all court reporters was $45,610 in 2006, according to the U.S. Department of Labor. Ten percent of reporters were paid less than $23,430 annually, and 10 percent had annual earnings of more than $77,770, also in 2006. Incomes can be even higher depending on the reporter's skill level, length of service, and the amount of time the reporter works. Official court reporters not only earn a salary, but also a per-page fee for transcripts. Freelance court reporters are paid by the job and also per page for transcripts.

Court reporters who work in small communities or as freelancers may not be able to work full-time. Successful court reporters with jobs in business environments may earn more than those in courtroom settings, but such positions carry less job security.

Those working for the government or full-time for private companies usually receive health insurance and other benefits, such as paid vacations and retirement pensions. Freelancers may or may not receive health insurance or other benefits, depending on the policies of their agencies.

WORK ENVIRONMENT

Offices and courtrooms are usually pleasant places to work. Under normal conditions, a court reporter can expect to work a standard 40 hours per week. During lengthy trials or other complicated proceedings, court reporters often work much longer hours. They must be on hand before and after the court is actually in session and must wait while a jury is deliberating. A court reporter often must be willing to work irregular hours, including some evenings. Court reporters must be able to spend long hours transcribing testimony with complete accuracy. There may be some travel involved, especially for freelance reporters and court reporters who are working for a traveling circuit judge. Normally, a court reporter will experience some down time without any transcript orders and then be hit all at once with several. This uneven workflow can cause the court reporter to have odd hours at times.

Court reporters spend time working with finances as well. Paperwork for record-keeping and tracking invoices, income, and expenses is part of the job.

Long hours of sitting in the same position can be tiring and court reporters may be bothered by eye and neck strain. There is also the risk of repetitive motion injuries, including carpal tunnel syndrome. The constant pressure to keep up and remain accurate can be stressful as well.

OUTLOOK

The U.S. Department of Labor predicts that employment of court reporters should grow much faster than the average for all occupations through 2016. Despite the rising number of criminal court cases and civil lawsuits, reduced budgets will limit employment opportunities for court reporters in local, state, and federal court systems. Job opportunities should be greatest in and around large metropolitan areas, but qualified court reporters should be able to find work in most parts of the country. There will be strong demand for court reporters who use their skills to produce captioning for live and taped television programs, which is a federal requirement for all television programming, and those who create real-time translations for the deaf and hard-of-hearing in legal and academic settings.

As always, job prospects will be best for those with the most training and experience. Because of the reliance on computers in many aspects of this job, computer experience and training are important. Court reporters who are certified—especially with the highest level of certification—will have the most opportunities to choose from.

As court reporters continue to use cutting-edge technology to make court transcripts more usable and accurate, the field itself should continue to grow.

FOR MORE INFORMATION

For information on digital/electronic court reporting and certification, contact

American Association of Electronic Reporters and Transcribers
23812 Rock Circle
Bothell, WA 98021-8573
Tel: 800-233-5306
Email: aaert@blarg.net
http://www.aaert.org

For information on certification and court reporting careers, contact

National Court Reporters Association
8224 Old Courthouse Road
Vienna, VA 22182-3808
Tel: 800-272-6272
Email: msic@ncrahq.org
http://www.ncraonline.org

For information on scholarships, contact

National Court Reporters Foundation
8224 Old Courthouse Road
Vienna, VA 22182-3808
Tel: 800-272-6272
Email: msic@ncrahq.org
http://ncraonline.org/Foundation

For tips on preparing for certification exams, and for career information, contact

National Verbatim Reporters Association
207 Third Avenue
Hattiesburg, MS 39401-3868
Tel: 601-582-4345
Email: nvra@aol.com
http://www.nvra.org

This organization represents court reporters who are employed at the federal level.

United States Court Reporters Association
4725 North Western Avenue, Suite 240
Chicago, IL 60625-2096
Tel: 800-628-2730
Email: uscra@uscra.org
http://www.uscra.org

CUSTOMER SERVICE REPRESENTATIVES

OVERVIEW

Customer service representatives, sometimes called *customer care representatives,* work with customers of one or many companies, assist with customer problems, or answer questions. Customer service representatives work in many different industries to provide "front-line" customer service in a variety of businesses. Most customer service representatives work in an office setting though some may work in the "field" to better meet customer needs. There are approximately 2.2 million customer service representatives employed in the United States.

THE JOB

Julie Cox is a customer service representative for Affina. Affina is a call center that handles customer service for a variety of companies. Cox works with each of Affina's clients and the call center operators to ensure that each call-in receives top customer service.

Customer service representatives often handle complaints and problems, and Cox finds that to be the case at the call center as well. While the operators who report to her provide customer service to those on the phone, Cox must oversee that customer service while also keeping in mind the customer service for her client, whatever business they may be in.

"I make sure that the clients get regular reports of the customer service calls and check to see if there are any recurring problems," says Cox.

One of the ways Cox observes if customer service is not being handled effectively is by monitoring the actual time spent on each phone call. If an operator spends a lot of time on a call, there is most likely a problem.

"Our customers are billed per minute," says Cox. "So we want to make sure their customer service is being handled well and efficiently."

Affina's call center in Columbus, Indiana, handles dozens of toll-free lines. While some calls are likely to be focused on complaints or questions, some are easier to handle. Cox and her staff handle calls from people simply wanting to order literature, brochures, or to find their nearest dealer location.

Customer service representatives work in a variety of fields and business, but one thing is common—the customer. All businesses depend on their customers to keep them in business, so customer service, whether handled internally or outsourced to a call center like Affina, is extremely important.

Some customer service representatives, like Cox, do most of their work on the telephone. Others may represent companies in the field, where the customer is actually using the product or service. Still other customer service representatives may specialize in Internet service, assisting customers over the World Wide Web via email or online chats.

Affina's call center is available to their clients 24 hours a day, seven days a week, so Cox and her staff must keep around-the-clock shifts. Not all customer service representatives work a varied schedule; many work a traditional daytime shift. However, customers have problems, complaints, and questions 24 hours a day, so many companies do staff their customer service positions for a longer number of hours, especially to accommodate customers during evenings and weekends.

REQUIREMENTS
High School

A high school diploma is required for most customer service representative positions. High school courses that emphasize communication, such as English and speech, will help you learn to communicate clearly. Any courses that require collaboration with others will also help to teach diplomacy and tact—two important aspects of customer service. Business courses will help you get a good overview of the business world, one that is dependent on customers and customer service. Computer skills are also very important.

Postsecondary Training

While a college degree is not necessary to become a customer service representative, certain areas of postsecondary training are helpful. Courses in business and organizational leadership will help to give you a better feel for the business world. Just as in high school, communications classes are helpful in learning to effectively talk with and meet the needs of other people.

These courses can be taken during a college curriculum or may be offered at a variety of customer service workshops or classes. Julie Cox is working as a customer service representative while she earns her business degree from a local college. Along with her college work, she has

SCHOOL SUBJECTS
Business, English, Speech

PERSONAL SKILLS
Communication/Ideas, Helping/Teaching

MINIMUM EDUCATION LEVEL
High school diploma

CERTIFICATION OR LICENSING
Voluntary

WORK ENVIRONMENT
Primarily Indoors, Primarily One Location

taken advantage of seminars and workshops to improve her customer service skills.

Bachelor's degrees in business and communications are increasingly required for managerial positions.

Certification or Licensing

Although it is not a requirement, customer service representative can become certified. The International Customer Service Association and HDI (formerly the Help Desk Institute) offer certification to customer service professionals. Contact these organizations for more information.

Other Requirements

"The best and the worst parts of being a customer service representative are the people," Julie Cox says. Customer service representatives should have the ability to maintain a pleasant attitude at all times, even while serving angry or demanding customers.

A successful customer service representative will most likely have an outgoing personality and enjoy working with people and assisting them with their questions and problems.

Because many customer service representatives work in offices and on the telephone, people with physical disabilities may find this career to be both accessible and enjoyable.

EXPLORING

Julie Cox first discovered her love for customer service while working in retail at a local department store.

Explore your ability for customer service by getting a job that deals with the public on a day-to-day basis. Talk with people who work with customers and customer service every day; find out what they like and dislike about their jobs.

There are other ways that you can prepare for a career in this field while you are still in school. Join your school's business club to get a feel for what goes on in the business world today. Doing volunteer work for a local charity or homeless shelter can help you decide if serving others is something that you'd enjoy doing as a career.

Evaluate the customer service at the businesses you visit. What makes that salesperson at The Gap better than the operator you talked with last week? Volunteer to answer phones at an agency in your town or city. Most receptionists in small companies and agencies are called on to provide customer service to callers. Try a nonprofit organization. They will welcome the help, and you will get a firsthand look at customer service.

EMPLOYERS

Customer service representatives are hired at all types of companies in a variety of areas. Industries that employ large numbers of customer service representatives include administrative and support services; retail trade establishments such as general merchandise stores and food and beverage stores; manufacturing, such as printing and related support activities; information, particularly the telecommunications industry; and wholesale trade. Because all businesses rely on customers, customer service is generally a high priority for those businesses. Some companies, like call centers, may employ a large number of customer service representatives to serve a multitude of clients, while small businesses may simply have one or two people who are responsible for customer service.

Approximately 30 percent of customer service representatives are employed in four states (California, Texas, Florida, and New York), but opportunities are available throughout the United States. In the United States, approximately 2.2 million workers are employed as customer service representatives.

STARTING OUT

You can become a customer service representative as an entry-level applicant, although some customer service representatives have first served in other areas of a company. This company experience may provide them with more knowledge and experience to answer customer questions. A college degree is not required, but any post-secondary training will increase your ability to find a job in customer service.

Ads for customer service job openings are readily available in newspapers and on Internet job search sites. With some experience and a positive attitude, it is possible to move into the position of customer service representative from another job within the company. Julie Cox started out at Affina as an operator and quickly moved into a customer service capacity.

ADVANCEMENT

Customer service experience is valuable in any business career path. Julie Cox hopes to combine her customer service experience with a business degree and move to the human resources area of her company.

It is also possible to advance to management or marketing jobs after working as a customer service representative. Businesses and their customers are inseparable, so most business professionals are experts at customer relations.

EARNINGS

Earnings vary based on location, level of experience, and size and type of employer. The U.S. Department of Labor reports the median annual income for all customer service representatives as $28,330 in 2006. Salaries ranged from less than $18,110 to more than $45,990. The Association of Support Professionals, which conducts salary surveys of tech support workers at software companies, reports that customer service representatives earned a median annual wage of $32,000 in 2007.

Other benefits vary widely according to the size and type of company in which representatives are employed. Benefits may include medical, dental, vision, and life insurance, 401(k) plans, or bonus incentives. Full-time customer service representatives can expect to receive vacation and sick pay, while part-time workers may not be offered these benefits.

WORK ENVIRONMENT

Customer service representatives work primarily indoors, although some may work in the field where the customers are using the product or service. They usually work in a supervised setting and report to a manager. They may spend many hours on the telephone, answering mail, or handling Internet communication. Many of the work hours involve little physical activity.

While most customer service representatives generally work a 40-hour workweek, others work a variety of shifts. Many businesses want customer service hours to coincide with the times that their customers are available to call or contact the business. For many companies, these times are in the evenings and on the weekends, so some customer service representatives work a varied shift and odd hours.

OUTLOOK

The U.S. Department of Labor predicts that employment for customer service representatives will grow much faster than the average for all occupations through 2016. This is a large field of workers and many replacement workers are needed each year as customer service reps leave this job for other positions, retire, or leave for other reasons. In addition, the Internet and e-commerce should increase the need for customer service representatives who will be needed to help customers navigate Web sites, answer questions over the phone, and respond to emails. Opportunities should be especially strong in the financial services, communications, and utilities industries.

For customer service representatives with specific knowledge of a product or business, the outlook is very good, as quick, efficient customer service is valuable in any business. Additional training and education and proficiency in a foreign language will also make finding a job as a customer service representative an easier task.

FOR MORE INFORMATION

For information on customer service and other support positions, contact

Association of Support Professionals
122 Barnard Avenue
Watertown, MA 02472-3414
Tel: 617-924-3944
http://www.asponline.com

For information on jobs, training, workshops, and salaries, contact

Customer Care Institute
17 Dean Overlook, NW
Atlanta, GA 30318-1663
Tel: 404-352-9291
Email: info@customercare.com
http://www.customercare.com

For information about the customer service industry, contact

HDI
102 South Tejon, Suite 1200
Colorado Springs, CO 80903-2242
Tel: 800-248-5667
Email: support@thinkhdi.com
http://www.thinkhdi.com

For information on international customer service careers and certification, contact

International Customer Service Association
401 North Michigan Avenue
Chicago, IL 60611-4255
Tel: 800-360-4272
Email: icsa@smithbucklin.com
http://www.icsa.com

DATABASE SPECIALISTS

OVERVIEW

Database specialists design, install, update, modify, maintain, and repair computer database systems to meet the needs of their employers. To do this work they need strong math skills, the ability to work with many variables at once, and a solid understanding of the organization's objectives. They consult with other management officials to discuss computer equipment purchases, determine requirements for various computer programs, and allocate access to the computer system to users. They might also direct training of personnel who use company databases regularly. Database specialists may also be called *database designers, database analysts, database managers,* or *database administrators* in some businesses; at other businesses, these designations represent separate jobs. All of these positions, however, fall under the umbrella category of database specialist. There are approximately 119,000 database specialists working in the United States.

THE JOB

So just what is a database and how is it used? It may be easiest to think of a database as being the computer version of the old-fashioned file cabinet that is filled with folders containing information. The database is the information, and the database specialist is the person who designs or adjusts programs that determine how the information is stored, how separate pieces of information relate and affect one another, and how the overall system should be organized. For example, a specialist may set up a retailer's customer database to have a separate "record" for each customer, in the same way that the retailer may have had a separate file folder in its file cabinet for each customer. In the retailer's sales database, each sale represented by an invoice will have a separate

SCHOOL SUBJECTS

Computer Science, Mathematics

PERSONAL SKILLS

Mechanical/Manipulative, Technical/Scientific

MINIMUM EDUCATION LEVEL

Bachelor's Degree

CERTIFICATION OR LICENSING

Voluntary

WORK ENVIRONMENT

Primarily Indoors, Primarily One Location

record. Each record contains many "fields" where specific pieces of information are entered. Examples of fields for a customer database might include customer number, customer name, address, city, state, ZIP code, phone, and contact person. Examples of fields in a sales database might include customer number, item purchased, quantity, price, date of purchase, and total. With information organized in separate fields, the retailer can easily sort customer records or invoices, just like filing folders in a file cabinet. In this way, the retailer could print a list of all its customers in Iowa, for example, or total sales for the month of April.

In the same way that records within a database can be sorted, databases themselves can be related to each other. The customer database can be related to the sales database by the common field: customer number. In this way, a business could print out a list of all purchases by a specific customer, for example, or a list of customers who purchased a specific product.

Database specialists are responsible for the flow of computer information within an organization. They make major decisions concerning computer purchases, system designs, and personnel training. Their duties combine general management ability with a detailed knowledge of computer programming and systems analysis.

The specific responsibilities of a database specialist are determined by the size and type of employer. For example, a database specialist for a telephone company may develop a system for billing customers, while a database specialist for a large store may develop a system for keeping track of in-stock merchandise. To do this work accurately, database specialists need a thorough

knowledge and understanding of the company's computer operations.

There are three main areas of the database specialist's work: planning what type of computer system a company needs; implementing and managing the system; and supervising computer room personnel.

To adequately plan a computer system, database specialists must have extensive knowledge of the latest computer technology and the specific needs of their company. They meet with high-ranking company officials and decide how to apply the available technology to the company's needs. Decisions include what type of hardware and software to order and how the data should be stored. Database specialists must be aware of the cost of the proposed computer system as well as the budget within which the company is operating. Long-term planning is also important. Specialists must ensure that the computer system can process not only the existing level of computer information received, but also the anticipated load and type of information the company could receive in the future. Such planning is vitally important since, even for small companies, computer systems can cost several hundred thousand dollars.

Implementing and managing a computer system entails a variety of technical and administrative tasks. Depending on the organization's needs, the specialist may modify a system already in place, develop a whole new system, or tailor a commercial system to meet these needs. To do this type of work, the database specialist must be familiar with accounting principles and mathematical formulas. Scheduling access to the computer is also a key responsibility. Sometimes, database specialists work with representatives from all of a company's departments to create a schedule. The specialist prioritizes needs and monitors usage so that each department can do its work. All computer usage must be documented and stored for future reference.

Safeguarding the computer operations is another important responsibility of database specialists. They must make plans in case a computer system fails or malfunctions so that the information stored in the computer is not lost. A duplication of computer files may be a part of this emergency planning. A backup system must also be employed so that the company can continue to process information. Database specialists must also safeguard a system so that only authorized personnel have access to certain information. Computerized information may be of vital importance to a company, and database specialists ensure that it does not fall into the wrong hands.

Database specialists may also be responsible for supervising the work of personnel in the computer department. They may need to train new computer personnel hires to use the company's database, and they may also need to train all computer personnel when an existing database is modified. At some organizations, specialists are also required to train all employees in the use of an upgraded or a new system. Therefore, specialists need the ability to translate technical concepts into everyday language.

Database specialists may be known by a number of different titles and have a variety of responsibilities, depending on the size and the needs of the organizations that employ them. According to an article in *Computerworld,* the title *database designer* indicates someone who works on database programming. These workers usually have a math or engineering background. The title *database administrator* indicates someone who primarily focuses on the performance of the database, making sure everything is running smoothly. They may also do routine jobs, such as adding new users to the system. The title *database analyst* indicates someone who primarily focuses on the business, its goals, products, and customers. They work on improving the database so that the organization can meet its goals. In large businesses or organizations, the many duties of the database specialist may be strictly divided among a number of specialists. In smaller organizations there may be only one database specialist, designer, manager, administrator, or analyst who is responsible for carrying out all the tasks mentioned above. No matter what their title is, however, all database specialists work with an operation that processes millions of bits of information at a huge cost. This work demands accuracy and efficiency in decision-making and problem-solving abilities.

REQUIREMENTS
High School

While you are in high school, take as many math, science, and computer classes as you can. These courses will provide you with the basis to develop your logical thinking skills and understanding of computers. Take electronics or other technical courses that will teach you about schematic drawing, working with electricity, and, again, develop logical thinking. You will also benefit from taking accounting courses and English classes, as you will need strong written and verbal communication skills.

Postsecondary Training

A bachelor's degree in computer science, computer information systems, database management or administration, or another computer-related discipline is recommended as the minimum requirement for those wishing

to work as database specialists. Some exceptions have been made for people without a degree but who have extensive experience in database administration. Taking this route to become a database specialist, however, is becoming increasingly rare. The employers of tomorrow will expect you to have at least a four-year degree. Courses in a bachelor's degree program usually include data processing, systems analysis methods, more detailed software and hardware concepts, management principles, and information systems planning. To advance in the field, you will probably need to complete further education. Many businesses today, especially larger companies, prefer database managers to have a master's degree in computer science or business administration. Some companies offer to help with or pay for their employees' advanced education, so you may want to consider this possibility when looking for an entry-level job.

Certification or Licensing

Some database specialists become certified for jobs in the computer field by passing an examination given by the Institute for Certification of Computing Professionals (ICCP). For further information, contact the ICCP at the address given at the end of this article. The ICCP, in cooperation with DAMA International, offers the certified data management professional designation to applicants who pass three examinations. In addition, specialists who want to keep their skills current may take training programs offered by database developers, such as Oracle. These training programs may also lead to certifications.

Other Requirements

Database specialists are strong logical and analytical thinkers. They excel at analyzing massive amounts of information and organizing it into a coherent structure composed of complicated relationships. They are also good at weighing the importance of each element of a system and deciding which ones can be omitted without diminishing the quality of the final project.

Specialists also need strong communication skills. This work requires contact with employees from a wide variety of jobs. Specialists must be able to ask clear, concise, and technical questions of people who are not necessarily familiar with how a database works.

As is true for all computer professionals, specialists should be motivated to keep up with technological advances and able to learn new things quickly. Those who are interested in working almost exclusively in one industry (for example, banking) should be willing to gain as much knowledge as possible about that specific field in addition to their computer training. With an understanding of both fields of knowledge, individuals are more easily able to apply computer technology to the specific needs of the company.

EXPLORING

There are a number of ways to explore your interest in this field while you are still in high school. "Start by reading books on the subject," says Scott Sciaretta, an internal database consultant for Choicepoint in Atlanta, Georgia. "There are hundreds of them at most bookstores."

You can also join your high school's computer club to work on computer projects and meet others interested in the field. Learn everything you can about computers by working with them regularly. Online sources can be particularly good for keeping up to date with new developments and learning from people who are actively involved in this work. Learn to use a commercial database program, either by teaching yourself or taking a class in it. The Association for Computing Machinery has a Special Interest Group on Management of Data (SIGMOD). The Resources page of SIGMOD's Web site (http://www.acm.org/sigmod) provides an index of public domain database software that you may want to check out.

You may also want to ask your school guidance counselor or a computer teacher to arrange for a database specialist to speak to your class at school or to arrange for a field trip to a company to see database specialists at work. Another option is to ask your school administrators about databases used by the school and try to interview any database specialists working in or for the school system. Similar attempts could be made with charities in your area that make use of computer databases for membership and client records as well as mailing lists.

Look for direct-experience opportunities, such as part-time work, summer internships, and even summer camps that specialize in computers. "Try to get a job as an intern in a database shop and learn by watching, mentoring, and grunt work," Sciaretta recommends. If you can't find such a position, you can still put your skills to work by offering to set up small databases, such as address books, recipe databases, or DVD libraries for friends or family members.

EMPLOYERS

Approximately 119,000 database administrators are employed in the United States today. Any business or organization that uses databases as a part of its operations hires database professionals. Database specialists work for investment companies, telecommunications firms, banks, insurance companies, publishing houses, hospitals, school systems, universities, and a host of other large and midsize businesses and nonprofit organizations. There are also many opportunities with federal, state, and city governments.

STARTING OUT

Most graduating college students work closely with their school's career services office to obtain information about job openings and interviews. Local and national employers often recruit college graduates on campus, making it much easier for students to talk with many diverse companies. Another good source of information is through summer internships, which are completed typically between junior and senior year. Many major companies in the computer field, such as Intel (http://www.intel.com/jobs/students) and Oracle (http://www.oracle.com/corporate/employment/college/opportunities/internships.html), have established undergraduate intern programs. This experience is valuable for two reasons. First, it gives students hands-on exposure to computer-related jobs. Second, it allows students to network with working computer professionals who may help them find full-time work after graduation. Interested individuals might also scan the classified ads or work with temporary agencies or headhunters to find entry-level and midlevel positions. Professional organizations, such as SIGMOD, and professional publications are other sources of information about job openings.

ADVANCEMENT

The job of database specialist is in itself a high-level position. Advancement will depend to some extent on the size of the business the specialist works for, with larger companies offering more opportunities for growth at the mid-level and senior levels of management. Scott Sciaretta explains his career path and advancement this way: "I got my first job in the field by internal promotion. Basically, I was doing some computer programming for my department on the side to automate a few of the menial tasks. My work got noticed, and I was given the job of running the company's computer department when the position opened. At my current level, the advancement opportunities are not easy. For me to advance I either need to expand my scope or work for a larger company, both of which are very feasible with hard work. However, salary advancements are easy and can be quite large. There are many opportunities for advancement from entry-level or junior positions."

Another factor influencing advancement is the interests of each individual. Generally, people fall into two categories: those who want to work on the business side and those who prefer to stay in a technical job. For individuals who want to get into the managerial side of the business, formal education in business administration is usually required, usually in the form of a master's degree in business administration. In upper-level management positions, specialists must work on cross-functional teams with professionals in finance, sales, personnel, purchasing, and operations. Superior database specialists at larger companies may also be promoted to executive positions.

Some database specialists prefer to stay on the technical side of the business. For them, the hands-on computer work is the best part of their job. Advancement for these workers will, again, involve further education in terms of learning about new database systems, gaining certification in a variety of database programs, or even moving into another technology area such as software design or networking.

As specialists acquire education and develop solid work experience, advancement will take the form of more responsibilities and higher wages. One way to achieve this is to move to a better-paying, more challenging database position at a larger company. Some successful database specialists become high-paid consultants or start their own businesses. Teaching, whether as a consultant or at a university or community college, is another option for individuals with high levels of experience.

EARNINGS

A fairly wide range of salaries exists for database specialists. Earnings vary with the size, type, and location of the organization as well as a person's experience, education, and job responsibilities. According to the U.S. Department of Labor, median annual earnings for database administrators were $64,670 in 2006. The lowest paid 10 percent earned less than $37,350, while the highest paid 10 percent earned more than $103,010. Robert Half International reported that starting salaries for database administrators ranged from $68,250 to $98,750 in 2007.

Benefits for database professionals depend on the employer; however, they usually include such items as health insurance, retirement or 401(k) plans, and paid vacation days.

WORK ENVIRONMENT

Database specialists work in modern offices, usually located next to the computer room. If they work as consultants, they may travel to client sites as little as once or twice per project or as often as every week. Most duties are performed at a computer at the individual's desk. Travel is occasionally required for conferences and visits to affiliated database locations. Travel requirements vary with employer, client, and level of position held. Database specialists may need to attend numerous meetings, especially during planning stages of a project. They work regular 40-hour weeks but may put in overtime as deadlines approach. During busy periods, the work can be quite stressful since accuracy is very important. Database specialists must therefore be able to work well under pressure and respond quickly to last-minute changes. Emergencies may also require specialists to work overtime or long hours without a break, sometimes through the night.

"I like what I do. It's kind of like playing," Scott Sciaretta says. "The hours are flexible. You get to work on and set up million-dollar systems. There also is a high degree of visibility from upper management. The downside is that I work lots of hours, including many weekends, and I have a never-ending list of work. The hardest part of the job is juggling the schedules and configurations for many projects at one time."

OUTLOOK

The use of computers and database systems in almost all business settings creates tremendous opportunities for well-qualified database personnel. Database specialists and computer support specialists are predicted by the U.S. Department of Labor to be among the fastest-growing occupations through 2016.

Employment opportunities for database specialists should be best in large urban areas because of the many businesses and organizations located there that need employees to work with their databases. Since smaller communities are also rapidly developing significant job opportunities, skilled workers can pick from a wide range of jobs throughout the country. Those with the best education and the most experience in computer systems and personnel management will find the best job prospects.

"The field of Unix systems and databases is wide open," notes Scott Sciaretta. "There is and will be greater demand for good talent than the industry can supply. Most companies are moving to larger databases, and the need for Oracle and Microsoft SQL Server database administrators in particular is a bottomless pit."

FOR MORE INFORMATION

For information on career opportunities or student chapters, contact

Association of Information Technology Professionals
401 North Michigan Avenue, Suite 2400
Chicago, IL 60611-4267
Tel: 800-224-9371
http://www.aitp.org

For information on certification, contact

DAMA International
19239 North Dale Mabry Highway, #132
Lutz, FL 33548-5067
Tel: 813-448-7786
Email: info@dama.org
http://www.dama.org

For information about scholarships, student membership, and careers, contact

IEEE Computer Society
1828 L Street, NW, Suite 1202
Washington, DC 20036-5104
Tel: 202-371-0101
Email: membership@computer.org
http://www.computer.org

For more information about computer certification, contact

Institute for Certification of Computing Professionals
2350 East Devon Avenue, Suite 115
Des Plaines, IL 60018-4610
Tel: 800-843-8227
Email: office@iccp.org
http://www.iccp.org

For more information on the Association for Computing Machinery's Special Interest Group on Management of Data, visit its Web site:

Special Interest Group on Management of Data
http://www.acm.org/sigmod

DENTAL ASSISTANTS

OVERVIEW

Dental assistants perform a variety of duties in the dental office, including helping the dentist examine and treat patients and completing laboratory and office work. They assist the dentist by preparing patients for dental exams, handing the dentist the proper instruments, taking and processing X rays, preparing materials for making impressions and restorations, and instructing patients in oral health care. They also perform administrative and clerical tasks so that the office runs smoothly and the dentist's time is available for working with patients. There are approximately 280,000 dental assistants employed in the United States.

THE JOB

Dental assistants help dentists as they examine and treat patients. They usually greet patients, escort them to the examining room, and prepare them by covering their clothing with paper or cloth bibs. They also adjust the headrest of the examination chair and raise the chair to the proper height. Many dental assistants take X rays of patients' teeth and process the film for the dentist to examine. They also obtain patients' dental records from the office files, so the dentist can review them before the examination.

During dental examinations and operations, dental assistants hand the dentist instruments as they are needed and use suction devices to keep the patient's mouth dry. When the examination or procedure is completed, assistants may give the patient after-care instructions for the teeth and mouth. They also provide instructions on infection-control procedures, preventing plaque buildup, and keeping teeth and gums clean and healthy between office visits.

Dental assistants also help with a variety of other clinical tasks. When a dentist needs a cast of a patient's teeth or mouth—used for diagnosing and planning the correction of dental problems—assistants may mix the necessary materials. They may also pour, trim, and polish these study casts. Some assistants prepare materials for making dental restorations, and many polish and clean patients' dentures. Some may perform the necessary laboratory work to make temporary dental replacements.

State laws determine which clinical tasks a dental assistant is able to perform. Dental assistants are not the same as *dental hygienists,* who are licensed to perform a wider variety of clinical tasks such as scaling and polishing teeth. Some states allow dental assistants to apply medications to teeth and gums, isolate individual teeth for treatment using rubber dams, and remove excess cement after cavities have been filled. In some states, dental assistants can actually put fillings in patients' mouths. Dental assistants may also check patients' vital signs, update and check medical histories, and help the dentist with any medical emergencies that arise during dental procedures.

Many dental assistants also perform clerical and administrative tasks. These include receptionist duties, scheduling appointments, managing patient records, keeping dental supply inventories, preparing bills for services rendered, collecting payments, and issuing receipts. Dental assistants often act as business managers who perform all nonclinical responsibilities such as hiring and firing auxiliary help, scheduling employees, and overseeing office accounting.

REQUIREMENTS

High School

Most dental assistant positions are entry-level. They usually require little or no experience and no education beyond high school. High school students who wish to work as dental assistants should take courses in general science, biology, health, chemistry, and business management. Typing is also an important skill for dental assistants.

Postsecondary Training

Dental assistants commonly acquire their skills on the job. Many, however, go on to receive training after high school at trade schools, technical institutes, and community and junior colleges that offer dental assisting programs. The armed forces also train some dental assistants. Students who complete two-year college programs receive associate's degrees, while those who complete one-year trade and technical school programs earn a certificate or diploma. Entrance requirements to these programs require a high school diploma and good grades in high school science, typing, and English. Some postsecondary schools require an interview or written examination, and some require that applicants pass physical and dental examinations. The American Dental Association's Commission on Dental Accreditation accredits about 269 of these programs. Some four- to six-month nonaccredited courses in dental assisting are also available from private vocational schools.

Accredited programs instruct students in dental assisting skills and theory through classes, lectures, and laboratory and preclinical experience. Students take courses in English, speech, and psychology as well as in the biomedical sciences, including anatomy, microbiology, and nutrition. Courses in dental science cover

SCHOOL SUBJECTS
Business, Health

PERSONAL SKILLS
Helping/teaching, Technical/Scientific

MINIMUM EDUCATION LEVEL
High School Diploma

CERTIFICATION OR LICENSING
Required by Some States

WORK ENVIRONMENT
Primarily Indoors, Primarily One Location

subjects such as oral anatomy and pathology, and dental radiography. Students also gain practical experience in chairside assisting and office management by working in dental schools and local dental clinics that are affiliated with their program.

Graduates of such programs may be assigned a greater variety of tasks initially and may receive higher starting salaries than those with high school diplomas alone.

Certification or Licensing

Dental assistants may wish to obtain certification from the Dental Assisting National Board, but this is usually not required for employment. Certified dental assistant (CDA) accreditation shows that an assistant meets certain standards of professional competence. To take the certification examination, assistants must be high school graduates who have taken a course in cardiopulmonary resuscitation and must have either a diploma from a formal training program accredited by the Commission on Dental Accreditation or two years of full-time work experience with a recommendation from the dentist for whom the work was done.

In more than 30 states dental assistants are allowed to take X rays (under a dentist's direction) only after completing a precise training program and passing a test. Completing the program for CDA certification fulfills this requirement. To keep their CDA credentials, however, assistants must either prove their skills through retesting or acquire further education.

Some states require dental assistants to be licensed or registered. This typically involves passing a written or practical examination or completing state-approved education courses.

Other Requirements

Dental assistants need a clean, well-groomed appearance and a pleasant personality. Manual dexterity and the ability to follow directions are also important.

EXPLORING

Students in formal training programs receive dental assisting experience as part of their training. High school students can learn more about the field by talking with assistants in local dentists' offices. The American Dental Assistants Association can put students in contact with dental assistants in their areas. Part-time, summer, and temporary clerical work may also be available in dentists' offices.

EMPLOYERS

Approximately 280,000 dental assistants are employed in the United States. Dental assistants are most likely to find employment in dental offices, whether it be a single dentist or a group practice with several dentists, assistants, and hygienists. Other places dental assistants may find jobs include dental schools, hospitals, public health departments, and U.S. Veterans Affairs and Public Health Service hospitals.

STARTING OUT

High school guidance counselors, family dentists, dental schools, dental placement agencies, and dental associations may provide applicants with leads about job openings. Students in formal training programs often learn of jobs through school career services offices.

ADVANCEMENT

Dental assistants may advance in their field by moving to larger offices or clinics, where they can take on more responsibility and earn more money. In small offices they may receive higher pay by upgrading their skills through education. Specialists in the dental field, who typically earn higher salaries than general dentists, often pay higher salaries to their assistants.

Further educational training is required for advancing to positions in dental assisting education. Dental assistants who wish to become dental hygienists must enroll in a dental hygiene program. Because many of these programs do not allow students to apply dental assisting courses toward graduation, dental assistants who think

they would like to move into hygienist positions should plan their training carefully.

In some cases, dental assistants move into sales jobs with companies that sell dental industry supplies and materials. Other areas that open to dental assistants include office management, placement services, and insurance companies.

EARNINGS

Dental assistants' salaries are determined by specific responsibilities, the type of office they work in, and the geographic location of their employer. Dental assistants had median annual earnings of $30,220 in 2006, according to the U.S. Department of Labor. The highest 10 percent earned more than $43,040 a year, while the lowest 10 percent earned less than $20,530 a year.

Salaried dental assistants in a private office typically receive paid vacation, health insurance, and other benefits. Part-time assistants in private offices often receive dental coverage, but do not typically receive other benefits.

WORK ENVIRONMENT

Dental assistants work in offices that are generally clean, modern, quiet, and pleasant. They are also well lighted and well ventilated. In small offices, dental assistants may work solely with dentists, while in larger offices and clinics they may work with dentists, other dental assistants, dental hygienists, and laboratory technicians. Although dental assistants may sit at desks to do office work, they spend a large part of the day beside the dentist's chair where they can reach instruments and materials.

About half of all dental assistants work 35- to 40-hour weeks, sometimes including Saturday hours, and approximately 35 percent of dental assistants work part time. Some part-time workers work in more than one dental office.

Taking X rays poses some risk because regular doses of radiation can be harmful to the body. However, all dental offices must have lead shielding and safety procedures that minimize the risk of exposure to radiation.

OUTLOOK

According to the U.S. Department of Labor, employment for dental assistants is expected to grow much faster than the average for all occupations through 2016, and is expected to be among the fastest-growing occupations. As the population grows, more people will seek dental services for preventive care and cosmetic improvements.

In addition, dentists who earned their dental degrees since the 1970s are more likely than other dentists to hire one or more assistants. Also, as dentists increase their knowledge of innovative techniques such as implantology and periodontal therapy, they generally delegate more routine tasks to assistants so they can make the best use of their time and increase profits.

Job openings will also be created through attrition as assistants leave the field or change jobs.

FOR MORE INFORMATION

For continuing education information and career services, contact

American Dental Assistants Association
35 East Wacker Drive, Suite 1730
Chicago, IL 60601-2211
Tel: 312-541-1550
http://www.dentalassistant.org

For education information, contact
American Dental Association
211 East Chicago Avenue
Chicago, IL 60611-2678
Tel: 312-440-2500
http://www.ada.org

For publications, information on dental schools, and scholarship information, contact
American Dental Education Association
1400 K Street, NW, Suite 1100
Washington, DC 20005-2415
Tel: 202-289-7201
Email: adea@adea.org
http://www.adea.org

For information on voluntary certification for dental assistants, contact
Dental Assisting National Board
444 North Michigan Avenue, Suite 900
Chicago, IL 60611-3985
Tel: 800-367-3262
http://www.dentalassisting.com

For information about continuing education, contact
National Association of Dental Assistants
900 South Washington Street, Suite G13
Falls Church, VA 22046-4009
Tel: 703-237-8616

DENTAL HYGIENISTS

OVERVIEW

Dental hygienists perform clinical tasks, serve as oral health educators in private dental offices, work in public health agencies, and promote good oral health by educating adults and children. Their main responsibility is to perform oral prophylaxis, a process of cleaning teeth by using sharp dental instruments, such as scalers and prophy angles. With these instruments, they remove stains and calcium deposits, polish teeth, and massage gums. There are approximately 167,000 dental hygienists employed in the United States.

THE JOB

In clinical settings, hygienists help prevent gum diseases and cavities by removing deposits from teeth and applying sealants and fluoride to prevent tooth decay. They remove tartar, stains, and plaque from teeth, take X rays and other diagnostic tests, place and remove temporary fillings, take health histories, remove sutures, polish amalgam restorations, and examine head, neck, and oral regions for disease.

Their tools include hand and rotary instruments to clean teeth, syringes with needles to administer local anesthetic (such as Novocain), teeth models to demonstrate home care procedures, and X-ray machines to take

SCHOOL SUBJECTS
Biology, Health

PERSONAL SKILLS
Helping/Teaching, Technical/Scientific

MINIMUM EDUCATION LEVEL
Associate's Degree

CERTIFICATION OR LICENSING
Required by All States

WORK ENVIRONMENT
Primarily Indoors, Primarily One Location

pictures of the oral cavity that the dentist uses to detect signs of decay or oral disease.

A hygienist also provides nutritional counseling and screens patients for oral cancer and high blood pressure. More extensive dental procedures are done by dentists. The hygienist is also trained and licensed to take and develop X rays. Other responsibilities depend on the employer.

Private dentists might require that the dental hygienist mix compounds for filling cavities, sterilize instruments, assist in surgical work, or even carry out clerical tasks such as making appointments and filling in insurance forms. The hygienist might well fill the duties of receptionist or office manager, functioning in many ways to assist the dentist in carrying out the day's schedule.

Although some of these tasks might also be done by a dental assistant, only the dental hygienist is licensed by the state to clean teeth. Licensed hygienists submit charts of each patient's teeth, noting possible decay or disease. The dentist studies these in making further diagnoses.

The *school hygienist* cleans and examines the teeth of students in a number of schools. The hygienist also gives classroom instruction on correct brushing and flossing of teeth, the importance of good dental care, and the effects of good nutrition. They keep dental records of students and notify parents of any need for further treatment.

Dental hygienists may be employed by local, state, or federal public health agencies. These hygienists carry out an educational program for adults and children, in public health clinics, schools, and other public facilities. A few dental hygienists may assist in research projects. For those with further education, teaching in a dental hygiene school may be possible.

Like all dental professionals, hygienists must be aware of federal, state, and local laws that govern hygiene practice. In particular, hygienists must know the types of infection control and protective gear that, by law, must be worn in the dental office to protect workers from infection. Dental hygienists, for example, must wear gloves, protective eyewear, and a mask during examinations. As with most health care workers, hygienists must be immunized against contagious diseases, such as hepatitis.

Dental hygienists are required by their state and encouraged by professional organizations to continue learning about trends in dental care, procedures, and regulations by taking continuing education courses. These may be held at large dental society meetings, colleges and universities, or in more intimate settings, such as a nearby dental office.

REQUIREMENTS
High School

The minimum requirement for admission to a dental hygiene school is graduation from high school. While in high school, you should follow a college preparatory program, which will include courses such as science, mathematics, history, English, and foreign language. It will also be beneficial for you to take health courses.

Postsecondary Training

Two levels of postsecondary training are available in this field. One is a four-year college program offering a bachelor's degree. More common is a two-year program leading to an associate's degree. The bachelor's degree is often preferred by employers, and more schools are likely to require completion of such a degree program in the future. There are about 286 accredited schools in the United States that offer one or both of these courses. Classroom work emphasizes general and dental sciences and liberal arts. Lectures are usually combined with laboratory work and clinical experience.

Certification or Licensing

After graduating from an accredited school, you must pass state licensing examinations, both written and clinical. The American Dental Association Joint Commission on National Dental Examinations administers the written part of the examination. This test is accepted by all states and the District of Columbia. The clinical part of the examination is administered by state or regional testing agencies.

Other Requirements

Aptitude tests sponsored by the American Dental Hygienists' Association are frequently required by dental hygiene schools to help applicants determine whether they will succeed in this field. Skill in handling delicate instruments, a sensitive touch, and depth perception are important attributes that are tested. To be a successful dental hygienist, you should be neat, clean, and personable.

EXPLORING

Work as a dental assistant can be a stepping-stone to a career as a dental hygienist. As a dental assistant, you could closely observe the work of a dental hygienist. You could then assess your personal aptitude for this work, discuss any questions with other hygienists, and enroll in a dental hygiene school where experience as a dental assistant would certainly be helpful.

You may be able to find part-time or summer work in high school as a dental assistant or clerical worker in a dentist's office. You also may be able to arrange to observe a dental hygienist working in a school or a dentist's office or visit an accredited dental hygiene school. The aptitude testing program required by most dental hygiene schools helps students assess their future abilities as dental hygienists.

EMPLOYERS

Approximately 167,000 dental hygienists are employed in the United States. Dental hygienists can find work in private dentist's offices, school systems, or public health agencies. Hospitals, industrial plants, and the armed forces also employ a small number of dental hygienists.

STARTING OUT

Once you have passed the National Board exams and a licensing exam in a particular state, you must decide on an area of work. Most dental hygiene schools maintain placement services for the assistance of their graduates, and finding a satisfactory position is usually not too difficult.

ADVANCEMENT

Opportunities for advancement, other than increases in salary and benefits that accompany experience in the field, usually require additional study and training. Educational advancement may lead to a position as an administrator, teacher, or director in a dental health program or to a more advanced field of practice. With further education and training, some hygienists may choose to go on to become dentists.

EARNINGS

The dental hygienist's income is influenced by such factors as education, experience, locale, and type of employer. Most dental hygienists who work in private dental offices are salaried employees, although some are paid a commission for work performed or a combination of salary and commission.

According to the U.S. Department of Labor, full-time hygienists earned a median annual salary of $62,800 in 2006. The lowest paid 10 percent of hygien-ists earned less than $40,450 annually, and the highest 10 percent earned $86,530 or more annually. Salaries in large metropolitan areas are generally somewhat higher than in small cities and towns. In addition, dental hygienists in research, education, or administration may earn higher salaries.

A salaried dental hygienist in a private office typically receives a paid two- or three-week vacation. Part-time or commissioned dental hygienists in private offices usually have no paid vacation.

WORK ENVIRONMENT

Working conditions for dental hygienists are pleasant, with well-lighted, modern, and adequately equipped facilities. Hygienists usually sit while working. State and federal regulations require that hygienists wear masks, protective eyewear, and gloves. Most hygienists do not wear any jewelry. They are required by government infection control procedures to leave their work clothes at work, so many dentists' offices now have laundry facilities to properly launder work clothes. They must also follow proper steril-izing techniques on equipment and instruments to guard against passing infection or disease.

More than 50 percent of all hygienists work part-time, or less than 35 hours a week. It is common practice among part-time and full-time hygienists to work in more than one office because many dentists schedule a hygienist to come in only two or three days a week. Hygienists frequently piece together part-time positions at several dental offices and substitute for other hygienists who take days off. About 88 percent of hygienists see eight or more patients daily, and 68 percent work in a single practice. Many private offices are open on Saturdays. The work hours of government employees are regulated by the particular agency.

OUTLOOK

The U.S. Department of Labor projects that employment of dental hygienists will grow much faster than the average for all occupations through 2016. In fact, the department predicts that dental hygienists will be among the fastest-growing occupations. The demand for dental hygienists is expected to grow as younger generations that grew up receiving better dental care keep their teeth longer.

Population growth, increased public awareness of proper oral home care, and the availability of dental insurance should result in the creation of more dental hygiene jobs. Moreover, as the population ages, there will be a special demand for hygienists to work with older people, especially those who live in nursing homes.

FOR MORE INFORMATION

For education information, contact

American Dental Association

211 East Chicago Avenue

Chicago, IL 60611-2678

Tel: 312-440-2500

http://www.ada.org

For publications, information on dental schools, and scholarship information, contact

American Dental Education Association

1400 K Street, NW, Suite 1100

Washington, DC 20005-2415

Tel: 202-289-7201

Email: adea@adea.org

http://www.adea.org

For career information and tips for dental hygiene students on finding a job, contact

American Dental Hygienists' Association

444 North Michigan Avenue, Suite 3400

Chicago, IL 60611-3980

Tel: 312-440-8900

Email: mail@adha.net

http://www.adha.org

DETECTIVES

OVERVIEW

Detectives are almost always plainclothes investigators who gather difficult-to-obtain information on criminal activity and other subjects. They conduct interviews and surveillance, locate missing persons and criminal suspects, examine records, and write detailed reports. Some make arrests and take part in raids. Detectives are employed by law enforcement agencies or operate their own private businesses. There are approximately 861,000 police detectives and 52,000 private detectives and investigators employed in the United States.

THE JOB

The job of a *police detective* begins after a crime has been committed. Uniformed police officers are usually the first to be dispatched to the scene of a crime, however, and it is police officers who are generally required to make out the initial crime report. This report is often the material with which a detective begins an investigation.

Detectives may also receive help early on from other members of the police department. *Evidence technicians are sometimes sent immediately to the scene of a crime to comb the area for physical* evidence. This step is important because most crime scenes contain physical evidence that could link a suspect to the crime. Fingerprints are the most common physical piece of evidence, but other clues, such as broken locks, broken glass, and footprints, as well as blood, skin, or hair traces, are also useful. If there is a suspect on the scene, torn clothing or any scratches, cuts, and bruises are noted. Physical evidence may then be tested by specially trained crime lab technicians.

It is after this initial stage that the case is assigned to a police detective. Police detectives may be assigned as many as two or three cases a day, and having 30 cases to handle at one time is not unusual. Because there is only a limited amount of time, an important part of a detective's work is to determine which cases have the greatest chance of being solved. The most serious offenses or those in which there is considerable evidence and obvious leads tend to receive the highest priority. All cases, however, are given at least a routine follow-up investigation.

Police detectives have numerous means of gathering additional information. For example, they contact and interview victims and witnesses, familiarize themselves with the scene of the crime and places where a suspect may spend time, and conduct surveillance operations. Detectives sometimes have informers who provide important leads. Because detectives must often work undercover, they wear ordinary clothes, not police uniforms. Also helpful are existing police files on other crimes, on known criminals, and on people suspected of criminal activity. If sufficient evidence has been collected, the police detective will arrest the suspect, sometimes with the help of uniformed police officers.

Once the suspect is in custody, it is the job of the police detective to conduct an interrogation. Questioning the suspect may reveal new evidence and help determine whether the suspect was involved in other unsolved crimes. Before finishing the case, the detective must prepare a detailed written report. Detectives are sometimes required to present evidence at the trial of the suspect.

Criminal investigation is just one area in which private investigators are involved. Some specialize, for example, in finding missing persons, while others may investigate insurance or computer fraud, gather information on the background of persons involved in divorce or child custody cases, administer lie detection tests, debug offices and telephones, or offer security services. Cameras, video equipment, tape and digital recorders, and lock picks are used in compliance with legal restrictions to obtain necessary information. Some private investigators work for themselves, but many others work for detective agencies or businesses. Clients include private individuals, corporations concerned with theft, insurance companies suspicious of fraud, department stores and other types of retail facilities that seek to prevent theft, and lawyers who want information for a case. Whoever the client, the private investigator is usually expected to provide a detailed report of the activities and results of the investigation.

REQUIREMENTS

High School

Because detectives work on a wide variety of cases, if you are interested in this field you are encouraged to take a diverse course load. English, American history, business law, government, psychology, sociology, chemistry, and physics are suggested, as are courses in journalism, computers, and a foreign language. The ability to type is often needed. To become a police detective, you must first have experience as a police officer. Hiring requirements for police officers vary, but most departments require at least a high school diploma.

Postsecondary Training

In some police departments a college degree may be necessary for some or all positions. Many colleges and universities offer courses or programs in police science, criminal justice, or law enforcement. Newly hired police officers are generally sent to a police academy for job training.

After gaining substantial experience in the department—usually about three to five years—and demonstrating the skills required for detective work, a police officer may be promoted to detective. In some police departments, candidates must first take a qualifying exam. For new detectives there is usually a training program, which may last from a few weeks to several months.

Private detective agencies usually do not hire individuals without previous experience. A large number of private investigators are former police officers. Those with no law enforcement experience who want to become private investigators can enroll in special private investigation schools, although these do not guarantee qualification for employment. A college degree is an admissions requirement at some private investigation schools. These schools teach skills essential to detective work, such as how to take and develop fingerprints, pick locks, test

SCHOOL SUBJECTS
English, Government, History

PERSONAL SKILLS
Leadership/Management, Technical/Scientific

MINIMUM EDUCATION LEVEL
High School Diploma

CERTIFICATION OR LICENSING
Voluntary (Certification), Required by Certain States (Licensing)

WORK ENVIRONMENT
Indoors and Outdoors, One Location with Some Travel

for the presence of human blood, investigate robberies, identify weapons, and take photographs. The length of these programs and their admissions requirements vary considerably. Some are correspondence programs, while others offer classroom instruction and an internship at a detective agency. Experience can also be gained by taking classes in law enforcement, police science, or criminal justice at a college or university.

Certification or Licensing

In almost all large cities the hiring of police officers must follow local civil service regulations. In such cases candidates generally must be at least 21 years old, U.S. citizens, and within the locally prescribed height and weight limits. Other requirements include 20/20 corrected vision and good hearing. Background checks are often done.

The civil service board usually gives both a written and physical examination. The written test is intended to measure a candidate's mental aptitude for police work, while the physical examination focuses on strength, dexterity, and agility.

The National Association of Legal Investigators awards the certified legal investigator designation to private detectives and investigators who specialize in cases that deal with negligence or criminal defense investigations. ASIS, a security industry trade organization, offers the professional certified investigator certification for detectives in private business or in law enforcement.

Private detectives and investigators must be licensed in all states except for Alabama, Alaska, Colorado, Idaho, Mississippi, Missouri, and South Dakota. In states with licensing requirements, generally applicants must pass a written examination and file a bond. Depending on the state, applicants may also need to have a minimum amount of experience, either as a police officer or as an apprentice under a licensed private investigator. An additional license is sometimes required for carrying a gun.

Other Requirements

Among the most important personal characteristics helpful for detectives are an inquisitive mind, good observation skills, a keen memory, and well-developed oral and written communication skills. The large amount of physical activity involved requires that detectives be in good shape. An excellent moral character is especially important.

EXPLORING

There are few means of exploring the field of detective work, and actual experience in the field prior to employment is unlikely. Some police departments, however, do hire teenagers for positions as police trainees and interns. If you are interested in becoming a detective, you should talk with your school guidance counselor, your local police department, local private detective agencies, a private investigation school, or a college or university offering police science, criminal justice, or law enforcement courses. In addition, the FBI operates an Honors Internship Program (http://www.fbijobs.gov/231.asp) for undergraduate and graduate students that exposes interns to a variety of investigative techniques.

EMPLOYERS

There are more than 861,000 police and detectives in the United States. A large percentage work for police departments (mainly at the local level) or other government agencies. Approximately 52,000 detectives work as private investigators, employed either for themselves, for a private detective firm, or for a business.

STARTING OUT

If you are interested in becoming a detective, you should contact your local police department, the civil service office or examining board, or private detective agencies in your area to determine hiring practices and any special requirements. Newspapers may list available jobs. If you

earn a college degree in police science, criminal justice, or law enforcement, you may benefit from your institution's career services or guidance office. Some police academies accept candidates not sponsored by a police department, and for some people this may be the best way to enter police work.

ADVANCEMENT

Advancement within a police department may depend on several factors, such as job performance, length of service, formal education and training courses, and special examinations. Large city police departments, divided into separate divisions with their own administrations, often provide greater advancement possibilities.

Because of the high dropout rate for private investigators, those who manage to stay in the field for more than five years have an excellent chance for advancement. Supervisory and management positions exist, and some private investigators start their own agencies.

EARNINGS

Median annual earnings of police detectives and criminal investigators were $58,260 in 2006, according to the U.S. Department of Labor. The lowest 10 percent earned $34,480 or less, while the highest 10 percent earned more than $92,590 annually. Mean annual earnings were $70,560 in federal government, $51,400 in state government, and $55,550 in local government. Compensation generally increases considerably with experience. Police departments generally offer better-than-average benefits, including health insurance, paid vacation, sick days, and pension plans.

Median annual earnings of salaried private detectives and investigators were $33,750 in 2006, according to the U.S. Department of Labor. The lowest 10 percent earned less than $19,720, and the highest 10 percent earned more than $64,380.

Private investigators who are self-employed have the potential for making much higher salaries. Hourly fees of $50 to $150 and even more, excluding expenses, are possible. Detectives who work for an agency may receive benefits, such as health insurance, but self-employed investigators must provide their own.

WORK ENVIRONMENT

The working conditions of a detective are diverse. Almost all of them work out of an office, where they may consult with colleagues, interview witnesses, read documents, or contact people on the telephone.

Their assignments bring detectives to a wide range of environments. Interviews at homes or businesses may be necessary. Traveling is also common. Rarely do jobs expose a detective to possible physical harm or death, but detectives are more likely than most people to place themselves in a dangerous situation.

Schedules for detectives are often irregular, and overtime, as well as night and weekend hours, may be necessary. At some police departments and detective agencies, overtime is compensated with additional pay or time off.

Although the work of a detective is portrayed as exciting in popular culture, the job has its share of monotonous and discouraging moments. For example, detectives may need to sit in a car for many hours waiting for a suspect to leave a building entrance only to find that the suspect is not there. Even so, the great variety of cases usually makes the work interesting.

OUTLOOK

Employment for police detectives is expected to increase faster than the average for all other occupations through 2016, according to the U.S. Department of Labor. Many openings will likely result from police detectives retiring or leaving their departments for other reasons.

Employment for private investigators is predicted to grow faster than the average for all careers through 2016, although it is important to keep in mind that law enforcement or comparable experience is often required for employment. The use of private investigators by insurance firms, restaurants, hotels, and other businesses is on the rise. Areas of particular growth include the investigation of the various forms of computer fraud, the conducting of employee background checks, the investigation of retail theft and fraud, and the prevention of industrial spying.

FOR MORE INFORMATION

For information on certification and colleges and universities that offer security-related courses and majors, contact
ASIS
1625 Prince Street
Alexandria, VA 22314-2818
Tel: 703-519-6200
http://www.asisonline.org

Contact the IACP for information about careers in law enforcement.
International Association of Chiefs of Police (IACP)
515 North Washington Street
Alexandria, VA 22314-2357

Tel: 703-836-6767
Email: information@theiacp.org
http://www.theiacp.org

For more information on private investigation, contact
National Association of Investigative Specialists
PO Box 82148
Austin, TX 78708-2148
Tel: 512-719-3595
http://www.pimall.com/nais/nais.j.html

For information on certification, contact
National Association of Legal Investigators
235 North Pine Street
Lansing, MI 48933-1021
Tel: 866-520-6254
Email: info@nalionline.org
http://www.nalionline.org

DIAGNOSTIC MEDICAL SONOGRAPHERS

OVERVIEW

Diagnostic medical sonographers, or *sonographers,* use advanced technology in the form of high-frequency sound waves similar to sonar to produce images of the internal body for analysis by radiologists and other physicians. There are approximately 46,000 diagnostic medical sonographers employed in the United States.

THE JOB

Sonographers work on the orders of a physician or radiologist. They are responsible for the proper selection and preparation of the ultrasound equipment for each specific exam. They explain the procedure to patients, recording any additional information that may be of later use to the physician. Sonographers instruct patients and assist them into the proper physical position so that the test may begin.

When the patient is properly aligned, the sonographer applies a gel to the skin that improves the diagnostic image. The sonographer selects the transducer, a microphone-shaped device that directs high-frequency sound waves into the area to be imaged, and adjusts

SCHOOL SUBJECTS
Biology, Chemistry

PERSONAL SKILLS
Helping/Teaching, Technical/Scientific

MINIMUM EDUCATION LEVEL
Associate's Degree

CERTIFICATION OR LICENSING
Recommended

WORK ENVIRONMENT
Primarily Indoors, Primarily One Location

equipment controls according to the proper depth of field and specific organ or structure to be examined. The transducer is moved as the sonographer monitors the sound wave display screen in order to ensure that a quality ultrasonic image is being produced. Sonographers must master the location and visualization of human anatomy to be able to clearly differentiate between healthy and pathological areas.

When a clear image is obtained, the sonographer activates equipment that records individual photographic views or sequences as real-time images of the affected area. These images are recorded on computer disk, magnetic tape, strip printout, film, or videotape. The sonographer removes the film after recording and prepares it for analysis by the physician. In order to be able to discuss the procedure with the physician, if asked, the sonographer may also record any further data or observations that occurred during the exam.

Sonographers can be trained in the following specialties: abdomen, breast, echocardiography, neurosonology, obstetrics/gynecology, ophthalmology, and vascular technology.

Other duties include updating patient records, monitoring and adjusting sonographic equipment to maintain accuracy, and, after considerable experience, preparing work schedules and evaluating potential equipment purchases.

REQUIREMENTS
High School

If you are interested in a career in sonography, you should take high-school courses in mathematics, biology, phys-

ics, anatomy and physiology, and, especially, chemistry. Also, take English and speech classes to improve your communication skills. In this career you will work with both patients and other medical professionals, and it will be important for you to be able to follow directions as well as explain procedures. Finally, take computer courses to familiarize yourself with using technology.

Postsecondary Training

Instruction in diagnostic medical sonography is offered by hospitals, colleges, universities, technical schools, and the armed forces in the form of hospital certificates, and two-year associate's and four-year bachelor's degree programs. Most sonographers enter the field after completing an associate's degree. The Joint Review Committee on Education in Diagnostic Medical Sonography (a division of the Commission on Accreditation of Allied Health Education Programs) has accredited 147 programs in the United States. Education consists of classroom and laboratory instruction, as well as hands-on experience in the form of internships in a hospital ultrasound department. Areas of study include patient care and medical ethics, general and cross-sectional anatomy, physiology and pathophysiology, applications and limitations of ultrasound, and image evaluation.

Certification or Licensing

After completing their degrees, sonographers may register with the American Registry for Diagnostic Sonography (ARDMS). Registration allows qualified sonographers to take the National Boards to gain certification, which, although optional, is frequently required by employers. Other licensing requirements may exist at the state level but vary greatly. Three registration categories are available to sonographers: registered diagnostic medical sonographer, registered diagnostic cardiac sonographer, and registered vascular technologist. The Society of Diagnostic Medical Sonography offers a certification designation, advanced practice sonographer, to ARDMS-registered sonographers who have five years of clinical experience, have a bachelor's degree, and who have met other requirements.

Students should also be aware of continuing education requirements that exist to keep sonographers at the forefront of current technology and diagnostic theory. They are required to maintain certification through continuing education classes, which vary from state to state. This continuing education, offered by hospitals and ultrasound equipment companies, is usually offered after regular work hours have ended.

Other Requirements

On a personal level, prospective sonographers need to be technically adept, detail-oriented, and precision-minded. You need to enjoy helping others and working with a variety of professionals as part of a team. You must be able to follow physician instructions, while maintaining a creative approach to imaging as you complete each procedure. Sonographers need to cultivate a professional demeanor, while still expressing empathy, patience, and understanding in order to reassure patients. This professionalism is also necessary because, in some instances, tragedy such as cancer, untreatable disease, or fetal death is revealed during imaging procedures. As a result, sonographers must be able to skillfully deflect questions better left to the radiologist or the attending physician. Clear communication, both verbal and written, is a plus for those who are part of a health care team.

EXPLORING

Although it is impossible for you to gain direct experience in sonography without proper education and certification, you can gain insight into duties and responsibilities by speaking directly to an experienced sonographer. You can visit a hospital, health maintenance organization, or other locations to view the equipment and facilities used and to watch professionals at work. You may also consider contacting teachers at schools of diagnostic medical sonography or touring their educational facilities. Guidance counselors or science teachers may also be able to arrange a presentation by a sonographer.

EMPLOYERS

Approximately 46,000 sonographers are employed in the United States. More than 50 percent of all sonographers are employed by hospitals. However, increasing employment opportunities exist in nursing homes, HMOs, medical and diagnostic laboratories, imaging centers, private physicians' offices, research laboratories, educational institutions, and industry.

STARTING OUT

Those interested in becoming diagnostic medical sonographers must complete a sonographic educational program such as one offered by teaching hospitals, colleges and universities, technical schools, and the armed forces. You should be sure to enroll in an accredited educational program as those who complete such a program stand the best chances for employment.

Voluntary registration with the American Registry for Diagnostic Sonography is key to gaining employment.

Most employers require registration with the ARDMS. Other methods of entering the field include responding to job listings in sonography publications, registering with employment agencies specializing in the health care field, contacting headhunters, or applying to the personnel offices of health care employers. The ARDMS offers a Web site, http://www.ultrasoundjobs.com, to help sonographers locate jobs in the field.

ADVANCEMENT

Many advancement areas are open to sonographers who have considerable experience, and most importantly, advanced education. Sonographers with a bachelor's degree stand the best chance to gain additional duties or responsibilities. Technical programs, teaching hospitals, colleges, universities, and, sometimes, in-house training programs can provide this further training. Highly trained and experienced sonographers can rise to the position of *chief technologist, administrator,* or *clinical supervisor,* overseeing sonography departments, choosing new equipment, and creating work schedules. Others may become *sonography instructors,* teaching ultrasound technology in hospitals, universities, and other educational settings. Other sonographers may gravitate toward marketing, working as *ultrasound equipment sales representatives* and selling ultrasound technology to medical clients. Sonographers involved in sales may market ultrasound technology for nonmedical uses to the plastics, steel, or other industries. Sonographers may also work as *machinery demonstrators,* traveling at the behest of manufacturers to train others in the use of new or updated equipment.

Sonographers may pursue advanced education in conjunction with or in addition to their sonography training. Sonographers may become certified in computer tomography, magnetic resonance imaging, nuclear medicine technology, radiation therapy, and cardiac catheterization. Others may become diagnostic cardiac sonographers or focus on specialty areas such as obstetrics/gynecology, neurosonography, peripheral vascular doppler, and ophthalmology.

EARNINGS

According to the U.S. Department of Labor, diagnostic medical sonographers earned a median annual income of $57,160 in 2006. The lowest paid 10 percent of this group, which included those just beginning in the field, made $40,960 or less. The highest paid 10 percent, which included those with experience and managerial duties, earned more than $77,520 annually. Mean earnings for those who worked in hospitals were $57,670 and for those employed in offices and clinics of medical doctors, $58,050.

Pay scales vary based on experience, educational level, and type and location of employer, with urban employers offering higher compensation than rural areas and small towns. Beyond base salaries, sonographers can expect to enjoy many fringe benefits, including paid vacation, sick and personal days, and health and dental insurance.

WORK ENVIRONMENT

A variety of work settings exist for sonographers, from health maintenance organizations to mobile imaging centers to clinical research labs or industry. In health care settings, diagnostic medical sonographers may work in departments of obstetrics/gynecology, cardiology, neurology, and others.

Sonographers enjoy a workplace that is clean, indoors, well lighted, quiet, and professional. Most sonographers work at one location, although mobile imaging sonographers and sales representatives can expect a considerable amount of travel.

The typical sonographer is constantly busy, seeing as many as 25 patients in the course of an eight-hour day. Overtime may also be required by some employers. The types of examinations vary by institution, but frequent areas include fetal ultrasounds, gynecological (i.e., uterus, ovaries), and abdominal (i.e., gallbladder, liver, and kidney) tests. Prospective sonographers should be aware of the occasionally repetitive nature of the job and the long hours usually spent standing. Daily duties may be both physically and mentally taxing. Although not exposed to harmful radiation, sonographers may nevertheless be exposed to communicable diseases and hazardous materials from invasive procedures. Universal safety standards exist to ensure the safety of the sonographer.

OUTLOOK

According to the U.S. Department of Labor, employment of diagnostic medical sonographers should grow faster than the average for all occupations through 2016. One reason for this growth is that sonography is a safe, nonradioactive imaging process. In addition, sonography has proved successful in detecting life-threatening diseases and in analyzing previously nonimageable internal organs. Sonography will play an increasing role in the fields of obstetrics/gynecology and cardiology. Furthermore, the aging population will create high demand for qualified technologists to operate diagnostic machinery. Approximately three out of four sonog-

raphers work in urban areas, and demand for qualified diagnostic medical sonographers exceeds the current supply in some areas of the country, especially rural communities, small towns, and some retirement areas. Those flexible about location and compensation will enjoy the best opportunities in current and future job markets.

A few important factors may slow growth. The health care industry is currently in a state of transition because of public and government debate concerning Medicare, universal health care, and the role of third-party payers in the system. Also, some procedures may prove too costly for insurance companies or government programs to cover. Hospital sonography departments will also be affected by this debate and continue to downsize. Some procedures will be done only on weekends, weeknights, or on an outpatient basis, possibly affecting employment opportunities, hours, and salaries of future sonographers. Conversely, nursing homes, HMOs, mobile imaging centers, and private physicians' groups will offer new employment opportunities to highly skilled sonographers.

Anyone considering a career in sonography should be aware that there is considerable competition for the most lucrative jobs. Those flexible in regard to hours, salary, and location and who possess advanced education stand to prosper in future job markets. Those complementing their sonographic skills with training in other imaging areas, such as magnetic resonance imaging, computer tomography, nuclear medicine technology, or other specialties, will best be able to meet the changing requirements and rising competition of future job markets.

FOR MORE INFORMATION

For information about available jobs and credentials, contact

American Registry for Diagnostic Sonography
51 Monroe Street, Plaza East One
Rockville, MD 20850-2400
Tel: 800-541-9754
http://www.ardms.org

For information regarding accredited programs of sonography, contact

Commission on Accreditation of Allied Health Education Programs
1361 Park Street
Clearwater, FL 33756-6039
Tel: 727-210-2350
Email: mail@caahep.org
http://www.caahep.org

For information regarding a career in sonography or to subscribe to the Journal of Diagnostic Medical Sonography, *contact*

Society of Diagnostic Medical Sonography
2745 Dallas Parkway, Suite 350
Plano, TX 75093-8730
Tel: 800-229-9506
http://www.sdms.org

ELECTRICIANS

OVERVIEW

Electricians design, assemble, install, test, and repair electrical fixtures and wiring. They work on a wide range of electrical and data communications systems that provide light, heat, refrigeration, air-conditioning, power, and the ability to communicate. There are approximately 705,000 electricians working in the United States.

THE JOB

Many electricians specialize in either construction or maintenance work, although some work in both fields. Electricians in construction are usually employed by electrical contractors. Other *construction electricians* work for building contractors or industrial plants, public utilities, state highway commissions, or other large organizations that employ workers directly to build or remodel their properties. A few are self-employed.

When installing electrical systems, electricians may follow blueprints and specifications or they may be told verbally what is needed. They may prepare sketches showing the intended location of wiring and equipment. Once the plan is clear, they measure, cut, assemble, and install plastic-covered wire or electrical conduit, which is a tube or channel through which heavier grades of electrical wire or cable are run. They strip insulation from wires, splice and solder wires together, and tape or cap the ends. They attach cables and wiring to the incoming electrical service and to various fixtures and machines that use electricity. They install switches, circuit breakers, relays, transformers, grounding leads, signal devices, and other electrical components. After the installation is complete, construction electricians test circuits for continuity and safety, adjusting the setup as needed.

Maintenance electricians do many of the same kinds of tasks, but their activities are usually aimed at preventing trouble before it occurs. They periodically inspect equipment and carry out routine service procedures, often according to a predetermined schedule. They repair or replace worn or defective parts and keep management informed about the reliability of the electrical systems. If any breakdowns occur, maintenance electricians return the equipment to full functioning as soon as possible so that the expense and inconvenience are minimal.

Maintenance electricians, also known as *electrical repairers,* may work in large factories, office buildings, small plants, or wherever existing electrical facilities and machinery need regular servicing to keep them in good working order. Many maintenance electricians work in manufacturing industries, such as those that produce automobiles, aircraft, ships, steel, chemicals, and industrial machinery. Some are employed by hospitals, municipalities, housing complexes, or shopping centers to do maintenance, repair, and sometimes installation work. Some work for or operate businesses that contract to repair and update wiring in residences and commercial buildings.

A growing number of electricians are involved in activities other than constructing and maintaining electrical systems in buildings. Many are employed to install computer wiring and equipment, telephone wiring, or the coaxial and fiber optics cables used in telecommunications and computer equipment. Electricians also work in power plants, where electric power is generated; in machine shops, where electric motors are repaired and rebuilt; aboard ships, fixing communications and navigation systems; at locations that need large lighting and power installations, such as airports and mines; and in numerous other settings.

SCHOOL SUBJECTS
Mathematics, Technical/Shop

PERSONAL SKILLS
Mechanical/Manipulative, Technical/Scientific

MINIMUM EDUCATION LEVEL
Apprenticeship

CERTIFICATION OR LICENSING
Required by Certain States

WORK ENVIRONMENT
Primarily Indoors, Primarily Multiple Locations

All electricians must work in conformity with the National Electrical Code as well as any current state and local building and electrical codes. (Electrical codes are standards that electrical systems must meet to ensure safe, reliable functioning.) In doing their work, electricians try to use materials efficiently, to plan for future access to the area for service and maintenance on the system, and to avoid hazardous and unsightly wiring arrangements, making their work as neat and orderly as possible.

Electricians use a variety of equipment ranging from simple hand tools such as screwdrivers, pliers, wrenches, and hacksaws to power tools such as drills, hydraulic benders for metal conduit, and electric soldering guns. They also use testing devices such as oscilloscopes, ammeters, and test lamps. Construction electricians often supply their own hand tools. Experienced workers may have hundreds of dollars invested in tools.

REQUIREMENTS
High School

If you are thinking of becoming an electrician, whether you intend to enter an apprenticeship or learn informally on the job, you should have a high school background that includes such courses as applied mathematics and science, shop classes that teach the use of various tools, and mechanical drawing. Electronics courses are especially important if you plan to become a maintenance electrician.

Postsecondary Training

Some electricians still learn their trade the same way electrical workers did many years ago—informally on the job while employed as helpers to skilled workers. Especially if that experience is supplemented with vocational or technical school courses, correspondence courses, or training received in the military, electrical helpers may in time become well-qualified crafts workers in some area of the field.

You should be aware, however, that most professionals believe that apprenticeship programs provide the best all-around training in this trade. Apprenticeships combine a series of planned, structured, supervised job experiences with classroom instruction in related subjects. Many programs are designed to give apprentices a variety of experiences by having them work for several electrical contractors doing different kinds of jobs. Typically, apprenticeships last four to five years and provides at least 144 hours of classroom instruction and 2,000 hours of on-the-job training each year. Completion of

an apprenticeship is usually a significant advantage in getting the better jobs in the field.

Applicants for apprenticeships generally need to be high school graduates, at least 18 years of age, in good health, and with at least average physical strength. Although local requirements vary, many applicants are required to take tests to determine their aptitude for the work.

Most apprenticeship programs are developed and conducted by state and national contractor associations such as the Independent Electrical Contractors Inc. and the union locals of the International Brotherhood of Electrical Workers. Some programs are conducted as cooperative efforts between these groups and local community colleges and training organizations. In either situation, the apprenticeship program is usually managed by a training committee. An agreement regarding in-class and on-the-job training is usually established between the committee and each apprentice.

Certification or Licensing

Some states and municipalities require that electricians be licensed. To obtain a license, electricians usually must pass a written examination on electrical theory, National Electrical Code requirements, and local building and electrical codes. Electronics specialists receive certification training and testing through the International Society of Certified Electronic Technicians.

Other Requirements

You will need to have good color vision because electricians need to be able to distinguish color-coded wires. Agility and manual dexterity are also desirable characteristics, as are a sense of teamwork, an interest in working outdoors, and a love of working with your hands.

Electricians may or may not belong to a union. While many electricians belong to such organizations as the International Brotherhood of Electrical Workers; the International Union of Electronic, Electrical, Salaried, Machine, and Furniture Workers-Communications Workers of America; the International Association of Machinists and Aerospace Workers; and other unions, an increasing number of electricians are opting to affiliate with independent (nonunion) electrical contractors.

EXPLORING

Hobbies such as repairing radios, building electronics kits, or working with model electric trains will help you understand how electricians work. In addition to sampling related activities like these, you may benefit by arranging to talk with an electrician about his or her job. With the help of a teacher or guidance counselor, it may be possible to contact a local electrical contracting firm and locate someone willing to give an insider's description of the occupation.

EMPLOYERS

Approximately 705,000 electricians are employed in the United States. Electricians are employed in almost every industry imaginable, from construction (which employs 68 percent of wage and salary workers) to telecommunications to health care to transportation and more. Most work for contractors, but many work for institutional employers that require their own maintenance crews, or for government agencies. Approximately 11 percent of electricians are self-employed.

STARTING OUT

People seeking to enter this field may either begin working as helpers or they may enter an apprenticeship program. Leads for helper jobs may be located by contacting electrical contractors directly or by checking with the local offices of the state employment service or in newspaper classified advertising sections. Students in trade and vocational programs may be able to find job openings through the career services office of their school.

If you are interested in an apprenticeship, you may start by contacting the union local of the International Brotherhood of Electrical Workers, the local chapter of Independent Electrical Contractors Inc., or the local apprenticeship training committee. Information on apprenticeship possibilities also can be obtained through the state employment service.

ADVANCEMENT

The advancement possibilities for skilled, experienced electricians depend partly on their field of activity. Those who work in construction may become supervisors, job site superintendents, or estimators for electrical contractors. Some electricians are able to establish their own contracting businesses, although in many areas contractors must obtain a special license. Another possibility for some electricians is to move, for example, from construction to maintenance work, or into jobs in the shipbuilding, automobile, or aircraft industry.

Many electricians find that after they are working in the field, they still need to take courses to keep abreast of new developments. Unions and employers may sponsor classes introducing new methods and materials or explaining changes in electrical code requirements. By taking skill-improvement courses, electricians may also improve their chances for advancement to better-paying positions.

EARNINGS

Most established, full-time electricians working for contractors average earnings about $21 per hour, or $43,680 per year for full-time work, according to the National Joint Apprenticeship Training Committee—and it is possible to make much more. According to the U.S. Department of Labor, median hourly earnings of electricians were $20.97 in 2006 ($43,610 annually). Wages ranged from less than $12.76 an hour for the lowest paid 10 percent to more than $34.95 an hour for the highest paid 10 percent, or from $26,530 to $72,700 yearly for full-time work. Beginning apprentices earn 40 to 50 percent of the base electrician's wage and receive periodic increases each year of their apprenticeship.

Overall, it's important to realize these wages can vary widely, depending on a number of factors, including geographic location, the industry in which an electrician works, prevailing economic conditions, union membership, and others. Wage rates for many electricians are set by contract agreements between unions and employers. In general, electricians working in cities tend to be better paid than those in other areas. Those working as telecommunications or residential specialists tend to make slightly less than those working as linemen or wiremen.

Electricians who are members of the International Brotherhood of Electrical Workers, the industry's labor union, are entitled to benefits including paid vacation days and holidays, health insurance, pensions to help with retirement savings, supplemental unemployment compensation plans, and so forth.

WORK ENVIRONMENT

Although electricians may work for the same contractor for many years, they work on different projects and at different work sites. In a single year, they may install wiring in a new housing project, rewire a factory, or install computer or telecommunications wiring in an office, for instance. Electricians usually work indoors, although some must do tasks outdoors or in buildings that are still under construction. The standard workweek is approximately 40 hours. In many jobs, overtime may be required. Maintenance electricians often have to work some weekend, holiday, or night hours because they must service equipment that operates all the time.

Electricians often spend long periods on their feet, sometimes on ladders or scaffolds or in awkward or uncomfortable places. The work can be strenuous. Electricians may have to put up with noise and dirt on the job.

They may risk injuries such as falls off ladders, electrical shocks, and cuts and bruises. By following established safety practices, most of these hazards can be avoided.

OUTLOOK

Employment of electricians will grow about as fast as the average for all occupations through 2016, according to the U.S. Department of Labor. Growth will result from an overall increase in both residential and commercial construction, as well as in power plant construction. In addition, growth will be driven by the ever-expanding use of electrical and electronic devices and equipment. Electricians will be called on to upgrade old wiring and to install and maintain more extensive wiring systems than have been necessary in the past. In particular, the use of sophisticated computer, telecommunications, and data-processing equipment and automated manufacturing systems is expected to lead to job opportunities for electricians. Electricians with experience in a wide variety of skills—including voice, data, and video wiring—will have the best employment options.

In addition to opportunities created by growth in the construction and residential industries and other fields, a large number of job openings will occur as a result of workers retiring or leaving the field for other occupations.

While the overall outlook for this occupational field is good, the availability of jobs will vary over time and from place to place. Construction activity fluctuates depending on the state of the local and national economy. Thus, during economic slowdowns, opportunities for construction electricians may not be plentiful. People working in this field need to be prepared for periods of unemployment between construction projects. Openings for apprentices also decline during economic downturns. Maintenance electricians are usually less vulnerable to periodic unemployment because they are more likely to work for one employer that needs electrical services on a steady basis. But if they work in an industry where the economy causes big fluctuations in the level of activity—such as automobile manufacturing, for instance—they may be laid off during recessions.

FOR MORE INFORMATION

For more information about the industry, contact
Independent Electrical Contractors
4401 Ford Avenue, Suite 1100
Alexandria, VA 22302-1432
Tel: 703-549-7351
Email: info@ieci.org
http://www.ieci.org

For information about the rules and benefits of joining a labor union, contact
International Brotherhood of Electrical Workers
900 Seventh Street, NW
Washington, DC 20001-3886
Tel: 202-833-7000
http://www.ibew.org
http://www.electrifyingcareers.com

For information on certification, contact
International Society of Certified Electronic Technicians
3608 Pershing Avenue
Fort Worth, TX 76107-4527
Tel: 800-946-0201
Email: info@iscet.org
http://www.iscet.org

For industry information, contact
National Electrical Contractors Association
3 Bethesda Metro Center, Suite 1100
Bethesda, MD 20814-6302
Tel: 301-657-3110
http://www.necanet.org

For background information on apprenticeship and training programs aimed at union workers, contact
National Joint Apprenticeship and Training Committee
301 Prince George's Boulevard, Suite D
Upper Marlboro, MD 20774-7401
Email: office@njatc.org
http://www.njatc.org

For information on careers, visit
ElectrifyingCareers.com
http://www.electrifyingcareers.com

ELEMENTARY SCHOOL TEACHERS

OVERVIEW

Elementary school teachers instruct students from the first through sixth or eighth grades. They develop teaching outlines and lesson plans, give lectures, facilitate discussions and activities, keep class attendance records, assign homework, and evaluate student progress. Most teachers work with one group of children throughout the day, teaching several subjects and supervising such activities as lunch and recess. Approximately 1.5 million elementary school teachers are employed in the United States.

THE JOB

Depending on the school, elementary school teachers teach grades one through six or eight. In smaller schools, grades may be combined. There are still a few one-room, one-teacher elementary schools in remote rural areas. However, in most cases, teachers instruct approximately 20–30 children of the same grade. They teach a variety of subjects in the prescribed course of study, including language, science, mathematics, and social studies. In the classroom, teachers use various methods to educate their students, such as reading to them, assigning group projects, and showing films for discussion. Teachers also use educational games to help their pupils come up with creative ways to remember lessons.

In the first and second grades, elementary school teachers cover the basic skills: reading, writing, counting, and telling time. With older students, teachers instruct history, geography, math, English, and handwriting. To capture attention and teach new concepts, they use arts and crafts projects, workbooks, music, and other interactive activities. In the upper grades, teachers assign written and oral reports and involve students in projects and competitions such as spelling bees, science fairs, and math contests. Although they are usually required to follow a curriculum designed by state or local administrators, teachers study new learning methods to incorporate into the classroom, such as using computers to surf the Internet.

"I utilize many different, some unorthodox, teaching tools," says Andrea LoCastro, a sixth-grade teacher in Clayton, New Jersey. "I have a lunchtime chess club. Students give up their recess to listen to classical music and play, or learn to play, chess." She has also found that role-playing activities keep her students interested in the various subjects. "We are studying ancient Greece," she says, "and I currently have my students writing persuasive essays as either part of Odysseus' legal team or the Cyclops' legal team. I intend to culminate the activity with a mock trial, Athenian style."

To create unique exercises and activities such as those LoCastro uses, teachers need to devote a fair amount of time to preparation outside of the classroom. They prepare daily lesson plans and assignments, grade papers and tests, and keep a record of each student's progress. Other responsibilities include communicating with parents through written reports and scheduled meetings,

SCHOOL SUBJECTS
English, Speech

PERSONAL SKILLS
Communication/Ideas, Helping/Teaching

MINIMUM EDUCATION LEVEL
Bachelor's Degree

CERTIFICATION OR LICENSING
Required by All States

WORK ENVIRONMENT
Primarily Indoors, Primarily One Location

keeping their classroom orderly, and decorating desks and bulletin boards to keep the learning environment visually stimulating.

Elementary school teachers may also teach music, art, and physical education, but these areas are often covered by specialized teachers. *Art teachers* develop art projects, procure supplies, and help students develop drawing, painting, sculpture, mural design, ceramics, and other artistic abilities. Some art teachers also teach students about the history of art and lead field trips to local museums. *Music teachers* teach music appreciation and history. They direct organized student groups such as choruses, bands, or orchestras, or guide music classes by accompanying them in singing songs or playing instruments. Often, music teachers are responsible for organizing school pageants, musicals, and plays. *Physical education teachers* help students develop physical skills such as coordination, strength, and stamina and social skills such as self-confidence and good sportsmanship. Physical education teachers often serve as sports coaches and may organize field days and intramural activities.

When working with elementary-aged children, teachers need to instruct social skills along with general school subjects. They serve as disciplinarians, establishing and enforcing rules of conduct to help students learn right from wrong. To keep the classroom manageable, teachers maintain a system of rewards and punishments to encourage students to behave, stay interested, and participate. In cases of classroom disputes, teachers must also be mediators, teaching their pupils to peacefully work through arguments.

Recent developments in school curricula have led to new teaching arrangements and methods. In some schools, one or more teachers work with students within a small age range instead of with particular grades. Other schools are adopting bilingual education, where students are instructed throughout the day in two languages by either a *bilingual teacher* or two separate teachers.

Many teachers find it rewarding to witness students develop and hone new skills and adopt an appreciation for learning. In fact, many teachers inspire their own students to later join the teaching profession themselves. "Teaching is not just a career," says LoCastro, "It is a commitment—a commitment to the 20-plus children that walk into your classroom door each September eager for enlightenment and fun."

REQUIREMENTS
High School

Follow your school's college preparatory program and take advanced courses in English, mathematics, science, history, and government to prepare for an education degree. Art, music, physical education, and extracurricular activities will contribute to a broad base of knowledge necessary to teach a variety of subjects. Composition, journalism, and communications classes are also important for developing your writing and speaking skills.

Postsecondary Training

All 50 states and the District of Columbia require public elementary education teachers to have a bachelor's degree in either education or in the subject they plan to teach. Prospective teachers must also complete an approved training program. In the United States, there are more than 500 accredited teacher education programs, which combine subject and educational classes with work experience in the classroom.

Though programs vary by state, courses cover how to instruct language arts, mathematics, physical science, social science, art, and music. Additionally, prospective teachers must take educational training courses, such as philosophy of education, child psychology, and learning methods. To gain experience in the classroom, student teachers are placed in a school to work with a full-time teacher. During this training period, student teachers observe the ways in which lessons are presented and the classroom is managed, learn how to keep records of attendance and grades, and gain experience in handling the class, both under supervision and alone.

Some states require prospective teachers to have master's degrees in education and specialized technology training to keep them familiar with more modern teaching methods using computers and the Internet.

Certification or Licensing

Public school teachers must be licensed under regulations established by the state in which they are teaching. If they relocate, teachers have to comply with any other regulations in their new state to be able to teach, though many states have reciprocity agreements that make it easier for teachers to change locations.

Licensure examinations test prospective teachers for competency in basic subjects such as mathematics, reading, writing, teaching, and other subject matter proficiency. In addition, many states are moving towards a performance-based evaluation for licensing. In this case, after passing the teaching examination, prospective teachers are given provisional licenses. Only after proving themselves capable in the classroom are they eligible for a full license.

Another growing trend spurred by recent teacher shortages is alternative licensure arrangements. For those who have a bachelor's degree but lack formal education courses and training in the classroom, states can issue a provisional license. These workers immediately begin teaching under the supervision of a licensed educator for one to two years and take education classes outside of their working hours. Once they have completed the required coursework and gained experience in the classroom, they are granted a full license. This flexible licensing arrangement has helped to bring additional teachers into school systems needing instructors.

Other Requirements

Many consider the desire to teach a calling. This calling is based on a love of children and a dedication to their welfare. If you want to become a teacher, you must respect children as individuals, with personalities, strengths, and weaknesses of their own. You must also be patient and self-disciplined to manage a large group independently. Teachers make a powerful impression on children, so they need to serve as good role models. "Treat students with kindness and understanding, rules and consequences," LoCastro suggests. "Be nice, yet strict. They'll love you for it."

EXPLORING

To explore the teaching career, look for leadership opportunities that involve working with children. You might find summer work as a counselor in a summer camp, as a leader of a scout troop, or as an assistant in a public park or community center. Look for opportunities to tutor younger students or coach children's athletic teams. Local community theaters may need directors and assistants for summer children's productions. Day care centers often hire high school students for late afternoon and weekend work.

EMPLOYERS

There are approximately 1.5 million elementary school teachers employed in the United States. Teachers are needed at public and private institutions, including parochial schools and Montessori schools, which focus more on the child's own initiatives. Teachers are also needed in day care centers that offer full-day elementary programs and charter schools, which are smaller, deregulated schools that receive public funding. Although rural areas maintain schools, more teaching positions are available in urban or suburban areas.

STARTING OUT

After obtaining a college degree, finishing the student teaching program, and becoming certified, prospective teachers have many avenues for finding a job. College career services offices and state departments of education maintain listings of job openings. Many local schools advertise teaching positions in newspapers. Another option is directly contacting the administration in the schools in which you'd like to work. While looking for a full-time position, you can work as a substitute teacher. In more urban areas with many schools, you may be able to find full-time substitute work.

ADVANCEMENT

As teachers acquire experience or additional education, they can expect higher wages and more responsibilities. Teachers with leadership skills and an interest in administrative work may advance to serve as principals or supervisors, though the number of these positions is limited and competition is fierce. Others may advance to work as *senior* or *mentor teachers* who assist less experienced staff. Another move may be into higher education, teaching education classes at a college or university. For most of these positions, additional education is required.

Other common career transitions are into related fields. With additional preparation, teachers can become librarians, reading specialists, or counselors.

"I intend to continue teaching as my career," says Andrea LoCastro. "I am not at all interested in moving up to administration. I will, however, pursue a master's in teaching after receiving tenure."

EARNINGS

According to the U.S. Department of Labor, the median annual salary for elementary school teachers was $45,570 in 2006. The lowest 10 percent earned $30,370 or less; the highest 10 percent earned $72,720 or more. Private school teachers generally earn less than public school teachers.

According to the American Federation of Teachers, beginning teachers earned an average salary of $31,753 a year in 2004–05.

Teachers often supplement their earnings through teaching summer classes, coaching sports, sponsoring a club, or other extracurricular work. More than half of all teachers belong to unions such as the American Federation of Teachers or the National Education Association. These unions bargain with schools over contract conditions such as wages, hours, and benefits. Depending on the state, teachers usually receive a retirement plan, sick leave, and health and life insurance. Some systems grant teachers sabbatical leave.

WORK ENVIRONMENT

Most teachers are contracted to work 10 months out of the year, with a two-month vacation during the summer. During their summer break, many continue their education to renew or upgrade their teaching licenses and earn higher salaries. Teachers in schools that operate year-round work eight-week sessions with one-week breaks in between and a five-week vacation in the winter.

Teachers work in generally pleasant conditions, although some older schools may have poor heating or electrical systems. The work can seem confining, requiring them to remain in the classroom throughout most of the day. Although the job is not overly strenuous, dealing with busy children all day can be tiring and trying. Teachers must stand for many hours each day, do a lot of talking, show energy and enthusiasm, and may have to handle discipline problems. But, according to Andrea LoCastro, problems with students are usually overshadowed by their successes. "Just knowing a child is learning something because of you is the most rewarding feeling, especially when you and the child have struggled together to understand it."

OUTLOOK

According to the *Occupational Outlook Handbook*, employment opportunities for elementary school teachers are expected to grow slightly faster than the average for all occupations through 2016. The need to replace retiring teachers will provide many opportunities nationwide.

The demand for teachers varies widely depending on geographic area. Inner-city schools characterized by poor working conditions and low salaries often suffer a shortage of teachers. In addition, more opportunities exist for those who specialize in a subject in which it is harder to attract qualified teachers, such as mathematics, science, bilingual education, or foreign languages.

The National Education Association believes it will be a difficult challenge to hire enough new teachers to meet rising enrollments and replace the large number of retiring teachers, primarily because of low teacher salaries. Higher salaries along with other necessary changes, such as smaller classroom sizes and safer schools, will be necessary to attract new teachers and retain experienced ones. Other challenges for the profession involve attracting more men into teaching. The percentage of male teachers continues to decline.

The demand for teachers varies widely depending on geographic area. The U.S. Department of Labor predicts that the following states will experience the largest increases in enrollment: Nevada, Arizona, Texas, and Georgia. Enrollments in the Midwest will remain steady, while enrollments in the Northeast will decline.

In order to improve education, drastic changes are being considered by some districts. Some private companies are managing public schools in the hope of providing better facilities, faculty, and equipment. Teacher organizations are concerned about taking school management away from communities and turning it over to remote corporate headquarters.

Charter schools and voucher programs are two other controversial alternatives to traditional public education. Publicly funded charter schools are not guided by the rules and regulations of traditional public schools. Some view these schools as places of innovation and improved educational methods; others see them as ill-equipped and unfairly funded with money that could better benefit local school districts. Vouchers, which exist only in a few cities, use public tax dollars to allow students to attend private schools. In theory, the vouchers allow for more choices in education for poor and minority students. Teacher organizations see some danger in giving public funds to unregulated private schools.

FOR MORE INFORMATION

For information about careers, education, and union membership, contact the following organizations

American Federation of Teachers
555 New Jersey Avenue, NW

Washington, DC 20001-2029
Tel: 202-879-4400
Email: online@aft.org
http://www.aft.org

National Council for Accreditation
   of Teacher Education
2010 Massachusetts Avenue, NW, Suite 500
Washington, DC 20036-1023
Tel: 202-466-7496
Email: ncate@ncate.org
http://www.ncate.org

National Education Association
1201 16th Street, NW
Washington, DC 20036-3290
Tel: 202-833-4000
http://www.nea.org

This Web site serves as a clearinghouse for men interested in becoming teachers.

MenTeach
http://www.menteach.org

EMERGENCY MEDICAL TECHNICIANS

OVERVIEW

Emergency medical technicians, often called *EMTs,* respond to medical emergencies to provide immediate treatment for ill or injured persons both on the scene and during transport to a medical facility. They function as part of an emergency medical team, and the range of medical services they perform varies according to their level of training and certification. There are approximately 201,000 emergency medical technicians employed in the United States.

THE JOB

EMTs provide on-site emergency care. Their goal is to rapidly identify the nature of the emergency, stabilize the patient's condition, and initiate proper medical procedures at the scene and en route to a hospital. Communities often take great pride in their emergency medical services, knowing that they are as well prepared as possible and that they can minimize the tragic consequences of mishandling emergencies.

The types of treatments an individual is able to give depend mostly on the level of training and certification he or she has completed. First responders, the lowest tier of workers in the emergency services, are qualified to provide basic care to the sick and injured since they are often the first to arrive on scene during an emergency. This designation is often held by firefighters, police officers, and other emergency services workers. The most common designation that EMTs hold is EMT-basic. A basic EMT can perform CPR, control bleeding, treat shock victims, apply bandages, splint fractures, and perform automatic defibrillation, which requires no interpretation of EKGs. They are also trained to deal with emotionally disturbed patients and heart attack, poisoning, and burn victims. The EMT-intermediate, which is the second level of training, is also prepared to start an IV, if needed, or use a manual defibrillator to apply electrical shocks to the heart in the case of a cardiac arrest. A growing number of EMTs are choosing to train for the highest level of certification—the EMT-paramedic. With this certification, the individual is permitted to perform more intensive treatment procedures. Often working in close radio contact with a doctor, he or she may give drugs intravenously or orally, interpret EKGs, perform endotracheal intubation, and use more complex life-support equipment.

In the case where a victim or victims are trapped, EMTs first give any medical treatment, and then remove the victim, using special equipment such as the Amkus Power Unit. They may need to work closely with the police or the fire department in the rescue attempt.

EMTs are sent in an ambulance to the scene of an emergency by a *dispatcher,* who acts as a communications channel for all aspects of emergency medical services. The dispatcher may also be trained as an EMT. It typically is the dispatcher who receives the call for help, sends out the appropriate medical resource, serves as the continuing link between the emergency vehicle and medical facility throughout the situation, and relays any requests for special assistance at the scene.

EMTs, who often work in two-person teams, must be able to get to an emergency scene in any part of their geographic area quickly and safely. For the protection of the public and themselves, they must obey the traffic laws that apply to emergency vehicles. They must be familiar with the roads and any special conditions affecting the choice of route, such as traffic, weather-related problems, and road construction.

Once at the scene, they may find victims who appear to have had heart attacks, are burned, trapped under

SCHOOL SUBJECTS
Biology, Health

PERSONAL SKILLS
Helping/Teaching, Technical/Scientific

MINIMUM EDUCATION LEVEL
Some Postsecondary Training

CERTIFICATION OR LICENSING
Required by All States

WORK ENVIRONMENT
Indoors and Outdoors, Primarily Multiple Locations

fallen objects, lacerated, in labor, poisoned, or emotionally disturbed. Because people who have been involved in an emergency are sometimes very upset, EMTs often have to exercise skill in calming both victims and bystanders. They must do their work efficiently and in a reassuring manner.

EMTs are often the first qualified personnel to arrive on the scene, so they must make the initial evaluation of the nature and extent of the medical problem. The accuracy of this early assessment can be crucial. EMTs must be on the lookout for any clues, such as medical identification emblems, indicating that the person has significant allergies, diabetes, epilepsy, or other conditions that may affect decisions about emergency treatment. EMTs must know what questions to ask bystanders or family members if they need more information about a patient.

Once they have evaluated the situation and the patient's condition, EMTs establish the priorities of required care. They administer emergency treatment under standing orders or in accordance with specific instructions received over the radio from a physician. For example, they may have to open breathing passages, perform cardiac resuscitation, treat shock, or restrain emotionally disturbed patients. The particular procedures and treatments that EMTs may carry out depend partly on the level of certification they have achieved.

People who must be transported to the hospital are put on stretchers or backboards, lifted into the ambulance, and secured for the ride. The choice of hospital is not always up to the EMTs, but when it is they must base the decision on their knowledge of the equipment and staffing needed by the patients. The receiving hospital's emergency department is informed by radio, either directly or through the dispatcher, of details such as the number of persons being transported and the nature of their medical problems. Meanwhile, EMTs continue to monitor the patients and administer care as directed by the medical professional with whom they are maintaining radio contact.

Once at the hospital, EMTs help the staff bring the patients into the emergency department and may assist with the first steps of in-hospital care. They supply whatever information they can, verbally and in writing, for the hospital's records. In the case of a patient's death, they complete the necessary procedures to ensure that the deceased's property is safeguarded.

After the patient has been delivered to the hospital, EMTs check in with their dispatchers and then prepare the vehicle for another emergency call. This includes replacing used linens and blankets; replenishing supplies of drugs, oxygen; and so forth. In addition, EMTs make sure that the ambulance is clean and in good running condition. At least once during the shift, they check the gas, oil, battery, siren, brakes, radio, and other systems.

REQUIREMENTS
High School

While still in high school, interested students should take courses in health and science, driver education, and English. To be admitted to a basic training program, applicants usually must be at least 18 years old and have a high school diploma and valid driver's license. Exact requirements vary slightly between states and training courses. Many EMTs first become interested in the field while in the U.S. Armed Forces, where they may have received training as medics.

Postsecondary Training

The standard basic training program for EMTs was designed by the U.S. Department of Transportation. It is taught in hospitals, community colleges, and police, fire, and health departments across the country. It is approximately 110 hours in length and constitutes the minimum mandatory requirement to become an EMT. In this course, you are taught how to manage common emergencies such as bleeding, cardiac arrest, fractures, and airway obstruction. You also learn how to use equipment such as stretchers, backboards, fracture kits, and oxygen delivery systems.

Successful completion of the basic EMT course opens several opportunities for further training. Among these are a two-day course on removing trapped victims and a five-day course on driving emergency vehicles. Another, somewhat longer course, trains dispatchers. Completion of these recognized training courses may be required for EMTs to be eligible for certain jobs in some areas.

Certification or Licensing

All 50 states have some certification requirement. Certification is only open to those who have completed the standard basic training course. Some states offer new EMTs the choice of the National Registry examination or the state's own certification examination. A majority of states accept national registration in place of their own examination for EMTs who relocate to their states.

After the training program has been successfully completed, the graduate has the opportunity to work toward becoming certified or registered with the National Registry of Emergency Medical Technicians (NREMT). All states have some sort of certification requirement of their own, but many of them accept registration in NREMT in place of their own certification. Applicants should check the specific regulations and requirements for their state.

At present, the NREMT recognizes four levels of competency: first responder, EMT-basic, EMT-intermediate, and EMT-paramedic. Although it is not always essential for EMTs to become registered with one of these ratings, you can expect better job prospects as you attain higher levels of registration.

Candidates for the first responder designation must have completed the standard Department of Transportation training program (or their state's equivalent) and pass both a state-approved practical examination and a written examination.

Candidates for the EMT-basic designation must have completed the standard Department of Transportation training program (or their state's equivalent), have six months' experience, have a current approved CPR credential for the professional rescuer, and pass both a state-approved practical examination and a written examination.

The EMT-intermediate level of competency requires all candidates to have current registration at the basic EMT-basic level. They must also have a certain amount of experience, have a current approved CPR credential for the professional rescuer, and pass both a written test and a practical examination.

To become registered as an EMT-paramedic, or EMT-P, the highest level of registration, candidates must be already registered at the basic or intermediate level. They must have completed a special EMT-P training program and pass both a written and practical examination. Because training is much more comprehensive and specialized than for other EMTs, EMT-Ps are prepared to make more physician-like observations and judgments.

Other Requirements

Anyone who is considering becoming an EMT should have a desire to serve people and be emotionally stable and clearheaded. You must inspire confidence with levelheadedness and good judgment. You must be efficient, neither wasting time nor hurrying through delicate work.

Prospective EMTs need to be in good physical condition. Other requirements include good manual dexterity and motor coordination; the ability to lift and carry up to 125 pounds; good visual acuity, with lenses for correction permitted; accurate color vision, enabling safe driving and immediate detection of diagnostic signs; and competence in giving and receiving verbal and written communication.

EXPLORING

Students in high school usually have little opportunity for direct experience with the emergency medical field. It may be possible to learn a great deal about the health-services field through a part-time, summer, or volunteer job in a hospital or clinic. Such service jobs can provide a chance to observe and talk to staff members concerned with emergency medical services.

High school health courses are a useful introduction to some of the concepts and terminology that EMTs use. You may also be able to take a first-aid class or training in cardiopulmonary resuscitation (CPR). Organizations such as the Red Cross can provide information on local training courses available.

EMPLOYERS

Approximately 201,000 emergency medical technicians are employed in the United States. EMTs are employed by fire departments, private ambulance services, police departments, volunteer emergency medical services squads, hospitals, industrial plants, or other organizations that provide prehospital emergency care.

STARTING OUT

A good source of employment leads for a recent graduate of the basic EMT training program is the school or agency that provided the training. You can also apply directly to local ambulance services, fire departments, and employment agencies.

In some areas, you may face stiff competition if you are seeking full-time paid employment immediately upon graduation. Although you may sometimes qualify for positions with fire and police departments, you are generally more likely to be successful in pursuing positions with private companies.

Volunteer work is an option for EMTs. Volunteers are likely to average eight to 12 hours of work per week. If you are a beginning EMT without prior work experience in the health field, you may find it advantageous to start your career as a part-time volunteer to gain experience.

Flexibility about the location of a job may help you gain a foothold on the career ladder. In some areas, salaried positions are hard to find because of a strong tradition of volunteer ambulance services. Therefore, if you are willing to relocate where the demand is higher, you should have a better chance of finding employment.

ADVANCEMENT

With experience, EMTs can gain more responsibility while retaining the same job. However, more significant advancement is possible if you move up through the progression of ratings recognized by the NREMT. These ratings acknowledge increasing qualifications, making higher paying jobs and more responsibility easier to obtain.

An avenue of advancement for some EMTs leads to holding an administrative job, such as supervisor, director, operations manager, or trainer. Another avenue of advancement might be further training in a different area of the health care field. Some EMTs eventually move out of the health care field entirely and into medical sales, where their familiarity with equipment and terminology can make them valuable employees.

EARNINGS

Earnings of EMTs depend on the type of employer and individual level of training and experience. Those working in the public sector, for police and fire departments, usually receive a higher wage than those in the private sector, working for ambulance companies and hospitals. Salary levels typically rise with increasing levels of skill, training, and certification.

According to the U.S. Department of Labor, median annual earnings of EMTs and paramedics were $27,070 in 2006. Salaries ranged from less than $17,300 for the lowest 10 percent to more than $45,280 for the highest 10 percent. For those who worked in local government the mean salary was $30,750, and in hospitals, $29,210.

Benefits vary widely depending on the employer but generally include paid holidays and vacations, health insurance, and pension plans.

WORK ENVIRONMENT

EMTs must work under all kinds of conditions, both indoors and outdoors, and sometimes in very trying circumstances. They must do their work regardless of extreme weather conditions and are often required to do fairly strenuous physical tasks such as lifting, climbing, and kneeling. They consistently deal with situations that many people would find upsetting and traumatic, such as deaths, accidents, and serious injuries.

EMTs usually work irregular hours, including some nights, weekends, and holidays. Those working for fire departments often put in 50 hours a week, while EMTs employed in hospitals work 40- to 60-hour weeks. EMTs employed by private ambulance services work 45 to 50 hours a week. Volunteer EMTs work much shorter hours.

An additional stress factor faced by EMTs is concern over contracting AIDS or other infectious diseases from bleeding patients. The actual risk of exposure is quite small, and emergency medical programs have implemented procedures to protect EMTs from exposure to the greatest possible degree; however, some risk of exposure does exist, and prospective EMTs should be aware of this.

In spite of the intensity of their demanding job, many EMTs derive enormous satisfaction from knowing that they are able to render such a vital service to the victims of sudden illness or injury.

OUTLOOK

Employment for EMTs is expected to grow faster than the average for all occupations through 2016, according to the U.S. Department of Labor. The proportion of older people, who most use emergency medical services, is growing in many communities, placing more demands on the emergency medical services delivery system and increasing the need for EMTs. There is also high turnover in this occupation (due to limited opportunities for advancement and modest pay), and many openings will occur as current EMTs leave the field.

The employment outlook for paid EMTs depends partly on the community in which they are seeking employment. Many communities perceive the advantages of high-quality emergency medical services and are willing and able to raise tax dollars to support them. In these communities, which are often larger, the employment outlook should remain favorable. Volunteer services are being phased out in these areas, and well-equipped emergency services operated by salaried EMTs are replacing them.

In some communities, however, particularly smaller ones, the employment outlook is not so favorable. Maintaining a high-quality emergency medical services delivery system can be expensive, and financial strains on some local governments could inhibit the growth of these services. Communities may not be able to support the level of emergency medical services that they would otherwise like to, and the employment prospects for EMTs may remain limited.

FOR MORE INFORMATION

For industry news and government affairs, contact
American Ambulance Association
8201 Greensboro Drive, Suite 300
McLean, VA 22102-3814
Tel: 800-523-4447
http://www.the-aaa.org

For educational programs and scholarship information, contact
National Association of Emergency Medical Technicians
PO Box 1400
Clinton, MS 39060-1400
Tel: 800-346-2368
Email: info@naemt.org
http://www.naemt.org

For information on testing for EMT certification, contact
National Registry of Emergency Medical Technicians
Rocco V. Morando Building
PO Box 29233
6610 Busch Boulevard
Columbus, OH 43229-1740
Tel: 614-888-4484
http://www.nremt.org

ENVIRONMENTAL ENGINEERS

OVERVIEW

Environmental engineers design, build, and maintain systems to control waste streams produced by municipalities or private industry. Such waste streams may be wastewater, solid waste, hazardous waste, or contaminated emissions to the atmosphere (air pollution). Environmental engineers typically are employed by the Environmental Protection Agency (EPA), by private industry, or by engineering consulting firms. There are about 54,000 environmental engineers employed in the United States.

THE JOB

There is a small pond in Crawford County, Illinois, which provides the habitat and primary food source for several different species of fish, frogs, turtles, insects, and birds, as well as small mammals. About a half-mile away is the Jack J. Ryan and Sons Manufacturing Company. For years, this plant has safely treated its wastewater—produced during the manufacturing process—and discharged it into the pond. Then one day, without warning, hundreds of dead fish wash up on the banks of the pond. What's going on? What should be done? It is the job of environmental engineers to investigate and design a system to make the water safe for the flora and fauna that depend on it for survival.

Environmental engineers who work for the federal or state Environmental Protection Agency (EPA) act as police officers or detectives. They investigate problems stemming from systems that aren't functioning properly. They have knowledge about wastewater treatment systems and have the authority to enforce environmental regulations.

The Crawford County pond is in the jurisdiction of the Champaign regional office of the Illinois Environmental Protection Agency (IEPA). There are three divisions: air, land, and water. An environmental engineer in the water division would be alerted to the fish kill at the pond and head out to the site to investigate. The engineer takes photographs and samples of the water and makes notes to document the problem. He or she considers the possibilities: Is it a discharge problem from Jack J. Ryan and Sons? If so, was there an upset in the process? A spill? A flood? Could a storage tank be leaking? Or is the problem further upstream? The pond is connected to other waterways, so could some other discharger be responsible for killing the fish?

The engineer visits Jack J. Ryan and Sons to talk to the production manager and ask if the plant has been doing anything differently lately. The investigation might include a tour of the plant or an examination of its plans. It might also include questioning other manufacturers further upstream, to see if they are doing something new that's caused the fish kill.

Once the problem has been identified, the environmental engineer and the plant officials can work together on the solution. For example, the production manager

---

SCHOOL SUBJECTS
Mathematics, Physics

PERSONAL SKILLS
Leadership/Management, Technical/Scientific

MINIMUM EDUCATION LEVEL
Bachelor's Degree

CERTIFICATION OR LICENSING
Recommended

WORK ENVIRONMENT
Primarily Indoors, Primarily Multiple Locations

---

at Jack J. Ryan and Sons reports that they've changed something in the manufacturing process to produce a new kind of die-cast part. They didn't know they were doing something wrong. The EPA engineer informs the company they'll be fined $10,000, and a follow-up investigation will be conducted to make sure it has complied with regulations.

Jack J. Ryan and Sons may have its own environmental engineer on staff. This engineer's job is to help keep the company in compliance with federal and state regulations while balancing the economic concerns of the company. At one time, industries' environmental affairs positions were often filled by employees who also had other positions in the plant. Since the late 1980s, however, these positions are held by environmental experts, including scientists, engineers, lawyers, and communications professionals.

In the Crawford County pond scenario, a Ryan and Sons environmental expert might get a call from an engineer at the IEPA: "There seems to be a fish kill at the pond near your plant. We've determined it's probably from a discharge from your plant." The Ryan and Sons expert looks at the plant's plans, talks to the production manager, and figures out a plan of action to bring the company into compliance.

Some companies rely on environmental engineering consulting firms instead of keeping an engineer on staff. Consulting firms usually provide teams that visit the plant, assess the problem, and design a system to get the plant back into compliance. Consulting firms not only know the technical aspects of waste control, but also have expertise in dealing with the government—filling out the required government forms, for example.

Broadly speaking, environmental engineers may focus on one of three areas: air, land, or water. Those who are concerned with air work on air pollution control, air quality management, and other specialties involved in systems to treat emissions. The private sector tends to have the majority of these jobs. Environmental engineers focused on land include landfill professionals, for whom environmental engineering and public health are key areas. Engineers focused on water work on activities similar to those described above.

A big area for environmental engineers is hazardous waste management. Expertise in designing systems and processes to reduce, recycle, and treat hazardous waste streams is very much in demand. This area tends to be the most technical of all the environmental fields and so demands more professionals with graduate and technical degrees.

Environmental engineers spend a lot of time on paperwork—including writing reports and memos and filling out forms. They also might climb a smokestack, wade in a creek, or go toe-to-toe with a district attorney in a battle over a compliance matter. If they work on company staffs, they may face frustration over not knowing what is going on in their own plants. If they work for the government, they might struggle with bureaucracy. If they work for a consultant, they may have to juggle the needs of the client (including the need to keep costs down) with the demands of the government.

REQUIREMENTS
High School

A bachelor's degree is mandatory to work in environmental engineering. At the high school level, the most important course work is in science and mathematics. It's also good to develop written communication skills. Competition to get into the top engineering schools is tough, so it's important to do well on your ACT or SAT tests.

Postsecondary Training

More than 55 colleges offer environmental degree programs that are accredited by the Accreditation Board for Engineering and Technology (http://www.abet.org). Another possibility is to earn a civil engineering, mechanical engineering, industrial engineering, or other traditional engineering degree with an environmental focus. You could also obtain a traditional engineering degree and learn the environmental knowledge on the job, or obtain a master's degree in environmental engineering.

Certification or Licensing

If your work as an engineer affects public health, safety, or property, you must register with the state. To obtain registration, you must have a degree from an accredited engineering program. Right before you get your degree (or soon after), you must pass an engineer-in-training (EIT) exam covering fundamentals of science and engineering. A few years after you've started your career, you also must pass an exam covering engineering practice. Additional certification is voluntary and may be obtained through such organizations as the American Academy of Environmental Engineers.

Other Requirements

Environmental engineers must like solving problems and have a good background in science and math. They must be able to, in the words of one engineer, "just get in there and figure out what needs to be done." Engineers must be able to communicate verbally and in writing with a variety of people from both technical and nontechnical backgrounds.

EXPLORING

A good way to explore becoming an environmental engineer is to talk to someone in the field. Contact your local EPA office, check the Yellow Pages for environmental consulting firms in your area, or ask a local industrial company if you can visit. The latter is not as far-fetched as you might think: Big industry has learned the value of earning positive community relations, and their outreach efforts may include having an open house for their neighbors in which one can walk through their plants, ask questions, and get a feel for what goes on there.

You cannot practice at being an environmental engineer without having a bachelor's degree. However, you can put yourself in situations in which you're around environmental engineers to see what they do and how they work. To do so, you may volunteer for the local chapter of a nonprofit environmental organization, do an internship with an environmental organization, or work first as an environmental technician, a job that requires less education (such as a two-year associate's degree or even a high school diploma).

Another good way to get exposure to environmental engineering is to familiarize yourself with professional journals. Two journals that may be available in your library include *Chemical & Engineering News,* which regularly features articles on waste management systems, and *Environmental Engineer* and *Pollution Engineering,* which features articles of interest to environmental engineers.

EMPLOYERS

Approximately 54,000 environmental engineers are employed in the United States. Environmental engineers most often work for the Environmental Protection Agency, in private industry, or at engineering consulting firms.

STARTING OUT

The traditional method of entering this field is by obtaining a bachelor's degree and applying directly to companies or to the EPA. School career services offices can assist you in these efforts.

ADVANCEMENT

After environmental engineers have gained work experience, there are several routes for advancement. Those working for the EPA can become a department supervisor or switch to private industry or consulting. In-house environmental staff members may rise to supervisory positions. Engineers with consulting firms may become project managers or specialists in certain areas.

Environmental careers are evolving at a breakneck speed. New specialties are emerging all the time. Advancement may take the form of getting involved at the beginning stages of a new subspecialty that suits an engineer's particular interests, experience, and expertise.

EARNINGS

The U.S. Department of Labor reports that median annual earnings of environmental engineers were $69,940 in 2006. Salaries ranged from less than $43,180 for the lowest paid 10 percent to more than $106,230 for the highest paid 10 percent. According to a 2007 salary survey by the National Association of Colleges and Employers, bachelor's degree candidates in environmental/environmental health received starting offers averaging $47,960 a year.

According to the American Academy of Environmental Engineers, engineers with a bachelor of science degree were receiving starting salaries ranging from $36,000 to $42,000 with some as much as $48,000 in the late 1990s. Those with a master's degree earned $40,000 to $45,000 and those with a Ph.D. earned $42,000 to $50,000. Licensed engineers with five years of experience can expect to earn from $50,000 to $60,000.

Fringe benefits vary widely depending on the employer. State EPA jobs may include, for example, two weeks of vacation, health insurance, tuition reimbursement, use of company vehicles for work, and similar perks. In-house or consulting positions may add additional benefits to lure top candidates.

WORK ENVIRONMENT

Environmental engineers split their time between working in an office and working out in the field. They may also spend time in courtrooms. Since ongoing education is crucial in most of these positions, engineers must attend training sessions and workshops and study new regulations, techniques, and problems. They usually work as part of a team that may include any of a number of different specialists. Engineers must also give presentations of technical information to those with both technical and nontechnical backgrounds.

OUTLOOK

The *Occupational Outlook Handbook* projects that employment for environmental engineers will grow much faster than the average for all occupations through 2016. Engineers will be needed to clean up existing hazards and help companies comply with government regulations. The shift toward prevention of problems and protecting public health should create job opportunities.

Jobs are available with all three major employers—the EPA, industry, and consulting firms. The EPA has long been a big employer of environmental engineers.

FOR MORE INFORMATION

For information on certification, careers, and salaries or a copy of Environmental Engineering Selection Guide *(which gives names of accredited environmental engineering programs and of professors who have board certification as environmental engineers), contact*

American Academy of Environmental Engineers
130 Holiday Court, Suite 100
Annapolis, MD 21401-7003
Tel: 410-266-3311
Email: info@aaee.net
http://www.aaee.net

For career guidance information contact
Junior Engineering Technical Society
1420 King Street, Suite 405
Alexandria, VA 22314-2794

Tel: 703-548-5387

Email: info@jets.org

http://www.jets.org

The following is a cross-disciplinary environmental association:

National Association of Environmental Professionals

PO Box 2086

Bowie, MD 20718-2086

Tel: 888-251-9902

http://www.naep.org

For information about the private waste services industry, contact

National Solid Wastes Management Association

4301 Connecticut Avenue, NW, Suite 300

Washington, DC 20008-2304

Tel: 202-244-4700

http://www.nswma.org

Contact the SCA for information about internships for high school students.

Student Conservation Association (SCA)

689 River Road

PO Box 550

Charlestown, NH 03603-0550

Tel: 603-543-1700

http://www.sca-inc.org

☐ ENVIRONMENTAL TECHNICIANS

. . . .

OVERVIEW

Environmental technicians, also known as *pollution control technicians*, conduct tests and field investigations to obtain soil samples and other data. Their research is used by engineers, scientists, and others who help clean up, monitor, control, or prevent pollution. An environmental technician usually specializes in air, water, or soil pollution. Although work differs by employer and specialty, technicians generally collect samples for laboratory analysis with specialized instruments and equipment; monitor pollution control devices and systems, such as smokestack air "scrubbers"; and perform various other tests and investigations to evaluate pollution problems. They follow strict procedures in collecting and recording data in order to meet the requirements of environmental laws.

In general, environmental technicians do not operate the equipment and systems designed to prevent pollution or remove pollutants. Instead, they test environmental conditions. In addition, some analyze and report on their findings.

There are approximately 37,000 environmental science and protection technicians, including health technicians, in the United States.

THE JOB

Environmental technicians usually specialize in one aspect of pollution control, such as water pollution, air pollution, or soil pollution. Sampling, monitoring, and testing are the major activities of the job. No matter what the specialty, environmental technicians work largely for or with government agencies that regulate pollution by industry.

Increasingly, technicians input their data into computers. Instruments used to collect water samples or monitor water sources may be highly sophisticated electronic devices. Technicians usually do not analyze the data they collect. However, they may report on what they know to scientists or engineers, either verbally or in writing.

Water pollution technicians monitor both industrial and residential discharge, such as from wastewater treatment plants. They help to determine the presence and extent of pollutants in water. They collect samples from lakes, streams, rivers, groundwater (the water under the earth), industrial or municipal wastewater, or other sources. Samples are brought to labs, where chemical and other tests are performed. If the samples contain harmful substances, remedial (cleanup) actions will need to be taken. These technicians also may perform various field tests, such as checking the pH, oxygen, and nitrate level of surface waters.

Some water pollution technicians set up monitoring equipment to obtain information on water flow, movement, temperature, or pressure and record readings from these devices. To trace flow patterns, they may inject dyes into the water.

Technicians have to be careful not to contaminate their samples, stray from the specific testing procedure, or otherwise do something to ruin the sample or cause faulty or misleading results.

Depending on the specific job, water pollution technicians may spend a good part of their time outdoors, in good weather and bad, aboard boats, and sometimes near unpleasant smells or potentially hazardous substances. Field sites may be in remote areas. In some cases, the technician may have to fly to a different part of the country, perhaps staying away from home for a long period of time.

Water pollution technicians play a big role in industrial wastewater discharge monitoring, treatment, and control. Nearly every manufacturing process produces wastewater, but U.S. manufacturers today are required to be more careful about what they discharge with their wastewater.

Some technicians specialize in groundwater, ocean water, or other types of natural waters. *Estuarine resource technicians,* for example, specialize in estuary waters, or coastal areas where fresh water and salt water come together. These bays, salt marshes, inlets, and other tidal water bodies support a wide variety of plant and animal life with ecologically complex relationships. They are vulnerable to destructive pollution from adjoining industries, cities and towns, and other sources. Estuarine resource technicians aid scientists in studying the resulting environmental changes. They may work in laboratories or aboard boats, or may use diving gear to collect samples directly.

Air pollution technicians collect and test air samples (for example, from chimneys of industrial manufacturing plants), record data on atmospheric conditions (such as determining levels of airborne substances from auto or industrial emissions), and supply data to scientists and engineers for further testing and analysis. In labs, air pollution technicians may help test air samples or re-create contaminants. They may use atomic absorption spectrophotometers, flame photometers, gas chromatographs, and other instruments for analyzing samples.

In the field, air pollution technicians may use rooftop sampling devices or operate mobile monitoring units or stationary trailers. The trailers may be equipped with elaborate automatic testing systems, including some of the same devices found in laboratories. Outside air is pumped into various chambers in the trailer where it is analyzed for the presence of pollutants. The results can be recorded by machine on 30-day rolls of graph paper or fed into a computer at regular intervals. Technicians set up and maintain the sampling devices, replenish the chemicals used in tests, replace worn parts, calibrate instruments, and record results. Some air pollution technicians specialize in certain pollutants or pollution sources. For example, *engine emission technicians* focus on exhaust from internal combustion engines.

Soil or *land pollution technicians* collect soil, silt, or mud samples and check them for contamination. Soil can become contaminated when polluted water seeps into the earth, such as when liquid waste leaks from a

SCHOOL SUBJECTS
Biology, Chemistry

PERSONAL SKILLS
Mechanical/Manipulative, Technical/Scientific

MINIMUM EDUCATION LEVEL
Some Postsecondary Training

CERTIFICATION OR LICENSING
Required for Certain Positions

WORK ENVIRONMENT
Indoors and Outdoors, One Location with Some Travel

landfill or other source into surrounding ground. Soil pollution technicians work for federal, state, and local government agencies, for private consulting firms, and elsewhere. (Some soil conservation technicians perform pollution control work.)

A position sometimes grouped with other environmental technicians is that of *noise pollution technician.* Noise pollution technicians use rooftop devices and mobile units to take readings and collect data on noise levels of factories, highways, airports, and other locations in order to determine noise exposure levels for workers or the public. Some test noise levels of construction equipment, chain saws, snow blowers, lawn mowers, or other equipment.

REQUIREMENTS
High School

In high school, key courses include biology, chemistry, and physics. Conservation or ecology courses also will be useful, if offered at your school. Math classes should include at least algebra and geometry, and taking English and speech classes will help to sharpen your communications skills. In addition, work on developing your computer skills while in high school, either on your own or through a class.

Postsecondary Training

Some technician positions call for a high school diploma plus employer training. As environmental work becomes more technical and complex, more positions are being filled by technicians with at least an associate's degree. To meet this need, many community colleges across the country have developed appropriate programs for environmental technicians. Areas of study include environmental engineering technologies, pollution control technologies, conservation, and ecology. Courses include meteorology, toxicology, source testing, sampling, and analysis, air quality management, environmental science, and statistics. Other training requirements vary by employer. Some experts advise attending school in the part of the country where you'd like to begin your career so you can start getting to know local employers before you graduate.

Certification or Licensing

Certification or licensing is required for some positions in pollution control, especially those in which sanitation, public health, a public water supply, or a sewage treatment system is involved. For example, the Institute of Professional Environmental Practice offers the qualified environmental professional and the environmental professional intern certifications. See the end of this article for contact information.

Other Requirements

Environmental technicians should be curious, patient, detail-oriented, and capable of following instructions. Basic manual skills are a must for collecting samples and performing similar tasks. Complex environmental regulations drive technicians' jobs; therefore, it's crucial that they are able to read and understand technical materials and to carefully follow any written guidelines for sampling or other procedures. Computer skills and the ability to read and interpret maps, charts, and diagrams are also necessary.

Technicians must make accurate and objective observations, maintain clear and complete records, and be exact in their computations. In addition, good physical conditioning is a requirement for some activities, for example, climbing up smokestacks to take emission samples.

EXPLORING

To learn more about environmental jobs, visit your local library and read some technical and general-interest publications in environmental science. This might give you an idea of the technologies being used and issues being discussed in the field today. You also can visit a municipal health department or pollution control agency in your community. Many agencies are pleased to explain their work to visitors.

School science clubs, local community groups, and naturalist clubs may help broaden your understanding of various aspects of the natural world and give you some experience. Most schools have recycling programs that enlist student help.

With the help of a teacher or career counselor, a tour of a local manufacturing plant using an air- or water-pollution abatement system also might be arranged. Many plants offer tours of their operations to the public. This may provide an excellent opportunity to see technicians at work.

As a high school student, it may be difficult to obtain summer or part-time work as a technician due to the extensive operations and safety training required for some of these jobs. However, it is worthwhile to check with a local environmental agency, nonprofit environmental organizations, or private consulting firms to learn of volunteer or paid support opportunities. Any hands-on experience you can get will be of value to a future employer.

EMPLOYERS

Approximately 37,000 environmental science and protection technicians are employed in the United States. Many jobs for environmental technicians are with the government agencies that monitor the environment, such as the Environmental Protection Agency (EPA), and the Departments of Agriculture, Energy, and Interior.

Water pollution technicians may be employed by manufacturers that produce wastewater, municipal wastewater treatment facilities, private firms hired to monitor or control pollutants in water or wastewater, and government regulatory agencies responsible for protecting water quality.

Air pollution technicians work for government agencies such as regional EPA offices. They also work for private manufacturers producing airborne pollutants, research facilities, pollution control equipment manufacturers, and other employers.

Soil pollution technicians may work for federal or state departments of agriculture and EPA offices. They also work for private agricultural groups that monitor soil quality for pesticide levels.

Noise pollution technicians are employed by private companies and by government agencies such as OSHA (Occupational Safety and Health Administration).

STARTING OUT

Graduates of two-year environmental programs are often employed during their final term by recruiters who visit their schools. Specific opportunities will vary depending on the part of the country, the segment of the environmental industry, the specialization of the technician (air, water, or land), the economy, and other factors. Many beginning technicians find the greatest number of positions available in state or local government agencies.

Most schools provide job-hunting advice and assistance. Direct application to state or local environmental agencies, employment agencies, or potential employers can also be a productive approach. If you hope to find employment outside your current geographic area, you may get good results by checking with professional organizations or by reading advertisements in technical journals, many of which have searchable job listings on the Internet.

ADVANCEMENT

The typical hierarchy for environmental work is technician (two years of postsecondary education or less), technologist (two years or more of postsecondary training), technician manager (perhaps a technician or technologist with many years of experience), and scientist or engineer (four-year bachelor of science degree or more, up to Ph.D. level).

In some private manufacturing or consulting firms, technician positions are used for training newly recruited professional staff. In such cases, workers with four-year degrees in engineering or physical science are likely to be promoted before those with two-year degrees. Employees of government agencies usually are organized under civil service systems that specify experience, education, and other criteria for advancement. Private industry promotions are structured differently and will depend on a variety of factors.

EARNINGS

Pay for environmental technicians varies widely depending on the nature of the work they do, training and experience required for the work, type of employer, geographic region, and other factors. Public-sector positions tend to pay less than private-sector positions.

Earnings of energy conservation technicians vary significantly based on the amount of formal training and experience. According to the U.S. Department of Labor, the average annual salary for environmental science and protection technicians was $38,090 in 2006. Salaries ranged from less than $23,600 to more than $60,700.

Technicians who worked for local government earned mean annual salaries of $43,050 in 2006; those who were employed by state government earned $43,810. Technicians who become managers or supervisors can earn $70,000 per year or more. Technicians who work in private industry or who further their education to secure teaching positions can also expect to earn higher than average salaries.

No matter which area they specialize in, environmental technicians generally enjoy fringe benefits such as paid vacation, holidays and sick time, and employer-paid training. Technicians who work full time (and some who work part-time) often receive health insurance benefits. Technicians who are employed by the federal government may get additional benefits, such as pension and retirement benefits.

WORK ENVIRONMENT

Conditions range from clean and pleasant indoor offices and laboratories to hot, cold, wet, bad-smelling, noisy, or even hazardous settings outdoors. Anyone planning a career in environmental technology should realize the possibility of exposure to unpleasant or unsafe conditions at least occasionally in his or her career. Employers often can minimize these negatives through special equipment and procedures. Most laboratories and manufacturing companies have safety procedures for potentially dangerous situations.

Some jobs involve vigorous physical activity, such as handling a small boat or climbing a tall ladder. For the most part, technicians need only to be prepared for moderate activity. Travel may be required; technicians go to urban, industrial, or rural settings for sampling.

Because their job can involve a considerable amount of repetitive work, patience and the ability to handle routine are important. Yet, particularly when environmental technicians are working in the field, they also have to be ready to use their resourcefulness and ingenuity to find the best ways of responding to new situations.

OUTLOOK

Demand for environmental technicians is expected to increase much faster than the average for all occupations through 2016, according to the U.S. Department of Labor. Those trained to handle increasingly complex technical demands will have the best employment prospects. Environmental technicians will be needed to collect soil, water, and air samples to measure the levels of pollutants; to monitor the private industry's compliance with environmental regulations; and to clean up contaminated sites. Most employment growth will occur in professional, scientific, and technical services.

Demand will be higher in some areas of the country than others depending on specialty; for example, air pollution technicians will be especially in demand in large cities, such as Los Angeles and New York, which face pressure to comply with national air quality standards. Amount of industrialization, stringency of state and local pollution control enforcement, health of local economy, and other factors also will affect demand by region and specialty. Perhaps the greatest factors affecting environmental work are continued mandates for pollution control by the federal government. As long as the federal government supports pollution control, environmental technicians will be needed.

FOR MORE INFORMATION

For job listings and certification information, contact
Air & Waste Management Association
420 Fort Duquesne Boulevard
One Gateway Center, Third Floor
Pittsburgh, PA 15222-1435
Tel: 412-232-3444
Email: info@awma.org
http://www.awma.org

For information on the engineering field and technician certification, contact
American Society of Certified Engineering Technicians
PO Box 1536
Brandon, MS 39043-1536
Tel: 601-824-8991
http://www.ascet.org

For information on environmental careers and student employment opportunities, contact
Environmental Protection Agency
Ariel Rios Building
1200 Pennsylvania Avenue, NW
Washington, DC 20460-0001
Tel: 202-260-2090
http://www.epa.gov

For information on certification, contact
Institute of Professional Environmental Practice
600 Forbes Avenue
339 Fisher Hall
Pittsburgh, PA 15282-0001
Email: ipep@duq.edu
http://www.ipep.org

For job listings and scholarship opportunities, contact
National Ground Water Association
601 Dempsey Road
Westerville, OH 43081-8978
Tel: 800-551-7379
Email: ngwa@ngwa.org
http://www.ngwa.org

For information on conferences and workshops, contact
Water Environment Federation
601 Wythe Street
Alexandria, VA 22314-1994
Tel: 800-666-0206
http://www.wef.org

EVENT PLANNERS

OVERVIEW

The duties of *event planners* are varied, and may include establishing a site for an event; making travel, hotel, and food arrangements; and planning the program and overseeing the registration. The planner may be responsible for negotiating, planning, and coordinating a major worldwide convention, or the planner may be involved with a small, in-house meeting involving only a few people. Some professional associations, government agencies, nonprofit organizations, political groups, and educational institutions hire event planners or have employees on staff who have these responsibilities. Many of these organizations and companies outsource their event planning responsibilities to firms that specialize in these services, such as marketing, public relations, and event planning firms. In addition, many event and meeting planners are independent consultants.

Some event planners' services are also used on a personal level to plan class or family reunions, birthday parties, weddings, or anniversaries. There are approximately 51,000 event planners employed in the United States.

THE JOB

Event planners have a variety of duties depending on their specific title and the firm they work for or the firms they work with. Generally, planners organize and plan an event such as a meeting, a special open house, a convention, or a specific celebration.

Meetings might consist of a small interdepartmental meeting, a board meeting, an all-employee meeting, an in-house training session, a stockholders' meeting, or a meeting with vendors or distributors. When planning for these events, meeting planners usually check the calendars of key executives to establish a meeting time that fits into their schedules. Planners reserve meeting rooms, training rooms, or outside facilities for the event. They visit outside sites to make sure they are appropriate for that specific event. Planners notify people of the time, place, and date of the event and set up registration procedures, if necessary. They arrange for food, room layout, audiovisual equipment, instructors, computers, sound equipment, and telephone equipment as required.

In some cases, a company may employ an in-house meeting planner who is responsible for small- to medium-sized events. When a large meeting, trade show, conference, open house, or convention is planned, the in-house event planner may contract with outside meeting planners to assist with specific responsibilities such as registration, catering, and display setup. Some companies have their own trade show or convention managers on staff.

Convention, trade show, or *conference managers* negotiate and communicate with other enterprises related to the convention or trade show industry such as hotel and catering sales staff, speaker's bureaus, and trade staff such as electricians or laborers who set up convention display areas. They may also be responsible for contracting the transportation of the equipment and supplies to and from the event site. The manager usually works with an established budget and negotiates fees with these enterprises and enters contracts with them. Additional contracts may also need to be negotiated with professionals to handle registration, marketing, and public relations for the event.

Managers and planners need to be aware of legal aspects of trade show set-ups such as fire code regulations, floor plan, and space limitations, and make sure they are within these guidelines. They often need to get these arrangements approved in writing. Good record keeping and communication skills are used daily. The convention manager may have staff to handle the sales, registration, marketing, logistics, or other specific aspects of the event, or these duties may be subcontracted to another firm.

Some convention planners are employed specifically by convention and visitors' bureaus, the tourism industry, or by exhibit halls or convention facilities. Their job responsibilities may be specific to one aspect of the show, or they may be required to do any or all of the above-mentioned duties. Some convention and trade show managers may work for the exposition center or

SCHOOL SUBJECTS
Business, English, Foreign Language

PERSONAL SKILLS
Communication/Ideas, Leadership/Management

MINIMUM EDUCATION LEVEL
Bachelor's Degree

CERTIFICATION OR LICENSING
Voluntary

WORK ENVIRONMENT
Primarily Indoors, One Location with Some Travel

association and be responsible for selling booth space at large events.

Special event coordinators are usually employed by large corporations who hold numerous special events or by firms who contract their special event planning services to companies, associations, or religious, political, or educational groups. A special event coordinator is responsible for planning, organizing, and implementing a special event such as an open house, an anniversary, the dedication of a new facility, a special promotion or sale, an ordination, a political rally, or a victory celebration. This coordinator works with the company or organization and determines the purpose of the special event, the type of celebration desired, the site, the budget, the attendees, the food and entertainment preferences, and the anticipated outcome. The special event planner then coordinates the vendors and equipment necessary to successfully hold this event. The coordinator works closely with the client at all times to ensure that the event is being planned as expected. Follow-up assessment of the event is usually part of the services offered by the special event coordinator.

Party planners are often employed by individuals, families, or small companies to help them plan a small party for a special occasion. Many party planners are independent contractors who work out of their homes or are employees of small firms. Party planners may help plan weddings, birthdays, christenings, bar or bat mitzvahs, anniversaries, or other events. They may be responsible for the entire event including the invitations, catering, decorating, entertainment, serving, and cleanup, or planners may simply perform one or two aspects such as contracting with a magician for a children's birthday party, recommending a menu, or greeting and serving guests.

REQUIREMENTS

High School

If you are interested in entering the field of event planning, you should take high school classes in business, English, and speech. Because many conferences and meetings are international in scope, you may also want to take foreign language and geography courses. In addition, computer science classes will be beneficial.

Postsecondary Training

Almost all coordinators and planners must have a four-year college degree to work for a company, corporation, convention, or travel center. Some institutions offer bachelor's degrees in meeting planning; however, degrees in business, English, communications, marketing, public relations, sales, or travel would also be a good fit for a career as a meetings manager, convention planner, or special event coordinator. Many directors and planners who become company heads have earned graduate degrees.

Some small firms, convention centers, or exhibit facilities may accept persons with associate's degrees or travel industry certification for certain planning positions. Party planners may not always need education beyond high school, but advancement opportunities will be more plentiful with additional education.

Certification or Licensing

There are some professional associations for planners that offer certification programs. For example, Meeting Professionals International offers the certification in meeting management designation. The International Association for Exhibition and Events offers the certified in exhibition management designation. The Convention Industry Council offers the certified meeting professional designation. The Society of Government Meeting Professionals offers the certified government meeting professional designation. (See "For More Information" at the end of this article for contact information.)

Other Requirements

To be an event planner, you must have excellent organizational skills, the ability to plan projects and events, and the ability to think creatively. You must be able to work well with people and anticipate their needs in advance. You should be willing to pitch in to get a job done even though it may not be part of your duties. In a situation where there is an unforeseen crisis, you need to react quickly and professionally. Planners should have good negotiating and communication skills and be assertive but tactful.

EXPLORING

High school guidance counselors can supply information on event planners or convention coordinators. Public and school librarians may also be able to provide useful books, magazines, and pamphlets. Searching the Internet for companies that provide event-planning services can give you an idea of the types of services that they offer. Professional associations related to the travel, convention, and meeting industries may have career information available to students. Some of these organizations are listed at the end of this article.

Attending local trade shows and conventions will provide insight into the operations of this industry. Also, some exhibit and convention halls may hire students to assist with various aspects of trade show operations. You can learn more about this profession by subscribing to magazines such as *Meetings & Conventions* (http://www. meetings-conventions.com).

Some party planners may hire assistants to help with children's birthday parties or other special events. Organize and plan a large family event, such as a birthday, anniversary, graduation, or retirement celebration. You will have to find a location, hire caterers or assign family members to bring specific food items, send invitations, purchase and arrange decorations, and organize entertainment, all according to what your budget allows.

You can also gain business experience through school activities. Join the business club, run for student council, or head up the prom committee to learn how to plan and carry out events.

EMPLOYERS

Approximately 51,000 event planners are employed in the United States. Many large corporations or institutions worldwide hire meeting managers, convention managers, or event planners to handle their specific activities. Although some companies may not have employees with the specific title of event planner or meeting manager, these skills are very marketable and these duties may be part of another job title. In many companies, these duties may be part of a position within the marketing, public relations, or corporate communications department.

Convention facilities, exhibit halls, training and educational institutions, travel companies, and health care facilities also hire event planners. Hotels often hire planners to handle meetings and events held within their facilities. Large associations usually maintain an event planning staff for one or more annual conventions or business meetings for their members.

Job opportunities are also available with companies that contract out event and meeting planning services. Many of these companies have positions that specialize in certain aspects of the planning service, such as travel coordinator, exhibit planner, facilities negotiator, or they have people who perform specific functions such as trade show display setup, registration, and follow-up reporting.

Planners interested in jobs with the convention and trade show industries or hotels may find that larger cities have more demand for planners and offer higher salaries.

Experienced meeting planners or convention managers may choose to establish their own businesses or independently contract out their services. Party planning may also be a good independent business venture.

STARTING OUT

An internship at a visitors and convention bureau, exhibit center, or with a travel agency or meeting planning company is a good way to meet and network with other people in this field. Attending trade shows might offer a chance to speak with people about the field and to discuss any contacts they might have.

Some colleges and universities may offer job placement for people seeking careers in meeting planning or in the convention and trade show industries. Professional associations related to these industries are also good contacts for someone starting out. Classified ads and trade magazines may also offer some job leads.

ADVANCEMENT

Advancement opportunities for people in the event planning field are good. Experienced planners can expect to move into positions of increased responsibility. They may become senior managers and executive directors of private businesses, hotels, convention facilities, exhibit halls, travel corporations, museums, or other facilities. They can advance within a corporation to a position with more responsibilities or they may go into the planning business for themselves. Planners who have established a good reputation in the industry are often recruited by other firms or facilities and can advance their careers with these opportunities.

EARNINGS

According to the U.S. Department of Labor, meeting and convention planners made a median annual salary of $42,180 in 2006. The lowest 10 percent earned less than $25,880, and the highest 10 percent earned more than $70,950.

Benefits may vary depending on the position and the employer but generally include vacation, sick leave, insurance, and other work-related benefits.

WORK ENVIRONMENT

Work environments vary with the planner's title and job responsibilities, but generally planners can expect to work in a business setting as part of a team. Usually, the planner's initial planning work is done in a clean environment with modern equipment prior to the opening of a convention or trade show. Working in convention and trade show environments, however, can be noisy, crowded, and distracting. In addition, the days can be long and may require standing for hours. If the planner is involved with supervising the setup or dismantling of a trade show or convention, the work can be dirty and physically demanding.

Although most facilities have crews that assist with setup, meeting planners occasionally get involved with last-minute changes and may need to do some physical lifting of equipment, tables, or chairs.

Event planners can usually expect to work erratic hours, often putting in long days prior to the event and the day the event is actually held. Travel is often part of the job requirements and may include working and/or traveling nights and on the weekends.

OUTLOOK

Job opportunities for event planners will continue to grow at a faster-than-average rate through 2016, according to the U.S. Department of Labor. The introduction of new technology enables more meetings to take place than ever before. Conventions, trade shows, meetings, and incentive travel support more than 1.5 million American jobs, according to the Professional Convention Management Association (PCMA). These events account for more than $80 billion in annual spending. Opportunities should be best for event planners employed by medical and pharmaceutical associations.

FOR MORE INFORMATION

For information on certification and event planning, contact the following organizations:

Convention Industry Council
1620 I Street, NW, 6th Floor

Washington, DC 20006-4005
Tel: 877-429-8634
http://www.conventionindustry.org

International Association for Exhibition and Events
PO Box 802425
Dallas, TX 75251-1313
Tel: 972-458-8002
http://www.iaem.org

Meeting Professionals International
3030 Lyndon B. Johnson Freeway, Suite 1700
Dallas, TX 75234-2759
Tel: 972-702-3000
Email: feedback@mpiweb.org
http://www.mpiweb.org

Society of Government Meeting Professionals
908 King Street, Lower Level
Alexandria, VA 22314-3047
Tel: 703-549-0892
http://www.sgmp.org

For information on careers in the field of event planning, contact the following organizations:

Professional Convention Management Association
2301 South Lake Shore Drive, Suite 1001
Chicago, IL 60616-1419
Tel: 877-827-7262
Email: administration@pcma.org
http://www.pcma.org

Society of Independent Show Organizers
7000 West Southwest Highway
Chicago Ridge, IL 60415
Tel: 877-YES-SISO
http://www.siso.org

FAST-FOOD WORKERS

OVERVIEW

Whether the restaurant's menu lists pizza, tacos, hamburgers, or fried chicken, a *fast-food worker* is responsible for serving each customer the correct order in an efficient, professional, and courteous manner. Fast-food workers may be employed by large chain restaurants or privately owned shops. Although most of these places serve only one kind of food, some establishments have a wide selection of dishes. In either type of restaurant, fast-food workers should be familiar with the menu, including prices, portion sizes, side dishes or condiments, and how the food is prepared.

THE JOB

Fast-food workers may have a variety of duties. Some fast-food establishments require employees to be familiar with all aspects of the restaurant: greeting and serving customers, cleanup and maintenance, and preparation of some of the simpler food items. Larger chain restaurants may institute this practice as a way of familiarizing the fast-food worker with the restaurant's needs as a whole, with the possibility of specialization later. Smaller restaurants, not having enough staff to allow specialization, may follow this pattern out of necessity.

Fast-food workers who are part of the kitchen staff may begin as assistants to the trained cooks. These assistants may help set up supplies, refill condiment containers, or do prep work such as slicing meats or vegetables. For the sake of sanitation as well as safety, these assistants also may be responsible for general cleanup duties in the kitchen area.

Kitchen staff employees who cook are responsible for preparing all food to meet the company's standards. In this regard, the food must be made consistently and neatly. *Cooks* must be agile and quick in their handling of food.

The *cashier* in a fast-food restaurant may be responsible for taking the customer's order, entering the order into the computer or cash register, taking payment, and returning proper change. In some fast-food establishments the cashier may act as *counter worker* and have additional tasks. These added duties can include filling the customer's order; selecting the various sandwiches, side orders, or beverages from those stations; and serving it to the customer on a tray or in a carryout container. It is often the cashier's duty to greet customers, welcoming them to the restaurant in a friendly and courteous way. Since these employees are responsible for interacting with customers, they are required to keep their immediate workstations clean and neat.

In addition to interacting with the customers, the counter worker must also be able to communicate effectively with the kitchen and managerial staff. The counter worker may have to tell the kitchen staff about a special order for a sandwich or shortages of certain food items. The counter worker may need to notify the manager about a problem with the register or a disgruntled customer. Since delays can take away from customer satisfaction and hurt the restaurant's business, the counter worker must be able to identify, communicate, and solve problems quickly.

Good fast-food employees develop professional attitudes and marketable work skills. They learn to work under pressure and to meet the work standards that their managers expect. A fast-food worker also learns tangible skills, such as working a cash register, cooking, and communicating. In the different areas of fast-food work, employees must be able to keep up the pace, show personal motivation, and be willing to work as part of a team.

Unlike some other types of work, however, the fast-food business is a no-nonsense job. A cashier or counter worker may handle hundreds of dollars a day. Cooks work over fryers and grills and handle knives and meat slicers. The work requires concentration and a professional attitude.

REQUIREMENTS

High School

If you are working a part-time job and are still in high school, you may find that courses such as home economics, advanced cooking, or health and sanitation may be helpful. As a fast-food worker making your way up the ranks of a restaurant, you may decide to pursue special training or education.

Postsecondary Training

If a fast-food employee is already working full-time at a large franchise and is interested in pursuing management training, there are many outlets for career preparation. Many franchises have their own training programs for future managers and franchise owners. McDonald's, Dunkin' Donuts, and Burger King all offer serious course work in such areas as maintaining restaurant equipment; hiring, training, and motivating employees; and purchasing supplies. Most other chain franchises offer employee instruction as well, so that the product and image of their restaurants are kept consistent and so that they may offer new franchise owners assistance in getting started in the business.

Other Requirements

For an entry-level position at a fast-food restaurant, you should be motivated, cheerful, and cooperative. The fast-food business requires a quick pace, especially during the breakfast and lunch rush periods. A motivated employee

SCHOOL SUBJECTS
Business, Family and Consumer Science

PERSONAL SKILLS
Following Instructions, Helping/Teaching

MINIMUM EDUCATION LEVEL
High School Diploma

CERTIFICATION OR LICENSING
None Available

WORK ENVIRONMENT
Indoors and Outdoors, Primarily One Location

is willing to work extra hard and offer help to a fellow employee during these times. When the restaurant is busy, paying close attention and thinking quickly are as necessary in accepting money and counting back change as they are in the handling of food.

You should be neat in appearance as well as have good work habits. Some fast-food restaurants require that their employees wear uniforms or follow a dress code. They also may dictate specific rules of behavior. Because such guidelines are important for both safety reasons and the atmosphere of the restaurant, employees must respect and follow them. Failure to do so may result in the employee being sent home or having his or her pay reduced. The good qualities and work habits that are found in reliable fast-food workers reflect the professional attitude that managers and franchise owners strive for in their restaurants.

EXPLORING

Course work in home economics and other classes that develop cooking skills can provide good preparation for the job of a fast-food worker. In addition, general business or management courses provide a solid basis for entry-level workers. Students should also look into opportunities for working in the school cafeteria or other food service area. Neighborhood restaurants and local hot dog or hamburger stands may also hire summer help.

Certain high schools offer cooperative work-study programs to students to assist them in gaining job experience. Such programs may offer concentrations in the food service industry or host lectures from community members already involved in the field.

EMPLOYERS

Fast-food workers may be employed by large chain restaurants or privately owned shops.

STARTING OUT

At some fast-food restaurants, more than 50 percent of the positions are for part-time employees. These restaurants rely heavily on their part-timers and are accustomed to planning their work schedules accordingly. Applying at restaurants that hire part-time or student help is a good way to enter this field. Even at smaller, privately owned establishments, the fast-food worker will be introduced to some of the common factors of the industry: working with and for a variety of people, keeping up a quick pace, and cooking, packaging, and serving food in a friendly way.

Local papers often advertise for help in neighborhood restaurants, and some fast-food establishments contact school counseling departments to post job openings. However, the majority of positions are available to those who walk in and fill out an application. Since entry-level positions open up and are filled quickly, applicants are advised to contact restaurants regularly if no openings are immediately available.

ADVANCEMENT

Because of the diversity in the restaurant business, there is ample opportunity for workers to find an area of interest or specialization. Fast-food workers may take advantage of manager-trainee opportunities or tuition assistance to move higher up within the company. Some fast-food workers use their experience to go on to other areas of food service, such as waiting tables or working as a restaurant host or manager. Others may decide to go to a vocational cooking school or pursue hotel and restaurant management careers.

EARNINGS

Like other entry-level workers with part-time jobs, fast-food workers can expect to begin at the minimum hourly wage: $5.85. If they work full time, this is a salary of $12,168 a year. Top fast-food cooks earned $9.99 an hour ($20,770 annually for full-time work) in 2006, according to the U.S. Department of Labor. The median hourly salary for fast-food cooks was $7.41 (full-time work at this rate is $15,410 a year) in 2006. Full-time food preparation workers (including fast-food workers) earned average hourly salaries of $7.24 per week (full-time work at this rate earns $15,050 a year) in 2006. The highest paid 10 percent of food preparation workers earned more than $10.16 per hour ($21,130 or

more a year full time), while the lowest paid 10 percent of food preparation workers earned $5.79 or less per hour ($12,050 or less a year full time).

Larger restaurant franchises often offer annual raises and bonuses. Restaurants that have late evening or all-night hours may compensate employees working those shifts with higher hourly wages. Sometimes employees earn additional compensation or time-and-a-half for working overtime or on holidays. Some restaurants and individually owned franchises offer bonuses for tuition assistance, as well as periodic bonuses.

WORK ENVIRONMENT

Fast-food restaurants need to meet the safety and sanitary standards enforced by local and state health departments. These agencies require an establishment to have proper lighting and adequate heating, cooling, and ventilation systems so employees can work in a comfortable environment.

Large fast-food franchises are often decorated pleasantly, incorporating the logo, color schemes, or trademark characters of their parent companies. They supply adequate and comfortable seating facilities, which are maintained according to corporate standards.

Fast-food employees may work shifts of five to nine hours and receive appropriate coffee and lunch breaks. These establishments often have private rooms, separated from the main dining rooms, for employees to eat lunches and relax.

Fast-food workers may have regular work hours (mornings only, for example) or floating schedules that require them to work a combination of evenings, afternoons, and weekends. Fast-food workers may be called in by their managers to work an extra shift or work overtime if another employee is ill or if the restaurant is very busy. Fast-food workers should be fairly flexible because their managers have no way to determine in advance how busy or understaffed the restaurant will be.

OUTLOOK

Employment for fast-food workers should increase faster than the average for all occupations through 2016, according to the U.S. Department of Labor. Americans are constantly on the move and will continue to eat at fast-food restaurants to save time and money. Job opportunities for all types of food and beverage workers are expected to be plentiful for the next decade or more. In fact, this career will offer among the largest number of job openings during this time period. Most openings will result from a need to replace workers who have left the field for other professions.

Entry-level jobs are not difficult to come by. Submitting an application and keeping in touch with managers for openings can lead to the beginning of a successful career in the fast-food industry. Owning a franchise is a popular business venture, but one that demands the recruitment and promotion of reliable, capable staff. Knowledge of the business from the bottom up is a definite advantage for franchise owners.

FOR MORE INFORMATION

Visit this association's Web site for information on the restaurant industry (including fast-food establishments), food safety, and government regulations.

National Restaurant Association
1200 17th Street, NW
Washington, DC 20036-3006
Tel: 800-424-5156
http://www.restaurant.org

This trade association offers information on food service employee requirements and training.

National Restaurant Association Educational Foundation
175 West Jackson Boulevard, Suite 1500
Chicago, IL 60604-2814
Tel: 800-765-2122
Email: info@restaurant.org
http://www.nraef.org

☐ FINANCIAL ANALYSTS

OVERVIEW

Financial analysts analyze the financial situation of companies and recommend ways for these companies to manage, spend, and invest their money. The goal of financial analysts is to help their employer or clients make informed, lucrative financial decisions. They assemble and evaluate the company's financial data and assess investment opportunities. They look at the company's financial history, the direction that company wants to take in the future, the company's place in the industry, and current and projected economic conditions. Financial analysts also conduct similar research on companies that might become investment opportunities. They write reports and compile spreadsheets that show the benefits of certain investments or selling certain securities.

SCHOOL SUBJECTS
Business, Computer Science, Mathematics

PERSONAL SKILLS
Communication/Ideas, Leadership/Management

MINIMUM EDUCATION LEVEL
Bachelor's Degree

CERTIFICATION OR LICENSING
Recommended

WORK ENVIRONMENT
Primarily Indoors, Primarily One Location

Among the businesses employing financial analysts are banks, brokerage firms, government agencies, mutual funds, and insurance and investment companies. There are approximately 221,000 financial analysts employed in the United States.

THE JOB

Financial analysts are sometimes called *investment analysts* or *security analysts*. The specific types, direction, and scope of analyses performed by financial analysts are many and varied, depending on the industry, the employer or client, and the analyst's training and years of experience. Financial analysts study their employer's or client's financial status and make financial and investment recommendations. To arrive at these recommendations, financial analysts examine the employer's or client's financial history and objectives, income and expenditures, risk tolerance, and current investments. Once they understand the employer's or client's financial standing and investment goals, financial analysts scout out potential investment opportunities. They research other companies, perhaps in a single industry, that their employer or client may want to invest in. This in-depth research consists of investigating the business of each company, including history, past and potential earnings, and products. Based on their findings, financial analysts may recommend that their employer or client buy stock in these companies. If the employer or client already holds stock in a particular company, financial analysts' research may indicate that stocks should be held or sold, or that more should be purchased.

Financial analysts work for companies in any number of industries, including banking, transportation, health care, technology, telecommunications, and energy. While investment options and concerns differ among these, financial analysts still apply the same basic analytic tools in devising investment strategies. They try to learn everything they can about the industry they are working in. They study the markets and make industry comparisons. They also research past performance and future trends of bonds and other investments.

Financial analysts compile many types of reports on their employer or client and on investment opportunities, such as profit-and-loss statements and quarterly outlook statements. They help to develop budgets, analyze and oversee cash flow, and perform cost-benefit analyses. They conduct risk analyses to determine what the employer or client can risk at a given time and/or in future. Another responsibility is to ensure that their employer or client meets any relevant tax or regulatory requirements. Financial analysts compile their work using various software programs, often developing financial models, such as charts or graphs, to display their data.

Companies that want to go public (sell company shares to individual investors for the first time) often ask financial analysts to make projections of future earnings as well as presentations for potential investors. Financial analysts also make sure that all paperwork is in order and compliant with Securities and Exchange Commission rules and regulations.

Entry-level financial analysts, usually working under direct supervision, mainly conduct research and compile statistical data. After a few years of experience, they become more involved in presenting reports. While a financial analyst generally offers recommendations, a senior financial analyst often has the authority to actually decide purchases or sales. Senior financial analysts implement a company's business plan. In larger companies, they also assist different departments in conducting their own financial analyses and business planning. Those in senior positions become supervisors as well, training junior financial analysts.

Many specialties fall under the job title of financial analyst. These specialties vary from employer to employer, and duties overlap between different types of analysts. In smaller firms a financial analyst may have extensive responsibility, while at larger firms a financial analyst may specialize in one of any number of areas. *Budget analysts,* often *accountants* or *controllers,* look at the operating costs of a company or its individual departments and prepare budget reports. *Credit analysts* examine credit records to determine the potential risk in extending credit or lending money. *Investment analysts* evaluate investment data so they can make suitable investment recommendations. *Mergers and acquisitions analysts* conduct research and make recommendations relating to company mergers and acquisitions. *Money market analysts* assess financial data and investment opportunities, giving advice specifically in the area of money markets. *Ratings analysts* explore a company's financial situation to determine whether or not it will be able to repay debts. *Risk analysts* focus on evaluating the risks of investments. The intent is to identify and then minimize a company's risks and losses. *Security analysts* specialize in studying securities, such as stocks and bonds. *Tax analysts* prepare, file, and examine federal, state, and local tax payments and returns for their employer or client and perhaps also for local affiliates. They analyze tax issues and keep up with tax law changes. *Treasury analysts* manage their company's or client's daily cash position, prepare cash journal entries, initiate wire transfers, and perform bank reconciliations.

Analysts are considered either *buy-side analysts,* who usually work for money management firms, or *sell-side analysts,* sometimes called *sales analysts* or *Wall Street analysts,* who usually work for brokerage firms.

Personal financial advisers have many similar responsibilities (assessing finances, projecting income, recommending investments), but these are performed on behalf of individuals rather than companies.

REQUIREMENTS
High School

Since financial analysts work with numbers and compile data, you should take as many math classes as are available. Accounting, business, economics, and computer classes will be helpful as well. A good grasp of computer spreadsheet programs such as Excel is vital. Take extra care as you research and write reports in any subject matter or in public speaking, and it will pay off later when you must conduct investment research and write and present investment recommendations.

Postsecondary Training

Most employers require that financial analysts hold a bachelor's degree in accounting, business administration, economics, finance, or statistics. Other possible majors include communications, international business, and public administration. Some companies will hire you if you hold a bachelor's degree in another discipline as long as you can demonstrate mathematical ability. In college, take business, economics, and statistics courses. Since computer technology plays such a big role in a financial analyst's work, computer classes can be helpful as well. English composition classes can prepare you for the writing you will need to do when preparing reports. Some employers require a writing sample prior to an interview.

Financial analysts generally continue to take courses to keep up with the ongoing changes in the world of finance, including international trade, state and federal laws and regulations, and computer technology. Proficiency in certain databases, presentation graphics, spreadsheets, and other software is expected. Some employers require their employees to have a master's degree.

Many top firms offer summer internship programs. Check company Web sites for the particulars, such as assignments and qualifications. An internship can provide you with helpful contacts and increase your chances of landing a job when you finish with college.

Certification or Licensing

Financial analysts can earn the title chartered financial analyst (CFA). While certification is not required, it is recommended. The CFA program, which is administered by the CFA Institute, consists of three levels of examinations. These rigorous exams deal with such topics as economics, financial statement analysis, corporate finance, and portfolio management. The CFA Institute states that a candidate may need to spend at least 250 hours studying to prepare for each level. The Motley Fool, a financial education company (http://www.fool.com), reported that about 50 percent of the candidates fail the first level. A candidate can take only one level per year, so a minimum of three years is required to become a CFA charterholder. If a candidate fails a level, it can be taken the next year. Candidates who do not successfully complete all three levels within seven years must reregister.

Before taking the exams, you must already have a bachelor's degree (or four years of professional experience). There is no required course of study. Prior to earning the CFA charter, you must have spent three years in a related field working in the investment decision-making process and you must first apply to become a member of the CFA Institute as well as a local society.

The CFA charter is recognized around the world as a standard in the finance industry. Many employers expect job seekers to be CFA charterholders.

For certain upper-level positions, some firms require that you have a certified public accountant license.

Other Requirements

Research, organizational, and communication skills are crucial for this job. Financial analysts conduct in-depth research, often looking for hard-to-find data. Organizational skills are important when it comes to compiling and presenting this data. Once you have explored a company's financial situation, you must communicate complicated ideas through presentations and/or written reports. You should be able to clearly communicate ideas, both verbally when making presentations and on paper when writing reports.

The work requires strong analytic skills, so a knack for numbers and attention to detail are also helpful. An interest in solving problems will go a long way. It is important that a financial analyst be accurate and thorough in preparing financial statements.

You should enjoy reading and be able to retain what you read, since it is important to keep up with what's happening in the industry and take it into account when offering financial solutions to employers or clients. Since many financial analysts must travel at a moment's notice to conduct research or complete a deal, flexibility is another important characteristic.

Financial analysts should be able to work well under pressure, as this line of work often demands long hours and entails strict deadlines. You should have good interpersonal skills and enjoy interacting with others. Deals or important contacts can be made at social functions or business conferences.

EXPLORING

There are many sources of information dealing with the financial services industry. Read publications such as *Barron's* (http://www.barrons.com), *Wall Street Journal* (http://www.wsj.com), *Forbes* (http://www.forbes.com), *BusinessWeek* (http://www.businessweek.com), *Fortune* (http://www.fortune.com), and *Financial Times* (http://www.ft.com). In either the print or online versions, you will find a wealth of information on stocks, mutual funds, finance, education, careers, salaries, global business, and more. You can also use these resources to conduct company research. You might have to become a subscriber to access certain sections online.

AnalystForum (http://www.analystforum.com) is a resource for chartered financial analysts and CFA candidates. While this site won't be of much use to you until you've launched your career, you can find links to financial, investment, and security analyst society sites. From within these societies, you can perhaps track down a professional who would be willing to do an information interview with you.

While in high school, you might volunteer to handle the bookkeeping for a school club or student government, or help balance the family checking account to become familiar with simple bookkeeping practices. Your school may have an investment club you can join. If not, ask a parent or teacher to help you research and analyze investment opportunities. Choose a specific industry (e.g., telecommunications, technology, or health care), study companies in that industry, and select and track several stocks that appear to have growth potential.

EMPLOYERS

Financial analysts work in the public and private sectors. Employers include banks, brokerage and securities firms, corporations, government agencies, manufacturers, mutual and pension funds, and financial management, insurance, investment, trust, and utility companies. Many financial analysts are self-employed.

According to the *Occupational Outlook Handbook*, more than 40 percent of financial analysts work for security and commodity brokers, banks and credit institutions, and insurance carriers. The rest work mainly for insurance carriers, computer and data processing services, and management and public relations firms.

Since financial analysts often work in Wall Street companies, many employers are found in New York City. They are also concentrated in other large cities but work in smaller cities as well. Approximately 221,000 financial analysts are employed in the United States.

STARTING OUT

Representatives from hiring companies (e.g., banks, brokerage firms, or investment companies) may visit college campuses to meet with students interested in pursuing careers as financial analysts. College career services offices will have details on such visits. Company Web sites may also offer campus recruiting schedules.

Gaining an entry-level position can be difficult. Some companies offer in-house training, but many don't. Beginning as a research assistant might be one way to break into the business. Read member profiles at association sites to see where members have worked as financial analysts. Explore those companies that look appealing.

Make contacts and network with other financial analysts. Your local CFA Institute society or chapter will probably hold regular meetings, affording ample networking opportunities. You can become a CFA Institute member whether or not you are a CFA charterholder, but

charterholders enjoy full member benefits, such as access to job postings. (Complete details, including listings for local societies and chapters, can be found at the CFA Institute's Web site, http://www.cfainstitute.org.) Also, internships can be an excellent way to make contacts and gain experience in the field.

As an interview tool, the New York Society of Security Analysts suggests that you compile an investment recommendation for potential clients to give them an idea of the kind of research you're capable of and how you present your data.

You can search for job ads online. One resource is the Jobsinthemoney.com network (http://www.jobsinthemoney.com). If you know what companies you'd like to work for, visit their Web sites. Chances are you will find online job listings there.

ADVANCEMENT

Financial analysts who accurately prepare their employer's or client's financial statements and who offer investment advice that results in profits will likely be rewarded for their efforts. Rewards come in the form of promotions and/or bonuses. Successful financial analysts may become senior financial analysts, sometimes in only three or four years. Some become portfolio or financial managers. Rather than simply making recommendations on their company's or client's investment policies, those who advance to a senior position have more decision-making responsibility.

Some financial analysts move on to jobs as investment bankers or advisors. Others become officers in various departments in their company. Positions include chief financial officer and vice president of finance. In time, some cultivate enough contacts to be able to start their own consulting firms.

EARNINGS

The U.S. Department of Labor reports that median annual earnings of financial analysts were $66,590 in 2006. Top earners (the top 10 percent) made more than $130,130, and the lowest salaries (the lowest 10 percent) were less than $40,340.

If the investments of financial analysts' employers or clients perform well, it is not uncommon for those financial analysts to receive a bonus in addition to their salary. With bonuses, skilled financial analysts can make much more than their base salary.

Benefits include paid vacation, health, disability, life insurance, and retirement or pension plans. Some employers also offer profit-sharing plans. Tuition reimbursement may also be available.

WORK ENVIRONMENT

Most financial analysts work in an office in a corporate setting. Frequently, they work alone (e.g., when conducting research or talking on the phone to clients). Some may work out of their homes. Much time is spent working on a computer, doing research and compiling data. Travel is frequently required—there are meetings and social functions to attend, clients to meet, and companies to research at their place of business. Because financial analysts spend much of their normal business hours talking or meeting with clients, they often conduct research after hours and generally work long days. It is not uncommon for financial analysts to clock well in excess of 50 hours per week.

OUTLOOK

The state of the economy and the stock market has a direct effect on the employment outlook for financial analysts. When the economy is doing well, companies are more likely to make investments, resulting in a need for financial analysts. When the economy is doing poorly, companies are less likely to make investments, and there will be less need for financial analysts. The *Occupational Outlook Handbook* (*OOH*), anticipating an increase in business investments, predicts much-faster-than-average employment growth in this field through 2016. The *OOH* notes, too, that international securities markets, the complexity of financial products, and business mergers and acquisitions demand financial analysts to sort through all the issues involved. Because of the close scrutiny analysts have been under, it might become more desirable for financial analysts to hold the CFA charter. Despite the prediction for excellent growth, competition for positions as financial analysts will be very strong since many people are interested in entering the field. Applicants with strong college grades in finance, accounting, and economics courses and an MBA or certification will have the best job prospects.

Individual investing will also affect the need for financial analysts, in that the more people invest in mutual funds [often through 401(k) plans], the greater the need there will be for financial analysts to recommend financial products to the mutual fund companies.

FOR MORE INFORMATION

This organization's Web site offers industry news and certification information.

Association for Financial Professionals
4520 East West Highway, Suite 750
Bethesda, MD 20814-3574
Tel: 301-907-2862
http://www.afponline.org

For complete CFA Institute information, including lists of institute societies, publications, news, conference details, and certification information, contact

CFA Institute
560 Ray C. Hunt Drive
Charlottesville, VA 22903-2981
Tel: 800-247-8132
Email: info@cfainstitute.orghttp://www.aimr.org

The NYSSA's Web site includes a list of top employers of financial analysts as well as an article on becoming a security analyst.

New York Society of Security Analysts (NYSSA)
1177 Avenue of the Americas, 2nd Floor
New York, NY 10036-2714
Tel: 800-248-0108
Email: staff@nyssa.org
http://www.nyssa.org

For information on laws and regulations pertaining to investors and the securities markets, contact

U.S. Securities and Exchange Commission
Office of Investor Education and Advocacy
100 F Street, NE
Washington, DC 20549-2000
Tel: 202-942-8088
Email: help@sec.gov
http://www.sec.gov

This Web site has links to financial, investment, and security analyst societies.

AnalystForum
http://www.analystforum.com

For issues of interest to senior finance executives, see

CFO.com
http://www.cfo.com

FINANCIAL PLANNERS

OVERVIEW

Financial planning is the process of establishing financial goals and creating ways to reach them. Certified *financial planners*, sometimes known as *personal financial advisors*, examine the assets of their clients and suggest what steps they need to take in the future to meet their goals. They

SCHOOL SUBJECTS

Business, Mathematics

PERSONAL SKILLS

Helping/Teaching, Leadership/Management

MINIMUM EDUCATION LEVEL

Bachelor's Degree

CERTIFICATION OR LICENSING

Recommended (Certification), Required for Certain Positions (Licensing)

WORK ENVIRONMENT

Primarily Indoors, Primarily One Location

take a broad approach to financial advice, which distinguishes them from other professional advisers, such as insurance agents, stockbrokers, accountants, attorneys, and real estate agents, each of whom typically focuses on only one aspect of a person's finances. Approximately 176,000 personal financial advisors are employed in the United States.

THE JOB

Financial planners advise their clients on many aspects of finance. Although they seem to be jacks-of-all-trades, certified financial planners do not work alone; they meet with their clients' other advisers, such as attorneys, accountants, trust officers, and investment bankers. Financial planners fully research their clients' overall financial picture. After meeting with the clients and their other advisers, certified financial planners analyze the data they have received and generate a written report that includes their recommendations on how the clients can best achieve their goals. This report details the clients' financial objectives, current income, investments, risk tolerance, expenses, tax returns, insurance coverage, retirement programs, estate plans, and other important information.

Financial planning is an ongoing process. The plan must be monitored and reviewed periodically so that adjustments can be made, if necessary, to assure that it continues to meet individual needs.

The plan itself is a set of recommendations and strategies for clients to use or ignore, according to The Princeton Review Online, and financial planners should be ready to answer hard questions about the integrity of the plans they map out. After all, they are dealing with all of the money and investments that people have worked a lifetime accruing.

People need financial planners for different things. Some might want life insurance, college savings plans, or estate planning. Sometimes these needs are triggered by changes in people's lives, such as retirement, death of a spouse, disability, marriage, birth of children, or job changes. Certified financial planners spend the majority of their time on the following topics: investment planning, retirement planning, tax planning, estate planning, and risk management. All of these areas require different types of financial knowledge, and planners are generally expected to be extremely competent in the disciplines of asset management, employee benefits, estate planning, insurance, investments, and retirement, according to the Certified Financial Planner Board of Standards. A financial planner must also have good interpersonal skills, since establishing solid client-planner relationships is essential to the planner's success. It also helps to have good communication skills, since even the best financial plan, if presented poorly to a client, can be rejected.

Clients drive the job of financial planners. The advice planners provide depends on their clients' particular needs, resources, and priorities. Many people think they cannot afford or do not need a comprehensive financial plan. Certified financial planners must have a certain amount of expertise in sales to build their client base.

Certified financial planners use various ways to develop their client lists, including telephone solicitation, giving seminars on financial planning to the general public or specific organizations, and networking with social contacts. Referrals from satisfied customers also help the business grow.

Although certified financial planners are trained in comprehensive financial planning, some specialize in one area, such as asset management, investments, or retirement planning. In most small or self-owned financial planning companies, they are generalists. However, in some large companies, planners might specialize in particular areas, including insurance, real estate, mutual funds, annuities, pensions, or business valuations.

REQUIREMENTS
High School

If financial planning sounds interesting to you, take as many business classes as possible as well as mathematics. Communication courses, such as speech or drama, will help put you at ease when talking in front of a crowd, something financial planners must do occasionally. English courses will help you prepare the written reports planners present to their clients.

Postsecondary Training

Earning a bachelor's degree starts financial planners on the right track, but it will help if your degree indicates skill with numbers, be it in science or business. A business administration degree with a specialization in financial planning or a liberal arts degree with courses in accounting, business administration, economics, finance, marketing, human behavior, counseling, and public speaking is excellent preparation for this sort of job.

Certification or Licensing

However, education alone will not motivate clients to turn over their finances to you. Many financial professionals are licensed on the state and federal levels in financial planning specialties, such as stocks and insurance. The Securities and Exchange Commission and most states have licensing requirements for investment advisers, a category under which most financial planners also fall. However, the government does not regulate most of the activities of planners. Therefore, to show credibility to clients, most financial planners choose to become certified as either a certified financial planner (CFP) or a chartered financial consultant (ChFC).

To receive the CFP mark of certification, offered by the CFP Board, candidates must meet what the board refers to as the four E's, which comprise the following:

Education: To be eligible to take the certification exam, candidates must meet education requirements in one of the following ways. The first option is to complete a CFP board-registered program in financial planning. The second is to hold a specific degree and professional credentials in one of several areas the board has approved of; these include certified public accountant, licensed attorney, chartered financial consultant, chartered life underwriter, chartered financial analyst, doctor of business administration, and Ph.D. in business or economics. Lastly, applicants may submit transcripts of their undergraduate or graduate education to the board for review. If the board feels the education requirements have been met, the candidate may sit for the exam. Applicants must also have a bachelor's degree in any area of study or program to obtain CFP certification. They do not need to have earned this degree at the time they take the examination, but must show proof of completion of this degree in order to complete the final stage of certification.

Examination: Once candidates have completed the education requirements, they may take the certification exam, which tests knowledge on various key aspects of financial planning.

Experience: Either before or after passing the certification exam, candidates must have three years of work experience.

Ethics: After candidates have completed the education, examination, and experience requirements, they must voluntarily ascribe to the CFP Board's Code of Ethics and Professional Responsibility and Financial Planning Practice Standards to be allowed to use the CFP mark. This voluntary agreement empowers the board to take action if a CFP licensee violates the code. Such violations could lead to disciplinary action, including permanent revocation of the right to use the CFP mark.

The American College offers the ChFC designation. To receive this designation, candidates must complete certain course work stipulated by The American College, meet experience requirements, and agree to uphold The American College's Code of Ethics and Procedures.

To maintain the CFP and the ChFC designations, professionals will need to meet continuing education and other requirements as determined by the CFP Board and The American College.

Other Requirements

Other factors that contribute to success as a financial planner include keeping up with continuing education, referrals from clients, specialization, people and communication skills, and a strong educational background.

EXPLORING

There is not much that students can do to explore this field, since success as a certified financial planner comes only with training and years on the job. However, you can check out the financial planning information available on the Internet to familiarize yourself with the terms used in the industry. You should also take as many finance and business classes as possible. Talking to certified financial planners will also help you gather information on the field.

EMPLOYERS

Approximately 176,000 personal financial advisors are employed in the United States. Financial planners are employed by financial planning firms across the country. Many of these firms are small, perhaps employing two to 15 people, and most are located in urban areas. A smaller, but growing, number of financial planners are employed by corporations, banks, credit unions, mutual fund companies, insurance companies, accounting or law firms, colleges and universities, credit counseling organizations, and brokerage firms. In addition, many financial planners are self-employed.

STARTING OUT

Early in their careers, financial planners work for banks, mutual fund companies, or investment firms and usually receive extensive on-the-job training. The job will deal heavily with client-based and research activities. Financial planners may start their own business as they learn personal skills and build their client base. During their first few years, certified financial planners spend many hours analyzing documents, meeting with other advisers, and networking to find new clients.

ADVANCEMENT

Those who have not changed their career track in five years can expect to have established some solid, long-term relationships with clients. Measured success at this point will be the planners' service fees, which will be marked up considerably from when they started their careers.

Those who have worked in the industry for 10 years usually have many clients and a six-figure income. Experienced financial planners can also move into careers in investment banking, financial consulting, and financial analysis. Because people skills are also an integral part of being a financial planner, consulting, on both personal and corporate levels, is also an option. Many planners will find themselves attending business school, either to achieve a higher income or to switch to one of the aforementioned professions.

EARNINGS

There are several methods of compensation for financial planners. Fee-only means that compensation is earned entirely from fees from consultation, plan development, or investment management. These fees may be charged on an hourly or project basis depending on clients' needs or on a percentage of assets under management. Commission-only compensation is received from the sale of financial products that clients agree to purchase to implement financial planning recommendations. There is no charge for advice or preparation of the financial plan. Fee-offset means that compensation received in the form of commission from the sale of financial products is offset against fees charged for the planning process. Combination fee/commission is a fee charged for consultation, advice, and financial plan preparation on an hourly, project, or percentage basis.

Planners might also receive commissions from recommended products targeted to achieve goals and objectives. Some planners work on a salary basis for financial services institutions such as banks, credit unions, and other related organizations.

The median annual gross income of certified financial planners was $283,079 in 2007, according to the 2007 *Survey of Trends in the Financial Planning Industry* conducted by the Financial Planning Association. These incomes were earned from financial plan writing, product sales, consulting, and related activities.

The U.S. Department of Labor reports that financial planners earned a median annual salary of $66,120 in 2006. The most-experienced financial planners with the highest level of education earned more than $114,260, while the least-experienced financial planners earned less than $32,340.

Firms might also provide beginning financial planners with a steady income by paying a draw, which is a minimum salary based on the commission and fees the planner can be expected to earn.

Some financial planners receive vacation days, sick days, and health insurance, but that depends on whether they work for financial institutions or on their own.

WORK ENVIRONMENT

Most financial planners work by themselves in offices or at home. Others work in offices with other financial planners. Established financial planners usually work the same hours as others in the business community. Beginners who are seeking customers probably work longer hours. Many planners accommodate customers by meeting with them in the evenings and on weekends. They might spend a lot of time out of the office meeting with current and prospective clients, attending civic functions, and participating in trade association meetings.

OUTLOOK

The employment of financial planners is expected to grow by 41 percent through 2016, according to the U.S. Department of Labor—or much faster than the average for all occupations. Employment is expected to grow rapidly in the future for a number of reasons. More funds should be available for investment, as personal income and inherited wealth grow. Demographics will also play a role; as increasing numbers of baby boomers turn 50, demand will grow for retirement-related investments. Most people, in general, are likely to turn to financial planners for assistance with retirement planning. Individual saving and investing for retirement are expected to become more important, as many companies reduce pension benefits and switch from defined-benefit retirement plans to defined-contribution plans, which shift the investment responsibility from the company to the individual. Furthermore, a growing number of individual investors are expected to seek advice from financial planners regarding the increasing complexity and array of investment alternatives for assistance with estate planning.

Due to the highly competitive nature of financial planning, many beginners leave the field because they are not able to establish a sufficient clientele. Once established, however, planners have a strong attachment to their occupation because of high earning potential and considerable investment in training. Job opportunities should be best for mature individuals with successful work experience.

FOR MORE INFORMATION

For more information about financial education and the ChFC designation, contact

The American College
270 South Bryn Mawr Avenue
Bryn Mawr, PA 19010-2105
Tel: 888-263-7265
Email: studentservices@theamericancollege.edu
http://www.theamericancollege.edu

To learn more about financial planning and to obtain a copy of the Guide to CFP Certification, *contact*

Certified Financial Planner Board of Standards
1425 K Street, NW, Suite 500
Washington, DC 20005-3686
Tel: 800-487-1497
Email: mail@CFPBoard.org
http://www.cfp.net

For information on financial planning, visit the FPA's Web site.

Financial Planning Association (FPA)
4100 East Mississippi Avenue, Suite 400
Denver, CO 80246-3053
Tel: 800-322-4237
http://www.fpanet.org

For more information on fee-only financial advisers, contact

National Association of Personal Financial Advisors
3250 North Arlington Heights Road, Suite 109
Arlington Heights, IL 60004-1574
Tel: 847-483-5400
Email: info@napfa.org
http://www.napfa.org

FOOD SERVICE WORKERS

OVERVIEW

Food service workers include waiters (the term *waiter* refers to both male and female servers) of many different types, as well as counter attendants, dining room attendants, hosts, fast-food workers, kitchen assistants, and others. These workers take customers' orders, serve food and beverages, make out customers' checks, and sometimes take payments. These basic duties, however, may vary greatly depending on the specific kind of food service establishment. There are approximately 6.9 million people working as waiters, helpers, attendants, hosts, and other food servers in the United States.

THE JOB

Food service workers have a variety of job duties depending on the size and kind of food establishment in which they are employed. In small restaurants, sandwich shops, grills, diners, fast-food outlets, and cafeterias, customers are usually looking for hot food and quick service. Informal waiters, servers, and lunchroom or coffee shop counter attendants work to satisfy patrons and give them the kind of attention that will make them repeat customers. They take customers' orders, serve food and beverages, calculate bills, and sometimes collect money. Between serving customers, waiters in small establishments may clear and clean tables and counters, replenish supplies,

SCHOOL SUBJECTS
Family and Consumer Science, Mathematics

PERSONAL SKILLS
Following Instructions, Helping/Teaching

MINIMUM EDUCATION LEVEL
High School Diploma

CERTIFICATION OR LICENSING
Required by All States

WORK ENVIRONMENT
Primarily Indoors, Primarily One Location

and set up table service for future customers. When business is slow, they spend some time cleaning the serving area and equipment such as coffee machines and blenders. *Combined food preparation and serving workers* work specifically at fast-food establishments. They are the people who take food and drink orders from customers at the counter or drive-through window. They also bring the ordered items to the customers and take payment. During quiet periods at the restaurant, they may be responsible for such chores as making coffee, cooking french fries, or cleaning tables. *Counter attendants* in lunchrooms, coffee shops, and diners often do some simple cooking tasks, such as making sandwiches, salads, and cold drinks and preparing ice cream dishes. They also may have to help with such tasks as cleaning kitchen equipment, sweeping and mopping floors, and carrying out trash. Other workers in this category include cafeteria counter attendants, supervisors, canteen operators, and fountain servers.

In larger and more formal restaurants, *waiters,* or *servers,* perform essentially the same services as those working in smaller establishments, but they usually have extra duties designed to make the dining experience more enjoyable. These duties may include seating the customers, presenting them with menus, suggesting choices from the menu, informing the customers of special preparations and seasonings of food, and sometimes suggesting beverages that would complement the meal. They check to see that the correct dinnerware and utensils are on the table and try to attend to any special requests the customers may have.

Servers in expensive restaurants serve food following more formal and correct procedures. *Captains, headwaiters, maitre d's,* and *hosts* or *hostesses* may greet and seat the guests, take reservations over the phone, and supervise the service of the waiters. *Wine stewards* assist customers in selecting wines from the restaurant's available stock.

Dining room attendants, also known as *waiters' assistants, buspersons,* or *bussers,* assist the waiters in their duties. They may clear and reset tables, carry soiled dishes to the dishwashing area, carry in trays of food, and clean up spilled food and broken dishes. In some restaurants, these attendants also serve water and bread and butter to customers. During slow periods, they may fill salt and pepper shakers, clean coffeepots, and do various other tasks. *Cafeteria attendants* clear and set tables, carry trays of dirty dishes to the kitchen, check supplies, and sometimes serve coffee to customers.

While dining room and cafeteria attendants assure clean and attractive table settings in the dining areas, *kitchen assistants* help maintain an efficient and hygienic kitchen area by cleaning food preparation and storage areas, sweeping and scrubbing floors, and removing garbage. They may also move supplies and equipment from storage to work areas, perform some simple food preparation, and wash the pots and pans used in cooking. To keep the kitchen operating smoothly, they maintain a steady supply of clean dishes by scraping food from plates, stacking dishes in and removing them from the dishwasher, polishing flatware, and removing water spots from glasses. *Dishwashers* wash dishes, cutlery, and cooking equipment and utensils.

Some food servers may be designated by the place in which they work or the type of specialized service they perform, such as carhops and dining car, room service, takeout, buffet, and club waiters.

REQUIREMENTS
High School

Applicants for jobs as waiters or other food service workers usually do not need a high school diploma. Most employers, however, favor applicants with some high school training, and graduation from high school is generally considered a personal asset, especially if you are planning a career in this industry. While in high school, take family and consumer science classes to learn about food preparation, storage, and presentation. Take basic math classes because you will frequently be dealing with money and will need to do addition, subtraction, and division. At some restaurants waiters carry a certain amount of money with them and make change for customers' bills right at the tables. To do this, you must make quick and accurate calculations in your head. English and speech classes should help you develop your communications skills, which are very important for waiters to have. If you have hopes of moving into management positions or owning your own food business someday, take business and accounting classes as well.

Postsecondary Training

Vocational schools may offer special training courses for waiters. Special courses are sometimes offered by restaurant associations in conjunction with schools or food agencies, and many employers seek persons who have had such training.

Smaller, more informal restaurants may hire servers who are without special training or previous experience. In these situations, the necessary skills are learned on the job. Larger restaurants and those with more formal dining atmospheres usually hire only experienced waiters. Almost without exception, food counter workers, waiters' assistants, and kitchen helpers learn their skills on the job.

Certification or Licensing

Food service workers almost always are required to obtain health certificates from the state department of public health that certify they are free from communicable diseases, as shown by physical examination and blood tests. This is required for the protection of the general public.

The principal union for waiters, food counter workers, waiters' assistants, and kitchen helpers is UNITE HERE; however, not all employees are union members.

Other Requirements

Food service workers generally must be free from any physical disabilities that would impair their movements on the job. They must possess strong physical stamina, because the work requires many long hours of standing and walking. Waiters and food counter workers need to have a congenial temperament, patience, and the desire to please and be of service to the public. All food service workers must be neat and clean in their personal hygiene and dress. Those who serve the public should present a pleasant appearance, be able to communicate well, and be able to use basic arithmetic skills to compute customers' checks. In some restaurants that specialize in the foods of a certain country, servers might need to speak a foreign language. A good memory and persuasive skills are additional personal assets for this occupation.

EXPLORING

Explore this work by getting part-time or summer work as a dining room attendant, counter worker, or waiter at a restaurant, grill, or coffee shop with a casual atmosphere. Volunteer opportunities that combine some type of food service and interaction with the public may also be available in your area. Meals on Wheels, shelters serving meals, and catering services are all sources to consult for volunteering opportunities.

Dealing with the public is a large aspect of food service work, so get experience in this area. If you are unable to find a food service position, get a part-time or summer job as a store clerk, cashier, or other worker directly involved with the public.

EMPLOYERS

Approximately 6.9 million people are employed as waiters, helpers, attendants, hosts, and other food servers in the United States. The food service industry is one of the largest and most active sectors of the nation's economy. Employers include small restaurants (such as grills, sandwich shops, tearooms, soda shops, and diners), larger restaurants, hotel dining rooms, ships, trains, hospitals, schools, factories, and many other establishments where food is served.

STARTING OUT

People usually enter this field by applying in person for open positions. Job openings are frequently listed in newspaper advertisements, or they may be located through local offices of the state employment service or private employment agencies. The private agencies may charge a percentage fee for their placement services. In some areas where food service workers are unionized, potential employees may seek job placement assistance by contacting union offices.

ADVANCEMENT

Employees may advance to better-paying jobs by transferring to larger and more formal restaurants. They also may gain better positions and higher pay as they obtain more training and experience.

In general, advancement in this field is limited. Nevertheless, waiters may earn promotions to positions as headwaiters, hosts or hostesses, captains, or other supervisors. A waiter may be promoted eventually to restaurant manager, depending on training, experience, and work performance record, as well as on the size and type of food establishment. Food counter workers can advance to cashiers, cooks, waiters, counter or fountain supervisors, or line supervisors in cafeterias. Large organizations, such as fast-food or other restaurant chains, may have management training programs or less formal on-the-job training for dependable workers who have leadership ability. Promotion opportunities are much more limited for waiters' assistants and kitchen helpers. Some of them become waiters, cooks' assistants, or short-order cooks; these promotions are more likely to happen in large restaurants and institutions. Some of these higher positions require reading, writing, and arithmetic skills, which employees seeking promotion should keep in mind.

Advancement usually involves greater responsibilities and higher pay. In some cases, a promotion may mean that the employee has the chance to earn more in service tips than in actual salary increases, depending on the size, type, and location of the establishment.

Some individuals may aspire to owning their own businesses or to entering into business partnerships after they have earned and reserved some capital and gained the necessary training and experience. Knowledge of the restaurant and food service business from the inside can be a definite advantage to someone opening or buying a restaurant.

EARNINGS

The earnings of food service workers are determined by a number of factors, such as the type, size, and location of the food establishment, union membership, experience and training of the workers, basic wages paid, and, in some cases, tips earned. Estimating the average wage scale is therefore difficult and has a wide margin of error. It should also be noted that two out of five food service workers, and half of waiters, worked part time, so the annual wages mentioned here would not be applicable for below full-time work.

Waiters depend a great deal on tips to supplement their basic wages, which in general are relatively small. According to the U.S. Department of Labor, waiters earned a median hourly wage of $7.14 (including tips) in 2006. At this pay rate, a person working a 40-hour workweek on a full-time basis would earn approximately $14,850 annually. The department also reports that the highest paid 10 percent of waiters earned more than $12.46 per hour (approximately $25,910 annually) in 2006. Tips, usually ranging from 15 to 20 percent of the customers' checks, often amount to more than the actual wages, especially in the larger metropolitan areas. Naturally, waiters working in busy, expensive restaurants earned the most.

The department also reports the following figures for full-time workers in various positions. (All earnings exclude tips.) Dining room and cafeteria attendants earned a median of $7.36 per hour in 2006, which is approximately $15,310 per year for full-time work. The lowest paid 10 percent earned less than $5.91 per hour, or approximately $12,290 annually. Most of these attendants' earnings come from wages, while a portion may come from tip pools that are shared with other members of the wait staff. Hosts and hostesses made a median of $7.78 per hour in 2006. This makes for an approximate yearly income of $16,170. Many hosts' and hostesses' earnings come from wages, but some may share in a tip pool with other dining room workers. Counter attendants at coffee shops, cafeterias, and other such establishments earned a median hourly wage of $7.76, or approximately $16,130 annually.

Another reason earnings vary so widely in this industry is because special laws govern the minimum wage that must be paid to tipped workers. While the federal minimum wage is $5.85, employers under certain circumstances are allowed to pay tipped workers less than this amount. The minimum an employer could pay tipped workers was $2.13 per hour. The yearly income for a full-time worker making this amount is approximately $4,430 without tips.

As a benefit, most businesses offer free or discounted meals to workers. Full-time workers often receive some benefits, such as health insurance and sick days.

WORK ENVIRONMENT

Working conditions for food service workers have improved greatly, as more restaurants have been air-conditioned and modernized and many laborsaving techniques have become available. This occupational group is still subject to certain work hazards, however. These may include burns from heat and steam; cuts and injuries from knives, glassware, and other equipment; and sometimes hard falls from rushing on slippery floors. The job also requires lifting heavy trays of food, dishes, and water glasses, as well as a great deal of bending and stooping. In some cases, employees may work near steam tables or hot ovens.

Working hours will vary with the place of employment. The majority of waiters work 40- to 48-hour weeks, while food counter workers, waiters' assistants, and kitchen helpers generally work fewer than 30 hours a week. Split shifts are common to cover rush hours; some employees may work the lunch and dinner shifts, for example, with a few hours off in between. This is good for students, of course, who can then plan their courses around work schedules.

Most food service workers have to work evenings, weekends, and holidays. Some holiday work may be rotated among all the employees. One day off per week is usually in the schedule. Benefits for food service workers usually include free or discounted meals during the hours when they work. Their place of employment often furnishes work uniforms.

Work in this field is physically strenuous, requiring long hours of standing and walking, carrying heavy trays or pots and pans, and lifting other types of equipment. Rush hours are hectic, particularly for those employees who serve the public, attending to several tables or customers at the same time. Hard-to-please customers can also add to the employee's stress level.

The operation of a restaurant or other food service depends on the teamwork of its employees. An even disposition and a sense of humor, especially under pressure, contribute greatly to the efficiency and pleasantness of the restaurant's operation. The ability to converse easily with customers is a major asset for those working directly with the public.

OUTLOOK

Because work schedules can be flexible, part-time work is often available, and because people need little or no training to do this work, the food service industry employs a substantial number of people. Additionally, the demand for restaurants and other eateries continues to grow as our population grows. In particular, the large and growing population of senior citizens, who often prefer to dine at restaurants offering table service from waiters, should mean a steady demand for those in this field. According to the U.S. Department of Labor, overall employment for those in food service should grow about as fast as the average for all careers through 2016. Employment of combined food preparation and serving workers (including those employed at fast-food restaurants) is expected to grow faster than the average as busy Americans continue to patronize these establishments to save time.

Overall, job opportunities in the field will be excellent. Many job openings will come from the need to replace workers who have left the field. Turnover is high in these jobs for a number of reasons, including the low pay, the long hours, and the large number of students and others who do this work on a temporary basis before moving on to other occupations. Some food service workers look for seasonal job opportunities in summer or winter resort areas. They may prefer to move with the seasonal trade because they can take advantage of the benefits the vacation area offers.

Jobs for beginning workers will be more plentiful in lower-priced restaurants, where employees usually work only a short time. More expensive and formal restaurants tend to hire only experienced workers. Because of the higher pay, better tips, and other benefits, the job turnover rate is lower in these establishments, which increases the competition for job openings.

The health of the economy and some world events also affect the health of this industry. In economic downturns, people tend to eat out less frequently and go to less expensive restaurants. Some events, such as the Olympics, can draw many visitors to an area and cause a small boom for eating establishments there. Other events, such as the threat of terrorism, can cause people in that area to dine out less frequently for a time. Both such positive and negative events, however, generally have only a short-term effect on the industry.

FOR MORE INFORMATION

For information on job opportunities and accredited education programs, contact

International Council on Hotel, Restaurant, and Institutional Education
2810 North Parham, Suite 230
Richmond, VA 23294-4422
Tel: 804-346-4800
http://chrie.org

For information on education, scholarships, and careers, contact

National Restaurant Association Educational Foundation
175 West Jackson Boulevard, Suite 1500
Chicago, IL 60604-2814
Tel: 800-765-2122
Email: info@nraef.org
http://www.nraef.org

For information on food service careers and programs in Canada, contact the following associations:

Canadian Restaurant and Foodservices Association
316 Bloor Street West
Toronto, ON M5S 1W5 Canada
Tel: 800-387-5649
Email: info@crfa.ca
http://www.crfa.ca

Canadian Society of Nutrition Management
PO Box 1473
Everett, ON L0M 1J0 Canada
Tel: 866-355-2766
Email: csnm@csnm.ca
http://www.csnm.ca

FORENSIC SCIENCE TECHNICIANS

OVERVIEW

Forensic science technicians apply scientific principles and methods to the analysis, identification, and classification of physical evidence relating to criminal (or suspected criminal) cases. They do much of their work in laboratories, where they subject evidence to tests and then record the results. They may travel to crime scenes to collect

SCHOOL SUBJECTS
Biology, Chemistry

PERSONAL SKILLS
Following Instructions, Technical/Scientific

MINIMUM EDUCATION LEVEL
Bachelor's Degree

CERTIFICATION OR LICENSING
None Available

WORK ENVIRONMENT
Primarily Indoors, Primarily Multiple Locations

evidence and record the physical facts of a site. Forensic science technicians may also be called upon to testify as expert witnesses and to present scientific findings in court. Approximately 13,000 forensic science technicians are employed in the United States.

THE JOB

Forensic science technicians, also called *criminalists,* use the instruments of science and engineering to examine physical evidence. They use spectroscopes, microscopes, gas chromatographs, infrared and ultraviolet light, microphotography, and other lab measuring and testing equipment to analyze fibers, fabric, dust, soils, paint chips, glass fragments, fire accelerants, paper and ink, and other substances in order to identify their composition and origin. They analyze poisons, drugs, and other substances found in bodies by examining tissue samples, stomach contents, and blood samples. They analyze and classify blood, blood alcohol, semen, hair, fingernails, teeth, human and animal bones and tissue, and other biological specimens. Using samples of the DNA in these materials, they can match a person with a sample of body tissue. They study documents to determine whether they are forged or genuine. They also examine the physical properties of firearms, bullets, and explosives.

At the scene of a crime (whether actual or suspected), forensic science technicians collect and label evidence. This painstaking task may involve searching for spent bullets or bits of an exploded bomb and other objects scattered by an explosion. They might look for footprints, fingerprints, and tire tracks, which must be recorded or preserved by plaster casting before they are wiped out. Since crime scenes must eventually be cleaned up, forensic science technicians take notes and photographs to preserve the arrangement of objects, bodies, and debris. They are sometimes called on later to reconstruct the scene of a crime by making a floor plan or map pinpointing the exact location of bodies, weapons, and furniture.

Forensic science technicians spend the bulk of their time in the laboratory working with physical evidence. They seldom have direct contact with persons involved in actual or suspected crimes or with police investigators except when collecting evidence and reporting findings. Forensic science technicians do not interpret their findings relative to the criminal investigation in which they are involved; that is the work of police investigators. The purpose of crime lab work is to provide reliable scientific analysis of evidence that can then be used in criminal investigations and, if needed later, in court proceedings.

REQUIREMENTS
High School

In high school, you can begin to prepare for a career in forensics by taking a heavy concentration of science courses, including chemistry, biology, physiology, and physics. Computer skills are also important, so be sure to take as many computer science classes as possible. A basic grounding in spoken and written communications will be useful because forensic science technicians must write very detailed reports and are sometimes called on to present their findings in court.

Postsecondary Training

Most employers require applicants to have a bachelor's degree in forensic science or a related field. A number of universities and community colleges in the United States offer programs in forensic science and various aspects of crime lab work. These courses are often spread throughout the school, in the anatomy, physiology, chemistry, or biology departments, or they may be grouped together as part of the criminal justice department. Additionally, some colleges may have separate forensic science departments. Visit the Web sites of the American Academy of Forensic Sciences (http://www.aafs.org) and the Council on Forensic Science Education (http://www.criminology.fsu.edu/COFSE/default.html) for lists of colleges and universities that offer classes and programs in forensic science.

Other Requirements

To be successful in this field, you should have an aptitude for scientific investigation, an inquiring and logical mind, and the ability to make precise measurements and observations. Patience and persistence are important qualities, as is a good memory. Forensic science technicians must constantly bear in mind that the accuracy of their lab investigations can have great consequences for others.

EXPLORING

A large community police department may have a crime lab of its own whose experts can give you specific information about their work and the preparation that helped them build their careers. Smaller communities often use the lab facilities of a larger city nearby or the state police. A school counselor or a representative of the local police may be able to help you arrange a tour of these labs. Lectures in forensic science given at universities or police conventions may also be open to students. Online services and Internet access may provide entry to forums devoted to forensic science and are good sources of information on the daily and professional experiences of people already active in this field.

EMPLOYERS

There are approximately 13,000 forensic science technicians employed in the United States. Forensic science technicians are typically employed by large police departments or state law enforcement agencies nationwide. They may also be employed by the federal government (including the FBI and the military) or a medical examiner's office.

STARTING OUT

Crime labs are maintained by the federal government and by state and local governments. Applications should be made directly to the personnel department of the government agency supporting the lab. Civil service appointments usually require applicants to take an examination. Such appointments are usually widely advertised well in advance of the application date. Those working for the FBI or other law enforcement agencies usually undergo background checks, which examine their character, background, previous employers, and family and friends.

ADVANCEMENT

In a large crime laboratory, forensic science technicians usually advance from an assistant's position to working independently at one or more special types of analysis. From there they may advance to a position as project leader or being in charge of all aspects of one particular investigation. In smaller labs, one technician may have to fill many roles. With experience, such a technician may progress to more responsible work but receive no advancement in title.

Crucial to advancement is further education. Forensic science technicians need to be familiar with scientific procedures such as gas chromatography, ultraviolet and infrared spectrophotometry, mass spectroscopy, electrophoresis, polarizing microscopy, light microscopy, and conventional and isoelectric focusing; knowledge of these analytical techniques and procedures is taught or more fully explored at the master's and doctorate levels. Other, more specific areas of forensics, such as DNA analysis, require advanced degrees in molecular biology and genetics.

EARNINGS

Earnings for forensic science technicians vary with the employer, geographic location, and educational and skill levels. Salaries for entry-level positions as research assistants or technicians working in local and regional labs range from $20,000 to $25,000. For those individuals with a bachelor's degree and two to five years of specialized experience, salaries range from $30,000 to $40,000. Salaries for those with advanced degrees range from $50,000 to well over $100,000 a year. The U.S. Department of Labor reports that the median hourly salary for forensic science technicians was $21.79 in 2006. For full-time employment, this means a median salary of approximately $45,330 a year.

Benefits for full-time workers include vacation and sick time, health, and sometimes dental, insurance, and pension or 401 (k) plans.

WORK ENVIRONMENT

Forensic science technicians usually perform the analytical portion of their work in clean, quiet, air-conditioned laboratories, but they are frequently required to travel to crime scenes to collect evidence or study the site to understand more fully the evidence collected by detectives. When gathering evidence and analyzing it, forensic science technicians need to be able to concentrate, sometimes in crowded, noisy situations. For this reason, technicians must be adaptable and able to work in a variety of environments, including dangerous or unpleasant places.

Many crime scenes are grisly and may be extremely distressing for beginning workers and even for more seasoned professionals. In addition, forensic science technicians who work with human remains will regularly view corpses, and, more often than not, these corpses will have been mutilated in some way or be in varying degrees of decomposition. Individuals interested in this field need to develop the detachment and objectivity necessary to view corpses and extract specimens for testing and analysis.

Simulating the precise conditions of a crime site for a full analysis is often crucial, so forensic science technicians often return to the site so that they can perform tests or functions outside of the controlled environment of their lab. When traveling to the scene of a crime, forensic science technicians may have to carry cases of tools, cameras, and chemicals. In order not to risk contaminating evidence, they must follow strict procedures (both in and out of the laboratory) for collecting and testing evidence; these procedures can be extremely time-consuming and thus require a great deal of patience. Forensic science technicians also need to be able to arrive at and present their findings impartially. In large labs, they often work as part of a team under the direction of a senior technologist. They may experience eyestrain and contact with strong chemicals, but little heavy physical work is involved.

OUTLOOK

The employment of forensic science technicians is expected to grow much faster than the average for all occupations through 2016, according to the U.S. Department of Labor. Population increases, a rising crime rate, and the greater emphasis on scientific methodology in crime investigation have increased the need for trained technicians. Forensic science technicians who are employed by state and local public safety departments should experience especially strong employment opportunities, although some government agencies may be under pressure to reduce staff because of budget problems. Forensic science technicians with a four-year degree in forensic science will enjoy the best employment prospects.

FOR MORE INFORMATION

For information on careers and colleges and universities that offer forensic science programs, contact

American Academy of Forensic Sciences
410 North 21st Street
Colorado Springs, CO 80904-2798
Tel: 719-636-1100
http://www.aafs.org

To learn more about forensic services at the FBI, visit the FBI Laboratory Division's Web site.

Federal Bureau of Investigation (FBI)
J. Edgar Hoover Building

935 Pennsylvania Avenue
Washington, DC 20535-0001
Tel: 202-324-3000
http://www.fbi.gov and http://www.fbi.gov/hq/lab/labhome.htm

For information on career paths, contact
Forensic Sciences Foundation
410 North 21st Street
Colorado Springs, CO 80904-2712
http://www.forensicsciencesfoundation.org/career_paths/careers.htm

For information on colleges and universities that offer forensic science programs, contact
Council on Forensic Science Education
http://www.criminology.fsu.edu/COFSE/default.html

GENERAL MAINTENANCE MECHANICS

OVERVIEW

General maintenance mechanics, sometimes called *maintenance technicians* or *building engineers,* repair and maintain machines, mechanical equipment, and buildings, and work on plumbing, electrical, and controls. They also do minor construction or carpentry work and routine preventive maintenance to keep the physical structures of businesses, schools, factories, and apartment buildings in good condition. They also maintain and repair specialized equipment and machinery found in cafeterias, laundries, hospitals, offices, and factories. There are approximately 1.4 million general maintenance mechanics employed in the United States, working in almost every industry.

THE JOB

General maintenance mechanics perform almost any task that may be required to maintain a building or the equipment in it. They may be called on to replace faulty electrical outlets, fix air-conditioning motors, install water lines, build partitions, patch plaster or drywall, open clogged drains, dismantle, clean, and oil machinery, paint windows, doors, and woodwork, repair institutional-size dishwashers or laundry machines, and see to many other problems. Because of the diverse nature of the responsibilities of maintenance mechanics, they have to know how to use a variety of materials and be skilled in the use of most hand tools and ordinary power tools. They also must be able to recognize when they cannot handle a problem and must recommend that a specialized technician be called.

General maintenance mechanics work in many kinds of settings. Mechanics who work primarily on keeping industrial machines in good condition may be called *factory maintenance workers* or *mill maintenance workers,* while those mechanics who concentrate on the maintenance of a building's physical structure may be called *building maintenance workers and technicians.*

Once a problem or defect has been identified and diagnosed, maintenance mechanics must plan the repairs. They may consult blueprints, repair manuals, and parts catalogs to determine what to do. They obtain supplies and new parts from a storeroom or order them from a distributor. They install new parts in place of worn or broken ones, using hand tools, power tools, and sometimes electronic test devices and other specialized equipment. In some situations, maintenance mechanics may fix an old part or even fabricate a new part. To do this, they may need to set up and operate machine tools, such as lathes or milling machines, and operate gas- or arc-welding equipment to join metal parts together.

One of the most important kinds of duties general maintenance mechanics perform is routine preventive maintenance to correct defects before machinery breaks down or a building begins to deteriorate. This type of maintenance keeps small problems from turning into large, expensive ones. Mechanics often inspect machinery on a regular schedule, perhaps following a checklist that includes such items as inspecting belts, checking fluid levels, replacing filters, oiling moving parts, and so forth. They keep records of the repair work done and the inspection dates. Repair and inspection records can be important evidence of compliance with insurance requirements and government safety regulations.

New buildings often have computer-controlled systems, so mechanics who work in them must have basic computer skills. For example, newer buildings might have light sensors that are electronically controlled and automatically turn lights on and off. The maintenance mechanic has to understand how to make adjustments and repairs.

In small establishments, one mechanic may be the only person working in maintenance, and thus may be responsible for almost any kind of repair. In large estab-

SCHOOL SUBJECTS
Mathematics, Technical/Shop

PERSONAL SKILLS
Mechanical/Manipulative, Technical/Scientific

MINIMUM EDUCATION LEVEL
High School Diploma

CERTIFICATION OR LICENSING
Voluntary

WORK ENVIRONMENT
Indoors and Outdoors, Primarily One Location

lishments, however, tasks may be divided among several mechanics. For example, one mechanic may be assigned to install and set up new equipment, while another may handle preventive maintenance.

REQUIREMENTS
High School

Many employers prefer to hire helpers or mechanics who are high school graduates, but a diploma is not always required. High school courses that will prepare you for this occupation include mechanical drawing, metal shop, electrical shop, woodworking, blueprint reading, general science, computer science, and applied mathematics.

Postsecondary Training

Some mechanics learn their skills by working as helpers to people employed in building trades, such as electricians or carpenters. Other mechanics attend trade or vocational schools that teach many of the necessary skills. Becoming fully qualified for a mechanic's job usually requires one to four years of on-the-job training or classroom instruction, or some combination of both.

Certification or Licensing

There are some certification and training programs open to maintenance mechanics. The BOMI Institute International, for example, offers the designation of systems maintenance technician (SMT) to applicants who have completed courses in boilers, heating systems, and applied mathematics; refrigeration systems and accessories; air handling, water treatment, and plumbing systems; electrical systems and illumination; and building control systems. Technicians who have achieved SMT status can go on and become certified as systems maintenance administrators by taking further classes in building design and maintenance, energy management, and supervision. The Association for Facilities Engineering offers the certified plant engineer and certified plant maintenance manager designations to applicants who pass an examination and satisfy job experience requirements. While not necessarily required for employment, employees with certification may become more valuable assets to their employers and may have better chances at advancement.

Other Requirements

General maintenance mechanics need to have good manual dexterity and mechanical aptitude. People who enjoy taking things apart and putting them back together are good candidates for this career. Since some of the work, such as reaching, squatting, and lifting, requires physical strength and stamina, reasonably good health is necessary. Mechanics also need the ability to analyze and solve problems and to work effectively on their own without constant supervision.

EXPLORING

Shop classes can give you a good indication of your mechanical aptitude and of whether or not you would enjoy maintenance work. The best way to experience the work these mechanics do, however, is to get a summer or part-time job as a maintenance helper in a factory, apartment complex, or similar setting. If such a job is not available, you might try talking with a maintenance mechanic to get a fuller, more complete picture of his or her responsibilities.

EMPLOYERS

General maintenance mechanics are employed in factories, hospitals, schools, colleges, hotels, offices, stores, malls, gas and electric companies, government agencies, and apartment buildings throughout the United States. Statistics from the U.S. Department of Labor indicate that there are approximately 1.4 million people in the field. Approximately 19 percent are employed in manufacturing industries, while 10 percent work for federal, state, and local governments. Others are employed in service industries, such as elementary and secondary schools, colleges and universities, hospitals and nursing homes, and hotels, office and apartment buildings, and utility companies.

STARTING OUT

General maintenance mechanics usually start as helpers to experienced mechanics and learn their skills on the job. Beginning helpers are given the simplest jobs, such as changing light bulbs or making minor drywall repairs. As general maintenance mechanics acquire skills, they are assigned more complicated work, such as troubleshooting malfunctioning machinery.

Job seekers in this field usually apply directly to potential employers. Information on job openings for mechanic's helpers can often be found through newspaper classified ads, school career services offices, and the local offices of the state employment service. Graduates of trade or vocational schools may be able to get referrals and information from their school's career services office. Union offices may also be a good place to learn about job opportunities.

ADVANCEMENT

Some general maintenance mechanics who are employed in large organizations may advance to supervisory positions. Another possibility is to move into one of the traditional building trades and become a craftworker, such as a plumber or electrician. In smaller organizations, opportunities for promotion are limited, although increases in pay may result from an employee's good performance and increased value to the employer.

EARNINGS

Earnings for general maintenance mechanics vary widely depending on skill, geographical location, and industry. The U.S. Department of Labor reports that general maintenance mechanics and repairers earned median annual salaries of $31,910 in 2006. Earnings ranged from less than $19,140 to more than $50,840.

Almost all maintenance mechanics receive a benefits package that includes health insurance, paid vacation, sick leave, and a retirement plan. Mechanics earn overtime pay for work in excess of 40 hours per week.

WORK ENVIRONMENT

General maintenance mechanics work in almost every industry and in a wide variety of facilities. In most cases, they work a 40-hour week. Some work evening or night shifts or on weekends; they may also be on call for emergency repairs. In the course of a single day, mechanics may do a variety of tasks in different parts of a building or in several buildings, and they may encounter different conditions in each spot. Sometimes they have to work in hot or cold conditions, on ladders, in awkward or cramped positions, among noisy machines, or in other uncomfortable places. Sometimes they must lift heavy weights. On the job, they must stay aware of potential hazards such as electrical shocks, burns, falls, and cuts and bruises. By following safety regulations and using tools properly, they can keep such risks to a minimum.

The mechanic who works in a small establishment may be the only maintenance worker and is often responsible for doing his or her job with little direct supervision. Those who work in larger establishments usually report to a maintenance supervisor who assigns tasks and directs their activities.

OUTLOOK

Employment of general maintenance mechanics is expected to grow about as fast as the average for all occupations through 2016, according to the U.S. Department of Labor. Although the rate of construction of new apartment and office buildings, factories, hotels, schools, and stores is expected to be slower than in the past, most of these facilities still require the services of maintenance mechanics. This is a large occupation with a high turnover rate, and employment opportunities are expected to be excellent. In addition to newly created jobs, many openings will arise as experienced mechanics transfer to other occupations or leave the labor force.

General maintenance mechanics who work for manufacturing companies may be subject to layoffs during bad economic times, when their employers are under pressure to cut costs. Most mechanics, however, are not usually as vulnerable to layoffs related to economic conditions.

FOR MORE INFORMATION

For information on certification, contact
Association for Facilities Engineering
12100 Sunset Hills Road, Suite 130
Reston, VA 20190-3221
Tel: 703-234-4066
Email: info@afe.org
http://www.afe.org

This organization provides education programs for commercial property professionals, including building engineers and technicians.
BOMA International
1101 15th Street, NW, Suite 800
Washington, DC 20005-5021
Tel: 202-408-2662

Email: info@boma.org
http://www.boma.org

For information on professional certifications, contact
BOMI International
One Park Place, Suite 475
Annapolis, MD 21401-3479
Tel: 800-235-2664
Email: Service@bomi.org
http://www.bomi-edu.org

For information on general maintenance careers in building maintenance and construction, contact
Mechanical Contractors Association of America
1385 Piccard Drive
Rockville, MD 20850-4329
Tel: 301-869-5800
http://www.mcaa.org/careers

HEALTH CARE MANAGERS

OVERVIEW

Health care managers, also known as *health services managers* and *health services administrators,* direct the operation of hospitals, nursing homes, and other health care organizations. They are responsible for facilities, services, programs, staff, budgets, and relations with

SCHOOL SUBJECTS
Business, English

PERSONAL SKILLS
Helping/Teaching, Leadership/Management

MINIMUM EDUCATION LEVEL
Bachelor's Degree

CERTIFICATION OR LICENSING
Voluntary (Certification), Required for Certain Positions (Licensing)

WORK ENVIRONMENT
Primarily Indoors, One Location with Some Travel

other organizations. There are approximately 262,000 health care managers employed in the United States.

THE JOB

Health care managers of hospitals and health care facilities organize and manage personnel, equipment, and auxiliary services. They hire and supervise personnel, handle budgets and fee schedules charged to patients, and establish billing procedures. In addition, they help plan space needs, purchase supplies and equipment, oversee building and equipment maintenance, and provide for mail, phones, laundry, and other services for patients and staff. In some health care institutions, many of these duties are delegated to assistants or to various department heads. These assistants may supervise operations in such clinical areas as surgery, nursing, dietary, or therapy and in such administrative areas as purchasing, finance, housekeeping, and maintenance.

The health services administrator works closely with the institution's governing board to develop plans and policies. Following the board's directions, the administrator may carry out large projects that expand and develop hospital services. Such projects include organizing fund-raising campaigns and planning new research projects.

Health services managers meet regularly with their staffs to discuss departmental goals and to address problems. Managers may organize training programs for nurses, interns, and others in cooperation with the medical staff and department heads. Health care executives also represent the health care facility at community or professional meetings.

REQUIREMENTS
High School

If you are interested in a career in health management, you should start preparing in high school by taking college preparatory classes. Because communication skills are important, take as many speech and writing classes as possible. Courses in health, business, mathematics, and computer science are also excellent choices to help you prepare for this career.

Postsecondary Training

The training required to qualify for this work depends, to a large extent, on the qualifications established by the individual employer or a facility's governing board. Most prefer people with a graduate degree in health services administration, long-term care administration, public

administration, health sciences, public health, or business administration. A few require that their chief executives be physicians, while others look for people with formal training in law or general business administration as well as experience in the health care field. The future health care administrator may have a liberal arts foundation with a strong background in the social sciences or business economics.

Specialized training in health services administration is offered at both graduate and undergraduate levels. The graduate program generally takes two years to complete. Graduate students split their time between studying in the classroom and working as an administrative resident in a program-approved health care facility. Successful completion of the course work, the residency, and perhaps a thesis is required to earn the master's degree. An optional third-year fellowship provides additional work experience supervised by a mentor. During this period, the individual may work in various hospital departments as an assistant to department heads.

Certification or Licensing

The American College of Health Care Administrators (ACHCA) offers voluntary certification to nursing home and assisted living administrators who meet educational and work experience requirements and pass an examination. Certification must be renewed every five years. Contact the ACHCA for more information.

Additionally, the American College of Healthcare Executives (ACHE) offers the certified healthcare executive designation to candidates who pass an examination and meet other requirements. Fellow status is available to certified healthcare executives with advanced experience and skills. Contact the ACHE for more information.

Licensure is not a requirement for health care services executives employed in hospitals. However, all states require nursing home administrators to be licensed. Most states use the licensing exam prepared by the National Association of Boards of Examiners of Long Term Care Administrators. Because requirements vary from state to state, those considering careers in nursing home administration should contact their state's licensing body for specific licensure requirements. Also, it should be noted that continuing education is now a condition of licensure in most states.

Other Requirements

Much of the work of health services managers consists of dealing with people—the hospital's governing board, the medical staff, the department heads and other employees, the patients and their families, and community leaders and businesses. Therefore, health care managers must be tactful and sympathetic.

In addition, administrators must be able to coordinate the health care facility's many related functions. They need to understand, for instance, financial operations, purchasing, organizational development, and public relations. They must also have the ability to make some decisions with speed and others with considerable study. And, of course, health services executives should have a deep interest in the care of sick and injured patients.

Special hospitals, such as mental hospitals, often employ administrators who are physicians in the facility's specialty.

EXPLORING

If you are considering a career as a health services manager, you should take advantage of opportunities in high school to develop some of the skills required in this line of work. Because administrators and other health care executives need strong leadership and communication skills, participation in clubs as a leader or active member and in debate and speech clubs is helpful. Working in your school's health center is also useful. Hospitals, nursing homes, and other health service facilities offer part-time work after school, on weekends, and during the summer. Health services executives are often willing to speak to interested students, but be sure to make an appointment first.

EMPLOYERS

Approximately 262,000 health care managers are employed in hospitals, HMOs, group medical practices, and centers for urgent care, cardiac rehabilitation, and diagnostic imaging. Opportunities are also plentiful in long-term care facilities, such as nursing homes, home health care agencies, adult day care programs, life care communities, and other residential facilities.

STARTING OUT

A student in training as an administrative resident or postgraduate fellow may be offered a job as an administrative assistant or department head by the hospital or health care facility where the residency is served. The hospital's administrator at the place of training also may assist the student in locating a job.

Job openings can also be found by contacting the university's career services office or through bulletins of state and national associations. Large professional society meetings may offer on-site notices of job openings. Positions in federal- and state-operated health care institutions are filled by the civil service or by political appointment. Appointments to armed forces hospitals are handled by the various branches of the services.

Although the majority of students prepare for this career with a four-year college program followed by graduate study, it is still possible to secure a health administration position through experience and training in subordinate jobs and working up the administrative ladder.

ADVANCEMENT

It is unusual to finish college and step into a position as an upper-level health services executive. Most new graduates first gain experience in a more specialized clinical or administrative area of a health care facility. There they can become accustomed to working with health care personnel, patients, information systems, budgets, and finances. This experience and/or graduate work often leads to promotion to department head. Those with graduate training can expect to achieve higher-level positions. Assistant administrator or vice president is often the next step and may lead to appointment as the hospital's chief executive.

EARNINGS

Salaries of health services executives depend on the type of facility, geographic location, the size of the administrative staff, the budget, and the policy of the governing board. The U.S. Department of Labor reports that the median annual earnings of medical and health services managers were $73,340 in 2006. Salaries ranged from less than $45,050 to more than $127,830. The U.S. Department of Labor reports that the mean salary of health care managers who worked in hospitals was $84,930 in 2006, and those who worked in nursing care facilities earned $71,480.

A *Modern Healthcare* survey reports the following median annual salaries for department managers in 2005: respiratory therapy, $74,700; home health care, $82,000; physical therapy, $83,700; medical imaging/diagnostic radiology, $96,000; medical records, $97,000; rehabilitation services $92,500; and nursing services, $103,400.

Some administrators receive free meals, housing, and laundry service, depending on the facility in which they are employed. They usually receive paid vacations and holidays, sick leave, hospitalization and insurance benefits, and pension programs. The executive benefits package nowadays often includes management incentive bonuses based on job performance ranging from $25,000 to $225,000.

WORK ENVIRONMENT

To perform efficiently as an executive, health services administrators usually work out of a large office. They must maintain good communication with the staff and members of various departments.

Most administrators work five and a half days a week, averaging about 55 to 60 hours. However, hours can be irregular because hospitals and other health care facilities operate around the clock; emergencies may require the manager's supervision any time of the day or night.

OUTLOOK

Because every hospital and numerous other health care facilities employ administrators, employment opportunities in health care will be good through 2016 as the industry continues to diversify and deal with the problems of financing health care for everyone. The U.S. Department of Labor predicts that employment will grow faster than the average for all occupations.

Not all areas will grow at the same rate, however. Changes in the health care system are taking place because of the need to control escalating costs. This will have the greatest impact on hospitals, traditionally the largest employer of health services executives. The number of hospitals is declining as separate companies are set up to provide services such as ambulatory surgery, alcohol and drug rehabilitation, or home health care. So, while hospitals may offer fewer jobs, many new openings are expected to be available in other health care settings. Employment will grow the fastest in offices and clinics of medical practitioners and home health care services. There will also be more opportunities with health care management companies that provide management services to hospitals and other organizations, as well as specific departments such as emergency, managed care contract negotiations, information management systems, and physician recruiting.

Many colleges and universities are reporting more graduates in health services administration than hospitals and other health care facilities can employ. As a result, competition for administrative jobs will be stiff. However, many starting executives can find jobs working in health care settings other than hospitals, or they may be offered jobs at the department head or staff levels.

With hospitals adopting a more business-like approach aimed at lowering costs and increasing earnings, demand for M.B.A. graduates should remain steady. Individuals who have strong people skills and business or management knowledge will find excellent opportunities as administrators in nursing homes and other long-term facilities.

FOR MORE INFORMATION

For information on state licensing, certification, and student resources, contact

American College of Health Care Administrators
12100 Sunset Hills Road, Suite 130
Reston, VA 20190-3221
Tel: 703-739-7900
http://www.achca.org

For general information on health care management, contact

American College of Healthcare Executives
One North Franklin Street, Suite 1700
Chicago, IL 60606-3529
Tel: 312-424-2800
Email: geninfo@ache.org
http://www.ache.org

For information on health care administration careers, scholarships, and accredited programs, contact

**Association of University Programs
in Health Administration**
2000 North 14th Street, Suite 780
Arlington, VA 22201-2543
Tel: 703-894-0940
Email: aupha@aupha.org
http://www.aupha.org

For information about employment opportunities in ambulatory care management and medical group practices, contact

Medical Group Management Association
104 Inverness Terrace East
Englewood, CO 80112-5306
Tel: 877-275-6462
Email: service@mgma.com
http://www.mgma.org

For information on licensure, contact

**National Association of Long Term Care Administrator
Boards**
1444 I Street, NW, #700
Washington, DC 20005-6542
Tel: 202-712-9040
Email: nab@bostrom.com
http://www.nabweb.org

For publications, news releases, and information from recent health care conferences, contact

National Health Council
1730 M Street, NW, Suite 500

Washington, DC 20036-4561
Tel: 202-785-3910
Email: info@nhcouncil.org
http://www.nationalhealthcouncil.org

For information about careers in health care office management, contact

Professional Association of Health Care Office Management
4700 West Lake Avenue
Glenview, IL 60025-1468
Tel: 800-451-9311
http://www.pahcom.com

For comprehensive information about the career of health care manager, visit

Make a Difference: Discover a Career in Healthcare Management!
http://www.healthmanagementcareers.org

HOME HEALTH CARE AIDES

OVERVIEW

Home health care aides, also known as *homemaker-home health aides* or *home attendants,* serve elderly and infirm persons by visiting them in their homes and caring for them. Working under the supervision of nurses or social workers, they perform various household chores that clients are unable to perform for themselves as well as attend to patients' personal needs. Although they work primarily with the elderly, home health care aides also attend to clients with disabilities or those needing help with small children. There are approximately 787,000 home health aides employed in the United States.

THE JOB

Home health care aides enable elderly persons to stay in their own homes. For some clients, just a few visits a week are enough to help them look after themselves. Although physically demanding, the work is often emotionally rewarding. Home care aides may not have access to equipment and facilities such as those found in hospitals, but they also don't have the hospital's frantic pace. Home care aides are expected to take the time to get to know their clients and their individual needs. They

---

SCHOOL SUBJECTS
Family and Consumer Science, Health

PERSONAL SKILLS
Following Instructions, Helping/Teaching

MINIMUM EDUCATION LEVEL
High School Diploma

CERTIFICATION OR LICENSING
Required for Certain Positions

WORK ENVIRONMENT
Primarily Indoors, Primarily Multiple Locations

---

perform their duties within the client's home environment, which often is a much better atmosphere than the impersonal rooms of a hospital.

In addition to the elderly, home health care aides assist people of any age who are recovering at home following hospitalization. They also help children whose parents are ill, disabled, or neglectful. Aides may be trained to supply care to people suffering from specific illnesses such as AIDS, Alzheimer's disease, or cancer, or patients with developmental disabilities who lack sufficient daily living skills.

Clients unable to feed themselves may depend on home care aides to shop for food, prepare their meals, feed them, and clean up after meals. Likewise, home health care aides may assist clients in dressing and grooming, including washing, bathing, cleaning teeth and nails, and fixing the clients' hair.

Massages, alcohol rubs, whirlpool baths, and other therapies and treatments may be a part of a client's required care. Home health care aides may work closely with a physician or home nurse in giving medications and dietary supplements and helping with exercises and other therapies. They may check pulses, temperatures, and respiration rates. Occasionally, they may change nonsterile dressings, use special equipment such as a hydraulic lift, or assist with braces or artificial limbs.

Home health care aides working in home care agencies are supervised by a registered nurse, physical therapist, or social worker who assigns them specific duties. Aides report changes in patients' conditions to the supervisor or case manager.

Household chores are often another aspect of the home health care aide's responsibilities. Light housekeeping, such as changing and washing bed linens, doing the laundry and ironing, and dusting, may be necessary. When a home care aide looks after the children of a disabled or neglectful parent, work may include making lunches for the children, helping them with their homework, or providing companionship and adult supervision in the evening.

Personal attention and comfort are important aspects of an aide's care. Home health care aides can provide this support by reading to children, playing checkers or a computer game, or visiting with an elderly client. Often just listening to a client's personal problems will help the client through the day. Because elderly people do not always have the means to venture out alone, a home health care aide may accompany an ambulatory patient to the park for an afternoon stroll or to the physician's office for an appointment.

REQUIREMENTS

High School

Many programs require only a high school diploma for entry-level positions. Previous or additional course work in home economics, cooking, sewing, and meal planning are very helpful, as are courses that focus on family living and home nursing.

Postsecondary Training

Health care agencies usually focus their training on first aid, hygiene, and the principles of health care. Cooking and nutrition, including meal preparation for patients with specific dietary needs, are often included in the program. Home health care aides may take courses in psychology and child development as well as family living. Because of the need for hands-on work, aides usually learn how to bathe, dress, and feed patients as well as how to help them walk upstairs or get up from bed. The more specific the skill required for certain patients, the more an agency is likely to have more comprehensive instruction.

Most agencies will offer free training to prospective employees. Such training may include instruction on how to deal with depressed or reluctant patients, how to prepare easy and nutritious meals, and tips on housekeeping. Specific course work on health and sanitation may also be required.

Certification or Licensing

Home Care University, a subsidiary of the National Association for Home Care and Hospice, offers the home care aide certification to applications who complete educational and skill requirements and pass a written examination. Contact the association for more information.

The federal government has enacted guidelines for home health aides whose employers receive reimbursement from Medicare. Federal law requires home health aides to pass a competency test covering 12 areas: communication skills; documentation of patient status and care provided; reading and recording vital signs; basic infection control procedures; basic body functions; maintenance of a healthy environment; emergency procedures; physical, emotional, and developmental characteristics of patients; personal hygiene and grooming; safe transfer techniques; normal range of motion and positioning; and basic nutrition.

Federal law suggests at least 75 hours of classroom and practical training supervised by a registered nurse. Training and testing programs may be offered by the employing agency, but they must meet the standards of the Centers for Medicare and Medicaid Services. Training programs vary depending upon state regulations.

Other Requirements

Caring for people in their own homes can be physically demanding work. Lifting a client for baths and exercise, helping a client up and down stairs, performing housework, and aiding with physical therapy all require that an aide be in good physical condition. Aides do not have the equipment and facilities of a hospital to help them with their work, and this requires adaptability and ingenuity. Oftentimes they must make do with the resources available in a typical home.

An even temperament and a willingness to serve others are important characteristics for home health care aides. People in this occupation should be friendly, patient, sensitive to others' needs, and tactful. At times an aide will have to be stern in dealing with uncooperative patients or calm and understanding with those who are angry, confused, despondent, or in pain. Genuine warmth and respect for others are important attributes. Cheerfulness and a sense of humor can go a long way in establishing a good relationship with a client, and a good relationship can make working with the client much easier.

Home health care aides must be willing to follow instructions and abide by the health plan created for each patient. Aides provide an important outreach service, supporting the care administered by the patient's physician, therapist, or social worker. They are not trained medical personnel, however, and must know the limits of their authority.

EXPLORING

Home health care aides are employed in many different areas. Interested students can learn more about the work by contacting local agencies and programs that provide home care services and requesting information on the organization's employment guidelines or training programs. Visiting the county or city health department and contacting the personnel director may provide useful information as well. Often, local organizations sponsor open houses to inform the community about the services they provide. This could serve as an excellent opportunity to meet the staff involved in hiring and program development and to learn about job opportunities. In addition, it may be possible to arrange to accompany a home health care aide on a home visit.

EMPLOYERS

Approximately 787,000 home health aides are employed in the United States. The primary employers of home health care aides are local social service agencies that provide home care services. Such agencies often have training programs for prospective employees. Home health care aides might also find employment with hospitals that operate their own community outreach programs. Most hospitals, however, hire home health care aides through agencies.

STARTING OUT

Some social service agencies enlist the aid of volunteers. By contacting agencies and inquiring about such openings, aspiring home care aides can get an introduction to the type of work this profession requires. Also, many agencies or nursing care facilities offer free training to prospective employees.

Checking the local Yellow Pages for agencies that provide health care to the aged and disabled or family service organizations can provide a list of employment prospects. Nursing homes, public and private health care facilities, and local chapters of the Red Cross and United Way are likely to hire entry-level employees. The National Association for Home Care and Hospice can also supply information on reputable agencies and departments that employ home care aides.

ADVANCEMENT

As home health care aides develop their skills and deepen their experience, they may advance to management or supervisory positions. Those who find greater enjoyment working with clients may branch into more specialized care and pursue additional training. Additional experience and education often bring higher pay and increased responsibility.

Aides who wish to work in a clinic or hospital setting may return to school to complete a nursing degree. Other related occupations include social worker, physical or occupational therapist, and dietitian. Along with a desire for advancement, however, must come the willingness to meet additional education and experience requirements.

EARNINGS

Earnings for home health care aides are comparable to the salaries of nursing and psychiatric aides and nurse assistants. Depending on the agency, considerable flexibility exists in working hours and patient load. For many aides who begin as part-time employees, the starting salary is usually the minimum hourly wage. For full-time aides with significant training or experience, earnings may be around $6 to $8 per hour. According to the U.S. Department of Labor, median hourly earnings of home health aides were $9.34 in 2006. Wages ranged from less than $7.06 to more than $13.00 an hour.

Aides are usually paid only for the time worked in the home. They normally are not paid for travel time between jobs.

Vacation policies and benefits packages vary with the type and size of the employing agency. Many full-time home health care aides receive one week of paid vacation following their first year of employment, and they often receive two weeks of paid vacation each year thereafter. Full-time aides may also be eligible for health insurance and retirement benefits. Some agencies also offer holiday or overtime compensation.

WORK ENVIRONMENT

Health aides in a hospital or nursing home setting work at a much different pace and in a much different environment than the home health care aide. With home care, aides can take the time to sit with their clients and get to know them. Aides spend a certain amount of time with each client and can perform their responsibilities without the frequent distractions and demands of a hospital. Home surroundings differ from situation to situation. Some homes are neat and pleasant, while others are untidy and depressing. Some patients are angry, abusive, depressed, or otherwise difficult; others are pleasant and cooperative.

Because home health care aides usually have more than one patient, the hours an aide works can fluctuate based on the number of clients and types of services needed. Many clients may be ill or have disabilities. Some may be elderly and have no one else to assist them with light housekeeping or daily errands. These differences can dictate the type of responsibilities a home care aide has for each patient.

Working with the infirm or disabled can be a rewarding experience as aides enhance the quality of their clients' lives with their help and company. However, the personal strains—on the clients as well as the aides—can make the work challenging and occasionally frustrating. There can be difficult emotional demands that aides may find exhausting. Considerable physical activity is involved in this line of work, such as helping patients to walk, dress, or take care of themselves. Traveling from one home to another and running various errands for patients can also be tiring and time-consuming, or it can be a pleasant break.

OUTLOOK

As government and private agencies develop more programs to assist the dependent, the need for home health care aides will continue to grow. Because of the physical and emotional demands of the job, there is high turnover and, therefore, frequent job openings for home health care aides.

Also, the number of people 70 years of age and older is expected to increase substantially, and many of them will require at least some home care. Rising health care costs are causing many insurance companies to consider alternatives to hospital treatment, so many insurance providers now cover home care services. In addition, hospitals and nursing homes are trying to balance the demand for their services and their limitations in staff and physical facilities. The availability of home health care aides can allow such institutions as hospitals and nursing homes to offer quality care to more people. The U.S. Department of Labor projects that employment of home health aides will grow much faster than the average for all occupations through 2016.

FOR MORE INFORMATION

For certification information and statistics on the home health care industry, visit the association's Web site:

National Association for Home Care and Hospice
228 Seventh Street, SE
Washington, DC 20003-4306
Tel: 202-547-7424
http://www.nahc.org

For information on caring for the elderly, visit
ElderWeb
http://www.elderweb.com

HUMAN RESOURCES WORKERS

OVERVIEW

Human resources workers, also known as *personnel and labor relations specialists,* formulate policy and organize and conduct programs relating to all phases of personnel activity. *Labor relations specialists* serve as mediators between employees and the employer. They represent management during the collective-bargaining process when contracts with employees are negotiated. They also represent the company at grievance hearings, required when a worker feels management has not fulfilled its end of an employment contract. There are approximately 868,000 human resources workers employed in the United States.

THE JOB

Human resources workers are the liaison between the management of an organization and its employees. They see that management makes effective use of employees' skills, while at the same time improving working conditions for employees and helping them find fulfillment in their jobs. Most positions in this field involve heavy contact with people, at both management and nonmanagement levels.

Both human resources workers and labor relations specialists are experts in employer-employee relations, although the labor relations specialists concentrate on matters pertaining to union members. Human resources workers interview job applicants and select or recommend those who seem best suited to the company's needs. Their choices for hiring and advancement must follow the guidelines for equal employment opportunity and affirmative action established by the federal government. Human resources workers also plan and maintain programs for wages and salaries, employee benefits, and training and career development.

In small companies, one person often handles all the personnel work. This is the case for Susan Eckerle, human resources manager for Crane Federal Credit Union. She is responsible for all aspects of personnel management for 50 employees who work at three different locations. "I handle all hiring, employee relations counseling, corrective action, administration of benefits, and termination," she says. When Eckerle started working for the credit union, there was no specific human resources department. Therefore, much of her time is spent establishing policies and procedures to ensure that personnel matters run smoothly and consistently. "I've had to write job descriptions, set up interview procedures, and write the employee handbook," she says. "In addition, we don't have a long-term disability plan, and I think we need one. So I've been researching that."

Although Eckerle handles all phases of the human resources process, this is not always the case. The personnel department of a large organization may be staffed by many specialists, including recruiters, interviewers, job analysts, and specialists in charge of benefits, training, and labor relations. In addition, a large personnel department might include *personnel clerks* and *assistants* who issue forms, maintain files, compile statistics, answer inquiries, and do other routine tasks.

Human resources managers and *employment managers* are concerned with the overall functioning of the personnel department and may be involved with hiring, employee orientation, record keeping, insurance reports, wage surveys, budgets, grievances, and analyzing statistical data and reports. *Industrial relations directors* formulate the policies to be carried out by the various department managers.

Of all the human resources workers, the one who first meets new employees is often the recruiter. Companies depend on *personnel recruiters* to find the best employees available. To do this, recruiters develop sources through contacts within the community. In some cases, they travel extensively to other cities or to college campuses to meet with college career services directors, attend campus job fairs, and conduct preliminary interviews with potential candidates.

Employment interviewers interview applicants to fill job vacancies, evaluate their qualifications, and recommend hiring the most promising candidates. They sometimes administer tests, check references and backgrounds, and arrange for indoctrination and training. They must also be familiar and current with guidelines for equal employment opportunity (EEO) and affirmative action.

In very large organizations, the complex and sensitive area of EEO is handled by specialists who may be called *EEO representatives, affirmative-action coordinators,* or *job development specialists.* These specialists develop employment opportunities and on-the-job training programs for minority or disadvantaged applicants; devise systems or set up representative committees through which grievances can be investigated and resolved as they come up; and monitor corporate practices to pre-

SCHOOL SUBJECTS
Business, Psychology

PERSONAL SKILLS
Communications/Ideas, Leadership/Management

MINIMUM EDUCATION LEVEL
Bachelor's Degree

CERTIFICATION OR LICENSING
Recommended

WORK ENVIRONMENT
Primarily Indoors, One Location with Some Travel

vent possible EEO violations. Preparing and submitting EEO statistical reports is also an important part of their work.

Job analysts are sometimes also called *compensation analysts* and *position classifiers.* They study all of the jobs within an organization to determine job and worker requirements. Through observation and interviews with employees, they gather and analyze detailed information about job duties and the training and skills required. They write summaries describing each job, its specifications, and the possible route to advancement. Job analysts classify new positions as they are introduced and review existing jobs periodically. These job descriptions, or position classifications, form a structure for hiring, training, evaluating, and promoting employees, as well as for establishing an equitable pay system.

Occupational analysts conduct technical research on job relationships, functions, and content; worker characteristics; and occupational trends. The results of their studies enable business, industry, and government to utilize the general workforce more effectively.

Developing and administering the pay system is the primary responsibility of the *compensation manager.* With the assistance of other specialists on the staff, compensation managers establish a wage scale designed to attract, retain, and motivate employees. A realistic and fair compensation program takes into consideration company policies, government regulations concerning minimum wages and overtime pay, rates currently being paid by similar firms and industries, and agreements with labor unions. The compensation manager is familiar with all these factors and uses them to determine the compensation package.

Training specialists prepare and conduct a wide variety of education and training activities for both new and existing employees. Training specialists may work under the direction of an *education and training manager*. Training programs may cover such special areas as apprenticeship programs, sales techniques, health and safety practices, and retraining displaced workers. The methods chosen by training specialists for maximum effectiveness may include individual training, group instruction, lectures, demonstrations, meetings, or workshops, using such teaching aids as handbooks, demonstration models, multimedia programs, and reference works. These specialists also confer with management and supervisors to determine the needs for new training programs or revision of existing ones, maintain records of all training activities, and evaluate the success of the various programs and methods. Training instructors may work under the direction of an education and training manager. *Coordinators of auxiliary personnel* specialize in training nonprofessional nursing personnel in medical facilities.

Training specialists may help individuals establish career development goals and set up a timetable in which to strengthen job-related skills and learn new ones. Sometimes this involves outside study paid for by the company or rotation to jobs in different departments of the organization. The extent of the training program and the responsibilities of the training specialists vary considerably, depending on the size of the firm and its organizational objectives.

Benefits programs for employees are handled by *benefits managers* or *employee-welfare managers*. The major part of such programs generally involves insurance and pension plans. Since the enactment of the Employee Retirement Income Security Act (ERISA), reporting requirements have become a primary responsibility for personnel departments in large companies. The retirement program for state and local government employees is handled by *retirement officers*. In addition to regular health insurance and pension coverage, employee benefit packages have often grown to include such things as dental insurance, accidental death and disability insurance, automobile insurance, homeowner's insurance, profit sharing and thrift/savings plans, and stock options. The expertise of benefits analysts and administrators is extremely important in designing and carrying out the complex programs. These specialists also develop and coordinate additional services related to employee welfare, such as car pools, child care, cafeterias and lunchrooms, newsletters, annual physical exams, recreation and physical fitness programs, and counseling. Personal and financial counseling for employees close to retirement age is growing especially important.

In some cases—especially in smaller companies—the personnel department is responsible for administering the occupational safety and health programs. The trend, however, is toward establishing a separate safety department under the direction of a safety engineer, industrial hygienist, or other safety and health professionals.

Human resources departments may have access to resources outside the organization. For example, *employer relations representatives* promote the use of public employment services and programs among local employers. *Employee-health maintenance program specialists* help set up local government-funded programs among area employers to provide assistance in treating employees with alcoholism or behavioral medical problems.

In companies where employees are covered by union contracts, labor relations specialists form the link between union and management. Prior to negotiation of a collective-bargaining agreement, *labor relations managers* counsel management on their negotiating position and provide background information on the provisions of the current contract and the significance of the proposed changes. They also provide reference materials and statistics pertaining to labor legislation, labor market conditions, prevailing union and management practices, wage and salary surveys, and employee benefit programs. This work requires that labor relations managers be familiar with sources of economic and wage data and have an extensive knowledge of labor law and collective-bargaining trends. In the actual negotiation, the employer is usually represented by the director of labor relations or another top-level official, but the members of the company's labor relations staff play an important role throughout the negotiations.

Specialists in labor relations, or union-management relations, usually work for unionized organizations, helping company officials prepare for collective-bargaining sessions, participating in contract negotiations, and handling day-to-day labor relations matters. A large part of the work of labor relations specialists is analyzing and interpreting the contract for management and monitoring company practices to ensure their adherence to the terms. Of particular importance is the handling of grievance procedures. To investigate and settle grievances, these specialists arrange meetings between workers who raise a complaint, managers and supervisors, and a union representative. A grievance, for example, may concern seniority rights during a layoff. Labor relations disputes are sometimes investigated and resolved by *professional conciliators* or *mediators*. Labor relations work requires keeping up to date on developments in labor law, including arbitration decisions, and maintaining close contact with union officials.

Government human resources workers do essentially the same work as their counterparts in business, except that they deal with public employees whose jobs are subject to civil service regulations. Much of government personnel work concentrates on job analysis, because civil service jobs are strictly classified as to entry requirements, duties, and wages. In response to the growing importance of training and career development in the public sector, however, an entire industry of educational and training consultants has sprung up to provide similar services for public agencies. The increased union strength among government workers has resulted in a need for more highly trained labor relations specialists to handle negotiations, grievances, and arbitration cases on behalf of federal, state, and local agencies.

REQUIREMENTS
High School
. . . .

To prepare for a career as a human resources worker, you should take high school classes that will help prepare you for college. A solid background in the basics—math, science, and English—should be helpful in college-level work. You might especially focus on classes that will help you understand and communicate easily with people. Psychology, English, and speech classes are all good choices. Business classes can help you understand the fundamental workings of the business world, which is also important. Finally, foreign language skills could prove very helpful, especially in areas where there are large numbers of people who speak a language other than English.

Postsecondary Training
. . . .

High school graduates may start out as personnel clerks and advance to a professional position through experience, but such situations are becoming rare. Most employers require human resources workers to have a college degree. After high school, Susan Eckerle attended a four-year college and received a bachelor's degree in retail management, with a minor in psychology. She says that if she were starting over now, however, she would get a degree in human resources instead.

There is little agreement as to what type of undergraduate training is preferable for human resources work. Some employers favor college graduates who have majored in human resources, human resources administration, or industrial and labor relations, while others prefer individuals with a general business background. Another opinion is that human resources workers should have a well-rounded liberal arts education, with a degree in psychology, sociology, counseling, or education. A master's degree in business administration is also considered suitable preparation. Students interested in personnel work with a government agency may find it an asset to have a degree in personnel administration, political science, or public administration.

Individuals preparing for a career as a human resources worker will benefit from a wide range of courses. Classes might include business administration, public administration, psychology, sociology, political science, and statistics. For prospective labor relations specialists, valuable courses include labor law, collective bargaining, labor economics, labor history, and industrial psychology.

Work in labor relations may require graduate study in industrial or labor relations. While not required for entry-level jobs, a law degree is a must for those who conduct contract negotiations, and a combination of industrial relations courses and a law degree is especially desirable. For a career as a professional arbitrator, a degree in industrial and labor relations, law, or personnel management is required.

Certification or Licensing
. . . .

Some organizations for human resources professionals offer certification programs, which usually consist of a series of classes and a test. For example, the International Foundation of Employee Benefits Plans offers the certified employee benefit specialist designation to candidates who complete a series of college-level courses and pass exams on employee benefits plans. Other organizations that offer certification include the American Society for Training and Development, the Society for Human Resource Management, and WorldatWork Society of Certified Professionals. Though voluntary, certification is highly recommended and can improve chances for advancement.

Other Requirements
. . . .

Human resources workers must be able to communicate effectively and clearly both in speech and in writing and deal comfortably and easily with people of different levels of education and experience. "You've got to be people oriented," says Eckerle. "You have to love people and like working with them. That is huge."

Objectivity and fair-mindedness are also necessary in this job, where you often need to consider matters from both the employee's and the employer's point of view. "Being the liaison between management and employees can put you in a tough spot sometimes," Eckerle says. "You're directly between the two poles, and you have to be able to work with both sides."

These workers cooperate as part of a team; at the same time, they must be able to handle responsibility individually. Eckerle says it is important to be organized because you are often responsible for tracking many different things regarding many different people. "You can't be sloppy in your work habits, because you're dealing with a lot of important information and it all has to be processed correctly," she says.

EXPLORING

If you enjoy working with others, you can find helpful experience in managing school teams, planning banquets or picnics, working in your dean's or counselor's office, or reading books about personnel practices in businesses. You might also contact and interview the personnel director of a local business to find out more about the day-to-day responsibilities of this job. Part-time and summer employment in firms that have a personnel department are very good ways to explore the personnel field. Large department stores usually have personnel departments and should not be overlooked as a source of temporary work.

EMPLOYERS

Human resources workers hold approximately 868,000 jobs, with close to 90 percent employed in the private sector. Of those specialists who work in the private sector, 13 percent work in administrative and support services; 10 percent work in professional, scientific, and technical services; 9 percent in finance and insurance firms; 9 percent in health care; and 7 percent in manufacturing. The companies that are most likely to hire human resources workers are the larger ones, which have more employees to manage.

STARTING OUT

Career services counselors at colleges and universities can help graduates find employment. Also, large companies often send recruiters to campuses looking for promising job applicants. Otherwise, interested individuals may apply directly to local companies.

While still in high school, you may apply for entry-level jobs as personnel clerks and assistants. Private employment agencies and local offices of the state employment service are other possible sources for work. In addition, newspaper want ads often contain listings of many personnel jobs.

Beginners in personnel work are trained on the job or in formal training programs, where they learn how to classify jobs, interview applicants, or administer employee benefits. Then they are assigned to specialized areas in the personnel department. Some people enter the labor relations field after first gaining experience in general personnel work, but it is becoming more common for qualified individuals to enter that field directly.

ADVANCEMENT

After trainees have mastered basic personnel tasks, they are assigned to specific areas in the department to gain specialized experience. In time, they may advance to supervisory positions or to manager of a major part of the personnel program, such as training, compensation, or EEO/affirmative action. Advancement may also be achieved by moving into a higher position in a smaller organization. A few experienced employees with exceptional ability ultimately become top executives with titles such as director of human resources or director of labor relations. As in most fields, employees with advanced education and a proven track record are the most likely to advance in human resources positions.

EARNINGS

Jobs for human resources workers pay salaries that vary widely depending on the nature of the business and the size and location of the firm, as well as on the individual's qualifications and experience.

According to a survey conducted by the National Association of Colleges and Employers, an entry-level human resources specialist with a bachelor's degree in human resources, including labor and industrial relations, earned $41,680 annually in 2007.

The U.S. Department of Labor (DOL) reports that median annual earnings of human resources, training, and labor relations specialists were $52,270 in 2006. Salaries ranged from less than $26,000 to more than $88,630. The DOL reports the following mean salaries for human resources professionals by industry: federal government, $72,240; local government, $52,960; employment services, $47,760; and business, professional, labor, political, and similar organizations, $46,260. Human resources managers earned salaries that ranged from less than $51,810 to $114,860 or more in 2006.

Benefits for human resources workers depend on the employer; however, they usually include such items as health insurance, retirement or 401(k) plans, and paid vacation days.

WORK ENVIRONMENT

Human resources employees work under pleasant conditions in modern offices. Personnel specialists are seldom required to work more than 35 or 40 hours per week, although they may do so if they are developing a program or special project. The specific hours you work as a human resources specialist may depend upon which company you work for. "I work Monday through Friday," says Susan Eckerle, "but if you work for a company that has weekend hours, you'll probably have to work some weekends too. If you never work weekends, you won't know your employees."

Labor relations specialists often work longer hours, especially when contract agreements are being prepared and negotiated. The difficult aspects of the work may involve firing people, taking disciplinary actions, or handling employee disputes.

OUTLOOK

The U.S. Department of Labor predicts that there will be faster-than-average growth through 2016 for human resources, training, and labor relations managers and specialists. The Department of Labor also predicts especially strong growth for training and development specialists and employment, recruitment, and placement specialists.

Competition for jobs will continue to be strong, however, as there will be an abundance of qualified applicants. Opportunities will be best in the private sector as businesses continue to increase their staffs as they begin to devote more resources to increasing employee productivity, retraining, safety, and benefits. Employment should also be strong with consulting firms that offer personnel and benefits and compensation services to businesses that cannot afford to have their own extensive staffs. As jobs change with new technology, more employers will need training specialists to teach new skills. Human resources jobs may be affected by the trend in corporate downsizing and restructuring. Applicants who are certified will have the best prospects for employment.

FOR MORE INFORMATION

For information on standards and procedures in arbitration, contact
American Arbitration Association
1633 Broadway, 10th Floor

New York, NY 10019-6705
Tel: 212-716-5800
http://www.adr.org

For information on certification, contact
American Society for Training and Development
1640 King Street, Box 1443
Alexandria, VA 22313-2043
Tel: 703-683-8100
http://www.astd.org

For information about certification, contact
International Foundation of Employee Benefits Plans
PO Box 69
Brookfield, WI 53008-0069
Tel: 888-334-3327
http://www.ifebp.org

For information on training, job opportunities, and human resources publications, contact
International Public Management Association for Human Resources
1617 Duke Street
Alexandria, VA 22314-3406
Tel: 703-549-7100
http://www.ipma-hr.org

For general information on labor relations, contact
Labor and Employment Relations Association
University of Illinois—Urbana-Champaign
121 Labor and Industrial Relations Building
504 East Armory
Champaign, IL 61820-6221
Tel: 217-333-0072
Email: LERAoffice@uiuc.edu
http://www.irra.uiuc.edu

For information on certification and to use an interactive career-mapping tool, visit the society's Web site:
Society for Human Resource Management
1800 Duke Street
Alexandria, VA 22314-3494
Tel: 800-283-SHRM
http://www.shrm.org

For news and information on compensation and benefits administration and certification, contact
WorldatWork
14040 North Northsight Boulevard
Scottsdale, AZ 85260-3601
Tel: 877-951-9191
http://www.worldatwork.org

❏ HUMAN SERVICES WORKERS

OVERVIEW

Under the supervision of social workers, psychologists, sociologists, and other professionals, *human services workers* offer support to families, the elderly, the poor, and others in need. They teach life and communication skills to people in mental health facilities or substance abuse programs. Employed by agencies, shelters, halfway houses, and hospitals, they work individually with clients or in group counseling. They also direct clients to social services and benefits. There are approximately 339,000 human services workers employed in the United States.

THE JOB

A group of teenagers in a large high school are concerned about the violence that threatens them every day. They have seen their friends and classmates hurt in the school's hallways, on the basketball court, and in the parking lot. In a place built for their education, they fear for their safety, and each of them has something to say about it. They have something to say to the administration, to the parents, and, most of all, to the kids who carry guns and knives to school. Human services workers come to their aid. Human services workers step in to support the efforts of social workers, psychologists, and other professional agencies or programs. Human services workers

SCHOOL SUBJECTS
Health, Sociology

PERSONAL SKILLS
Communication/Ideas, Helping/Teaching

MINIMUM EDUCATION LEVEL
Some Postsecondary Training

CERTIFICATION OR LICENSING
None Available

WORK ENVIRONMENT
Primarily Indoors, Primarily One Location

may work in a school, a community center, a housing project, or a hospital. They may work as aides, assistants, technicians, or counselors. In the case of the high school students who want to improve conditions in their school, human services workers serve as group leaders under the supervision of a school social worker, meeting with some of the students to discuss their fears and concerns. They also meet with administrators, faculty, and parents. Eventually, they conduct a school-wide series of group discussions—listening, taking notes, offering advice, and most important, empowering people to better their communities and their lives.

The term "human services" covers a wide range of careers, from counseling prison inmates to counseling the families of murder victims; from helping someone with a disability find a job to caring for the child of a teenage mother during the school day. From one-on-one interaction to group interaction, from paperwork to footwork, the human services worker is focused on improving the lives of others.

As society changes, so do the concerns of human services workers. New societal problems (such as the rapid spread of AIDS among teenagers and the threat of gang violence) require special attention, as do changes in the population (such as the increasing number of elderly people living on their own and the increasing number of minimum-wage workers unable to fully provide for their families). New laws and political movements also affect human services workers because many social service programs rely heavily on federal and state aid. Although government policy makers are better educated than the policy makers of years past, social service programs are more threatened than ever before. Despite all these changes in society and the changes in the theories of social work, some things stay the same—human services workers care about the well-being of individuals and communities. They are sensitive to the needs of diverse groups of people, and they are actively involved in meeting the needs of the public.

Human services workers have had many of the same responsibilities throughout the years. They offer their clients counseling, representation, emotional support, and the services they need. Although some human services workers assist professionals with the development and evaluation of social programs, policy analysis, and other administrative duties, most work directly with clients.

This direct work can involve aid to specific populations, such as ethnic groups, women, and the poor. Many human services workers assist poor people in numerous ways. They interview clients to identify needed services. They care for clients' children during job or medical appointments and offer clients emotional support. They determine whether clients are eligible for food stamps, Medicaid, or other welfare programs. In some food stamp programs, aides advise low-income family members how to plan, budget, shop for, and prepare balanced meals, often accompanying or driving clients to the store and offering suggestions on the most nutritious and economical food to purchase.

Some aides serve tenants in public housing projects. They are employed by housing agencies or other groups to help tenants relocate. They inform tenants of the use of facilities and the location of community services, such as recreation centers and clinics. They also explain the management's rules about sanitation and maintenance. They may at times help resolve disagreements between tenants and landlords.

Members of specific populations call on the aid of human services workers for support, information, and representation. The human services worker can provide these clients with counseling and emotional support and direct them to support groups and services. Social workers work with human services workers to reach out to the people; together, they visit individuals, families, and neighborhood groups to publicize the supportive services available.

Other clients of human services workers are those experiencing life-cycle changes. Children, adolescents, and the elderly may require assistance in making transitions. Human services workers help parents find proper day care for their children. They educate young mothers about how to care for an infant. They counsel children struggling with family problems or peer pressure. They offer emotional support to gay, lesbian, and bisexual teenagers and involve them in support groups. Some programs help the elderly stay active and help them prepare meals and clean their homes. They also assist the elderly in getting to and from hospitals and community centers and stay in touch with these clients through home visits and telephone calls.

Some human services workers focus on specific problems, such as drug and alcohol abuse. Human services workers assist in developing, organizing, and conducting programs dealing with the causes of and remedies for substance abuse. Workers may help individuals trying to overcome drug or alcohol addiction to master practical skills, such as cooking and doing laundry, and teach them ways to communicate more effectively with others. Domestic violence is also a problem receiving more attention, as more and more people leave abusive situations. Shelters for victims require counselors, assistants, tutors, and day care personnel for their children.

Human services workers may also teach living and communication skills in homeless shelters and mental health facilities.

Record keeping is an important part of the duties of human services workers, because records may affect a client's eligibility for future benefits, the proper assessment of a program's success, and the prospect of future funding. Workers prepare and maintain records and case files of every person with whom they work. They record clients' responses to the various programs and treatment. They must also track costs in group homes in order to stay within budget.

REQUIREMENTS
High School

Some employers hire people with only a high school education, but these employees might find it hard to move beyond clerical positions. Interested high school students should plan to attend a college or university and should take classes in English, mathematics, political science, psychology, and sociology.

Postsecondary Training

Certificate and associate's degree programs in human services or mental health are offered at community and junior colleges, vocational-technical institutes, and other postsecondary institutions. It is also possible to pursue a bachelor's degree in human services. Almost 500 human services education programs exist; academic programs such as these prepare students for occupations in the human services. Because the educators at these colleges and universities stay in regular contact with the social work employers in their area, the programs are continually revised to meet the changing needs of the field. Students are exposed early and often to the kinds of situations they may encounter on the job.

Undergraduate and graduate programs typically include courses in psychology, sociology, crisis intervention, family dynamics, therapeutic interviewing, rehabilitation, and gerontology.

Other Requirements

Many people perform human services work because they want to make a difference in their community. They may also like connecting on a personal level with other people, offering them emotional support, helping them sort out problems, and teaching them how to care for themselves and their families. A genuine interest in the lives and concerns of others and a sensitivity to their situations are important to a human services worker. An artistic background can also be valuable in human services. Some programs in mental health facilities, domestic violence shelters, and other group homes use art therapy. Painting, music, dance, and creative writing are sometimes incorporated into counseling sessions, providing a client with alternative modes of expression.

In addition to the rewarding aspects of the job, a human services worker must be prepared to take on difficult responsibilities. The work can be very stressful. The problems of some populations—such as prison inmates, battered women and children, substance abusers, and the poor—can seem insurmountable. Their stories and day-to-day lives can seem tragic. Even if human services workers are not counseling clients, they are working directly with clients on some level. Just helping a person fill out an application or prepare a household budget requires a good disposition and the ability to be supportive. Clients may not welcome help and may not even care about their own well-being. In these cases, a human services worker must remain firm but supportive and encouraging. Patience is very important, whatever the area of human service.

The workload for a human services worker can also be overwhelming. An agency with limited funding cannot always afford to hire the number of employees it needs. A human services worker employed by an understaffed agency will probably be overworked. This can sometimes result in employee burnout.

EXPLORING

To get an idea of the requirements of human service, you can volunteer your time to a local human services agency or institution. Church organizations also involve young people in volunteer work, as do the Red Cross, the Boy Scouts, and the Girl Scouts. Volunteer work could include reading to blind or elderly people and visiting nursing homes and halfway homes. You might get involved organizing group recreation programs at the YMCA or YWCA or performing light clerical duties in an office. You could also encourage any high school organizations to which you belong to become actively involved in charity work.

Some members of high school organizations also perform social services within their own schools, educating classmates on the dangers of gangs, unsafe sex, and substance abuse. By being actively involved in your community, you can gain experience in human services as well as build up a history of volunteer service that will impress future employers.

EMPLOYERS

Approximately 339,000 human services workers are employed in the United States. They are employed in a variety of settings, including agency offices, community centers, group homes, halfway houses, mental health facilities, hospitals, shelters, and the private homes of clients.

STARTING OUT

Students may find jobs through their high school counselors or local and state human services agencies. Sometimes summer jobs and volunteer work can develop into full-time employment upon graduation. Employers try to be selective in their hiring because many human services jobs involve direct contact with people who are impaired and therefore vulnerable to exploitation. Experience with helping others is a definite advantage.

ADVANCEMENT

Job performance has some bearing on pay raises and advancement for human services workers. However, career advancement almost always depends on formal education, such as a bachelor's or master's degree in social work, counseling, rehabilitation, or some other related field. Many employers encourage their workers to further their education and some may even reimburse part of the costs of school. In addition, many employers provide in-service training such as seminars and workshops.

EARNINGS

Salaries of human services workers depend in part on their employer and amount of experience. According to the U.S. Department of Labor, median annual earnings of social and human service assistants were $25,580 in 2006. Salaries ranged from less than $16,180 to more than $40,780.

Benefits for full-time workers include vacation and sick time, health, and sometimes dental, insurance, and pension or 401(k) plans.

WORK ENVIRONMENT

Most human services workers work a standard 40-hour week, spending time both in the office and in the field interviewing clients and performing other support services. Some weekend and evening work may be required, but compensatory time off is usually granted. Workers in residential settings generally work in shifts. Because group homes need 24-hour staffing, workers usually work some evenings and weekends.

Work conditions are affected by the size and location of the town in which the work is found. The societal problems of large, urban areas are different from those of small, rural areas. In a city, human services workers deal with issues of crime, racism, gang warfare, and violence in the schools. These problems can exist in smaller communities as well, but human services workers in rural areas focus more on work with the elderly and the poor. Rural communities typically have an older population, with people living deeper in the country and farther from public and private services. This can require more transportation time. The social services in rural areas, because of lower salaries and poorer facilities, typically have trouble attracting workers.

Offices and facilities may be clean and cheerful, or they may be dismal, cramped, and inadequately equipped. While out in the field with clients, workers may also find themselves in dangerous, squalid areas. In a large city, workers can rely on public transportation, whereas workers in a rural community must often drive long distances.

OUTLOOK

Employment for human services workers will grow much faster than the average for all occupations through 2016, according to the U.S. Department of Labor. The best opportunities will be in job-training programs, residential care facilities, and private social service agencies, which include such services as adult daycare and meal delivery programs. Correctional facilities are also expected to employ many more human services workers. Because counseling inmates and offenders can be undesirable work, there are a number of high-paying jobs available in that area.

New ideas in treating people with disabilities or mental illness also influence employment growth in group homes and residential care facilities. Public concern for the homeless—many of whom are former mental patients who were released under service reductions in the 1980s—as well as for troubled teenagers, and those with substance abuse problems, is likely to bring about new community-based programs and group residences.

Job prospects in public agencies are not as bright as they once were because of fiscal policies that tighten eligibility requirements for federal welfare and other payments. State and local governments are expected to remain major employers, however, as the burden of providing social services such as welfare, child support, and nutrition programs is shifted from the federal government to the state and local level. In larger cities, such as New York or Washington, D.C., jobs in the public sector will be more plentiful than in smaller cities because of the higher demand. There is also a higher burnout rate in the larger cities, resulting in more job opportunities as people vacate their positions for other careers.

FOR MORE INFORMATION

For more information on careers in counseling, contact
American Counseling Association
5999 Stevenson Avenue
Alexandria, VA 22304-3304
Tel: 800-347-6647
http://www.counseling.org

To access the online publication Choices: Careers in Social Work, *visit the NASW's Web site:*
National Association of Social Workers (NASW)
750 First Street, NE, Suite 700
Washington, DC 20002-4241
http://www.socialworkers.org

For information on student memberships, scholarships, and master's degree programs in human services, visit the NOHS's Web site:
National Organization for Human Services (NOHS)
90 Madison Street, Suite 206
Denver, CO 80206-5418
Tel: 303-320-5430
Email: info@nationalhumanservices.org
http://www.nohse.com

For information on employment with government human service agencies, contact
U.S. Department of Health and Human Services
200 Independence Avenue, SW
Washington, DC 20201-0004
Tel: 877-696-6775
http://www.hhs.gov

The following is a job search Web site for social services and social work positions.
SocialService.Com
http://www.socialservice.com

INDUSTRIAL ENGINEERS

OVERVIEW

Industrial engineers use their knowledge of various disciplines—including systems engineering, management science, operations research, and fields such as ergonomics—to determine the most efficient and cost-effective methods for industrial production. They are responsible for designing systems that integrate materials, equipment, information, and people in the overall production process. Approximately 201,000 industrial engineers are employed in the United States.

THE JOB

Industrial engineers are involved with the development and implementation of the systems and procedures that are utilized by many industries and businesses. In general, they figure out the most effective ways to use the three basic elements of any company: people, facilities, and equipment.

Although industrial engineers work in a variety of businesses, the main focus of the discipline is in manufacturing, also called industrial production. Primarily, industrial engineers are concerned with process technology, which includes the design and layout of machinery and the organization of workers who implement the required tasks.

Industrial engineers have many responsibilities. With regard to facilities and equipment, engineers are involved

---

SCHOOL SUBJECTS
Computer Science, Mathematics

PERSONAL SKILLS
Leadership/Management, Technical/Scientific

MINIMUM EDUCATION LEVEL
Bachelor's Degree

CERTIFICATION OR LICENSING
Required by Certain States

WORK ENVIRONMENT
Primarily Indoors, Primarily One Location

---

in selecting machinery and other equipment and then in setting them up in the most efficient production layout. They also develop methods to accomplish production tasks, such as the organization of an assembly line. In addition, they devise systems for quality control, distribution, and inventory.

Industrial engineers are responsible for some organizational issues. For instance, they might study an organization chart and other information about a project and then determine the functions and responsibilities of workers. They devise and implement job evaluation procedures as well as articulate labor-utilization standards for workers. Engineers often meet with managers to discuss cost analysis, financial planning, job evaluation, and salary administration. Not only do they recommend methods for improving employee efficiency but they may also devise wage and incentive programs.

Industrial engineers evaluate ergonomic issues, the relationship between human capabilities and the physical environment in which they work. For example, they might evaluate whether machines are causing physical harm or discomfort to workers or whether the machines could be designed differently to enable workers to be more productive.

REQUIREMENTS
High School

To prepare for a college engineering program, concentrate on mathematics (algebra, trigonometry, geometry, calculus), physical sciences (physics, chemistry), social sciences (economics, sociology), and English. Engineers often have to convey ideas graphically and may need to visualize processes in three-dimension, so courses in graphics, drafting, or design are also helpful. In addition, round out your education with computer science, history, and foreign language classes. If honors-level courses are available to you, be sure to take them.

Postsecondary Training

A bachelor's degree from an accredited institution is usually the minimum requirement for all professional positions. The Accreditation Board for Engineering and Technology (ABET) accredits schools offering engineering programs, including industrial engineering. A listing of accredited colleges and universities is available on the ABET's Web site (http://www.abet.org), and a visit there should be one of your first stops when you are deciding on a school to attend. Colleges and universities offer either four- or five-year engineering programs.

Because of the intensity of the curricula, many students take heavy course loads and attend summer sessions in order to finish in four years.

During your junior and senior years of college, you should consider your specific career goals, such as in which industry to work. Third- and fourth-year courses focus on such subjects as facility planning and design, work measurement standards, process design, engineering economics, manufacturing and automation, and incentive plans.

Many industrial engineers go on to earn a graduate degree. These programs tend to involve more research and independent study. Graduate degrees are usually required for teaching positions.

Certification or Licensing

Licensure as a professional engineer is recommended since an increasing number of employers require it. Even those employers who do not require licensing will view it favorably when considering new hires or when reviewing workers for promotion. Licensing requirements vary from state to state. In general, however, they involve having graduated from an accredited school, having four years of work experience, and having passed the eight-hour Fundamentals of Engineering exam and the eight-hour Principles and Practice of Engineering exam. These exams are offered by the National Council of Examiners for Engineering and Surveying (http://www.ncees.org). Depending on your state, you can take the Fundamentals exam shortly before your graduation from college or after you have received your bachelor's degree. At that point you will be an engineer-in-training. Once you have fulfilled all the licensure requirements, you receive the designation professional engineer.

Other Requirements

Industrial engineers enjoy problem solving and analyzing things as well as being a team member. The ability to communicate is vital since engineers interact with all levels of management and workers. Being organized and detail-minded is important because industrial engineers often handle large projects and must bring them in on time and on budget. Since process design is the cornerstone of the field, an engineer should be creative and inventive.

EXPLORING

Try joining a science or engineering club, such as the Junior Engineering Technical Society (JETS). JETS offers academic competitions in subjects such as computer fundamentals, mathematics, physics, and English. It also conducts design contests in which students learn and apply science and engineering principles. JETS also offers the *Pre-Engineering Times*, a publication that will be useful if you are interested in engineering. It contains information on engineering specialties, competitions, schools, scholarships, and other resources. Visit http://www.jets.org/publications/petimes.cfm to read the publication. You also might read some engineering books for background on the field or magazines such as *Industrial Engineer*, a magazine published by the Institute of Industrial Engineers (IIE). Selected articles from *Industrial Engineer* can be viewed on the IIE's Web site, http://www.iienet.org.

EMPLOYERS

Approximately 201,000 industrial engineers are employed in the United States. Although a majority of industrial engineers are employed in the manufacturing industry, related jobs are found in almost all businesses, including aviation, aerospace, transportation, communications, electric, gas and sanitary services, government, finance, insurance, real estate, wholesale and retail trade, construction, mining, agriculture, forestry, and fishing. Also, many work as independent consultants.

STARTING OUT

The main qualification for an entry-level job is a bachelor's degree in industrial engineering. Accredited college programs generally have job openings listed in their career services offices. Entry-level industrial engineers find jobs in various departments, such as computer operations, warehousing, and quality control. As engineers gain on-the-job experience and familiarity with departments, they may decide on a specialty. Some may want to continue to work as process designers or methods engineers, while others may move on to administrative positions.

Some further examples of specialties include work measurement standards, shipping and receiving, cost control, engineering economics, materials handling, management information systems, mathematical models, and operations. Many who choose industrial engineering as a career find its appeal in the diversity of sectors that are available to explore.

ADVANCEMENT

After having worked at least three years in the same job, an industrial engineer may have the basic credentials needed for advancement to a higher position. In general, positions in operations and administration are considered high-level jobs, although this varies from company to company. Engineers who work in these areas tend to earn larger salaries than those who work in warehousing or cost control, for example. If one is interested in moving to a different company, it is considered easier to do so within the same industry.

Industrial engineering jobs are often considered stepping-stones to management positions, even in other fields. Engineers with many years' experience frequently are promoted to higher level jobs with greater responsibilities. Because of the field's broad exposure, industrial engineering employees are generally considered better prepared for executive roles than are other types of engineers.

EARNINGS

According to the U.S. Department of Labor, the median annual wage for industrial engineers in 2006 was $68,620. The lowest paid 10 percent of all industrial engineers earned less than $44,790 annually. However, as with most occupations, salaries rise as more experience is gained. Very experienced engineers can earn more than $100,980. According to a survey by the National Association of Colleges and Employers, the average starting salary for industrial engineers with a bachelor's degree was $55,067 in 2007, with a master's degree, $64,759 a year; and with a Ph.D., $77,364.

Benefits for full-time industrial engineers include vacation and sick time, health and dental insurance, and pension or 401 (k) plans.

WORK ENVIRONMENT

Industrial engineers usually work in offices at desks and computers, designing and evaluating plans, statistics, and other documents. Overall, industrial engineering is ranked above other engineering disciplines for factors such as employment outlook, salary, and physical environment. However, industrial engineering jobs are considered stressful because they often entail tight deadlines and demanding quotas, and jobs are moderately competitive. Most engineers work an average of 40 hours per week.

Industrial engineers generally collaborate with other employees, conferring on designs and procedures, as well as with business managers and consultants. Although they spend most of their time in their offices, they frequently must evaluate conditions at factories and plants, where noise levels are often high.

OUTLOOK

The U.S. Department of Labor anticipates that employment for industrial engineers will grow faster than the average for all occupations through 2016. The demand for industrial engineers will continue as manufacturing and other companies strive to make their production processes more effective and competitive. Engineers who transfer or retire will create the highest percentage of openings in this field.

FOR MORE INFORMATION

For a list of ABET-accredited engineering schools, contact
Accreditation Board for Engineering and Technology (ABET)
111 Market Place, Suite 1050
Baltimore, MD 21202-7116
Tel: 410-347-7700
http://www.abet.org

For comprehensive information about careers in industrial engineering, contact
Institute of Industrial Engineers
3577 Parkway Lane, Suite 200
Norcross, GA 30092-2833
Tel: 800-494-0460
http://www.iienet.org

Visit the JETS Web site for membership information and to read the online brochure Industrial Engineering.
Junior Engineering Technical Society (JETS)
1420 King Street, Suite 405
Alexandria, VA 22314-2750
Tel: 703-548-5387
Email: info@jets.org
http://www.jets.org

INTERIOR DESIGNERS AND DECORATORS

OVERVIEW

Interior designers and *interior decorators* evaluate, plan, and design the interior areas of residential, commercial, and industrial structures. In addition to helping clients select equipment and fixtures, these professionals supervise the coordination of colors and materials, obtain estimates and costs within the client's budget, and oversee the execution and installation of the project. They also often advise clients on architectural requirements, space planning, and the function and purpose of the environment.

There are currently approximately 72,000 interior designers working in the United States. These specialists are employed by interior design or architectural firms, department stores, furniture stores, hotel chains, and large corporations.

THE JOB

The terms "interior designer" and "interior decorator" are sometimes used interchangeably. However, there is an important distinction between the two. Interior designers plan and create the overall design for interior spaces, while interior decorators focus on the decorative aspects of the design and furnishing of interiors. A further distinction concerns the type of interior space on which the design or decorating professional works. Specifically, *residential designers* focus on individual homes, while *contract* or *commercial designers* specialize in office buildings, industrial complexes, hotels, hospitals, restaurants, schools, factories, and other nonresidential environments.

Interior designers and decorators perform a wide variety of services, depending on the type of project and the clients' requirements. A job may range from designing and decorating a single room in a private residence to coordinating the entire interior arrangement of a huge building complex. In addition to planning the interiors of new buildings, interior professionals also redesign existing interiors.

Design and decorating specialists begin by evaluating a project. They first consider how the space will be used. In addition to suiting the project's functional requirements, designs must address the needs, desires, tastes, and budget of the client as well. The designer often works closely with the architect in planning the complete layout of rooms and use of space. The designer's plans must work well with the architect's blueprints and comply with other building requirements. Design work of this kind is usually done in connection with the building or renovation of large structures.

Interior professionals may design the furniture and accessories to be used on a project, or they might work with materials that are already available. They select and plan the arrangement of furniture, draperies, floor coverings, wallpaper, paint, and other decorations. They make their decisions only after considering general style, scale of furnishings, colors, patterns, flow, lighting, safety, communication, and a host of other factors. They must also be familiar with local, state, and federal laws as well as building codes and other related regulations.

Although interior designers and decorators may consult with clients throughout the conceptual phase of the design project, they usually make a formal presentation once the design has been formulated. Such presentations may include sketches, scaled floorplans, drawings, models, color charts, photographs of furnishings, and samples of materials for upholstery, draperies, and wall coverings. Designers and decorators also usually provide a cost estimate of furnishings, materials, labor, transportation, and incidentals required to complete the project.

Once plans have been approved by the client, the interior designer and decorator assembles materials—drapery fabrics, upholstery fabrics, new furniture, paint, and wallpaper—and supervises the work, often acting as agent for the client in contracting the services of craftworkers and specifying custom-made merchandise. Interior professionals must be familiar with many materials used in furnishing. They must know when certain materials are suitable, how they will blend with other materials, and how they will wear. They must also be familiar with historical periods influencing design and have a knack for using and combining the best contributions of these designs of the past. Since designers and decorators supervise the work done from their plans, they should know something about painting, carpet laying, carpentry, cabinet making, and other craft areas. In addition, they must

SCHOOL SUBJECTS
Art, Business

PERSONAL SKILLS
Artistic, Communication/Ideas

MINIMUM EDUCATION LEVEL
Associate's Degree

CERTIFICATION OR LICENSING
Required by Certain States

WORK ENVIRONMENT
Primarily Indoors, Primarily Multiple Locations

be able to buy materials and services at reasonable prices while producing quality work.

Some designers and decorators specialize in a particular aspect of interior design, such as furniture, carpeting, or artwork. Others concentrate on particular environments, such as offices, hospitals, restaurants, or transportation, including ships, aircraft, and trains. Still others specialize in the renovation of old buildings. In addition to researching the styles in which rooms were originally decorated and furnished, these workers often supervise the manufacture of furniture and accessories to be used.

Considerable paperwork is involved in interior design and decoration, much of it related to budgets and costs. Interior professionals must determine quantities and make and obtain cost estimates. In addition, designers and decorators write up and administer contracts, obtain permits, place orders, and check deliveries carefully. All of this work requires an ability to attend to detail in the business aspect of interior design.

REQUIREMENTS
High School

Although formal training is not always necessary in the field of interior design, it is becoming increasingly important and is usually essential for advancement. Most architectural firms, department stores, and design firms accept only professionally trained people, even for beginning positions.

If you're considering a career as an interior designer or decorator, classes in home economics, art history, design, fine arts, and drafting will prove to be valuable. Since interior design is both an art and a business, such courses as marketing, advertising, accounting, management, and general business are important as well.

Postsecondary Training

Professional schools offer two- or three-year certificates or diplomas in interior design. Colleges and universities award undergraduate degrees in four-year programs, and graduate study is also available. The Council for Interior Design Accreditation (CIDA) accredits bachelor's degree programs in interior design. There are 145 accredited interior design programs offered through art, architecture, and home economics schools in the United States and Canada. The National Association of Schools of Art and Design also accredits colleges and universities with programs in art and design. College students interested in entering the interior design field should take courses

in art history, architectural drawing and drafting, fine arts, furniture design, codes and standards of design, and computer-aided design, as well as classes that focus on the types of materials primarily used, such as fibers, wood, metals, and plastics. Knowledge of lighting and electrical equipment as well as furnishings, art pieces, and antiques, is important.

In addition to art and industry-specific areas of study, courses in business and management are vital to aspiring interior designers and decorators. Learning research methods will help you stay abreast of government regulations and safety standards. You should also have some knowledge of zoning laws, building codes, and other restrictions. Finally, keeping up with product performance and new developments in materials and manufacture is an important part of the ongoing education of the interior designer and decorator.

Art historians, people with architecture or environmental planning experience, and others with qualifications in commercial or industrial design may also qualify for employment in interior design.

Certification or Licensing

Currently, 23 states, the District of Columbia, and Puerto Rico require licensing for interior designers, according to the U.S. Department of Labor. Each of these states has its own requirements for licensing and regulations for practice, so it's important to contact the specific state in order to find out how one can apply. To become eligible for registration or licensing in these jurisdictions, applicants must satisfy experience and education requirements and take the National Council for Interior Design Qualification (NCIDQ) Examination.

To prepare students for this examination, the NCIDQ offers the Interior Design Experience Program. Program participants are required to complete 3,520 hours of documented experience in the following categories: Programming, Schematic Design, Design Development, Contract Documents, Contract Administration, and Professional Practice. According to the council, this experience may be achieved through "working directly in a competency area, by observing others who are engaged in such work, or by attending lectures, seminars, and continuing education courses." Students who have completed at least 96 semester credits hours (or 144 quarter credits hours of education) in a CIDA-accredited interior design program are eligible to participate.

Additionally, the National Kitchen and Bath Association offers several certifications to designers who specialize in kitchen and bath design.

Other Requirements

First and foremost, interior designers and decorators need to have artistic talent, including an eye for color, proportion, balance, and detail, and have the ability to visualize. Designers must be able to render an image clearly and carry it out consistently. At the same time, artistic taste and knowledge of current and enduring fashion trends are essential.

In addition, interior designers need to be able to supervise craftworkers and work well with a variety of other people, including clients and suppliers. Designers should be creative, analytical, and ethical. They also need to be able to focus on the needs of clients, develop a global view, and have an appreciation of diversity. Finally, precision, patience, perseverance, enthusiasm, and attention to detail are vital.

EXPLORING

If you're thinking about becoming an interior designer or decorator, there are several ways to learn about the field. Courses in home economics or any of the fine arts, offered either at school or through a local organization, can give you a taste of some of the areas of knowledge needed by interior designers.

To get a sense of the actual work done by design specialists, you may be able to find a part-time or summer job in a department or furniture store. Such experience will enable you to learn more about the materials used in interior design and decorating and to see the store's interior design service in action. Since the business aspects of interior design are just as important as the creative side, any kind of general selling or business experience will prove to be valuable. As a salesperson at any type of store, for example, you'll learn how to talk to customers, write up orders, close sales, and much more.

In addition to learning about interior design itself, knowledge of auxiliary and support industries will be useful as well. To get a firsthand look at associated fields, you may want to arrange a visit to a construction site, examine an architect's blueprints, talk to someone who specializes in lighting, or tour a furniture manufacturing plant.

Ultimately, the best way to learn about interior design or decorating is to talk to a design professional. While interviewing an interior designer or decorator will be interesting and enlightening, finding a mentor who is doing the type of work that you may want to do in the future is ideal. Such a person can suggest other activities that may be of interest to you as you investigate the interior design field, provide you with the names of trade magazines and/or books that can shed some light on the industry, and serve as a resource for questions you might have.

EMPLOYERS

Approximately 72,000 interior designers and decorators are employed in the United States. Interior designers and decorators can be found wherever there is a need to style or beautify the interior environment of a building. The main professional areas in which they work are residential, government, commercial, retail, hospitality, education and research, health care, and facilities management.

In addition to "traditional" interior design and decorating opportunities, some professionals design theater, film, and television settings. A few designers become teachers, lecturers, or consultants, while others work in advertising and journalism.

The majority of interior designers and decorators work either for themselves or for companies employing fewer than five people. Since the industry is not dominated by giant conglomerates or even mid-sized firms, employment opportunities are available all across the United States, as well as abroad, in cities both large and small.

STARTING OUT

Most large department stores and design firms with established reputations hire only trained interior designers and decorators. More often than not, these employers look for prospective employees with a good portfolio and a bachelor of fine arts degree. Many schools, however, offer apprenticeship or internship programs in cooperation with professional studios or offices of interior design. These programs make it possible for students to apply their academic training in an actual work environment prior to graduation.

After graduating from a two- or three-year training program (or a four-year university), the beginning interior professional must be prepared to spend one to three years as an assistant to an experienced designer or decorator before achieving full professional status. This is the usual method of entering the field of interior design and gaining membership in a professional organization.

Finding work as an assistant can often be difficult, so be prepared to take any related job. Becoming a sales clerk for interior furnishings, a shopper for accessories or fabrics, or even a receptionist or stockroom assistant can help you get a foot in the door and provide valuable experience as well.

ADVANCEMENT

While advancement possibilities are available, competition for jobs is intense and interior designers and decorators must possess a combination of talent, personality, and business sense to reach the top. Someone just starting out in the field must take a long-range career view, accept jobs that offer practical experience, and put up with long hours and occasionally difficult clients. It usually takes three to six years of practical, on-the-job experience in order to become a fully qualified interior designer or decorator.

As interior professionals gain experience, they can move into positions of greater responsibility and may eventually be promoted to such jobs as design department head or interior furnishings coordinator. Professionals who work with furnishings in architectural firms often become more involved in product design and sales. Designers and decorators can also establish their own businesses. Consulting is another common area of work for the established interior professional.

EARNINGS

Interior designers earned median annual salaries of $42,260 in 2006, according to the U.S. Department of Labor. The highest paid 10 percent earned more than $78,760, while the lowest paid 10 percent earned less than $24,270 annually. The U.S. Department of Labor reports the following mean salaries for interior designers by specialty: architectural and engineering services, $50,300; specialized design services, $50,190; and furniture stores, $43,330. In general, interior designers and decorators working in large urban areas make significantly more than those working in smaller cities.

Designers and decorators at interior design firms can earn a straight salary, a salary plus a bonus or commission, or a straight commission. Such firms sometimes pay their employees a percentage of the profits as well. Self-employed professionals may charge an hourly fee, a flat fee, or a combination of the two depending on the project. Some designers and decorators charge a percentage on the cost of materials bought for each project.

The benefits enjoyed by interior designers and decorators, like salaries and bonuses, depend on the particular employer. Benefits may include paid vacations, health and life insurance, paid sick or personal days, employee-sponsored retirement plans, and an employer-sponsored 401(k) program.

WORK ENVIRONMENT

Working conditions for interior designers and decorators vary, depending on where they are employed. While professionals usually have an office or a studio, they may spend the day at a department store, architecture firm, or construction site working with the decorating materials sold by the firm and the clients who have purchased them. In addition, designers often go on-site to consult with and supervise the projects being completed by various craftworkers.

Whether designers or decorators are employed by a firm or operate their own businesses, much of their time is spent in clients' homes and businesses. While more and more offices are using the services of interior designers and decorators, the larger part of the business still lies in the area of home design. Residential designers and decorators work intimately with customers, planning, selecting materials, receiving instructions, and sometimes subtly guiding the customers' tastes and choices in order to achieve an atmosphere that is both aesthetic and functional.

While designers and decorators employed by department stores, furniture stores, or design firms often work regular 40-hour weeks, self-employed professionals usually work irregular hours—including evenings and weekends—in order to accommodate their clients' schedules. Deadlines must be met, and if there have been problems and delays on the job, the designer or decorator must work hard to complete the project on schedule. In general, the more successful the individual becomes, the longer and more irregular the hours.

The interior professional's main objective is ultimately to please the customer and thus establish a good reputation. Customers may be difficult at times. They may often change their minds, forcing the designer or decorator to revise plans. Despite difficult clients, the work is interesting and provides a variety of activities.

OUTLOOK

Employment opportunities are expected to be good for interior designers and decorators through 2016, according to the U.S. Department of Labor. However, since the services of design professionals are in many ways a luxury, the job outlook is heavily dependent on the economy. In times of prosperity, there is a steady increase in jobs. When the economy slows down, however, opportunities in the field decrease markedly.

Marketing futurist Faith Popcorn predicts that people will be staying home more (cocooning) and that there will be an increase in what she calls "fantasy adventure." This trend is based on people's desire to stay at home but, at the same time, feel like they are in exotic, remote places. In the future, Popcorn sees homes containing rooms designed like Las Vegas-style resorts, African plains, and other interesting destinations. Both cocooning and fantasy adventure will further add to the many opportunities that will be available to interior designers.

According to the International Interior Designers Association's Industry Advisory Council (IAC), a number of trends specific to the industry will also positively influence the employment outlook for interior designers and decorators. Clients in all market areas, for example, will develop an appreciation for the value of interior design work as well as increased respect for the interior professional's expertise. In addition, businesses, ever mindful of their employees' safety, health, and general welfare, will rely more heavily on designers to create interior atmospheres that will positively impact workplace performance.

The IAC also notes the importance of technology in the field of interior design. In addition to affecting the design of homes, technology will impact the production of design materials as well as create the need for multidisciplinary design. Professionals both familiar and comfortable with technology will definitely have an edge in an ever-competitive job market. Finally, the IAC points to the continued importance of education and research in the field of interior design. According to Allison Carll-White, former director of the International Interior Designers Association's Research and Education Forum, design organizations will have to offer programs focusing on basic interior design in order to attract talented students to the profession.

While competition for good designing and decorating positions is expected to be fierce, especially for those lacking experience, there is currently a great need for industrial interior designers in housing developments, offices, restaurants, hospital complexes, senior care facilities, hotels, and other large building projects. In addition, as construction of houses increases, there will be many projects available for residential designers and decorators. Designers with strong knowledge of ergonomics and green design will also enjoy excellent job prospects. Those who specialize in one aspect of interior design, such as kitchen or bath design, may have better employment prospects in this highly competitive field.

FOR MORE INFORMATION

For industry trends, career guidance, and other resources, contact
American Society of Interior Designers
608 Massachusetts Avenue, NE
Washington, DC 20002-6006
Tel: 202-546-3480
http://www.asid.org

For a list of accredited interior design programs, contact
Council for Interior Design Accreditation
146 Monroe Center, NW, Suite 1318
Grand Rapids, MI 49503-2822
Tel: 616-458-0400
Email: info@accredit-id.org
http://www.accredit-id.org

For information on continuing education, publications, and a list of accredited graduate programs in interior design, contact
Interior Design Educators Council
7150 Winton Drive, Suite 300
Indianapolis, IN 46268-4398
Tel: 317-328-4437
Email: info@idec.org
http://www.idec.org

For information on the industry, contact
International Interior Design Association
222 Merchandise Mart, Suite 567
Chicago, IL 60654-1103
Tel: 888-799-4432
Email: iidahq@iida.org
http://www.iida.com

For information on accredited interior design programs, contact
National Association of Schools of Art and Design
11250 Roger Bacon Drive, Suite 21
Reston, VA 20190-5248
Tel: 703-437-0700
Email: info@arts-accredit.org
http://nasad.arts-accredit.org

For information on the Interior Design Experience Program, contact
National Council for Interior Design Qualification
1200 18th Street, NW, Suite 1001
Washington, DC 20036-2506
Tel: 202-721-0220
Email: info@ncidq.org
http://www.ncidq.org

For information on certification, contact
National Kitchen and Bath Association
687 Willow Grove Street
Hackettstown, NJ 07840-1713
Tel: 800-843-6522
http://www.nkba.org

For useful information about interior design, visit
Dezignare Interior Design Collective
http://dezignare.com

For useful career information, visit
Careers in Interior Design
http://www.careersininteriordesign.com

INTERPRETERS AND TRANSLATORS

OVERVIEW

An *interpreter* translates spoken passages of a foreign language into another specified language. The job is often designated by the language interpreted, such as Spanish or Japanese. In addition, many interpreters specialize according to subject matter. For example, *medical interpreters* have extensive knowledge of and experience in the health care field, while *court or judiciary interpreters* speak both a second language and the "language" of law. *Interpreters for the deaf* aid in the communication between people who are unable to hear and those who can.

In contrast to interpreters, *translators* focus on written materials, such as books, plays, technical or scientific papers, legal documents, laws, treaties, and decrees. A *sight translator* performs a combination of interpreting and translating by reading printed material in one language while reciting it aloud in another.

In the United States, approximately 41,000 interpreters and translators currently work full time.

THE JOB

Although interpreters are needed for a variety of languages and different venues and circumstances, there are only two basic systems of interpretation: simultaneous and consecutive. Spurred in part by the invention and development of electronic sound equipment, simultaneous interpretation has been in use since the charter of the United Nations (UN).

Simultaneous interpreters are able to convert a spoken sentence instantaneously. Some are so skilled that they are able to complete a sentence in the second language at almost the precise moment that the speaker is conversing in the original language. Such interpreters are usually familiar with the speaking habits of the speaker and can anticipate the way in which the sentence will be completed. The interpreter may also make judgments about the intent of the sentence or phrase from the speaker's gestures, facial expressions, and inflections. While working at a fast pace, the interpreter must be careful not to summarize, edit, or in any way change the meaning of what is being said.

In contrast, *consecutive interpreters* wait until the speaker has paused to convert speech into a second language. In this case, the speaker waits until the interpreter has finished before resuming the speech. Since every sentence is repeated in consecutive interpretation, this method takes longer than simultaneous interpretation.

In both systems, interpreters are placed so that they can clearly see and hear all that is taking place. In formal situations, such as those at the UN and other international conferences, interpreters are often assigned to a glass-enclosed booth. Speeches are transmitted to the booth, and interpreters, in turn, translate the speaker's words into a microphone. Each UN delegate can tune in the voice of the appropriate interpreter. Because of the difficulty of the job, these simultaneous interpreters usually work in pairs, each working 30-minute shifts.

All international conference interpreters are simultaneous interpreters. Many interpreters, however, work in situations other than formal diplomatic meetings. For

SCHOOL SUBJECTS
English, Foreign Language, Speech

PERSONAL SKILLS
Communication/Ideas, Helping/Teaching

MINIMUM EDUCATION LEVEL
Bachelor's Degree

CERTIFICATION OR LICENSING
Recommended

WORK ENVIRONMENT
Primarily Indoors, Primarily Multiple Locations

example, interpreters are needed for negotiations of all kinds, as well as for legal, financial, medical, and business purposes. Court or judiciary interpreters, for example, work in courtrooms and at attorney–client meetings, depositions, and witness-preparation sessions.

Other interpreters serve on call, traveling with visitors from foreign countries who are touring the United States. Usually, these language specialists use consecutive interpretation. Their job is to make sure that whatever the visitors say is understood and that they also understand what is being said to them. Still other interpreters accompany groups of U.S. citizens on official tours abroad. On such assignments, they may be sent to any foreign country and might be away from the United States for long periods of time.

Interpreters also work on short-term assignments. Services may be required for only brief intervals, such as for a special conference or single interview with press representatives.

While interpreters focus on the spoken word, translators work with written language. They read and translate novels, plays, essays, nonfiction and technical works, legal documents, records and reports, speeches, and other written material. Translators generally follow a certain set of procedures in their work. They begin by reading the text, taking careful notes on what they do not understand. To translate questionable passages, they look up words and terms in specialized dictionaries and glossaries. They may also do additional reading on the subject to understand it better. Finally, they write translated drafts in the target language.

REQUIREMENTS
High School

If you are interested in becoming an interpreter or translator, you should take a variety of English courses, because most translating work is from a foreign language into English. The study of one or more foreign languages is vital. If you are interested in becoming proficient in one or more of the Romance languages, such as Italian, French, or Spanish, basic courses in Latin will be valuable.

While you should devote as much time as possible to the study of at least one foreign language, other helpful courses include speech, business, cultural studies, humanities, world history, geography, and political science. In fact, any course that emphasizes the written and/or spoken word will be valuable to aspiring interpreters or translators. In addition, knowledge of a particular subject matter in which you may have interest, such as

health, law, or science, will give you a professional edge if you want to specialize. Finally, courses in typing and word processing are recommended, especially if you want to pursue a career as a translator.

Postsecondary Training

Because interpreters and translators need to be proficient in grammar, have an excellent vocabulary in the chosen language, and have sound knowledge in a wide variety of subjects, employers generally require that applicants have at least a bachelor's degree. Scientific and professional interpreters are best qualified if they have graduate degrees.

In addition to language and field-specialty skills, you should take college courses that will allow you to develop effective techniques in public speaking, particularly if you're planning to pursue a career as an interpreter. Courses such as speech and debate will improve your diction and confidence as a public speaker.

Hundreds of colleges and universities in the United States offer degrees in languages. In addition, educational institutions now provide programs and degrees specialized for interpreting and translating. Georgetown University (http://www.georgetown.edu/departments/linguistics) offers both undergraduate and graduate programs in linguistics. Graduate degrees in interpretation and translation may be earned at the University of California–Santa Barbara (http://www.ucsb.edu), the University of Puerto Rico (http://www.upr.clu.edu), and the Monterey Institute of International Studies (http://www.miis.edu/languages.html). Many of these programs include both general and specialized courses, such as medical interpretation and legal translation.

Academic programs for the training of interpreters can be found in Europe as well. The University of Geneva's School of Translation and Interpretation (http://www.unige.ch/en) is highly regarded among professionals in the field.

Certification or Licensing

Although interpreters and translators need not be certified to obtain jobs, employers often show preference to certified applicants. Certification in Spanish, Haitian, Creole, and Navajo is also required for interpreters who are employed by federal courts. State and local courts often have their own specific certification requirements. The National Center for State Courts has more information on certification for these workers. Interpreters for the deaf who pass an examination may qualify for either comprehensive or legal certification by the Registry of Interpreters for the Deaf.

The U.S. Department of State has a three-test requirement for interpreters. These include simple consecutive interpreting (escort), simultaneous interpreting (court/seminar), and conference-level interpreting (international conferences). Applicants must have several years of foreign language practice, advanced education in the language (preferably abroad), and be fluent in vocabulary for a very broad range of subjects.

Foreign language translators may be granted certification by the American Translators Association (ATA) upon successful completion of required exams. ATA certification is available for translators who translate the following languages into English: Arabic, Croatian, Danish, Dutch, French, German, Hungarian, Japanese, Polish, Portuguese, Russian, and Spanish. Certification is also available for translators who translate English into the following languages: Chinese, Croatian, Dutch, Finnish, French, German, Hungarian, Italian, Japanese, Polish, Portuguese, Russian, Spanish, and Ukrainian.

Other Requirements

Interpreters should be able to speak at least two languages fluently, without strong accents. They should be knowledgeable of not only the foreign language but also of the culture and social norms of the region or country in which it is spoken. Both interpreters and translators should read daily newspapers in the languages in which they work to keep current in both developments and usage.

Interpreters must have good hearing, a sharp mind, and a strong, clear, and pleasant voice. They must be able to be precise and quick in their translation. In addition to being flexible and versatile in their work, both interpreters and translators should have self-discipline and patience. Above all, they should have an interest in and love of language.

Finally, interpreters must be honest and trustworthy, observing any existing codes of confidentiality at all times. The ethical code of interpreters and translators is a rigid one. They must hold private proceedings in strict confidence. Ethics also demands that interpreters and translators not distort the meaning of the sentences that are spoken or written. No matter how much they may agree or disagree with the speaker or writer, interpreters and translators must be objective in their work. In addition, information they obtain in the process of interpretation or translation must never be passed along to unauthorized people or groups.

EXPLORING

If you have an opportunity to visit the United Nations, you can watch the proceedings to get some idea of the techniques and responsibilities of the job of the interpreter. Occasionally, an international conference session is televised, and you can observe work of the interpreters. You should note, however, that interpreters who work at these conferences are in the top positions of the vocation. Not everyone may aspire to such jobs. The work of interpreters and translators is usually less public, but not necessarily less interesting.

If you have adequate skills in a foreign language, you might consider traveling in a country in which the language is spoken. If you can converse easily and without a strong accent and can interpret to others who may not understand the language well, you may have what it takes to work as an interpreter or translator.

For any international field, it is important that you familiarize yourself with other cultures. You can even arrange to correspond regularly with a pen pal in a foreign country. You may also want to join a school club that focuses on a particular language, such as the French Club or the Spanish Club. If no such clubs exist, consider forming one. Student clubs can allow you to hone your foreign-language speaking and writing skills and learn about other cultures.

Finally, participating on a speech or debate team enables you to practice your public speaking skills, increase your confidence, and polish your overall appearance by working on eye contact, gestures, facial expressions, tone, and other elements used in public speaking.

EMPLOYERS

There are approximately 41,000 interpreters and translators working full-time in the United States. Although many interpreters and translators work for government or international agencies, some are employed by private firms. Large import-export companies often have interpreters or translators on their payrolls, although these employees generally perform additional duties for the firm. International banks, companies, organizations, and associations often employ both interpreters and translators to facilitate communication. In addition, translators and interpreters work at publishing houses, schools, bilingual newspapers, radio and television stations, airlines, shipping companies, law firms, and scientific and medical operations.

While translators are employed nationwide, a large number of interpreters find work in New York and Washington, D.C. Among the largest employers of interpreters and translators are the United Nations, the World Bank, the U.S. Department of State, the Bureau of the Census, the CIA, the FBI, the Library of Congress, the Red Cross, the YMCA, and the armed forces.

Finally, many interpreters and translators work independently in private practice. These self-employed professionals must be disciplined and driven, since they must handle all aspects of the business such as scheduling work and billing clients.

STARTING OUT

Most interpreters and translators begin as part-time freelancers until they gain experience and contacts in the field. Individuals can apply for jobs directly to the hiring firm, agency, or organization. Many of these employers advertise available positions in the classified section of the newspaper or on the Internet. In addition, contact your college career services office and language department to inquire about job leads.

While many opportunities exist, top interpreting and translating jobs are hard to obtain since the competition for these higher profile positions is fierce. You may be wise to develop supplemental skills that can be attractive to employers while refining your interpreting and translating techniques. The United Nations (UN), for example, employs administrative assistants who can take shorthand and transcribe notes in two or more languages. The UN also hires tour guides who speak more than one language. Such positions can be initial steps toward your future career goals.

ADVANCEMENT

Competency in language determines the speed of advancement for interpreters and translators. Job opportunities and promotions are plentiful for those who have acquired great proficiency in languages. However, interpreters and translators need to constantly work and study to keep abreast of the changing linguistic trends for a given language. The constant addition of new vocabulary for technological advances, inventions, and processes keep languages fluid. Those who do not keep up with changes will find that their communication skills become quickly outdated.

Interpreters and translators who work for government agencies advance by clearly defined grade promotions. Those who work for other organizations can aspire to become chief interpreters or chief translators, or reviewers who check the work of others.

Although advancement in the field is generally slow, interpreters and translators will find many opportunities to succeed as freelancers. Some can even establish their own bureaus or agencies.

EARNINGS

Earnings for interpreters and translators vary depending on experience, skills, number of languages used, and employers. In government, trainee interpreters and translators generally begin at the GS-5 rating, earning from $26,264 to $34,139 a year in 2008. Those with a college degree can start at the higher GS-7 level, earning from $32,534 to $42,290. With an advanced degree, trainees begin at the GS-9 ($39,795 to $51,738), GS-10 ($43,824 to $56,973), or GS-11 level ($48,148 to $62,593).

Interpreters who are employed by the United Nations work under a salary structure called the Common System. In 2008, UN short-term interpreters (workers employed for a duration of 60 days or less) had daily gross pay of $494.50 (Grade I) or $322.50 (Grade II). UN short-term translators and revisers had daily gross pay of $197.10 (Translator I), $242.05 (Translator II), $286.80 (Translator III/Reviser I), $323.20 (Translator IV/Reviser II), or $359.60 (Reviser III).

The U.S. Department of Labor reports the following mean annual salaries for interpreters and translators by specialty in 2006: junior colleges, $45,800; general medical and surgical hospitals, $38,430; local government, $35,200; and elementary and secondary schools, $33,680.

Interpreters employed by nonprofit organizations had median annual incomes of $47,690 in 2006, according to *Compensation in Nonprofit Organizations 2006*, a report from Abbott, Langer & Associates.

Interpreters and translators who work on a freelance basis usually charge by the word, the page, the hour, or the project. Freelance interpreters for international conferences or meetings can earn between $300 and $500 a day from the U.S. government.

By the hour, freelance translators usually earn between $15 and $35; however, rates vary depending on the language and the subject matter. Book translators work under contract with publishers. These contracts cover the fees that are to be paid for translating work as well as royalties, advances, penalties for late payments, and other provisions.

Interpreters and translators working in a specialized field have high earning potential. According to the National Association of Judiciary Interpreters and Translators, the federal courts pay $305 per day for court interpreters. Most work as freelancers, earning annual salaries from $30,000 to $100,000 a year.

Interpreters who work for the deaf also may work on a freelance basis, earning anywhere from $12 to $40 an hour, according to the Registry of Interpreters for the Deaf. Those employed with an agency, government organization, or school system can earn up to $30,000 to start; in urban areas, $40,000 to $50,000 a year.

Depending on the employer, interpreters and translators often enjoy such benefits as health and life insurance, pension plans, and paid vacation and sick days.

WORK ENVIRONMENT

Interpreters and translators work under a wide variety of circumstances and conditions. As a result, most do not have typical nine-to-five schedules.

Conference interpreters probably have the most comfortable physical facilities in which to work. Their glass-enclosed booths are well lit and temperature controlled. Court or judiciary interpreters work in courtrooms or conference rooms, while interpreters for the deaf work at educational institutions as well as a wide variety of other locations.

Interpreters who work for escort or tour services are often required to travel for long periods of time. Their schedules are dictated by the group or person for whom they are interpreting. A freelance interpreter may work out of one city or be assigned anywhere in the world as needed.

Translators usually work in offices, although many spend considerable time in libraries and research centers. Freelance translators often work at home, using their own personal computers, modems, dictionaries, and other resource materials.

While both interpreting and translating require flexibility and versatility, interpreters in particular, especially those who work for international congresses or courts, may experience considerable stress and fatigue. Knowing that a great deal depends upon their absolute accuracy in interpretation can be a weighty responsibility.

OUTLOOK

Employment for interpreters and translators is expected to grow much faster than the average for all occupations through 2016, according to the U.S. Department of Labor. However, competition for available positions will be fierce. With the explosion of such technologies as the Internet, lightning-fast modems, and videoconferencing, global communication has taken great strides. In short, the world has become smaller, so to speak, creating a demand for professionals to aid in the communication between people of different languages and cultural backgrounds.

In addition to new technological advances, demographic factors will fuel demand for translators and interpreters. Although some immigrants who come to the United States assimilate easily with respect to culture and language, many have difficulty learning English. As immigration to the United States continues to increase, interpreters and translators will be needed to help immigrants function in an English-speaking society. According to Ann Macfarlane, past president of the American Translators Association, "community interpreting" for immigrants and refugees is a challenging area requiring qualified language professionals.

Another demographic factor influencing the interpreting and translating fields is the growth in overseas travel. Americans on average are spending an increasing amount of money on travel, especially to foreign countries. The resulting growth of the travel industry will create a need for interpreters to lead tours, both at home and abroad.

In addition to leisure travel, business travel is spurring the need for more translators and interpreters. With workers traveling abroad in growing numbers to attend meetings, conferences, and seminars with overseas clients, interpreters and translators will be needed to help bridge both the language and cultural gaps.

While no more than a few thousand interpreters and translators are employed in the largest markets (the federal government and international organizations), other job options exist. The medical field, for example, provides a variety of jobs for language professionals, translating such products as pharmaceutical inserts, research papers, and medical reports for insurance companies. There will also be strong demand for interpreters in health care settings such as hospitals, outpatient treatment centers, and large offices of physicians due to the steady increase in immigrants to the United States who do not speak English as their primary language. Opportunities exist for qualified individuals in law, trade and business, tourism, recreation, and the government (including homeland security; interpreters and translators who are fluent in Middle Eastern and North African languages will have especially strong employment opportunities).

The U.S. Department of Labor predicts that employment growth will be limited for conference interpreters and literary translators.

FOR MORE INFORMATION

For information on careers in literary translation, contact
American Literary Translators Association
University of Texas-Dallas
800 West Campbell Road, Mail Station JO51
Richardson, TX 75080-3021
http://www.literarytranslators.org

For more on the translating and interpreting professions, including information on accreditation, contact

American Translators Association
225 Reinekers Lane, Suite 590
Alexandria, VA 22314-2875
Tel: 703-683-6100
Email: ata@atanet.org
http://www.atanet.org

For more information on court interpreting, contact

National Association of Judiciary Interpreters and Translators
1707 L Street, NW, Suite 507
Washington, DC 20036-4201
Tel: 202-293-0342
Email: headquarters@najit.org
http://www.najit.org

For information on interpreter training programs for working with the deaf, contact

Registry of Interpreters for the Deaf
333 Commerce Street
Alexandria, VA 22314-2801
Tel: 703-838-0030
Email: membership@rid.org
http://www.rid.org

LICENSED PRACTICAL NURSES

OVERVIEW

Licensed practical nurses (LPNs), a specialty of the nursing profession, are sometimes called *licensed vocational nurses.* LPNs are trained to assist in the care and treatment of patients. They may assist registered nurses and physicians or work under various other circumstances. They perform many of the general duties of nursing and may be responsible for some clerical duties. LPNs work in hospitals, public health agencies, nursing homes, or in home health. Approximately 749,000 licensed practical nurses are employed in the United States.

THE JOB

Licensed practical nurses work under the supervision of a registered nurse, or a physician. They are responsible

---

SCHOOL SUBJECTS
Biology, Chemistry

PERSONAL SKILLS
Helping/Teaching, Technical/Scientific

MINIMUM EDUCATION LEVEL
Some Postsecondary Training

CERTIFICATION OR LICENSING
Voluntary (Certification), Required by All States (Licensing)

WORK ENVIRONMENT
Primarily Indoors, Primarily Multiple Locations

---

for many general duties of nursing such as administering prescribed drugs and medical treatments to patients, taking patients' temperatures and blood pressures, assisting in the preparation of medical examination and surgery, and performing routine laboratory tests. LPNs help with therapeutic and rehabilitation sessions; they may also participate in the planning, practice, and evaluation of a patient's nursing care.

A primary duty of an LPN is to ensure that patients are clean and comfortable, and that their needs, both physical and emotional, are met. They sometimes assist patients with daily hygiene such as bathing, brushing teeth, and dressing. Many times they provide emotional comfort by simply talking with the patient.

LPNs working in nursing homes have duties similar to those employed by hospitals. They provide bedside care, administer medications, develop care plans, and supervise nurse assistants. Those working in doctors' offices and clinics are sometimes required to perform clerical duties such as keeping records, maintaining files and paperwork, as well as answering phones and tending the appointment book. Home health LPNs, in addition to their nursing duties, may sometimes prepare and serve meals to their patients.

REQUIREMENTS
High School

Some LPN programs do not require a high school diploma, but it is highly recommended, particularly if you want to be eligible for advancement opportunities. To prepare for a career as an LPN, you should study biology, chemistry, physics, and science while in high school. English and mathematics courses are also helpful.

Postsecondary Training

Those interested in a career as an LPN usually enroll in a practical nursing program after graduating from high school. There are about 1,500 state-approved programs in the United States that provide practical nursing training. According to the U.S. Department of Labor, 60 percent of all LPNs graduate from a technical or vocational school and 30 percent from a community or junior college. The remainder are enrolled in colleges, hospital programs, or high schools. Most programs last 12 months, with time spent for both classroom study and supervised clinical care. Courses include basic nursing concepts, anatomy, physiology, medical-surgical nursing, pediatrics, obstetrics, nutrition, and first aid. Clinical practice is most often in a hospital setting.

Certification or Licensing

The National Federation of Licensed Practical Nurses offers voluntary certification for LPNs who specialize in IV therapy or gerontology. The National Association for Practical Nurse Education and Service offers voluntary certification for LPNs who specialize in long-term care or pharmacology. Contact these organizations for more information.

All 50 states require graduates of a state-approved practical nursing program to take a licensing examination that has been developed by the National Council of State Boards of Nursing.

Other Requirements

Stamina, both physical and mental, is a must for this occupation. LPNs may be assigned to care for heavy or immobile patients or patients confused with dementia. Patience, and a caring, nurturing attitude, are valuable qualities to possess in order to be a successful LPN. As part of a health care team, they must be able to follow orders and work under close supervision.

EXPLORING

High school students can explore an interest in this career by reading books or by checking out Web sites devoted to the nursing field. You should also take advantage of any information available in your school career center. An excellent way to learn more about this career firsthand is to speak with the school nurse or local public health nurse. Visits to the local hospital

can give you a feel for the work environment. Volunteer work at a hospital, community health center, or even the local Red Cross chapter can provide valuable experience. Some high schools offer membership in Future Nurses organizations.

EMPLOYERS

Approximately 749,000 licensed practical nurses are employed in the United States. The U.S. Department of Labor reports that 26 percent of LPNs work in hospitals, 26 percent work in nursing facilities, and 12 percent work in physicians' offices and clinics. Others are employed by home health care agencies, public health agencies, schools, residential care facilities, temp agencies, and government agencies.

STARTING OUT

After they fulfill licensing requirements, LPNs should check with human resource departments of hospitals, nursing homes, and clinics for openings. Employment agencies that specialize in health professions, and state employment agencies are other ways to find employment, as are school career services centers. Newspaper classified ads, nursing associations, and professional journals are great sources of job opportunities.

ADVANCEMENT

About 40 percent of LPNs use their license and experience as a stepping-stone for other occupations in the health field, many of which offer more responsibility and higher salaries. Some LPNs, for example, with additional training, become medical technicians, surgical attendants, optometric assistants, or psychiatric technicians. Many LPNs return to school to become registered nurses. Hospitals often offer LPNs the opportunity for more training, seminars, workshops, and clinical sessions to sharpen their nursing skills.

EARNINGS

According to the U.S. Department of Labor, LPNs earned an average of $36,550 annually in 2006. Ten percent earned less than $26,380, and 10 percent earned more than $50,480. Many LPNs are able to supplement their salaries with overtime pay and shift differentials. About 19 percent of all LPNs work part time.

Licensed practical nurses who are employed full time also usually receive fringe benefits, such as paid sick, holiday, and vacation time, medical coverage, 401(k) plans, and other perks depending on the employer.

WORK ENVIRONMENT

Most LPNs work 40-hour weeks, less if part time. As with other health professionals, they may be asked to work during nights, weekends, or holidays to provide 24-hour care for their patients. Nurses are usually given pay differentials for these shifts.

LPNs employed in hospitals and nursing homes, as well as in clinics, enjoy clean, well-lighted, and generally comfortable work environments. The nature of their work calls for LPNs to be on their feet for most of the shift—providing patient care, dispensing medication, or assisting other health personnel.

OUTLOOK

Employment for LPNs is expected to grow faster than the average for all occupations through 2016, according to the U.S. Department of Labor. A growing elderly population requiring long-term health care is the primary factor for the demand for qualified LPNs. Traditionally, hospitals have provided the most job opportunities for LPNs. However, this source will only provide a moderate number of openings in the future. Inpatient population is not expected to increase significantly. Also, in many hospitals, certified nursing attendants are increasingly taking over many of the duties of LPNs.

Employment for LPNs in most non-hospital settings is expected to be even stronger. The increasing number of people age 65 and over and technological innovations that allow for more treatments at home will create much-faster-than-average employment opportunities for LPNs who work in home health care services.

Faster-than-average employment growth is predicted for LPNs in nursing homes. Due to advanced medical technology, people are living longer, though many will require medical assistance. Private medical practices will also be excellent job sources because many medical procedures are now being performed on an outpatient basis in doctors' offices.

FOR MORE INFORMATION

For information on education programs and careers, contact

American Association of Colleges of Nursing
One Dupont Circle, NW, Suite 530
Washington, DC 20036-1135
Tel: 202-463-6930
http://www.aacn.nche.edu

For information on licensing, contact
National Council of State Boards of Nursing
111 East Wacker Drive, Suite 2900
Chicago, IL 60601-4277
Tel: 312-525-3600
Email: info@ncsbn.org
http://www.ncsbn.org

For career and certification information, contact the following organizations:
National Association for Practical Nurse Education and Service
1940 Duke Street, Suite 200
Alexandria, VA 22314-3452
Tel: 703-933-1003
Email: napnes@napnes.org
http://www.napnes.org

National Federation of Licensed Practical Nurses
605 Poole Drive
Garner, NC 27529-5203
Tel: 919-779-0046
http://www.nflpn.org

Discover Nursing, sponsored by Johnson & Johnson Services, provides information on nursing careers, nursing schools, and scholarships.
Discover Nursing
http://www.discovernursing.com

MAKEUP ARTISTS

OVERVIEW

Makeup artists prepare actors for performances on stage and before cameras. They read scripts and consult with directors, producers, and technicians to design makeup effects for each individual character. They apply makeup and prosthetics and build and style wigs. They also create special makeup effects. Approximately 2,100 theatrical and performance makeup artists are employed In the United States.

THE JOB

Some of makeup artist Vincent Guastini's creations have involved turning Alanis Morissette into God and Matt Damon and Ben Affleck into angels. These effects for the film *Dogma* hearken back to the earliest examples of theatrical makeup, back to the Middle Ages when makeup effects were used to represent God, angels, and devils. But Guastini is not relying on the simple symbolic face painting of the past; this production demanded that

SCHOOL SUBJECTS
Art, Theater/Dance

PERSONAL SKILLS
Artistic, Communication/Ideas

MINIMUM EDUCATION LEVEL
Some Postsecondary Training

CERTIFICATION OR LICENSING
None Available

WORK ENVIRONMENT
Indoors and Outdoors, Primarily Multiple Locations

he design complicated animatronic wings, detailed rubber masks, and radio-controlled mechanical creatures. With a crew of some of the top makeup artists in the business, Guastini created effects using rubber, plastic, fiberglass, latex paints, radio-control units from model airplanes, and steel cables. "As well as," Guastini says, "the old standby of a makeup kit filled with grease paints, makeup, rubber glues, brushes, and powders."

From a seven-foot-tall alien for the film *Metamorphosis: The Alien Factor* to the animatronic killer doll Chucky in *Child's Play III,* Guastini has created some very bizarre and disturbing effects. "Movies like *Star Wars* and horror movies left an impact on me as a kid," Guastini says, citing his inspirations. He is also called upon to create less extreme transformations with makeup; his production company worked on *The Last of the Mohicans,* which involved applying wounds and prosthetics to hundreds of actors and extras. Other movies that Guastini has worked on include *Man on the Moon, Requiem for a Dream, Virus,* and Stephen King's *Thinner.* Not every project involves prosthetics and special effects. Makeup artists also apply "clean" makeup, which is a technique of applying foundations and powders to keep actors and models looking natural under the harsh lighting of stage and film productions. Makeup artists accent, or downplay, an actor's natural features. They conceal an actor's scars, skin blemishes, tattoos, and wrinkles, as well as apply these things when needed for the character. Having read the script and met with the director and technicians, makeup artists take into consideration many factors: the age of the characters, the setting of the production, the time period, lighting effects, and other details that deter-

mine how an actor should appear. Historical productions require a great deal of research to learn about the hair and clothing styles of the time. Makeup artists also style hair; apply wigs, bald caps, beards, and sideburns; and temporarily color hair. In many states, however, makeup artists are limited in the hair services they can perform; some productions bring in locally licensed cosmetologists for hair cutting, dye jobs, and perms.

After much preparation, the makeup artist becomes an important backstage presence during a production. Throughout the making of a film, makeup artists arrive early for work every day. On the set of *Dogma,* preparing an actor's makeup took four to six hours. "We were always the first to arrive and the last to leave the set," Guastini says of his crew of artists. Makeup artists are required to maintain the actors' proper makeup throughout filming and to help the actors remove the makeup at the end of the day. With the aid of fluorescent lighting, makeup artists apply the makeup, and they keep their eyes on the monitors during filming to make sure the makeup looks right. Guastini's production crew is also responsible for the mechanical creatures they create. "We must do constant repairs and upkeep on any mechanical creatures, making sure they're in working order," Guastini says.

Most makeup artists for film are in business for themselves, contracting work from studios, production companies, and special effects houses on a freelance basis. They may supplement their film work with projects for TV, video, commercials, industrial films, and photo shoots for professional photographers. Makeup artists for theater may also work freelance or be employed fulltime by a theater or theater troupe. Makeup artists for theater find work with regional theaters, touring shows, and recreational parks.

REQUIREMENTS
High School

Does becoming a makeup artist sound interesting to you? If so, there are a number of classes you can take in high school to help prepare you for this profession. Take all the art classes you can, including art history if this is offered at your school. Photography courses will help you understand the use of light and shadow. Courses in illustration, painting, and drawing will help you to develop the skills you'll need for illustrating proposed makeup effects. Learning about sculpting is important, as creating special makeup effects with rubber, prosthetics, and glue is often much like sculpting from clay. Other helpful classes for you to take are anatomy and chemistry. Anatomy will give you an understanding of the human body, and chemistry will give you insight into the products you will be using. If your school offers drama classes, be sure to take these. In drama class you will gain an understanding of all the different elements—such as scripts, actors, and location—needed for a production. Computer classes will give you exposure to this technology, which you may use in the future to design projects. Try experimenting with makeup and special effects on your own. Take photographs of your efforts in order to build a portfolio of your work. Finally, because this work is typically done on a freelance basis and you will need to manage your business accounts, it will be helpful to take math, business, and accounting classes.

Postsecondary Training

There are a number of postsecondary educational routes you can take to become a makeup artist. If you have experience and a portfolio to show off your work, you may be able to enter the business right out of high school. This route is not always advisable, however, because your chances for establishing a successful freelance career without further training are slim. You must be very ambitious, enthusiastic, and capable of seeking out successful mentors willing to teach you the ropes. This can mean a lot of time working for free or for very little pay.

Another route you can take is to get specific training for makeup artistry through vocational schools. One advantage of this route is that after graduating from the program, you will be able to use the school's career services office, instructors, and other graduates as possible networking sources for jobs. Probably the most highly respected schools for makeup artists in film are the Joe Blasco schools, which have several locations across the country. Topics you might study at a Joe Blasco school include beauty makeup, old age makeup, bald cap, hairwork, and monster makeup. Some people in the business have cosmetology degrees, also offered by vocational schools. A cosmetology course of study, however, is not typically geared toward preparing you for makeup artistry work in the entertainment industry.

A third route you can take is to get a broad-based college or university education that results in either a bachelor's or master's degree. Popular majors for makeup artists include theater, art history, film history, photography, and fashion merchandising. In addition to makeup courses, it is important to take classes in painting, illustration, computer design, and animation. A master of fine arts degree in theater or filmmaking will allow you to gain hands-on experience in production as well as working with a faculty of practicing artists.

Other Requirements

Patience and the ability to get along well with people are important for a makeup artist—throughout a film production, the actors will spend many hours in the makeup chair. Though many actors will be easy to work with, you may have to put up with much irritability, as well as overwhelming egos. Producers and directors can also be difficult to work with. And, as you gain more experience, you may have more knowledge about filmmaking than some of the producers of the projects. This may put you in frustrating situations, and you may see time wasted in costly mistakes.

Attention to detail is important; you must be quick to spot any makeup problems before they are filmed. Such responsibilities can be stressful—a whole production team will be relying on you to properly apply makeup that will look good on film. If your work isn't up to par, the whole production will suffer. Work as a makeup artist requires as much creativity and ingenuity as any other filmmaking task. The directors and actors rely on the makeup artists to come up with interesting makeup effects and solutions to filming problems. "It's important to be original in your work," Vincent Guastini advises. Guastini is also an example of the importance of ambition and dedication—within five years of graduating high school, he began work on his first motion picture. A year after that first assignment, he had developed a list of clients and put together a team of special effects artists. Because of the tough, competitive nature of the entertainment industry, makeup artists must be persistent and enthusiastic in their pursuit of work.

As a makeup artist, you may want to consider joining a union. The International Alliance of Theatrical Stage Employees, Moving Picture Technicians, Artists and Allied Crafts of the United States, Its Territories, and Canada represents workers in theater, film, and television production. Hair stylists, makeup artists, engineers, art directors, and set designers are some of the professionals who belong to the 500 local unions affiliated with the alliance. Union membership is not required of most makeup artists for film and theater, but it can help individuals negotiate better wages, benefits, and working conditions. Theaters in larger cities may require union membership of makeup artists, while smaller, regional theaters across the country are less likely to require membership.

EXPLORING

High school drama departments or local community theaters can provide you with great opportunities to explore the makeup artist's work. Volunteer to assist with makeup during a stage production and you will learn about the materials and tools of a makeup kit, as well as see your work under stage lights. A high school video production team or film department may also offer you opportunities for makeup experience.

Most states have their own film commissions that are responsible for promoting film locales and inviting film productions to the local area. These film commissions generally need volunteers and may have internships for students. By working for a film commission, you will learn about productions coming to your state and may have the chance to work on the production. Film industry publications such as *Variety* (http://www.variety.com) can alert you to internship opportunities.

The summer is a great time for students interested in stage production to gain firsthand experience. There are probably local productions in your area, but summer theaters often promote positions nationally. The Theatre Communications Group publishes a directory of nonprofit professional theaters across the country. Its bimonthly publication, *ARTSEARCH*, provides information on summer theater positions and internships.

Finally, explore this career by reading other publications for the field. For example, check out *Make-Up Artist Magazine* (http://www.makeupmag.com), a bimonthly publication with profiles of makeup artists for film as well as how-to columns and product information.

EMPLOYERS

Approximately 2,100 theatrical and performance makeup artists are employed in the United States. Although makeup artists work in a wide variety of circumstances, from theater to television to movies, they usually are self-employed, contracting individual jobs. Theater troupes, touring shows, and amusement parks may hire makeup artists on to their staffs, but in the film industry, makeup artists work on a freelance basis. Large cities and metropolitan areas will provide the majority of jobs for makeup artists, particularly those cities associated with thriving theaters, movie or television studios, fashion photography, and modeling/talent agencies. Although there may be some jobs in smaller towns, they probably will be mostly along the lines of industrial films, corporate videos, and photographic shoots—not very promising for those who wish to make a living in this line of work. Those who aspire to work exclusively as makeup artists gravitate toward the big cities.

STARTING OUT

You should keep a photographic record of all the work you do for theater and film productions, including photos of any drawings or sculptures you have done for art

classes. It's important to have a portfolio to send along with your resume to effects shops, makeup departments, and producers. "Be prepared to work for free or for little money at the start," Vincent Guastini advises, "just to hook up with the right person who will hire you the next time out." To build a portfolio of photographs, experiment in art classes and at home with makeup and special effects, and photograph the results. Check with local TV studios about work in their makeup departments. Locally produced newscasts, children's programming, documentaries, and commercials offer opportunities for makeup artists. Commercials are often quick productions (between one and three days) with small casts, and they pay well. Department stores hire makeup artists to demonstrate and sell cosmetic products in department stores, which may be a starting position for those who want to earn a salary while getting on-the-job training and practice.

Because of the freelance nature of the business, you will be going from project to project. This requires you to constantly seek out work. Read industry trade magazines like *Variety*, and don't be shy about submitting your portfolio to producers and studios. Self-promotion will be an important part of your success as a makeup artist.

ADVANCEMENT

Many makeup artists start as assistants or volunteers on a production, making contacts and connections. They eventually take on projects for which they are in charge of makeup departments and designing makeup effects. They may also establish their own production companies and make their own films or stage their own plays. "I would love to direct someday," Vincent Guastini says about his future, "or produce a film, but the project the first time out should be a really solid, visually exciting film that incorporates my current talents."

Successful, experienced makeup artists can pick and choose their projects and work as much as they like. In the early years, makeup artists must frequently take on a variety of different projects just for the money; however, as they become established in the field and develop a solid reputation, they can concentrate on projects specific to their interests.

EARNINGS

Makeup artists usually contract with a production, negotiating a daily rate. This rate can vary greatly from project to project, depending on the budget of the production, the prestige of the project, and other factors. Even well-established makeup artists occasionally forgo payment to work on the low-budget independent productions of filmmakers they respect.

Independent contractors don't draw steady, yearly salaries. This means they may work long hours for several weeks, then, upon completion of a production, go without work for several weeks. Unless makeup artists are part of the union, they may have to provide all their own health insurance. An experienced makeup artist can make around $300 a day on a film with a sizable budget; some of the top makeup artists in the business command around $1,000 a day. Theatrical makeup artists can make comparable daily wages on Broadway, or in a theater in a large city; some small theaters, however, may only pay around $50 a day.

Because of such variables as the unsteady nature of the work, the makeup artist's experience, and even where he or she works, the yearly incomes for these individuals vary widely. Some makeup artists may show yearly earnings little higher than those resulting from the minimum wage. Others may have annual income in the hundreds of thousands of dollars. The U.S. Department of Labor reports that theater and performance makeup artists had median annual salaries of $31,820 in 2006. Salaries ranged from less than $14,500 to more than $70,750.

WORK ENVIRONMENT

Long hours, deadlines, and tight budgets can result in high stress on a movie set. Because makeup artists move from production to production, they work with different groups of people all the time, and in different locales and settings. Although this allows makeup artists the opportunity to travel, it may also make a makeup artist feel displaced. While working on a production, they may have to forgo a social life, working long hours to design effects and prepare the actors for filming. The workdays may be twice as long as in the average workplace, and those work hours may be a stressful combination of working hurriedly then waiting.

For those passionate about the work, however, any uncomfortable or frustrating conditions are easily overlooked. "I like creating something from nothing and seeing it alive and moving," Vincent Guastini says in regard to the creatures he has constructed for special effects. He also appreciates the travel and variety. "I like the people I meet," he says, "and the job is always different no matter the project or effect."

When working for the theater, the conditions are generally more controlled. With the exception of outdoor productions, theatrical makeup artists work in the dressing and makeup rooms of theaters and concert halls. The work can be very stressful, however, as the actors hurry to prepare for live productions.

OUTLOOK

Makeup artists will find their opportunities increasing in the film and television industries. Digital TV has made it possible for hundreds of cable channels to be piped into our homes. The original programming needed to fill the schedules of these new channels results in jobs for makeup artists. Makeup effects artists will find challenging and well-paying work as the film industry pushes the envelope on special effects. These makeup artists may be using computers more and more, as digital design becomes an important tool in creating film effects.

Funding for theaters, some of which comes from the National Endowment for the Arts, is always limited and may be reduced during economic downturns or when productions are unpopular. During these times many theaters may be unable to hire the cast and crew needed for new productions. There has been a revived interest in Broadway, however, due to highly successful musicals like *Rent*, *The Lion King*, and *Wicked*. This interest could result in better business for traveling productions, as well as regional theaters across the country.

There will be a continuing need for makeup artists in still photography to prepare models for catalog and magazine shoots.

FOR MORE INFORMATION

For information on the alliance, a union representing more than 110,000 members in entertainment and related fields in the United States and Canada, contact

International Alliance of Theatrical Stage Employees, Moving Picture Technicians, Artists and Allied Crafts of the United States, Its Territories, and Canada
1430 Broadway, 20th Floor
New York, NY 10018-3348
Tel: 212-730-1770
http://www.iatse-intl.org

For information about how to order a copy of or subscription to Make-Up Artist Magazine, *contact*

Make-Up Artist Magazine
4018 NE 112th Avenue, Suite D-8
Vancouver, WA 98682-5703
Tel: 800-805-6648
http://www.makeupmag.com

For information about theater jobs and a sample copy of ARTSEARCH, *contact*

Theatre Communications Group
520 Eighth Avenue, 24th Floor
New York, NY 10018-4156
Tel: 212-609-5900

Email: tcg@tcg.org
http://www.tcg.org

For information about the Joe Blasco schools and careers in makeup artistry, visit

Joe Blasco Professional Make-Up Artist Training Centers
http://www.joeblasco.com

MANAGEMENT ANALYSTS AND CONSULTANTS

OVERVIEW

Management analysts and consultants analyze business or operating procedures to devise the most efficient methods of accomplishing work. They gather and organize information about operating problems and procedures and prepare recommendations for implementing new systems or changes. They may update manuals outlining established methods of performing work and train personnel in new applications. There are approximately 678,000 management analysts and consultants employed in the United States.

THE JOB

Management analysts and consultants are called in to solve any of a vast array of organizational problems. They are often needed when a rapidly growing small company needs a better system of control over inventories and expenses.

The role of the consultant is to come into a situation in which a client is unsure or inexpert and to recommend actions or provide assessments. There are many different types of management analysts and consultants. In general, they all require knowledge of general management, operations, marketing, logistics, materials management and physical distribution, finance and accounting, human resources, electronic data processing and systems, and management science.

Management analysts and consultants may be called in when a major manufacturer must reorganize its corporate structure when acquiring a new division. For example, they assist when a company relocates to another state by coordinating the move, planning the new facility, and training new workers.

The work of management analysts and consultants is quite flexible—it varies from job to job. In general, man-

agement analysts and consultants collect, review, and analyze data, make recommendations, and assist in the implementation of their proposals. Some projects require several consultants to work together, each specializing in a different area. Other jobs require the analysts to work independently.

Public and private organizations use management analysts for a variety of reasons. Some organizations lack the resources necessary to handle a project. Other organizations, before they pursue a particular course of action, will consult an analyst to determine what resources will be required or what problems will be encountered. Some companies seek outside advice on how to resolve organizational problems that have already been identified or to avoid troublesome problems that could arise.

Firms providing consulting practitioners range in size from solo practitioners to large international companies employing hundreds of people. The services are generally provided on a contract basis. A company will choose a consulting firm that specializes in the area that needs assistance, and then the two firms negotiate the conditions of the contract. Contract variables include the proposed cost of the project, staffing requirements, and the deadline.

After getting a contract, the analyst's first job is to define the nature and extent of the project. He or she analyzes statistics, such as annual revenues, employment, or expenditures. He or she may also interview employees and observe the operations of the organization on a day-to-day basis.

The next step for the analyst is to use his or her knowledge of management systems to develop solutions. While preparing recommendations, he or she must take into account the general nature of the business, the relationship of the firm to others in its industry, the firm's internal organization, and the information gained through data collection and analysis.

Once they have decided on a course of action, management analysts and consultants usually write reports of their findings and recommendations and present them to the client. They often make formal oral presentations about their findings as well. Some projects require only reports; others require assistance in implementing the suggestions.

REQUIREMENTS
High School

High school courses that will give you a general preparation for this field include business, mathematics, and computer science. Management analysts and consultants must pass on their findings through written or oral presentations, so be sure to take English and speech classes, too.

Postsecondary Training

Employers generally prefer to hire management analysts and consultants with a master's degree in business or public administration, or at least a bachelor's degree and several years of appropriate work experience. Many college majors provide a suitable education for this occupation because of the diversity of problem areas addressed by management analysts and consultants. These include many areas in the computer and information sciences, engineering, business and management, education, communications, marketing and distribution, and architecture and environmental design.

When hired directly from school, management analysts and consultants often participate in formal company training programs. These programs may include instruction on policies and procedures, computer systems and software, and management practices and principles. Regardless of their background, most management analysts and consultants routinely attend conferences to keep abreast of current developments in the field.

Certification and Licensing

The Institute of Management Consultants USA, in cooperation with the Association of Internal Management Consultants, offers the certified management consultant designation to those who pass an examination and meet minimum educational and experience criteria. Certification is voluntary, but may provide an additional advantage to job seekers.

Other Requirements

Management analysts and consultants are often responsible for recommending layoffs of staff, so it is important that they learn to deal with people diplomatically. Their job requires a great deal of tact, enlisting cooperation while exerting leadership, debating their points, and pointing out errors. Consultants must be quick thinkers, able to refute objections with finality. They also must be able to make excellent presentations.

A management analyst must also be unbiased and analytical, with a disposition toward the intellectual side of business and a natural curiosity about the way things work best.

EXPLORING

The reference departments of most libraries include business areas that will have valuable research tools such

SCHOOL SUBJECTS
Business, Computer Science, Speech

PERSONAL SKILLS
Communication/Ideas, Leadership/Management

MINIMUM EDUCATION LEVEL
Bachelor's Degree

CERTIFICATION OR LICENSING
Voluntary

WORK ENVIRONMENT
Primarily Indoors, Primarily Multiple Locations

as encyclopedias of business consultants and "who's who" of business consultants. These books should list management analysis and consulting firms across the country, describing their annual sales and area of specialization, like industrial, high tech, small business, and retail. After doing some research, you can call or write to these firms and ask for more information.

For more general business exploration, see if your school has a business or young leaders club. If there is nothing of the sort, you may want to explore Junior Achievement, a nationwide association that connects young business-minded students with professionals in the field for mentoring and career advice. Visit http://www.ja.org for more information.

EMPLOYERS

About 27 percent of the 678,000 management analysts and consultants in the United States are self-employed. Federal, state, and local governments employ many of the others. The Department of Defense employs the majority of those working for the federal government. The remainder work in the private sector for companies providing consulting services. Although management analysts and consultants are found throughout the country, the majority are concentrated in major metropolitan areas.

STARTING OUT

Most government agencies offer entry-level analyst and consultant positions to people with bachelor's degrees and no work experience. Many entrants are also career changers who were formerly mid- and upper-level managers. With 27 percent of the practicing management consultants self-employed, career changing is a common route into the field.

Anyone with some degree of business expertise or an expert field can begin to work as an independent consultant. The number of one- and two-person consulting firms in this country is well over 100,000. Establishing a wide range of appropriate personal contacts is by far the most effective way to get started in this field. Consultants have to sell themselves and their expertise, a task far tougher than selling a tangible product the customer can see and handle. Many consultants get their first clients by advertising in newspapers, magazines, and trade or professional periodicals. After some time in the field, word-of-mouth advertising is often the primary method of attracting new clients.

ADVANCEMENT

A new consultant in a large firm may be referred to as an *associate* for the first couple of years. The next progression is to *senior associate,* a title that indicates three to five years' experience and the ability to supervise others and do more complex and independent work. After about five years, the analyst who is progressing well may become an *engagement manager* with the responsibility to lead a consulting team on a particular client project. The best managers become *senior engagement managers,* leading several study teams or a very large project team. After about seven years, those who excel will be considered for appointment as *junior partners* or *principals.* Partnership involves responsibility for marketing the firm and leading client projects. Some may be promoted to senior partnership or *director,* but few people successfully run this full course. Management analysts and consultants with entrepreneurial ambition may open their own firms.

EARNINGS

Salaries and hourly rates for management analysts and consultants vary widely, according to experience, specialization, education, and employer. In 2006, management analysts and consultants had median annual earnings of $68,050, according to the U.S. Department of Labor. The lowest 10 percent earned less than $39,840, and the highest 10 percent earned more than $128,330.

Many consultants can demand between $400 and $1,000 per day. Their fees are often well over $40 per hour. Self-employed management consultants receive no fringe benefits and generally have to maintain their own office, but their pay is usually much higher than salaried consultants. They can make more than $2,000 per day or $250,000 in one year from consulting just two days per week.

Typical benefits for salaried analysts and consultants include health and life insurance, retirement plans, vacation and sick leave, profit sharing, and bonuses for outstanding work. All travel expenses are generally reimbursed by the employer.

WORK ENVIRONMENT

Management analysts and consultants generally divide their time between their own offices and the client's office or production facility. They can spend a great deal of time on the road.

Most management analysts and consultants work at least 40 hours per week plus overtime depending on the project. The nature of consulting projects—working on location with a single client toward a specific goal—allows these professionals to totally immerse themselves in their work. They sometimes work 14- to 16-hour days, and six- or seven-day workweeks can be fairly common.

While self-employed, consultants may enjoy the luxury of setting their own hours and doing a great deal of their work at home; the trade-off is sacrificing the benefits provided by the large firms. Their livelihood depends on the additional responsibility of maintaining and expanding their clientele on their own.

Although those in this career usually avoid much of the potential tedium of working for one company all day, every day, they face many pressures resulting from deadlines and client expectations. Because the clients are generally paying generous fees, they want to see dramatic results, and the management analyst can feel the weight of this.

OUTLOOK

Employment of management analysts is expected to grow much faster than the average for all occupations through 2016, according to the U.S. Department of Labor. Industry and government agencies are expected to rely more and more on the expertise of these professionals to improve and streamline the performance of their organizations. Many job openings will result from the need to replace personnel who transfer to other fields or leave the labor force.

Competition for management consulting jobs will be strong. Employers can choose from a large pool of applicants who have a wide variety of educational backgrounds and experience. The challenging nature of this job, coupled with high salary potential, attracts many. A graduate degree, experience and expertise in the industry, as well as a knack for public relations, are needed to stay competitive.

Trends that have increased the growth of employment in this field include advancements in information technology and e-commerce, the growth of international business, and fluctuations in the economy that have forced businesses to streamline and downsize.

The Department of Labor predicts that opportunities will be best at very large consulting firms that have expertise in international business and in smaller firms that focus on providing consulting services in specific areas such as biotechnology, engineering, information technology, health care, marketing, and human resources.

FOR MORE INFORMATION

For industry information, contact the following organizations

American Institute of Certified Public Accountants
1211 Avenue of the Americas
New York, NY 10036-8775
Tel: 212-596-6200
http://www.aicpa.org

American Management Association
1601 Broadway
New York, NY 10019-7434
Tel: 877-566-9441
http://www.amanet.org

Association of Management Consulting Firms
380 Lexington Avenue, Suite 1700
New York, NY 10168-0002
Tel: 212-551-7887
Email: info@amcf.org
http://www.amcf.org

For information on certification, contact
Association of Internal Management Consultants
824 Caribbean Court
Marco Island, FL 34145-3422
Tel: 239-642-0580
Email: info@aimc.org
http://www.aimc.org

For information on certification, contact
Institute of Management Consultants USA
2025 M Street, NW, Suite 800
Washington, DC 20036-3309
Tel: 800-221-2557
Email: office@imcusa.org
http://www.imcusa.org

MARINE SERVICES TECHNICIANS

OVERVIEW

Marine services technicians inspect, maintain, and repair marine vessels, from small boats to large yachts. They work on vessels' hulls, engines, transmissions, navigational equipment, and electrical, propulsion, and refrigeration systems. Depending on their specialty, they may also be known as *motorboat mechanics, marine electronics technicians,* or *fiberglass technicians.* Marine services technicians may work at boat dealerships, boat repair shops, boat engine manufacturers, or marinas. Naturally, jobs are concentrated near large bodies of water and coastal areas.

THE JOB

Marine services technicians work on the more than 16 million boats and other watercraft owned by people in the United States. They test and repair boat engines, transmissions, and propellers; rigging, masts, and sails; and navigational equipment and steering gear. They repair or replace defective parts and sometimes make new parts to meet special needs. They may also inspect and replace internal cabinets, refrigeration systems, electrical systems and equipment, sanitation facilities, hardware, and trim.

Workers with specialized skills often have more specific titles. For example, *motorboat mechanics* work on

---

SCHOOL SUBJECTS
Mathematics, Technical/Shop

PERSONAL SKILLS
Following Instructions, Mechanical/Manipulative

MINIMUM EDUCATION LEVEL
Some Postsecondary Training

CERTIFICATION OR LICENSING
Required for Certain Positions

WORK ENVIRONMENT
Indoors and Outdoors, One Location with Some Travel

boat engines—those that are inboard, outboard, and inboard/outboard. Routine maintenance tasks include lubricating, cleaning, repairing, and adjusting parts.

Motorboat mechanics often use special testing equipment, such as engine analyzers, compression gauges, ammeters, and voltmeters, as well as other computerized diagnostic equipment. Technicians must know how to disassemble and reassemble components and refer to service manuals for directions and specifications. Motorboat workers often install and repair electronics, sanitation, and air-conditioning systems. They need a set of general and specialized tools, often provided by their employers; many mechanics gradually acquire their own tools, often spending up to thousands of dollars on this investment.

Marine electronics technicians work with vessels' electronic safety and navigational equipment, such as radar, depthsounders, loran (long-range navigation), autopilots, and compass systems. They install, repair, and calibrate equipment for proper functioning. Routine maintenance tasks include checking, cleaning, repairing, and replacing parts. Electronics technicians check for common causes of problems, such as loose connections and defective parts. They often rely on schematics and manufacturers' specification manuals to troubleshoot problems. These workers also must have a set of tools, including hand tools such as pliers, screwdrivers, and soldering irons. Other equipment, often supplied by their employers, includes voltmeters, ohmmeters, signal generators, ammeters, and oscilloscopes.

Technicians who are *field repairers* go to the vessel to do their work, perhaps at the marina dock. *Bench repairers,* on the other hand, work on equipment brought into shops.

Some technicians work only on vessel hulls. These are usually made of either wood or fiberglass. *Fiberglass repairers* work on fiberglass hulls, of which most pleasure crafts today are built. They reinforce damaged areas of the hull, grind damaged pieces with a sander, or cut them away with a jigsaw and replace them using resin-impregnated fiberglass cloth. They finish the repaired sections by sanding, painting with a gel-coat substance, and then buffing.

REQUIREMENTS
High School

Most employers prefer to hire applicants who have a high school diploma. If you are interested in this work, take mathematics classes and shop classes in metals, woodwork, and electronics while you are in high school. These classes will give you experience completing detailed and precise work. Shop classes will also give you experience using a variety of tools and reading blueprints. Take computer classes; you will probably be using this tool throughout your career for such things as diagnostic and design work. Science classes, such as physics, will also be beneficial to you. Finally, don't forget to take English classes. These classes will help you hone your reading and research skills, which will be needed when you consult technical manuals for repair and maintenance information throughout your career.

Postsecondary Training

Many marine services technicians learn their trade on the job. They find entry-level positions as general boatyard workers, doing such jobs as cleaning boat bottoms, and work their way into the position of service technician. Or they may be hired as trainees. They learn how to perform typical service tasks under the supervision of experienced mechanics and gradually complete more difficult work. The training period may last for about three years.

Other technicians decide to get more formal training and attend vocational or technical colleges for classes in engine repair, electronics, and fiberglass work. Some schools, such as Cape Fear Community College in North Carolina and Washington County Community College in Maine, have programs specifically for marine technicians (see For More Information). These schools often offer an associate's degree in areas such as applied science. Classes students take may include mathematics, physics, electricity, schematic reading, and circuit theory. Boat manufacturers and other types of institutions, such as the American Boatbuilders and Repairers Association, Mystic Seaport Museum, and the WoodenBoat School, offer skills training through less formal courses and seminars that often last several days or a few weeks. The military services can also provide training in electronics.

Certification or Licensing

Those who test and repair marine radio transmitting equipment must have a general radio-telephone operator license from the Federal Communications Commission (445 12th Street, SW, Washington, DC 20554-0001, Tel: 888-225-5322, http://www.fcc.gov).

Certification for technicians in the marine electronics industry is voluntary, and is administered by the National Marine Electronics Association. There are four grades of certification for workers in this industry: the certified marine electronic technician (CMET) designation for technicians with one year of experience, the advanced CMET designation for those with three years of experience, the senior CMET designation for those with 10 years of experience, and the lifetime CMET designation for those who have passed the advanced CMET exam, have a minimum of 10 years as a senior CMET, and who are approved by a majority vote of the certification committee. Basic certification is by written examination and the employer's verification as to the technician's proficiency in the repair of basic radar, voice SSB, VHF, depth sounders, and autopilots. The higher degrees of certification are earned by meeting all previous grade requirements plus satisfactorily completing a factory training course or having the employer attest to the technician's proficiency in repairing advanced equipment.

Other Requirements

Most technicians work outdoors some of the time, and they are often required to test-drive the vessels they work on. This is considered an added benefit by many workers. Some workers in this field maintain that one of the most important qualities for a technician is a pleasant personality. Boat owners are often very proud of and attached to their vessels, so workers need to have both respect and authority when communicating with customers.

Technicians also need to be able to adapt to the cyclical nature of this business. They are often under a lot of pressure in the summer months, when most boat owners are enjoying the water and calling on technicians for service. On the other hand, they often have gaps in their work during the winter; some workers receive unemployment compensation at this time.

Motorboat technicians' work can sometimes be physically demanding, requiring them to lift heavy outboard motors or other components. Electronics technicians, on the other hand, must be able to work with delicate parts, such as wires and circuit boards. They should have good eyesight, color vision, and good hearing (to listen for malfunctions revealed by sound).

Some marine services technicians may be required to provide their own hand tools. These tools are usually acquired over a period of time, but the collection may cost the mechanic hundreds if not thousands of dollars.

EXPLORING

This field lends itself to a lot of fun ways to explore job opportunities. Of course, having a boat of your own and working on it is one of the best means of preparation. If friends, neighbors, or relatives have boats, take trips with them and see how curious you are about what makes

the vessel work. Offer to help do repairs to the boat, or at least watch while repairs are made and routine maintenance jobs are done. Clean up the deck, sand an old section of the hull, or polish the brass. If a boat just isn't available to you, try to find some type of engine to work on. Even working on an automobile engine will give you a taste of what this type of work is like.

Some high schools have co-op training programs through which students can look for positions with boat-related businesses, such as boat dealerships or even marinas. Check with your guidance counselor about this possibility. You also can read trade magazines such as *Boating Industry* (http://www.boating-industry.com) and the online forum *Professional Boatbuilder* (http://www.proboat.com). These periodicals offer information monthly or bimonthly on the pleasure boat industry, as well as on boat design, construction, and repair.

EMPLOYERS

Marine services technicians are employed by boat retailers, boat repair shops, boat engine manufacturers, boat rental firms, resorts, and marinas. The largest marinas are in coastal areas, such as Florida, New York, California, Texas, Massachusetts, and Louisiana; smaller ones are located near lakes and water recreation facilities such as campgrounds. Manufacturers of large fishing vessels also employ technicians for on-site mechanical support at fishing sites and competitive events. These workers often follow professionals on the fishing circuit, traveling from tournament to tournament maintaining the vessels.

STARTING OUT

A large percentage of technicians get their start by working as general boatyard laborers—cleaning boats, cutting grass, painting, and so on. After showing interest and ability, they can begin to work with experienced technicians and learn skills on the job. Some professional organizations, such as Marine Trades Association of New Jersey and Michigan Boating Industries Association, offer scholarships for those interested in marine technician training.

For those technicians who have attended vocational or technical colleges, career services offices of these schools may have information about job openings.

ADVANCEMENT

Many workers consider management and supervisory positions as job goals. After working for a number of years on actual repairs and maintenance, many technicians like to manage repair shops, supervise other workers, and deal with customers more directly. These positions require less physical labor but more communication and management skills. Many workers like to combine both aspects by becoming self-employed; they may have their own shops, attract their own jobs, and still get to do the technical work they enjoy.

Advancement often depends on an individual's interests. Some become marina managers, manufacturers' salespersons, or field representatives. Others take a different direction and work as *boat brokers,* selling boats. *Marine surveyors* verify the condition and value of boats; they are independent contractors hired by insurance companies and lending institutions such as banks.

EARNINGS

According to the U.S. Department of Labor, the median yearly earnings of motorboat mechanics were $33,210 in 2006. The middle 50 percent earned between $26,330 and $41,610. Salaries ranged from less than $20,680 to more than $50,750 a year.

Technicians in small shops tend to receive few fringe benefits, but larger employers often offer paid vacations, sick leave, and health insurance. Some employers provide uniforms and tools and pay for work-related training. Many technicians who enjoy the hands-on work with boats claim that the best benefit is to take repaired boats out for test-drives.

WORK ENVIRONMENT

Technicians who work indoors often are in well-lit and ventilated shops. The work is cleaner than that on cars because there tends to be less grease and dirt on marine engines; instead, workers have to deal with water scum, heavy-duty paint, and fiberglass. In general, marine work is similar to other types of mechanical jobs, where workers encounter such things as noise when engines are being run and potential danger with power tools and chemicals. Also similar to other mechanics' work, sometimes technicians work alone on a job and at other times they work on a boat with other technicians. Unless a technician is self-employed, his or her work will likely be overseen by a supervisor of some kind. For any repair job, the technician may have to deal directly with customers.

Some mechanics, such as those who work at marinas, work primarily outdoors—and in all kinds of weather. In boats with no air conditioning, the conditions in the summer can be hot and uncomfortable. Technicians often have to work in tight, uncomfortable places to perform repairs. Sailboats have especially tight access to inboard engines.

There is often a big demand for service just before Memorial Day and the Fourth of July. In the summer workweeks can average 60 hours. But in winter the week can involve less than 40 hours of work, with layoffs common at this time of year. In the warmer climates of the United States, work tends to be steadier throughout the year.

OUTLOOK

According to the U.S. Department of Labor, employment opportunities for small engine mechanics, including marine services technicians, are expected to grow about as fast as the average for all occupations through 2016. As boat design and construction become more complicated, the outlook will be excellent for technicians who complete formal training programs. Most marine craft purchases are made by the over-40 age group, which is expected to increase over the next decade. The growth of this population segment should help expand the market for motorboats and increase the demand for qualified mechanics.

The availability of jobs will be related to the health of the pleasure boat industry. According to *Boating Industry,* there are 10,000 marine retailers in the United States and 1,500 boatyards that repair hulls and engines. One interesting demographic trend that will influence job opportunities is the shift of the population to the South and West, where warm-weather seasons are longer and thus attract more boating activity.

An increase in foreign demand for U.S. pleasure vessels will mean more opportunities for workers in this field. U.S. manufacturers are expected to continue to develop foreign markets and establish more distribution channels. However, legislation in the United States may require boat operator licenses and stricter emission standards, which might lead to a decrease in the number of boats sold and maintained here.

FOR MORE INFORMATION

For industry information, contact

American Boatbuilders and Repairers Association
50 Water Street
Warren, RI 02885-3034
Tel: 401-247-0318
http://www.abbra.org

To find out whether there is a marine association in your area, contact

Marine Retailers Association of America
PO Box 1127
Oak Park, IL 60304-0127

Tel: 708-763-9210
Email: mraa@mraa.com
http://www.mraa.com

For information on certification, the industry, and membership, contact
National Marine Electronics Association
7 Riggs Avenue
Severna Park, MD 21146-3819
Tel: 410-975-9425
Email: info@nmea.org
http://www.nmea.org

For educational information, contact the following:
Cape Fear Community College
411 North Front Street
Wilmington, NC 28401-3910
Tel: 910-362-7000
http://cfcc.edu

Washington County Community College
Eastport Campus
16 Deep Cove Road
Eastport, ME 04631-3218
Tel: 800-210-6932
Email: admissions@wctc.org
http://www.wccc.me.edu/abeast.html

MARKETING RESEARCH ANALYSTS

OVERVIEW

Marketing research analysts collect, analyze, and interpret data in order to determine potential demand for a product or service. By examining the buying habits, wants, needs, and preferences of consumers, research analysts are able to recommend ways to improve products, increase sales, and expand customer bases. There are approximately 234,000 marketing research analysts employed in the United States.

THE JOB

Marketing researchers collect and analyze all kinds of information in order to help companies improve their products, establish or modify sales and distribution

---

SCHOOL SUBJECTS
Business, Mathematics

PERSONAL SKILLS
Following Instructions, Technical/Scientific

MINIMUM EDUCATION LEVEL
Bachelor's Degree

CERTIFICATION OR LICENSING
None Available

WORK ENVIRONMENT
Primarily Indoors, Primarily One Location

---

policies, and make decisions regarding future plans and directions. In addition, research analysts are responsible for monitoring both in-house studies and off-site research, interpreting results, providing explanations of compiled data, and developing research tools.

One area of marketing research focuses on company products and services. In order to determine consumer likes and dislikes, research analysts collect data on brand names, trademarks, product design, and packaging for existing products, items being test-marketed, and those in experimental stages. Analysts also study competing products and services that are already on the market to help managers and strategic planners develop new products and create appropriate advertising campaigns.

In the sales methods and policy area of marketing research, analysts examine firms' sales records and conduct a variety of sales-related studies. For example, information on sales in various geographical areas is analyzed and compared to previous sales figures, changes in population, and total and seasonal sales volume. By analyzing this data, marketing researchers can identify peak sales periods and recommend ways to target new customers. Such information helps marketers plan future sales campaigns and establish sales quotas and commissions.

Advertising research is closely related to sales research. Studies on the effectiveness of advertising in different parts of the country are conducted and compared to sales records. This research is helpful in planning future advertising campaigns and in selecting the appropriate media to use.

Marketing research that focuses on consumer demand and preferences solicits opinions of the people who use the products or services being considered. In addition to actually conducting opinion studies, marketing researchers often design the ways to obtain the information. They write scripts for telephone interviews, develop direct-mail questionnaires and field surveys, and design focus group programs.

Through one or a combination of these studies, market researchers are able to gather information on consumer reaction to the need for and style, design, price, and use of a product. The studies attempt to reveal who uses various products or services, identify potential customers, or get suggestions for product or service improvement. This information is helpful for forecasting sales, planning design modifications, and determining changes in features.

Once information has been gathered, marketing researchers analyze the findings. They then detail their findings and recommendations in a written report and often orally present them to management as well.

A number of professionals compose the marketing research team. The *project supervisor* is responsible for overseeing a study from beginning to end. The *statistician* determines the sample size—or the number of people to be surveyed—and compares the number of responses. The project supervisor or statistician, in conjunction with other specialists (such as *demographers* and *psychologists*), often determines the number of interviews to be conducted as well as their locations. *Field interviewers* survey people in various public places, such as shopping malls, office complexes, and popular attractions. *Telemarketers* gather information by placing calls to current or potential customers, to people listed in telephone books, or to those who appear on specialized lists obtained from list houses. Once questionnaires come in from the field, *tabulators* and *coders* examine the data, count the answers, code noncategorical answers, and tally the primary counts. The marketing research analyst then analyzes the returns, writes up the final report, and makes recommendations to the client or to management.

Marketing research analysts must be thoroughly familiar with research techniques and procedures. Sometimes the research problem is clearly defined, and information can be gathered readily. Other times, company executives may know only that a problem exists as evidenced by a decline in sales. In these cases, the market research analyst is expected to collect the facts that will aid in revealing and resolving the problem.

REQUIREMENTS
High School

Most employers require their marketing research analysts to hold at least a bachelor's degree, so a college prepara-

tory program is advised. Classes in English, marketing, economics, mathematics, psychology, and sociology are particularly important. Courses in computing are especially useful, since a great deal of tabulation and statistical analysis is required in the marketing research field.

Postsecondary Training

A bachelor's degree is essential for careers in marketing research. Majors in marketing, business administration, statistics, computer science, history, or economics provide a good background for most types of research positions. In addition, course work in sociology and psychology is helpful for those who are leaning toward consumer demand and opinion research. Since quantitative skills are important in various types of industrial or analytic research, students interested in these areas should take statistics, econometrics, survey design, sampling theory, and other mathematics courses.

Many employers prefer that a marketing research analyst hold a master's degree as well as a bachelor's degree. A master's of business administration, for example, is frequently required on projects calling for complex statistical and business analysis. Graduate work at the doctorate level is not necessary for most positions, but it is highly desirable for those who plan to become involved in advanced research studies.

Certification and Licensing

The Marketing Research Association offers certification for marketing research analysts. Contact the association for more information.

Other Requirements

To work in this career, you should be intelligent, detail oriented, and accurate; have the ability to work easily with words and numbers; and be particularly interested in solving problems through data collection and analysis. In addition, you must be patient and persistent, since long hours are often required when working on complex studies.

As part of the market research team, you must be able to work well with others and have an interest in people. The ability to communicate, both orally and in writing, is also important, since you will be responsible for writing up detailed reports on the findings in various studies and presenting recommendations to management.

EXPLORING

You can find many opportunities in high school to learn more about the necessary skills for the field of marketing research. For example, experiments in science, problems in student government, committee work, and other school activities provide exposure to situations similar to those encountered by marketing research analysts.

You can also seek part-time employment as a survey interviewer at local marketing research firms. Gathering field data for consumer surveys offers valuable experience through actual contact with both the public and marketing research supervisors. In addition, many companies seek a variety of other employees to code, tabulate, and edit surveys; monitor telephone interviews; and validate the information entered on written questionnaires. You can search for job listings in local newspapers and on the Web or apply directly to research organizations.

EMPLOYERS

Approximately 234,000 marketing research analysts are employed in the United States. Large corporations, industrial firms, advertising agencies, data collection businesses, and private research organizations that handle local surveys for companies on a contract basis employ marketing research analysts. While many marketing research organizations offer a broad range of services, some firms subcontract parts of an overall project out to specialized companies. For example, one research firm may concentrate on product interviews, while another might focus on measuring the effectiveness of product advertising. Similarly, some marketing analysts specialize in one industry or area. For example, agricultural marketing specialists prepare sales forecasts for food businesses, which use the information in their advertising and sales programs.

Although many smaller firms located all across the country outsource studies to marketing research firms, these research firms, along with most large corporations that employ marketing research analysts, are located in such big cities as New York or Chicago. Approximately 90 percent of salaried marketing research analysts are employed in private industry, but opportunities also exist in government and academia, as well as at hospitals, public libraries, and a variety of other types of organizations.

STARTING OUT

Students with a graduate degree in marketing research and experience in quantitative techniques have the best chances of landing jobs as marketing research analysts. Since a bachelor's degree in marketing or business is usually not sufficient to obtain such a position, many employees without postgraduate degrees start out as research assistants, trainees, interviewers, or questionnaire editors. In such positions, those aspiring to the job

of research analyst can gain valuable experience conducting interviews, analyzing data, and writing reports.

Use your college career services office, the Web, and help wanted sections of local newspapers to look for job leads. Another way to get into the marketing research field is through personal and professional contacts. Names and telephone numbers of potential employers may come from professors, friends, or relatives. Finally, students who have participated in internships or have held marketing research-related jobs on a part-time basis while in school or during the summer may be able to obtain employment at these firms or at similar organizations.

ADVANCEMENT

Most marketing research professionals begin as *junior analysts* or *research assistants*. In these positions, they help in preparing questionnaires and related materials, training survey interviewers, and tabulating and coding survey results. After gaining sufficient experience in these and other aspects of research project development, employees are often assigned their own research projects, which usually involve supervisory and planning responsibilities. A typical promotion path for those climbing the company ladder might be from assistant researcher to marketing research analyst to assistant manager and then to manager of a branch office for a large private research firm. From there, some professionals become market research executives or research directors for industrial or business firms.

Since marketing research analysts learn about all aspects of marketing on the job, some advance by moving to positions in other departments, such as advertising or sales. Depending on the interests and experience of marketing professionals, other areas of employment to which they can advance include data processing, teaching at the university level, statistics, economics, and industrial research and development.

In general, few employees go from starting positions to executive jobs at one company. Advancement often requires changing employers. Therefore, marketing research analysts who want to move up the ranks frequently go from one company to another, sometimes many times during their careers.

EARNINGS

Beginning salaries in marketing research depend on the qualifications of the employee, the nature of the position, and the size of the firm. Interviewers, coders, tabulators, editors, and a variety of other employees usually get paid by the hour and may start at $6 or more per hour. The U.S. Department of Labor reported that in 2006, median annual earnings of market research analysts were $58,820. The middle 50 percent earned salaries that ranged from $42,190 to $84,070. Salaries ranged from less than $32,250 to more than $112,510. Experienced analysts working in supervisory positions at large firms can earn even higher earnings. Market research directors earn up to $200,000.

Because business or industrial firms employ most marketing research workers, they receive typical fringe benefit packages, including health and life insurance, pension plans, and paid vacation and sick leave.

WORK ENVIRONMENT

Marketing research analysts usually work a 40-hour week. Occasionally, overtime is necessary in order to meet project deadlines. Although they frequently interact with a variety of marketing research team members, analysts also do a lot of independent work, analyzing data, writing reports, and preparing statistical charts.

While most marketing research analysts work in offices located at the firm's main headquarters, those who supervise interviewers may go into the field to oversee work. In order to attend conferences, meet with clients, or check on the progress of various research studies, many market research analysts find that regular travel is required.

OUTLOOK

The U.S. Department of Labor predicts that employment for marketing research analysts will grow faster than the average for all occupations through 2016. Increasing competition among producers of consumer goods and services and industrial products, combined with a growing awareness of the value of marketing research data, will contribute to opportunities in the field. Opportunities will be best for those with graduate degrees who seek employment in marketing research firms, companies that design computer systems and software, financial services organizations, health care institutions, advertising firms, manufacturing firms that produce consumer goods, and insurance companies.

While many new graduates are attracted to the field, creating a competitive situation, the best jobs and the highest pay will go to those individuals who hold a master's degree or doctorate in marketing research, statistics, economics, or computer science.

FOR MORE INFORMATION

For information on college chapters, internship opportunities, and financial aid opportunities, contact
American Advertising Federation
1101 Vermont Avenue, NW, Suite 500

Washington, DC 20005-6306
Tel: 202-898-0089
Email: aaf@aaf.org
http://www.aaf.org

For information on graduate programs, contact
American Association for Public Opinion Research
PO Box 14263
Lenexa, KS 66285-4263
Tel: 913-895-4601
Email: info@aapor.org
http://www.aapor.org

For information on advertising agencies, contact
American Association of Advertising Agencies
405 Lexington Avenue, 18th Floor
New York, NY 10174-1801
Tel: 212-682-2500
http://www.aaaa.org

For career resources and job listings, contact
American Marketing Association
311 South Wacker Drive, Suite 5800
Chicago, IL 60606-6629
Tel: 800-262-1150
http://www.marketingpower.com

For comprehensive information on market and opinion research, contact
Council for Marketing and Opinion Research
110 National Drive, 2nd Floor
Glastonbury, CT 06033-1212
Tel: 860-657-1881
Email: information@cmor.org
http://www.cmor.org

For information on graduate programs in marketing, contact
Council of American Survey Research Organizations
170 North Country Road, Suite 4
Port Jefferson, NY 11777-2606
Tel: 631-928-6954
Email: casro@casro.org
http://www.casro.org

For information on education and training, contact
Marketing Research Association
110 National Drive, 2nd Floor
Glastonbury, CT 06033-1212
Tel: 860-682-1000
Email: email@mra-net.org
http://www.mra-net.org

For career information, visit

Careers Outside the Box: Survey Research: A Fun, Exciting, Rewarding Career

http://www.casro.org/careers

MASSAGE THERAPISTS

SCHOOL SUBJECTS

Health, Physical Education

PERSONAL SKILLS

Helping/Teaching, Mechanical/Manipulative

MINIMUM EDUCATION LEVEL

Some Postsecondary Training

CERTIFICATION OR LICENSING

Recommended (Certification), Required by Certain States (Licensing)

WORK ENVIRONMENT

Primarily Indoors, Primarily One Location

OVERVIEW

Massage therapy is a broad term referring to a number of health-related practices, including Swedish massage, sports massage, Rolfing, Shiatsu and acupressure, trigger point therapy, and reflexology. Although the techniques vary, most *massage therapists* (or *massotherapists*) press and rub the skin and muscles. Relaxed muscles, improved blood circulation and joint mobility, reduced stress and anxiety, and decreased recovery time for sprains and injured muscles are just a few of the potential benefits of massage therapy. Massage therapists are sometimes called *bodyworkers*. The titles *masseur* and *masseuse*, once common, are now rare among those who use massage for therapy and rehabilitation. There are approximately 118,000 massage therapists employed in the United States.

THE JOB

Massage therapists work to produce physical, mental, and emotional benefits through the manipulation of the body's soft tissue. Auxiliary methods, such as the movement of joints and the application of dry and steam heat, are also used. Among the potential physical benefits are the release of muscle tension and stiffness, reduced blood pressure, better blood circulation, a shorter healing time for sprains and pulled muscles, increased flexibility and greater range of motion in the joints, and reduced swelling from edema (excess fluid buildup in body tissue). Massage may also improve posture, strengthen the immune system, and reduce the formation of scar tissue.

Mental and emotional benefits include a relaxed state of mind, reduced stress and anxiety, clearer thinking, and a general sense of well-being. Physical, mental, and emotional health are all interconnected: Being physically fit and healthy can improve emotional health, just as a positive mental attitude can bolster the immune system to help the body fight off infection. A release of muscle tension also leads to reduced stress and anxiety, and

physical manipulation of sore muscles can help speed the healing process.

There are many different approaches a massage therapist may take. Among the most popular are Swedish massage, sports massage, Rolfing, Shiatsu and acupressure, and trigger point therapy.

In Swedish massage the traditional techniques are effleurage, petrissage, friction, and tapotement. Effleurage (stroking) uses light and hard rhythmic strokes to relax muscles and improve blood circulation. It is often performed at the beginning and end of a massage session. Petrissage (kneading) is the rhythmic squeezing, pressing, and lifting of a muscle. For friction, the fingers, thumb, or palm or heel of the hand are pressed into the skin with a small circular movement. The massage therapist's fingers are sometimes pressed deeply into a joint. Tapotement (tapping), in which the hands strike the skin in rapid succession, is used to improve blood circulation.

During the session the client, covered with sheets, lies undressed on a padded table. Oil or lotion is used to smooth the skin. Some massage therapists use aromatherapy, adding fragrant essences to the oil to relax the client and stimulate circulation. Swedish massage may employ a number of auxiliary techniques, including the use of rollers, belts, and vibrators; steam and dry heat; ultraviolet and infrared light; and saunas, whirlpools, steam baths, and packs of hot water or ice.

Sports massage is essentially Swedish massage used in the context of athletics. A light massage generally is given before an event or game to loosen and warm the muscles. This reduces the chance of injury and may improve performance. After the event the athlete is massaged more deeply to alleviate pain, reduce stiffness, and promote healing.

Rolfing, developed by American Ida Rolf, involves deep, sometimes painful massage. Intense pressure is applied to various parts of the body. Rolfing practitioners believe that emotional disturbances, physical pain, and other problems can occur when the body is out of alignment—for example, as a result of poor posture. This method takes 10 sessions to complete.

Like the ancient Oriental science of acupuncture, Shiatsu and acupressure are based on the concept of meridians, or invisible channels of flowing energy in the body. The massage therapist presses down on particular points along these channels to release blocked energy and untie knots of muscle tension. For this approach the patient wears loosely fitted clothes, lies on the floor or on a futon, and is not given oil or lotion for the skin.

Trigger point therapy, a neuromuscular technique, focuses in on a painful area, or trigger point, in a muscle. A trigger point might be associated with a problem in another part of the body. Using the fingers or an instrument, such as a rounded piece of wood, concentrated pressure is placed on the irritated area in order to "deactivate" the trigger point.

All of these methods of massage can be altered and intermingled depending on the client's needs. Massage therapists can be proficient in one or many of the methods, and usually tailor a session to the individual.

REQUIREMENTS
High School

Since massage therapists need to know more than just technical skills, many practitioners use the basic knowledge learned in high school as a foundation to build a solid career in the field. During your high school years, you should take fundamental science courses, such as chemistry, anatomy, and biology. These classes will give you a basic understanding of the human body and prepare you for the health and anatomy classes you will take while completing your postsecondary education. English, psychology, and other classes relating to communications and human development will also be useful as the successful massage therapist is able to express his or her ideas with clients as well as understand the clients' reactions to the therapy. If you think you might wish to run your own massage therapy business someday, computer and business courses are essential. Finally, do not neglect your own physical well-being. Take physical education

and health courses to strengthen your body and your understanding of your own conditioning.

Postsecondary Training

The best way to become a successful massage therapist is to attend an accredited massage therapy school after you have finished high school. There are more than 300 state-accredited massage schools located throughout the United States. More than 85 of these schools are accredited or approved by the Commission on Massage Therapy Accreditation (COMTA), a major accrediting agency for massage therapy programs and an affiliate of the American Massage Therapy Association (AMTA). COMTA-accredited and -approved schools must provide at least 500 hours of classroom instruction. (The average massage therapist has 688 hours of initial training, according to the American Massage Therapy Association.) Studies should include such courses as anatomy, physiology, theory and practice of massage therapy, and ethics. In addition, students should receive supervised hands-on experience. Most programs offer students the opportunity to participate at clinics, such as those providing massage services at hospices, hospitals, and shelters, or at school clinics that are open to the general public.

Massage therapy training programs typically take about a year to complete. Students can specialize in particular disciplines, such as infant massage or rehabilitative massage. Basic first aid and cardiopulmonary resuscitation (CPR) must also be learned. When choosing a school, you should pay close attention to the philosophy and curricula of the program, since a wide range of program options exists. Also, keep in mind that licensure requirements for massage therapists vary by state. For example, some state medical boards require students to have completed more than 500 hours of instruction before they can be recognized as massage therapists. Part of your process for choosing a school, therefore, should include making sure that the school's curriculum will allow you to meet your state's requirements.

Certification or Licensing

Currently, 38 states and the District of Columbia regulate the practice of massage therapy, requiring licensure, certification, or registration. Because requirements for licensing, certification, registration, and even local ordinances vary, however, you will need to check with your state's department of regulatory agencies to get specifics for your area. Typically, requirements include completing an accredited program and passing a written test and a demonstration of massage therapy techniques.

The National Certification Board for Therapeutic Massage and Bodywork offers two national certification examinations for massage therapists: the National Certification Examination for Therapeutic Massage and Bodywork and the National Certification Examination for Therapeutic Massage. To learn more about each exam, visit http://www.ncbtmb.com. Certification is highly recommended, since it demonstrates a therapist's high-level of education and achievement. Certification may also make a therapist a more desirable candidate for job openings.

Other Requirements

Physical requirements of massage therapists generally include the ability to use their hands and other tools to rub or press on the client's body. Manual dexterity is usually required to administer the treatments, as is the ability to stand for at least an hour at a time. Special modifications or accommodations can often be made for people with different abilities.

If you are interested in becoming a massage therapist, you should be, above all, nurturing and caring. Constance Bickford, a certified massage therapist in Chicago, thinks that it is necessary to be both flexible and creative: easily adaptable to the needs of the client, as well as able to use different techniques to help the client feel better. Listening well and responding to the client is vital, as is focusing all attention on the task at hand. Massage therapists need to tune in to their client rather than zone out, thinking about the grocery list or what to cook for supper. An effective massage is a mindful one, where massage therapist and client work together toward improved health.

To be a successful massage therapist, you should also be trustworthy and sensitive. Someone receiving a massage may feel awkward lying naked in an office covered by a sheet, listening to music while a stranger kneads his or her muscles. A good massage therapist will make the client feel comfortable in what could potentially be perceived as a vulnerable situation.

Therapists considering opening up their own business should be prepared for busy and slow times. In order to both serve their clients well and stay in business, they should be adequately staffed during rush seasons, and must be financially able to withstand dry spells.

EXPLORING

The best way to become familiar with massage therapy is to get a massage. Look for a certified therapist in your area and make an appointment for a session. If you can afford it, consider going to several different therapists who offer different types of massage. Also, ask if you can set up an information interview with one of the therapists. Explain that you are interested in pursuing this career and come to the interview prepared to ask questions. What is this massage therapist's educational background? Why was he or she drawn to the job? What is the best part of this work? By talking to a massage therapist, you may also have the chance to develop a mentoring relationship with him or her.

A less costly approach is to find a book on massage instruction at a local public library or bookstore. Massage techniques can then be practiced at home. Books on self-massage are available. Many books discuss in detail the theoretical basis for the techniques. Videos that demonstrate massage techniques are available as well.

Consider volunteering at a hospice, nursing home, or shelter. This work will give you experience in caring for others and help you develop good listening skills. It is important for massage therapists to listen well and respond appropriately to their clients' needs. The massage therapist must make clients feel comfortable, and volunteer work can help foster the skills necessary to achieve this.

EMPLOYERS

Approximately 118,000 massage therapists are employed in the United States. After graduating from an accredited school of massage therapy, there are a number of possibilities for employment. Doctors' offices, hospitals, clinics, health clubs, resorts, country clubs, cruise ships, community service organizations, and nursing homes, for example, all employ massage therapists. Some chiropractors have a massage therapist on staff to whom they can refer patients. A number of massage therapists run their own businesses. Most opportunities for work will be in larger, urban areas with population growth, although massage therapy is slowly spreading to more rural areas as well.

STARTING OUT

There are a number of resources you can use to locate a job. The AMTA offers job placement information to certified massage therapists who belong to the organization. Massage therapy schools have career services offices. Newspapers often list jobs. Some graduates are able to enter the field as self-employed massage therapists, scheduling their own appointments and managing their own offices.

Networking is a valuable tool in maintaining a successful massage therapy enterprise. Many massage therapists get clients through referrals, and often rely on word of mouth to build a solid customer base. Beginning massage therapists might wish to consult businesses about arranging onsite massage sessions for their employees.

Health fairs are also good places to distribute information about massage therapy practices and learn about other services in the industry. Often, organizers of large sporting events will employ massage therapists to give massages to athletes at the finish line. These events may include marathons and runs or bike rides held to raise money for charitable organizations.

ADVANCEMENT

For self-employed massage therapists, advancement is measured by reputation, the ability to attract clients, and the fees charged for services. Health clubs, country clubs, and other institutions have supervisory positions for massage therapists. In a community service organization, massage therapists may be promoted to the position of health service director. Licensed massage therapists often become instructors or advisors at schools for massage therapy. They may also make themselves available to advise individuals or companies on the short- and long-term benefits of massage therapy, and how massage therapy can be introduced into professional work environments.

EARNINGS

The earnings of massage therapists vary greatly with the level of experience and location of practice. Therapists in New York and California, for example, typically charge higher rates than those in other parts of the country. Some entry-level massage therapists earn as little as minimum wage (ending up with a yearly income of around $12,170), but with experience, a massage therapist can charge from $45 to $70 for a one-hour session.

The U.S. Department of Labor reports that massage therapists earned a median salary of $33,400 a year in 2006. The lowest 10 percent earned $15,550 or less, while the highest 10 percent earned $70,360 or more.

The American Massage Therapy Association reports that massage therapists charge an average of $60 for a one-hour massage. Those with earnings at the high end typically worked in higher paying geographic areas (such as large cities), had years of experience, and had built up a large clientele.

Approximately 64 percent of all massage therapists are self employed, and self-employed therapists are not paid for the time spent on bookkeeping, maintaining their offices, waiting for customers to arrive, and looking for new clients. In addition, they must pay a self-employment tax and provide their own benefits. With membership in some national organizations, self-employed massage therapists may be eligible for group life, health, liability, and renter's insurance through the organization's insurance agency.

Massage therapists employed by a health club usually get free or discounted memberships to the club. Those who work for resorts or on cruise ships can get free or discounted travel and accommodations, in addition to full access to facilities when not on duty. Massage therapists employed by a sports team often get to attend the team's sporting events.

WORK ENVIRONMENT

Massage therapists work in clean, comfortable settings. Because a relaxed environment is essential, the massage room may be dim, and soft music, scents, and oils are often used. Since massage therapists may see a number of people per day, it is important to maintain a hygienic working area. This involves changing sheets on the massage table after each client, as well as cleaning and sterilizing any implements used, and washing hands frequently.

Massage therapists employed by businesses may use a portable massage chair—that is, a padded chair that leaves the client in a forward-leaning position ideal for massage of the back and neck. Some massage therapists work out of their homes or travel to the homes of their clients.

The workweek of a massage therapist is typically 35 to 40 hours, which may include evenings and weekends. On average, 19 hours per week are spent with clients, and the other hours are spent making appointments and taking care of other business-related details.

Since the physical work is sometimes demanding, massage therapists need to take measures to prevent repetitive stress disorders, such as carpal tunnel syndrome. Also, for their own personal safety, massage therapists who work out of their homes or have odd office hours need to be particularly careful about scheduling appointments with unknown clients.

OUTLOOK

The industry predicts a strong employment outlook for massage therapists through the next several years. The growing acceptance of massage therapy as an important health care discipline has led to the creation of additional jobs for massage therapists in many sectors. Opportunities should be strongest for women, as clients—both male and female—report that they are more comfortable working with female massage therapists. Approximately 84 percent of massage therapists are women.

One certified massage therapist points to sports massage as one of the fastest-growing specialties in the field. The increasing popularity of professional sports has given massage therapists new opportunities to work as key members of a team's staff. Their growing presence in sports has made massage therapy more visible to the public, spreading the awareness of the physical benefits of massage.

Massages aren't just for athletes. According to a survey by the American Massage Therapy Association, 24 percent of Americans surveyed in June 2007 had a massage in the past 12 months. The survey found that people are getting massages not just for medical reasons, but to relax and reduce stress.

There is a growing opportunity for massage therapists in the corporate world. Many employers eager to hold on to good employees offer perks, such as workplace massages. As a result, many massage therapists are working as mobile business consultants.

FOR MORE INFORMATION

For information on careers and education programs, contact

American Massage Therapy Association
500 Davis Street
Evanston, IL 60201-4695
Tel: 877-905-2700
Email: info@amtamassage.org
http://www.amtamassage.org

For information on careers in the field (including the brochure, Your Massage & Bodywork Career), *state board requirements, and training programs, contact*

Associated Bodywork and Massage Professionals
1271 Sugarbush Drive
Evergreen, CO 80439-9766
Tel: 800-458-2267
Email: expectmore@abmp.com
http://www.abmp.com
http://www.massagetherapy.com

For information on accreditation and programs, contact
Commission on Massage Therapy Accreditation
1007 Church Street, Suite 302
Evanston, IL 60201-5912
Tel: 847-869-5039
Email: info@comta.org
http://www.comta.org

For information about state certification and education requirements, contact

National Certification Board for Therapeutic Massage and Bodywork
1901 South Meyers Road, Suite 240
Oakbrook Terrace, IL 60181-5243
Tel: 800-296-0664
Email: info@ncbtmb.com
http://www.ncbtmb.com

MEDICAL ASSISTANTS

OVERVIEW

Medical assistants help physicians in offices, hospitals, and clinics. They keep medical records, help examine and treat patients, and perform routine office duties to allow physicians to spend their time working directly with patients. Medical assistants are vitally important to the smooth and efficient operation of medical offices. There are approximately 417,000 medical assistants employed in the United States.

THE JOB

Depending on the size of the office, medical assistants may perform clerical or clinical duties, or both. The larger the office, the greater the chance that the assistant will specialize in one type of work.

SCHOOL SUBJECTS
Biology, Mathematics

PERSONAL SKILLS
Helping/Teaching, Technical/Scientific

MINIMUM EDUCATION LEVEL
Some Postsecondary Training

CERTIFICATION OR LICENSING
Voluntary

WORK ENVIRONMENT
Primarily Indoors, Primarily One Location

In their clinical duties, medical assistants help physicians by preparing patients for examination or treatment. They may check and record patients' blood pressure, pulse, temperature, height, and weight. Medical assistants often ask patients questions about their medical histories and record the answers in the patient's file. In the examining room, the medical assistant may be responsible for arranging medical instruments and handing them to the physician as requested during the examination. Medical assistants may prepare patients for X rays and laboratory examinations, as well as administer electrocardiograms. They may apply dressings, draw blood, and give injections. Medical assistants also may give patients instructions about taking medications, watching their diet, or restricting their activities before laboratory tests or surgery. In addition, medical assistants may collect specimens such as throat cultures for laboratory tests and may be responsible for sterilizing examining room instruments and equipment.

Medical assistants prepare examining rooms for patients and keep examining and waiting rooms clean and orderly. After each examination, they straighten the examining room and dispose of used linens and medical supplies. Sometimes medical assistants keep track of office and medical supply inventories and order necessary supplies. They may deal with pharmaceutical and medical supply company representatives when ordering supplies.

At other times, medical assistants may perform a wide range of administrative tasks. *Medical secretaries* and *medical receptionists* also perform administrative activities in medical offices, but these workers are distinguished from medical assistants by the fact that they rarely perform clinical functions. The administrative and clerical tasks that medical assistants may complete include typing case histories and operation reports; keeping office files, X rays, and other medical records up to date; keeping the office's financial records; preparing and sending bills and receiving payments; and transcribing dictation from the physician. Assistants may also answer the telephone, greet patients, fill out insurance forms, schedule appointments, take care of correspondence, and arrange for patients to be admitted to the hospital. Most medical assistants use word processors and computers for most record-keeping tasks.

Some medical assistants work in ophthalmologists' offices, where their clinical duties involve helping with eye examinations and treatments. They use special equipment to test and measure patients' eyes and check for disease. They administer eye drops and dressings and teach patients how to insert and care for contact lenses. They may maintain surgical instruments and help

physicians during eye surgery. Other medical assistants work as *optometric assistants*, who may be required to prepare patients for examination and assist them in eyewear selection; *chiropractor assistants*, whose duties may include treatment and examination of patients' muscular and skeletal problems; and *podiatric assistants*, who assist podiatrists during examinations and surgery, take and develop X rays, and make castings of patients' feet.

REQUIREMENTS
High School

Medical assistants usually need a high school diploma, but in many cases receive specific training on the job. High school courses in the sciences, especially biology, are helpful, as are courses in algebra, English, bookkeeping, typing, computers, and office practices.

Postsecondary Training

Formal training for medical assistants is available at many trade schools, community and junior colleges, and universities. College programs generally award an associate's degree and take two years to complete. Other programs can last as long as a year and award a diploma or certificate. Prior to enrolling in any school program, you should check its curriculum and verify its accreditation.

Schools for medical assistants may be accredited by either the Commission on Accreditation of Allied Health Education Programs, which has approved approximately 500 medical and ophthalmic programs; the Accrediting Bureau of Health Education Schools, which has accredited approximately 170 medical assisting programs; or the Committee on Accreditation for Ophthalmic Medical Personnel, which has accredited approximately 11 ophthalmic medical assisting programs and three programs in ophthalmic clinical assisting. Coursework includes biology, anatomy, physiology, and medical terminology, as well as typing, transcribing, shorthand, record keeping, and computer skills. Perhaps most importantly, these programs provide supervised, hands-on clinical experience in laboratory techniques, first-aid procedures, proper use of medical equipment, and clinical procedures. You also learn administrative duties and procedures in medical offices and receive training in interpersonal communications and medical ethics.

Certification or Licensing

Voluntarily certification is available from certain professional organizations. The registered medical assistant credential is awarded by American Medical Technologists, and the American Association of Medical Assistants awards a credential for certified medical assistant. Ophthalmic assistants can receive the following designations from the Joint Commission on Allied Health Personnel in Ophthalmology: certified ophthalmic assistant, corporate certified ophthalmic assistant, certified ophthalmic technician, and certified ophthalmic medical technologist. The American Society of Podiatric Medical Assistants offers the podiatric medical assistant, certified designation. Medical assistants generally do not need to be licensed. Some states require medical assistants to pass a test or take a course before they can perform certain tasks like taking X rays.

Other Requirements

To be a successful medical assistant, you must be able to interact with patients and other medical personnel and be able to follow detailed directions. In addition, you must be dependable and compassionate and have the desire to help people. Medical assistants must also respect patients' privacy by keeping medical information confidential. Overall, medical assistants who help patients feel at ease in the doctor's office and other medical settings and have good communication skills and a desire to serve should do well in this job.

EXPLORING

Students in postsecondary school medical assistant programs will have the chance to explore the field through the supervised clinical experience required by the various programs. Others may wish to gain additional experience by volunteering at hospitals, nursing homes, or clinics to get a feel for the work involved in a medical environment. You may want to talk with the medical assistants in your own or other local physicians' offices to find out more about the work they do.

EMPLOYERS

About 417,000 medical assistants are employed in physicians' offices, clinics, hospitals, health maintenance organizations, and other medical facilities. Approximately 62 percent work in private doctors' offices and 12 percent work in hospitals. Another 11 percent work in optometrists', podiatrists', and chiropractors' offices and other health care facilities.

STARTING OUT

Students enrolled in college or other postsecondary school medical assistant programs may learn of available positions through their school career services offices. High school guidance counselors may have information about positions for students about to graduate. Newspaper want ads and state employment offices are other good places to look for leads. You may also wish to call local physicians' offices to find out about unadvertised openings.

ADVANCEMENT

Experienced medical assistants may be able to move into managerial or administrative positions without further education, but moving into a more advanced clinical position, such as nursing, requires more education. As more and more clinics and group practices open, more office managers will be needed, and these are positions that well-qualified, experienced medical assistants may be able to fill. As with most occupations, today's job market gives medical assistants with computer skills more opportunities for advancement.

EARNINGS

The earnings of medical assistants vary widely, depending on experience, skill level, and location. According to the U.S. Department of Labor, median annual earnings of medical assistants were $26,290 in 2006. The lowest 10 percent earned less than $18,860, and the highest 10 percent earned more than $36,840 a year. Mean annual earnings of medical assistants who worked in offices of physicians were $27,290 and in hospitals they were $28,740.

Medical assistants usually receive six or seven paid holidays a year, as well as annual paid vacation days. They often receive health and life insurance, a retirement plan, sick leave, and uniform allowances.

WORK ENVIRONMENT

Most medical assistants work in pleasant, modern surroundings. The average medical assistant works 40 hours a week, including some Saturday and evening hours. Sterilizing equipment and handling medical instruments require care and attentiveness. As most professionals in the health sciences will attest, working with people who are ill may be upsetting at times, but it can also have many personal rewards.

OUTLOOK

Employment for medical assistants will grow much faster than the average for all occupations through 2016, according to the U.S. Department of Labor. Most openings will occur to replace workers who leave their jobs, but many will be the result of a predicted surge in the number of physicians' offices, clinics, and other outpatient care facilities. The growing number of elderly Americans who need medical treatment is also a factor for this increased demand for health services. In addition, new and more complex paperwork for medical insurance, malpractice insurance, government programs, and other purposes will create a growing need for assistants in medical offices.

Many physicians prefer experienced and formally trained medical assistants, so these workers will have the best employment outlook. Word-processing skills, computer skills, and formal certification are all definite assets.

FOR MORE INFORMATION

For information on accreditation and testing, contact

Accrediting Bureau of Health Education Schools
7777 Leesburg Pike, Suite 314-North
Falls Church, VA 22043-2411
Tel: 703-917-9503
Email: info@abhes.org
http://www.abhes.org

For career and certification information, contact the following organizations

American Association of Medical Assistants
20 North Wacker Drive, Suite 1575
Chicago, IL 60606-2963
Tel: 312-899-1500
http://www.aama-ntl.org

American Medical Technologists
10700 West Higgins Road
Park Ridge, IL 60018-3707
Tel: 847-823-5169
http://www.amt1.com

For information on podiatric medical assisting careers and certification, contact

American Society of Podiatric Medical Assistants
2124 South Austin Boulevard
Cicero, IL 60804-2012
Tel: 888-882-7762
http://www.aspma.org

For information on accredited programs, contact

Commission on Accreditation of Allied Health Education Programs
1361 Park Street
Clearwater, FL 33756-6039
Tel: 727-210-2350
http://www.caahep.org

For information on accredited programs and certification, contact

Joint Commission on Allied Health Personnel in Ophthalmology
2025 Woodlane Drive
St. Paul, MN 55125-2998
Tel: 800-284-3937
Email: jcahpo@jcahpo.org
http://www.jcahpo.org/newsite/index.htm

MEDICAL LABORATORY TECHNICIANS

OVERVIEW

Medical laboratory technicians perform routine tests in medical laboratories. These tests help physicians and other professional medical personnel diagnose and treat disease. Technicians prepare samples of body tissue; perform laboratory tests, such as urinalysis and blood counts; and make chemical and biological analyses of cells, tissue, blood, or other body specimens. They usually work under the supervision of a medical technologist or a laboratory director. Medical laboratory technicians may work in many fields, or specialize in one specific medical area, such as cytology (the study of cells), hematology (the study of blood, especially on the cellular level), serology (the study and identification of antibodies found in the blood), or histology (the study of body tissue). There are approximately 319,000 medical laboratory technicians and technologists employed in the United States.

THE JOB

Medical laboratory technicians may be generalists in the field of laboratory technology; that is, they may be trained to carry out many different kinds of medical laboratory work. Alternatively, they may specialize in one type of medical laboratory work, such as cytology, hematology, blood bank technology, serology, or histology. The following paragraphs describe the work of generalists and those in the specialty fields of cytology, histology, and blood bank technology.

Medical laboratory technicians who work as generalists perform a wide variety of tests and laboratory procedures in chemistry, hematology, urinalysis, blood banking, serology, and microbiology. By performing these tests and procedures, they help to develop vital data on the blood, tissues, and fluids of the human body. This data is then used by physicians, surgeons, pathologists, and other medical personnel to diagnose and treat patients.

The tests and procedures that these technicians perform are more complex than the routine duties assigned to laboratory assistants, but do not require specialized knowledge like those performed by more highly trained medical technologists. In general, medical laboratory technicians work with only limited supervision. This means that while the tests they perform may have well-established procedures, the technicians themselves must exercise independent judgment. For instance, they must be able to discriminate between very similar colors or shapes, correct their own errors using established strategies, and monitor ongoing quality control measures.

To carry out these responsibilities, medical laboratory technicians need a sound knowledge of specific techniques and instruments and must be able to recognize factors that potentially influence both the procedures they use and the results they obtain.

In their work, medical laboratory technicians frequently handle test tubes and other glassware and use precision equipment, such as microscopes and automated blood analyzers. (Blood analyzers determine the levels of certain blood components like cholesterol, sugar, and hemoglobin.) Technicians also are often responsible for making sure machines are functioning and supplies are adequately stocked.

Medical laboratory technicians who specialize in cytology are usually referred to as cytotechnicians. *Cytotechnicians* prepare and stain body cell samplings using special dyes that accentuate the delicate patterns of the cytoplasm, and structures such as the nucleus. Mounted on slides, the various features of the specimen then stand out brightly under a microscope. Using microscopes that magnify cells perhaps 1,000 times, cytotechnicians screen out normal samplings and set aside those with minute irregularities (in cell size, shape, and color) for further study by a pathologist.

Medical laboratory technicians specializing in histology are usually referred to as *histologic technicians* or *tissue technicians*. Histology is the study of the structure and chemical composition of the tissues, and histologic technicians are mainly concerned with detecting tissue abnormalities and assisting in determining appropriate treatments for the disease conditions associated with the abnormalities.

Medical laboratory technicians who specialize in blood bank technology perform a wide variety of routine tests related to running blood banks, offering transfusion

SCHOOL SUBJECTS
Biology, Chemistry

PERSONAL SKILLS
Following Instructions, Technical/Scientific

MINIMUM EDUCATION LEVEL
Some Postsecondary Training

CERTIFICATION OR LICENSING
Required by Certain States

WORK ENVIRONMENT
Primarily Indoors, Primarily One Location

services, and investigating blood diseases and reactions to transfusions. Examples of tasks frequently performed by medical laboratory technicians specializing in this field include donor screening, determining blood types, performing tests of patients' blood counts, and assisting physicians in the care of patients with blood-related problems.

REQUIREMENTS
High School

To be hired as a medical laboratory technician, you must have a high school diploma and one or two years of postsecondary training. No specific kind of high school training is required; however, you must be able to meet the admissions requirements of institutions offering post-high school training. In general, courses in biology, chemistry, mathematics, English, and computer science will be most helpful in a career as a medical laboratory technician.

Postsecondary Training

After high school, prospective technicians enroll in one- or two-year training programs accredited by the Commission on Accreditation of Allied Health Education Programs, the Accrediting Bureau of Health Education Schools, or the National Accrediting Agency for Clinical Laboratory Sciences, which fully accredits approximately 470 programs. One-year programs include both classroom work and practical laboratory training and focus on areas such as medical ethics and conduct, medical terminology, basic laboratory solutions and media, manipulation of cytological and histological specimens, blood collecting techniques, and introductions to basic hematology, serology, blood banking, and urinalysis.

To earn an associate's degree, you must complete a two-year post-high school program. Like certificate programs, associate's degree programs include classroom instruction and practical training. Courses are taught both on campus and in local hospitals. On-campus courses focus on general knowledge and basic skills in laboratory testing associated with hematology, serology, chemistry, microbiology, and other pertinent biological and medical areas. The clinical training program focuses on basic principles and skills required in medical diagnostic laboratory testing.

Certification or Licensing

Students who have earned an associate's degree are eligible for certification from several different agencies, including the Board of Registry of the American Society for Clinical Pathology, the American Medical Technologists, the National Credentialing Agency for Laboratory Personnel, and the American Association of Bioanalysts.

Prospective medical laboratory technicians who think they might want to specialize in cytology or blood bank technology should definitely consider the two-year program, which will best prepare them for the additional education they may need later.

In addition to completing the educational programs described above, prospective technicians need to pass an examination after graduation to receive certification. In some states, this certificate is all that is required for employment. In other states, state licensure is also required. School officials are the best source of information regarding state requirements.

Other Requirements

Besides fulfilling the academic requirements, medical laboratory technicians must have good manual dexterity, normal color vision, the ability to follow instructions, and a tolerance for working under pressure.

EXPLORING

It is difficult for people interested in a career in medical laboratory technology to gain any direct experience through part-time employment. There are some other ways, however, to learn more about this career on a first-hand basis. Perhaps the best way is to arrange a visit to a hospital, blood bank, or commercial medical laboratory to see technicians at work at their jobs. Another way

to learn about this kind of work in general, and about the training required in particular, is to visit an accredited school of medical laboratory technology to discuss career plans with an admissions counselor at the school. You can also write to the sources listed at the end of this article for more reading material on medical laboratory technology or visit their Web sites. Finally, you should remember that high school science courses with laboratory sections will give you exposure to some of the kinds of work you might do later in your career.

EMPLOYERS

Medical laboratory technicians are employed where physicians work, such as in hospitals, clinics, offices of physicians, blood blanks, and commercial medical laboratories. Approximately 319,000 medical laboratory technicians and technologists are employed in the United States, with more than half working in hospitals.

STARTING OUT

Graduates of medical laboratory technology schools usually receive assistance from faculty and school career services offices to find their first jobs. Hospitals, laboratories, and other facilities employing medical laboratory technicians may notify local schools of job openings. Often the hospital or laboratory at which you receive your practical training will offer full-time employment after graduation. Positions may also be secured using the various registries of certified medical laboratory workers. Newspaper job advertisements and commercial placement agencies are other sources of help in locating employment.

ADVANCEMENT

Medical laboratory technicians often advance by returning to school to earn a bachelor's degree. This can lead to positions as medical technologists, histological technologists, cytotechnologists, or specialists in blood bank technology.

Other technicians advance by gaining more responsibility while retaining the title of technician. For instance, with experience, these workers can advance to supervisory positions or other positions assigning work to be done by other medical laboratory workers. Medical laboratory technicians may also advance by training to do very specialized or complex laboratory or research work.

EARNINGS

Salaries of medical laboratory technicians vary according to employer and geographical area. According to the U.S. Department of Labor, median annual earnings of medical and clinical laboratory technicians were $32,840 in 2006. Salaries ranged from less than $21,830 to more than $50,250. Fifty percent of workers in this field earned between $26,430 and $41,020 annually in 2006. Medical laboratory technicians who go on to earn their bachelor's degrees and certification as medical technologists can expect an increase in annual earnings.

Most medical laboratory technicians receive paid vacations and holidays, sick leave, health insurance, and retirement benefits.

WORK ENVIRONMENT

Medical laboratory technicians work in clean, well-lit, and usually air-conditioned settings. There may, however, be unpleasant odors and some infectious materials involved in the work. In general, there are few hazards associated with these odors and materials as long as proper methods of sterilization and handling of specimens, materials, and equipment are used.

Medical laboratory technicians often spend much of their days standing or sitting on stools. A 40-hour, five-day week is normal, although those working in hospitals can expect some evening and weekend work.

Medical laboratory technicians derive satisfaction from knowing their work is very important to patients and their physicians. Although the work involves new patient samples, it also involves some very repetitive tasks that some people may find trying. Additionally, the work must often be done under time pressure, even though it is often very painstaking.

Another factor that aspiring medical laboratory technicians should keep in mind is that advancement opportunities are limited, although they do exist. To maximize their chances for advancement, medical laboratory technicians must consider getting additional training.

OUTLOOK

The U.S. Department of Labor predicts that employment for medical laboratory technicians will grow faster than the average for all occupations through 2016. Competition for jobs, however, may be strong. One reason for this increased competition is the overall national effort to control health care costs. Hospitals, where most medical laboratory technicians are employed, will seek to control costs in part through cutting down on the amount of laboratory testing they do and, consequently, the personnel they require.

Despite such cutbacks, though, the overall amount of medical laboratory testing will probably increase, as much of medical practice today relies on high-quality laboratory testing. However, because of the increased use of automation, this increase in laboratory testing probably will not lead to an equivalent growth in employment.

One other technological factor that will influence employment in this field is the development of laboratory-testing equipment that is easier to use. This means that some testing that formerly had to be done in hospitals can now be done in physicians' offices and other non-hospital settings. This development will slow growth in hospital laboratory employment; however, it should increase the number of technicians hired by medical groups and clinics, medical and diagnostic laboratories, and other ambulatory health care services such as blood and organ banks. In addition, equipment that is easier to use may also lead to technicians being able to do more kinds of testing, including some tests that used to be done only by medical technologists.

Medical laboratory testing is an absolutely essential element in today's medicine. For well-trained technicians who are flexible in accepting responsibilities and willing to continue their education throughout their careers, employment opportunities should be excellent.

FOR MORE INFORMATION

For information on accreditation, contact
Accrediting Bureau of Health Education Schools
7777 Leesburg Pike, Suite 314-North
Falls Church, VA 22043-2411
Tel: 703-917-9503
Email: info@abhes.org
http://www.abhes.org

For information on certification, contact
American Association of Bioanalysts
906 Olive Street, Suite 1200
St. Louis, MO 63101-1434
Tel: 314-241-1445
Email: aab@aab.org
http://www.aab.org

For career and certification information, contact
American Medical Technologists
10700 West Higgins Road, Suite 150
Rosemont, IL 60018-3707
Tel: 847-823-5169

Email: mail@amt1.com

http://www.amt1.com

For information on clinical laboratory careers and certification, contact

American Society for Clinical Laboratory Science

6701 Democracy Boulevard, Suite 300

Bethesda, MD 20817-7500

Tel: 301-657-2768

Email: ascls@ascls.org

http://www.ascls.org

For information on certification, contact

American Society for Clinical Pathology

33 West Monroe, Suite 1600

Chicago IL 60603-5308

Tel: 800-267-2727

Email: info@ascp.org

http://www.ascp.org

For information on careers, contact

Clinical Laboratory Management Association

989 Old Eagle School Road, Suite 815

Wayne, PA 19087-1704

Tel: 610-995-2640

http://www.clma.org

For information on accredited programs, contact

Commission on Accreditation of Allied Health Education Programs

1361 Park Street

Clearwater, FL 33756-6039

Tel: 727-210-2350

Email: mail@caahep.org

http://www.caahep.org

For information on accredited programs, contact

National Accrediting Agency for Clinical Laboratory Sciences

8410 West Bryn Mawr Avenue, Suite 670

Chicago, IL 60631-3402

Tel: 773-714-8880

Email: info@naacls.org

http://www.naacls.org

For information on certification, contact

National Credentialing Agency for Laboratory Personnel

PO Box 15945-289

Lenexa, KS 66285

Tel: 913-895-4613

Email: nca-info@goamp.com

http://www.nca-info.org

☐ MEDICAL RECORD TECHNICIANS

OVERVIEW

In any hospital, clinic, or other health care facility, permanent records are created and maintained for all the patients treated by the staff. Each patient's medical record describes in detail his or her condition over time. Entries include illness and injuries, operations, treatments, outpatient visits, and the progress of hospital stays. *Medical record technicians* compile, code, and maintain these records. They also tabulate and analyze data from groups of records in order to assemble reports. They review records for completeness and accuracy; assign codes to the diseases, operations, diagnoses, and treatments according to detailed standardized classification systems; and post the codes on the medical record. They transcribe medical reports; maintain indices of patients, diseases, operations, and other categories of information; compile patient census data; and file records. In addition, they may direct the day-to-day operations of the medical records department. They maintain the flow of records and reports to and from other departments, and sometimes assist medical staff in special studies or research that draws on information in the records. There are approximately 170,000 medical record technicians employed in the United States.

THE JOB

A patient's medical record consists of all relevant information and observations of any health care workers who have dealt with the patient. It may contain, for example, several diagnoses, X-ray and laboratory reports, electrocardiogram tracings, test results, and drugs prescribed. This summary of the patient's medical history is very important to the physician in making speedy and correct decisions about care. Later, information from the record is often needed in authenticating legal forms and insurance claims. The medical record documents the adequacy and appropriateness of the care received by the patient and is the basis of any investigation when the care is questioned in any way.

Patterns and trends can be traced when data from many records are considered together. These types of statistical reports are used by many different groups. Hospital administrators, scientists, public health agencies, accrediting and licensing bodies, people who evaluate the effectiveness of current programs or plan future ones, and medical reimbursement organizations are examples of some groups that rely on health care statistics. Medical records can provide the data to show whether a new treatment or medication really works, the relative effectiveness of alternative treatments or medications, or patterns that yield clues about the causes or methods of preventing certain kinds of disease.

Medical record technicians are involved in the routine preparation, handling, and safeguarding of individual records as well as the statistical information extracted from groups of records. Their specific tasks and the scope of their responsibilities depend a great deal on the size and type of the employing institution. In large organizations, there may be a number of technicians and other employees working with medical records. The technicians may serve as assistants to the medical record administrator as needed or may regularly specialize in some particular phase of the work done by the department. In small facilities, however, technicians often carry out the whole range of activities and may function fairly independently, perhaps bearing the full responsibility for all day-to-day operations of the department. A technician in a small facility may even be a department director. Sometimes technicians handle medical records and also spend part of their time helping out in the business or admitting office.

Whether they work in hospitals or other settings, medical record technicians must organize, transfer, analyze, preserve, and locate vast quantities of detailed information when needed. The sources of this information include physicians, nurses, laboratory workers, and other members of the health care team.

In a hospital, a patient's cumulative record goes to the medical record department at the end of the hospital stay. A technician checks over the information in the file to be sure that all the essential reports and data are included and appear accurate. Certain specific items must be supplied in any record, such as signatures, dates, the patient's physical and social history, the results of physical examinations, provisional and final diagnoses, periodic progress notes on the patient's condition during the hospital stay, medications prescribed and administered, therapeutic treatments, surgical procedures, and an assessment of the outcome or the condition at the time of discharge. If any item is missing, the technician sends the record to the person who is responsible for supplying the information. After all necessary information has been received and the record has passed the review, it is considered the official document describing the patient's case.

The record is then passed to a *medical record coder*. Coders are responsible for assigning a numeric code

SCHOOL SUBJECTS
Computer Science, Health, English

PERSONAL SKILLS
Following Instructions, Technical/Scientific

MINIMUM EDUCATION LEVEL
Associate's Degree

CERTIFICATION OR LICENSING
Recommended

WORK ENVIRONMENT
Primarily Indoors, Primarily One Location

to every diagnosis and procedure listed in a patient's file. Most hospitals in the United States use a nationally accepted system for coding. The lists of diseases, procedures, and conditions are published in classification manuals that medical records personnel refer to frequently. By reducing information in different forms to a single consistent coding system, the data contained in the record is rendered much easier to handle, tabulate, and analyze. It can be indexed under any suitable heading, such as by patient, disease, type of surgery, physician attending the case, and so forth. Cross-indexing is likely to be an important part of the medical record technician's job. Because the same coding systems are used nearly everywhere in the United States, the data may be used not only by people working inside the hospital, but may also be submitted to one of the various programs that pool information obtained from many institutions.

After the information on the medical record has been coded, technicians may use a packaged computer program to assign the patient to one of several hundred diagnosis-related groupings, or DRGs. The DRG for the patient's stay determines the amount of money the hospital will receive if the patient is covered by Medicare or one of the other insurance programs that base their reimbursement on DRGs.

Because information in medical records is used to determine how much hospitals are paid for caring for patients, the accuracy of the work done by medical records personnel is vital. A coding error could cause the hospital or patient to lose money.

Another vital part of the job concerns filing. Regardless of how accurately and completely information is gathered and stored, it is worthless unless it can be retrieved promptly. If paper records are kept, technicians are usually responsible for preparing records for storage, filing them, and getting them out of storage when needed. In some organizations, technicians supervise other personnel who carry out these tasks.

In many health care facilities, computers, rather than paper, are used for nearly all the medical record keeping. In such cases, medical and nursing staff make notes on an electronic chart. They enter patient-care information into computer files, and medical record technicians access the information using their own terminals. Computers have greatly simplified many traditional routine tasks of the medical records department, such as generating daily hospital census figures, tabulating data for research purposes, and updating special registries of certain types of health problems, such as cancer and stroke.

In the past, some medical records that were originally on paper were later photographed and stored on microfilm, particularly after they were a year or two old. Medical record technicians may be responsible for retrieving and maintaining those films. It is not unusual for a health care institution to have a combination of paper and microfilm files as well as computerized record storage, reflecting the evolution of technology for storing information.

Confidentiality and privacy laws have a major bearing on the medical records field. The laws vary in different states for different types of data, but in all cases, maintaining the confidentiality of individual records is of major concern to medical records workers. All individual records must be in secure storage but also be available for retrieval and specified kinds of properly authorized use. Technicians may be responsible for retrieving and releasing this information. They may prepare records to be released in response to a patient's written authorization, a subpoena, or a court order. This requires special knowledge of legal statutes and often requires consultation with attorneys, judges, insurance agents, and other parties with legitimate rights to access information about a person's health and medical treatment.

Medical record technicians may participate in the quality assurance, risk management, and utilization review activities of a health care facility. In these cases, they may serve as *data abstractors* and data analysts, reviewing records against established standards to ensure quality of care. They may also prepare statistical reports for the medical or administrative staff that reviews appropriateness of care.

With more specialized training, medical record technicians may participate in medical research activities by maintaining special records, called registries, related to such areas as cancer, heart disease, transplants, or adverse outcomes of pregnancies. In some cases, they are required to abstract and code information from records of patients with certain medical conditions. These technicians also may prepare statistical reports and trend analyses for the use of medical researchers.

REQUIREMENTS

High School

If you are contemplating a career in medical records, you should take as many high school English classes as possible, because technicians need both written and verbal communication skills to prepare reports and communicate with other health care personnel. Basic math or business math is very desirable because statistical skills are important in some job functions. Biology courses will help to familiarize yourself with the terminology that medical record technicians use. Other science courses, computer training, typing, and office procedures are also helpful.

Postsecondary Training

Most employers prefer to hire medical record technicians who have completed a two-year associate's degree program accredited by the American Medical Association's Commission on Accreditation for Health Informatics and Information Management Education and the American Health Information Management Association (AHIMA). There are approximately 245 of these accredited programs available throughout the United States, mostly offered in junior and community colleges. They usually include classroom instruction in such subjects as anatomy, physiology, medical terminology, medical record science, word processing, medical aspects of recordkeeping, statistics, computers in health care, personnel supervision, business management, English, and office skills.

In addition to classroom instruction, the student is given supervised clinical experience in the medical records departments of local health care facilities. This provides students with practical experience in performing many of the functions learned in the classroom and the opportunity to interact with health care professionals.

Certification or Licensing

Medical record technicians who have completed an accredited training program are eligible to take a national qualifying examination to earn the credential of registered health information technician (RHIT). Most health care institutions prefer to hire individuals with an RHIT credential as it signifies that they have met the standards established by the AHIMA as the mark of a qualified health professional. AHIMA also offers certification to medical coders and health information administrators. Specialized certifications in medical coding are also available from the American Academy of Professional Coders.

Other Requirements

Medical records are extremely detailed and precise. Sloppy work could have serious consequences in terms of payment to the hospital or physician, validity of the patient records for later use, and validity of research based on data from medical records. Therefore, a prospective technician must have the capacity to do consistently reliable and accurate routine work. Records must be completed and maintained with care and attention to detail. You may be the only person who checks the entire record, and you must understand the responsibility that accompanies this task.

The technician needs to be able to work rapidly as well as accurately. In many medical record departments, the workload is very heavy, and you must be well organized and efficient in order to stay on top of the job. You must be able to complete your work accurately, in spite of interruptions, such as phone calls and requests for assistance. You also need to be discreet, as you will deal with records that are private and sometimes sensitive.

Computer skills also are essential, and some experience in transcribing dictated reports may be useful.

EXPLORING

To learn more about this and other medical careers, you may be able to find summer, part-time, or volunteer work in a hospital or other health care facility. Sometimes such jobs are available in the medical records area of an organization. You may also be able to arrange to talk with someone working as a medical record technician or administrator. Faculty and counselors at schools that offer medical record technician training programs may also be good sources of information. You also can learn more about this profession by reading journals and other literature available at a public library.

EMPLOYERS

Although two out of five of the 170,000 medical record technicians employed in the United States work in hospitals, many work in other health care settings, including health maintenance organizations (HMOs), industrial clinics, skilled nursing facilities, rehabilitation centers, large group medical practices, ambulatory

care centers, and state and local government health agencies. Technicians also work for computer firms, consulting firms, and government agencies. Records are maintained in all these facilities, although record-keeping procedures vary.

Not all medical record technicians are employed in a single health care facility; some serve as consultants to several small facilities. Other technicians do not work in health care settings at all. They may be employed by health and property liability insurance companies to collect and review information on medical claims. A few are self-employed, providing medical transcription services.

STARTING OUT

Most successful medical record technicians are graduates of two-year accredited programs. Graduates of these programs should check with their schools' career services offices for job leads. Those who have taken the accrediting exam and have become certified can use the AHIMA's resume referral service.

You may also apply directly to the personnel departments of hospitals, nursing homes, outpatient clinics, and surgery centers. Many job openings are also listed in the classified advertising sections of local newspapers and with private and public employment agencies.

ADVANCEMENT

Medical record technicians may be able to achieve some advancement and salary increase without additional training simply by taking on greater responsibility in their job function. With experience, technicians may move to supervisory or department head positions, depending on the type and structure of the employing organization. Another means of advancing is through specialization in a certain area of the job. Some technicians specialize in coding, particularly Medicare coding or tumor registry. With a broad range of experience, a medical record technician may be able to become an independent consultant. Generally, technicians with an associate's degree and the RHIT designation are most likely to advance.

More assured job advancement and salary increase come with the completion of a bachelor's degree in medical record administration. The bachelor's degree, along with AHIMA accreditation, makes the technician eligible for a supervisory position, such as department director. Because of a general shortage of medical record administrators, hospitals often assist technicians who are working toward a bachelor's degree by providing flexible scheduling and financial aid or tuition reimbursement.

EARNINGS

The salaries of medical record technicians are greatly influenced by the location, size, and type of employing institution, as well as the technician's training and experience. According to the AHIMA, beginning technicians with an associate's degree can earn from $20,000 to $30,000 annually. Those who have earned a bachelor's degree can expect to earn between $30,000 and $50,000 a year. With five years of experience, technicians can earn up to $75,000 annually.

According to the U.S. Department of Labor, the median annual earnings of medical record and health information technicians were $28,030 in 2006. Salaries ranged from less than $19,060 to more than $45,260.

In general, medical record technicians working in large urban hospitals make the most money, and those in rural areas make the least. Like most hospital employees, medical record technicians usually receive paid vacations and holidays, life and health insurance, and retirement benefits.

WORK ENVIRONMENT

Medical records departments are usually pleasantly clean, well-lit, and air-conditioned areas. Sometimes, however, paper or microfilm records are kept in cramped, out-of-the-way quarters. Although the work requires thorough and careful attention to detail, there may be a constant bustle of activity in the technician's work area, which can be disruptive. The job is likely to involve frequent routine contact with nurses, physicians, hospital administrators, other health care professionals, attorneys, and insurance agents. On occasion, individuals with whom the technicians may interact are demanding or difficult. In such cases, technicians may find that the job carries a high level of frustration.

A 40-hour workweek is the norm, but because hospitals operate on a 24-hour basis, the job may regularly include night or weekend hours. Part-time work is sometimes available.

The work is extremely detailed and may be tedious. Some technicians spend the majority of their day sitting at a desk, working on a computer. Others may spend hours filing paper records or retrieving them from storage.

In many hospital settings, the medical record technician experiences pressure caused by a heavy workload. As the demands for health care cost containment and productivity increase, medical record technicians may be required to produce a significantly greater volume of high-quality work in shorter periods of time.

Nonetheless, the knowledge that their work is significant for patients and medical research can be personally very satisfying for medical record technicians.

OUTLOOK

Employment prospects through 2016 are very good. The U.S. Department of Labor predicts that employment in this field will grow faster than the average for all careers. The demand for well-trained medical record technicians will grow rapidly and will continue to exceed the supply. This expectation is related to the health care needs of a population that is both growing and aging and the trend toward more technologically sophisticated medicine and greater use of diagnostic procedures. It is also related to the increased requirements of regulatory bodies that scrutinize both costs and quality of care of health care providers. Because of the fear of medical malpractice lawsuits, doctors and other health care providers are documenting their diagnoses and treatments in greater detail. Also, because of the high cost of health care, insurance companies, government agencies, and courts are examining medical records with a more critical eye. These factors combine to ensure a healthy job outlook for medical record technicians.

Opportunities will be best in offices of physicians, particularly in large group practices, nursing and residential care facilities, home health care services, and outpatient care centers.

Technicians with associate's degrees and RHIT status will have the best prospects, and the importance of such qualifications is likely to increase.

FOR MORE INFORMATION

For information on training and certification, contact
American Academy of Professional Coders
2480 South 3850 West, Suite B
Salt Lake City, UT 84120-7208
Tel: 800-626-2633
Email: info@aapc.com
http://www.aapc.com

For information on earnings, careers in health information management, and accredited programs, contact
American Health Information Management Association
233 North Michigan Avenue, 21st Floor
Chicago, IL 60601-5800
Tel: 312-233-1100
Email: info@ahima.org
http://www.ahima.org

For a list of schools offering accredited programs in health information management, contact
Commission on Accreditation for Health Informatics and Information Management Education
233 North Michigan Avenue, 21st Floor
Chicago, IL 60601-5800
http://www.cahiim.org

For information on a career as a cancer registrar, contact
National Cancer Registrars Association
1340 Braddock Place, Suite 203
Alexandria, VA 22314-1651
Tel: 703-299-6640
http://www.ncra-usa.org

MEDICAL SECRETARIES

SCHOOL SUBJECTS
Mathematics, Physics

PERSONAL SKILLS
Leadership/Management, Technical/Scientific

MINIMUM EDUCATION LEVEL
Bachelor's Degree

CERTIFICATION OR LICENSING
Recommended

WORK ENVIRONMENT
Primarily Indoors, Primarily Multiple Locations

OVERVIEW

Medical secretaries perform administrative and clerical work in medical offices, hospitals, or private physicians' offices. They answer phone calls, order supplies, handle correspondence, bill patients, complete insurance forms, and transcribe dictation. Medical secretaries also handle bookkeeping, greet patients, schedule appointments, arrange hospital admissions, and schedule surgeries. There are approximately 408,000 medical secretaries employed throughout the United States.

THE JOB

Medical secretaries play important roles in the health care profession. They transcribe dictation, prepare correspondence, and assist physicians or medical scientists with reports, speeches, articles, and conference proceedings. Medical secretaries also record simple medical histories, arrange for patients to be hospitalized, and order supplies. Most need to be familiar with insurance rules, billing practices, and hospital or laboratory procedures.

Doctors rely on medical secretaries to keep administrative operations under control. Secretaries are the information clearinghouses for the office. They schedule appointments, handle phone calls, organize and maintain paper and electronic files, and produce correspondence for the office. Medical secretaries must have basic technical skills to operate office equipment such as facsimile machines, photocopiers, and switchboard systems. Increasingly, they use computers to run spreadsheet, word-processing, database-management, or desktop publishing programs.

REQUIREMENTS
High School

Most employers require medical secretaries to have a high school diploma and be able to type between 60 and 90

words per minute. In order to handle more specialized duties, you must be familiar with medical terms and procedures and be able to use medical software programs. In addition, you need to have basic math skills and strong written and verbal communication skills to write up correspondence and handle patient inquiries. English, speech, and health classes will help you prepare for this career.

Postsecondary Training

One- and two-year programs are offered by many vocational, community, and business schools covering the skills needed for secretarial work. For more specialized training, some schools offer medical secretarial programs, covering the basics such as typing, filing, and accounting, as well as more specialized courses on medical stenography, first aid, medical terminology, and medical office procedures.

Certification or Licensing

Certification is not required for a job as a medical secretary, but obtaining it may bring increased opportunities, earnings, and responsibility. The International Association of Administrative Professionals offers the certified professional secretary (CPS) and certified administrative professional (CAP) designations. To achieve CPS or CAP certification, you must meet certain experience requirements and pass a rigorous exam covering a number of general secretarial topics.

Other Requirements

To succeed as a medical secretary, you must be trustworthy and use discretion when dealing with confidential medical records. You must also have a pleasant and confident personality for handling the public and a desire to help others in a dependable and conscientious manner.

EXPLORING

The best way to learn about this career is to speak with an experienced medical secretary about his or her work. Ask your school guidance counselor to set up an information interview with a medical secretary, or arrange a tour of a medical facility so you can see secretaries in action.

EMPLOYERS

Approximately 408,000 medical secretaries are employed in the United States. Medical secretaries work in private physicians' offices, hospitals, outpatient clinics, emergency care facilities, research laboratories, and large health organizations, such as the Mayo Medical Clinic. The Mayo Clinic branches, located in Florida, Minnesota, and Arizona, employ more than 1,000 medical secretaries who work for nearly 1,200 physicians and scientists. A majority of medical secretaries work with one or two physicians practicing in a clinical outpatient care setting. The remainder provide support to physicians and scientists in clinical and research laboratories, hospitals, or Mayo Clinic's medical school.

STARTING OUT

To find work in this field, you should apply directly to hospitals, clinics, and physicians' offices. Potential positions might be listed with school or college career services offices or in newspaper want ads. Networking with medical secretaries is another inside track to job leads, because employers tend to trust employee recommendations.

ADVANCEMENT

Promotions for secretaries who work in doctors' offices are usually limited to increases in salary and responsibilities. Medical secretaries employed by clinics or hospitals can advance to executive positions, such as senior secretary, clerical supervisor, or office manager; or into more administrative jobs, such as medical records clerk, administrative assistant, or unit manager.

EARNINGS

The U.S. Department of Labor reports that medical secretaries earned a median annual salary of $28,090 in 2006. Salaries ranged from less than $19,750 to more than $40,870. The mean salary in 2006 for medical secretaries employed in physicians' offices was $28,560; in hospitals, $28,440; and in dentist offices, $33,930.

Most employers offer vacation, sick leave, and medical benefits. Many also include life, dental, and vision care insurance, retirement benefits, and profit sharing.

WORK ENVIRONMENT

Medical secretaries usually work 40 hours a week, Monday through Friday, during regular business hours. However, some work extended hours one or two days a week, depending on the physician's office hours. They do their work in well-lit, pleasant surroundings, but could encounter stressful emergency situations.

OUTLOOK

While the demand for secretaries in the general sector is expected to grow as fast as the average for all occupations, the U.S. Department of Labor projects a higher demand for medical secretaries, expecting the occupation to grow faster than the average for all occupations through 2016.

Health services are demanding more from their support personnel and are increasing salary levels accordingly. Technological advances are making secretaries more productive and able to handle the duties once done by managers or other staff. The distribution of work has shifted; secretaries receive fewer requests for typing and filing jobs. Instead, they do more technical work requiring computer skills beyond keyboarding. The job outlook appears brightest for those who are up to date on the latest programs and technological advances.

FOR MORE INFORMATION

For information on professional certification, contact
International Association of Administrative Professionals
PO Box 20404
10502 NW Ambassador Drive
Kansas City, MO 64195-0404
Tel: 816-891-6600
Email: service@iaap-hq.org
http://www.iaap-hq.org

The Mayo Clinic is a major employer of medical secretaries. Visit its Web site for more information.
Mayo Clinic
http://www.mayoclinic.org/jobs

NAIL TECHNICIANS

OVERVIEW

Nail technicians clean, shape, and polish fingernails and toenails. They groom cuticles and apply cream to hands and arms (feet and calves in the case of pedicures). They apply a variety of artificial nails and provide ongoing maintenance. Many nail technicians are skilled in "nail art" and decorate clients' nails with stencils, glitter, and ornaments. Nail technicians may also call themselves *manicurists, pedicurists, nail sculpturists,* or *nail artists.* There are approximately 78,000 nail technicians working in the United States.

THE JOB

Nail technicians generally work at a manicurist table and chair or stool across from their clients. Their work implements include finger bowls, electric heaters, wet sanitizer containers, alcohol, nail sticks and files, cuticle instruments, emery boards and buffers, tweezers, nail polishes and removers, abrasives, creams and oils, and nail dryers.

Standard manicure procedure involves removing old polish, shaping nails, softening and trimming cuticles and applying cuticle cream, cleansing and drying hands and nails, applying polish and topcoat, and applying hand lotion. As an extra service, lotion is often massaged into the wrists and arms as well as the hands. Technicians should always follow a sanitary cleanup procedure at their stations following each manicure, including sanitizing instruments and table, discarding used materials, and washing and drying their hands.

A man's manicure is a more conservative procedure than a woman's; the process is similar, but most men prefer to have a dry polish or to have their nails buffed.

Pedicuring has become a popular and important salon service, especially when fashion and weather dictate open-toed shoe styles. The procedure for a pedicure is much like that of a manicure, with the set-up involving a low stool for the technician and an ottoman for the client's feet.

Nail technicians also provide other services, including the application of artificial nails. A number of techniques are employed, depending on the individual client's preferences and nail characteristics. These include nail wrapping, nail sculpturing, nail tipping, press-on nails, and nail dipping. Technicians also repair broken nails and do "fill-ins" on artificial nails as the real nails grow out.

SCHOOL SUBJECTS
English, Health, Speech

PERSONAL SKILLS
Communication/Ideas, Following Instructions

MINIMUM EDUCATION LEVEL
High School Diploma

CERTIFICATION OR LICENSING
Voluntary

WORK ENVIRONMENT
Primarily Indoors, Primarily One Location

Nail technicians must take care to use only new or sanitized instruments to prevent the spread of disease. The rapid growth of this industry has been accompanied by an increased awareness of the many ways in which viral, fungal, and bacterial infections can be spread. Many states have passed laws regarding the use of various instruments. Although nail technicians may be exposed to such contagious diseases as athlete's foot and ringworm, the use of gloves is not a practical solution due to the level of precision required in a nail technician's work. For this reason, nail technicians must be able to distinguish between skin or nail conditions that can be treated in the salon and disorders and diseases that require medical attention. In so doing, educated and honest nail technicians can contribute to the confidence, health, and well-being of their customers.

REQUIREMENTS
High School

Many states require that nail technicians be high school graduates, although a few states require only an eighth- or tenth-grade education. If you are interested in becoming a nail technician, consider taking health and anatomy classes in high school. These classes will give you a basis for understanding skin and nail conditions. Since many nail technicians are self-employed, you may benefit from taking business classes that teach you how a successful business is run. Take art classes, such as painting, drawing, or sculpting, which will allow you to work with your hands and develop a sense of color and design. Finally, do not forget to take English or communication classes.

These courses will help you hone your speaking and writing skills, skills that you will need when dealing with the public. Some high schools with vocational programs may offer cosmetology courses. Such courses may include the study of bacteriology, sanitation, and mathematics. These specialized courses can be helpful in preparing students for their future work. You will need to check with your high school about the availability of such a vocational program.

Postsecondary Training

Your next step on the road to becoming a nail technician is to attend a cosmetology or nail school. Some states have schools specifically for nail technician training; in other states, the course work must be completed within the context of a full cosmetology program. Nail technology courses generally require between 100 and 500 clock hours of training, but requirements can vary widely from state to state. Because of these variations, make sure the school you choose to attend will allow you to meet the educational requirements of the state in which you hope to work. When the required course work has been completed, the student must pass an examination that usually includes a written test and a practical examination to demonstrate mastery of required skills. A health certificate is sometimes required.

Course work in nail schools (or nail technician programs in cosmetology schools) reflects that students are expected to learn a great deal more than just manicuring; typical courses of study encompass a broad array of subjects. The course outline at Pivot Point International (with affiliated schools throughout the United States) includes bacteriology, sanitation, and aseptic control procedures; diseases and disorders of the nail; anatomy (of the nails, hands, and feet); nail styling and artificial nail techniques; spa manicures and pedicures; aromatherapy; reflexology; state law; advertising and sales; and people skills. Course work also includes working on live models so that each student graduates with hands-on experience in each service studied.

Certification or Licensing

Most states require nail technicians to be licensed. Usually a fee is charged to take the exam, and another fee is assessed before receiving the license. Exams usually include both written and practical tests. Many states now offer special nail technician licenses (sometimes called limited or specialty certificates), which require anywhere from 100 to 500 hours of schooling in a licensed cosmetology or nail school. In states where no limited certificates are offered, a student must complete cosmetology school (substantially more hours than required for a specialty), become licensed as a cosmetologist, and then specialize in nail technology. Some states offer special licenses for manicurist managers and nail technician instructors; these require substantially more hours of schooling than do nail technician licenses. Reciprocity agreements exist in some states that enable a nail technician to work in another state without being retested. Some states require that nail technicians be 16 or 18 years old in order to be licensed. You will need to find out the licensing requirements for the state in which you hope to work. Associations and state boards of health can often supply this information.

Other Requirements

Nail technicians must have good vision and manual dexterity, as their work is very exacting in nature. Creativity and artistic talents are helpful, especially in those technicians who perform nail art, which can include painting designs and applying various decorative items to nails. A steady hand is important, and nail technicians should also have an eye for form and color.

Since nail technicians provide services to a wide variety of people, the personality and attitude of a nail technician to a large extent ultimately determine his or her success. While some clients are easy to please, others are demanding and even unreasonable; a nail technician who is able to satisfy even the most difficult customers will be positioned to develop a large, loyal following. Nail technicians who are punctual, courteous, respectful, and patient will enjoy a distinct competitive advantage over others in the industry that lack these qualities. Tact, professionalism, and competence are important. Knowledge and practice of proper sanitizing techniques should be clearly visible to clients. Naturally, hygiene and grooming are of paramount importance in this profession, and a nail technician's own hands and nails should be perfectly groomed; this is one's best form of advertisement and can help foster confidence in prospective and new clients.

A confident, outgoing personality can be a great boon to a nail technician's success. Customers may readily accept recommendations for additional nail services from a persuasive, knowledgeable, and competent nail technician who appears genuinely interested in the customer's interests. Nail technicians who can successfully sell their services will enjoy increased business.

Unlike most careers in the cosmetology field, nail technicians are not required to be on their feet all day. Nail technology is a good choice for those interested in the beauty industry who prefer to be able to work in a seated, comfortable position.

EXPLORING

If you are considering a career as a nail technician, a good avenue of exploration is to call a cosmetology or nail school and ask for an opportunity to tour the facilities, observe classes, and question instructors. Another enjoyable option is for you to make an appointment with a nail technician for a manicure or pedicure. By receiving one of these services yourself, you will have the opportunity to visit the place of business, take in the atmosphere, and experience the procedure. In addition, you'll have the opportunity to talk to someone who can answer your questions about this line of work. Explain that you are interested in becoming a nail technician, and you may find that you can develop a mentoring relationship with this professional technician. A part-time job in a beauty salon that offers nail services may also help you determine your interest in various aspects of the beauty industry. Part-time positions for non-technicians in nail salons, though, may prove difficult to find.

EMPLOYERS

There are about 78,000 nail technicians employed in the United States. As with cosmetologists and other personal appearance workers, approximately 46 percent of nail technicians are self-employed. They may rent a "booth" or chair at a salon; some may own their own nail salons. A growing number of nail technicians are employed by nail salons, which are rapidly increasing in number in many areas of the country. Beauty shops and department store salons also employ nail technicians, but most have only one or two on staff (very large salons have more). Since nail services represent one of the fastest-growing segments of the cosmetology industry, there is good potential for those wishing to open their own businesses in the nail industry.

STARTING OUT

In most states, graduating from an accredited cosmetology or nail school that meets the state's requirements for licensing is the vehicle for entry into this field. Nearly all cosmetology schools assist graduates with the process of finding employment. Want ads and personal visits to salons and shops are also productive means of finding a job.

ADVANCEMENT

Advancement in the nail technology industry most often takes the form of establishing a large, loyal clientele. Other opportunities include owning one's own nail salon. This can be a highly profitable endeavor if one has the proper business skills and savvy; the cost of materials and overhead can be relatively low, and, in addition to the earnings realized from services performed for their customers, the owners typically receive half of their operators' earnings.

Some technicians choose to advance by becoming nail instructors in cosmetology or nail schools or becoming inspectors for state cosmetology boards.

Nail technicians who constantly strive to increase their knowledge and proficiency in a wide array of nail services will have a competitive advantage and will be positioned to secure a large and varied clientele.

EARNINGS

Income for nail technicians can vary widely, depending on the skill, experience, and clientele of the nail technician, the type and location of the shop or salon, the tipping habits of the clientele, and the area of the country. The U.S. Department of Labor reports the median annual income for nail technicians was $19,190 in 2006. (This income includes tips.) The lowest paid 10 percent earned $14,210 or less, while the highest paid 10 percent earned $31,910 or more. Salary.com, a provider of compensation information, reports that nationwide manicurists had yearly earnings ranging from approximately $16,031 to $23,007 in 2008. Those working in large metropolitan areas may have slightly higher earnings, but the cost of living is also higher there. According to findings by *NAILS Magazine*, which surveyed professionals in 2007, nail technicians serviced on average between 21 and 40 clients per week and charged on average approximately $17.53 for a basic manicure. Given these figures, a technician who works 50 weeks a year (with two weeks off for vacation) would earn $18,407 to $35,060. The magazine also reports the average cost of a booth rental was $380 per month, with an average of $4,560 per year. Deducting this charge from the technician's earnings leaves the technician with a base income of approximately $13,847 to $30,500. Tips have not been figured into this income, and they may raise earnings by several thousand dollars per year.

The importance of the talents and personality of the nail technician cannot be underestimated when evaluating potential earnings. Those who hold themselves to the highest levels of professionalism, express a genuine interest in clients' well-being, and provide the highest quality service quickly develop loyal clienteles, and these nail technicians will realize earnings that far exceed the averages.

Those technicians who work in beauty shops are less likely than those in nail salons to have appointments scheduled throughout the day; however, customers in beauty salons often pay more and tip better for these services. Also, there is less competition within the beauty shop setting, as the majority of beauty salons employ only one or two nail technicians.

Owning one's own nail salon can be very profitable, as the cost of equipment is relatively low. In addition to taking home one's own earnings from servicing clients, the owner also generally gets half of the income generated by the shop's other operators. Nail salons are a prime example of a small business with tremendous potential for success.

Except for those nail technicians who work in department stores or large salons, most do not enjoy much in the way of benefits; few nail technicians receive health and life insurance or paid vacations.

WORK ENVIRONMENT

Nail technicians work indoors in bright, well-ventilated, comfortable environments. Unlike most careers in the cosmetology industry that require operators to be on their feet most of the day, nail technicians perform their work seated at a table.

Many nail technicians work five-day weeks including Saturdays, which are a high-volume business day in this industry. Working some evenings may be helpful in building one's clientele, as a large percentage of customers are working professionals. Nail technicians often enjoy some flexibility in their hours, and many enjoy successful part-time careers.

A large number of nail technicians are self-employed; they may rent a space in a beauty or nail salon. Often, nail technicians must provide their own supplies and tools. Nail technicians are exposed to a certain amount of chemicals and dust, but this is generally manageable in well-ventilated work surroundings. Those who work in full-service salons may be exposed to additional chemicals and odors.

Inherent in the nature of a nail technician's work is the constant company of others. A nail technician who is not a "people person" will find this line of work most challenging. But since most people who choose this career enjoy the company of others, they find the opportunity to talk with and get to know people to be one of the most satisfying and enjoyable aspects of their work.

OUTLOOK

The nail business (a multibillion dollar industry) has been growing rapidly for years. Nail salons and day spas offering nail services continue to crop up everywhere, and nail technicians represent one of the fastest-growing segments of the various specialized service providers in the beauty industry. According to the U.S. Department of Labor, employment for nail technicians should grow much faster than the average for all occupations through 2016.

Once a mark of feminine status, nail services are now sought and enjoyed by a wide variety of people, both male and female. Helen Barkan, whose clients have dubbed her the "Nail Doctor," has been a nail technician and salon owner in the Deerbrook Mall in Deerfield, Illinois, for the past 24 years, and she has been doing nails for more years than she'll reveal. Barkan, whose straightforward services focus on helping clients grow strong, healthy nails (she doesn't do artificial nails), says, "Many of my clients have been coming to me for more than 20 years. I've always been willing to spend a little extra time and go the extra mile for my customers, and at one time I worked seven days a week. My clients are important to me, and they know that." Barkan has watched the industry change dramatically over the decades. Today, approximately one-third of Barkan's customers are men, and they come for manicures and pedicures alike. Clearly, there is a market for all kinds of nail services, from the most basic hand and nail care to the most involved procedures and outlandish styles.

FOR MORE INFORMATION

This magazine has information on the latest nail technologies, fashions, safety matters, and industry news.
NAILS Magazine
3520 Challenger Street
Torrance, CA 90503-1640
Tel: 310-533-2400
http://www.nailsmag.com

This organization accredits cosmetology schools nationally and can provide information on licensed training schools.
National Accrediting Commission of Cosmetology Arts and Sciences
4401 Ford Avenue, Suite 1300
Alexandria, VA 22302-1432

Tel: 703-600-7600

http://www.naccas.org

This organization of nail technicians, stylists, salon owners, and other professionals can provide industry and education information.

National Cosmetology Association

401 North Michigan Avenue, 19th Floor

Chicago, IL 60611-4274

Tel: 312-527-6765

http://www.salonprofessionals.org

This Web site for beauty professionals has a list of state licensing requirements for nail technicians.

BeautyTech

http://www.beautytech.com/nailtech

For information on careers in the beauty industry, visit

Careers in Beauty

http://www.beautyschools.org/associations/7485/
careersinbeauty.cfm

NURSE ASSISTANTS

OVERVIEW

Nurse assistants (also called *nurse aides, orderlies,* or *hospital attendants*) work under the supervision of nurses and handle much of the personal care needs of the patients. This allows the nursing staff to perform their primary duties more effectively and efficiently. Nurse assistants help move patients, assist in patients' exercise and nutrition needs, and oversee patients' personal hygiene. Nurse assistants may also be required to take patients to other areas of the hospital for treatment, therapy, or diagnostic testing. They are required to keep charts of their work with patients for review by other medical personnel and to comply with required reporting. There are about 1.4 million nurse assistants in the United States, and about 52 percent of them are employed in nursing homes and residential care facilities.

THE JOB

Nurse assistants generally help nurses care for patients in hospital or nursing home settings. Their duties include tending to the daily care of the patients, including bath-

SCHOOL SUBJECTS
Biology, Health

PERSONAL SKILLS

Following Instructions, Helping/Teaching

MINIMUM EDUCATION LEVEL

High School Diploma

CERTIFICATION OR LICENSING

Required for Certain Positions

WORK ENVIRONMENT

Primarily Indoors, Primarily Multiple Locations

ing them, helping them with their meals, and checking their body temperature and blood pressure. In addition, they often help persons who need assistance with their personal hygiene needs and answer their call lights when they need immediate assistance.

The work can be strenuous, requiring the lifting and moving of patients. Nurse assistants must work with partners or in groups when performing the more strenuous tasks to ensure their safety as well as the patient's. Some requirements of the job can be as routine as changing sheets and helping a patient or resident with phone calls, while other requirements can be as difficult and unattractive as assisting a resident with elimination and cleaning up a resident or patient who has vomited.

Nurse assistants may be called upon to perform the more menial and unappealing tasks of health and personal care, but they also have the opportunity to develop meaningful relationships with patients. In a nursing home, nursing assistants work closely with residents, often gaining their trust and friendship.

REQUIREMENTS
High School

Although a high school diploma is not always required to work as a nurse assistant, there are a number of high school classes that can help you do this work. Communication skills are valuable for a nurse assistant to have, so take English classes. Science courses, such as biology and anatomy, and family and consumer science, health, and nutrition classes are also helpful. Some high schools offer courses directly related to nurse assistant training.

These classes may include body mechanics, infection control, and resident/patient rights.

Postsecondary Training

Nurse assistants are not required to have a college degree, but they may have to complete a short training course at a community college or vocational school. These training courses, usually taught by a registered nurse, teach basic nursing skills and prepare students for the state certification exam. Nurse assistants typically begin the training courses after getting their first job as an assistant, and the course work is often incorporated into their on-the-job training.

Many people work as nurse assistants as they pursue other medical professions such as a premedical or nursing program.

Certification or Licensing

Some states require nurse assistants to be certified no matter where they work. The Omnibus Budget Reconciliation Act of 1987 requires nurse assistants working in nursing homes to undergo special training. Nursing homes can hire inexperienced workers as nurse assistants, but they must have at least 75 hours of training and pass a competency evaluation program within four months of being hired. Those who fulfill these requirements are then certified.

Other Requirements

You must care about the patients in your care, and you must show a genuine understanding and compassion for the ill, people with disabilities, and the elderly. Because of the rigorous physical demands placed on you, you should be in good health and have good work habits. Along with good physical health, you should have good mental health and a cheerful disposition. The job can be emotionally demanding, requiring patience and stability. You should be able to work as a part of a team and also be able to take orders and follow through on your responsibilities.

EXPLORING

Because a high school diploma is frequently not required of nursing aides, many high school students are hired by nursing homes and hospitals for part-time work. Job opportunities may also exist in a hospital or nursing home kitchen, introducing you to diet and nutrition. These jobs will give you an opportunity to become familiar with the hospital and nursing home environments.

Also, volunteer work can familiarize you with the work nurses and nurse assistants perform, as well as introduce you to basic medical terminology.

EMPLOYERS

Approximately 52 percent of the 1.4 million nurse assistants in the United States are employed in nursing homes and residential care facilities, and another 29 percent work in hospitals. Others are employed in halfway houses, retirement centers, homes for persons with disabilities, and private homes. Approximately 23 percent of nurse assistants work part time—8 percent higher than the average for all workers.

STARTING OUT

Because of the high demand for nurse assistants, you can apply directly to the health facilities in your area, contact your local employment office, or check your local newspaper's help wanted ads.

ADVANCEMENT

For the most part, there is not much opportunity for advancement with this job. To advance in a health care facility requires additional training. After becoming familiar with the medical and nursing home environments and gaining some knowledge of medical terminology, some nurse assistants enroll in nursing programs or pursue other medically related careers.

Many facilities are recognizing the need to retain good health care workers and are putting some training and advancement programs in place for their employees.

EARNINGS

Salaries for most health care professionals vary by region, population, and size and kind of institution. The pay for nurse assistants in a hospital is usually more than in a nursing home.

According to the U.S. Department of Labor, nurse assistants earned median hourly wages of $10.67 in 2006. For full-time work at 40 hours per week, this hourly wage translates into a yearly income of approximately $22,180. The lowest paid 10 percent earned less than $7.78 per hour (approximately $16,190 per year), and the highest paid 10 percent earned more than $14.99 per hour (approximately $31,190 annually).

Benefits are usually based on the hours worked, length of employment, and the policies of the facility. Some offer paid vacation and holidays, medical or hospital insurance, and retirement plans. Some also provide free meals to their workers.

WORK ENVIRONMENT

The work environment in a health care or long-term care facility can be hectic at times and very stressful. Some patients may be uncooperative and may actually be combative. Often there are numerous demands that must be met at the same time. Nurse assistants are required to be on their feet most of the time, and they often have to help lift or move patients. Most facilities are clean and well lighted, but nurse assistants do have the possibility of exposure to contagious diseases, although using proper safety procedures minimizes their risk.

Nurse assistants generally work a 40-hour workweek, with some overtime. The hours and weekly schedule may be irregular, depending on the needs of the institution. Nurse assistants are needed around the clock, so work schedules may include night shift or swing-shift work.

OUTLOOK

There will continue to be many job opportunities for nurse assistants; the U.S. Department of Labor predicts that this occupation will grow faster than the average for all occupations through 2016. Because of the physical and emotional demands of the job, and because of the lack of advancement opportunities, there is a high employee turnover rate. Additional opportunities may be available as different types of care facilities are developed and as facilities try to curb operating costs. Opportunities will be best in nursing and residential care facilities.

In addition, more nurse assistants will be required as government and private agencies develop more programs to assist people with disabilities, dependent people, and the increasing aging population.

FOR MORE INFORMATION

For information and statistics on the home health care industry, visit the association's Web site:

National Association for Home Care and Hospice
228 Seventh Street, SE
Washington, DC 20003-4306
Tel: 202-547-7424
http://www.nahc.org

For additional information on nurse assistant careers and training, contact

National Network of Career Nursing Assistants
3577 Easton Road
Norton, OH 44203-5661
Tel: 330-825-9342
Email: cnajeni@aol.com
http://www.cna-network.org

☐ OCCUPATIONAL THERAPISTS

OVERVIEW

Occupational therapists (OTs) select and direct therapeutic activities designed to develop or restore maximum function to individuals with disabilities. There are approximately 99,000 occupational therapists employed in the United States.

THE JOB

Occupational therapists use a wide variety of activities to help clients attain their goals for productive, independent living. These goals include developing maximum self-sufficiency in activities of daily living, such as eating, dressing, writing, using a telephone and other communication resources, as well as functioning in the community and the workplace.

In developing a therapeutic program for a client, the occupational therapist often works as a member of a team that can include physicians, nurses, psychiatrists, physical therapists, speech therapists, rehabilitation counselors, social workers, and other specialists. OTs use creative, educational, and recreational activities, as well as human ingenuity, in helping people achieve their full potential, regardless of their disabilities. Each therapy program is designed specifically for the individual client.

Occupational therapists help clients explore their likes and dislikes, their abilities, and their creative, educational,

---

SCHOOL SUBJECTS
Biology, Health

PERSONAL SKILLS
Helping/Teaching, Mechanical/Manipulative

MINIMUM EDUCATION LEVEL
Bachelor's Degree

CERTIFICATION OR LICENSING
Required

WORK ENVIRONMENT
Primarily Indoors, Primarily One Location

and recreational experiences. Therapists help people choose activities that have the most appeal and value for them. For example, an activity may be designed to promote greater dexterity for someone with arthritic fingers. Learning to use an adapted computer might help a young person with a spinal cord injury to succeed in school and career goals. The therapist works with the clients' interests and helps them develop practical skills and functional independence.

The occupational therapist may work with a wide range of clients. They may assist a client in learning to use an artificial limb. Another client may have suffered a stroke or other neurological disability, and the therapist works with the client to redevelop the client's motor functions or re-educate his or her muscle function. Therapists may assist in the growth and development of premature infants, or they may work with disabled children, helping them learn motor skills or develop skills and tools that will aid them in their education and social interaction.

Some therapists also conduct research to develop new types of therapies and activities and to measure the effectiveness of a therapy program. They may also design and make special equipment or splints to help clients perform their activities.

Other duties may include supervision of volunteer workers, student therapists, and occupational therapy assistants who give instruction in a particular skill. Therapists must prepare reports to keep members of the professional team informed.

Chief occupational therapists in a hospital may teach medical and nursing students the principles of occupational therapy. Many occupational therapists have administrative duties such as directing different kinds of occupational therapy programs, coordinating patient activities, and acting as consultants or advisors to local and state health departments, mental health authorities, and the division of vocational rehabilitation.

REQUIREMENTS
High School

Since you will need to get a college degree, taking college preparatory classes in high school is a must. Courses such as biology, chemistry, and health will expose you to the science fields. Other courses, such as art and social sciences, will help give you an understanding of other aspects of your future work. Also important is a strong background in English. Remember, occupational therapy is a career oriented toward helping people. To be able to work with many different people with dif-

ferent needs, you will need excellent communication skills. Also keep in mind that college admission officers will look favorably at any experience you have had working in the health care field, either in volunteer or paid positions.

Postsecondary Training

As an undergraduate, you should take courses that emphasize the biological and behavioral sciences. Your studies should include classes on anatomy, physiology, neurology, psychology, human growth and development, and sociology.

Anyone wishing to receive the professional credential, occupational therapist, registered (OTR), from the National Board for Certification in Occupational Therapy (NBCOT) must have completed at least a master's degree in the field. Graduate programs are accredited by the Accreditation Council for Occupational Therapy Education, which is a part of the American Occupational Therapy Association (AOTA). Visit http://www.aota.org/Educate/Schools.aspx for a list of accredited programs.

The AOTA recommends that students interested in pursuing graduate study in occupational therapy first earn bachelor's degrees in biology, kinesiology, psychology, sociology, anthropology, liberal arts, or anatomy.

Graduate occupational therapy programs cover general medical and surgical conditions and interpretation of the principles and practice of occupational therapy in pediatrics, psychiatry, orthopedics, general medicine, and surgery. In addition, emphasis is put on research and critical thinking. Management and administration are also covered in graduate programs.

In addition to classroom work, you must complete fieldwork requirements. According to the AOTA, students need to complete the equivalent of 24 weeks of supervised experience working with clients. This may be done on a full-time basis or a part-time (but not less than half-time) schedule. This training must be completed in order to qualify for professional certification.

In addition to these full-time study options, there are a limited number of part-time and evening programs that allow prospective occupational therapists to work in another field while completing their requirements in occupational therapy.

Certification or Licensing

All states and the District of Columbia regulate the practice of occupational therapy through certification and licensing. National certification is granted by the

NBCOT. In order to take the NBCOT exam, you must graduate from an accredited program and complete the clinical practice period. Those who pass this written test are given the designation, occupational therapist, registered, and may use the initials OTR after their names. Initial certification is good for five years and must be renewed every five years after that. Many hospitals and other employers require that their occupational therapists have the OTR designation. In addition, the NBCOT offers several specialty certifications, such as board certified in pediatrics. To receive a specialty certification, you must fulfill education and experience requirements as well as pass an exam.

License requirements generally include graduation from an accredited program, passing the NBCOT certification exam, payment of license fees, and, in some cases, passing an exam covering state statutes and regulations. License renewal requirements vary by state.

Other Requirements

In order to succeed as an occupational therapist, you should enjoy working with people. You should have a patient, calm, and compassionate temperament and have the ability to encourage and inspire your clients. Like your clients, you may encounter frustrating situations as a therapist. For example, it can be difficult and stressful when a client does not respond to treatment as you had hoped. In such situations, occupational therapists need to be persistent, not giving up on the client. Imagination and creativity are also important at such times, because you may need to think of new ways to address the client's problem and create new methods or tools for the client to use.

EXPLORING

While in high school, you should meet with occupational therapists, visit the facilities where they work, and gain an understanding of the types of equipment and skills they use. Many hospitals and occupational therapy facilities and departments also have volunteer opportunities, which will give you strong insight into this career.

EMPLOYERS

There are approximately 99,000 occupational therapists at work in hospitals, schools, nursing homes, home health agencies, mental health centers, adult day care programs, outpatient clinics, and residential care facilities. The profession has seen a growing number of therapists becoming self-employed, in either solo or group practice or in consulting firms.

STARTING OUT

Your school's career services office is usually the best place to start your job search as a newly graduated occupational therapist. You may also apply directly to government agencies (such as the U.S. Public Health Service), private hospitals, and clinics. In addition, the AOTA can provide job seekers with assistance through its employment bulletins.

ADVANCEMENT

Newly graduated occupational therapists usually begin as staff therapists and may qualify as senior therapists after several years on the job. The U.S. Army, Navy, Air Force, Coast Guard, and the U.S. Public Health Service commission occupational therapists; other branches of the federal service give civil service ratings. Experienced therapists may become directors of occupational therapy programs in large hospitals, clinics, or workshops, or they may become teachers. Some positions are available as program coordinators and as consultants with large institutions and agencies.

A few colleges and health agencies offer advanced courses in the treatment of special disabilities, such as those resulting from cerebral palsy. Some institutions provide in-service programs for therapists.

EARNINGS

According to the U.S. Department of Labor, median salaries for occupational therapists were $60,470 in 2006. The lowest 10 percent earned $40,840 or less a year in 2006, and the top 10 percent earned more than $89,450. The AOTA reports that its members earned median annual salaries of $55,800 in 2006.

Salaries for occupational therapists often vary according to where they work. In areas where the cost of living is higher, occupational therapists generally receive higher pay. Occupational therapists employed in public schools earn salaries that vary by school district. In some states, they are classified as teachers and are paid accordingly.

Therapists employed at hospitals and government and public agencies generally receive full benefit packages that include vacation and sick pay, health insurance, and retirement benefits. Self-employed therapists and those who run their own businesses must provide their own benefits.

WORK ENVIRONMENT

Occupational therapists work in occupational therapy workshops or clinics. As mentioned earlier, these workshops or clinics can be found at a variety of locations, such as hospitals, long-term care facilities, schools, and adult day care centers. No matter what the location, though, these workshops and clinics are well-lighted, pleasant settings. Generally, therapists work eight-hour days and 40-hour weeks, with some evening work required in a few organizations.

OUTLOOK

Opportunities for occupational therapists are expected to be highly favorable through 2016 and will grow much faster than the average for all other careers, according to the *Occupational Outlook Handbook.* This growth will occur as a result of the increasing number of middle-aged and elderly people that require therapeutic services. Acute hospital, orthopedic, and rehabilitation settings will provide strong employment opportunities since the elderly are often treated in these places. Additionally, the U.S. Department of Labor reports that driver rehabilitation and fall-prevention training for the elderly are practice areas that are growing in popularity.

The demand for occupational therapists is also increasing because of growing public interest in and government support for people with disabilities and for occupational therapy programs helping people attain the fullest possible functional status. The demand for rehabilitative and long-term care services is expected to grow strongly over the next decade. There will be numerous opportunities for work with mental health clients, children, and the elderly, as well as with those with disabling conditions.

As the health care industry continues to be restructured, there should be many more opportunities for occupational therapists in nontraditional settings. This factor and proposed changes in the laws should create an excellent climate for therapists wishing to enter private practice. Home health care will experience strong growth in the next decade.

FOR MORE INFORMATION
Visit the AOTA's Web site to find out about accredited occupational therapy programs, career information, and news related to the field.

American Occupational Therapy Association (AOTA)
4720 Montgomery Lane
PO Box 31220
Bethesda, MD 20824-1220
Tel: 301-652-2682
http://www.aota.org

For information on certification requirements, contact
**National Board for Certification
   in Occupational Therapy**
12 South Summit Avenue, Suite 100
Gaithersburg, MD 20877-4150
Tel: 301-990-7979
http://www.nbcot.org

OCCUPATIONAL THERAPY ASSISTANTS AND AIDES

OVERVIEW
Occupational therapy assistants (also called OTAs) help people with mental, physical, developmental, or emotional limitations using a variety of activities to improve basic motor functions and reasoning abilities. They work under the direct supervision of an occupational therapist, and their duties include helping to plan, implement, and evaluate rehabilitation programs designed to regain patients' self-sufficiency and to restore their physical and mental functions. There are 25,000 occupational therapy assistants employed in the United States. *Occupational therapy aides* help OTAs and occupational therapists by doing such things as clerical work, preparing therapy equipment for a client's use, and keeping track of supplies. Approximately 8,000 occupational therapy aides are employed in the United States.

THE JOB
Occupational therapy is used to help provide rehabilitation services to persons with mental, physical, emotional, or developmental disabilities. The goal of occupational therapy is to improve a patient's quality of life by compensating for limitations caused by age, illness, or injury. It differs from physical therapy because it focuses not only on physical rehabilitation, but also on psychological well-being. Occupational therapy emphasizes improvement of the activities of daily living—including such functions as personal hygiene, dressing, eating, and cooking.

Occupational therapy assistants, under the supervision of the therapist, implement patient care plans and activities. They help patients improve mobility and productivity using a variety of activities and exercises. They may use adaptive techniques and equipment to help patients perform tasks many take for granted. A reacher, a long-handled device that pinches and grabs small items, may be used to pick up keys from the floor or a book from the shelf. Therapy assistants may have patients mix ingredients for a cake or flip a grilled cheese sandwich using a special spatula. Activities such as dancing, playing cards, or throwing a ball are fun, yet they help improve mobility and give the patients a sense of self-esteem. Therapists evaluate an activity, minimize the number of steps, and streamline movement so the patient will be less fatigued.

Assistants may also help therapists evaluate a patient's progress, change care plans as needed, make therapy appointments, and complete paperwork.

Occupational therapy aides are responsible for materials and equipment used during therapy. They assemble and clean equipment and make certain the therapists and assistants have what they need for a patient's therapy session. A therapy aide's duties are more clerical in nature. They answer telephones, schedule appointments, order supplies and equipment, and complete insurance forms and other paperwork.

REQUIREMENTS
High School

According to the U.S. Department of Labor, most occupational therapy aides receive on-the-job training, while occupational therapy assistants require further education after high school. For either position, however, a high school diploma is a must. Prepare for these careers by taking classes in biology, health, and social sciences. Anyone interested in doing this work must also be able to communicate clearly, follow directions, and work as part of a team. English or communication classes can help you improve on these skills.

In addition, admissions officers at postsecondary programs are favorably impressed if you have experience in the health care field. If you cannot find a paid job, consider volunteering at a local hospital or nursing home during your high school years.

Postsecondary Training

While occupational therapy aides receive on-the-job training, occupational therapy assistants must have either an associate's degree or certificate from an accredited OTA program. Programs are accredited by the Accreditation Council for Occupational Therapy Edu-

---

SCHOOL SUBJECTS
Health, Psychology

PERSONAL SKILLS
Helping/Teaching, Mechanical/Manipulative

MINIMUM EDUCATION LEVEL
Associate's Degree (Assistants), High School Diploma (Aides)

CERTIFICATION OR LICENSING
Required (Assistants), None Available (Aides)

WORK ENVIRONMENT
Primarily Indoors, Primarily One Location

---

cation (ACOTE), which is part of the American Occupational Therapy Association (AOTA). Approximately 126 programs are fully accredited by the ACOTE; in addition, a number of programs are on "inactive status," meaning that they are not currently accepting new students but may reactivate (begin accepting students again) in the future. A full listing of programs, as well as their contact information, is available at http://www. aota.org/Students/Schools.aspx.

Generally, programs take two years to complete. Studies include courses such as human anatomy, psychology of adjustment, biology, human kinesiology, therapeutic media, and techniques. Most schools also require their students to take a number of general classes as well to round out their education. These may be courses such as English, business math, and management. In addition to class work, you will be required to complete a period of supervised fieldwork, which will give you hands-on experience with occupational therapy.

Certification or Licensing

Occupational therapy aides do not require certification or licensing. Occupational therapy assistants must pass the certifying test of the National Board for Certification in Occupational Therapy. After passing this test, assistants receive the designation certified occupational therapy assistant. Licensure requirements for assistants vary by state, so you will need to check with the licensing board of the state in which you want to work for specific information.

Other Requirements

Occupational therapy assistants and aides must be able to take directions. OTAs should have a pleasant disposition, strong people skills, and a desire to help those in need. Assistants must also be patient and responsible. Aides, too, should be responsible. They also need to be detail oriented in order to keep track of paperwork and equipment. It is important for assistants and aides to work well as a team.

EXPLORING

A visit to your local hospital's occupational therapy department is the best way to learn about this field. Speak with occupational therapists, assistants, and aides to gain an understanding of the work they do. Also, the AOTA and other related organizations might be able to provide career information. School guidance and job centers, and the library, are good information sources.

EMPLOYERS

There are approximately 25,000 occupational therapy assistants and 8,000 occupational therapy aides employed in the United States. Approximately 29 percent of all assistants and aides work in a hospital setting, 23 percent are employed by occupational therapists, and 21 percent work in nursing and residential care facilities. Others work in community care facilities for the elderly, offices of physicians, home health care services, outpatient rehabilitation centers, and state government agencies.

STARTING OUT

The career services department of your local community college or technical school can provide a listing of jobs available in the occupational therapy field. Job openings are usually posted in hospital human resource departments. Professional groups are also a good source of information; for example, the AOTA's Web site has an employment page for members.

ADVANCEMENT

After some experience, occupational therapy assistants can be promoted to *lead assistant*. Lead assistants are responsible for making work schedules of other assistants and for the training of occupational therapy students. Since occupational therapy assistants work under the supervision of an occupational therapist, there is little room for advancement. Aides may return to school and train to become occupational therapy assistants. Some assistants and aides return to school to become occupational therapists. Some shift to other health care careers.

EARNINGS

According to the U.S. Department of Labor, the median yearly income of occupational therapy assistants was $42,060 in 2006. Salaries ranged from less than $26,050 to $58,270 or more annually. Naturally, experience, location, and type of employer all factor into the salaries paid.

The importance of education cannot be overlooked, as assistants tend to earn more than aides. Median annual earnings of occupational therapist aides were $25,020 in 2006, according to the U.S. Department of Labor. Salaries ranged from less than $17,060 to $44,130 or more annually.

Benefits for full-time workers depend on the employer. They generally include health and life insurance, paid sick and vacation time, holiday pay, and a retirement plan.

WORK ENVIRONMENT

Most occupational therapy assistants and aides work during the day, although depending on the place of employment, some evening or weekend work may be required. Most therapy is done in a hospital or clinic setting that is clean, well lighted, and generally comfortable.

Occupational therapy assistants often use everyday items, settings, and activities to help rehabilitate their patients. Such props include kitchen settings, card games, dancing, or exercises. Therapy assistants should be in good physical shape, since heavy lifting—of patients as well as equipment—is a daily part of the job. Therapy assistants should also have stamina, since they are on their feet for much of the day.

OUTLOOK

According to the *Occupational Outlook Handbook*, employment for occupational therapy assistants and aides will grow much faster than the average for all careers through 2016. However, only a small number of new jobs will actually be available due to the size of these occupations. Occupational growth will stem from an increased number of people with disabilities and elderly people. Although more people are living well into their 70s, 80s, and in some cases, 90s, they often need the kinds of services occupational therapy provides. Medical technology has greatly improved, saving many lives that in the past would be lost through accidents, stroke, or other illnesses. Such people need rehabilitation therapy as they recuperate. Hospitals and employers are hiring more therapy assistants to help with the workload and to reduce costs.

Occupational therapy aides with just a high school diploma will face increasingly strong competition for jobs as more aides pursue advanced education.

FOR MORE INFORMATION

For additional information on careers, education, and news related to the field, contact

American Occupational Therapy Association
4720 Montgomery Lane
PO Box 31220
Bethesda, MD 20824-1220
Tel: 301-652-2682
http://www.aota.org

For information on certification, contact

National Board for Certification in Occupational Therapy
12 South Summit Avenue, Suite 100
Gaithersburg, MD 20877-4150
Tel: 301-990-7979
http://www.nbcot.org

☐ OFFICE CLERKS

OVERVIEW

Office clerks perform a variety of clerical tasks that help an office run smoothly, including file maintenance, mail sorting, and record-keeping. In large companies, office clerks might have specialized tasks such as inputting data into a computer, but in most cases, clerks are flexible and have many duties including typing, answering telephones, taking messages, responding to emails, making photocopies, and preparing mailings. Office clerks usually work under close supervision, often with experienced clerks directing their activities. There are approximately 3.2 million office clerks employed in the United States.

THE JOB

Office clerks usually perform a variety of tasks as part of their overall job responsibility. They may type or file bills, statements, and business correspondence. They may stuff envelopes, answer telephones, respond to emails, and sort mail. Office clerks also enter data into computers, run errands, and operate office equipment such as photocopiers, fax machines, and switchboards. In the course of an average day, an office clerk usually performs a combination of these and other clerical tasks, spending an hour or so on one task and then moving on to another as directed by an office manager or other supervisor.

SCHOOL SUBJECTS
Business, Mathematics

PERSONAL SKILLS
Communication/Ideas, Following Instructions

MINIMUM EDUCATION LEVEL
High School Diploma

CERTIFICATION OR LICENSING
Voluntary

WORK ENVIRONMENT
Primarily Indoors, Primarily One Location

An office clerk may work with other office personnel, such as a bookkeeper or accountant, to maintain a company's financial records. The clerk may type and mail invoices and sort payments as they come in, keep payroll records, or take inventories. With more experience, the clerk may be asked to update customer files to reflect receipt of payments and verify records for accuracy.

Office clerks often deliver messages from one office worker to another, an especially important responsibility in larger companies. Clerks may relay questions and answers from one department head to another. Similarly, clerks may relay messages from people outside the company or employees who are outside of the office to those working in house. Office clerks may also work with other personnel on individual projects, such as preparing a yearly budget or making sure a mass mailing gets out on time.

Administrative clerks assist in the efficient operation of an office by compiling business records; providing information to sales personnel and customers; and preparing and sending out bills, policies, invoices, and other business correspondence. Administrative clerks may also keep financial records and prepare the payroll. *File clerks* review and classify letters, documents, articles, and other information and then file this material so it can be quickly retrieved at a later time. They contribute to the smooth distribution of information at a company.

Some clerks have titles that describe where they work and the jobs they do. For example, *congressional-district aides* work for the elected officials of their U.S. congressional district. *Police clerks* handle routine office procedures in police stations, and *concrete products dispatchers* work with construction firms on building projects.

REQUIREMENTS

High School

To prepare for a career as an office clerk, you should take courses in English, mathematics, and as many business-related subjects, such as keyboarding and bookkeeping, as possible. Community colleges and vocational schools often offer business education courses that provide training for general office workers.

Postsecondary Training

A high school diploma is usually sufficient for beginning office clerks, although business courses covering office machine operation and bookkeeping are also helpful. To succeed in this field, you should have computer skills, the ability to concentrate for long periods of time on repetitive tasks, good English and communication skills, and mathematical abilities. Legible handwriting is also a necessity.

Certification or Licensing

The International Association of Administrative Professionals offers certification for administrative professionals (including office clerks). Contact the association for more information.

Other Requirements

To find work as an office clerk, you should have an even temperament, strong communication skills, and the ability to work well with others. You should find systematic and detailed work appealing. Other personal qualifications include dependability, trustworthiness, and a neat personal appearance.

EXPLORING

You can gain experience by taking on clerical or bookkeeping responsibilities with a school club or other organization. In addition, some school work-study programs may provide opportunities for part-time on-the-job training with local businesses. You may also be able to get a part-time or summer job in a business office by contacting businesses directly or enlisting the aid of a guidance counselor. Training in the operation of business machinery (computers, word processors, and so on) may be available through evening courses offered by business schools and community colleges.

EMPLOYERS

Approximately 3.2 million office clerks are employed throughout the United States. Major employers include local government; utility companies; health care companies; finance and insurance agencies; real estate firms; professional, scientific, and technical services companies; and other large firms. Smaller companies also hire office workers and sometimes offer a greater opportunity to gain experience in a variety of clerical tasks.

STARTING OUT

To secure an entry-level position, you should contact businesses or government agencies directly. Newspaper ads and temporary-work agencies are also good sources for finding jobs in this area. Most companies provide on-the-job training, during which company policies and procedures are explained.

ADVANCEMENT

Office clerks usually begin their employment performing more routine tasks such as delivering messages and sorting and filing mail. With experience, they may advance to more complicated assignments and assume a greater responsibility for the entire project to be completed. Those who demonstrate the desire and ability may move to other clerical positions, such as secretary or receptionist. Clerks with good leadership skills may become group managers or supervisors. To be promoted to a professional occupation such as accountant, a college degree or other specialized training is usually necessary.

The high turnover rate that exists among office clerks increases promotional opportunities. The number and kind of opportunities, however, usually depend on the place of employment and the ability, education, and experience of the employee.

EARNINGS

Salaries for office clerks vary depending on the size and geographic location of the company and the skills of the worker. According to the U.S. Department of Labor, the median salary for full-time office clerks was $23,710 in 2006. The lowest paid 10 percent earned less than $14,850, while the highest paid group earned more than $37,600. The Department of Labor reports that office clerks earned the following mean salaries by industry in 2006: local government, $27,500; general medical and surgical hospitals, $26,910; colleges, universities, and professional schools, $25,680; and elementary and secondary schools, $25,410.

Full-time workers generally also receive paid vacations, health insurance, sick leave, and other benefits.

WORK ENVIRONMENT

As is the case with most office workers, office clerks work an average 40-hour week. They usually work in comfortable surroundings and are provided with modern equipment. Although clerks have a variety of tasks and responsibilities, the job itself can be fairly routine and repetitive. Clerks often interact with accountants and other office personnel and may work under close supervision.

OUTLOOK

Approximately 3.2 million people hold jobs as office clerks. Although employment of clerks is expected to grow only about as fast as the average through 2016, there will still be many jobs available due to the vastness of this field and a high turnover rate. With the increased use of data processing equipment and other types of automated office machinery, more and more employers are hiring people proficient in a variety of office tasks. According to OfficeTeam, the following industries show the strongest demand for qualified administrative staff: technology, financial services, construction, and manufacturing.

Because they are so versatile, office workers can find employment in virtually any kind of industry, so their overall employment does not depend on the fortunes of any single sector of the economy. In addition to private companies, the federal government should continue to be a good source of jobs. Office clerks with excellent computer skills, proficiency in office machinery, strong communication skills, and the ability to perform many tasks at once will be in strong demand. Temporary and part-time work opportunities should also increase, especially during busy business periods.

FOR MORE INFORMATION

For information on seminars, conferences, and news on the industry, contact

Association of Executive and Administrative Professionals
900 South Washington Street, Suite G-13
Falls Church, VA 22046-4009
Tel: 703-237-8616
http://www.naesaa.com

For information on certification, contact

International Association of Administrative Professionals
10502 NW Ambassador Drive, PO Box 20404
Kansas City, MO 64195-0404
Tel: 816-891-6600
http://www.iaap-hq.org

For free office career and salary information, visit the following Web site:

OfficeTeam
http://www.officeteam.com

PARALEGALS

OVERVIEW

Paralegals, also known as *legal assistants*, assist in trial preparations, investigate facts, prepare documents such as affidavits and pleadings, and, in general, do work customarily performed by lawyers. Approximately 238,000 paralegals and legal assistants work in law firms, businesses, and government agencies all over the United States; the majority work with lawyers and legislators.

THE JOB

A paralegal's main duty is to do everything a lawyer needs to do but does not have time to do. Although the lawyer assumes responsibility for the paralegal's work, the paralegal may take on all the duties of the lawyer except for setting fees, appearing in court, accepting cases, and giving legal advice.

Paralegals spend much of their time in law libraries, researching laws and previous cases and compiling facts to help lawyers prepare for trial. Paralegals often interview witnesses as part of their research as well. After analyzing the laws and facts that have been compiled for a particular client, the paralegal often writes a report that the lawyer may use to determine how to proceed with the case. If a case is brought to trial, the paralegal helps prepare legal arguments and draft pleadings to be filed in court. They also organize and store files and correspondence related to cases.

SCHOOL SUBJECTS
Computer Science, English, Government

PERSONAL SKILLS
Communication/Ideas, Following Instructions

MINIMUM EDUCATION LEVEL
Some Postsecondary Training

CERTIFICATION OR LICENSING
Voluntary

WORK ENVIRONMENT
Primarily Indoors, Primarily Multiple Locations

Not all paralegal work centers on trials. Many paralegals work for corporations, agencies, schools, and financial institutions. *Corporate paralegals* create and maintain contracts, mortgages, affidavits, and other documents. They assist with corporate matters, such as shareholder agreements, contracts, and employee benefit plans. Another important part of a corporate paralegal's job is to stay on top of new laws and regulations to make sure the company is operating within those parameters.

Some paralegals work for the government. They may prepare complaints or talk to employers to find out why health or safety standards are not being met. They often analyze legal documents, collect evidence for hearings, and prepare explanatory material on various laws for use by the public. For example, a *court administrator paralegal* is in charge of keeping the courthouse functioning; tasks include monitoring personnel, handling the case load for the court, and general administration.

Other paralegals are involved in community or public-service work. They may help specific groups, such as poor or elderly members of the community. They may file forms, research laws, and prepare documents. They may represent clients at hearings, although they may not appear in court on behalf of a client.

Many paralegals work for large law firms, agencies, and corporations and specialize in a particular area of law. Some work for smaller firms and have a general knowledge of many areas of law. Paralegals have varied duties, and an increasing number use computers in their work.

REQUIREMENTS
High School

While in high school, take a broad range of subjects, including English, social studies or government, computer science, and languages, especially Spanish and Latin. Because legal terminology is used constantly, word origins and vocabulary should be a focus.

Postsecondary Training

Requirements for paralegals vary by employer. Some paralegals start out as legal secretaries or clerical workers and gradually are given more training and responsibility. The majority, however, choose formal training and education programs.

Formal training programs usually range from one to three years and are offered in a variety of educational settings: four-year colleges and universities, law schools, community and junior colleges, business schools, proprietary schools, and paralegal associations. Admission requirements vary, but good grades in high school and college are always an asset. There are approximately 1,000 paralegal programs, about 260 of which have been approved by the American Bar Association. The National Federation of Paralegal Associations reports that 84 percent of all paralegals receive formal paralegal education.

Some paralegal programs require a bachelor's degree for admission; others do not require any college education. In either case, those who have a college degree usually have an edge over those who do not.

Certification or Licensing

Paralegals are not required to be licensed or certified. Instead, when lawyers employ paralegals, they often follow guidelines designed to protect the public from the practice of law by unqualified persons.

Paralegals may, however, opt to be certified. To do so, they may take and pass an extensive two-day test conducted by the National Association of Legal Assistants (NALA) Certifying Board. Paralegals who pass the test may use the title certified legal assistant (CLA) after their names. CLAs who prefer to be referred to as "certified paralegals" can use the certified paralegal designation. The NALA also offers an advanced certified paralegal designation to experienced paralegals who complete education requirements. Several specialized courses are available including Contracts Management/Contracts Administration, Discovery, Social Security Disability, and Trial Practice.NALS, an association for legal professionals, offers a basic and an advanced certification for legal professionals and the professional paralegal certification for paralegals. Contact the association for more information.

In 1994, the National Federation of Paralegal Associations established the Paralegal Advanced Competency Exam as a means for paralegals who meet education and experience requirements to acquire professional recognition. Paralegals who pass this exam and maintain the continuing education requirement may use the designation *registered paralegal*.

The American Alliance of Paralegals offers the American Alliance certified paralegal designation to applicants who have least five years of experience as a paralegal and meet educational criteria.

Other Requirements

Communication skills, both verbal and written, are vital to working as a paralegal. You must be able to turn research into reports that a lawyer or corporate executive can use. You must also be able to think logically and learn new laws and regulations quickly. Research skills, computer skills, and people skills are other necessities.

EXPLORING

If you are interested in a career as a paralegal, but you are not positive yet, do not worry. There are several ways you can explore the career of a paralegal. Colleges, universities, and technical schools have a wealth of information available for the asking. Elizabeth Houser, a practicing paralegal, recommends contacting schools that have paralegal programs directly. "Ask questions. They are helpful and will give you a lot of information about being a paralegal," she says.

Look for summer or part-time employment as a secretary or in the mailroom of a law firm to get an idea of the nature of the work. If paid positions are not available, offer yourself as a volunteer to the law offices in town. Ask your guidance counselor to help you set up a volunteer/internship agreement with a lawyer.

Talk to your history or government teacher about organizing a trip to a lawyer's office and a courthouse. Ask your teacher to set aside time for you to talk to paralegals working there and to their supervising attorneys.

If you have access to a computer, search the World Wide Web for information on student organizations that are affiliated with the legal profession. You can also contact the organizations listed at the end of this article for general information.

EMPLOYERS

Paralegals and legal assistants hold approximately 238,000 jobs in the United States. The majority (70 percent) work for lawyers in law offices or in law firms. Other paralegals work for the government, namely for the Federal Trade Commission, Justice Department, Treasury Department, Internal Revenue Service, Department of the Interior, and many other agencies and offices. Paralegals also work in the business community. Anywhere legal matters are part of the day-to-day work, paralegals are usually handling them. Paralegals fit in well in business because many smaller corporations must deal with legal regulations but don't necessarily need an attorney or a team of lawyers.

Paralegals in business can be found all over the country. Larger cities employ more paralegals who focus on the legal side of the profession, and government paralegals will find the most opportunities in state capitals and Washington, D.C.

STARTING OUT

Although some law firms promote legal secretaries to paralegal status, most employers prefer to hire individuals who have completed paralegal programs. To have the best opportunity at getting a quality job in the paralegal field, you should attend a paralegal school. In addition to providing a solid background in paralegal studies, most schools help graduates find jobs. Even though the job market for paralegals is expected to grow rapidly over the next 10 years, those with the best credentials will get the best jobs.

For Elizabeth Houser, the internship program was the springboard to her first paralegal position. "The paralegal program of study I took required an internship. I was hired directly from that internship experience."

The National Federation of Paralegal Associations recommends using job banks that are sponsored by paralegal associations across the country. For paralegal associations that may be able to help, see the addresses listed at the end of this article. Many jobs for paralegals are posted on the Internet as well.

ADVANCEMENT

There are no formal advancement paths for paralegals. There are, however, some possibilities for advancement, as large firms are beginning to establish career programs for paralegals.

For example, a person may be promoted from a paralegal to a head legal assistant who supervises others. In addition, a paralegal may specialize in one area of law, such as environmental, real estate, or medical malpractice. Many paralegals also advance by moving from small to large firms.

Expert paralegals who specialize in one area of law may go into business for themselves. Rather than work for one firm, these freelance paralegals often contract their services to many lawyers. Some paralegals with bachelor's degrees enroll in law school to train to become lawyers.

Paralegals can also move horizontally by taking their specialized knowledge of the law into another field, such as insurance, occupational health, or law enforcement.

EARNINGS

Salaries vary greatly for paralegals. The size and location of the firm and the education and experience of the employee are some factors that determine the annual earnings of paralegals.

The U.S. Department of Labor reports that paralegals and legal assistants had median annual earnings of $43,040 in 2006. The highest 10 percent earned more than $67,540, while the lowest 10 percent earned less than $27,450. According to the Department of Labor, paralegals and legal assistants earned the following mean annual salaries in 2006 by industry: federal government, $57,590; local government, $44,580; legal services, $43,950; and state government, $40,870.

Benefits for paralegals depend on the employer; however, they usually include such items as health insurance, retirement or 401(k) plans, and paid vacation days.

WORK ENVIRONMENT

Paralegals often work in pleasant and comfortable offices. Much of their work is performed in a law library. Some paralegals work out of their homes in special employment situations. When investigation is called for, paralegals may travel to gather information. Most paralegals work a 40-hour week, although long hours are sometimes required to meet court-imposed deadlines. Longer hours—sometimes as much as 90 hours per week—are usually the normal routine for paralegals starting out in law offices and firms.

Many of the paralegal's duties involve routine tasks, so they must have a great deal of patience. However, paralegals may be given increasingly difficult assignments over time. Paralegals are often unsupervised, especially as they gain experience and a reputation for quality work. Elizabeth Houser does much of her work unsupervised. "You get to put a lot of yourself into what you do and that provides a high level of job satisfaction," she says.

OUTLOOK

Employment for paralegals is expected to grow much faster than the average for all occupations through 2016, according to the U.S. Department of Labor. One reason for the expected rapid growth in the profession is the financial benefits of employing paralegals. The paralegal, whose duties fall between those of the legal secretary and those of the attorney, helps make the delivery of legal services more cost effective to clients. The growing need for legal services among the general population and the increasing popularity of prepaid legal plans is creating a tremendous demand for paralegals in private law firms. In the private sector, paralegals can work in banks, insurance companies, real estate and title insurance firms, and corporate legal departments. In the public sector, there is a growing need for paralegals in the courts and community legal service programs, government agencies, and consumer organizations.

The growth of this occupation, to some extent, is dependent on the economy. Businesses are less likely to pursue litigation cases when profit margins are down, thus curbing the need for new hires.

FOR MORE INFORMATION

For information on certification, contact

American Alliance of Paralegals
16815 East Shea Boulevard, Suite 110, No. 101
Fountain Hills, AZ, 85268-6667
http://www.aapipara.org

For information regarding accredited educational facilities, contact

American Association for Paralegal Education
19 Mantua Road
Mt. Royal, NJ 08061-1006
Tel: 856-423-2829
Email: info@aafpe.org
http://www.aafpe.org

For general information about careers in the law field, contact

American Bar Association
Standing Committee on Paralegals
321 North Clark Street
Chicago, IL 60610-7598
Tel: 800-285-2221
http://www.abanet.org/legalservices/paralegals

For career information, contact

Association of Legal Administrators
75 Tri-State International, Suite 222
Lincolnshire, IL 60069-4435
Tel: 847-267-1252
http://www.alanet.org

For information on certification and careers in law, contact

NALS . . . the association for legal professionals
314 East 3rd Street, Suite 210
Tulsa, OK 74120-2409
Tel: 918-582-5188
Email: info@nals.org
http://www.nals.org

For information about educational and licensing programs, certification, and paralegal careers, contact

National Association of Legal Assistants
1516 South Boston Avenue, Suite 200
Tulsa, OK 74119-4013
Tel: 918-587-6828

Email: nalanet@nala.org
http://www.nala.org

For information about almost every aspect of becoming a paralegal, contact

National Federation of Paralegal Associations
PO Box 2016
Edmonds, WA 98020-9516
Tel: 425-967-0045
Email: info@paralegals.org
http://www.paralegals.org

For information about employment networks and school listings, contact

National Paralegal Association
PO Box 406
Solebury, PA 18963-0406
Tel: 215-297-8333
Email: admin@nationalparalegal.org
http://www.nationalparalegal.org

PHARMACISTS

OVERVIEW

Pharmacists are health professionals responsible for the dispensation of prescription and nonprescription medications. They act as consultants to health practitioners and the general public concerning possible adverse drug reactions and interactions, and may also give advice relating to home medical supplies and durable health care equipment. The role of the pharmacist has evolved into that of consultant and medicinal expert, because of the expanded duties of pharmacy technicians and the increasing time restrictions placed on health maintenance organization physicians. There are approximately 243,000 pharmacists in the United States.

THE JOB

Pharmacists need a thorough knowledge of drug products. Most importantly, they need to understand how drugs work for people who are sick, how the drugs interact with a person's body as well as illness, and how different drugs may interact with each other. In addition to dispensing drugs according to orders from physicians, dentists, and other health care practitioners, pharmacists advise these professionals on the appro-

---

SCHOOL SUBJECTS
Chemistry, Mathematics

PERSONAL SKILLS
Following Instructions, Technical/Scientific

MINIMUM EDUCATION LEVEL
Doctorate

CERTIFICATION OR LICENSING
Recommended (Certification), Required by All States (Licensing)

WORK ENVIRONMENT
Primarily Indoors, Primarily One Location

---

priate selection and use of medications. They monitor how long patients have been taking a medication and provide information to patients and doctors when a generic brand of a drug is available. Pharmacist Shreen Beshures, who has been involved in the pharmacy business since high school, explains that part of her work includes "print[ing] recommendations to the doctors for a reduction in the number of medications [or] a more cost-effective medication." In addition to advising doctors and other health professionals, pharmacists talk with patients or customers about medications, explaining what the medications are supposed to do and how to use them properly. Pharmacists working in retail locations, such as a neighborhood drugstore, may also find that customers come to them with questions about symptoms. They may recommend nonprescription products such as headache remedies, vitamins, and cough syrups. All pharmacists keep records of drugs and medications dispensed to each person in order to identify duplicate drugs or combinations of drugs that can cause adverse reactions or side effects.

In conjunction with these duties, pharmacists are required to maintain their licenses through continuing education, though education requirements vary by location. Some states may require this education in the form of correspondence (written responses to educational material), or conferences and seminars. Some states may also require continuing education in particular disease topics and treatment.

Pharmacists' duties vary somewhat depending on where they are employed. About 62 percent of pharmacists work for community retail pharmacies, such as a local drugstore pharmacy, a chain drugstore pharmacy, or a grocery store pharmacy. These pharmacists fill prescription orders, contact doctors and other health care professional by phone when clarification about a prescription is needed, and have frequent interaction with the public. In addition to pharmaceutical duties, they sell merchandise unrelated to health, hire and supervise other workers, and oversee the general operation of the pharmacy.

Pharmacists who work at hospitals or clinics prepare sterile solutions or special mixtures, dispense medications on-site, and complete administrative duties. They work closely with the medical staff, suggesting what medications to use, explaining their effects, and sometimes demonstrating how to give medications. They also keep precise records of what type and amount of medications each patient is on, keep track of supplies in the pharmacy, and buy new supplies as necessary. They may also interact with patients, meeting with them before their discharge to discuss what medications they will use at home. At a large hospital or clinic employing a number of pharmacists, a supervising pharmacist may also be responsible for arranging schedules and overseeing the work of others.

Many pharmacists are employed by large pharmaceutical manufacturers. They may work in one of several capacities. Some engage in research to help develop new drugs or to improve or find new uses for old ones. Others supervise the preparation of ingredients that go into the tablets, capsules, ointments, solutions, or other dosage forms produced by the manufacturer. Others test or standardize the raw or refined chemicals that eventually will go into the finished drug. Some may assist with advertising the company's products, to make sure that nothing untruthful or misleading is said about a product in professional literature. Some pharmacists may prepare literature on new products for pharmaceutical or technical journals. Others write material for package inserts.

Pharmacists employed by government agencies may work in a number of different kinds of positions. They may be inspectors who monitor drug manufacturing firms, hospitals, wholesalers, or community pharmacies. They may work in research with agencies such as the FDA, testing the effectiveness of new drugs, or they may work with agencies involved with narcotics and other controlled substances.

Other opportunities for pharmacists include teaching at schools of pharmacy, working in the armed forces, and working for Health Maintenance Organizations (HMOs) or insurance companies. Some pharmacists write or edit reports for journals, draft technical papers, and staff professional associations. An increasing number of pharmacists—senior care pharmacists—are employed by nursing homes and other long-term care facilities to provide and monitor drug therapy for the elderly. Some pharmacists complete additional education to become patent attorneys or experts in pharmaceutical law.

All pharmacists must be diligent in maintaining clean and ordered work areas. They must be exceedingly precise in their calculations and possess a high degree of concentration in order to reduce the risk of error as they compound and assemble prescriptions. Additionally, pharmacists must be proficient with a variety of technical devices and computer systems. However, more and more drug products are shipped in finished form by the pharmaceutical manufacturer. The actual compounding of prescription medications, therefore, is taking a smaller amount of time.

REQUIREMENTS
High School

If you are thinking of becoming a pharmacist, you should take college preparatory courses in high school and concentrate in the areas of mathematics and science. It is especially important that you take biology, chemistry, and physics to prepare for this work. Additionally, you should take English, speech, and a foreign language, because good communications skills will be important as you progress through college, job interviews, and eventual employment as a pharmacist. If working as a community pharmacist sounds interesting to you, consider taking business and accounting courses to prepare yourself for working in and running a drugstore.

Postsecondary Training

To become a pharmacist, you will need to earn the degree Doctor of Pharmacy (Pharm.D.) from a school accredited by the Accreditation Council for Pharmacy Education. The Pharm.D. has replaced the bachelor of pharmacy degree (B.Pharm.), which is no longer awarded. The doctorate degree generally takes six years to complete. The first year or two of study does not take place in a school of pharmacy but rather in a general college setting. You will take pre-pharmacy classes such as chemistry, organic chemistry, biology, physics, calculus, statistics, English, and social sciences. After you have completed this work you will need to gain admission to a school of pharmacy. You may apply to a school of pharmacy that is part of the university where you completed your pre-pharmacy work, or you may apply to a school of pharmacy that is not part of your undergraduate school. In addition to completing pre-pharmacy courses, some schools of pharmacy require applicants to take the Pharmacy College Admissions Test (PCAT).

In pharmacy school, you will take courses such as the principles of pharmacology, biochemistry, pharmacy law and ethics, and pharmaceutical care. In addition, your education should include an internship, sometimes known as a clerkship, in which you work under the supervision of a professional pharmacist. When deciding on a school to attend, you should consult the Accreditation Council for Pharmacy Education's annual Directory of Accredited Professional Programs of Colleges and Schools of Pharmacy for accredited programs. It is available on the council's Web site http://www.acpe-accredit.org/deans/schools.asp.

Certification or Licensing

Pharmacists who specialize in a specific health care discipline can obtain voluntary certification. Currently the Board of Pharmaceutical Specialties recognizes and offers certification in five areas: nuclear pharmacy (involving the use of radioactive drugs), nutrition support pharmacy (involving care of patients with special needs in receiving nutrition), oncology pharmacy (involving care of patients with cancer), pharmacotherapy (involving the safe, economic, and proper use of drug therapies), and psychiatric pharmacy (involving the care of those with psychiatric-related illnesses). Pharmacists who specialize in geriatric health care may receive the certified geriatric pharmacist designation from the Commission for Certification in Geriatric Pharmacy (http://www.ccgp.org).

Practicing pharmacists are required to be licensed in all 50 states, the District of Columbia, and all U.S. territories. Applicants for licensure must have graduated from an accredited pharmacy program, completed an internship under a licensed pharmacist, and passed their state's or a multistate board examination.

Other Requirements

You will need good people skills to deal with patients, other pharmacy workers, and other health care professionals. A good bedside manner (a kind, comforting approach), like that required of doctors, will help you in a hospital or nursing home setting, particularly as pharmacists' responsibilities expand to include counseling and advising. You should also be very organized, and have an eye for detail—doctors, nurses, and patients will all be relying on you to keep accurate drug records.

EXPLORING

To explore this job, talk to a local pharmacist about his or her work. Volunteer at a hospital or clinic in your area to get hands-on experience working in a medical environment. You can also try to get a paid part-time or summer job at a nutrition and vitamin store where you'll have the opportunity to learn about dietary supplements, vitamins, and herbal remedies.

While in high school, Shreen Beshures got a part-time job as a pharmacy technician in a neighborhood drugstore. She advises those considering this career to "get a part-time job in a drugstore or . . . at a pharmacy in a hospital to see if it's really what you want to do." Of course, if you get a job at a pharmacy, do not expect to be in the back mixing medications with a mortar and pestle. Nevertheless, you can benefit by working in a position such as stock clerk, salesclerk, or delivery person. Any one of these jobs will give you the chance to observe firsthand the kind of work that pharmacists do, see how they interact with customers, and gain experience working with customers yourself. After you have demonstrated responsibility and interest, you may even have the opportunity to assist in the pharmacy—entering data in customer computer records, taking inventory on equipment, bottles, and vials, and preparing labels.

Depending on where you live, it may also be possible for you to get an internship through the National Association of Chain Drug Stores Foundation's chain community pharmacy internship program. For more information, visit http://www.nacdsfoundation.org.

EMPLOYERS

Approximately 62 percent of pharmacists work in community pharmacies—there are approximately 39,000 pharmacies operated by chain drugstores, supermarkets, and mass merchants, and there are another 18,000 independent pharmacies. Approximately 23 percent of pharmacists work in hospitals. Pharmacists can also find work at mail order pharmacies, pharmaceutical companies, and agencies of the federal government. Some pharmacists are self-employed and fill-in as "temps" at a number of different community pharmacies. There are approximately 243,000 pharmacists working in the United States.

STARTING OUT

"I had always wanted to go to medical school," Shreen Beshures says, "but wasn't sure. I took pre-med classes in college, which were also pre-pharmacy, and decided to transfer to a pharmacy school in New York." Once you are ready to graduate from pharmacy school, the career services office of your college or university should be one source of information about job openings. Internships also provide the opportunity to make professional contacts, and you may hear about an open position through these contacts. A number of placement services involved in the health care field work with pharmacists, placing them in the jobs they want. Newspaper advertisements and associations, such as the American Society of Health-System Pharmacists, can also provide information on job openings. Once you have become licensed, you may apply directly to a community, hospital, or clinic pharmacy that interests you. Though the level of work is the same for beginning pharmacists as it is for experienced pharmacists, you may have to work long hours, evenings, and weekends until you've gained some seniority with the pharmacy.

ADVANCEMENT

Community pharmacists may enjoy advancement to supervisory positions. The hospital pharmacist may advance to the position of chief pharmacist or director of pharmacy services after accumulating several years of experience.

Pharmacists who are employed by drug manufacturing firms may anticipate increases in both salary and responsibility as they gain experience and increase their value to their firms.

Pharmacists who acquire advanced degrees and education may become *pharmacologists,* who study the effects of drugs on the body.

EARNINGS

The earnings of salaried pharmacists are largely determined by the location, size, and type of employer as well as by the duties and responsibilities of the individual pharmacist. Pharmacists who own or manage pharmacies often earn considerably more than other pharmacists. According to the U.S. Department of Labor, pharmacists earned a median yearly income of $94,520 in 2006. The lowest paid 10 percent earned less than $67,860 per year, while the highest paid 10 percent made more than $119,480 during that same time. The Department of Labor also reports that pharmacists earned the following mean salaries in 2006 by type of employer: health and personal care stores, $95,140; other general merchandise stores, $94,450; department stores, $94,170; grocery stores, $92,690; and general medical and surgical hospitals, $92,550.

Pharmacists, in addition to salary, enjoy fringe benefits such as paid vacation, medical and dental insurance, overtime, and sometimes bonuses and profit sharing, depending on the size and type of employer. Because of the high demand for pharmacists who will work odd hours in community drugstores, temp pharmacists can often negotiate for benefits, as well.

WORK ENVIRONMENT

A pharmacy is usually a pleasant place to work. Pharmacies should be well lighted, well ventilated, and kept in a clean and orderly fashion. Many chain-owned pharmacies now provide 18- or 24-hour operations.

Hospital pharmacies are efficient, orderly, and busy with a variety of important activities. The physicians, nurses, technicians, and other medical personnel with whom the pharmacist works are usually intelligent and concerned people. These pharmacies are also usually in operation 18 or 24 hours a day.

The two most unfavorable conditions of the pharmacist's practice are long hours and the necessity to stay on one's feet. It is not unusual to be on duty at least 48 hours a week. Most state laws covering the practice of pharmacy require that there be a pharmacist on duty at all times when the pharmacy is open. Most pharmacies employ at least two pharmacists because it is customary to remain open at least 12 hours a day. Many pharmacies are also open at least part of the time on Sundays. Despite the requirements of the job, most pharmacists appreciate being involved in health care. "I'm an integral part of the health care system," Shreen Beshures says, "preventing medication errors and aiding nurses and physicians with medications."

Pharmacists who operate their own pharmacies have financial responsibilities. Many pharmacies do better than one to two million dollars in gross sales each year in business. They must hire employees, maintain an adequate inventory, and keep records. They must make rent or mortgage payments and pay insurance premiums and taxes. The growing influence of third-party prescription programs has forced pharmacists to spend considerable amounts of time processing claims, maintaining government records, and explaining benefit plans to customers. Many community pharmacy owners complain of restrictions placed on them by government agencies, insurance companies, and HMOs that they claim hinders their ability to compete with chain competitors.

OUTLOOK

The U.S. Department of Labor predicts that employment for pharmacists will grow much faster than the average for all occupations through 2016. Reasons for this increase include the growing middle-aged and senior population (generally the largest consumers of medications), technical and scientific advances that will make more drugs available and affordable, and even the advertising of medications that informs consumers of the variety of medicines available, resulting in their asking for these drugs.

Opportunities should be good in community pharmacies, hospital pharmacies, and mail-order pharmacies. Even better employment is expected in assisted-living facilities and home care settings.

The role of the pharmacist is expected to expand. Pharmacists will be more involved in counseling their patients and in advising physicians on the drugs to prescribe. Pharmacists will make house calls and see patients in doctor's offices. They will also be studying more complex medications and sorting out drug information on the Internet.

The Department of Labor predicts that pharmacists will have good opportunities in managed care settings as they will be increasingly relied on to study trends and patterns in the use of medications and analyze the benefits and costs of various drug treatments. Drug companies will also need pharmacists to work in research and development and sales and marketing. Pharmaceutical informatics—the use of information technology to improve the care of patients—is another rapidly growing subspecialty.

FOR MORE INFORMATION

For information on careers, contact
Academy of Managed Care Pharmacy
100 North Pitt Street, Suite 400
Alexandria, VA 22314
Tel: 800-827-2627
http://www.amcp.org

For more information about pharmacy education, contact
Accreditation Council for Pharmacy Education
20 North Clark Street, Suite 2500
Chicago, IL 60602-5109

Tel: 312-664-3575
Email: info@acpe-accredit.org
http://www.acpe-accredit.org

For information on educational programs, contact
American Association of Colleges of Pharmacy
1727 King Street
Alexandria VA 22314-2700
Tel: 703-739-2330
Email: mail@aacp.org
http://www.aacp.org

For information about student membership and publications, and for news about the industry, visit the APhA's Web site, or contact
American Pharmacists Association (APhA)
1100 15th Street NW, Suite 400
Washington, DC 20005-1707
Tel: 202-628-4410
http://www.aphanet.org

For information on different areas of pharmacy practice and career opportunities, contact
American Society of Health-System Pharmacists
7272 Wisconsin Avenue
Bethesda, MD 20814-4836
Tel: 301-657-3000
http://www.ashp.org

For more information about pharmacy specialties, visit the BPS's Web site.
Board of Pharmaceutical Specialties (BPS)
1100 15th Street, NW, Suite 400
Washington, DC 20005-1707
Tel: 202-429-7591
http://www.bpsweb.org

For information on pharmacy careers and industry facts, contact
National Association of Chain Drug Stores
413 North Lee Street
Alexandria, VA 22314-2301
Tel: 703-549-3001
http://www.nacds.org

For information on state boards of pharmacy, contact
National Association of Boards of Pharmacy
1600 Feehanville Drive
Mount Prospect, IL 60056-6014
Tel: 847-391-4406
http://www.nabp.net

For information about careers in independent pharmacy, internships, scholarships, and to read America's Pharmacist *magazine, contact*

National Community Pharmacists Association
100 Daingerfield Road
Alexandria, VA 22314-6302
Tel: 800-544-7447
Email: info@ncpanet.org
http://www.ncpanet.org

PHARMACY TECHNICIANS

OVERVIEW

Pharmacy technicians provide technical assistance for pharmacists and work under their direct supervision. They usually work in chain or independent drug stores, hospitals, community ambulatory care centers, home health care agencies, nursing homes, and the pharmaceutical industry. They perform a wide range of technical support functions and tasks related to the pharmacy profession. They maintain patient records; count, package, and label medication doses; prepare and distribute sterile products; and fill and dispense routine orders for stock supplies such as over-the-counter products. There are approximately 285,000 pharmacy technicians employed in the United States.

SCHOOL SUBJECTS
Biology, Chemistry

PERSONAL SKILLS
Following Instructions, Technical/Scientific

MINIMUM EDUCATION LEVEL
Some Postsecondary Training

CERTIFICATION OR LICENSING
Voluntary

WORK ENVIRONMENT
Primarily Indoors, Primarily One Location

THE JOB

The roles of the pharmacist and pharmacy technician expanded greatly in the 1990s. The pharmacist's primary responsibility is to ensure that medications are used safely and effectively through clinical patient counseling and monitoring. In order to provide the highest quality of pharmaceutical care, pharmacists now focus on providing clinical services. As a result, pharmacy technicians' duties have evolved into a more specialized role known as pharmacy technology. Pharmacy technicians perform more of the manipulative functions associated with dispensing prescriptions. Their primary duties are drug-product preparation and distribution, but they are also concerned with the control of drug products. Technicians assemble, prepare, and deliver requested medication. Technicians are responsible for record keeping, and they record drug-related information on specified forms, frequently doing this part of the work on computers. Depending on a technician's experience, he or she may order pharmaceuticals and take inventory of controlled substances, such as Valium and Ritalin.

Technicians who work in hospitals have the most varied responsibilities of all pharmacy technicians. In a hospital, technicians fill total parenteral nutrition preparations and standard and chemotherapy IVs (intravenous solutions) for patients under doctors' orders. Other duties that a hospital pharmacy technician may be required to do include filling "stat," or immediate, orders and delivering them; preparing special emergency carts stocked with medications; and monitoring defibrillators and resuscitation equipment. In an emergency, pharmacy technicians respond with doctors and nurses, rushing the cart and other equipment to the emergency site. They also keep legal records of the events that occur during an emergency. Technicians work in the hospital's outpatient pharmacy, which is similar to a commercial drugstore, and assist the pharmacist in dispensing medication.

Tamara Britton works as a technician in a hospital. Because the hospital pharmacy is open 24 hours a day, Tamara has worked all three shifts. Her work involves using a computer to create labels for large IV bags and "piggybacks" (small-volume IV bags). She stacks the IVs on carts, then delivers them to the appropriate nurse stations. She also delivers medications through a process known as "tubing and shagging." Two "tubes," or lines, (similar to those at a bank's drive-through) run through the entire hospital to every nurse unit. "Shagging" is the process of placing the nurse unit's medications in baggies; the meds are then shot through the tubes to the proper units. Tamara also prepares drug carts with the aid of a RxOBOT; this robotic arm is in a glassed-off room, and fills the drawers of the carts with the correct medication for individual patients. Britton places coded labels on the drawers of the carts. She explains, "I put the drawers with labels facing Robota (we named her) and a conveyor belt takes them in the room for Robota to fill with all of the patients' existing meds for the day. The tray, after filling, drops down to a lower conveyor belt that brings the drawer back to me, which I replace in the cart."

As their roles increase, trained technicians have become more specialized. Some specialized types of pharmacy technicians include *narcotics control pharmacy technicians, operating room pharmacy technicians, emergency room pharmacy technicians, nuclear pharmacy technicians,* and *home health care pharmacy technicians.* Specially trained pharmacy technicians are also employed as *data entry technicians, lead technicians, supervisors,* and *technician managers.*

REQUIREMENTS
High School

You should take courses in mathematics and science (especially chemistry and biology), because you will be dealing with patient records and drug dosages. Health classes can help you get a basic understanding of the health care industry and various medical treatments. Take English and speech classes to help you develop your writing and communication skills. You will be using a computer a lot to maintain records and prepare labels, so take courses in computer fundamentals.

Postsecondary Training

In the past, pharmacy technicians received most of their training on the job in hospital and community pharmacy-training programs. Since technician functions and duties have changed greatly in recent years, most pharmacy technicians today receive their education through formal training programs offered through community colleges, vocational/technical schools, hospital community pharmacies, and government programs throughout the United States. Program length usually ranges from six months to two years, and leads to a certificate, diploma, or associate's degree in pharmacy technology. A high school diploma usually is required for entry into a training program. The American Society of Health-System Pharmacists (ASHP) is the national accrediting organization for pharmacy technician training programs. The ASHP can provide you with information on approved programs across the country (see address at end of this article).

In a pharmacy technician training program, you will receive classroom instruction and participate in supervised clinical apprenticeships in health institutions and community pharmacies. Courses include introduction to pharmacy and health care systems, pharmacy laws and ethics, medical terminology, chemistry, and microbiology. Most pharmacy technicians continue their education even after their formal training ends by reading professional journals and attending training or informational seminars, lectures, review sessions, and audiovisual presentations.

Certification or Licensing

At least three states license pharmacy technicians and all 50 states have adopted, the National Pharmacy Technician Certification Examination, a written, standardized test for voluntary certification of technicians. Those who pass the test can use the certified pharmacy technician designation. Some states, including Texas and Louisiana, require certification of pharmacy technicians. To receive certification from the Pharmacy Technician Certification Board, you will be tested on such subjects as the top 200 drugs in use by the medical profession. After receiving certification, you will be required to complete 20 hours of continuing education every two years as part of the qualifications for recertification. The Institute for the Certification of Pharmacy Technicians also offers a national certification examination. Even though certification is not required in every state, it is recommended to enhance your credentials, demonstrate to employers your commitment to the profession, and possibly qualify you for higher pay.

Other Requirements

You must be precision-minded, honest, and mature as you are depended on for accuracy and high levels of quality control, especially in hospitals. "I pay attention to details," Tamara Britton says, "and try to catch all my own mistakes before a pharmacist checks my work." You need good communications skills in order to successfully interact with pharmacists, supervisors, and other technicians. You must be able to follow written and oral instructions precisely because a wide variety of people, including physicians, nurses, pharmacists, and patients, rely on your actions. You also need some computer aptitude in order to effectively record pharmaceutical data.

EXPLORING

Ask your school's guidance or career counselor to help you arrange for a pharmacy technician to talk to a group of students interested in this career. Your counselor may also be able to help you arrange for an information interview with a pharmacy technician. During such an interview you will meet one-on-one with the technician and ask him or her about the work. Volunteer work at a local hospital or nursing home will provide you with an excellent opportunity to be in an environment similar to the one in which many professional technicians work. As a volunteer, you can hone your communication skills and learn about medical settings by interacting with both patients and medical staff. You may even have the opportunity to meet and talk with pharmacy technicians. Finally, look for a part-time or summer job at a local retail pharmacy. Although your duties may be limited to stocking the shelves, working the cash register, or making deliveries, you will still gain valuable experience by working in this environment and interacting with trained pharmacists and technicians. By doing this, you may even be able to find a mentor who is willing to give you advice about education and the pharmacy technician career.

EMPLOYERS

Approximately 285,000 pharmacy technicians are employed in the United States. Most opportunities for pharmacy technicians are in retail. According to the National Association of Chain Drug Stores, there are approximately 39,000 pharmacies operated by traditional chain pharmacy companies, mass merchants, and supermarkets, as well as nearly 18,000 independent pharmacies. Technicians also work in hospitals and long-term care facilities as well as in clinics at military bases, prisons, and colleges. Technicians are also finding work with home health care agencies, mail-order and Internet pharmacies, and with the federal government.

STARTING OUT

In some cases you may be able to pursue education and certification while employed as a pharmacy technician. Some chain drugstores pay the certification fees for their techs and also reward certified techs with higher hourly pay. This practice will probably increase—industry experts predict a need for pharmacists and technicians as more chain drugstores open across the country, and more pharmacies offer 24-hour service.

Pharmacy technicians often are hired by the hospital or agency where they interned. If you don't find employment this way, you can use employment agencies or newspaper ads to help locate job openings. Tamara Britton found her hospital job in the classifieds. "There was an ad that said 'use your data entry skills and become a

pharmacy technician.' They tested me on data entry and then interviewed me and gave me the job. They trained me on all I needed to know to do the job."

ADVANCEMENT

Depending on where they are employed, technicians may direct or instruct newer pharmacy technicians, make schedules, or move to purchasing or computer work. Some hospitals have a variety of tech designations, based on experience and responsibility, with a corresponding increase in pay. Some pharmacy techs return to school to pursue a degree in pharmacy.

EARNINGS

According to the U.S. Department of Labor, pharmacy technicians had median annual earnings of $25,630 in 2006. The lowest paid 10 percent of technicians earned less than $17,800, while the highest paid 10 percent made $36,720 or more. Pharmacy technicians earned the following mean salaries in 2006 by type of employer: federal government, $35,350; general medical and surgical hospitals, $29,720; grocery stores, $26,730; and electronic shopping and mail-order houses, $26,460.

Benefits that technicians receive depend on their employers but generally include medical and dental insurance, retirement savings plans, and paid sick, personal, and vacation days.

WORK ENVIRONMENT

Pharmacy technicians work in clean, well-lit, pleasant, and professional surroundings. They may wear scrubs or other uniforms in hospitals, especially in the IV room. In a retail drugstore, a technician may be allowed to wear casual clothing along with a smock. Most pharmacy settings are extremely busy, especially hospital and retail. "I feel like I'm part of a system," Tamara Britton says, "to help the sick get better and maybe keep people from dying." The job of pharmacy technician, like any other occupation that demands skill, speed, and accuracy, can be stressful. Because most hospitals, nursing homes, health care centers, and retail pharmacies are open between 16 and 24 hours a day, multiple shifts, weekend, and holiday hours usually are required.

OUTLOOK

The U.S. Department of Labor projects much-faster-than-average employment growth for pharmacy technicians through 2016. As the role of the pharmacist shifts to consultation, more technicians will be needed to assemble and dispense medications. Furthermore, new employment avenues and responsibilities will mirror that of the expanding and evolving role of the pharmacist. A strong demand is emerging for technicians with specialized training to work in specific areas, such as emergency room and nuclear pharmacy. An increasing number of pharmacy technicians will be needed as the number of older Americans (who, on average, require more prescription medication than younger generations) continues to rise.

Those who want to work as pharmacy technicians should be aware that in the future they may need more education to gain certification because of the growing number of complex medications and new drug therapies on the market. Mechanical advances in the pharmaceutical field, such as robot-picking devices and automatic counting equipment, may eradicate some of the duties pharmacy technicians previously performed, yet there will remain a need for skilled technicians to clean and maintain such devices. Traditionally, pharmacists have been required to check the work of technicians; however, in some states, hospitals are allowing techs to check the work of other techs.

FOR MORE INFORMATION

Contact the AAPT for more information on membership and continuing education.

American Association of Pharmacy Technicians (AAPT)
PO Box 1447
Greensboro, NC 27402-1447
Tel: 877-368-4771
Email: aapt@pharmacytechnician.com
http://www.pharmacytechnician.com

For more information on accredited pharmacy technician training programs, contact

American Society of Health-System Pharmacists
7272 Wisconsin Avenue
Bethesda, MD 20814-4836
Tel: 301-657-3000
http://www.ashp.org

For information on certification, contact

Institute for the Certification of Pharmacy Technicians
2536 South Old Highway 94, Suite 214
St. Charles, MO 63303-5612
Email: info@icptmail.org
http://www.nationaltechexam.org

For industry information and employment opportunities in retail, contact

National Association of Chain Drug Stores
413 North Lee Street

Alexandria, VA 22314-2301
Tel: 703-549-3001
http://www.nacds.org

For information on careers, contact

National Pharmacy Technician Association
PO Box 683148
Houston, TX 77268-3148
Tel: 888-247-8700
http://www.pharmacytechnician.org

To learn more about certification and training, contact

Pharmacy Technician Certification Board
1100 15th Street, NW, Suite 730
Washington, DC 20005-1707
Tel: 800-363-8012
http://www.ptcb.org

Pharmacy Week *is a newsletter for professionals and pharmacy students. Check out its Web site for articles, industry news, job listings, and continuing education information.*

Pharmacy Week
http://www.pharmacyweek.com

PHYSICAL THERAPISTS

OVERVIEW

Physical therapists, formerly called *physiotherapists,* are health care specialists who restore mobility, alleviate pain and suffering, and work to prevent permanent disability for their patients. They test and measure the functions of the musculoskeletal, neurological, pulmonary, and cardiovascular systems and treat problems in these systems caused by illness, injury, or birth defect. Physical therapists provide preventive, restorative, and rehabilitative treatment for their patients. Approximately 173,000 physical therapists are licensed to practice in the United States.

THE JOB

To initiate a program of physical therapy, the physical therapist consults the individual's medical history, examines the patient and identifies problems, confers with the physician or other health care professionals involved in the patient's care, establishes objectives and

SCHOOL SUBJECTS
Biology, Chemistry

PERSONAL SKILLS
Helping/Teaching, Mechanical/Manipulative

MINIMUM EDUCATION LEVEL
Master's Degree

CERTIFICATION OR LICENSING
Required by All States

WORK ENVIRONMENT
Primarily Indoors, Primarily One Location

treatment goals that are consistent with the patient's needs, and determines the methods for accomplishing the objectives.

Treatment goals established by the physical therapist include preventing disability, relieving pain, and restoring function. In the presence of illness or injury, the ultimate goal is to assist the patient's physical recovery and reentry into the community, home, and work environment at the highest level of independence and self-sufficiency possible.

To aid and maintain recovery, the physical therapist also provides education to involve patients in their own care. The educational program may include exercises, posture reeducation, and relaxation practices. In many cases, the patient's family is involved in the educational program to provide emotional support or physical assistance as needed. These activities evolve into a continuum of self-care when the patient is discharged from the physical therapy program.

Physical therapists provide care for many types of patients of all ages. This includes working with burn victims to prevent abnormal scarring and loss of movement, with stroke victims to regain movement and independent living, with cancer patients to relieve discomfort, and with cardiac patients to improve endurance and achieve independence. Physical therapists also provide preventive exercise programs, postural improvement, and physical conditioning to individuals who perceive the need to promote their own health and well-being.

Physical therapists should have a creative approach to their work. No two patients respond the same way to

exactly the same kind of treatment. The challenge is to find the right way to encourage the patient to make progress, to respond to treatment, to feel a sense of achievement, and to refuse to become discouraged if progress is slow.

Many physical therapists acquire specialized knowledge through clinical experience and educational preparation in specialty areas of practice, such as cardiopulmonary physical therapy, clinical electrophysiologic physical therapy, neurologic physical therapy, orthopedic physical therapy, pediatric physical therapy, geriatric physical therapy, and sports physical therapy.

REQUIREMENTS
High School

While you are in high school you can begin to prepare for this career by taking college preparatory classes. These should include biology, chemistry, physics, health, and mathematics. Because so much of this work involves direct contact with clients, you should improve your people skills as well as your communication skills by taking psychology, sociology, and English classes. Also, take computer science courses so that you are computer literate. Statistics, history, and a foreign language are also beneficial.

Postsecondary Training

Physical therapists attain their professional skills through extensive education that takes place both in the classroom and in clinical settings. You should attend a school accredited by the Commission on Accreditation in Physical Therapy Education (CAPTE) to receive the most thorough education. CAPTE now only accredits schools offering postbaccalaureate degrees (master's and doctorate degrees), and you will need one of these degrees to practice physical therapy. Previously, CAPTE had accredited bachelor's degree programs; however, this change was made to give students an appropriate amount of time to study liberal arts as well as a physical therapy curriculum. Course work should include classes in the humanities as well as those geared for the profession, such as anatomy, human growth and development, and therapeutic procedures. Clinical experience is done as supervised fieldwork in such settings as hospitals, home care agencies, and nursing homes. According to the APTA, there are 43 accredited programs offering master's degrees and 166 offering doctorates in physical therapy. Visit the APTA's Web site (http://www.apta.org) for a listing of accredited programs.

Certification or Licensing

Specialist certification of physical therapists, while not a requirement for employment, is a desirable advanced credential. The American Board of Physical Therapy Specialties, an appointed group of the American Physical Therapy Association, certifies physical therapists who demonstrate specialized knowledge and advanced clinical proficiency in a specialty area of physical therapy practice and who pass a certifying examination. The seven areas of specialization are cardiovascular and pulmonary, clinical electrophysiologic, neurologic, orthopaedics, pediatrics, geriatrics, and sports.

Upon graduating from an accredited physical therapy educational program, all physical therapists must successfully complete a national examination. Other licensing requirements vary by state. You will need to check with the licensing board of the state in which you hope to work for specific information.

Other Requirements

Successful physical therapists enjoy working with people and helping others to feel better, both physically and emotionally. They need creativity and patience to determine a treatment plan for each client and to help them achieve treatment goals. Physical therapists must also be committed to lifelong learning because new developments in technology and medicine mean that therapists must continually update their knowledge. It is also a plus to have a positive attitude and an outgoing personality.

EXPLORING

Your first step in exploring this field could be to talk with a physical therapist in your community about the work. Your school guidance counselor should be able to help you arrange for such an information interview. Hands-on experience is important to get because schools that you apply to will take this into consideration. This experience will also help you decide how well you like working with people who are sometimes in pain or confused. One possibility is to volunteer at a physical therapy program. If such an opening is not available, try volunteering at a local hospital, nursing home, or other care facility to gain experience working in these settings. You can also look for volunteer opportunities or summer jobs at camps for the disabled. Paid

part-time positions may also be available as a hospital orderly or aide to a physical therapist.

EMPLOYERS

Hospitals employ about 60 percent of physical therapists. According to the U.S. Department of Labor, the rest work in settings such as offices of physicians, private physical therapy offices, community health centers, sports facilities, nursing homes, home health care, and schools. Physical therapists may be involved in research or teach at colleges and universities. Veterans Administration hospitals and other government agencies also hire physical therapists. Some physical therapists are self-employed. Approximately 173,000 physical therapists are employed in the United States.

STARTING OUT

Physical therapy graduates may obtain jobs through their college career services offices or by answering ads in any of a variety of professional journals. They can apply in person or send letters and resumes to hospitals, medical centers, rehabilitation facilities, and other places that hire physical therapists. Some find jobs through the APTA.

ADVANCEMENT

In a hospital or other health care facility, one may rise from being a staff physical therapist to being the chief physical therapist and then director of the department. Administrative responsibilities are usually given to those physical therapists who have had several years of experience plus the personal qualities that prepare them for undertaking this kind of assignment.

After serving in a hospital or other institution for several years, some physical therapists open up their own practices or go into a group practice, with both often paying higher salaries.

EARNINGS

Salaries for physical therapists depend on experience and type of employer. Physical therapists earned an annual average salary of $66,200 in 2006, according to the U.S. Department of Labor. Fifty percent averaged between $55,030 and $78,080; the top 10 percent earned $94,810 or more a year. In 2006, the top-paying industries for physical therapists were child day care services, $81,310; home health care services, $75,670; employment services, $69,290; and nursing care facilities, $68,870.

Salaried physical therapists also enjoy fringe benefits such as paid vacation, 401 (k) savings plans, and medical and dental insurance.

WORK ENVIRONMENT

The typical physical therapist works approximately 40 hours each week, including Saturdays. Patient sessions may be brief or may last an hour or more. Usually, treatment is on an individual basis, but occasionally therapy may be given in groups when the patients' problems are similar.

OUTLOOK

Employment for physical therapists is expected to grow much faster than the average for all occupations through 2016, according to the U.S. Department of Labor. One reason for this strong growth is the fact that the median age of the American population is rising, and this older demographic group develops a higher number of medical conditions that cause physical pain and disability. The Department of Labor reports that employment should be especially strong in acute hospital, orthopedic, and rehabilitation settings, where elderly patients are most often treated. Also, advances in medical technology save more people, who then require physical therapy. For example, as more trauma victims and newborns with birth defects survive, the need for physical therapists will rise. Another reason is the public's growing interest in physical fitness, which has resulted in an increasing number of athletic injuries requiring physical therapy. In industry and fitness centers, a growing interest in pain and injury prevention also has created new opportunities for physical therapists.

Employment prospects for physical therapists should continue to be good into the next decade. If enrollment in accredited physical therapy programs remains at the current level, there will be more openings for physical therapists than qualified individuals to fill them.

FOR MORE INFORMATION

The APTA offers the brochure A Future in Physical Therapy, *a directory of accredited schools, certification, and general career information.*

American Physical Therapy Association (APTA)
1111 North Fairfax Street
Alexandria, VA 22314-1488
Tel: 800-999-2782
http://www.apta.org

For information on accredited programs, contact
**Commission on Accreditation in
    Physical Therapy Education**
http://www.apta.org/CAPTE

PHYSICAL THERAPY ASSISTANTS

OVERVIEW

Physical therapy assistants help to restore physical function in people with injury, birth defects, or disease. They assist physical therapists with a variety of techniques, such as exercise, massage, heat, and water therapy.

Physical therapy assistants work directly under the supervision of physical therapists. They teach and help patients improve functional activities required in their daily lives, such as walking, climbing, and moving from one place to another. The assistants observe patients during treatments, record the patients' responses and progress, and report these to the physical therapist, either orally or in writing. They fit patients for and teach them to use braces, artificial limbs, crutches, canes, walkers, wheelchairs, and other devices. They may make physical measurements to assess the effects of treatments or to evaluate patients' range of motion, length and girth of body parts, and vital signs. Physical therapy assistants act as members of a team and regularly confer with other members of the physical therapy staff. There are approximately 60,000 physical therapy assistants employed in the United States.

THE JOB

Physical therapy personnel work to prevent, diagnose, and rehabilitate, to restore physical function, prevent permanent disability as much as possible, and help people achieve their maximum attainable performance. For many patients, this objective involves daily living skills, such as eating, grooming, dressing, bathing, and other basic movements that unimpaired people do automatically without thinking.

Physical therapy may alleviate conditions such as muscular pain, spasm, and weakness, joint pain and stiffness, and neuromuscular incoordination. These conditions may be caused by any number of disorders, including fractures, burns, amputations, arthritis, nerve or muscular injuries, trauma, birth defects, stroke, multiple sclerosis, and cerebral palsy. Patients of all ages receive physical therapy services; they may be severely disabled or they may need only minimal therapeutic intervention.

Physical therapy assistants always work under the direction of a qualified physical therapist. Other members of the health team may be a physician or surgeon, nurse, occupational therapist, psychologist, or vocational counselor. Each of these practitioners helps establish and achieve realistic goals consistent with the patient's individual needs. Physical therapy assistants help perform tests to evaluate disabilities and determine the most suitable treatment for the patient; then, as the treatment progresses, they routinely report the patient's condition to the physical therapist. If they observe a patient having serious problems during treatment, the assistants notify the therapist as soon as possible. Physical therapy assistants generally perform complicated therapeutic procedures decided by the physical therapist; however, assistants may initiate routine procedures independently.

These procedures may include physical exercises, which are the most varied and widely used physical treatments. Exercises may be simple or complicated, easy or strenuous, active or passive. Active motions are performed by the patient alone and strengthen or train muscles. Passive exercises involve the assistant moving the body part through the motion, which improves mobility of the joint but does not strengthen muscle. For example, for a patient with a fractured arm, both active and passive exercise may be appropriate. The passive exercises may be designed to maintain or increase the range of motion in the shoulder, elbow, wrist, and finger joints, while active resistive exercises strengthen muscles weakened by disuse. An elderly patient who has suffered a stroke may need guided exercises aimed at keeping the joints mobile, regaining the function of a limb, walking, or climbing stairs. A child with cerebral palsy who would otherwise never walk may be helped to learn coordination exercises that enable crawling, sitting balance, standing balance, and, finally, walking.

Patients sometimes perform exercises in bed or immersed in warm water. Besides its usefulness in alleviating stiffness or paralysis, exercise also helps to improve circulation, relax tense muscles, correct posture, and aid the breathing of patients with lung problems.

Other treatments that physical therapy assistants may administer include massages, traction for patients with neck or back pain, ultrasound and various kinds of heat treatment for diseases such as arthritis that inflame joints or nerves, cold applications to reduce swelling, pain, or hemorrhaging, and ultraviolet light.

Physical therapy assistants train patients to manage devices and equipment that they either need temporarily or permanently. For example, they instruct patients how to walk with canes or crutches using proper gait and maneuver well in a wheelchair. They also teach patients how to apply, remove, care for, and cope with splints, braces, and artificial body parts.

SCHOOL SUBJECTS
Biology, Health

PERSONAL SKILLS
Helping/Teaching, Mechanical/Manipulative

MINIMUM EDUCATION LEVEL
Associate's Degree

CERTIFICATION OR LICENSING
Required by Certain States

WORK ENVIRONMENT
Primarily Indoors, Primarily One Location

Physical therapy personnel must often work on improving the emotional state of patients, preparing them psychologically for treatments. The overwhelming sense of hopelessness and lack of confidence that afflict many disabled patients can reduce the patients' success in achieving improved functioning. The health team must be attuned to both the physical and nonphysical aspects of patients to assure that treatments are most beneficial. Sometimes physical therapy personnel work with patients' families to educate them on how to provide simple physical treatments and psychological support at home.

In addition, physical therapy assistants may perform office duties: They schedule patients, keep records, handle inventory, and order supplies. These duties may also be handled by *physical therapy aides*. Aides may also be required to keep treatment areas clean and ready for each new patient's therapy, as well as transport patients, when necessary, to and from treatment areas.

REQUIREMENTS
High School

Does this work sound interesting to you? If so, you can prepare for it while still in high school by taking biology, health, and mathematics classes. Psychology, sociology, and even social studies classes will be helpful, because they will give you an understanding of people. And, since you will be working so closely with clients as well as other professionals, you will need excellent communication skills. Therefore, take English courses and other classes that will improve these skills, such as speech. It is also a good idea to take computer science classes since almost all employers require their employees to have computer communication skills.

Postsecondary Training

In order to do this work, you will need a degree from an accredited physical therapy assistant program. Accreditation is given by the Commission on Accreditation in Physical Therapy Education (CAPTE), which is part of the American Physical Therapy Association (APTA). These programs, leading to an associate's degree, are usually offered at community and junior colleges. Typically lasting two years, the programs combine academic instruction with a period of supervised clinical practice in a physical therapy setting. According to the APTA, there are 233 accredited schools offering assistant programs as well as several programs in development. Information about these programs can be found on APTA's Web site, http://www.apta.org. The first year of study is typically taken up with general course work, while the second year is focused on professional classes. Classes you can expect to take include mathematics, biology, applied physical sciences, psychology, human growth and development, and physical therapist assistant procedures such as massage, therapeutic exercise, and heat and cold therapy.

In recent years, admission to accredited programs has been fairly competitive, with three to five applicants for each available opening.

Some physical therapy assistants begin their careers while in the armed forces, which operate training programs. While these programs are not sufficient for state licensure and do not award degrees, they can serve as an excellent introduction to the field for students who later enter more complete training programs.

Certification or Licensing

More than 40 states require regulation of physical therapy assistants in the form of registration, certification, or licensure. Typically, graduation from an CAPTE-accredited program and passing a written exam are needed for licensing. Because requirements vary by state, you will need to check with your state's licensure board for specific information. Physical therapy aides are not typically licensed.

Other Requirements

Physical therapy assistants must have stamina, patience, and determination, but at the same time they must be able to establish personal relationships quickly and successfully. They should genuinely like and understand people, both under normal conditions and under the stress of illness. An outgoing personality is highly desirable as is the ability to instill confidence and enthusiasm in patients. Much of the work of physical retraining and restoring is very repetitive, and assistants may not perceive any progress for long periods of time. At times patients may seem unable or unwilling to cooperate. In such cases, assistants need boundless patience, to appreciate small gains and build on them. When restoration to good health is not attainable, physical therapist assistants must help patients adjust to a different way of life and find ways to cope with their situation. Creativity is an asset to devising methods that help disabled people achieve greater self-sufficiency. Assistants should be flexible and open to suggestions offered by their coworkers and willing and able to follow directions closely.

Because the job can be physically demanding, physical therapy assistants must be reasonably strong and enjoy physical activity. Manual dexterity and good coordination are needed to adjust equipment and assist patients. Assistants should be able to lift, climb, stoop, and kneel.

EXPLORING

While still in high school, you can experience this work by getting summer or part-time employment or by volunteering in the physical therapy department of a hospital or clinic. Also, many schools, both public and private, have volunteer assistance programs for work with disabled students. You can also gain direct experience by working with disabled children in a summer camp.

These opportunities will provide you with direct job experience that will help you determine if you have the personal qualities necessary for this career. If you are unable to get direct experience, you should talk to a physical therapist or physical therapy assistant during career-day programs at your high school. It may also be possible for you to arrange to visit a physical therapy department, watch the staff at work, and ask questions.

EMPLOYERS

Physical therapy assistants are employed in hospitals, rehabilitation centers, schools for those with disabilities, nursing homes, community and government health agencies, physicians' or physical therapists' offices, and facilities for the mentally disabled. There are approximately 60,000 physical therapy assistants and 46,000 physical therapy aides employed in the United States.

STARTING OUT

One good way to find a job is to access the resources available at the career services office of your educational institution. Alternatively, you can apply to the physical therapy departments of local hospitals, rehabilitation centers, extended-care facilities, and other potential employers. Openings are listed in the classified ads of newspapers, professional journals, and with private and public employment agencies. In locales where training programs have produced many physical therapy assistants, competition for jobs may be keen. In such cases, you may want to widen your search to areas where there is less competition, especially suburban and rural areas.

ADVANCEMENT

With experience, physical therapy assistants are often given greater responsibility and better pay. In large health care facilities, supervisory possibilities may open up. In small institutions that employ only one physical therapist, the physical therapist assistant may eventually take care of all the technical tasks that go on in the department, within the limitations of his or her training and education.

Physical therapy assistants with degrees from accredited programs are generally in the best position to gain advancement in any setting. They sometimes decide to earn a postbaccalaureate degree in physical therapy and become fully qualified physical therapists.

EARNINGS

Salaries for physical therapy assistants vary considerably depending on geographical location, employer, and level of experience. Physical therapy assistants earned median annual salaries of $41,360 in 2006, according to the U.S. Department of Labor. The lowest 10 percent earned less than $26,190; the highest 10 percent earned more than $57,220. According to Salary.com, the national average median salary for physical therapy assistants in 2008 was $41,291. Salaries ranged from less than $33,154 to $49,183 or more.

Fringe benefits vary, although they usually include paid holidays and vacations, health insurance, and pension plans.

WORK ENVIRONMENT

Physical therapy is generally administered in pleasant, clean, well-lighted, and well-ventilated surroundings. The space devoted to physical therapy services is often large, in order to accommodate activities such as gait training and exercises and procedures requiring equipment. Some procedures are given at patients' bedsides.

In the physical therapy department, patients come and go all day, many in wheelchairs, on walkers, canes, crutches, or stretchers. The staff tries to maintain a purposeful, harmonious, congenial atmosphere as they and the patients work toward the common goal of restoring physical efficacy.

The work can be exhausting. Physical therapy assistants may be on their feet for hours at a time, and they may have to move heavy equipment, lift patients, and help them to stand and walk. Most assistants work daytime hours, five days a week, although some positions require evening or weekend work. Some assistants work on a part-time basis.

The combined physical and emotional demands of the job can exert a considerable strain. Prospective assistants would be wise to seek out some job experience related to physical therapy so that they have a practical understanding of their psychological and physical capacities. By exploring their suitability for the work, they can make a better commitment to the training program.

Job satisfaction can be great for physical therapy assistants as they can see how their efforts help to make people's lives much more rewarding.

OUTLOOK

Employment prospects are very good for physical therapy assistants; the U.S. Department of Labor predicts that employment will grow much faster than the average for all careers through 2016. Many new positions for physical therapy assistants and aides are expected to open up as hospital programs that aid the disabled expand and as long-term facilities seek to offer residents more adequate services.

A major contributing factor is the increasing number of Americans aged 65 and over. This group tends to suffer a disproportionate amount of the accidents and chronic illnesses that necessitate physical therapy services. Many from the baby boom generation are reaching the age common for heart attacks, thus creating a need for more cardiac and physical rehabilitation. Legislation that requires appropriate public education for all disabled children also may increase the demand for physical therapy services. As more adults engage in strenuous physical exercise, more musculoskeletal injuries will result, thus increasing demand for physical therapy services.

FOR MORE INFORMATION

For additional education and career information, contact

American Physical Therapy Association
1111 North Fairfax Street
Alexandria, VA 22314-1488
Tel: 800-999-2782
http://www.apta.org

For information on accredited programs, contact

Commission on Accreditation in Physical Therapy Education
Email: accreditation@apta.org
http://www.apta.org/CAPTE

PHYSICIAN ASSISTANTS

OVERVIEW

Physician assistants (PAs) practice medicine under the supervision of licensed doctors of medicine or osteopathy, providing various health care services to patients. Much of the work they do was formerly limited to physicians. There are approximately 66,000 physician assistants employed in the United States.

THE JOB

Physician assistants help physicians provide medical care to patients. PAs may be assigned a variety of tasks; they may take medical histories of patients, do complete routine physical examinations, order laboratory tests, draw blood samples, give injections, decide on diagnoses, choose treatments, and assist in surgery. Although the duties of PAs vary by state, they always work under the supervision and direction of a licensed physician. The extent of the PA's duties depends on the specific laws of the state and the practices of the supervising physician, as well as the experience and abilities of the PA. PAs work in a variety of health care settings, including hospitals, clinics, physician's offices, and federal, state, and local agencies.

More than 34 percent of all PAs specialize in family/general medicine, general internal medicine, and general pediatrics. Nearly 25 percent of PAs are in general surgery or surgical subspecialties, more than 10 percent specialize in emergency medicine, and more than 11 percent are in internal medicine subspecialties.

All 50 states, the District of Columbia, and Guam allow PAs to prescribe medicine to patients; Indiana is the only state that does not authorize PAs to prescribe medication. Physician assistants may be known by other occupational titles such as *child health associates*, *MEDEX*, *physician associates*, *anesthesiologist's assistants*, or *surgeon's assistants*.

PAs are skilled professionals who assume a great deal of responsibility in their work. By handling various medical tasks for their physician employers, PAs allow physicians more time to diagnose and treat more severely ill patients.

REQUIREMENTS

High School

Since a physician assistant needs to be good with numbers and understand how the human body works, anyone interested in this job can begin preparing in high school by taking math classes and science classes, such as biology and chemistry, as well as health classes. English and social science classes, such as psychology, will also help you improve your communication skills and give you an understanding of people.

Also, keep in mind that it's not too early to gain some experience in the health care field. Many postsecondary institutions take into consideration an applicant's hands-on experience when deciding whom to accept, so look for paid or volunteer positions in your community.

Postsecondary Training

Most states require that PAs complete an educational program approved by the Accreditation Review Commission on Education for the Physician Assistant (http://www.arc-pa.org). There are approximately 140 fully or provisionally accredited PA programs. Admissions requirements vary, but two years of college courses in science or health, and some health care experience, are usually the minimum requirements. The American Academy of Physician Assistants (AAPA) reports that a majority of all students accepted, however, have their bachelor's or master's degrees. Most educational programs last 24 to 32 months, although some last only one year and others may last as many as three years.

The first six to 24 months of most programs involve classroom instruction in human anatomy, physiology, microbiology, clinical pharmacology, applied psychology, clinical medicine, and medical ethics. In the last months of most programs, students engage in supervised clinical work, usually including assignments, or rotations, in various branches of medicine, such as family practice, pediatrics, and emergency medicine.

Graduates of these programs may receive a certificate, an associate's degree, a bachelor's degree, or a master's degree; most programs, however, offer graduates a bachelor's degree. The one MEDEX program that presently exists (at the University of Washington, http://www.washington.edu/medicine/som/depts/medex) lasts only 18 months. It is designed for medical corpsmen, registered nurses, and others who have had extensive patient-care experience. MEDEX students usually obtain most of their clinical experience by working with a physician who will hire them after graduation.

PA programs are offered in a variety of educational and health care settings, including colleges and universities, medical schools and centers, hospitals, and the armed forces. State laws and regulations dictate the scope of the PA's duties, and, in all but a few states, PAs must be graduates of an approved training program.

Certification or Licensing

Currently, all states require that PAs be certified by the National Commission on Certification of Physician Assistants (NCCPA). To become certified, applicants must be graduates of an accredited PA program and pass the Physician Assistant National Certifying Examination (PANCE). The examination consists of three parts: The first part tests general medical knowledge, the second section tests the PA's specialty—either primary care or surgery—and the third part tests for practical clinical knowledge. After successfully completing the examination, physician assistants can use the credential, physician assistant-certified.

Once certified, PAs are required to complete 100 hours of continuing medical education courses every two years, and in addition must pass a recertification examination every six years. Besides NCCPA certification, most states also require that PAs register with the state medical board. State rules and regulations vary greatly concerning the work of PAs, and applicants are advised to study the laws of the state in which they wish to practice.

Licensing for physician assistants varies by state. New graduates should contact their state's licensing board to find out about specific requirements. Some states grant temporary licenses to physician assistants who have applied for the PANCE. For permanent licensure, most states require verification of certification or an official record of their exam scores.

SCHOOL SUBJECTS
Biology, Health

PERSONAL SKILLS
Helping/Teaching, Technical/Scientific

MINIMUM EDUCATION LEVEL
Some Postsecondary Training

CERTIFICATION OR LICENSING
Required by All States

WORK ENVIRONMENT
Primarily Indoors, Primarily Multiple Locations

Other Requirements

To be a successful physician assistant, you must be able to work well with many different kinds of people, from the physician who supervises you to the many different patients you see every day. In addition to being a caring individual, you should also have a strong desire to continue learning in order to keep up with the latest medical procedures and recertification requirements. Since ill individuals depend on a physician assistant's decisions, anyone interested in this job should have leadership skills and self-confidence as well as compassion.

EXPLORING

If you are interested in exploring the profession, talk with school guidance counselors, practicing PAs, PA students, and various health care employees at local hospitals and clinics. You can also obtain information by contacting one of the organizations listed at the end of this chapter. Working as a volunteer in a hospital, clinic, or nursing home is a good way to get exposure to the health care profession. In addition, while in college, you may be able to obtain summer jobs as a hospital orderly, nurse assistant, or medical clerk. Such jobs can help you assess your interest in and suitability for work as a PA before you apply to a PA program.

EMPLOYERS

PAs work in a variety of health care settings. According to the AAPA, 55 percent of all PAs are employed by single physicians or group practices; 23 percent are employed by hospitals; and 9 percent work for some type of government agency with the Department of Veterans' Affairs being the largest government employer of PAs. They are also employed by clinics, nursing homes, long-term care facilities, and prisons. Many areas lacking quality medical care personnel, such as remote rural areas and the inner city, are hiring PAs to meet their needs. Approximately 66,000 physician assistants are employed in the United States.

STARTING OUT

PAs must complete their formal training programs before entering the job market. Once they complete their studies, PA students can utilize the placement services of their schools to locate jobs. PAs may also seek employment at hospitals, clinics, medical offices, or other health care settings. Information about jobs with the federal government can be obtained by contacting the Office of Personnel Management's Web site at http://www.usajobs.opm.gov.

ADVANCEMENT

Since the PA profession is still quite new, formal lines of advancement have not yet been established. There are still several ways to advance. Hospitals, for example, do not employ head PAs. Those with experience can assume more responsibility at higher pay, or they move on to employment at larger hospitals and clinics. Some PAs go back to school for additional education to practice in a specialty area, such as surgery, urology, or ophthalmology.

EARNINGS

Salaries of PAs vary according to experience, specialty, and employer. The U.S. Department of Labor reports that the lowest paid 10 percent of all physician assistants earned less than $43,100 in 2006, and the highest paid 10 percent earned $102,230 or more. The department also reports that physician assistants employed in offices and clinics of medical doctors had mean annual earnings of $74,130 in 2006, while those employed in hospitals earned $71,300. The median annual average salary for all PAs was $82,223 in 2007, according to the 2007 AAPA Physician Assistant Census Survey. PAs are well compensated compared with other occupations that have similar training requirements. Most PAs receive health and life insurance among other benefits.

WORK ENVIRONMENT

Most work settings are comfortable and clean, although, like physicians, PAs spend a good part of their day standing or walking. The workweek varies according to the employment setting. A few emergency room PAs may work 24-hour shifts, twice a week; others work 12-hour shifts, three times a week. PAs who work in physicians' offices, hospitals, or clinics may have to work weekends, nights, and holidays. PAs employed in clinics, however, usually work five-day, 40-hour weeks.

OUTLOOK

Employment for physician assistants, according to the U.S. Department of Labor, is expected to increase much faster than the average for all occupations through 2016 as the health care industry uses more physician assistants to reduce costs. Opportunities will be best in rural areas and inner city clinics—settings which often have trouble attracting the most qualified candidates.

The role of the PA in delivering health care has also expanded over the past decade. PAs have taken on new duties and responsibilities, and they now work in a variety of health care settings. The Department of Labor reports that physician assistants should have good opportunities in hospitals, academic medical centers, public clinics, prisons, and inpatient teaching hospitals.

FOR MORE INFORMATION

For more information on PA careers, educational programs, and scholarships, contact
American Academy of Physician Assistants
950 North Washington Street
Alexandria, VA 22314-1552
Tel: 703-836-2272
Email: aapa@aapa.org
http://www.aapa.org

For information on certification, contact
National Commission on Certification of Physician Assistants
12000 Findley Road, Suite 200
Duluth, GA 30097-1409
Tel: 678-417-8100
Email: nccpa@nccpa.net
http://www.nccpa.net

For industry information and to subscribe ($35 fee) to the PA Programs Directory, contact
Physician Assistant Education Association
300 North Washington Street, Suite 505
Alexandria, VA 22314-2544
Tel: 703-548-5538
Email: info@paeaonline.org
http://www.paeaonline.org

❑ PHYSICIANS

OVERVIEW

Physicians diagnose, prescribe medicines for, and otherwise treat diseases and disorders of the human body. A physician may also perform surgery and often specializes in one aspect of medical care and treatment. Physicians hold either a doctor of medicine (M.D.) or osteopathic medicine (D.O.) degree. Approximately 633,000 M.D.'s and D.O.'s are employed in the United States.

THE JOB

The greatest number of physicians are in private practice. They see patients by appointment in their offices and examining rooms, and visit patients who are confined to the hospital. In the hospital, they may perform operations or give other kinds of medical treatment. Some physicians also make calls on patients at home if the patient is not able to get to the physician's office or if the illness is an emergency.

Slightly more than 12 percent of physicians are general practitioners or family practitioners. They see patients of all ages and both sexes and will diagnose and treat those ailments that are not severe enough or unusual enough to require the services of a specialist. When special problems arise, however, the general practitioner will refer the patient to a specialist.

Not all physicians are engaged in private practice. Some are in academic medicine and teach in medical schools or teaching hospitals. Some are engaged only in research. Some are salaried employees of health maintenance organizations or other prepaid health care plans. Some are salaried hospital employees.

Some physicians, often called *medical officers*, are employed by the federal government, in such positions as public health, or in the service of the Department of Veterans Affairs. State and local governments also employ physicians for public health agency work. A large number of physicians serve with the armed forces, both in this country and overseas.

Industrial physicians or *occupational physicians* are employed by large industrial firms for two main reasons: to prevent illnesses that may be caused by certain kinds of work and to treat accidents or illnesses of employees. Although most industrial physicians may roughly be classified as general practitioners because of the wide variety of illnesses that they must recognize and treat, their knowledge must also extend to public health techniques and to understanding such relatively new hazards

as radiation and the toxic effects of various chemicals, including insecticides.

A specialized type of industrial or occupational physician is the *flight surgeon*. Flight surgeons study the effects of high-altitude flying on the physical condition of flight personnel. They place members of the flight staff in special low-pressure and refrigeration chambers that simulate high-altitude conditions and study the reactions on their blood pressure, pulse and respiration rate, and body temperature.

Another growing specialty is the field of nuclear medicine. Some large hospitals have a nuclear research laboratory, which functions under the direction of a *chief of nuclear medicine*, who coordinates the activities of the lab with other hospital departments and medical personnel. These physicians perform tests using nuclear isotopes and use techniques that let physicians see and understand organs deep within the body.

M.D.'s may become specialists in any of the 40 different medical care specialties, including allergy and immunology, anesthesiology, dermatology, emergency medicine, family medicine, internal medicine, medical genetics, neurology, nuclear medicine, obstetrics and gynecology, ophthalmology, otolaryngology, pathology, pediatrics, physical medicine and rehabilitation, preventive medicine, psychiatry, radiation oncology, radiology, and urology.

REQUIREMENTS
High School

The physician is required to devote many years to study before being admitted to practice. Interested high school

---

SCHOOL SUBJECTS
Biology, Health

PERSONAL SKILLS
Helping/Teaching, Technical/Scientific

MINIMUM EDUCATION LEVEL
Medical Degree

CERTIFICATION OR LICENSING
Required by All States

WORK ENVIRONMENT
Primarily Indoors, Primarily Multiple Locations

students should enroll in a college preparatory course, and take courses in English, languages (especially Latin), the humanities, social studies, and mathematics, in addition to courses in biology, chemistry, and physics.

Postsecondary Training

To begin a career as a physician you need to first enter a liberal arts program in an accredited undergraduate institution. Some colleges offer a premedical course, but a good general education, with as many science courses as possible and a major in biology or chemistry is considered adequate preparation for the study of medicine. Courses should include physics, biology, inorganic and organic chemistry, English, mathematics, and the social sciences.

College students should begin to apply to medical schools early in their senior year, so it is advisable to begin your research into schools as early as your freshman year. There are 126 accredited schools of medicine and 20 accredited schools of osteopathic medicine in the country. For more information, consult a copy of *Medical School Admission Requirements, United States and Canada,* available from the Association of American Medical Colleges or from your college library. It is an annual publication updated each spring. Read carefully the admissions requirements of the several medical schools to which you hope to apply to avoid making mistakes in choosing a graduate program.

Some students may be admitted to medical school after only three years of study in an undergraduate program. There are a few medical schools that award the bachelor's degree at the end of the first year of medical school study. This practice is becoming less common as more students seek admission to medical schools. Most premedical students plan to spend four years in an undergraduate program and to receive the bachelor's degree before entering the four-year medical school program.

During your second or third year in college, you should arrange with an adviser to take the Medical College Admission Test (MCAT). This test is given each spring and each fall at certain selected sites. Your adviser should know the date, place, and time; or you may contact the Association of American Medical Colleges. All medical colleges in the United States require this test for admission, and a student's MCAT score is one of the factors that is weighed in the decision to accept or reject any applicant. Because the test does not evaluate medical knowledge, most college students who are enrolled in liberal arts programs should not find it to be unduly difficult. The examination covers four areas: verbal facility, quantitative ability, knowledge of the humanities and social sciences, and knowledge of biology, chemistry, and physics.

You are encouraged to apply to at least three institutions to increase your chances of being accepted by one of them. Approximately 45 percent of qualified applicants to medical schools are admitted each year. To facilitate this process, the American Medical College Application Service (AMCAS) will check, copy, and submit applications to the medical schools you specify. More information about this service may be obtained from the AMCAS, premedical advisers, and medical schools.

In addition to the traditional medical schools, there are several schools of basic medical sciences that enroll medical students for the first two years (preclinical experience) of medical school. They offer a preclinical curriculum to students similar to that which is offered by a regular medical school. At the end of the two-year program, you can then apply to a four-year medical school for the final two years of instruction.

Although high scholarship is a determining factor in admitting a student to a medical school, it is actually only one of the criteria considered. By far the greatest number of successful applicants to medical schools are "B" students. Because admission is also determined by a number of other factors, including a personal interview, other qualities in addition to a high scholastic average are considered desirable for a prospective physician. High on the list of desirable qualities are emotional stability, integrity, reliability, resourcefulness, and a sense of service.

The average student enters medical school at age 21 or 22. Then you begin another four years of formal schooling. During the first two years of medical school, studies include human anatomy, biochemistry, physiology, pharmacology, psychology, microbiology, pathology, medical ethics, and laws governing medicine. Most instruction in the first two years is given through classroom lectures, laboratories, seminars, independent research, and the reading of textbook material and other types of literature. You also learn to take medical histories, examine patients, and recognize symptoms.

During the last two years in medical school, you become actively involved in the treatment process. You spend a large proportion of the time in the hospital as part of a medical team headed by a teaching physician who specializes in a particular area. Others on the team may be interns or residents. You are closely supervised as you learn techniques such as how to take a patient's medical history, how to conduct a physical examination, how to work in the laboratory, how to make a diagnosis, and how to keep all the necessary records.

As you rotate from one medical specialty to another, you obtain a broad understanding of each field. You are assigned to duty in internal medicine, pediatrics, psychiatry, obstetrics and gynecology, surgery, and other specialties.

In addition to this hospital work, you continue to take course work. You are responsible for assigned studies and also for some independent study.

Most states require all new M.D.'s to complete at least one year of postgraduate training, and a few require an internship plus a one-year residency. If you decide to specialize, you will spend from three to seven years in advanced residency training plus another two or more years of practice in the specialty. Then you must pass a specialty board examination to become a board-certified M.D. The residency years are stressful—residents often work 24-hour shifts and put in up to 80 hours per week.

For a teaching or research career, you may also earn a master's degree or a Ph.D. in a biology or chemistry subfield, such as biochemistry or microbiology.

Certification or Licensing

After receiving the M.D. degree, the new physician is required to take an examination to be licensed to practice. Every state requires such an examination. It is conducted through the board of medical examiners in each state. Some states have reciprocity agreements with other states so that a physician licensed in one state may be automatically licensed in another without being required to pass another examination. This is not true throughout the United States, however, so it is wise to find out about licensing procedures before planning to move. Board certification is also available in a variety of medical specialties. Those seeking to become board certified participate in residencies that last up to seven years and must pass an examination by a member board of the American Board of Medical Specialties or the American Osteopathic Association.

Other Requirements

You must have some plan for financing your long and costly education. You face a period of at least eight years after college when you will not be self-supporting. While still in school, you may be able to work only during summer vacations, because the necessary laboratory courses of the regular school year are so time consuming that little time is left for activities other than the preparation of daily lessons. Some scholarships and loans are available to qualified students.

If you work directly with patients you need to have great sensitivity to their needs. Interpersonal skills are important, even in isolated research laboratories, since you must work and communicate with other scientists. Since new technology and discoveries happen at such a rapid rate, you must continually pursue further education to keep up with new treatments, tools, and medicines.

EXPLORING

One of the best introductions to a career in health care is to volunteer at a local hospital, clinic, or nursing home. In this way it is possible to get a feel for what it is like to work around other health care professionals and patients and possibly determine exactly where your interests lie. As in any career, reading as much as possible about the profession, talking with a high school counselor, and interviewing those working in the field are other important ways to explore your interest. You can also visit Tomorrow's Doctors (http://www.aamc.org/students/start.htm), a Web site created by the Association of American Medical Colleges to help educate students about the field.

EMPLOYERS

There are about 633,000 M.D.'s and D.O.'s working in the United States. Physicians can find employment in a wide variety of settings, including hospitals, nursing homes, managed-care offices, prisons, schools and universities, research laboratories, trauma centers, clinics, and public health centers. Some are self-employed in their own or group practices. In the past, many physicians went into business for themselves, either by starting their own practice or by becoming a partner in an existing one. Few physicians—about 17 percent—are choosing to follow this path today. There are a number of reasons for this shift. Often, the costs of starting a practice or buying into an existing practice are too high. Most are choosing to take salaried positions with hospitals or groups of physicians.

Jobs for physicians are available all over the world, although licensing requirements may vary. In Third World countries, there is great demand for medical professionals of all types. Conditions, supplies, and equipment may be poor and pay is minimal, but there are great rewards in terms of experience. Many doctors fulfill part or all of their residency requirements by practicing in other countries.

Physicians interested in teaching may find employment at medical schools or university hospitals. There are also positions available in government agencies such as the Centers for Disease Control, the National Institutes of Health, and the Food and Drug Administration.

Pharmaceutical companies and chemical companies hire physicians to research and develop new drugs, instruments, and procedures.

STARTING OUT

There are no shortcuts to entering the medical profession. Requirements are an M.D. degree, a licensing examination, a one- or two-year internship, and a period of residency that may extend as long as five years (and seven years if they are pursuing board certification in a specialty).

Upon completing this program, which may take up to 15 years, physicians are then ready to enter practice. They may choose to open a solo private practice, enter a partnership practice, enter a group practice, or take a salaried job with a managed-care facility or hospital. Salaried positions are also available with federal and state agencies, the military, including the Department of Veterans Affairs, and private companies. Teaching and research jobs are usually obtained after other experience is acquired.

Most M.D.'s practice in urban areas near hospitals and universities.

ADVANCEMENT

Physicians who work in a managed-care setting or for a large group or corporation can advance by opening a private practice. The average physician in private practice does not advance in the accustomed sense of the word. Their progress consists of advancing in skill and understanding, in numbers of patients, and in income. They may be made a fellow in a professional specialty or elected to an important office in the American Medical Association or American Osteopathic Association. Teaching and research positions may also increase a physician's status.

Some physicians may become directors of a laboratory, managed-care facility, hospital department, or medical school program. Some may move into hospital administration positions.

A physician can achieve recognition by conducting research in new medicines, treatments, and cures, and publishing their findings in medical journals. Participation in professional organizations can also bring prestige.

A physician can advance by pursuing further education in a subspecialty or a second field such as biochemistry or microbiology.

EARNINGS

Physicians have among the highest average earnings of any occupational group. The level of income for any individual physician depends on a number of factors, such as region of the country, economic status of the patients, and the physician's specialty, skill, experience, professional reputation, and personality. The median income in 2008 for family practice physicians was $147,516 per year, according to Physician Search's annual survey. Pediatricians had median earnings of $149,754, and internal medicine physicians earned $160,318. Depending on area of practice, most physicians with at least three years of experience earned between $111,000 and $500,000 annually in 2008, with some surgical specialties paying more than $850,000 per year. According to the U.S. Department of Labor, the mean income in 2006 for family practitioners was $149,850; general surgeons, $184,150; anesthesiologists, $184,340; and obstetricians/gynecologists, $178,040. Physicians who are employed by the Department of Veterans Affairs earned starting salaries of about $110,000 or more based on years of experience and location of practice.

In 2006–07, the average first-year resident received a stipend of about $44,747 a year, depending on the type of residency, the size of the hospital, and the geographic area. Fifth-year residents earned about $52,372 a year. If the physician enters private practice, earnings during the first year may not be impressive. As the patients increase in number, however, earnings will also increase.

Salaried doctors usually earn fringe benefits such as health and dental insurance, paid vacations, and the opportunity to participate in retirement plans.

WORK ENVIRONMENT

The offices and examining rooms of most physicians are well equipped, attractive, well lighted, and well ventilated. There is usually at least one nurse-receptionist on the physician's staff, and there may be several nurses, a laboratory technician, one or more secretaries, a bookkeeper, or receptionist.

Physicians usually see patients by appointments that are scheduled according to individual requirements. They may reserve all mornings for hospital visits and surgery. They may see patients in the office only on certain days of the week.

Physicians spend much of their time at the hospital performing surgery, setting fractures, working in the emergency room, or visiting patients.

Physicians in private practice have the advantages of working independently, but more than one-third of all physicians worked an average of 60 hours or more per week in 2006. Also, they may be called from their homes or offices in times of emergency. Telephone calls may come at any hour of the day or night. It is difficult for physicians to plan leisure-time activities, because their plans may change without notice. One of the advantages of group practice is that members of the group rotate emergency duty.

The areas in most need of physicians are rural hospitals and medical centers. Because the physician is normally working alone, and covering a broad territory, the workday can be quite long with little opportunity for vacation. Because placement in rural communities has become so difficult, some towns are providing scholarship money to students who pledge to work in the community for a number of years.

Physicians in academic medicine or in research have regular hours, work under good physical conditions, and often determine their own workload. Teaching and research physicians alike are usually provided with the best and most modern equipment.

OUTLOOK

The U.S. Department of Labor reports that employment in this field is expected to grow faster than the average for all occupations through 2016. Population growth, particularly among the elderly, is a factor in the demand for physicians. Another factor contributing to the predicted increase is the widespread availability of medical insurance, through both private plans and public programs. More physicians will also be needed for medical research, public health, rehabilitation, and industrial medicine. New technology will allow physicians to perform more procedures to treat ailments once thought incurable.

Employment opportunities will be good for family practitioners and internists, geriatric and preventive care specialists, as well as general pediatricians. Rural and low-income areas are in need of more physicians, and there is a short supply of general surgeons and psychiatrists.

The shift in health care delivery from hospitals to outpatient centers and other nontraditional settings to contain rising costs may mean that more and more physicians will become salaried employees.

There will be considerable competition among newly trained physicians entering practice, particularly in large cities. Physicians willing to locate to inner cities and rural areas—where physicians are scarce—should encounter little difficulty.

FOR MORE INFORMATION

Visit the AAFP's Web site to access career information and other resources.

American Academy of Family Physicians (AAFP)
PO Box 11210
Shawnee Mission, KS 66207-1210
Tel: 800-274-2237
Email: contactcenter@aafp.org
http://www.aafp.org

For general information on health care careers, contact
American Medical Association
515 North State Street
Chicago, IL 60610-4320
Tel: 800-621-8335
http://www.ama-assn.org

For a list of accredited U.S. and Canadian medical schools and other education information, contact
Association of American Medical Colleges
2450 N Street, NW
Washington, DC 20037-1126
Tel: 202-828-0400
http://www.aamc.org

For information on careers and educational paths, visit
Tomorrow's Doctors
http://www.aamc.org/students/start.htm

PLUMBERS AND PIPEFITTERS

OVERVIEW

Plumbers and *pipefitters* assemble, install, alter, and repair pipes and pipe systems that carry water, steam, air, or other liquids and gases for sanitation and industrial purposes as well as other uses. Plumbers also install plumbing fixtures, appliances, and heating and refrigerating units. There are approximately 569,000 plumbers and pipefitters working in the United States.

SCHOOL SUBJECTS

Chemistry, Physics

PERSONAL SKILLS

Following Instructions, Mechanical/Manipulative

MINIMUM EDUCATION LEVEL

Apprenticeship

CERTIFICATION OR LICENSING

Required by Certain States

WORK ENVIRONMENT

Primarily Indoors, Primarily Multiple Locations

THE JOB

Because little difference exists between the work of the plumber and the pipefitter in most cases, the two are often considered to be one trade. However, some craftsworkers specialize in one field or the other, especially in large cities.

The work of pipefitters differs from that of plumbers mainly in its location and the variety and size of pipes used. Plumbers work primarily in residential and commercial buildings, whereas pipefitters are generally employed by large industrial concerns—such as oil refineries, refrigeration plants, and defense establishments—where more complex systems of piping are used. Plumbers assemble, install, and repair heating, water, and drainage systems, especially those that must be connected to public utilities systems. Some of their jobs include replacing burst pipes and installing and repairing sinks, bathtubs, water heaters, hot water tanks, garbage disposal units, dishwashers, and water softeners. Plumbers also may work on septic tanks, cesspools, and sewers. During the final construction stages of both commercial and residential buildings, plumbers install heating and air-conditioning units and connect radiators, water heaters, and plumbing fixtures.

Most plumbers follow set procedures in their work. After inspecting the installation site to determine pipe location, they cut and thread pipes, bend them to required angles by hand or machines, and then join them by means of welded, brazed, caulked, soldered, or threaded joints. To test for leaks in the system, they fill the pipes with water or air. Plumbers use a variety of tools, including hand tools such as wrenches, reamers, drills, braces and

bits, hammers, chisels, and saws; power machines that cut, bend, and thread pipes; gasoline torches; and welding, soldering, and brazing equipment.

Specialists include diesel engine pipefitters, *steamfitters* (who install pipe systems that facilitate the movement of gases or liquids under high pressure), *sprinklerfitters* (who install automatic fire sprinkler systems), ship- and boat-building coppersmiths, industrial-gas fitters, gas-main fitters, prefab plumbers, and pipe cutters.

REQUIREMENTS
High School

A high school diploma is especially important for getting into a good apprenticeship program. High school preparation should include courses in mathematics, chemistry, and physics, as well as some shop courses.

Postsecondary Training

To qualify as a plumber, a person must complete either a formal apprenticeship or an informal on-the-job training program. To be considered for the apprenticeship program, individuals must pass an examination administered by the state employment agency and have their qualifications approved by the local joint labor-management apprenticeship committee.

The apprenticeship program for plumbers consists of four or five years of carefully planned activity combining direct training with at least 144 hours of formal classroom instruction each year. The program is designed to give apprentices diversified training by having them work for several different plumbing or pipefitting contractors.

On-the-job training, on the other hand, usually consists of working for five or more years under the guidance of an experienced craftsworker. Trainees begin as helpers until they acquire the necessary skills and knowledge for more difficult jobs. Frequently, they supplement this practical training by taking trade (or correspondence) school courses.

Certification or Licensing

A license is required for plumbers in many places. To obtain this license, plumbers must pass a special examination to demonstrate their knowledge of local building codes as well as their all-around knowledge of the trade. To become a plumbing contractor in most places, a master plumber's license must be obtained.

Other Requirements

To be successful in this field, you should like to solve a variety of problems and should not object to being called on during evenings, weekends, or holidays to perform emergency repairs. As in most service occupations, plumbers should be able to get along well with all kinds of people. You should be a person who works well alone, but who can also direct the work of helpers and enjoy the company of those in the other construction trades.

EXPLORING

Although opportunities for direct experience in this occupation are rare for those in high school, there are ways to explore the field. Speaking to an experienced plumber or pipefitter will give you a clearer picture of day-to-day work in this field. Pursuing hobbies with a mechanical aspect will help you determine how much you like such hands-on work.

EMPLOYERS

Plumbers and pipefitters hold about 569,000 jobs. Approximately 55 percent work for plumbing, heating, and air-conditioning contractors engaged in new construction, repair, modernization, or maintenance work. Approximately 12 percent of plumbers and pipefitters are self-employed.

STARTING OUT

Applicants who wish to become apprentices usually contact local plumbing, heating, and air-conditioning contractors who employ plumbers, the state employment service bureau, or the local branch of the United Association of Journeymen and Apprentices of the Plumbing and Pipe Fitting Industry of the United States and Canada. Individual contractors or contractor associations often sponsor local apprenticeship programs. Apprentices very commonly go on to permanent employment with the firms with which they apprenticed.

ADVANCEMENT

If plumbers have certain qualities, such as the ability to deal with people and good judgment and planning skills, they may progress to such positions as supervisor or job estimator for plumbing or pipefitting contractors. If they work for a large industrial company, they may advance to the position of job superintendent. Many plumbers go into business for themselves. Eventually they may expand their activities and become contractors, employing other workers.

EARNINGS

Plumbers and pipefitters had median earnings of $42,770 in 2006, according to the U.S. Department of Labor. Wages ranged from less than $25,580 to $72,360 or more. Pay rates for apprentices usually start at 50 percent of the experienced worker's rate, and increase by 5 percent every six months until a rate of 95 percent is reached. Benefits for union workers usually include health insurance, sick time, and vacation pay, as well as pension plans.

WORK ENVIRONMENT

Most plumbers have a regular 40-hour workweek with extra pay for overtime. Unlike most of the other building trades, this field is little affected by seasonal factors. The work of the plumber is active and strenuous. Standing for prolonged periods and working in cramped or uncomfortable positions are often necessary. Possible risks include falls from ladders, cuts from sharp tools, and burns from hot pipes or steam. Working with clogged pipes and toilets can also be smelly.

OUTLOOK

Employment opportunities for plumbers (especially those with welding skills) are expected to be very good through 2016, according to the U.S. Department of Labor. This is one of the largest and top-paying careers in the construction industry, and many opportunities will be available. Construction projects are usually only short-term in nature and more plumbers will find steady work in renovation, repair, and maintenance. Since pipework is becoming more important in large industries, more workers will be needed for installation and maintenance work, especially where refrigeration and air-conditioning equipment are used. Pipefitters and steamfitters will enjoy good prospects as a result of the need for continued maintenance, as well as new construction, of factories, office buildings, and power plants. Changes in state laws regarding fire protection in businesses and homes should increase employment demand for sprinklerfitters. Employment opportunities fluctuate with local economic conditions, although the plumbing industry is less affected by economic trends than other construction trades.

FOR MORE INFORMATION

For more information about becoming a plumber or pipefitter, contact the following organizations:

Plumbing-Heating-Cooling Contractors Association
180 South Washington Street
PO Box 6808

Falls Church, VA 22046-2900
Tel: 800-533-7694
http://www.phccweb.org

United Association of Journeymen and Apprentices of the Plumbing and Pipe Fitting Industry of the United States and Canada
901 Massachusetts Avenue, NW
Washington, DC 20001-4397
Tel: 202-628-5823
http://www.ua.org

For information on state apprenticeship programs, visit
Employment & Training Administration
U.S. Department of Labor
http://www.doleta.gov

PRESCHOOL TEACHERS

OVERVIEW

Preschool teachers promote the general education of children under the age of five. They help students develop physically, socially, and emotionally, work with them on language and communications skills, and help cultivate their cognitive abilities. They also work with families to support parents in raising their young children and reinforcing skills at home. They plan and lead

---

SCHOOL SUBJECTS
Art, English, Family and Consumer Science

PERSONAL SKILLS
Communication/Ideas, Helping/Teaching

MINIMUM EDUCATION LEVEL
Some Postsecondary Training

CERTIFICATION OR LICENSING
Required for Certain Positions

WORK ENVIRONMENT
Primarily Indoors, Primarily One Location

---

activities developed in accordance with the specific ages and needs of the children they teach. It is the goal of all preschool teachers to help students develop the skills, interests, and individual creativity that they will use for the rest of their lives. Many schools and districts consider kindergarten teachers, who teach students five years of age, to be preschool teachers. For the purposes of this article, kindergarten teachers will be included in this category. There are approximately 430,000 preschool teachers and 170,000 kindergarten teachers in the United States.

THE JOB

Preschool teachers plan and lead activities that build on children's abilities and curiosity and aid them in developing skills and characteristics that help them grow. Because children develop at varying skill levels as well as have different temperaments, preschool teachers need to develop a flexible schedule with time allowed for music, art, playtime, academics, rest, and other activities.

Preschool teachers plan activities that encourage children to develop skills appropriate to their developmental needs. For example, they plan activities based on the understanding that a three-year-old child has different motor skills and reasoning abilities than a five-year-old child. They work with the youngest students on learning the days of the week and the recognition of colors, seasons, and animal names and characteristics; they help older students with number and letter recognition and even simple writing skills. Preschool teachers help children with basic, yet important, tasks like tying shoelaces and washing hands before eating. Attention to the individual needs of each child is vital: Preschool teachers need to be aware of these needs and capabilities, and when possible, adapt activities to the specific needs of the individual child. Self-confidence and the development of communication skills are encouraged in preschools. For example, teachers may give children simple art projects, such as finger painting, and have children show and explain their finished projects to the rest of the class. Show and tell, or "sharing time" as it is often called, gives students opportunities to speak and listen to others.

"A lot of what I teach is based on social skills," says June Gannon, a preschool teacher in Amherst, New Hampshire. "During our circle time, we say hello to one another, sing songs, have show and tell, talk about the weather and do calendar events. We then move on to language arts, which may include talking to children about rules, good listening, helping, sharing, etc., using puppets, work papers, games, and songs."

Preschool teachers adopt many parental responsibilities for the children. They greet the children in the morning and supervise them throughout the day. Often these responsibilities can be quite demanding and complicated. In harsh weather, for example, preschool teachers contend not only with boots, hats, coats, and mittens, but with the inevitable sniffles, colds, and generally cranky behavior that can occur in young children. For most children, preschool is their first time away from home and family for an extended period of time. A major portion of a preschool teacher's day is spent helping children adjust to being away from home and encouraging them to play together. This is especially true at the beginning of the school year. They may need to gently reassure children who become frightened or homesick.

In both full-day and half-day programs, preschool teachers supervise snack time, helping children learn how to eat properly and clean up after themselves. Proper hygiene is also stressed. Other activities include storytelling, music, and simple arts and crafts projects. Full-day programs involve a lunch period and at least one nap period. Programs usually have high-energy activities interspersed with calmer ones. Even though the children take naps, preschool teachers must be energetic throughout the day, ready to face with good cheer the many challenges and demands of young children.

Preschool teachers also work with the parents of each child. It is not unusual for parents to come to preschool and observe a child or go on a field trip with the class, and preschool teachers often take these opportunities to discuss the progress of each child as well as any specific problems or concerns. Scheduled meetings are available for parents who cannot visit the school during the day. Solutions to fairly serious problems are worked out in tandem with the parents, often with the aid of the director of the preschool, or in the case of an elementary school kindergarten, with the principal or headmaster.

Kindergarten teachers usually have their own classrooms, made up exclusively of five-year-olds. Although these teachers don't have to plan activities for a wide range of ages, they need to consider individual developmental interests, abilities, and backgrounds represented by the students. Kindergarten teachers usually spend more time helping students with academic skills than do other preschool teachers. While a teacher of a two-, three-, and four-year-old classroom may focus more on socializing and building confidence in students through play and activities, kindergarten teachers often develop activities that help five-year-olds acquire the skills they will need in grade school, such as introductory activities on numbers, reading, and writing.

REQUIREMENTS
High School

To prepare for this type of career, you should take developmental psychology, home economics, and classes that involve child care, such as family and consumer science. You'll also need a fundamental understanding of the general subjects you'll be introducing to preschool students, so take English, science, and math. Also, take classes in art, music, and theater to develop creative skills.

Postsecondary Training

Specific education requirements for preschool and kindergarten teachers vary from state to state and also depend on the specific guidelines of the school or district. Many schools and child care centers require preschool teachers to have a bachelor's degree in education or a related field, but others accept adults with a high school diploma and some childcare experience. Some preschool facilities offer on-the-job training to their teachers, hiring them as assistants or aides until they are sufficiently trained to work in a classroom alone. A college degree program should include coursework in a variety of liberal arts subjects, including English, history, and science as well as nutrition, child development, psychology of the young child, and sociology.

Several groups offer on-the-job training programs for prospective preschool teachers. For example, the American Montessori Society offers a career program for aspiring preschool teachers. This program requires a three-month classroom training period followed by one year of supervised on-the-job training.

Certification or Licensing

In some states, licensure may be required. Many states accept the child development associate credential (awarded by the Council for Professional Recognition) or an associate or bachelor's degree as sufficient requirements for work in a preschool facility. Individual state boards of education can provide specific licensure information. Kindergarten teachers working in public elementary schools almost always need teaching certification similar to that required by other elementary school teachers in the school. Other types of licensure or certification may be required, depending upon the school or district. These may include first-aid or cardiopulmonary resuscitation (CPR) training.

Other Requirements

Because young children look up to adults and learn through example, it is especially important that you serve as a good role model in this profession. "Remember how important your job is," June Gannon says. "Everything you say and do will affect these children." Gannon also emphasizes being respectful of the children and keeping a sense of humor. "I have patience and lots of heart for children," Gannon says. "You definitely need both."

EXPLORING

Preschools, daycare centers, and other childcare programs often hire high school students for part-time positions as aides. You may also find many volunteer opportunities to work with children. Check with your library or local literacy program about tutoring children and reading to preschoolers. Summer day camps or religious schools with preschool classes also hire high school students as counselors or counselors-in-training. Discussing the field with preschool teachers and observing in their classes are other good ways to discover specific job information and explore your aptitude for this career.

EMPLOYERS

There are approximately 430,000 preschool teachers employed in the United States, as well as 170,000 kindergarten teachers. Six of every 10 mothers of children under the age of six are in the labor force, and the number is rising. Both government and the private sector are working to fill the enormous need for quality childcare. Preschool teachers will find many job opportunities in private and public preschools, including daycare centers, government-funded learning programs, churches, and Montessori schools. They may find work in a small center, or with a large preschool with many students and classrooms. Preschool franchises, like Primrose Schools and Kids 'R' Kids International, are also providing more opportunities for preschool teachers.

STARTING OUT

Before becoming a preschool teacher, June Gannon gained a lot of experience in child care. "I have worked as a special education aide and have taken numerous classes in childhood education," she says. "I am a sign language interpreter and have taught deaf children in a public school inclusion program."

If you hope to become a preschool teacher, you can contact child care centers, nursery schools, Head Start programs, and other preschool facilities to identify job opportunities. Often jobs for preschool teachers are listed in the classified section of newspapers. In addition, many school districts and state boards of education maintain job listings of available teaching positions. If no permanent positions are available at preschools, you may be able to find opportunities to work as a substitute teacher. Most preschools and kindergartens maintain a substitute list and refer to it frequently.

ADVANCEMENT

Many teachers advance by becoming more skillful in what they do. Skilled preschool teachers, especially those with additional training, usually receive salary increases as they become more experienced. A few preschool teachers with administrative ability and an interest in administrative work advance to the position of director. Administrators need to have at least a master's degree in child development or a related field and have to meet any state or federal licensing regulations. Some become directors of Head Start programs or other government programs. A relatively small number of experienced preschool teachers open their own facilities. This entails not only the ability to be an effective administrator but also the knowledge of how to operate a business. Kindergarten teachers sometimes have the opportunity to earn more money by teaching at a higher grade level in the elementary school. This salary increase is especially true when a teacher moves from a half-day kindergarten program to a full-day grade school classroom.

EARNINGS

Although there have been some attempts to correct the discrepancies in salaries between preschool teachers and other teachers, salaries in this profession tend to be lower than teaching positions in public elementary and high schools. Because some preschool programs are only in the morning or afternoon, many preschool teachers work only part time. As part-time workers, they often do not receive medical insurance or other benefits and may get paid minimum wage to start.

According to the U.S. Department of Labor, preschool teachers earned a median salary of $22,680 a year in 2006. Annual salaries for these workers ranged from less than $14,870 to $39,960 or more. The Department of Labor reports that kindergarten teachers (which are classified separately from preschool teachers) earned median annual salaries of $43,580 in 2006. The lowest 10 percent earned less than $28,590, while the highest 10 percent earned $71,410 or more.

WORK ENVIRONMENT

Preschool teachers spend much of their workday on their feet in a classroom or on a playground. Facilities vary from a single room to large buildings. Class sizes also vary; some preschools serve only a handful of children, while others serve several hundred. Classrooms may be crowded and noisy, but anyone who loves children will enjoy all the activity. "The best part about working with children," June Gannon says, "is the laughter, the fun, the enjoyment of watching the children grow physically, emotionally, and intellectually."

Many children do not go to preschool all day, so work may be part time. Part-time employees generally work between 18 and 30 hours a week, while full-time employees work 35–40 hours a week. Part-time work gives the employee flexibility, and for many, this is one of the advantages of the job. Some preschool teachers teach both morning and afternoon classes, going through the same schedule and lesson plans with two sets of students.

OUTLOOK

Employment for preschool teachers is expected to increase much faster than the average for all occupations through 2016, according to the U.S. Department of Labor. Employment for kindergarten teachers is expected to grow faster than the average during this same time span. Specific job opportunities vary from state to state and depend on demographic characteristics and level of government funding. Jobs should be available at private child-care centers, nursery schools, Head Start facilities, public and private kindergartens, and laboratory schools connected with universities and colleges. In the past, the majority of preschool teachers were female, and although this continues to be the case, more males are becoming involved in early childhood education.

One-third of all child-care workers leave their centers each year, often because of the low pay and lack of benefits. This will mean plenty of job openings for preschool teachers and possibly improved benefit plans, as centers attempt to retain qualified preschool teachers.

Employment for all teachers, including preschool teachers, will vary by region and state. The U.S. Department of Labor predicts that southern and western states, particularly Nevada, Arizona, Texas, and Georgia, will have strong increases in enrollments, while schools located in the Northeast will have declining enrollment.

FOR MORE INFORMATION

For information on training programs, contact
American Montessori Society
281 Park Avenue South, 6th Floor
New York, NY 10010-6102
Tel: 212-358-1250
http://www.amshq.org

For information about certification, contact
Council for Professional Recognition
2460 16th Street, NW
Washington, DC 20009-3575
Tel: 800-424-4310
http://www.cdacouncil.org

For general information on preschool teaching careers, contact
National Association for the Education of Young Children
1313 L Street, NW, Suite 500
Washington, DC 20005-4110
Tel: 800-424-2460
http://www.naeyc.org

For information about student memberships and training opportunities, contact
National Association of Child Care Professionals
PO Box 90723
Austin, TX 78709-0723
Tel: 800-537-1118
Email: admin@naccp.org
http://www.naccp.org

PROFESSIONAL ATHLETES

OVERVIEW

Professional athletes participate in individual sports such as tennis, figure skating, golf, running, or boxing, competing against others to win prizes and money, while others compete on teams in football, basketball, hockey, baseball, soccer, or other sports.

SCHOOL SUBJECTS
Health, Physical Education

PERSONAL SKILLS
Following Instructions

MINIMUM EDUCATION LEVEL
High School Diploma

CERTIFICATION OR LICENSING
None Available

WORK ENVIRONMENT
Indoors and Outdoors, Primarily Multiple Locations

THE JOB

Unlike amateur athletes who play or compete in amateur circles for titles or trophies only, professional athletes compete to win titles, championships, and series and are paid for their work.

Competitions are organized by local, regional, national, and international organizations and associations whose primary functions are to promote the sport and sponsor competitive events. Within a professional sport there are usually different levels of competition based on age, ability, and gender. There are often different designations and events within one sport. Professional baseball, for example, is made up of the two major leagues (American and National) each made up of three divisions, East, Central, and West; and the minor leagues (single-A, double-A, triple-A). All of these teams are considered professional because the players are compensated for their work, but the financial rewards are the greatest in the major leagues. Tennis, for example, consists of doubles and singles, while track and field contains many different events, from field events such as the javelin and shot putt, to track events such as the 110-meter dash and the two-mile relay race. Athletes in these individual sports earn prize monies by winning particular events or competitions.

Athletes train year-round, on their own or with a coach, friend, parent, or trainer. In addition to stretching and exercising the specific muscles used in any given sport, athletes concentrate on developing excellent eating and sleeping habits that will help them remain in top condition throughout the year. Although certain sports have a particular season, most professional athletes train rigorously all year, varying the type and duration of their workouts to develop strength, cardiovascular ability, flexibility, endurance, speed, and quickness, as well as to focus on technique and control. Often, an athlete's training focuses less on the overall game or program that the athlete will execute, than on specific areas or details of that game or program. Figure skaters, for example, won't simply keep going through their entire long programs from start to finish but instead will focus on the jumps, turns, and hand movements that refine the program. Similarly, sprinters don't keep running only the sprint distances they race in during a meet; instead, they vary their workouts to include some distance work, some sprints, a lot of weight training to build strength, and maybe some mental exercises to build control and focus while in the starter's blocks. Tennis players routinely spend hours just practicing their forehand, down-the-line shots.

Professional teams train for most of the year, but unlike athletes in individual sports, the athletes who are members of a team usually have more of an off-season. The training programs of professional athletes differs according to the season. Following an off-season, most team sports have a training season, in which they begin to focus their workouts after a period of relative inactivity to develop or maintain strength, cardiovascular ability, flexibility, endurance, speed, and quickness, as well as to focus on technique and control. During the season, the team coach, physician, trainers, and physical therapists organize specific routines, programs, or exercises to target game skills as well as individual athletic weaknesses, whether skill-related or from injury.

Most team members specialize in a specific area of the game. In gymnastics, for example, the entire six-member team trains on all of the gymnastic apparatuses—balance beam, uneven bars, vault, and floor exercise—but usually each of the six gymnasts excels in only one or two areas. Those gymnasts who do excel in all four events are likely to do well in the individual, all-around title, which is a part of the team competition. Team members in football, basketball, baseball, soccer, and hockey all assume different positions, some of which change depending on whether or not the team is trying to score a goal (offensive positions) or prevent the opposition from scoring one (defensive positions). During team practices, athletes focus on their specific role in a game, whether that is defensive, offensive, or both. For example, a baseball or softball pitcher will spend some time running bases and throwing to other positions, but the majority of his or her time will most likely be spent practicing pitching.

Athletes often watch videotapes or films of their previous practices or competitions to see where they can improve their performance. They also study what the other competitors are doing in order to prepare strategies for winning.

REQUIREMENTS
High School

Most professional athletes demonstrate tremendous skill and interest in their sport well before high school. High school offers student athletes the opportunity to gain experience in the field in a structured and competitive environment. Under the guidance of a coach, you can begin developing suitable training programs for yourself and learn about health, nutrition, and conditioning issues.

High school also offers the opportunity to experiment with a variety of sports and a variety of positions within a sport. Most junior varsity and some varsity high school teams allow you to try out different positions and begin to discover whether you have more of an aptitude for the defensive dives of a goalie, the strong serves of a tennis player, or for the forwards' front-line action. High school coaches will help you learn to expand upon your strengths and abilities and develop yourself more fully as an athlete. High school is also an excellent time to begin developing the concentration powers, leadership skills, and good sportsmanship necessary for success in the field.

People who hope to become professional athletes should take a full load of high school courses including four years of English, math, and science as well as health and physical education. A solid high school education will help ensure success in college (often the next step in becoming a professional athlete) and may help you in earning a college athletic scholarship (although most athletic scholarships do not cover the full cost of tuition—especially at private, four-year colleges). A high school diploma will certainly give you something to fall back on if an injury, a change in career goals, or other circumstance prevents you from earning a living as an athlete.

Some individual sports such as tennis and gymnastics have professional competitors who are high school students. Teenagers in this situation often have private coaches with whom they practice both before and after going to school, and others are home-schooled as they travel to competitions.

Postsecondary Training

There are no formal education requirements for sports, although certain competitions and training opportunities are only available to those enrolled in four-year colleges and universities. Collegiate-level competitions are where most athletes in this area hone their skills; they may also compete in international or national competitions outside of college, but the chance to train and receive an education isn't one many serious athletes refuse. In fact, outstanding ability in athletics is the way many students pay for their college educations. Given the chances of striking it rich financially, an education (especially a free one) is a wise investment and one fully supported by most professional sports organizations.

College athletes major in everything from communications to pre-med and enjoy careers as coaches, broadcasters, teachers, doctors, actors, and business people, to name a few. As with high school sports, college athletes must maintain certain academic standards in order to be permitted to compete in intercollegiate play.

Other Requirements

If you want to be a professional athlete, you must be fully committed to succeeding. You must work almost non-stop to improve your conditioning and skills and not give up when you don't succeed as quickly or as easily as you had hoped. And even then, because the competition is so fierce, the goal of earning a living as a professional athlete is still difficult to reach. For this reason, professional athletes must not get discouraged easily. They must have the self-confidence and ambition to keep working and keep trying. Professional athletes must also have a love for their sport that compels them to want to reach their fullest potential.

EXPLORING

If you are interested in pursuing a career in professional sports you should start participating in that sport as much and as early as possible. With some sports, an individual who is 15 years old may already be too old to realistically begin pursuing a professional career. By playing the sport and by talking to coaches, trainers, and athletes in the field, you can ascertain whether you like the sport enough to make it a career, determine if you have enough talent, and gain new insight into the field. You can also contact professional organizations and associations for information on how to best prepare for a career in their sport. Sometimes there are specialized training programs available, and the best way to find out is to get in contact with the people whose job it is to promote the sport.

EMPLOYERS

Professional athletes who compete in individual sports are not employed in the same manner as most workers. They do not work for employers, but choose the competitions or tournaments they wish to compete in. For example, a professional runner may choose to enter the Boston Marathon and then travel to Atlanta for the Peachtree Road Race.

Professional team athletes are employed by private and public ownership groups throughout the United States and Canada. At the highest male professional level, there are 32 National Football League franchises, 30 Major League Baseball franchises, 30 National Basketball Association franchises, 30 National Hockey League franchises, and 14 Major League Soccer franchises. The Women's National Basketball Association has 14 franchises, and the women's National Pro Fastpitch softball league has six teams.

STARTING OUT

Professional athletes must meet the requirements established by the organizing bodies of their respective sport. Sometimes this means meeting a physical requirement, such as age, height, or weight; and sometimes this means fulfilling a number of required stunts, or participating in a certain number of competitions. Professional organizations usually arrange it so that athletes can build up their skills and level of play by participating in lower-level competitions. College sports, as mentioned earlier, are an excellent way to improve one's skills while pursuing an education.

Most team sports have some official manner of establishing which teams acquire which players; often, this is referred to as a draft, although sometimes members of a professional team are chosen through a competition. Usually, the draft occurs between the college and professional levels of the sport. The National Basketball Association (NBA), for example, has its NBA College Draft. During the draft, the owners, general managers, and coaching staff of professional basketball teams choose players in an order based on the team's performance in the previous season. This means that the team with the worst record in the previous season has a greater chance of getting to choose first from the list of available players.

ADVANCEMENT

Professional athletes advance into the elite numbers of their sport by working and practicing hard, and by winning. Professional athletes usually obtain representation by sports agents in the behind-the-scenes deals that determine for which teams they will be playing and what they will be paid. These agents may also be involved with other key decisions involving commercial endorsements, personal income taxes, and financial investments of the athlete's revenues.

Professional athletes in team sports advance in three ways: when their team advances, when they are traded to better teams, and when they negotiate better contracts. In all three instances, this is achieved by the individual team member who works and practices hard, and who gives his or her best performance in game after game. Winning teams also receive a deluge of media attention that often creates celebrities out of individual players, which in turn provides these top players with opportunities for financially rewarding commercial endorsements.

Professional athletes do have other options, especially those who have graduated from a four-year college or university. Many go into some area of coaching, sports administration, management, or broadcasting. The professional athlete's unique insight and perspective can be a real asset in these careers. Other athletes simultaneously pursue other interests, some completely unrelated to their sport, such as education, business, social welfare, or the arts. Many continue to stay involved with the sport they have loved since childhood, coaching young children or volunteering with local school teams.

A college education can prepare all athletes for the day when their bodies can no longer compete at the top level, whether because of age or an unforeseen injury. Every athlete should be prepared to move into another career, related to the world of sports or not.

EARNINGS

Today, professional athletes can earn salaries that range from $250,000 to $10 million or more annually. Top players or athletes in each sport also earn large fees for endorsements and advertising, usually for sports-related products and services, but increasingly for products or services completely unrelated to their sport. Such salaries and other incomes are not representative of the whole field of professional athletes, but are only indicative of the fantastic revenues a small percentage of athletes with extraordinary talent can hope to earn. The U.S. Department of Labor reports that athletes had median annual earnings of $41,060 in 2006. Ten percent earned less than $14,570 while the top 25 percent earned $94,040 or more.

Perhaps the only caveat to the financial success of an elite athlete is the individual's character or personality. An athlete with a bad temper or prone to unsportsmanlike behavior may still be able to set records or win games, but he or she won't necessarily be able to cash in on commercial endorsements. Advertisers are notoriously fickle about the spokespeople they choose to endorse products; some athletes have lost million-dollar accounts because of their bad behavior on and off the field of play.

WORK ENVIRONMENT

Athletes compete in many different conditions, according to the setting of the sport (indoors or outdoors) and the rules of the organizing or governing bodies. Track-and-field athletes often compete in hot or rainy conditions, but at any point, organizing officials can call off the meet, or postpone competition until better weather. Indoor events are less subject to cancellation. However, since it is in the best interests of an organization not to risk the athletes' health, any condition that might adversely affect the outcome of a competition is usually reason enough to cancel or postpone it. An athlete, on the other hand, may withdraw from competition if he or she is injured or ill. Nerves and fear are not good reasons to default on a competition and part of ascending into the ranks of professional athletes means learning to cope with the anxiety that competition brings. Some athletes actually thrive on the nervous tension.

In order to reach the elite level of any sport, athletes must begin their careers early. Most professional athletes have been honing their skills since they were quite young. Athletes fit hours of practice time into an already full day; many famous players practiced on their own in the hours before school, as well as for several hours after school during team practice. Competitions are often far from the young athlete's home, which means they must travel on a bus or in a van with the team and coaching staff. Sometimes young athletes are placed in special training programs far from their homes and parents. They live with other athletes training for the same sport or on the same team and only see their parents for holidays and vacations. The separation from a child's parents and family can be difficult; often an athlete's family decides to move to be closer to the child's training facility.

The expenses of a sport can be overwhelming, as is the time an athlete must devote to practice and travel to and from competitions. Although most high school athletic programs pay for many expenses, if the athlete wants additional training or private coaching, the child's parents must come up with the extra money. Sometimes, young athletes can get official sponsors or they might qualify for an athletic scholarship from the training program. In addition to specialized equipment and clothing, the athlete must sometimes pay for a coach, travel expenses, competition fees and, depending on the sport, time at the facility or gym where he or she practices. Gymnasts, for example, train for years as individuals, and then compete for positions on national or international teams. Up until the time they are accepted (and usually during their participation in the team), these gymnasts must pay for their expenses—from coach to travel to uniforms to room and board away from home.

Even with the years of hard work, practice, and financial sacrifice that most athletes and their families must endure, there is no guarantee that an athlete will achieve the rarest of the rare in the sports world—financial reward. An athlete needs to truly love the sport at which he or she excels, and also have a nearly insatiable ambition and work ethic.

OUTLOOK

The outlook for professional athletes will vary depending on the sport, its popularity, and the number of athletes currently competing. On the whole, the outlook for the field of professional sports is healthy, but the number of jobs will not increase dramatically. Some sports, however, may experience an increase in popularity, which will translate into greater opportunities for higher salaries, prize monies, and commercial endorsements. Some individual sports—such as golf or tennis—may add new tournaments, which may increase employment opportunities for athletes in these sports.

FOR MORE INFORMATION

Individuals interested in becoming professional athletes should contact the professional organizations for the sport in which they would like to compete. Ask for information on requirements, training centers, and coaches. The following organization may also be able to provide further information:

American Alliance for Health, Physical Education, Recreation, and Dance
1900 Association Drive
Reston, VA 20191-1598
Tel: 800-213-7193
http://www.aahperd.org

For a free brochure and information on the Junior Olympics and more, contact
Amateur Athletic Union
PO Box 22409
Lake Buena Vista, FL 32830-2409
Tel: 407-934-7200
http://www.aausports.org

For information on opportunities for women in sports, contact
National Association for Girls and Women in Sports
1900 Association Drive
Reston, VA 20191-1598
http://www.aahperd.org/nagws

For information on careers in sports and physical education, contact

National Association for Sport and Physical Education
1900 Association Drive
Reston, VA 20191-1598
Tel: 800-213-7193
Email: naspe@aahperd.org
http://www.aahperd.org/naspe

For information on union membership, contact the following organizations:

Major League Baseball Players Association
http://mlbplayers.mlb.com

National Basketball Players Association
http://www.nbpa.com

National Football League Players Association
http://www.nflplayers.com

National Hockey League Players' Association
http://www.nhlpa.com

PROPERTY AND REAL ESTATE MANAGERS

OVERVIEW

Property and real estate managers plan and supervise the activities that affect land and buildings. Most of them manage rental properties, such as apartment buildings, office buildings, and shopping centers. Others manage the services and commonly owned areas of condominiums and community associations. Approximately 329,000 property and real estate managers are employed in the United States.

THE JOB

Most property and real estate managers are responsible for day-to-day management of residential and commercial real estate and usually manage several properties at one time. Acting as the owners' agents and advisers, they supervise the marketing of space, negotiate lease agreements, direct bookkeeping activities, and report to owners on the status of the property. They also negoti-

ate contracts for trash removal and other services and hire the maintenance and on-site management personnel employed at the properties.

Some managers buy and develop real estate for companies that have widespread retail operations, such as franchise restaurants and hotel chains, or for companies that build such projects as shopping malls and industrial parks.

On-site managers are based at the properties they manage and may even live on the property. Most of them are responsible for apartment buildings and work under the direction of property managers. They train, supervise, and assign duties to maintenance staffs; inspect the properties to determine what maintenance and repairs are needed; schedule routine service of heating and air-conditioning systems; keep records of operating costs; and submit cost reports to the property managers or owners. They deal with residents on a daily basis and are responsible for handling their requests for service and repairs, resolving complaints concerning other tenants, and enforcing rules and lease restrictions.

Apartment house managers work for property owners or property management firms and are usually on-site managers. They show apartments to prospective tenants, negotiate leases, collect rents, handle tenants' requests, and direct the activities of maintenance staffs and outside contractors.

Building superintendents are responsible for operating and maintaining the facilities and equipment of such properties as apartment houses and office buildings. At small properties, the superintendent may be the only on-site manager and report directly to property managers; at larger properties, superintendents may report to on-site managers and supervise maintenance staffs.

Housing project managers direct the operation of housing projects provided for such groups as military families, low-income families, and welfare recipients. The housing is usually subsidized by the government and may consist of single-family homes, multiunit dwellings, or house trailers.

Condominium managers are responsible to unit-owner associations and manage the services and commonly owned areas of condominium properties. They submit reports to the association members, supervise collection of owner assessments, resolve owners' complaints, and direct the activities of maintenance staffs and outside contractors. In some communities, such as planned unit developments, homeowners belong to associations that employ managers to oversee the homeowners' jointly used properties and facilities.

Real estate asset managers work for institutional owners such as banks and insurance companies. Their responsibilities are larger in scope. Rather than manage day-to-day property operations, asset managers usually have an advisory role regarding the acquisition, rehabilitation, refinancing, and disposition of properties in a particular portfolio, and they may act for the owner in making specific business decisions, such as selecting and supervising site managers, authorizing operating expenditures, reviewing and approving leases, and monitoring local market conditions.

Specialized property and real estate managers perform a variety of other types of functions. *Market managers* direct the activities of municipal, regional, or state markets where wholesale fruit, vegetables, or meat are sold. They rent space to buyers and sellers and direct the supervisors who are responsible for collecting fees, maintaining and cleaning the buildings and grounds, and enforcing sanitation and security rules. *Public events facilities rental managers* negotiate contracts with organizations that wish to lease arenas, auditoriums, stadiums, or other facilities that are used for public events. They solicit new business and renewals of established contracts, maintain schedules to determine the availability of the facilities for bookings, and oversee operation and maintenance activities.

Real estate firm managers direct the activities of the *sales agents* who work for real estate firms. They screen and hire sales agents and conduct training sessions. They confer with agents and clients to resolve such problems as adjusting selling prices and determining who is responsible for repairs and closing costs. *Business opportunity-and-property-investment brokers* buy and sell business enterprises and investment properties on a commission or speculative basis. They investigate such factors as the financial ratings of businesses that are for sale, the desirability of a property's location for various types of businesses, and the condition of investment properties.

Businesses employ real estate managers to find, acquire, and develop the properties they need for their operations and to dispose of properties they no longer need. Real estate agents often work for companies that operate retail merchandising chains, such as fast-food restaurants, gasoline stations, and apparel shops. They locate sites that are desirable for their companies' operations and arrange to purchase or lease them. They also review their companies' holdings to identify properties that are no longer desirable and then negotiate to dispose of them. (*Real estate sales agents* also may be called real estate agents, but they are not involved in property man-

---

SCHOOL SUBJECTS
Business, English, Mathematics

PERSONAL SKILLS
Communication/Ideas, Leadership/Management

MINIMUM EDUCATION LEVEL
Bachelor's Degree

CERTIFICATION OR LICENSING
Voluntary (Certification), Required for Certain Positions (Licensing)

WORK ENVIRONMENT
Primarily Indoors, Primarily Multiple Locations

---

agement.) *Land development managers* are responsible for acquiring land for such projects as shopping centers and industrial parks. They negotiate with local governments, property owners, and public interest groups to eliminate obstacles to their companies' developments, and they arrange for architects to draw up plans and construction firms to build the projects.

REQUIREMENTS
High School

High school students interested in this field should enroll in college preparatory programs that include classes in business, mathematics, speech, and English.

Postsecondary Training

Most employers prefer college graduates for property and real estate management positions. They prefer degrees in real estate, business management, finance, and related fields, but they also consider liberal arts graduates. In some cases, inexperienced college graduates with bachelor's or master's degrees enter the field as assistant property managers.

Many property and real estate managers attend training programs offered by various professional and trade associations. Employers often send their managers to these programs to improve their management skills and expand their knowledge of such subjects as operation and maintenance of building mechanical systems, insurance and risk management, business and real estate law, and accounting and financial concepts. Many managers attend these programs voluntarily to prepare for advancement to positions with more responsibility.

Certification or Licensing

Certification or licensing is not required for most property managers. Managers who have appropriate experience, complete required training programs, and achieve satisfactory scores on written exams, however, can earn certification and such professional designations as certified property manager and accredited residential manager (which are offered by the Institute of Real Estate Management) and real property administrator and facilities management administrator (which are offered by BOMI International). Such designations are usually looked upon favorably by employers as a sign of a person's competence and dedication. Other organizations that offer certification include the Community Associations Institute and the National Board of Certification for Community Association Managers.

The federal government requires certification for managers of public housing that is subsidized by federal funds. Business opportunity-and-property-investment brokers must hold state licenses, and some states require real estate managers to hold licenses.

Other Requirements

Property and real estate managers must be skilled in both oral and written communications and be adept at dealing with people. They need to be good administrators and negotiators, and those who specialize in land development must be especially resourceful and creative to arrange financing for their projects. Managers for small rental or condominium complexes may be required to have building repair and maintenance skills as well as business management skills.

EXPLORING

If you are interested in property and real estate management, participate in activities that help you develop management skills, such as serving as an officer in an organization or participating in Junior Achievement (http://www.ja.org) projects. Part-time or summer jobs in sales or volunteer work that involves contact with the public would be good experience.

You may be able to tour apartment complexes, shopping centers, and other real estate developments and should take advantage of any opportunities to talk with property and real estate managers about their careers.

EMPLOYERS

Approximately 329,000 people in the United States are employed as property and real estate managers. About 36 percent work for real estate agents and brokers, lessors of real estate, or property management firms. Others work for real estate developers, government agencies that manage public buildings, corporations with large property holdings used for their retail operations, real estate investors, and mining and oil companies. Many are self-employed as developers, apartment building owners, property management firm owners, or owners of full-service real estate businesses. More than 50 percent of all property and real estate managers are self-employed.

STARTING OUT

Students who are about to graduate from college can obtain assistance from their career services offices in finding their first job. You can also apply directly to property management firms and check ads in the help wanted sections of local newspapers. Property and real estate managers often begin as on-site managers for small apartment house complexes, condominiums, or community associations. Some property managers begin as real estate agents or in another position in a real estate firm and later move into property management.

ADVANCEMENT

With experience, entry-level property and site managers may transfer to larger properties or they may become assistant property managers, working closely with property managers and acquiring experience in a variety of management tasks. Assistant managers may advance to property manager positions, in which they most likely will be responsible for several properties. As they advance in their careers, property managers may manage larger or more complex operations, specialize in managing specific types of property, or possibly establish their own companies.

To be considered for advancement, property managers must demonstrate the ability to deal effectively with tenants, contractors, and maintenance staff. They must be capable administrators and possess business skills, initiative, good organization, and excellent communication skills.

EARNINGS

Managers of residential and commercial rental real estate are usually compensated by a fee based on the gross rental income of the properties. Managers of condominiums and other homeowner-occupied properties also are usually paid on a fee basis. Site managers and others employed by a management company are typically salaried.

According to the U.S. Department of Labor, annual earnings for all property managers in 2006 ranged from less than $20,140 to $95,170 or more. The median annual salary for property managers in 2006 was $43,070.

Property and real estate managers usually receive such benefits as medical and health insurance. On-site apartment building managers may have rent-free apartments, and many managers have the use of company automobiles. In addition, managers involved in land development may receive a small percentage of ownership in their projects.

WORK ENVIRONMENT

Property and real estate managers usually work in offices but may spend much of their time at the properties they manage. On-site apartment building managers often leave their offices to inspect other areas, check maintenance or repair work, or resolve problems reported by tenants.

Many apartment managers must live in the buildings they manage so they can be available in emergencies, and they may be required to show apartments to prospective tenants at night or on weekends. Property and real estate managers may attend evening meetings with property owners, association boards of directors, or civic groups interested in property planned for development. Real estate managers who work for large companies frequently travel to inspect their companies' property holdings or locate properties their companies might acquire.

OUTLOOK

Employment of property and real estate managers is expected to increase faster than the average for all occupations through 2016, according to the U.S. Department of Labor. Job openings are expected to occur as older, experienced managers transfer to other occupations or leave the labor force. The best opportunities will be for college graduates with degrees in real estate, business administration, and related fields and professional certifications.

In the next decade, many of the economy's new jobs are expected to be in wholesale and retail trade, finance, insurance, real estate, and other service industries. Growth in these industries will bring a need for more office and retail properties and for people to manage them.

In housing, there will be a greater demand for apartments because of the high cost of owning a home. New home developments also are increasingly organized with

community or homeowner associations that require managers. In addition, more owners of commercial and multiunit residential properties are expected to use professional managers to help make their properties more profitable. The growing number of people age 65 and over will create a need for the construction of assisted-living and retirement communities, and managers will be needed to oversee these facilities.

FOR MORE INFORMATION

For information on certification, contact
BOMI International
One Park Place, Suite 475
Annapolis, MD 21401-3479
Tel: 800-235-2664
Email: service@bomi-edu.org
http://www.bomi-edu.org

For information on educational programs, contact
Building Owners and Managers Association International
1101 15th Street, NW, Suite 800
Washington, DC 20005-5021
Tel: 202-408-2662
Email: info@boma.org
http://www.boma.org

For information on certification, contact
Community Associations Institute
225 Reinekers Lane, Suite 300
Alexandria, VA 22314-2875
Tel: 888-224-4321
http://www.caionline.org

For information on training programs, certification, and industry research, contact
Institute of Real Estate Management
430 North Michigan Avenue
Chicago, IL 60611-4011
Tel: 800-837-0706
Email: custserv@irem.org
http://www.irem.org

This organization is devoted to the multifamily housing industry and represents developers, owners, managers, and suppliers.
National Apartment Association
4300 Wilson Boulevard, Suite 400
Arlington, VA 22203-4168
Tel: 703-518-6141
http://www.naahq.org

For information on certification, contact
National Board of Certification for Community Association Managers
225 Reinekers Lane, Suite 310
Alexandria, VA 22314-2856
Tel: 703-836-6902
Email: info@nbccam.org
http://www.nbccam.org

For information on property management in Canada, contact
Canadian Real Estate Association
200 Catherine Street, 6th Floor
Ottawa, ON K2P 2K9 Canada
Tel: 613-237-7111
Email: info@crea.ca
http://crea.ca

PSYCHOLOGISTS

OVERVIEW

Psychologists teach, counsel, conduct research, or administer programs to understand people and help people understand themselves. Psychologists examine individual and group behavior through testing, experimenting, and studying personal histories.

Psychologists normally hold doctorates in psychology. Unlike psychiatrists, they are not medical doctors and

SCHOOL SUBJECTS
Biology, Psychology, Sociology

PERSONAL SKILLS
Helping/Teaching, Technical/Scientific

MINIMUM EDUCATION LEVEL
Master's Degree

CERTIFICATION OR LICENSING
Voluntary (Certification), Required for Certain Positions (Licensing)

WORK ENVIRONMENT
Primarily Indoors, Primarily One Location

cannot prescribe medication. Approximately 166,000 psychologists are employed in the United States.

THE JOB

Psychology is both a science and a profession. As a science, it is a systematic approach to the understanding of people and their behavior; as a profession, it is the application of that understanding to help solve human problems. Psychology is a rapidly growing field, and psychologists work on a great variety of problems.

The field of psychology is so vast that no one person can become an expert in all of its specialties. The psychologist usually concentrates on one specialty. Many specialists use overlapping methodologies, theories, and treatments.

Many psychologists teach some area of basic psychology in colleges and universities. They are also likely to conduct research and supervise graduate student work in an area of special interest.

Clinical psychologists concern themselves with people's mental and emotional disorders. They assess and treat problems ranging from normal psychological crises, such as adolescent rebellion or middle-age loss of self-esteem, to extreme conditions, such as severe depression and schizophrenia.

Some clinical psychologists work almost exclusively with children. They may be staff members at a child guidance clinic or a treatment center for children at a large general hospital. *Child psychologists* and other clinical psychologists may engage in private practice, seeing clients at offices. Clinical psychologists comprise the largest group of specialists.

Developmental psychologists study how people develop from birth through old age. They describe, measure, and explain age-related changes in behavior, stages of emotional development, universal traits and individual differences, and abnormal changes in development. Many developmental psychologists teach and do research in colleges and universities. Some specialize in programs for children in day care centers, preschools, hospitals, or clinics. Others (known as *geropsychologists*) specialize in programs for the elderly.

Social psychologists study how people interact with one other, and how individuals are affected by their environment. Social psychology has developed from four sources: sociology, cultural anthropology, psychiatry, and psychology. Social psychologists are interested in individual and group behavior. They study the ways groups influence individuals and vice versa. They study different kinds of groups: ethnic, religious, political, educational, family, and many others. The social psychologist has devised ways to research group nature, attitudes, leadership patterns, and structure.

Counseling psychologists work with people who have problems they find difficult to face alone. These clients are not usually mentally or emotionally ill, but they are emotionally upset, anxious, or struggling with some conflict within themselves or their environment. By helping people solve their problems, make decisions, and cope with everyday stresses, the counseling psychologist actually is working in preventive mental health.

School psychologists frequently do diagnosis and remediation. They may engage primarily in preventive and developmental psychology. Many school psychologists are assigned the duty of testing pupils surmised to be exceptional. Other school psychologists work almost entirely with children who have proven to be a problem to themselves or to others and who have been referred for help by teachers or other members of the school system. Many school psychologists are concerned with pupils who reveal various kinds of learning disabilities. School psychologists may also be called upon to work with relationship problems between parents and children.

Industrial-organizational psychologists are concerned with the relation between people and work. They deal with organizational structure, worker productivity, job satisfaction, consumer behavior, personnel training and development, and the interaction between humans and machines. Industrial-organizational psychologists may work with a sales department to help salespeople become more effective. Some study assembly line procedures and suggest changes to reduce monotony and increase worker responsibility. Others plan various kinds of tests to help screen applicants for employment. Industrial-organizational psychologists conduct research to determine qualities that seem to produce the most efficient employees or help management develop programs to identify staff with management potential. They may be asked to investigate and report on certain differences of opinion between a supervisor and one of the workers. Some may design training courses to indoctrinate new employees or counsel older employees on career development or retirement preparation.

Other industrial psychologists, referred to as *engineering psychologists,* help engineers and technicians design systems that require workers or consumers and machines to interact. They also develop training aids for those systems.

Consumer psychologists are interested in consumer reactions to products or services. These psychologists may be asked to determine the kinds of products the public will buy. They may study, for instance, whether people prefer big cars or little cars. They might be asked to make decisions about the most appealing ways to present a product through advertising. Many of today's most established advertising, promotion, and packaging practices have been influenced by the opinions and advice of consumer psychologists. Consumer psychologists also try to improve product acceptability and safety in addition to helping the consumer make better decisions.

Psychometrists work with intelligence, personality, and aptitude tests used in clinics, counseling centers, schools, and businesses. They administer tests, score them, and interpret results as related to standard norms. Psychometrists also study methods and techniques used to acquire and evaluate psychological data. They may devise new, more reliable tests. These specialists are usually well trained in mathematics, statistics, and computer programming and technology.

The *educational psychologist* is concerned primarily with how people teach, learn, and evaluate learning. Many educational psychologists are employed on college or university faculties, and they also conduct research into learning theory. Educational psychologists are also interested in the evaluation of learning.

Experimental or *research psychologists* conduct scientific experiments on particular aspects of behavior, either animal or human. Much experimental study is done in learning, in physiological psychology (the relationship of behavior to physiological processes), and in comparative psychology (sometimes called animal psychology). Many experimental psychological studies are carried out with animals, partly because their environments can be carefully controlled.

Many psychologists of all kinds find that writing skills are helpful. They may write up the results of research efforts for a scholarly journal. Psychologists prepare papers for presentation at professional association meetings and sometimes write books or articles. As consultants or industrial psychologists, they may write instruction manuals. Educational psychologists may prepare test manuals.

Some psychologists become administrators who direct college or university psychology departments or personnel services programs in a school system or industry. Some become agency or department directors of research in scientific laboratories. They may be promoted to department head in a state or federal government agency. *Chief psychologists* in hospitals or psychiatric centers plan psychological treatment programs, direct professional and nonprofessional personnel, and oversee psychological services provided by the institution.

REQUIREMENTS
High School

Because you will need to continue your education beyond high school in order to become a psychologist, you should enroll in college preparatory courses. Your class schedule should concentrate on English courses, computer science, mathematics, and sciences. Algebra, geometry, and calculus are important to take, as are biology, chemistry, and physics. You should take social science courses, such as psychology and sociology. You should also take a modern foreign language, such as French or German, because reading comprehension of these languages is one of the usual requirements for obtaining the doctorate degree.

Postsecondary Training

A doctorate in psychology (Ph.D. or Psy.D.) is recommended. Some positions are available to people with a master's degree, but they are jobs of lesser responsibility and lower salaries than those open to people with a doctorate.

Psychology is an obvious choice for your college major, but not all graduate programs require entering students to have a psychology bachelor's degree. Nevertheless, your college studies should include a number of psychology courses, such as experimental psychology, developmental psychology, and abnormal psychology. You should also take classes in statistics as well as such classes as English, foreign language, and history to complete a strong liberal arts education.

Master's degree programs typically take two years to complete. Course work at this level usually involves statistics, ethics, and industrial and organizational content. If you want to work as a school psychologist, you will need to complete a supervised, year-long internship at a school after receiving your degree.

Some doctoral programs accept students with master's degrees; in other cases, students enter a doctoral program with only a bachelor's degree. Because entrance requirements vary, you will need to research the programs you are interested in to find out their specific requirements. The doctorate degree typically takes between four and seven years to complete for those who begin their studies with only the bachelor's degree. Coursework will include studies in various areas of psychology and research (including work in quantitative research methods). Those who focus on research often complete a yearlong postdoctoral fellowship. Those who want to work as clinical, counseling, or school psychologists must complete a one-year supervised internship. Frequently those who

are interested in clinical, counseling, or school psychology will get the Psy.D., because this degree emphasizes clinical rather than research work. In addition, those interested in these three areas should attend a program accredited by the American Psychological Association (APA). The National Association of School Psychologists also approves advanced degree programs in school psychology.

Unlike psychiatrists, psychologists do not need to attend medical school.

Certification or Licensing

The American Board of Professional Psychology offers voluntary specialty certification in 13 areas, including clinical psychology, clinical neuropsychology, and counseling, forensic, organizational, business, and school psychology. Requirements for certification include having a doctorate in psychology, professional experience, appropriate postdoctoral training, and the passing of an examination. Those who fulfill these requirements receive the designation of diplomate.

The National Association of School Psychologists awards the nationally certified school psychologist designation to applicants who complete educational requirements, an internship, and pass an examination. About 29 states recognize this designation.

Psychologists in independent practice or those providing any type of patient care, such as clinical, counseling, and school psychologists, must be licensed or certified by the state in which they practice. Some states require the licensing of industrial/organizational psychologists. Because requirements vary, you will need to check with your state's licensing board for specific information.

Other Requirements

Because psychology is such a broad field, various personal attributes apply to different psychology positions. Those involved in research, for example, should be analytical, detail oriented, and have strong math and writing skills. Those working with patients should be "people persons," able to relate to others, and have excellent listening skills. No matter what their area of focus, however, all psychologists should be committed to lifelong learning since our understanding of humans is constantly evolving.

To be a psychologist, one must have a desire to help people understand themselves and others. A basic curiosity is required as well as a fascination with the way the human mind works.

EXPLORING

If you are interested in psychology, explore the field by taking psychology classes in high school and reading all you can about the subject, including biographies of and works by noted psychologists. In addition, make an appointment to talk about the profession with a psychologist who may work at a nearby school, college, hospital, or clinic. Use the Internet to learn more about mental health issues by visiting Web sites, such as that of Mental Health America at http://www.nmha.org or the APA at http://www.apa.org.

If being involved with patient care interests you, gain experience in the health care field by volunteering at a local hospital or clinic. In addition, volunteer opportunities may exist at local nursing homes, where you will also have the chance to work with clients needing some type of assistance. If doing research work sounds appealing to you, consider joining your school's science club, which may offer the opportunity to work on projects, document the process, and work as part of a team.

EMPLOYERS

Approximately 166,000 psychologists are employed in the United States. Clinical psychologists may teach at colleges or universities. Or, clinical psychologists may work with patients in a private practice or a hospital, where they provide therapy after evaluation through special tests.

Many developmental psychologists teach and research in colleges and universities. Some specialize in programs for children in day care centers, preschools, hospitals, or clinics. About 34 percent of psychologists are self-employed.

Social psychologists often teach and conduct research in colleges or universities. They also work for agencies of the federal or state government or in private research firms. Some work as consultants. An increasing number of social psychologists work as researchers and personnel managers in such nontraditional settings as advertising agencies, corporations, and architectural and engineering firms.

Counseling psychologists work in college or university counseling centers; they also teach in psychology departments. They may be in private practice. Or they may work at a community health center, a marriage counseling agency, or a federal agency such as the Department of Veterans Affairs.

Consumer psychologists study consumer reactions to products or services. They are hired by advertising, promotion, and packaging companies.

Psychometrists may be employed in colleges and universities, testing companies, private research firms, or government agencies.

Educational psychologists may work for test publishing firms devising and standardizing tests of ability, aptitude, personal preferences, attitudes, or characteristics.

STARTING OUT

Those entering the field with only a bachelor's degree will face strong competition for few jobs. The university career services office or a psychology professor may be able to help such a student find a position assisting a psychologist at a health center or other location. Positions beyond the assistant level, however, will be very difficult to attain. Those graduating from master's or doctorate degree programs will find more employment opportunities. Again, university career services offices may be able to provide these graduates with assistance. In addition, contacts made during an internship may offer job leads. Joining professional organizations and networking with members is also a way to find out about job openings. In addition, these organizations, such as the APA, often list job vacancies in their publications for members.

ADVANCEMENT

For those who have bachelor's or master's degrees, the first step to professional advancement is to complete a doctorate degree. After that, advancement will depend on the area of psychology in which the person is working. For example, a psychologist teaching at a college or university may advance through the academic ranks from instructor to professor. Some college teachers who enjoy administrative work become department heads.

Psychologists who work for state or federal government agencies may, after considerable experience, be promoted to head a section or department. School psychologists might become directors of pupil personnel services. Industrial psychologists can rise to managerial or administrative positions.

After several years of experience, many psychologists enter private practice or set up their own research or consulting firms.

EARNINGS

Because the psychology field offers so many different types of employment possibilities, salaries for psychologists vary greatly. In addition, the typical conditions affecting salaries, such as the person's level of education, professional experience, and location, also apply. The U.S. Department of Labor reports that clinical, counseling, and school psychologists earned median salaries of $59,440 in 2006. Salaries ranged from less than $35,280 to $102,730 or more. The department also reports the following mean annual earnings for clinical, counseling, and school psychologists by employer: offices of other health practitioners, $80,400; elementary/secondary schools, $64,140; individual and family services, $57,730; and outpatient care centers, $55,820. Industrial-organizational psychologists earned salaries that ranged from less than $48,380 to $139,620 or more, with an average salary of $86,420 in 2006.

Benefits for full-time workers include vacation and sick time, health, and sometimes dental, insurance, and pension or 401(k) plans. Self-employed psychologists must provide their own benefits.

WORK ENVIRONMENT

Psychologists work under many different conditions. Those who work as college or university teachers usually have offices in a building on campus and access to a laboratory in which they carry out experiments.

Offices of school psychologists may be located in the school system headquarters. They may see students and their parents at those offices, or they might work in space set aside for them in several schools within the school district that they may visit regularly.

Psychologists in military service serve in this country or overseas. They may be stationed in Washington, D.C., and assigned to an office job, or they may be stationed with other military personnel at a post or, more likely, in a military hospital.

Psychologists employed in government work in such diverse places as public health or vocational rehabilitation agencies, the Department of Veterans Affairs, the Peace Corps, the U.S. Department of Education, or a state department of education. Their working conditions depend largely on the kind of jobs they have. They may be required to travel a lot or to produce publications. They may work directly with people or be assigned entirely to research.

Some psychologists are self-employed. Most work as clinical psychologists and have offices where they see clients individually. Others work as consultants to business firms. Self-employed psychologists rent or own their office spaces and arrange their own work schedules.

OUTLOOK

The U.S. Department of Labor projects that employment for psychologists will grow faster than the average for all occupations through 2016, with the largest increase in schools, hospitals, social service agencies, mental health centers, substance abuse treatment clinics, consulting firms, and private companies. Increased emphasis on health maintenance and illness prevention as well as growing interest in psychological services for special groups, such as children, the elderly, or returning military veterans, will create demand for psychologists. Many of these areas depend on government funding, however, and could be adversely affected in an economic downswing when spending is likely to be curtailed. Many openings should be available in business and industry, and the outlook is very good for psychologists who are in full-time independent practice.

Prospects look best for those with doctorates in applied areas, such as clinical, counseling, health, industrial/organizational, and school psychology, and for those with extensive technical training in quantitative research methods and computer applications. Postdoctorates are becoming increasingly crucial in the fields of research psychology that deal with behavior based on biology.

Competition for jobs will be tougher for those with master's (except in industrial-organizational psychology, which will experience much-faster-than-average growth) or bachelor's degrees. Most job candidates with bachelor's degrees, in fact, will not be able to find employment in the psychology field beyond assistant-level jobs at such places as rehabilitation centers. Some may work as high school psychology teachers if they meet state teaching certification requirements.

FOR MORE INFORMATION

For information on specialty certification, contact
American Board of Professional Psychology
300 Drayton Street, 3rd Floor
Savannah, GA 31401-4443
Tel: 800-255-7792
Email: office@abpp.org
http://www.abpp.org

For more on careers in psychology and mental health issues, contact
American Psychological Association
750 First Street, NE
Washington, DC 20002-4242
Tel: 800-374-2721
http://www.apa.org

For licensing information, visit the following Web site:
Association of State and Provincial Psychology Boards
PO Box 241245
Montgomery, AL 36124-1245
Tel: 334-832-4580
Email: asppb@asppb.org
http://www.asppb.org

For more information on certification and becoming a school psychologist, including graduate school information, contact

National Association of School Psychologists
4340 East-West Highway, Suite 402
Bethesda, MD 20814-4468
Tel: 866-331-NASP
Email: center@nasweb.org
http://www.nasponline.org

For a list of Canadian psychology departments providing graduate programs, contact

Canadian Psychological Association
141 Laurier Avenue West, Suite 702
Ottawa, ON K1P 5J3 Canada
Tel: 613-237-2144
Email: cpa@cpa.ca
http://www.cpa.ca

For a whimsical introduction to psychology, visit
ePsych
http://epsych.msstate.edu

☐ PUBLIC RELATIONS SPECIALISTS

OVERVIEW

Public relations (PR) specialists develop and maintain programs that present a favorable public image for an individual or organization. They provide information to the target audience (generally, the public at large) about the client, its goals and accomplishments, and any further plans or projects that may be of public interest.

PR specialists may be employed by corporations, government agencies, nonprofit organizations, or almost any type of organization. Many PR specialists hold positions in public relations consulting firms or work for advertising agencies. There are approximately 243,000 public relations specialists in the United States.

THE JOB

Public relations specialists are employed to do a variety of tasks. They may be employed primarily as writers, creating reports, news releases, and booklet texts.

SCHOOL SUBJECTS
Business, English, Journalism

PERSONAL SKILLS
Communication/Ideas, Leadership/Management

MINIMUM EDUCATION LEVEL
Bachelor's Degree

CERTIFICATION OR LICENSING
Voluntary

WORK ENVIRONMENT
Primarily Indoors, One Location with Some Travel

Others write speeches or create copy for radio, TV, or film sequences. These workers often spend much of their time contacting the press, radio, and TV as well as magazines on behalf of the employer. Some PR specialists work more as *editors* than writers, fact-checking and rewriting employee publications, newsletters, shareholder reports, and other management communications.

Specialists may choose to concentrate in graphic design, using their background knowledge of art and layout to develop brochures, booklets, and photographic communications. Other PR workers handle special events, such as press parties, convention exhibits, open houses, or anniversary celebrations.

PR specialists must be alert to any and all company or institutional events that are newsworthy. They prepare news releases and direct them toward the proper media. Specialists working for manufacturers and retailers are concerned with efforts that will promote sales and create goodwill for the firm's products. They work closely with the marketing and sales departments in announcing new products, preparing displays, and attending occasional dealers' conventions.

A large firm may have a *director of public relations* who is a vice president of the company and in charge of a staff that includes writers, artists, researchers, and other specialists. Publicity for an individual or a small organization may involve many of the same areas of expertise but may be carried out by a few people or possibly even one person.

Many PR workers act as consultants (rather than staff) of a corporation, association, college, hospital, or other institution. These workers have the advantage of being able to operate independently, state opinions objectively, and work with more than one type of business or association.

PR specialists are called upon to work with the public opinion aspects of almost every corporate or institutional problem. These can range from the opening of a new manufacturing plant to a college's dormitory dedication to a merger or sale of a company.

Public relations professionals may specialize. *Lobbyists* try to persuade legislators and other office holders to pass laws favoring the interests of the firms or people they represent. *Fund-raising directors* develop and direct programs designed to raise funds for social welfare agencies and other nonprofit organizations.

Early in their careers, public relations specialists become accustomed to having others receive credit for their behind-the-scenes work. The speeches they draft will be delivered by company officers, the magazine articles they prepare may be credited to the president of the company, and they may be consulted to prepare the message to stockholders from the chairman of the board that appears in the annual report.

REQUIREMENTS
High School

While in high school, take courses in English, journalism, public speaking, humanities, and languages because public relations is based on effective communication with others. Courses such as these will develop your skills in written and oral communication as well as provide a better understanding of different fields and industries to be publicized.

Postsecondary Training

Most people employed in public relations service have a college degree. Major fields of study most beneficial to developing the proper skills are public relations, English, and journalism. Some employers feel that majoring in the area in which the public relations person will eventually work is the best training. A knowledge of business administration is most helpful as is a native talent for selling. A graduate degree may be required for managerial positions. People with a bachelor's degree in public relations can find staff positions with either an organization or a public relations firm.

More than 200 colleges and about 100 graduate schools offer degree programs or special courses in public relations. In addition, many other colleges offer at least courses in the field. Public relations programs are sometimes administered by the journalism or communication departments of schools. In addition to courses in theory and techniques of public relations, interested individuals may study organization, management and administration, and practical applications and often specialize in areas such as business, government, and nonprofit organizations. Other preparation includes courses in creative writing, psychology, communications, advertising, and journalism.

Certification or Licensing

The Public Relations Society of America and the International Association of Business Communicators accredit public relations workers who have at least five years of experience in the field and pass a comprehensive examination. Such accreditation is a sign of competence in this field, although it is not a requirement for employment.

Other Requirements

Today's public relations specialist must be a businessperson first, both to understand how to perform successfully in business and to comprehend the needs and goals of the organization or client. Additionally, the public relations specialist needs to be a strong writer and speaker, with good interpersonal, leadership, and organizational skills.

EXPLORING

Almost any experience in working with other people will help you to develop strong interpersonal skills, which are crucial in public relations. The possibilities are almost endless. Summer work on a newspaper or trade paper or with a radio or television station may give insight into communications media. Working as a volunteer on a political campaign can help you to understand the ways in which people can be persuaded. Being selected as a page for the U.S. Congress or a state legislature will help you grasp the fundamentals of government processes. A job in retail will help you to understand some of the principles of product presentation. A teaching job will develop your organization and presentation skills. These are just some of the jobs that will let you explore areas of public relations.

You can also visit The Museum of Public Relations online at http://www.prmuseum.com to read about pioneers in the industry.

EMPLOYERS

Public relations specialists hold about 243,000 jobs. Workers may be paid employees of the organization they represent or they may be part of a public relations firm that works for organizations on a contract basis. Others are involved in fund-raising or political campaigning. Public relations may be done for a corporation, retail business, service company, utility, association, nonprofit organization, or educational institution.

Most PR firms are located in large cities that are centers of communications. New York, Chicago, San Francisco, Los Angeles, and Washington, D.C., are good places to start a search for a public relations job. Nevertheless, there are many good opportunities in cities across the United States.

STARTING OUT

There is no clear-cut formula for getting a job in public relations. Individuals often enter the field after gaining preliminary experience in another occupation closely allied to the field, usually some segment of communications, and frequently, in journalism. Coming into public relations from newspaper work is still a recommended route. Another good method is to gain initial employment as a public relations trainee or intern, or as a clerk, secretary, or research assistant in a public relations department or a counseling firm.

ADVANCEMENT

In some large companies, an entry-level public relations specialist may start as a trainee in a formal training program for new employees. In others, new employees may expect to be assigned to work that has a minimum of responsibility. They may assemble clippings or do rewrites on material that has already been accepted. They may make posters or assist in conducting polls or surveys, or compile reports from data submitted by others.

As workers acquire experience, they are typically given more responsibility. They write news releases, direct polls or surveys, or advance to writing speeches for company officials. Progress may seem to be slow, because some skills take a long time to master.

Some advance in responsibility and salary in the same firm in which they started. Others find that the path to advancement is to accept a more rewarding position in another firm.

The goal of many public relations specialists is to open an independent office or to join an established consulting firm. To start an independent office requires a large outlay of capital and an established reputation in the field. However, those who are successful in operating their own consulting firms probably attain the greatest financial success in the public relations field.

EARNINGS

Public relations specialists had median annual earnings of $47,350 in 2006, according to the U.S. Department of Labor. Salaries ranged from less than $28,080 to more than $89,220. The Department of Labor reports the following 2006 mean salaries for public relations specialists by type of employer: advertising and related services, $60,330; management of companies and enterprises, $59,420; business, professional, labor, political, and similar organizations, $59,310; colleges and universities, $46,310; and local government, $49,610.

Many PR workers receive a range of fringe benefits from corporations and agencies employing them, including bonus/incentive compensation, stock options, profit sharing/pension plans/401(k) programs, medical benefits, life insurance, financial planning, maternity/paternity leave, paid vacations, and family college tuition. Bonuses can range from 5 to 100 percent of base compensation and often are based on individual and/or company performance.

WORK ENVIRONMENT

Public relations specialists generally work in offices with adequate secretarial help, regular salary increases, and expense accounts. They are expected to make a good appearance in tasteful, conservative clothing. They must have social poise, and their conduct in their personal life is important to their firms or their clients. The public relations specialist may have to entertain business associates.

The PR specialist seldom works conventional office hours for many weeks at a time; although the workweek may consist of 35 to 40 hours, these hours may be supplemented by evenings and even weekends when meetings must be attended and other special events covered. Time behind the desk may represent only a small part of the total working schedule. Travel is often an important and necessary part of the job.

The life of the PR worker is so greatly determined by the job that many consider this a disadvantage. Because the work is concerned with public opinion, it is often difficult to measure the results of performance and to sell the worth of a public relations program to an employer or client. Competition in the consulting field is keen, and if a firm loses an account, some of its personnel may be affected. The demands it makes for anonymity will be considered by some as one of the profession's less inviting aspects. Public relations involves much more hard work and a great deal less glamour than is popularly supposed.

OUTLOOK

Employment of public relations professionals is expected to grow faster than average for all occupations through 2016, according to the U.S. Department of Labor. Competition will be keen for beginning jobs in public relations because so many job seekers are enticed by the perceived glamour and appeal of the field; those with both education and experience, as well as proficiency in one or more foreign languages, will have an advantage.

Most large companies have some sort of public relations resource, either through their own staff or through the use of a firm of consultants. Most are expected to expand their public relations activities, creating many new jobs. More smaller companies are hiring public relations specialists, adding to the demand for these workers. Additionally, as a result of recent corporate scandals, more public relations specialists will be hired to help improve the images of companies and regain the trust of the public. The U.S. Department of Labor predicts that the advertising industry will offer the best employment opportunities for public relations specialists through 2016.

FOR MORE INFORMATION

For information on accreditation, contact

**International Association of
    Business Communicators**
One Hallidie Plaza, Suite 600
San Francisco, CA 94102-2842
Tel: 415-544-4700
http://www.iabc.com

For statistics, salary surveys, and information on accreditation and student membership, contact

Public Relations Society of America
33 Maiden Lane, 11th Floor
New York, NY 10038-5150
Tel: 212-460-1400
Email: prssa@prsa.org (student membership)
http://www.prsa.org

This professional association for public relations professionals offers an accreditation program and opportunities for professional development.

Canadian Public Relations Society
4195 Dundas Street West, Suite 346
Toronto, ON M8X 1Y4 Canada
Tel: 416-239-7034
Email: admin@cprs.ca
http://www.cprs.ca

RADIOLOGIC TECHNOLOGISTS

OVERVIEW

Radiologic technologists operate equipment that creates images of a patient's body tissues, organs, and bones for the purpose of medical diagnoses and therapies. These images allow physicians to know the exact nature of a patient's injury or disease, such as the location of a broken bone or the confirmation of an ulcer.

Before an X-ray examination, radiologic technologists may administer drugs or chemical mixtures to the patient to better highlight internal organs. They place the patient in the correct position between the X-ray source and film and protect body areas that are not to be exposed to radiation. After determining the proper duration and intensity of the exposure, they operate the controls to beam X rays through the patient and expose the photographic film.

They may operate computer-aided imaging equipment that does not involve X rays and may help to treat diseased or affected areas of the body by exposing the patient to specified concentrations of radiation for prescribed times. Radiologic technologists and technicians hold about 196,000 jobs in the United States.

THE JOB

All radiological work is done at the request of and under the supervision of a physician. Just as a prescription is required for certain drugs to be dispensed or administered, so must a physician's request be issued before a patient can receive any kind of imaging procedure.

There are four primary disciplines in which radiologic technologists may work: radiography (taking X-ray pictures or radiographs), nuclear medicine, radiation therapy, and sonography. In each of these medical imaging methods, the technologist works under the direction of a physician who specializes in interpreting the pictures produced by X rays, other imaging techniques, or radiation therapy. Technologists can work in more than one of these areas. Some technologists specialize in working with a particular part of the body or a specific condition.

X-ray pictures, or radiographs, are the most familiar use of radiologic technology. They are used to diagnose and determine treatment for a wide variety of afflictions, including ulcers, tumors, and bone fractures. Chest X-ray pictures can determine whether a person has a lung disease. Radiologic technologists who operate X-ray equipment first help the patient prepare for the radiologic examination. After explaining the procedure, they may administer a substance that makes the part of the body being imaged more clearly visible on the film. (Note: Digital imaging technology is increasingly being used by imaging facilities today and may eventually replace film.) They make sure that the patient is not wearing jewelry or other metal that would obstruct the X rays. They position the person sitting, standing, or lying down so that the correct view of the body can be radiographed, and then they cover adjacent areas with lead shielding to prevent unnecessary exposure to radiation.

The technologist positions the X-ray equipment at the proper angle and distance from the part to be radiographed and determines exposure time based on the location of the particular organ or bone and thickness of the body in that area. The controls of the X-ray machine are set to produce pictures of the correct density, contrast, and detail. Placing the photographic film closest to the body part being x-rayed, the technologist takes the requested images, repositioning the patient as needed. Typically, there are standards regarding the number of views to be taken of a given body part. The film is then developed for the radiologist or other physician to interpret.

In a fluoroscopic examination (a more complex imaging procedure that examines the gastrointestinal area), a beam of X rays passes through the body and onto a fluorescent screen, enabling the physician to see the internal organs in motion. For these, the technologist first prepares a solution of barium sulfate to be administered to the patient, either rectally or orally, depending on the exam. The barium sulfate increases the contrast between the digestive tract and surrounding organs, making the image clearer. The technologist follows the physician's guidance in positioning the patient, monitors the machine's controls, and takes any follow-up radiographs as needed.

Radiologic technologists may learn other imaging procedures such as computed tomography (CT) scanning, which uses X rays to get detailed cross-sectional images of the body's internal structures, and MRI, which uses radio waves, powerful magnets, and computers to obtain images of body parts. These diagnostic procedures are becoming more common and usually require radiologic technologists to undergo additional on-the-job training.

Other specialties within the radiography discipline include mammography and cardiovascular interventional technology. In addition, some technologists may focus on radiography of joints and bones, or they may be involved in such areas as angiocardiography (visualiza-

SCHOOL SUBJECTS
Biology, Mathematics

PERSONAL SKILLS
Helping/Teaching, Technical/Scientific

MINIMUM EDUCATION LEVEL
Some Postsecondary Training

CERTIFICATION OR LICENSING
Voluntary (Certification), Required by Certain States (Licensing)

WORK ENVIRONMENT
Primarily Indoors, Primarily One Location

tion of the heart and large blood vessels) or neuroradiology (the use of radiation to diagnose diseases of the nervous system).

Radiologic technologists perform a wide range of duties, from greeting patients and putting them at ease by explaining the procedures to developing the finished film. Their administrative tasks include maintaining patients' records, recording equipment usage and maintenance, organizing work schedules, and managing a radiologist's private practice or hospital's radiology department. Some radiologic technologists teach in programs to educate other technologists.

REQUIREMENTS
High School

If this career interests you, take plenty of math and science classes in high school. Biology, chemistry, and physics classes will be particularly useful to you. Take computer classes to become comfortable working with this technology. English classes will help you improve your communication skills. You will need these skills both when interacting with the patients and when working as part of a health care team. Finally, consider taking photography classes. Photography classes will give you experience with choosing film, framing an image, and developing photographs.

Postsecondary Training

After high school, you will need to complete an education program in radiography. Programs range in length from one to four years. Depending on length, the programs award a certificate, associate's degree, or bachelor's degree. Two-year associate's degree programs are the most popular option.

Educational programs are available in hospitals, medical centers, colleges and universities, and vocational and technical institutes. It is also possible to get radiologic technology training in the armed forces.

The Joint Review Committee on Education in Radiologic Technology (http://www.jrcert.org) accredits training programs. To enter an accredited program, you must be a high school graduate; some programs require one or two years of higher education. Courses in radiologic technology education programs include anatomy, physiology, patient care, physics, radiation protection, medical ethics, principles of imaging, medical terminology, radiobiology, and pathology. For some supervisory or administrative jobs in this field, a bachelor's or master's degree may be required.

Certification or Licensing

Radiologic technologists can become certified through the American Registry of Radiologic Technologists (ARRT) after graduating from an accredited program in radiography, radiation therapy, or nuclear medicine. After becoming certified, many technologists choose to register with the ARRT. Registration is an annual procedure required to maintain the certification. Registered technologists meet the following three criteria: They agree to comply with the ARRT rules and regulations, comply with the ARRT standards of ethics, and meet continuing education requirements. Only technologists who are currently registered can designate themselves as ARRT registered technologists and use the initials RT after their names. Although registration and certification are voluntary, many jobs are open only to technologists who have acquired these credentials.

In addition to being registered in the various imaging disciplines, radiologic technologists can receive advanced qualifications in each of the four radiography specializations: mammography, CT, MRI, and cardiovascular interventional technology. As the work of radiologic technologists grows increasingly complex and employment opportunities become more competitive, the desirability of registration and certification will also grow.

An increasing number of states have set up licensing requirements for radiologic technologists. As of 2007, 40 states and Puerto Rico require radiologic technologists to be licensed. You will need to check with the state in which you hope to work about specific requirements there.

Other Requirements

Radiologic technologists should be responsible individuals with a mature and caring nature. They should be personable and enjoy interacting with all types of people, including those who are very ill. A compassionate attitude is essential to deal with patients who may be frightened or in pain.

EXPLORING

There is no way to gain direct experience in this profession without the appropriate qualifications. However, it is possible to learn about the duties of radiologic technologists by talking with them and observing the facilities and equipment they use. It is also possible to participate in information interviews with teachers of radiologic technology. Ask your guidance counselor or a science teacher to help you contact local hospitals or schools with radiography programs to locate technologists who are willing to talk to an interested student.

As with any career in health care, volunteering at a local hospital, clinic, or nursing home provides an excellent opportunity for you to explore your interest in the field. Most hospitals are eager for volunteers, and working in such a setting will give you a chance to see health care professionals in action as well as to have some patient contact.

EMPLOYERS

There are approximately 196,000 radiologic technologists working in the United States. According to the U.S. Department of Labor, more than 60 percent of these technologists work in hospitals. Radiologic technologists also find employment in doctors' offices and clinics, at medical and diagnostic laboratories, and in outpatient care centers.

STARTING OUT

With more states regulating the practice of radiologic technology, certification by the appropriate accreditation body for a given specialty is quickly becoming a necessity for employment. If you get your training from a school that lacks accreditation or if you learn on the job, you may have difficulty in qualifying for many positions, especially those with a wide range of assignments. If you are enrolled in a hospital educational program, you may be able to get a job with the hospital upon completion of the program. If you are in a degree program, get help in finding a job through your school's career services office.

ADVANCEMENT

More than 60 percent of all radiologic technologists are employed in hospitals where there are opportunities for advancement to administrative and supervisory positions such as chief technologist or technical administrator. Other technologists develop special clinical skills in advanced imaging procedures, such as CT scanning or MRI. Some radiologic technologists qualify as instructors. Radiologic technologists who hold bachelor's degrees have more opportunities for advancement. The technologist who wishes to become a teacher or administrator will find that a master's degree and considerable experience are necessary.

EARNINGS

Salaries for radiologic technologists compare favorably with those of similar health care professionals. According to the U.S. Department of Labor, median annual earnings of radiologic technologists and technicians were $48,170 in 2006. The lowest paid 10 percent, which typically includes those just starting out in the field, earned less than $32,750. The highest paid 10 percent, which typically includes those with considerable experience, earned more than $68,920.

Mean annual earnings of radiologic technologists and technicians who worked in medical and diagnostic laboratories were $52,440 in 2006. Those who worked in hospitals earned a mean salary of $49,640, and those who worked in offices and clinics of medical doctors earned $47,420.

Most technologists take part in their employers' vacation and sick leave provisions. In addition, most employers offer benefits such as health insurance and pensions.

WORK ENVIRONMENT

Full-time technologists generally work eight hours a day, 40 hours a week. In addition, they may be on call for some night emergency duty or weekend hours, which pays in equal time off or additional compensation.

In diagnostic radiologic work, technologists perform most of their tasks while on their feet. They move around a lot and often are called upon to lift patients who need help in moving.

Great care is exercised to protect technologists from radiation exposure. Each technologist wears a badge that measures radiation exposure, and records are kept of total exposure accumulated over time. Other routine precautions include the use of safety devices (such as lead aprons, lead gloves, and other shielding) and the use of disposable gowns, gloves, and masks. Careful attention to safety procedures has greatly reduced or eliminated radiation hazards for the technologist.

Radiologic technology is dedicated to conserving life and health. Technologists derive satisfaction from their work, which helps promote health and alleviate human suffering. Those who specialize in radiation therapy need to be able to handle the close relationships they inevitably develop while working with very sick or dying people over a period of time.

OUTLOOK

Overall, employment for radiologic technologists is expected to grow faster than the average for all occupations through 2016, according to the U.S. Department of Labor. Two major reasons for this growth are the development of new technologies, which are making many imaging modalities less expensive and more apt to be performed by radiologic technicians, and the increasing elderly population in the United States, which will create a need for radiologic technologists' services. The demand for qualified technologists in some areas of the country far exceeds the supply. This shortage is particularly acute in rural areas and small towns. Those who are willing to relocate to these areas may have increased job prospects. Radiologic technologists who are trained to do more than one type of imaging procedure will also find that they have increased job opportunities. Finally, those specializing in sonography are predicted to have more opportunities than those working only with radiographs. One reason for this is ultrasound's increasing popularity due to its lack of possible side effects.

In the years to come, increasing numbers of radiologic technologists will be employed in settings outside of hospitals, such as physicians' offices, clinics, health maintenance organizations, laboratories, government agencies, and diagnostic imaging centers. This pattern will be part of the overall trend toward lowering health care costs by delivering more care outside of hospitals. Nevertheless, hospitals will remain the major employers of radiologic technologists for the near future. Because of the increasing importance of radiologic technology in the diagnosis and treatment of disease, it is unlikely that hospitals will do fewer radiologic procedures than in the past. Instead, they try to do more on an outpatient basis and on weekends and evenings. This should increase the demand for part-time technologists and thus open more opportunities for flexible work schedules.

FOR MORE INFORMATION

For information on certification and educational programs, contact

American Registry of Radiologic Technologists
1255 Northland Drive
St. Paul, MN 55120-1155
Tel: 651-687-0048
http://www.arrt.org

For information about the field, a catalog of educational products, and to access its job bank, contact

American Society of Radiologic Technologists
15000 Central Avenue, SE
Albuquerque, NM 87123-3909
Tel: 800-444-2778
Email: customerinfo@asrt.org
http://www.asrt.org

For career information, contact

Society of Diagnostic Medical Sonography
2745 Dallas Parkway, Suite 350
Plano, TX 75093-8730
Tel: 800-229-9506
http://www.sdms.org

For career and education information, contact

Canadian Association of Medical Radiation Technologists
1000-85 Albert Street,
Ottawa, ON K1P 6A4 Canada
Tel: 613-234-0012
http://www.camrt.ca

REGISTERED NURSES

OVERVIEW

Registered nurses (RNs) help individuals, families, and groups to improve and maintain health and to prevent disease. They care for the sick and injured in hospitals and other health care facilities, physicians' offices, private homes, public health agencies, schools, camps, and industry. Some registered nurses are employed in private practice. RNs hold about 2.5 million jobs in the United States.

THE JOB

Registered nurses work under the direct supervision of nursing departments and in collaboration with physi-

cians. Fifty-nine percent of all nurses work in hospitals, where they may be assigned to general, operating room, or maternity room duty. They may also care for sick children or be assigned to other hospital units, such as emergency rooms, intensive care units, or outpatient clinics. There are many different kinds of RNs. The following paragraphs detail some of the many opportunities in registered nursing.

General duty nurses work together with other members of the health care team to assess the patient's condition and to develop and implement a plan of health care. These nurses may perform such tasks as taking patients' vital signs, administering medication and injections, recording the symptoms and progress of patients, changing dressings, assisting patients with personal care, conferring with members of the medical staff, helping prepare a patient for surgery, and completing any number of duties that require skill and understanding of patients' needs.

Surgical nurses oversee the preparation of the operating room and the sterilization of instruments. They assist surgeons during operations and coordinate the flow of patient cases in operating rooms.

Critical care nurses provide highly skilled direct patient care to critically ill patients needing intense medical treatment. Contrary to previously held beliefs that critical care nurses work only in intensive care units or cardiac care units of hospitals, today's critical care nurses work in the emergency departments, post-anesthesia recovery units, pediatric intensive care units, burn units, and neonatal intensive care units of medical facilities, as well as in other units that treat critically ill patients.

Maternity nurses, or *neonatal nurses*, help in the delivery room, take care of newborns in the nursery, and teach mothers how to feed and care for their babies.

The activities of staff nurses are directed and coordinated by *head nurses* and *charge nurses*. Heading up the entire nursing program in the hospital is the *nursing service director*, who administers the nursing program to maintain standards of patient care. The *nursing service director* advises the medical staff, department heads, and the hospital administrator in matters relating to nursing services and helps prepare the department budget.

Private duty nurses may work in hospitals or in a patient's home. They are employed by the patient they are caring for or by the patient's family. Their service is designed for the individual care of one person and is carried out in cooperation with the patient's physician.

Office nurses usually work in the office of a dentist, physician, or health maintenance organization (HMO). An office nurse may be one of several nurses on the staff or the only staff nurse. If a nurse is the only staff member, this person may have to combine some clerical duties with those of nursing, such as serving as receptionist, making appointments for the doctor, helping maintain patient records, sending out monthly statements, and attending to routine correspondence. If the physician's staff is a large one that includes secretaries and clerks, the office nurse will concentrate on screening patients, assisting with examinations, supervising the examining rooms, sterilizing equipment, providing patient education, and performing other nursing duties.

Occupational health nurses, or *industrial nurses,* are an important part of many large firms. They maintain a clinic at a plant or factory and are usually occupied in rendering preventive, remedial, and educational nursing services. They work under the direction of an industrial physician, nursing director, or nursing supervisor. They may advise on accident prevention, visit employees on the job to check the conditions under which they work, and advise management about the safety of such conditions. At the plant, they render treatment in emergencies.

School nurses may work in one school or in several, visiting each for a part of the day or week. They may supervise the student clinic, treat minor cuts or injuries, or give advice on good health practices. They may examine students to detect conditions of the eyes or teeth that require attention. They also assist the school physician.

Community health nurses, also called *public health nurses,* require specialized training for their duties. Their job usually requires them to spend part of the time traveling from one assignment to another. Their duties may differ greatly from one case to another. For instance, in one day they may have to instruct a class of expectant mothers, visit new parents to help them plan proper care for the baby, visit an aged patient requiring special care, and conduct a class in nutrition. They usually possess many varied nursing skills and often are called upon to resolve unexpected or unusual situations.

Home health care nurses, also called *visiting nurses,* provide home-based health care under the direction of a physician. They care for persons who may be recovering from an accident, illness, surgery, cancer, or childbirth. They may work for a community organization, a private health care provider, or they may be independent nurses who work on a contract basis.

While home health care nurses care for patients expecting to recover, *hospice nurses* care for people who are in the final stages of a terminal illness. Typically, a hospice patient has less than six months to live. Hospice nurses provide medical and emotional support to the patients and their families and friends. Hospice care usually takes place in the patient's home, but patients

---

SCHOOL SUBJECTS
Biology, Chemistry, Health

PERSONAL SKILLS
Helping/Teaching, Technical/Scientific

MINIMUM EDUCATION LEVEL
Some Postsecondary Training

CERTIFICATION OR LICENSING
Required

WORK ENVIRONMENT
Primarily Indoors, Primarily Multiple Locations

---

may also receive hospice care in a hospital room, nursing home, or a relative's home.

Administrators in the community health field include *nursing directors, educational directors,* and *nursing supervisors.* Some nurses go into nursing education and work with nursing students to instruct them on theories and skills they will need to enter the profession. Nursing instructors may give classroom instruction and demonstrations or supervise nursing students on hospital units. Some instructors eventually become nursing school directors, university faculty, or deans of a university degree program. Nurses also have the opportunity to direct staff development and continuing education programs for nursing personnel in hospitals.

Advanced practice nurses are nurses with training beyond that required to have the RN designation. There are four primary categories of nurses included in this category: *nurse-midwives, clinical nurse specialists, nurse anesthetists,* and *nurse practitioners.*

Some nurses are consultants to hospitals, nursing schools, industrial organizations, and public health agencies. They advise clients on such administrative matters as staff organization, nursing techniques, curricula, and education programs. Other administrative specialists include *educational directors* for the state board of nursing, who are concerned with maintaining well-defined educational standards, and *executive directors* of professional nurses' associations, who administer programs developed by the board of directors and the members of the association.

Some nurses choose to enter the armed forces. All types of nurses, except private duty nurses, are represented in the military services. They provide skilled nursing care to active-duty and retired members of the armed forces and their families. In addition to basic nursing skills, *military nurses* are trained to provide care in various environments, including field hospitals, on-air evacuation flights, and onboard ships. Military nurses actively influence the development of health care through nursing research. Advances influenced by military nurses include the development of the artificial kidney (dialysis unit) and the concept of the intensive care unit.

REQUIREMENTS
High School

If you are interested in becoming a registered nurse, you should take high school mathematics and science courses, including biology, chemistry, and physics. Health courses will also be helpful. English and speech courses should not be neglected because you must be able to communicate well with patients.

Postsecondary Training

There are three basic kinds of training programs that you may choose from to become a registered nurse: associate's degree, diploma, and bachelor's degree. The choice of which of the three training programs to pursue depends on your career goals. A bachelor's degree in nursing is required for most supervisory or administrative positions, for jobs in public health agencies, and for admission to graduate nursing programs. A master's degree is usually necessary to prepare for a nursing specialty or to teach. For some specialties, such as nursing research, a Ph.D. is essential.

There are approximately 709 bachelor's degree programs in nursing in the United States. It requires four (in some cases, five) years to complete. The graduate of this program receives a bachelor of science in nursing (B.S.N.) degree. The associate degree in nursing (A.D.N.) is awarded after completion of a two-year study program that is usually offered in a junior or community college. There are approximately 850 A.D.N. programs in the United States. You receive hospital training at cooperating hospitals in the general vicinity of the community college. The diploma program, which usually lasts three years, is conducted by hospitals and independent schools, although the number of these programs is declining. At the conclusion of each of these programs, you become a graduate nurse, but not, however, a registered nurse. To obtain the RN designation you must pass a licensing examination required in all states.

Nurses can pursue postgraduate training that allows them to specialize in certain areas, such as emergency room, operating room, premature nursery, or psychiatric nursing. This training is sometimes offered through hospital on-the-job training programs.

Certification or Licensing

Voluntary certification is available for a variety of registered nursing specialties, and certification may be required for the four advanced practice nursing specialties. Contact professional nursing associations in your specialty for more information on certification.

All states and the District of Columbia require a license to practice nursing. To obtain a license, graduates of approved nursing schools must pass a national examination. Nurses may be licensed by more than one state. In some states, continuing education is a condition for license renewal. Different titles require different education and training levels.

Other Requirements

You should enjoy working with people, especially those who may experience fear or anger because of an illness. Patience, compassion, and calmness are qualities needed by anyone working in this career. In addition, you must be able to give directions as well as follow instructions and work as part of a health care team. Anyone interested in becoming a registered nurse should also have a strong desire to continue learning, because new tests, procedures, and technologies are constantly being developed within medicine.

EXPLORING

You can explore your interest in nursing in a number of ways. Read books on careers in nursing and talk with high school guidance counselors, school nurses, and local public health nurses. Visit hospitals to observe the work and talk with hospital personnel to learn more about the daily activities of nursing staff.

Some hospitals now have extensive volunteer service programs in which high school students may work after school, on weekends, or during vacations in order both to render a valuable service and to explore their interests in nursing. There are other volunteer work experiences available with the Red Cross or community health services. Camp counseling jobs sometimes offer related experiences. Some schools offer participation in Future Nurses programs.

The Internet is full of resources about nursing. Check out Discover Nursing (http://www.discovernursing. com), Nursing Net (http://www.nursingnet.org), and the American Nursing Association's Nursing World (http:// www.nursingworld.org).

EMPLOYERS

Approximately 2.5 million registered nurses are employed in the United States. Hospitals account for 59 percent of jobs for registered nurses. Nurses are also employed by managed-care facilities, long-term care facilities, clinics, industry, home health care, schools, camps, and government agencies. Twenty-one percent of nurses work part time.

STARTING OUT

The only way to become a registered nurse is through completion of one of the three kinds of educational programs, plus passing the licensing examination. Registered nurses may apply for employment directly to hospitals, nursing homes, home care agencies, temporary nursing agencies, companies, and government agencies that hire nurses. Jobs can also be obtained through school career services offices, by signing up with employment agencies specializing in placement of nursing personnel, or through the state employment office. Other sources of jobs include nurses' associations, professional journals, and newspaper want ads.

ADVANCEMENT

Increasingly, administrative and supervisory positions in the nursing field go to nurses who have earned at least the bachelor of science degree in nursing. Nurses with many years of experience who are graduates of a diploma program may achieve supervisory positions, but requirements for such promotions have become more difficult in recent years and in many cases require at least the B.S.N. degree.

Nurses with bachelor's degrees are usually those who are hired as public health nurses. Nurses with master's degrees are often employed as clinical nurse specialists, faculty, instructors, supervisors, or administrators.

RNs can pursue further education to become advanced practice nurses, who have greater responsibilities and command higher salaries.

EARNINGS

According to the U.S. Department of Labor, registered nurses had median annual earnings of $57,280 in 2006. Salaries ranged from less than $40,250 to more than $83,440. Earnings of RNs vary according to employer. In 2006, those who worked at hospitals earned $60,970; at offices of physicians, $59,170; in home health care services, $56,810; and at nursing care facilities, $53,690.

Salary is determined by several factors: setting, education, and work experience. Most full-time nurses are given flexible work schedules as well as health and life insurance; some are offered education reimbursement and year-end bonuses. A staff nurse's salary is often limited only by the amount of work he or she is willing to take on. Many nurses take advantage of overtime work and shift differentials. About 7 percent of all nurses hold more than one job.

WORK ENVIRONMENT

Most nurses work in facilities that are clean and well lighted and where the temperature is controlled, although some work in rundown inner-city hospitals in less-than-ideal conditions. Usually, nurses work eight-hour shifts. Those in hospitals generally work any of three shifts: 7:00 A.M. to 3:00 P.M.; 3:00 P.M. to 11:00 P.M.; or 11:00 P.M. to 7:00 A.M.

Nurses spend much of the day on their feet, either walking or standing. Handling patients who are ill or infirm can also be very exhausting. Nurses who come in contact with patients with infectious diseases must be especially careful about cleanliness and sterility. Although many nursing duties are routine, many responsibilities are unpredictable. Sick persons are often very demanding, or they may be depressed or irritable. Despite this, nurses must maintain their composure and should be cheerful to help the patient achieve emotional balance.

Community health nurses may be required to visit homes that are in poor condition or very dirty. They may also come in contact with social problems, such as family violence. The nurse is an important health care provider and in many communities the sole provider.

Both the office nurse and the industrial nurse work regular business hours and are seldom required to work overtime. In some jobs, such as where nurses are on duty in private homes, they may frequently travel from home to home and work with various cases.

OUTLOOK

The nursing field is the largest of all health care occupations, and employment prospects for nurses are excellent. The U.S. Department of Labor projects that employment for registered nurses will grow much faster than the average for all professions through 2016. Opportunities will be strongest in the following sectors: offices of physicians and home health care services, where employment is expected to increase by 39 percent through 2016; outpatient care centers (except mental health and substance abuse), 34 percent growth; and employment services, 27 percent growth.

There has been a serious shortage of nurses in recent years. Many nurses leave the profession within five years because of unsatisfactory working conditions, including low pay, severe understaffing, high stress, physical demands, mandatory overtime, and irregular hours. The shortage will also be exacerbated by the increasing numbers of baby-boomer-aged nurses who are expected to retire, creating more open positions than there are graduates of nursing programs.

The much-faster-than-average job growth in this field is also a result of improving medical technology that will allow for treatments of many more diseases and health conditions. Nurses will be in strong demand to work with the rapidly growing population of senior citizens in the United States.

Approximately 59 percent of all nursing jobs are found in hospitals. However, because of administrative cost cutting, increased nurse's workload, and rapid growth of outpatient services (such as those that provide same-day surgery, chemotherapy, and rehabilitation), hospital nursing jobs will experience slower growth as compared to other settings within the nursing profession. Despite this prediction, there should continue to be a need for RNs in critical care units, emergency departments, and operating rooms. These settings, which often are stressful and involve overtime and night and weekend shifts, frequently have shortages of RNs.

Employment in home care and nursing homes is expected to grow rapidly. Though more people are living well into their 80s and 90s, many need the kind of long-term care available at a nursing home. Also, because of financial reasons, patients are being released from hospitals sooner and admitted into nursing homes. Many nursing homes have facilities and staff capable of caring for long-term rehabilitation patients, as well as those afflicted with Alzheimer's. Many nurses will also be needed to help staff the growing number of outpatient facilities, such as HMOs, group medical practices, and ambulatory surgery centers.

Registered nurses with a bachelor's degree or higher—especially those who work as advanced practice nurses—will have the strongest employment prospects.

Nursing specialties will be in great demand. There are, in addition, many part-time employment possibilities, with about 21 percent of RNs working part time.

FOR MORE INFORMATION

Visit the AACN's Web site to access a list of member schools and to read the online pamphlet Your Nursing Career: A Look at the Facts.

American Association of Colleges of Nursing (AACN)
One Dupont Circle, Suite 530
Washington, DC 20036-1110
Tel: 202-463-6930
http://www.aacn.nche.edu

For information about opportunities as an RN, contact the following organizations:

American Nurses Association
8515 Georgia Avenue, Suite 400
Silver Spring, MD 20910-3492
Tel: 800-274-4262
http://www.nursingworld.org

American Society of Registered Nurses
1001 Bridgeway, Suite 411
Sausalito, CA 94965-2104
Tel: 415-331-2700
Email: office@asrn.org
http://www.asrn.org

For information about state-approved programs and information on nursing, contact the following organizations:

National League for Nursing
61 Broadway
New York, NY 10006-2701
Tel: 800-669-1656
http://www.nln.org

National Organization for Associate Degree Nursing
7794 Grow Drive
Pensacola, FL 32514-7072
Tel: 850-484-6948
Email: noadn@noadn.org
http://www.noadn.org

Discover Nursing, sponsored by Johnson & Johnson Health Care Systems, provides information on nursing careers, nursing schools, and scholarships.

Discover Nursing
http://www.discovernursing.com

REHABILITATION COUNSELORS

OVERVIEW

Rehabilitation counselors provide counseling and guidance services to people with disabilities to help them resolve life problems and to train for and locate work that is suitable to their physical and mental abilities, interests, and aptitudes. There are approximately 141,000 rehabilitation counselors working in the United States.

THE JOB

Rehabilitation counselors work with people with disabilities to identify barriers to medical, psychological, personal, social, and vocational functioning and to develop a plan of action to remove or reduce those barriers.

Clients are referred to rehabilitation programs from many sources. Sometimes they seek help on their own initiative; sometimes their families bring them in. They may be referred by a physician, hospital, or social worker, or they may be sent by employment agencies, schools, or accident commissions. A former employer may seek help for the individual.

The counselor's first step is to determine the nature and extent of the disability and evaluate how that disability interferes with work and other life functions. This determination is made from medical and psychological reports as well as from family history, educational background, work experience, and other evaluative information.

The next step is to determine a vocational direction and plan of services to overcome the handicaps to employment or independent living.

The rehabilitation counselor coordinates a comprehensive evaluation of a client's physical functioning abilities and vocational interests, aptitudes, and skills. This information is used to develop vocational or independent-living goals for the client and the services necessary to reach those goals. Services that the rehabilitation counselor may coordinate or provide include physical and mental restoration, academic or vocational training, vocational counseling, job analysis, job modification or reasonable accommodation, and job placement. Limited financial assistance in the form of maintenance or transportation assistance may also be provided.

| **SCHOOL SUBJECTS** |
| Psychology, Sociology |
| **PERSONAL SKILLS** |
| Helping/Teaching, Technical/Scientific |
| **MINIMUM EDUCATION LEVEL** |
| Bachelor's Degree |
| **CERTIFICATION OR LICENSING** |
| Recommended |
| **WORK ENVIRONMENT** |
| Primarily Indoors, Primarily One Location |

The counselor's relationship with the client may be as brief as a week or as long as several years, depending on the nature of the problem and the needs of the client.

REQUIREMENTS

High School

To prepare for becoming a rehabilitation counselor, take your high school's college prep curriculum. These classes should include several years of mathematics and science, such as biology and chemistry. To begin to gain an understanding of people and societies, take history, psychology, and sociology classes. English classes are important to take because you will need excellent communication skills for this work. Some of your professional responsibilities will include documenting your work and doing research to provide your clients with helpful information; to do these things you will undoubtedly be working with computers. Therefore, you should take computer science classes so that you are skilled in using them. In addition, you may want to consider taking speech and a foreign language, both of which will enhance your communication skills.

Postsecondary Training

Although some positions are available for people with a bachelor's degree in rehabilitation counseling, these positions are usually as aides and offer limited advancement opportunities. Most employers require the rehabilitation counselors working for them to hold master's degrees.

Before receiving your master's, you will need to complete a bachelor's degree with a major in behavioral sciences, social sciences, or a related field. Another option is to complete an undergraduate degree in rehabilitation counseling. The Council for Accreditation of Counseling and Related Educational Programs has accredited 212 institutions that offer programs in counselor education. If you decide on an undergraduate degree in rehabilitation, it is recommended you attend an accredited program. Keep in mind, however, that even if you get an undergraduate degree in rehabilitation, you will still need to attend a graduate program to qualify for most counselor positions. No matter which undergraduate program you decide on, you should concentrate on courses in sociology, psychology, physiology, history, and statistics as well as courses in English and communications. Several universities now offer courses in various aspects of physical therapy and special education training. Courses in sign language, speech therapy, and a foreign language are also beneficial.

More than 100 graduate programs in rehabilitation counseling have been accredited by the Council on Rehabilitation Education, and to receive the most thorough education, it is recommended you attend one of these. A typical master's program usually lasts two years. Studies include courses in medical aspects of disability, psychosocial aspects of disability, testing techniques, statistics, personality theory, personality development, abnormal psychology, techniques of counseling, occupational information, and vocational training and job placement. A supervised internship is also an important aspect of a program.

Certification or Licensing

The regulation of counselors is required in 49 states and the District of Columbia. This regulation may be in the form of credentialing, registry, certification, or licensure. Regulations, however, vary by state and sometimes by employer. For example, an employer may require certification even if the state does not. You will need to check with your state's licensing board as well as your employer for specific information about your circumstances.

Across the country, many employers now require their rehabilitation counselors to be certified by the Commission on Rehabilitation Counselor Certification (CRCC). The purpose of certification is to provide assurance that professionals engaged in rehabilitation counseling meet set standards and maintain those standards through continuing education. To become certified, counselors must pass an extensive written examination to demonstrate their knowledge of rehabilitation counseling. The CRCC requires the master's degree as the minimum educational level for certification. Applicants who meet these certification requirements receive the designation of certified rehabilitation counselor.

Most state government rehabilitation agencies require future counselors to meet state civil service and merit system regulations. The applicant must take a competitive written examination and may also be interviewed and evaluated by a special board.

Other Requirements

The most important personal attribute required for rehabilitation counseling is the ability to get along well with other people. Rehabilitation counselors work with many different kinds of clients and must be able to see situations and problems from their client's point of view. They must be both patient and persistent. Rehabilitation may be a slow process with many delays and setbacks. The counselor must maintain a calm, positive manner even when no progress is made.

EXPLORING

To explore a career in which you work with people with disabilities, you should look for opportunities to volunteer or work in this field. One possibility is to be a counselor at a children's camp for disabled youngsters. You can also volunteer with a local vocational rehabilitation agency or an organization such as Easter Seals or Goodwill. Other possibilities include reading for the blind or leading a hobby or craft class at an adult day care center. And don't forget volunteer opportunities at a local hospital or nursing home. Even if your only responsibility is to escort people to the X-ray department or talk to patients to cheer them up, you will gain valuable experience interacting with people who are facing challenging situations.

EMPLOYERS

Approximately 141,000 rehabilitation counselors are employed in the United States. Counselors work in a variety of settings. About three-quarters of rehabilitation counselors work for state agencies; some also work for local and federal agencies. Employment opportunities are available in rehabilitation centers, mental health agencies, developmental disability agencies, sheltered workshops, training institutions, and special schools.

STARTING OUT

School career services offices are the best places for the new graduate to begin the career search. In addition, the National Rehabilitation Counseling Association and the American Rehabilitation Counseling Association (a division of the American Counseling Association) are sources for employment information. The new counselor may also apply directly to agencies for available positions. State and local vocational rehabilitation agencies employ about 10,000 rehabilitation counselors. The Department of Veterans Affairs employs several hundred people to assist with the rehabilitation of disabled veterans. Many rehabilitation counselors are employed by private for-profit or nonprofit rehabilitation programs and facilities. Others are employed in industry, schools, hospitals, and other settings, while others are self-employed.

ADVANCEMENT

The rehabilitation counselor usually receives regular salary increases after gaining experience in the job. He or she may move from relatively easy cases to increasingly challenging ones. Counselors may advance into such positions as administrator or supervisor after several years of counseling experience. It is also possible to find related counseling and teaching positions, which may represent an advancement in other fields.

EARNINGS

The U.S. Department of Labor reports that median annual earnings of rehabilitation counselors in 2006 were $29,200. Salaries ranged from less than $19,260 to more than $53,170.

Rehabilitation counselors employed by the federal government generally start at the GS-9 or GS-11 level. In 2008, basic GS-9 salary was $39,975. Those with master's degrees generally began at the GS-11 level, with a salary of $48,148 in 2008. Salaries for federal government workers vary according to the region of the country in which they work. Those working in areas with a higher cost of living receive additional locality pay.

Counselors employed by government and private agencies and institutions generally receive health insurance, pension plans, and other benefits, including vacation, sick, and holiday pay. Self-employed counselors must provide their own benefits.

WORK ENVIRONMENT

Rehabilitation counselors work approximately 40 hours each week and do not usually have to work during evenings or weekends. They work both in the office and in the field. Depending on the type of training required, lab space and workout or therapy rooms may be available. Rehabilitation counselors must usually keep detailed accounts of their progress with clients and write reports.

They may spend many hours traveling about the community to visit employed clients, prospective employers, trainees, or training programs.

OUTLOOK

The passage of the Americans with Disabilities Act of 1990 increased the demand for rehabilitation counselors. As more local, state, and federal programs are initiated that are designed to assist people with disabilities and as private institutions and companies seek to comply with this new legislation, job prospects are promising. Budget pressures may serve to limit the number of new rehabilitation counselors hired by government agencies; however, the overall outlook remains excellent.

The U.S. Department of Labor predicts that employment for all counselors will grow much faster than the average for all careers through 2016. Some of this growth can be attributed to the advances in medical technology that are saving more lives. In addition, more employers are offering employee assistance programs that provide mental health services.

FOR MORE INFORMATION

For general information on careers in rehabilitation counseling, contact
American Rehabilitation Counseling Association
5999 Stevenson Avenue
Alexandria, VA 22304-3300
Tel: 800-545-2223
http://www.arcaweb.org

For information on certification, contact
Commission on Rehabilitation Counselor Certification
300 North Martingale Road, Suite 460
Schaumburg, IL 60173-2088
Tel: 847-944-1325
Email: info@crccertification.com
http://www.crccertification.com

For listings of CORE-approved programs as well as other information, contact
Council on Rehabilitation Education (CORE)
300 North Martingale Road, Suite 460
Schaumburg, IL 60173-2088
Tel: 847-944-1345
http://www.core-rehab.org

For information on a variety of resources, contact
**National Clearinghouse of Rehabilitation
    Training Materials**
Utah State University

6524 Old Main Hill
Logan, UT 84322-6524
Tel: 866-821-5355
Email: ncrtm@usu.edu
http://ncrtm.org

To learn about government legislation, visit the NRA's Web site.

National Rehabilitation Association (NRA)
633 South Washington Street
Alexandria, VA 22314-4109
Tel: 703-836-0850
Email: info@nationalrehab.org
http://www.nationalrehab.org

The NRCA is a division of the National Rehabilitation Association. For news on legislation, employment, and other information, contact

National Rehabilitation Counseling Association (NRCA)
PO Box 4480
Manassas, VA 20108-4480
Tel: 703-361-2077
Email: NRCAOFFICE@aol.com
http://nrca-net.org

RESPIRATORY THERAPISTS

OVERVIEW

Respiratory therapists, also known as respiratory care practitioners, evaluate, treat, and care for patients with deficiencies or abnormalities of the cardiopulmonary (heart/lung) system by either providing temporary relief from chronic ailments or administering emergency care where life is threatened. They are involved with the supervision of other respiratory care workers in their area of treatment.

Working under a physician's direction, these workers set up and operate respirators, mechanical ventilators, and other devices. They monitor the functioning of the equipment and the patients' response to the therapy and maintain the patients' charts. They also assist patients with breathing exercises, and inspect, test, and order repairs for respiratory therapy equipment. They may demonstrate procedures to trainees and other health care personnel. Approximately 122,000 respiratory therapists are employed in the United States.

THE JOB

Respiratory therapists treat patients with various cardiorespiratory problems. They may provide care that affords temporary relief from chronic illnesses such as asthma or emphysema, or they may administer life-support treatment to victims of heart failure, stroke, drowning, or shock. These specialists often mean the difference between life and death in cases involving acute respiratory conditions, as may result from head injuries or drug poisoning. Adults who stop breathing for longer than three to five minutes rarely survive without serious brain damage, and an absence of respiratory activity for more than nine minutes almost always results in death. Respiratory therapists carry out their duties under a physician's direction and supervision. Therapists set up and operate special devices to treat patients who need temporary or emergency relief from breathing difficulties. The equipment may include respirators, positive-pressure breathing machines, or environmental control systems. Aerosol inhalants are administered to confine medication to the lungs. Respiratory therapists often treat patients who have undergone surgery because anesthesia depresses normal respiration, thus the patients need some support to restore their full breathing capability and to prevent respiratory illnesses.

In evaluating patients, therapists test the capacity of the lungs and analyze the oxygen and carbon dioxide concentration and potential of hydrogen (pH), a measure of the acidity or alkalinity level of the blood. To measure lung capacity, therapists have patients breathe into an instrument that measures the volume and flow of air during inhalation and exhalation. By comparing the reading with the norm for the patient's age, height, weight, and gender, respiratory therapists can determine whether lung deficiencies exist. To analyze oxygen, carbon dioxide, and pH levels, therapists draw an arterial blood sample, place it in a blood gas analyzer, and relay the results to a physician.

Respiratory therapists watch equipment gauges and maintain prescribed volumes of oxygen or other inhalants. Besides monitoring the equipment to be sure it is operating properly, they observe the patient's physiological response to the therapy and consult with physicians in case of any adverse reactions. They also record pertinent identification and therapy information on each patient's chart and keep records of the cost of materials and the charges to the patients.

Therapists instruct patients and their families on how to use respiratory equipment at home, and they may demonstrate respiratory therapy procedures to trainees and other health care personnel. Their responsibilities include inspecting and testing equipment. If it is faulty, they either make minor repairs themselves or order major repairs.

Respiratory therapy workers include therapists, technicians, and assistants. Differences between respiratory therapists' duties and those of other respiratory care workers' include supervising technicians and assistants, teaching new staff, and bearing primary responsibility for the care given in their areas. At times the respiratory therapist may need to work independently and make clinical judgments on the type of care to be given to a patient. Although *respiratory technicians* can perform many of the same activities as a therapist (for example, monitoring equipment, checking patient responses, and giving medicine), they do not make independent decisions about what type of care to give. *Respiratory assistants* clean, sterilize, store, and generally take care of the equipment but have very little contact with patients.

REQUIREMENTS
High School

To prepare for a career in this field while you are still in high school, take health and science classes, including biology, chemistry, and physics. Mathematics and statistics classes will also be useful to you since much of this work involves using numbers and making calculations. Take computer science courses to become familiar with using technical and complex equipment and to become familiar with programs you can use to document your work. Since some of your responsibilities may include working directly with patients to teach them therapies, take English classes to improve your communication skills. Studying a foreign language may also be useful.

Postsecondary Training

Formal training is necessary for entry to this field. Training is offered at the postsecondary level by hospitals, medical schools, colleges and universities, trade schools, vocational-technical institutes, and the armed forces. The Committee on Accreditation for Respiratory Care and the Commission on Accreditation of Allied Health Education Programs (CAAHEP) have accredited more than 375 programs nationwide. A listing of these programs is available on the CAAHEP's Web site, http://www.caahep.org. To be eligible for a respiratory therapy program, you must have graduated from high school.

Accredited respiratory therapy programs combine class work with clinical work. Programs vary in length, depending on the degree awarded. A certificate program

SCHOOL SUBJECTS
Health, Mathematics

PERSONAL SKILLS
Helping/Teaching, Technical/Scientific

MINIMUM EDUCATION LEVEL
Associate's Degree

CERTIFICATION OR LICENSING
Recommended

WORK ENVIRONMENT
Primarily Indoors, Primarily One Location

generally takes one year to complete, an associate's degree usually takes two years, and a bachelor's degree program typically takes four years. In addition, it is important to note that some advanced-level programs will prepare you for becoming a registered respiratory therapist (RRT), while entry-level programs will prepare you for becoming a certified respiratory therapist (CRT). RRT-prepared graduates will be eligible for jobs as respiratory therapists once they have been certified. CRT-prepared graduates, on the other hand, are only eligible for jobs as respiratory technicians after certification. The areas of study for both therapists and technicians cover human anatomy and physiology, chemistry, physics, microbiology, and mathematics. Technical studies include courses such as patient evaluation, respiratory care pharmacology, pulmonary diseases, and care procedures.

Certification and Licensing

The National Board for Respiratory Care (NBRC) offers voluntary certification to graduates of accredited programs. The certifications, as previously mentioned, are registered respiratory therapist (RRT) and certified respiratory therapist (CRT). You must have at least an associate's degree to be eligible to take the CRT exam. Anyone desiring certification must take the CRT exam first. After successfully completing this exam, those who are eligible can take the RRT exam. CRTs who meet further education and experience requirements can qualify for the RRT credential. There are also specialty designations available in pulmonary function technology and neonatal/pediatric respiratory care.

Certification is highly recommended because most employers require this credential. Those who are designated CRT or are eligible to take the exam are qualified for technician jobs that are entry-level or generalist positions. Employers usually require those with supervisory positions or those in intensive care specialties to have the RRT (or RRT eligibility).

More than 40 states regulate respiratory care personnel through licensing or certification. Requirements vary, so you will need to check with your state's regulatory board for specific information. The NBRC's Web site provides helpful contact information for state licensure agencies at http://www.nbrc.org/StateLicAgencies.htm.

Other Requirements

Respiratory therapists must enjoy working with people. You must be sensitive to your patients' physical and psychological needs because you will be dealing with people who may be in pain or who may be frightened. The work of this occupational group is of great significance. Respiratory therapists are often responsible for the lives and well being of people already in critical condition. You must pay strict attention to detail, be able to follow instructions and work as part of a team, and remain cool in emergencies. Mechanical ability and manual dexterity are necessary to operate much of the respiratory equipment.

EXPLORING

Those considering advanced study may obtain a list of accredited educational programs in respiratory therapy by visiting the Web site of the Commission on Accreditation of Allied Health Education Programs (http://www.caahep.org). Formal training in this field is available in hospitals, vocational-technical institutes, private trade schools, and other non-collegiate settings as well. Local hospitals can provide information on training opportunities. School vocational counselors may be sources of additional information about educational matters and may be able to set up interviews with or lectures by a respiratory therapy practitioner from a local hospital.

Hospitals are excellent places to obtain part-time and summer employment. They have a continuing need for helpers in many departments. Even though the work may not be directly related to respiratory therapy, you will gain knowledge of the operation of a hospital and may be in a position to get acquainted with respiratory therapists and observe them as they carry out their duties. If part-time or temporary work is not available, you may wish to volunteer your services.

EMPLOYERS

Nearly four out of five respiratory therapy jobs were in hospital departments of respiratory care, anesthesiology, or pulmonary medicine. The rest are employed by oxygen equipment rental companies, ambulance services, nursing homes, home health agencies, and physicians' offices. Many respiratory therapists (12 percent, as opposed to 5 percent in other occupations) hold a second job.

STARTING OUT

Graduates of CAAHEP-accredited respiratory therapy training programs may use their school's career services offices to help them find jobs. Otherwise, they may apply directly to the individual local health care facilities.

ADVANCEMENT

Many respiratory therapists start out as assistants or technicians. With appropriate training courses and experience, they advance to the therapist level. Respiratory therapists with sufficient experience may be promoted to assistant chief or chief therapist. With graduate education, they may be qualified to teach respiratory therapy at the college level or move into administrative positions such as director.

EARNINGS

Respiratory therapists earned a median salary of $47,420 in 2006, according to the U.S. Department of Labor. The lowest 10 percent earned less than $35,200, and the highest 10 percent earned more than $64,190.

Hospital workers receive benefits that include health insurance, paid vacations and sick leave, and pension plans. Some institutions provide additional benefits, such as uniforms and parking, and offer free courses or tuition reimbursement for job-related courses.

WORK ENVIRONMENT

Respiratory therapists generally work in extremely clean, quiet surroundings. They usually work 35 to 40 hours a week, which may include nights and weekends because hospitals are in operation 24 hours a day, seven days a week. The work requires long hours of standing and may be very stressful during emergencies.

A possible hazard is that the inhalants these employees work with are highly flammable. The danger of fire is minimized, however, if the workers test equipment regularly and are strict about taking safety precautions. As do workers in many other health occupations, respiratory therapists run a risk of catching infectious diseases. Careful adherence to proper procedures minimizes the risk.

OUTLOOK

Employment for respiratory therapists is expected to grow at a much-faster-than-average rate through 2016, despite the fact that efforts to control rising health care costs has reduced the number of job opportunities in hospitals.

The increasing demand for therapists is the result of several factors. The fields of neonatal care and gerontology are growing, and there are continuing advances in treatments for victims of heart attacks and accidents and for premature babies. Also, there is a greater incidence of cardiopulmonary and AIDS-related diseases, coupled with more advanced methods of diagnosing and treating them.

Employment opportunities for respiratory therapists should be very favorable in the rapidly growing field of home health care, although this area accounts for only a small number of respiratory therapy jobs. In addition to jobs in home health agencies and hospital-based home health programs, there should be numerous openings for respiratory therapists in offices of physicians, equipment rental companies, and in firms that provide respiratory care on a contract basis.

FOR MORE INFORMATION

For information on scholarships, continuing education, job listings, and careers in respiratory therapy, contact

American Association for Respiratory Care
9425 North MacArthur Boulevard, Suite 100
Irving, TX 75063-4706
Tel: 972-243-2272
Email: info@aarc.org
http://www.aarc.org

For more information on allied health care careers as well as a listing of accredited programs, contact

Commission on Accreditation of Allied Health Education Programs
1361 Park Street
Clearwater, FL 33756-6039
Tel: 727-210-2350
Email: caahep@caahep.org
http://www.caahep.org

For a list of accredited training programs, contact

Committee on Accreditation for Respiratory Care
1248 Harwood Road
Bedford, TX 76021-4244
Tel: 817-283-2835
Email: info@coarc.com
http://www.coarc.com

For information on licensing and certification, contact

National Board for Respiratory Care
18000 West 105th Street
Olathe, KS 66061-7543
Tel: 913-895-4900
http://www.nbrc.org

RETAIL SALES WORKERS

OVERVIEW

Retail sales workers assist customers with purchases by identifying their needs, showing or demonstrating merchandise, receiving payment, recording sales, and wrapping their purchases or arranging for their delivery. They are sometimes called *sales clerks*, *retail clerks*, or *salespeople*. There are approximately 4.5 million retail salespersons employed in the United States.

THE JOB

Salespeople work in more than a hundred different types of retail establishments in a variety of roles. Some, for example, work in small specialty shops where, in addition to waiting on customers, they might check inventory, order stock from sales representatives (or by telephone or mail), place newspaper display advertisements, prepare window displays, and rearrange merchandise for sale.

SCHOOL SUBJECTS
English, Mathematics, Speech

PERSONAL SKILLS
Communication/Ideas, Helping/Teaching

MINIMUM EDUCATION LEVEL
High School Diploma

CERTIFICATION OR LICENSING
Voluntary

WORK ENVIRONMENT
Primarily Indoors, Primarily One Location

Other salespeople may work in specific departments, such as the furniture department, of a large department store. The employees in a department work in shifts to provide service to customers six or seven days a week. To improve their sales effectiveness and knowledge of merchandise, they attend regular staff meetings. Advertising, window decorating, sales promotion, buying, and market research specialists support the work of retail salespeople.

Whatever they are selling, the primary responsibility of retail sales workers is to interest customers in the merchandise. This might be done by describing the product's features, demonstrating its use, or showing various models and colors. Some retail sales workers must have specialized knowledge, particularly those who sell such expensive, complicated products as stereos, appliances, and personal computers.

In addition to selling, most retail sales workers make out sales checks; receive cash, checks, and charge payments; bag or package purchases; and give change and receipts. Depending on the hours they work, retail sales workers might have to open or close the cash register. This might include counting the money in the cash register; separating charge slips, coupons, and exchange vouchers; and making deposits at the cash office. The sales records they keep are normally used in inventory control. Sales workers are usually held responsible for the contents of their registers, and repeated shortages are cause for dismissal in many organizations.

Sales workers must be aware of any promotions the store is sponsoring and know the store's policies and procedures, especially on returns and exchanges. Also, they often must recognize possible security risks and know how to handle such situations.

Consumers often form their impressions of a store by its sales force. To stay ahead in the fiercely competitive retail industry, employers are increasingly stressing the importance of providing courteous and efficient service. When a customer wants an item that is not on the sales floor, for example, the sales worker might be expected to check the stockroom and, if necessary, place a special order or call another store to locate the item.

REQUIREMENTS
High School

Employers generally prefer to hire high school graduates for most sales positions. Such subjects as English, speech, and mathematics provide a good background for these jobs. Many high schools and two-year colleges have special programs that include courses in merchandising, principles of retailing, and retail selling.

Postsecondary Training

In retail sales, as in other fields, the level of opportunity tends to coincide with the level of a person's education. In many stores, college graduates enter immediately into on-the-job training programs to prepare them for management assignments. Successful and experienced workers who do not have a degree might also qualify for these programs. Useful college courses include economics, business administration, and marketing. Many colleges offer majors in retailing. Executives in many companies express a strong preference for liberal arts graduates, especially those with some business courses or a master's degree in business administration.

Certification and Licensing

The National Retail Federation offers the following voluntary designations to sales workers who successfully pass an assessment and meet other requirements: national professional certification in sales, national professional certification in customer service, and basics of retail credential. Contact the federation for more information.

Other Requirements

The retail sales worker must be in good health. Many selling positions require standing most of the day. The sales worker must have stamina to face the grueling pace of busy times, such as weekends and the Christmas season, while at the same time remaining pleasant and effective. Personal appearance is important. Salespeople should be neat and well groomed and have an outgoing personality.

A pleasant speaking voice, natural friendliness, tact, and patience are all helpful personal characteristics. The sales worker must be able to converse easily with strangers of all ages. In addition to interpersonal skills, sales workers must be equally good with figures. They should be able to add and subtract accurately and quickly and operate cash registers and other types of business machines.

Most states have established minimum standards that govern retail employment. Some states set a minimum age of 14, require at least a high school diploma, or prohibit more than eight hours of work a day or 48 hours in any six days. These requirements are often relaxed during the Christmas season.

EXPLORING

Because of its seasonal nature, retailing offers numerous opportunities for temporary or part-time sales experience. Most stores add extra personnel for the Christmas season. Vacation areas may hire sales employees, usually high school or college students, on a seasonal basis. Fewer sales positions are available in metropolitan areas during the summer, as this is frequently the slowest time of the year.

Many high schools and junior colleges have developed "distributive education" programs that combine courses in retailing with part-time work in the field. The distributive education student may receive academic credit for this work experience in addition to regular wages. Store owners cooperating in these programs often hire students as full-time personnel upon completion of the program.

EMPLOYERS

About 4.5 million people are employed as sales workers in retail stores of all types and sizes. There are many different types of retail establishments, ranging from small specialty shops that appeal to collectors to large retailers that sell everything from eyeglasses to DVD players. Department stores, building material and garden equipment stores, clothing and accessories stores, other general merchandise stores, and motor vehicle and parts dealers employ the largest number of retail salespersons. Retail sales workers can have just one or two coworkers or well over 100, depending on the size of the establishment.

STARTING OUT

If they have openings, retail stores usually hire beginning salespeople who come in and fill out an application. Major department stores maintain extensive personnel departments, while in smaller stores the manager might do the hiring. Occasionally, sales applicants are given an aptitude test.

Young people might be hired immediately for sales positions. Often, however, they begin by working in the stockroom as clerks, helping to set up merchandise displays, or assisting in the receiving or shipping departments. After a while they might be moved up to a sales assignment.

Training varies with the type and size of the store. In large stores, the beginner might benefit from formal training courses that cover sales techniques, store policies, the mechanics of recording sales, and an overview of the entire store. Programs of this type are usually followed by on-the-job sales supervision. The beginner in a small store might receive personal instruction from the manager or a senior sales worker, followed by supervised sales experience.

College graduates and people with successful sales experience often enter executive training programs (sometimes referred to as flying squads because they move rapidly through different parts of the store). As they rotate through various departments, the trainees are exposed to merchandising methods, stock and inventory control, advertising, buying, credit, and personnel. By spending time in each of these areas, trainees receive a broad retailing background designed to help them as they advance into the ranks of management.

ADVANCEMENT

Large stores have the most opportunities for promotion. Retailing, however, is a mobile field, and successful and experienced people can readily change employment. This is one of the few fields where, if the salesperson has the necessary initiative and ability, advancement to executive positions is possible regardless of education.

When first on the job, sales workers develop their career potential by specializing in a particular line of merchandise. They become authorities on a certain product line, such as sporting equipment, women's suits, or building materials. Many good sales workers prefer the role of the *senior sales worker* and remain at this level. Others might be asked to become supervisor of a section. Eventually they might develop into a *department manager, floor manager, division or branch manager*, or *general manager*.

People with sales experience often enter related areas, such as buying. Other retail store workers advance into support areas, such as personnel, accounting, public relations, and credit.

Young people with ability find that retailing offers the opportunity for unusually rapid advancement. One study revealed that half of all retail executives are under 35 years of age. It is not uncommon for a person under 35 to be in charge of a retail store or department with an annual sales volume of over $1,000,000. Conversely, a retail executive who makes bad merchandising judgments might quickly be out of a job.

EARNINGS

Most beginning sales workers start at the federal minimum wage, which is $5.85 an hour. Wages vary greatly, depending primarily on the type of store and the degree of skill required. Businesses might offer higher wages to attract and retain workers. Some sales workers make as much as $12 an hour or more.

Department stores or retail chains might pay more than smaller stores. Higher wages are paid for positions requiring a greater degree of skill. Many sales workers also receive a commission (often 4 to 8 percent) on their sales or are paid solely on commission. According to the U.S. Department of Labor, median hourly earnings of retail salespersons, including commission, were $9.50 in 2006. A yearly salary for full-time work therefore averages $19,760. Wages ranged from less than $6.79 ($14,120 a year) to more than $18.48 an hour ($38,430 a year). Sales workers earned the following mean hourly wages by industry sector: new and used car dealerships, $21.23; building material and supplies dealers, $12.50; clothing stores, $9.68; and department stores, $9.43.

Salespeople in many retail stores are allowed a discount on their own purchases, ranging from 10 to 25 percent. This privilege is sometimes extended to the worker's family. Meals in the employee cafeterias maintained by large stores might be served at a price that is below cost. Many stores provide sick leave, medical and life insurance, and retirement benefits for full-time workers. Most stores give paid vacations.

WORK ENVIRONMENT

Retail sales workers generally work in clean, comfortable, well-lighted areas. Those with seniority have reasonably good job security. When business is slow, stores might curtail hiring and not fill vacancies that occur. Most stores, however, are able to weather mild recessions in business without having to release experienced sales workers. During periods of economic recession, competition among salespeople for job openings can become intense.

With nearly two million retail stores across the country, sales positions are found in every region. An experienced salesperson can find employment in almost any state. The vast majority of positions, however, are located in large cities or suburban areas.

The five-day, 40-hour workweek is the exception rather than the rule in retailing. Most salespeople can expect to work some evening and weekend hours, and longer than normal hours might be scheduled during Christmas and other peak periods. In addition, most retailers restrict the use of vacation time between Thanksgiving and early January. Most sales workers receive overtime pay during Christmas and other rush seasons. Part-time salespeople generally work at peak hours of business, supplementing the full-time staff. Because competition in the retailing business is keen, many retailers work under pressure. The sales worker might not be directly involved but will feel the pressures of the industry in subtle ways. The sales worker must be able to adjust to alternating periods of high activity and dull monotony. No two days—or even customers—are alike. Because some customers are hostile and rude, salespeople must learn to exercise tact and patience at all times.

OUTLOOK

About 4.5 million people are employed as sales workers in retail stores of all types and sizes. The employment of sales personnel should grow about as fast as the average for all occupations through 2016, according to the U.S. Department of Labor. Turnover among sales workers is much higher than average, which will create good employment opportunities in this large field. Many of the expected employment opportunities will stem from the need to replace workers. Other positions will result from existing stores' staffing for longer business hours or reducing the length of the average employee workweek. Employment opportunities are predicted to be the strongest at warehouse clubs and retail supercenters, according to the U.S. Department of Labor.

As drug, variety, grocery, and other stores have rapidly converted to self-service operations, they will need fewer sales workers. At the same time, many products, such as stereo components, cell phones, electrical appliances, computers, and sporting goods, do not lend themselves to self-service operations. These products require extremely skilled sales workers to assist customers and explain the benefits of various makes and models. On balance, as easy-to-sell goods will be increasingly marketed in self-service stores, the demand in the future will be strongest for sales workers who are knowledgeable about particular types of products.

During economic recessions, sales volume and the resulting demand for sales workers generally decline. Purchases of costly items, such as cars, appliances, and furniture, tend to be postponed during difficult economic times. In areas of high unemployment, sales of all types of goods might decline. Since turnover of sales workers is usually very high, however, employers often can cut payrolls simply by not replacing all those who leave.

There should continue to be good opportunities for temporary and part-time workers, especially during the holidays. Stores are particularly interested in people who, by returning year after year, develop good sales backgrounds.

FOR MORE INFORMATION

For information on certification and educational programs in the retail industry, contact

National Retail Federation
325 7th Street, NW, Suite 1100
Washington, DC 20004-2818
Tel: 800-673-4692
http://www.nrf.com

SALES REPRESENTATIVES

OVERVIEW

Sales representatives, also called *sales reps*, sell the products and services of manufacturers and wholesalers. They look for potential customers or clients such as retail stores, other manufacturers or wholesalers, government agencies, hospitals, and other institutions; explain or demonstrate their products to these clients; and attempt to make a sale. The job may include follow-up calls and visits to ensure the customer is satisfied.

Sales representatives work under a variety of titles. Those employed by manufacturers are typically called *manufacturers' sales workers* or *manufacturers' representatives*. Those who work for wholesalers are sometimes called *wholesale trade sales workers* or *wholesale sales representatives*. A *manufacturers' agent* is a self-employed salesperson who agrees to represent the products of various companies. A *door-to-door sales worker* usually represents just one company and sells products directly to consumers, typically in their homes. Approximately 2 million people work as manufacturers' and wholesale sales representatives in the United States.

THE JOB

Manufacturers' representatives and wholesale sales representatives sell goods to retail stores, other manufacturers and wholesalers, government agencies, and various institutions. They usually do so within a specific geographical area. Some representatives concentrate on just a few products. An electrical appliance salesperson, for example, may sell 10 to 30 items ranging from food freezers and air-conditioners to waffle irons and portable heaters. Representatives of drug wholesalers, however, may sell as many as 50,000 items.

The duties of sales representatives usually include locating and contacting potential new clients, keeping a regular correspondence with existing customers, determining their clients' needs, and informing them of pertinent products and prices. They also travel to meet with clients, show them samples or catalogs, take orders, arrange for delivery, and possibly provide installation. A sales representative also must handle customer complaints, keep up to date on new products, and prepare reports. Many salespeople attend trade conferences, where they learn about products and make sales contacts.

SCHOOL SUBJECTS
Business, Mathematics, Speech

PERSONAL SKILLS
Communication/Ideas, Helping/Teaching

MINIMUM EDUCATION LEVEL
High School Diploma

CERTIFICATION OR LICENSING
Voluntary

WORK ENVIRONMENT
Indoors and Outdoors, Primarily Multiple Locations

Finding new customers is one of sales representatives' most important tasks. Sales representatives often follow leads suggested by other clients, from advertisements in trade journals, and from participants in trade shows and conferences. They may make "cold calls" to potential clients. Sales representatives frequently meet with and entertain prospective clients during evenings and weekends.

Representatives who sell highly technical machinery or complex office equipment often are referred to as *sales engineers* or *industrial sales workers*. Because their products tend to be more specialized and their clients' needs more complex, the sales process for these workers tends to be longer and more involved. Before recommending a product, they may, for example, carefully analyze a customer's production processes, distribution methods, or office procedures. They usually prepare extensive sales presentations that include information on how their products will improve the quality and efficiency of the customer's operations.

Some sales engineers, often with the help of their company's research and development department, adapt products to a customer's specialized needs. They may provide the customer with instructions on how to use the new equipment or work with installation experts who provide this service. Some companies maintain a sales assistance staff to train customers and provide specific information. This permits sales representatives to devote a greater percentage of their time to direct sales contact.

Other sales workers, called *detail people*, do not engage in direct selling activities but strive instead to create a better general market for their companies' products. A detail person for a drug company, for example, may call on physicians and hospitals to inform them of new products and distribute samples.

The particular products sold by the sales representative directly affect the nature of the work. Salespeople who represent sporting goods manufacturers may spend most of their time driving from town to town calling on retail stores that carry sporting equipment. They may visit with coaches and athletic directors of high schools and colleges. A representative in this line may be a former athlete or coach who knows intimately the concerns of his or her customers.

Food manufacturers and wholesalers employ large numbers of sales representatives. Because these salespeople usually know the grocery stores and major chains that carry their products, their main focus is to ensure the maximum sales volume. Representatives negotiate with retail merchants to obtain the most advantageous store and shelf position for displaying their products. They encourage the store or chain to advertise their products, sometimes by offering to pay part of the advertising costs or by reducing the selling price to the merchant so that a special sale price can be offered to customers. Representatives check to make sure that shelf items are neatly arranged and that the store has sufficient stock of their products.

Sales transactions can involve huge amounts of merchandise, sometimes worth millions of dollars. For example, in a single transaction, a washing-machine manufacturer, construction company, or automobile manufacturer may purchase all the steel products it needs for an extended period of time. Salespeople in this field may do much of their business by telephone because the product they sell is standardized and, to the usual customer, requires no particular description or demonstration.

Direct, or door-to-door, selling has been an effective way of marketing various products, such as appliances and housewares, cookware, china, tableware and linens, foods, drugs, cosmetics and toiletries, costume jewelry, clothing, and greeting cards. Like other sales representatives, door-to-door sales workers find prospective buyers, explain and demonstrate their products, and take orders. Door-to-door selling has waned in popularity, and Internet-based selling has taken over much of the door-to-door market.

Several different arrangements are common between companies and their door-to-door sales workers. Under the direct company plan, for example, a sales representative is authorized to take orders for a product, and the company pays the representative a commission for each completed order. Such workers may be employees of the company and may receive a salary in addition to a commission, or they may be independent contractors. They usually are very well trained. Sales workers who sell magazine subscriptions may be hired, trained, and supervised by a *subscription crew leader*, who assigns representatives to specific areas, reviews the orders they take, and compiles sales records.

Under the exhibit plan a salesperson sets up an exhibit booth at a place where large numbers of people are expected to pass, such as a state fair, trade show, or product exposition. Customers approach the booth and schedule appointments with the salespersons for later demonstrations at home.

The dealer plan allows a salesperson to function as the proprietor of a small business. The salesperson, or dealer, purchases the product wholesale from the company and then resells it to consumers at the retail price, mainly through door-to-door sales.

Under various group plans, a customer is contacted by a salesperson and given the opportunity to sponsor a sales event. In the party plan, for example, the sales representative arranges to demonstrate products at the home of a customer, who then invites a group of friends for the party. The customer who hosts the party receives free or discounted merchandise in return for the use of the home and for assembling other potential customers for the salesperson.

Finally, the COD plan allows representatives to sell products on a cash-on-delivery (COD) basis. In this method, the salesperson makes a sale, perhaps collecting an advance deposit, and sends the order to the company. The company, in turn, ships the merchandise directly to the customer, who in this case makes payment to the delivery person, or to the salesperson. The product is then delivered to the customer and the balance collected.

Whatever the sales plan, door-to-door sales workers have some advantages over their counterparts in retail stores. Direct sellers, for example, do not have to wait for the customer to come to them; they go out and find the buyers for their products. The direct seller often carries only one product or a limited line of products and thus is much more familiar with the features and benefits of the merchandise. In general, direct sellers get the chance to demonstrate their products where they will most likely be used—in the home.

There are drawbacks to this type of selling. Many customers grow impatient or hostile when salespeople come to their house unannounced and uninvited. It may take several visits to persuade someone to buy the product. In a brief visit, the direct seller must win the confidence of the customer, develop the customer's interest in a product or service, and close the sale.

REQUIREMENTS
High School

A high school diploma is required for most sales positions, although an increasing number of salespeople are graduates of two- or four-year colleges. In high school, take classes such as business, mathematics, psychology, speech, and economics that will teach you to deal with customers and financial transactions.

Postsecondary Training

Some areas of sales work require specialized college work. Those in engineering sales, for example, usually have a college degree in a relevant engineering field. Other fields that demand specific college degrees include chemical sales (chemistry or chemical engineering), office systems (accounting or business administration), and pharmaceuticals and drugs (biology, chemistry, or pharmacy). Those in less technical sales positions usually benefit from course work in English, speech, psychology, marketing, public relations, economics, advertising, finance, accounting, and business law. Approximately 53 percent of sales representatives had an associate degree or higher in 2006, according to the U.S. Department of Labor.

Certification or Licensing

The Manufacturers' Representatives Educational Research Foundation offers several certification designations for sales representatives who are employed by manufacturers. Contact the foundation for more information.

Other Requirements

To be a successful sales representative, you should enjoy working with people. You should also be self-confident and enthusiastic, and self-disciplined. You must be able to handle rejection since only a small number of your sales contacts will result in a sale.

EXPLORING

If you are interested in becoming a sales representative, try to get part-time or summer work in a retail store. Working as a telemarketer also is useful. Some high schools and junior colleges offer programs that combine classroom study with work experience in sales.

Various opportunities exist to gain experience in direct selling. You can take part in sales drives for school or community groups, for instance.

Occasionally manufacturers hire college students for summer assignments. These temporary positions provide an opportunity for the employer and employee to appraise each other. A high percentage of students hired for these specialized summer programs become career employees after graduation. Some wholesale warehouses also offer temporary or summer positions.

EMPLOYERS

In the United States, 2 million people work as manufacturers' and wholesale sales representatives. Nearly 60 percent of these salespeople work in wholesale, many as sellers of machinery. Many others work in mining and manufacturing. Food, drugs, electrical goods, hardware, and clothing are among the most common products sold by sales representatives.

STARTING OUT

Firms looking for sales representatives sometimes list openings with high school and college career services offices, as well as with public and private employment agencies. In many areas, professional sales associations refer people to suitable openings. Contacting companies directly also is recommended. A list of manufacturers and wholesalers can be found in telephone books and industry directories, which are available at public libraries.

Although some high school graduates are hired for manufacturers' or wholesale sales jobs, many join a company in a nonselling position, such as office, stock, or shipping clerk. This experience allows an employee to learn about the company and its products. From there, he or she eventually may be promoted to a sales position.

Most new representatives complete a training period before receiving a sales assignment. In some cases new salespeople rotate through several departments of an organization to gain a broad exposure to the company's products. Large companies often use formal training programs lasting two years or more, while small organizations frequently rely on supervised sales experience.

Direct selling usually is an easy field to enter. Direct sale companies advertise for available positions in newspapers, in sales workers' specialty magazines, and on television and radio. Many people enter direct selling through contacts they have had with other door-to-door sales workers. Most firms have district or area representatives who interview applicants and arrange the necessary training. Part-time positions in direct selling are common.

ADVANCEMENT

New representatives usually spend their early years improving their sales ability, developing their product knowledge, and finding new clients. As sales workers gain experience they may be shifted to increasingly large territories or more difficult types of customers. In some organizations, experienced sales workers narrow their focus. For example, an office equipment sales representative may work solely on government contracts.

Advancement to management positions, such as *regional* or *district manager*, also is possible. Some representatives, however, choose to remain in basic sales. Because of commissions, they often earn more money than their managers do, and many enjoy being in the field and working directly with their customers.

A small number of representatives decide to become manufacturers' agents, or self-employed salespeople who handle products for various organizations. Agents perform many of the same functions as sales representatives but usually on a more modest scale.

Door-to-door sales workers also have advancement possibilities. Some are promoted to supervisory roles and recruit, train, and manage new members of the sales force. Others become *area, branch*, or district *managers*. Many managers of direct selling firms began as door-to-door sales workers.

EARNINGS

Many beginning sales representatives are paid a salary while receiving their training. After assuming direct responsibility for a sales territory, they may receive only a commission (a fixed percentage of each dollar sold). Also common is a modified commission plan (a lower rate of commission on sales plus a low base salary). Some companies provide bonuses to successful representatives.

Because manufacturers' and wholesale sales representatives typically work on commission, salaries vary widely. Some made as little as $26,030 a year in 2006, according to the U.S. Department of Labor. The most successful representatives earned more than $121,850. However, the median annual salaries for sales representatives working with technical and scientific products were $64,440, and $45,400, including commissions, for those working in other aspects of wholesale and manufacturing. Most sales representatives make between $35,000 and $71,000 a year.

Earnings can be affected by changes in the economy or industry cycles, and great fluctuations in salary from year to year or month to month are common. Employees who travel usually are reimbursed for transportation, hotels, meals, and client entertainment expenses. Door-to-door sales workers usually earn a straight commission on their sales, ranging from 10 to 40 percent of an item's suggested retail price.

Sales engineers earned salaries that ranged from less than $47,010 to $127,680 or more in 2006, according to the Department of Labor.

Sales representatives typically receive vacation days, medical and life insurance, and retirement benefits. However, manufacturers' agents and some door-to-door sales workers do not receive benefits.

WORK ENVIRONMENT

Salespeople generally work long and irregular hours. Those with large territories may spend all day calling and meeting customers in one city and much of the night traveling to the place where they will make the next day's calls and visits. Sales workers with a small territory may do little overnight travel but, like most sales workers, may spend many evenings preparing reports, writing up orders, and entertaining customers. Several times a year, sales workers may travel to company meetings and participate in trade conventions and conferences. Irregular working hours, travel, and the competitive demands of the job can be disruptive to ordinary family life.

Sales work is physically demanding. Representatives often spend most of the day on their feet. Many carry heavy sample cases or catalogs. Occasionally, sales workers assist a customer in arranging a display of the company's products or moving stock items. Many door-to-door sellers work in their own community or nearby areas, although some cover more extensive and distant territories. They often are outdoors in all kinds of weather. Direct sellers must treat customers, even those who are rude or impatient, with tact and courtesy.

OUTLOOK

Employment for manufacturers' and wholesale sales representatives is expected to grow about as fast as the average for all careers through 2016, according to the U.S. Department of Labor. Because of continued economic growth and an increasing number of new products on the market, more sales representatives will be needed to explain, demonstrate, and sell these products to customers. The Department of Labor notes that job opportunities will be better for wholesale and manufacturing sales representatives who specialize in technical and scientific products, although competition for in-house sales positions with wholesalers will be stiff, and jobs will go to applicants with the most experience and technical knowledge.

Independent sales workers, who are paid exclusively on a commission basis, should have strong employment opportunities.

Future opportunities will vary greatly depending upon the specific product and industry. For example, as giant food chains replace independent grocers, fewer salespeople will be needed to sell groceries to individual stores. By contrast, greater opportunities will probably exist in the air-conditioning field, and advances in consumer electronics and computer technology also may provide many new opportunities.

FOR MORE INFORMATION

For a list of marketing programs and detailed career information, contact

Direct Marketing Association
Educational Foundation
1120 Avenue of the Americas
New York, NY 10036-6700
Tel: 212-768-7277
http://www.the-dma.org

For referrals to industry trade associations, contact
Manufacturers' Agents National Association
One Spectrum Pointe, Suite 150
Lake Forest, CA 92630-2282
Tel: 877-626-2776
Email: MANA@MANAonline.org
http://www.manaonline.org

❑ SECURITY CONSULTANTS AND GUARDS

OVERVIEW

Security consultants and *security guards* protect public and private property against theft, fire, vandalism, illegal entry, and acts of violence. They may work for commercial or government organizations or private individuals. More than one million security workers are employed in the United States.

SCHOOL SUBJECTS
Business, Psychology

PERSONAL SKILLS
Communication/Ideas, Mechanical/Manipulative

MINIMUM EDUCATION LEVEL
Bachelor's Degree (Security Consultants), High School Diploma (Security Guards)

CERTIFICATION OR LICENSING
Recommended

WORK ENVIRONMENT
Indoors and Outdoors, One Location with Some Travel

THE JOB

A security consultant is engaged in protective service work. Anywhere that valuable property or information is present or people are at risk, a security consultant may be called in to devise and implement security plans that offer protection. Security consultants may work for a variety of clients, including large stores, art museums, factories, laboratories, data processing centers, and political candidates. They are involved in preventing theft, vandalism, fraud, kidnapping, and other crimes. Specific job responsibilities depend on the type and size of the client's company and the scope of the security system required.

Security consultants always work closely with company officials or other appropriate individuals in the development of a comprehensive security program that will fit the needs of individual clients. After discussing goals and objectives with the relevant company executives, consultants study and analyze the physical conditions and internal operations of a client's operation. They learn much by simply observing day-to-day operations.

The size of the security budget also influences the type of equipment ordered and methods used. For example, a large factory that produces military hardware may fence its property and place electronic surveillance equipment around the perimeter of the fence. They may also install perimeter alarms and use passkeys to limit access to restricted areas. A smaller company may use only entry-control mechanisms in specified areas. The consultant may recommend sophisticated technology, such as closed-circuit surveillance or ultrasonic motion detectors, alone or in addition to security personnel. Usually, a combination of electronic and human resources is used.

Security consultants not only devise plans to protect equipment but also recommend procedures on safeguarding and possibly destroying classified material. Increasingly, consultants are being called on to develop strategies to safeguard data processing equipment. They may have to develop measures to safeguard transmission lines against unwanted or unauthorized interceptions.

Once a security plan has been developed, the consultant oversees the installation of the equipment, ensures that it is working properly, and checks frequently with the client to ensure that the client is satisfied. In the case of a crime against the facility, a consultant investigates the nature of the crime (often in conjunction with police or other investigators) and then modifies the security system to safeguard against similar crimes in the future.

Many consultants work for security firms that have several types of clients, such as manufacturing and telecommunications plants and facilities. Consultants may handle a variety of clients or work exclusively in a particular area. For example, one security consultant may be assigned to handle the protection of nuclear power plants and another to handle data processing companies.

Security consultants may be called on to safeguard famous individuals or persons in certain positions from kidnapping or other type of harm. They provide security services to officers of large companies, media personalities, and others who want their safety and privacy protected. These consultants, like bodyguards, plan and review client travel itineraries and usually accompany the client on trips, checking accommodations and appointment locations along the way. They often check the backgrounds of people who will interact with the client, especially those who see the client infrequently.

Security consultants are sometimes called in for special events, such as sporting events and political rallies, when there is no specific fear of danger but rather a need for overall coordination of a large security operation. The consultants oversee security preparation—such as the stationing of appropriate personnel at all points of entry and exit—and then direct specific responses to any security problems.

Security officers develop and implement security plans for companies that manufacture or process material for the federal government. They ensure that their clients' security policies comply with federal regulations in such categories as the storing and handling of classified documents and restricting access to authorized personnel only.

Security guards have various titles, depending on the type of work they do and the setting in which they work. They may be referred to as *patrollers* (who are assigned to cover a certain area), *bouncers* (who eject unruly people from places of entertainment), *gaming surveillance officers* (who monitor for illegal activities, such as theft or cheating at casinos), *armored car guards* (who transport money and other valuables to and from financial instructions), *golf-course rangers* (who patrol golf courses), or *gate tenders* (who work at security checkpoints).

Many security guards are employed during normal working hours in public and commercial buildings and other areas with a good deal of pedestrian traffic and public contact. Others patrol buildings and grounds outside normal working hours, such as at night and on weekends. Guards usually wear uniforms and may carry a nightstick. Guards who work in situations where they may be called upon to apprehend criminal intruders are usually armed. They may also carry a flashlight, a whistle, a two-way radio, and a watch clock, which is used to record the time at which they reach various checkpoints.

Guards in public buildings may be assigned to a certain post or they may patrol an area. In museums, art galleries, and other public buildings, guards answer visitors' questions and give them directions; they also enforce rules against smoking, touching art objects, and so forth. In commercial buildings, guards may sign people in and out after hours and inspect packages being carried out of the building. *Bank guards* observe customers carefully for any sign of suspicious behavior that may signal a possible robbery attempt. In department stores, security guards often work with *undercover detectives* to watch for theft by customers or store employees. Guards at large public gatherings such as sporting events and conventions keep traffic moving, direct people to their seats, and eject unruly spectators. Guards employed at airports limit access to boarding areas to passengers only. They make sure people entering passenger areas have valid tickets and observe passengers and their baggage as they pass through X-ray machines and metal detection equipment.

After-hours guards are usually employed at industrial plants, defense installations, construction sites, and transport facilities such as docks and railroad yards. They make regular rounds on foot or, if the premises are very large, in motorized vehicles. They check to be sure that no unauthorized persons are on the premises, that doors and windows are secure, and that no property is missing. They may be equipped with walkie-talkies to report in at intervals to a central guard station. Sometimes guards perform custodial duties, such as turning on lights and setting thermostats.

In a large organization, a *security officer* is often in charge of the guard force; in a small organization, a single worker may be responsible for all security measures. As more businesses purchase advanced electronic security systems to protect their properties, more guards are being assigned to stations where they monitor perimeter security, environmental functions, communications, and other systems. In many cases, these guards maintain radio contact with other guards patrolling on foot or in motor vehicles. Some guards use computers to store information on matters relevant to security such as visitors or suspicious occurrences during their time on duty.

Security guards work for government agencies or for private companies hired by government agencies. Their task is usually to guard secret or restricted installations domestically or in foreign countries. They spend much of their time patrolling areas, which they may do on foot, on horseback, or in automobiles or aircraft. They may monitor activities in an area through the use of surveillance cameras and video screens. Their assignments usually include detecting and preventing unauthorized activities, searching for explosive devices, standing watch during secret and hazardous experiments, and performing other routine police duties within government installations.

Security guards are usually armed and may be required to use their weapons or other kinds of physical force to prevent some kinds of activities. They are usually not, however, required to remove explosive devices from an installation. When they find such devices, they notify a bomb disposal unit, which is responsible for removing and then defusing or detonating the device.

REQUIREMENTS
High School

A high school diploma is preferred for security guards and required for security consultants, who should also go on to obtain a college degree. Security guards must be high school graduates. In addition, they should expect to receive from three to six months of specialized training in security procedures and technology. If you would like to be a security guard, you should take mathematics courses while in high school to ensure that you can perform basic arithmetic operations with different units of measure; compute ratios, rates, and percentages; and interpret charts and graphs.

You should take English courses to develop your reading and writing skills. You should be able to read manuals, memos, textbooks, and other instructional materials and write reports with correct spelling, grammar, and punctuation. You should also be able to speak to small groups with poise and confidence.

Postsecondary Training

Most companies prefer to hire security consultants who have at least a college degree. An undergraduate or associate's degree in criminal justice, business administration, or related field is best. Course work should be broad and include business management, communications, computer courses, sociology, and statistics. As the security consulting field becomes more competitive, many consultants choose to get a master's in business administration or other graduate degree.

Although there are no specific educational or professional requirements, many security guards have had previous experience with police work or other forms of crime prevention. It is helpful if a person develops an expertise in a specific area. For example, if you want to work devising plans securing data processing equipment, it is helpful to have previous experience working with computers.

Some security guards receive on-the-job training. The American Society for Industrial Security International recommends that security guards receive at least 48 hours of training within the first 100 days of employment and pass a written or performance examination covering topics such as crime prevention, the use of force, and emergency response procedures.

Certification or Licensing

Many security consultants earn the certified protection professional designation. To be eligible for certification, a consultant must pass a written test and meet work and educational experience requirements. Information on certification is available from ASIS International, a professional organization to which many security consultants belong.

Virtually every state has licensing or registration requirements for security guards who work for contract security agencies. Registration generally requires that a person newly hired as a guard be reported to the licensing authorities, usually the state police department or special state licensing commission. To be granted a license, individuals generally must be 18 years of age, have no convictions for perjury or acts of violence, pass a background investigation, and complete classroom training on a variety of subjects, including property rights, emergency procedures, and capture of suspected criminals.

Other Requirements

For security guards, general good health (especially vision and hearing), alertness, emotional stability, and the ability to follow directions are important characteristics. Military service and experience in local or state police departments are assets. Prospective guards should have clean police records. Some employers require applicants to take a polygraph examination or a written test that indicates honesty, attitudes, and other personal qualities. Most employers require applicants and experienced workers to submit to drug screening tests as a condition of employment.

For some hazardous or physically demanding jobs, guards must be under a certain age and meet height and weight standards. For top-level security positions in facilities such as nuclear power plants or vulnerable information centers, guards may be required to complete a special training course. They may also need to fulfill certain relevant academic requirements.

Guards employed by the federal government must be U.S. armed forces veterans, have some previous experience as guards, and pass a written examination. Many positions require experience with firearms. In many situations, guards must be bonded.

Security guards need good eyesight and should be in good physical shape, able to lift at least 50 pounds, climb ladders, stairs, poles, and ropes, and maintain their balance on narrow, slippery, or moving surfaces. They should be able to stoop, crawl, crouch, and kneel with ease.

EXPLORING

Part-time or summer employment as a *clerk* with a security firm is an excellent way to gain insight into the skills and temperament needed to become a security consultant. Discussions with professional security consultants are another way of exploring career opportunities in this field. You may find it helpful to join a safety patrol at school.

If you are interested in a particular area of security consulting, such as data processing, for example, you can join a club or association to learn more about the field. This is a good way to make professional contacts.

Opportunities for part-time or summer work as security guards are not generally available to high school students. You may, however, work as a lifeguard, on a safety patrol, and as a school hallway monitor, which can provide helpful experience.

EMPLOYERS

Security services is one of the largest employment fields in the United States. Over one million persons are employed in the security industry in the United States. Industrial security firms and guard agencies (including guard and armored car services), also called contract security firms, employ over half of all guards, while the remainder are in-house guards employed by various establishments such as hospitals, schools, food services and drinking places, hotels, manufacturing firms, department stores, residential and nonresidential buildings, and government agencies.

STARTING OUT

People interested in careers in security services generally apply directly to security companies. Some jobs may be available through state or private employment services. People interested in security technician positions should apply directly to government agencies.

Beginning security personnel receive varied amounts of training. Training requirements are generally increasing as modern, highly sophisticated security systems become more common. Many employers give newly hired security guards instruction before they start the job and also provide several weeks of on-the-job training. Guards receive training in protection, public relations, report writing, crisis deterrence, first aid, and drug control.

Those employed at establishments that place a heavy emphasis on security usually receive extensive formal training. For example, guards at nuclear power plants may undergo several months of training before being placed on duty under close supervision. Guards may be taught to use firearms, administer first aid, operate alarm systems and electronic security equipment, handle emergencies, and spot and deal with security problems.

Many of the less strenuous guard positions are filled by older people who are retired police officers or armed forces veterans. Because of the odd hours required for many positions, this occupation appeals to many people seeking part-time work or second jobs.

Most entry-level positions for security consultants are filled by those with a bachelor's or associate's degree in criminal justice, business administration, or a related field. Those with a high school diploma and some experience in the field may find work with a security consulting firm, although they usually begin as security guards and become consultants only after further training.

Because many consulting firms have their own techniques and procedures, most require entry-level personnel to complete an on-the-job training program, during the course of which they learn company policies.

ADVANCEMENT

In most cases, security guards receive periodic salary increases, and guards employed by larger security companies or as part of a military-style guard force may increase their responsibilities or move up in rank. A guard with outstanding ability, especially with some college education, may move up to the position of chief guard, gaining responsibility for the supervision and training of an entire guard force in an industrial plant or a department store, or become director of security services for a business or commercial building. A few guards with management skills open their own contract security guard agencies; other guards become licensed private detectives. Experienced guards may become bodyguards for political figures, executives, and celebrities, or choose to enter a police department or other law enforcement agency. Additional training may lead to a career as a corrections officer.

Increased training and experience with a variety of security and surveillance systems may lead security guards into higher-paying security consultant careers. Security consultants with experience may advance to management positions or they may start their own private consulting firms. Instruction and training of security personnel is another advancement opportunity for security guards, consultants, and technicians.

EARNINGS

Earnings for security consultants vary greatly depending on the consultant's training and experience. Entry-level consultants with bachelor's degrees commonly start at $26,000 to $32,000 per year. Consultants with graduate degrees begin at $34,000 to $41,000 per year, and experienced consultants may earn $50,000 to $100,000 per year or more. Many consultants work on a per-project basis, with rates of $75 per hour or more.

Average starting salaries for security guards and technicians vary according to their level of training and experience, and the location where they work. Median annual earnings for security guards were $21,530 in 2006, according to the U.S. Department of Labor. Experienced security guards earned more than $35,840 per year in 2006, while the least-experienced security guards earned less than $15,030 annually.

Mean annual earnings for security guards employed by local government agencies were $27,820 in 2006, according to the U.S. Department of Labor.

The location of the work also affects earnings, with higher pay in locations with a higher cost of living. Government employees typically enjoy good job security and generous benefits. Benefits for positions with private companies vary significantly.

WORK ENVIRONMENT

Consultants usually divide their time between their offices and a client's business. Much time is spent ana-lyzing various security apparatuses and developing security proposals. The consultant talks with a variety of employees at a client's company, including the top officials, and discusses alternatives with other people at the consulting firm. A consultant makes a security proposal presentation to the client and then works with the client on any modifications. Consultants must be sensitive to budget issues and develop security systems that their clients can afford.

Consultants may specialize in one type of security work (nuclear power plants, for example) or work for a variety of large and small clients, such as museums, data processing companies, and banks. Although there may be a lot of travel and some work may require outdoor activity, there will most likely be no strenuous work. A consultant may oversee the implementation of a large security system but is not involved in the actual installation process. A consultant may have to confront suspicious people but is not expected to do the work of a police officer.

Security guards and technicians may work indoors or outdoors. In high-crime areas and industries vulnerable to theft and vandalism, there may be considerable physical danger. Guards who work in museums, department stores, and other buildings and facilities remain on their feet for long periods of time, either standing still or walking while on patrol. Guards assigned to reception areas or security control rooms may remain at their desks for the entire shift. Much of their work is routine and may be tedious at times, yet guards must remain constantly alert during their shift. Guards who work with the public, especially at sporting events and concerts, may have to confront unruly and sometimes hostile people. Bouncers often confront intoxicated people and are frequently called upon to intervene in physical altercations.

Many companies employ guards around the clock in three shifts, including weekends and holidays, and assign workers to these shifts on a rotating basis. The same is true for security technicians guarding government facilities and installations. Those with less seniority will likely have the most erratic schedules. Many guards work alone for an entire shift, usually lasting eight hours. Lunches and other meals are often taken on the job, so that constant vigilance is maintained.

OUTLOOK

Employment for guards and other security personnel is expected to increase faster than the average for all careers through 2016, according to the U.S. Department of Labor, as crime rates rise with the overall population growth. Public concern about crime, vandalism, and terrorism continues to grow. Many job openings will be created as a result of the high turnover of workers in this field.

A factor adding to this demand is the trend for private security firms to perform duties previously handled by police officers, such as courtroom security. Private security companies employ security technicians to guard many government sites, such as nuclear testing facilities. Private companies also operate many training facilities for government security technicians and guards, as well as provide police services for some communities.

Employment of gaming surveillance officers is expected to grow much faster than the average for all occupations through 2016, according to the Department of Labor. More states are legalizing gambling and states where gambling already is legal are building more casinos. This will create demand for more consultants and guards with experience in the gaming industry.

FOR MORE INFORMATION

For information on educational programs and certification procedures, contact

ASIS International
1625 Prince Street
Alexandria, VA 22314-2818
Tel: 703-519-6200
Email: asis@asisonline.org
http://www.asisonline.org

For information on union membership, contact

Security, Police, and Fire Professionals of America
25510 Kelly Road
Roseville, MI 40866-4932
Tel: 800-228-7492
http://www.spfpa.org

SOCIAL WORKERS

OVERVIEW

Social workers help people and assist communities in solving problems. These problems include poverty, racism, discrimination, physical and mental illness, addiction, and abuse. They counsel individuals and families, they lead group sessions, they research social problems, and they develop policy and programs. Social workers are dedicated to empowering people and helping them to preserve their dignity and worth. Approximately 595,000 social workers are employed in the United States.

THE JOB

After months of physical abuse from her husband, a young woman has taken her children and moved out of her house. With no job and no home, and fearing for her safety, she looks for a temporary shelter for herself and her children. Once there, she can rely on the help of social workers who will provide her with a room, food, and security. The social workers will offer counseling and emotional support to help her address the problems in her life. They will involve her in group sessions with other victims of abuse. They will direct her to job training programs and other employment services. They will set up interviews with managers of low-income housing. As the woman makes efforts to improve her life, the shelter will provide day care for the children. All these resources exist because the social work profession has long been committed to empowering people and improving society.

The social worker's role extends even beyond the shelter. If the woman has trouble getting help from other agencies, the social worker will serve as an advocate, stepping in to ensure that she gets the aid to which she is entitled. The woman may also qualify for long-term assistance from the shelter, such as a second-step program in which a social worker offers counseling and other support over several months. The woman's individual experience will also help in the social worker's research of the problem of domestic violence; with that research, the social worker can help the community come to a better understanding of the problem and can direct society toward solutions. Some of these solutions may include the development of special police procedures for domestic disputes, or court-ordered therapy groups for abusive spouses.

Direct social work practice is also known as clinical practice. As the name suggests, direct practice involves working directly with the client by offering counseling, advocacy, information and referral, and education. Indirect practice concerns the structures through which the direct practice is offered. Indirect practice (a practice consisting mostly of social workers with Ph.D. degrees) involves program development and evaluation, administration, and policy analysis. The vast majority of the 150,000 members of the National Association of Social Workers (NASW) work in direct service roles.

Because of the number of problems facing individuals, families and communities, social workers find jobs in a wide variety of settings and with a variety of client groups. Some of these areas are discussed in the following paragraphs:

Health/mental health care. Mental health care has become one of the leading areas of social work employment. These jobs are competitive and typically go to more experienced social workers. Settings include community mental health centers, where social workers serve persistently mentally ill people and participate in outreach services; state and county mental hospitals, for long-term, inpatient care; facilities of the Department of Veterans Affairs, involving a variety of mental health care programs for veterans; and private psychiatric hospitals, for patients who can pay directly. Social workers also work with patients who have physical illnesses. They help individuals and their families adjust to the illness and the changes that illness may bring to their lives. They confer with physicians and with other members of the medical team to make plans about the best way to help the patient. They explain the treatment and its anticipated outcome to both the patient and the family. They help the patient adjust to the possible prospect of long hospitalization and isolation from the family.

Child care/family services. Efforts are being made to offer a more universal system of care that would incorporate child care, family services, and community service. Child care services include day care homes, child care centers, and Head Start centers. Social workers in this setting attempt to address all the problems children face from infancy to late adolescence. They work with families to detect problems early and intervene when necessary. They research the problems confronting children and families, and they establish new services or adapt existing services to address these problems. They provide parenting education to teenage parents, which can involve living with a teenage mother in a foster care situation, teaching parenting skills, and caring for the baby while the mother attends school. Social workers alert employers to employees' needs for daytime child care.

Social workers in this area of service are constantly required to address new issues. In recent years, for example, social workers have developed services for families composed of different cultural backgrounds, services for children with congenital disabilities resulting from the mother's drug use, and disabilities related to HIV or AIDS.

Geriatric social work. Within this field, social workers provide individual and family counseling services in order to assess the older person's needs and strengths. Social workers help older people locate transportation and housing services. They also offer adult day care services, or adult foster care services that match older people with families. Adult protective services protect

SCHOOL SUBJECTS
Health, Psychology

PERSONAL SKILLS
Communication/Ideas, Helping/Teaching

MINIMUM EDUCATION LEVEL
Bachelor's Degree

CERTIFICATION OR LICENSING
Required by All States

WORK ENVIRONMENT
Primarily Indoors, Primarily Multiple Locations

older people from abuse and neglect, and respite services allow family members time off from the care of an older person. A little-recognized problem is the rising incidence of HIV/AIDS among the elderly; 25 percent of all HIV/AIDS patients are aged 50 or over.

School social work. In schools, social workers serve students and their families, teachers, administrators, and other school staff members. Education, counseling, and advocacy are important aspects of school social work. With education, social workers attempt to prevent alcohol and drug abuse, teen pregnancy, and the spread of HIV/AIDS and other sexually transmitted diseases. They provide multicultural and family life education. They counsel students who are discriminated against because of their sexual orientation or racial, ethnic, or religious background. They also serve as advocates for these students, bringing issues of discrimination before administrators, school boards, and student councils.

A smaller number of social workers are employed in the areas of *social work education* (a field composed of the professors and instructors who teach and train students of social work); *group practice* (in which social workers facilitate treatment and support groups); and *corrections* (providing services to inmates in penal institutions). Social workers also offer counseling, occupational assistance, and advocacy to those with addictions and disabilities, to the homeless, and to women, children, and the elderly who have been in abusive situations.

Client groups expand and change as societal problems change. Social work professionals must remain aware of the problems affecting individuals and communities in order to offer assistance to as many people as possible.

Computers have become important tools for social workers. Client records are maintained on computers, allowing for easier collection and analysis of data. Interactive computer programs are used to train social workers, as well as to analyze case histories (such as for an individual's risk of HIV infection).

REQUIREMENTS
High School

To prepare for a social work career, you should take courses in high school that will improve your communications skills, such as English, speech, and composition. On a debate team, you could further develop your skills in communication as well as research and analysis. History, social studies, and sociology courses are important in understanding the concerns and issues of society. Although some work is available for those with only a high school diploma or associate's degree (as a social work aide or social services technician), the most opportunities exist for people with degrees in social work.

Postsecondary Training

There are approximately 458 accredited B.S.W. (bachelor's in social work) programs and 181 accredited M.S.W. (master's in social work) programs accredited by the Council on Social Work Education. The Group for the Advancement of Doctoral Education lists 74 doctoral programs for Ph.D.'s in social work or D.S.W.'s (doctor of social work). The Council on Social Work Education requires that five areas be covered in accredited bachelor's degree social work programs: human behavior and the social environment; social welfare policy and services; social work practice; research; and field practicum. Most programs require two years of liberal arts study followed by two years of study in the social work major. Also, students must complete a field practicum of at least 400 hours. Graduates of these programs can find work in public assistance or they can work with the elderly or with people with mental or developmental disabilities.

Although no clear lines of classification are drawn in the social work profession, most supervisory and administrative positions require at least an M.S.W. degree. Master's programs are organized according to fields of practice (such as mental health care), problem areas (substance abuse), population groups (the elderly), and practice roles (practice with individuals, families, or communities). They are usually two-year programs that require at least 900 hours of field practice. Most positions in mental health care facilities require an M.S.W. Doc-

toral degrees are also available and prepare students for research and teaching. Most social workers with doctorates go to work in community organizations.

Certification or Licensing

Licensing, certification, or registration of social workers is required by all states. To receive the necessary licensing, a social worker will typically have to gain a certain amount of experience and also pass an exam. The certification programs help to identify those social workers who have gained the knowledge and experience necessary to meet national standards.

The National Association of Social Workers offers three voluntary credentials and 10 specialty certifications (seven for M.S.W.s and three for B.S.W.s). These credentials are particularly valuable for social workers in private practice, as some health insurance providers require them for reimbursement purposes. Contact the association for more information.

Other Requirements

Social work requires great dedication. As a social worker, you have the responsibility of helping whole families, groups, and communities, as well as focusing on the needs of individuals. Your efforts will not always be supported by society at large; sometimes you must work against a community's prejudice, disinterest, and denial. You must also remain sensitive to the problems of your clients, offering support, and not moral judgment or personal bias. The only way to effectively address new social problems and new client groups is to remain open to the thoughts and needs of all human beings. Assessing situations and solving problems requires clarity of vision and a genuine concern for the well-being of others.

With this clarity of vision, your work will be all the more rewarding. Social workers have the satisfaction of making a connection with other people and helping them through difficult times. Along with the rewards, however, the work can cause a great deal of stress. Hearing repeatedly about the deeply troubled lives of prison inmates, the mentally ill, abused women and children, and others can be depressing and defeating. Trying to convince society of the need for changes in laws and services can be a long, hard struggle. You must have perseverance to fight for your clients against all odds.

EXPLORING

As a high school student, you may find openings for summer or part-time work as a receptionist or file clerk with a local social service agency. If there are no opportunities for paid employment, you could work as a volunteer. You can also gain good experience by working as a counselor in a camp for children with physical, mental, or developmental disabilities. Your local YMCA, park district, or other recreational facility may need volunteers for group recreation programs, including programs designed for the prevention of delinquency. By reporting for your high school newspaper, you'll have the opportunity to interview people, conduct surveys, and research social change, all of which are important aspects of the social work profession.

You could also volunteer a few afternoons a week to read to people in retirement homes or to the blind. Work as a tutor in special education programs is sometimes available to high school students.

EMPLOYERS

Approximately 595,000 social workers are employed in the United States. Social workers can be employed in direct or clinical practice, providing individual and family counseling services, or they may work as administrators for the organizations that provide direct practice. Social workers are employed by community health and mental health centers; hospitals and mental hospitals; child care, family services, and community service organizations, including day care and Head Start programs; elderly care programs, including adult protective services and adult day care and foster care; prisons; shelters and halfway houses; schools; courts; and nursing homes.

STARTING OUT

Most students of social work pursue a master's degree and in the process learn about the variety of jobs available. They also make valuable connections through faculty and other students. Through the university's career services office or an internship program, a student will learn about job openings and potential employers.

A social work education in an accredited program will provide you with the most opportunities, and the best salaries and chances for promotion, but practical social work experience can also earn you full-time employment. A part-time job or volunteer work will introduce you to social work professionals who can provide you with career guidance and letters of reference. Agencies with limited funding may not be able to afford to hire social workers with M.S.W.'s and therefore will look for applicants with a great deal of experience and lower salary expectations.

ADVANCEMENT

More attractive and better-paying jobs tend to go to those with more years of practical experience. Dedication to your job, an extensive resume, and good references will lead to advancement in the profession. Also, many social work programs offer continuing education workshops, courses, and seminars. These refresher courses help practicing social workers to refine their skills and to learn about new areas of practice and new methods and problems. The courses are intended to supplement your social work education, not substitute for a bachelor's or master's degree. These continuing education courses can lead to job promotions and salary increases.

EARNINGS

The more education a social worker has completed, the more money he or she stands to make in the profession. The area of practice also determines earnings; the areas of mental health, group services, and community organization and planning provide higher salaries, while elderly and disabled care generally provide lower pay. Salaries also vary among regions. Social workers on the east and west coasts earn higher salaries than those in the Midwest. During their first five years of practice, social workers' salaries generally increase faster than in later years.

The median salary for child, family, and school social workers was $37,480 in 2006, according to the U.S. Department of Labor. The top 10 percent earned more than $62,530, while the lowest 10 percent earned less than $24,480. Medical and public health social workers' salaries ranged from less than $27,280 to more than $64,070 with a median salary of $43,040 in 2006, and mental health and substance abuse workers earned between $22,490 and $57,630 with a median salary of $35,410.

Most full-time positions provide life and medical insurance, pension plans, and paid vacation and holidays.

WORK ENVIRONMENT

Social workers do not always work at a desk. When they do, they may be interviewing clients, writing reports, or conferring with other staff members. Depending on the size of the agency, office duties such as typing letters, filing, and answering phones may be performed by an aide or volunteer. Social workers employed at shelters or halfway houses may spend most of their time with clients, tutoring, counseling, or leading groups.

Some social workers have to drive to remote areas to make a home visit. They may go into inner-city neighborhoods, schools, courts, or jails. In larger cities, domestic violence and homeless shelters are sometimes located in rundown or dangerous areas. Most social workers are involved directly with the people they serve and must carefully examine the client's living conditions and family relations. Although some of these living conditions can be pleasant and demonstrate a good home situation, others can be squalid and depressing.

Advocacy involves work in a variety of different environments. Although much of this work may require making phone calls and sending emails, faxes, and letters, it also requires meetings with clients' employers, directors of agencies, local legislators, and others. It may sometimes require testifying in court as well.

OUTLOOK

The field of social work is expected to grow much faster than the average for all occupations through 2016, according to the U.S. Department of Labor. The greatest factor for this growth is the increased number of older people who are in need of social services. Social workers that specialize in gerontology will find many job opportunities in nursing homes, hospitals, and home health care agencies. The needs of the future elderly population are likely to be different from those of the present elderly. Currently, the elderly appreciate community living, while subsequent generations may demand more individual care.

Schools will also need more social workers to deal with issues such as teenage pregnancies, children from single-parent households, and any adjustment problems recent immigrants may have. The trend to integrate students with disabilities into the general school population will require the expertise of social workers to make the transition smoother. However, job availability in schools will depend on funding given by state and local sources.

To help control costs, hospitals are encouraging early discharge for some of their patients. Social workers will be needed by hospitals to help secure health services for patients in their homes. There is also a growing number of people with physical disabilities or impairments staying in their own homes, requiring home health care workers. Opportunities for social workers in nursing homes, long-term care facilities, and hospices should also increase.

Employment for mental health and substance abuse social workers is expected to grow 30 percent by 2016; it is the fastest-growing subspecialty in the field. The field of substance abuse social work should be especially strong as courts increasingly place substance abusers in treatment programs instead of prison or as a condition of their sentencing or probation.

Increased availability of health insurance funding and the growing number of people able to pay for professional help will create opportunities for those in private practice. Many businesses hire social workers to help in employee assistance programs, often on a contractual basis.

Poverty is still a main issue that social workers address. Families are finding it increasingly challenging to make ends meet on wages that are just barely above the minimum. The problem of fathers who do not make their court-ordered child support payments forces single mothers to work more than one job or rely on welfare. An increased awareness of domestic violence has also focused attention on the fact that many homeless and unemployed people are women who have left abusive situations. Besides all this, working with the poor is often considered unattractive, leaving many social work positions in this area unfilled.

Competition for jobs in urban areas will remain strong. However, there is still a shortage of social workers in rural areas; these areas usually cannot offer the high salaries or modern facilities that attract large numbers of applicants.

The social work profession is constantly changing. The survival of social service agencies, both private and public, depends on shifting political, economic, and workplace issues.

Social work professionals are worried about the threat of declassification. Because of budget constraints and a need for more workers, some agencies have lowered their job requirements. When unable to afford qualified professionals, they hire those with less education and experience. This downgrading raises questions about quality of care and professional standards. Just as in some situations low salaries push out the qualified social worker, so do high salaries. In the area of corrections, attractive salaries (up to $40,000 for someone with a two-year associate's degree) have resulted in more competition from other service workers.

Liability is another growing concern. If a social worker, for example, tries to prove that a child has been beaten or attempts to remove a child from his or her home, the worker can potentially be sued for libel. At the other extreme, a social worker can face criminal charges for failure to remove a child from an abusive home. More social workers are taking out malpractice insurance.

FOR MORE INFORMATION

For information on social work careers and educational programs, contact

Council on Social Work Education
1725 Duke Street, Suite 500
Alexandria, VA 22314-3457
Tel: 703-683-8080
Email: info@cswe.org
http://www.cswe.org

To access the online publication Choices: Careers in Social Work, *contact*

National Association of Social Workers
750 First Street, NE, Suite 700
Washington, DC 20002-4241
Tel: 202-408-8600
Email: membership@naswdc.org
http://www.naswdc.org

For information on educational programs in Canada, contact

Canadian Association of Schools of Social Work
1398 Star Top Road
Ottawa, ON K1B 4V7 Canada
Tel: 613-792-1953
Email: cassw@cassw-acess.ca
http://www.cassw-acess.ca

For career information and job listings available in Canada, contact

Canadian Association of Social Workers
383 Parkdale Avenue, Suite 402
Ottawa, ON K1Y 4R4 Canada
Tel: 613-729-6668
Email: casw@casw-acts.ca
http://www.casw-acts.ca

SOFTWARE DESIGNERS

OVERVIEW

Software designers create new ideas and design prepackaged and customized computer software. Software designers devise applications such as word processors, front-end database programs, and spreadsheet programs that make it possible for computers to complete given tasks and to solve problems. Once a need in the market has been identified, software designers first conceive of the program on a global level by outlining what the program will do. Then they write the specifications from which programmers code computer commands to perform the given functions.

THE JOB

Without software, computer hardware would have nothing to do. Computers need to be told exactly what to do, and software is the set of codes that gives the computer those instructions. It comes in the form of the familiar prepackaged software that you find in a computer store, such as games, word processing, spreadsheet, and desktop publishing programs, and in customized applications designed to fit specific needs of a particular business. Software designers are the initiators of these complex programs. Computer programmers then create the software by writing the code that carries out the directives of the designer.

Software designers must envision every detail of what an application will do, how it will do it, and how it will look (the user interface). A simple example is how a home accounting program is created. The software designer first lays out the overall functionality of the program, specifying what it should be able to do, such as balancing a checkbook, keeping track of incoming and outgoing bills, and maintaining records of expenses. For each of these tasks, the software designer will outline the design details for the specific functions that he or she has mandated, such as what menus and icons will be used, what each screen will look like, and whether there will be

---

SCHOOL SUBJECTS
Computer Science, Mathematics

PERSONAL SKILLS
Communication/Ideas, Technical/Scientific

MINIMUM EDUCATION LEVEL
Bachelor's Degree

CERTIFICATION OR LICENSING
Voluntary

WORK ENVIRONMENT
Primarily Indoors, Primarily One Location

help or dialog boxes to assist the user. For example, the designer may specify that the expense record part of the program produce a pie chart that shows the percentage of each household expense in the overall household budget. The designer can specify that the program automatically display the pie chart each time a budget assessment is completed or only after the user clicks on the appropriate icon on the toolbar.

Some software companies specialize in building custom-designed software. This software is highly specialized for specific needs or problems of particular businesses. Some businesses are large enough that they employ in-house software designers who create software applications for their computer systems. A related field is software engineering, which involves writing customized complex software to solve specific engineering or technical problems of a business or industry.

Whether the designer is working on a mass-market or a custom application, the first step is to define the overall goals for the application. This is typically done in consultation with management if working at a software supply company, or with the client if working on a custom-designed project. Then, the software designer studies the goals and problems of the project. If working on custom-designed software, the designer must also take into consideration the existing computer system of the client. Next, the software designer works on the program strategy and specific design detail that he or she has envisioned. At this point, the designer may need to write a proposal outlining the design and estimating time and cost allocations. Based on this report, management or the client decides if the project should proceed.

Once approval is given, the software designer and the programmers begin working on writing the software program. Typically, the software designer writes the specifications for the program, and the applications programmers write the programming codes.

In addition to the duties involved in design, a software designer may be responsible for writing a user's manual or at least writing a report for what should be included in the user's manual. After testing and debugging the program, the software designer will present it to management or to the client.

REQUIREMENTS
High School

If you are interested in a career in computer science, you should take as many computer, math, and science courses as possible; they provide fundamental math and computer knowledge and teach analytical thinking skills. Classes that focus on schematic drawing and flowcharts are also very valuable. English and speech courses will help you improve your communication skills, which are very important to software designers who must make formal presentations to management and clients. Also, many technical/vocational schools offer programs in software programming and design. The qualities developed by these classes, plus imagination and an ability to work well under pressure, are key to success in software design.

Postsecondary Training

A bachelor's degree in computer science, software development, or software design plus one year's experience with a programming language is required for most software designers.

In the past, the computer industry has tended to be pretty flexible about official credentials; demonstrated computer proficiency and work experience have often been enough to obtain a good position. However, as more people enter the field, competition has increased, and job requirements have become more stringent. Technical knowledge alone does not suffice in the field of software design anymore. In order to be a successful software designer, you should have at least a peripheral knowledge of the field for which you intend to design software, such as business, education, or science. Individuals with degrees in education and subsequent teaching experience are much sought after as designers for educational software. Those with bachelor's degrees in computer science with a minor in business or accounting have an excellent chance for employment in designing business or accounting software.

Certification or Licensing

Certification in software development is offered by companies such as Sun Microsystems, Hewlett-Packard, IBM, Novell, and Oracle. While not required, certification tells employers that your skills meet industry education and training standards.

Additionally, the Institute of Electrical and Electronics Engineers Computer Society offers the designation, certified software development professional, to individuals who have a bachelor's degree, a minimum of 9,000 hours of software engineering experience within at least six of 11 knowledge areas, and pass an examination.

Other Requirements

Software design is project- and detail-oriented, and therefore, you must be patient and diligent. You must also enjoy problem-solving challenges and be able to work under a deadline with minimal supervision. As a software designer, you should also possess good communication skills for consulting both with management and with clients who will have varying levels of technical expertise.

Software companies are looking for individuals with vision and imagination to help them create new and exciting programs to sell in the ever-competitive software market. Superior technical skills and knowledge combined with motivation, imagination, and exuberance will make you an attractive candidate.

EXPLORING

Spending a day with a professional software designer or applications programmer will allow you to experience firsthand what this work entails. School guidance counselors can often help you organize such a meeting.

If you are interested in computer industry careers in general, you should learn as much as possible about computers. Keep up with new technology by talking to other computer users and by reading related magazines, such as *Computer* (http://www.computer.org/computer). You will also find it helpful to join computer clubs and use online services and the Internet to find more information about this field.

Advanced students can put their design ideas and programming knowledge to work by designing and programming their own applications, such as simple games and utility programs.

EMPLOYERS

Software designers are employed throughout the United States. Opportunities are best in large cities and suburbs where business and industry are active. Programmers who develop software systems work for software manufacturers, many of whom are in Silicon Valley, in northern California. There are also concentrations of software manufacturers in Boston, Chicago, and Atlanta, among other places. Designers who adapt and tailor the software to meet specific needs of end-users work for those end-user companies, many of which are scattered across the country.

STARTING OUT

Software design positions are regarded as some of the most interesting, and therefore the most competitive, in the computer industry. Some software designers are promoted from an entry-level programming position. Software design positions in software supply companies and large custom software companies will be difficult to secure straight out of college.

Entry-level programming and design jobs may be listed in the help wanted sections of newspapers. Employment agencies and online job banks are other good sources.

Students in technical schools or universities should take advantage of the campus career services office. They should check regularly for internship postings, job listings, and notices of on-campus recruitment. Career services offices are also valuable resources for resume tips and interviewing techniques. Internships and summer jobs with such corporations are always beneficial and provide experience that will give you the edge over your competition. General computer job fairs are also held throughout the year in larger cities.

There are many online career sites that post job openings, salary surveys, and current employment trends. The Web also has online publications that deal specifically with computer jobs. You can also obtain information from computer organizations such as the IEEE Computer Society. Because this is such a competitive field, you will need to show initiative and creativity that will set you apart from other applicants.

ADVANCEMENT

Those software designers who demonstrate leadership may be promoted to *project team leader*. Project team leaders develop new software projects and oversee the work done by software designers and applications programmers. With experience as a project team leader, a motivated software designer may be promoted to a position as a *software manager* who runs projects from an even higher level. Individuals with a knack for spotting trends in the software market are also likely to advance.

EARNINGS

Salaries for software designers vary with the size of the company and by location. Salaries may be slightly higher in areas where there is a large concentration of computer companies, such as the Silicon Valley in northern California and parts of Washington, Oregon, and the East Coast.

The National Association of Colleges and Employers reports that average starting salaries for graduates with a doctoral degree in computer science were $93,050 in

2005. Graduates with a bachelor's degree in computer science averaged $53,396 in 2007.

Median salaries for computer and information scientists (which include software designers) were $93,950 in 2006, according to the U.S. Department of Labor. Salaries ranged from less than $53,590 to $144,880 or more annually. At the managerial level, salaries are even higher and can reach $160,000 or more.

Most designers work for large companies, which offer a full benefits package that includes health insurance, vacation and sick time, and a profit sharing or retirement plan.

WORK ENVIRONMENT

Software designers work in comfortable environments. Many computer companies are known for their casual work atmosphere; employees generally do not have to wear suits, except during client meetings. Overall, software designers work standard weeks. However, they may be required to work overtime near a deadline. It is common in software design to share office or cubicle space with two or three coworkers, which is typical of the team approach to working. As a software designer or applications programmer, much of the day is spent in front of the computer, although a software designer will have occasional team meetings or meetings with clients.

Software design can be stressful work for several reasons. First, the market for software is very competitive and companies are pushing to develop more innovative software and to get it on the market before competitors do. For this same reason, software design is also very exciting and creative work. Second, software designers are given a project and a deadline. It is up to the designer and team members to budget their time to finish in the allocated time. Finally, working with programming languages and so many details can be very frustrating, especially when the tiniest glitch means the program will not run. For this reason, software designers must be patient and diligent.

OUTLOOK

Employment in software design is expected to grow much faster than the average for all occupations through 2016, according to the *Occupational Outlook Handbook*. Employment will increase as technology becomes more sophisticated and organizations continue to adopt and integrate these technologies, making for plentiful job openings. Hardware designers and systems programmers are constantly developing faster, more powerful, and more user-friendly hardware and operating systems.

As long as these advancements continue, the industry will need software designers to create software to use these improvements.

Business may have less need to contract for custom software as more prepackaged software arrives on the market that allows users with minimal computer skills to "build" their own software using components that they customize. However, the growth in the retail software market is expected to make up for this loss in customized services.

The expanding integration of Internet technologies by businesses has resulted in a rising demand for a variety of skilled professionals who can develop and support a variety of Internet applications.

FOR MORE INFORMATION

For information on internships, student membership, and the student magazine Crossroads, *contact*
Association for Computing Machinery
2 Penn Plaza, Suite 701
New York, NY 10121-0701
Tel: 800-342-6626
Email: SIGS@acm.org
http://www.acm.org

For information on career opportunities for women in computing, contact
Association for Women in Computing
41 Sutter Street, Suite 1006
San Francisco, CA 94104-5414
Tel: 415-905-4663
Email: info@awc-hq.org
http://www.awc-hq.org

For information on scholarships, certification, student membership, and to read Careers in Computer Science and Computer Engineering, *visit the IEEE's Web site.*
IEEE Computer Society
1828 L Street, NW, Suite 1202
Washington, DC 20036-5104
Tel: 202-371-0101
Email: membership@computer.org
http://www.computer.org

For industry information, contact the following organization
Software & Information Industry Association
1090 Vermont Avenue, NW, Sixth Floor
Washington, DC 20005-4095
Tel: 202-289-7442
http://www.siia.net

SOFTWARE ENGINEERS

OVERVIEW

Software engineers customize existing software programs to meet the needs and desires of a particular business or industry. First, they spend considerable time researching, defining, and analyzing the problem at hand. Then, they develop software programs to resolve the problem on the computer. There are about 857,000 software engineers employed in the United States.

THE JOB

Every day, businesses, scientists, and government agencies encounter difficult problems that they cannot solve manually, either because the problem is just too complicated or because it would take too much time to calculate the appropriate solutions. For example, astronomers receive thousands of pieces of data every hour from probes and satellites in space as well as from telescopes here on Earth. If they had to process the information themselves, compile careful comparisons with previous years' readings, look for patterns or cycles, and keep accurate records of the origin of the data, it would be so cumbersome and lengthy a project as to make it next to impossible. They can, however, process the data with the extensive help of computers. Computer software engineers define and analyze specific problems in business or science and help develop computer software applications that effectively solve them. The software engineers who work in the field of astronomy are well versed in its concepts, but many other kinds of software engineers exist as well.

Software engineers fall into two basic categories. *Systems software engineers* build and maintain entire computer systems for a company. *Applications software engineers* design, create, and modify general computer applications software or specialized utility programs.

Engineers who work on computer systems research how a company's departments and their respective computer systems are organized. For example, there might be customer service, ordering, inventory, billing, shipping, and payroll recordkeeping departments. Systems software engineers suggest ways to coordinate all these parts. They might set up intranets or networks that link computers within the organization and ease communication.

Some applications software engineers develop packaged software applications, such as word processing,

SCHOOL SUBJECTS
Computer Science, Mathematics

PERSONAL SKILLS
Mechanical/Manipulative, Technical/Scientific

MINIMUM EDUCATION LEVEL
Bachelor's Degree

CERTIFICATION OR LICENSING
Recommended

WORK ENVIRONMENT
Primarily Indoors, Primarily One Location

graphic design, or database programs, for software development companies. Other applications engineers design customized software for individual businesses or organizations. For example, a software engineer might work with an insurance company to develop new ways to reduce paperwork, such as claim forms, applications, and bill processing. Applications engineers write programs using programming languages like C++ and Java.

Software engineers sometimes specialize in a particular industry such as the chemical industry, insurance, or medicine, which requires knowledge of that industry in addition to computer expertise. Some engineers work for consulting firms that complete software projects for different clients on an individual basis. Others work for large companies that hire full-time engineers to develop software customized to their needs.

Both systems and applications software engineering involve extremely detail-oriented work. Since computers do only what they are programmed to do, engineers have to account for every bit of information with a programming command. Software engineers are thus required to be very well organized and precise. In order to achieve this, they generally follow strict procedures in completing an assignment.

First, they interview clients and colleagues to determine exactly what they want the final program to accomplish. Defining the problem by outlining the goal can sometimes be difficult, especially when clients have little technical training. Then, engineers evaluate the software applications already in use by the client to understand how and why they are failing to fulfill the needs of the operation. After this period of fact gathering, the engineers use methods of scientific analysis and mathematical models to develop possible solutions to the problems. These analytical methods help them predict and measure the outcomes of different proposed designs.

When they have developed a clear idea of what type of program is required to fulfill the client's needs, they draw up a detailed proposal that includes estimates of time and cost allocations. Management must then decide if the project will meet their needs, is a good investment, and whether or not it will be undertaken.

Once a proposal is accepted, both software engineers and technicians begin work on the project. They verify with hardware engineers that the proposed software program can be completed with existing hardware systems. Typically, the engineer writes program specifications and the technician uses his or her knowledge of computer languages to write preliminary programming. Engineers focus most of their effort on program strategies, testing procedures, and reviewing technicians' work.

Software engineers are usually responsible for a significant amount of technical writing, including project proposals, progress reports, and user manuals. They are required to meet regularly with clients to keep project goals clear and learn about any changes as quickly as possible.

When the program is completed, the software engineer organizes a demonstration of the final product to the client. Supervisors, management, and users are generally present. Some software engineers may offer to install the program, train users on it, and make arrangements for ongoing technical support.

Software engineering technicians assist engineers in completing projects. They are usually knowledgeable in analog, digital, and microprocessor electronics and programming techniques. Technicians know enough about program design and computer languages to fill in details left out by engineers or programmers, who conceive of the program from a large-scale perspective. Technicians might also test new software applications with special diagnostic equipment.

REQUIREMENTS
High School

If you are interested in pursuing this career, take as many computer, math, and science courses as possible, because they provide fundamental math and computer knowledge and teach analytical thinking skills. Classes that rely on schematic drawing and flowcharts are also very valuable. English and speech courses will help you improve your communication skills, which are very important for software engineers.

Postsecondary Training

As more and more well-educated professionals enter the industry, most employers now require a bachelor's degree. A typical degree concentration for an applications software engineer is software engineering or computer science. Systems software engineers typically pursue a concentration in computer science or computer information systems.

Obtaining a postsecondary degree is usually considered challenging and even difficult. In addition to natural ability, you should be hard working and determined to succeed. If you plan to work in a specific technical field, such as medicine, law, or business, you should receive some formal training in that particular discipline.

Certification or Licensing

The Institute of Electrical and Electronics Engineers Computer Society offers the designation, certified software development professional, to individuals who have a bachelor's degree, a minimum of 9,000 hours of software engineering experience within at least six of 11 knowledge areas, and pass an examination. The Institute for Certification of Computing Professionals also offers basic certifications to computer professionals.

Another option if you're interested in software engineering is to pursue commercial certification. These programs are usually run by computer companies that wish to train professionals to work with their products. Classes are challenging and examinations can be rigorous. New programs are introduced every year.

Other Requirements

As a software engineer, you will need strong communications skills in order to be able to make formal business presentations and interact with people having different levels of computer expertise. You must also be detail oriented and work well under pressure.

EXPLORING

Try to spend a day with a working software engineer in order to experience firsthand what their job is like. School guidance counselors can help you arrange such a visit. You can also talk to your high school computer teacher for more information.

In general, you should be intent on learning as much as possible about computers and computer software. You should learn about new developments by reading trade magazines and talking to other computer users. You also can join computer clubs and surf the Internet for information about working in this field.

EMPLOYERS

About 857,000 computer software engineers are employed in the United States. Approximately 507,000 work with applications and 350,000 work with systems software. Software engineering is done in many fields, including medical, industrial, military, communications, aerospace, scientific, and other commercial businesses. More than 29 percent of software engineers—the largest concentration in the field—work in computer systems design and related services.

STARTING OUT

As a technical, vocational, or university student of software engineering, you should work closely with your schools' career services offices, as many professionals find their first position through on-campus recruiting. Career services office staff are well trained to provide tips on resume writing, interviewing techniques, and locating job leads.

Individuals not working with a school career services office can check the classified ads for job openings. They also can work with a local employment agency that places computer professionals in appropriate jobs. Many openings in the computer industry are publicized by word of mouth, so you should stay in touch with working computer professionals to learn who is hiring. In addition, these people may be willing to refer you directly to the person in charge of recruiting.

ADVANCEMENT

Software engineers who demonstrate leadership qualities and thorough technical know-how may become project team leaders who are responsible for full-scale software development projects. Project team leaders oversee the work of technicians and engineers. They determine the overall parameters of a project, calculate time schedules and financial budgets, divide the project into smaller tasks, and assign these tasks to engineers. Overall, they do both managerial and technical work.

Software engineers with experience as project team leaders may be promoted to a position as *software manager,* running a large research and development department. Managers oversee software projects with a more encompassing perspective; they help choose projects to be undertaken, select project team leaders and engineering teams, and assign individual projects. In some cases, they may be required to travel, solicit new business, and contribute to the general marketing strategy of the company.

Many computer professionals find that their interests change over time. As long as individuals are well qualified and keep up to date with the latest technology, they are usually able to find positions in other areas of the computer industry.

EARNINGS

Software engineers with a bachelor's degree in computer engineering earned starting salaries of $56,201 in 2007, according to the National Association of Colleges and Employers. Computer engineers specializing in applications earned median annual salaries of $79,780 in 2006, according to the U.S. Department of Labor. The lowest 10 percent averaged less than $49,350, and the highest 10 percent earned $119,770 or more annually. Software engineers specializing in systems software earned median salaries of $85,370 in 2006. The lowest paid 10 percent averaged $53,580 annually, and the highest paid engineers made $125,750 per year. Experienced software engineers can earn more than $150,000 a year. When software engineers are promoted to project team leader or software manager, they earn even more. Software engineers generally earn more in geographical areas where there are clusters of computer companies, such as the Silicon Valley in northern California.

Most software engineers work for companies that offer extensive benefits, including health insurance, sick leave, and paid vacation. In some smaller computer companies, however, benefits may be limited.

WORK ENVIRONMENT

Software engineers usually work in comfortable office environments. Overall, they usually work 40-hour weeks, but their hours depend on the nature of the employer and expertise of the engineer. In consulting firms, for example, it is typical for software engineers to work long hours and frequently travel to out-of-town assignments.

Software engineers generally receive an assignment and a time frame within which to accomplish it; daily work details are often left up to the individuals. Some engineers work relatively lightly at the beginning of a project, but work a lot of overtime at the end in order to catch up. Most engineers are not compensated for overtime. Software engineering can be stressful, especially when engineers must work to meet deadlines. Working with programming languages and intense details is often frustrating. Therefore, software engineers should be patient, enjoy problem-solving challenges, and work well under pressure.

OUTLOOK

The field of software engineering is expected to be one of the fastest-growing occupations through 2016, according to the U.S. Department of Labor. Demands made on computers increase every day and from all industries. Rapid growth in the computer systems design and related industries will account for much of this growth. In addition, businesses will continue to implement new and innovative technology to remain competitive, and they will need software engineers to do this. Software engineers will also be needed to handle ever-growing capabilities of computer networks, e-commerce, and wireless technologies, as well as the security features needed to protect such systems from outside attacks. Outsourcing of jobs in this field to foreign countries will temper growth somewhat, but overall the future of software engineering is very bright.

Since technology changes so rapidly, software engineers are advised to keep up on the latest developments. While the need for software engineers will remain high, computer languages will probably change every few years and software engineers will need to attend seminars and workshops to learn new computer languages and software design. They also should read trade magazines, surf the Internet, and talk with colleagues about the field. These kinds of continuing education techniques help ensure that software engineers are best equipped to meet the needs of the workplace.

FOR MORE INFORMATION

For information on internships, student membership, and the student magazine Crossroads, *contact*

Association for Computing Machinery
2 Penn Plaza, Suite 701
New York, NY 10121-0701
Tel: 800-342-6626
Email: SIGS@acm.org
http://www.acm.org

For information on career opportunities for women in computing, contact

Association for Women in Computing
41 Sutter Street, Suite 1006
San Francisco, CA 94104-5414
Tel: 415-905-4663
Email: info@awc-hq.org
http://www.awc-hq.org

For certification information, contact

Institute for Certification of Computing Professionals
2350 East Devon Avenue, Suite 115
Des Plaines, IL 60018-4610

Tel: 800-843-8227
http://www.iccp.org

For information on scholarships, certification, student membership, and to read Careers in Computer Science and Computer Engineering, *visit the IEEE's Web site.*

IEEE Computer Society
1828 L Street, NW, Suite 1202
Washington, DC 20036-5104
Tel: 202-371-0101
Email: membership@computer.org
http://www.computer.org

For more information on careers in computer software, contact

Software & Information Industry Association
1090 Vermont Avenue, NW, Sixth Floor
Washington, DC 20005-4095
Tel: 202-289-7442
http://www.siia.net

SPORTS INSTRUCTORS AND COACHES

OVERVIEW

Sports instructors demonstrate and explain the skills and rules of particular sports, like golf or tennis, to individuals or groups. They help beginners learn basic rules, stances, grips, movements, and techniques of a game. Sports instructors often help experienced athletes to sharpen their skills.

Coaches work with a single, organized team or individual, teaching the skills associated with that sport. A coach prepares her or his team for competition. During the competition, he or she continues to give instruction from a vantage point near the court or playing field.

THE JOB

The specific job requirements of sports instructors and coaches varies according to the type of sport and athletes involved. For example, an instructor teaching advanced skiing at a resort in Utah will have different duties and responsibilities than an instructor teaching beginning swimming at a municipal pool. Nevertheless, all instructors and coaches are teachers. They must be very knowledgeable about rules and strategies for their respective sports. They must also have an effective teaching method that reinforces correct techniques and procedures so their students or players will be able to gain from that valuable knowledge. Also, instructors and coaches need to be aware of and open to new procedures and techniques. Many attend clinics or seminars to learn more about their sport or even how to teach more effectively. Many are also members of professional organizations that deal exclusively with their sport.

Safety is a primary concern for all coaches and instructors. Coaches and instructors make sure their students have the right equipment and know its correct use. A major component of safety is helping students feel comfortable and confident with their abilities. This entails teaching the proper stances, techniques, and movements of a game, instructing students on basic rules, and answering any questions.

While instructors may tutor students individually or in small groups, a coach works with all the members of a team. Both use lectures and demonstrations to show students the proper skills, and both point out students' mistakes or deficiencies.

Motivation is another key element in sports instruction. Almost all sports require stamina, and most coaches will tell you that psychological preparation is every bit as important as physical training.

Coaches and instructors also have administrative responsibilities. College coaches actively recruit new players to join their team. Professional coaches attend team meetings with owners and general managers to determine which players they will draft the next season. Sports instructors at health and athletic clubs schedule classes, lessons, and contests.

REQUIREMENTS

Training and educational requirements vary, depending on the specific sport and the ability level of students being instructed. Most coaches who are associated with schools have bachelor's degrees. Many middle and high school coaches are also teachers within the school. Most instructors need to combine several years of successful experience in a particular sport with some educational background, preferably in teaching. A college degree is becoming more important as part of an instructor's background.

High School

To prepare for college courses, high school students should take courses that teach human physiology. Biology, health, and exercise classes would all be helpful.

SCHOOL SUBJECTS
English, Physical Education

PERSONAL SKILLS
Communication/Ideas, Helping/Teaching

MINIMUM EDUCATION LEVEL
Some Postsecondary Training

CERTIFICATION OR LICENSING
Required in Certain Positions

WORK ENVIRONMENT
Indoors and Outdoors, Primarily Multiple Locations

Courses in English and speech are also important to improve or develop communication skills.

There is no substitute for developing expertise in a sport. If you can play the sport well and effectively explain to other people how they might play, you will most likely be able to get a job as a sports instructor. The most significant source of training for this occupation is gained while on the job.

Postsecondary Training

Postsecondary training in this field varies greatly. College and professional coaches often attended college as athletes, while others attended college and received their degrees without playing a sport. If you are interested in becoming a high school coach, you will need a college degree because you will most likely be teaching as well as coaching. At the high school level, coaches spend their days teaching everything from physical education to English to mathematics, and so the college courses these coaches take vary greatly. Coaches of some youth league sports may not need a postsecondary degree, but they must have a solid understanding of their sport and of injury prevention.

Certification or Licensing

Many facilities require sports instructors to be certified. Information on certification is available from any organization that deals with the specific sport in which one might be interested.

Since most high school coaches also work as teachers, those interested in this job should plan to obtain teacher certification in their state.

Other Requirements

Coaches have to be experts in their sport. They must have complete knowledge of the rules and strategies of the game, so that they can creatively design effective plays and techniques for their athletes. But the requirements for this job do not end here. Good coaches are able to communicate their extensive knowledge to the athletes in a way that not only instructs the athletes, but also inspires them to perform to their fullest potential. Therefore, coaches are also teachers.

"I think I'm good at my job because I love working with people and because I'm disciplined in everything I do," says Dawn Shannahan, former assistant girls' basketball and track coach at Leyden High School in Franklin Park, Illinois. Discipline is important for athletes, as they must practice plays and techniques over and over again. Coaches who cannot demonstrate and encourage this type of discipline will have difficulty helping their athletes improve. Shannahan adds, "I've seen coaches who are really knowledgeable about their sport but who aren't patient enough to allow for mistakes or for learning." Patience can make all the difference between an effective coach and one who is unsuccessful.

Similarly, Shannahan says, "A coach shouldn't be a pessimist. The team could be losing by a lot, but you have to stay optimistic and encourage the players." Coaches must be able to work under pressure, guiding teams through games and tournaments that carry great personal and possibly financial stakes for everyone involved.

EXPLORING

Try to gain as much experience as possible in all sports and a specific sport in particular. It is never too early to start. High school and college offer great opportunities to participate in sporting events either as a player, manager, trainer, or in intramural leagues.

Most communities have sports programs such as Little League baseball or track and field meets sponsored by a recreation commission. Get involved by volunteering as a coach, umpire, or starter.

Talking with sports instructors already working in the field is also a good way to discover specific job information and find out about career opportunities.

EMPLOYERS

Besides working in high schools, coaches are hired by colleges and universities, professional sports teams, individual athletes such as tennis players, and by youth leagues, summer camps, and recreation centers.

STARTING OUT

People with expertise in a particular sport, who are interested in becoming an instructor, should apply directly to the appropriate facility. Sometimes a facility will provide training.

For those interested in coaching, many colleges offer positions to *graduate assistant coaches*. Graduate assistant coaches are recently graduated players who are interested in becoming coaches. They receive a stipend and gain valuable coaching experience.

ADVANCEMENT

Advancement opportunities for both instructors and coaches depend on the individual's skills, willingness to learn, and work ethic. A sports instructor's success can be measured by their students' caliber of play and the number of students they instruct. Successful instructors may become well known enough to open their own schools or camps, write books, or produce how-to videos.

Some would argue that a high percentage of wins is the only criteria for success for professional coaches. However, coaches in the scholastic ranks have other responsibilities and other factors that measure success; for example, high school and college coaches must make sure their players are getting good grades. All coaches must try to produce a team that competes in a sportsmanlike fashion regardless of whether they win or lose.

Successful coaches are often hired by larger schools. High school coaches may advance to become college coaches, and the most successful college coaches often are given the opportunity to coach professional teams. Former players sometimes land assistant or head coaching positions.

EARNINGS

Earnings for sports instructors and coaches vary considerably depending on the sport and the person or team being coached. The coach of a Wimbledon champion commands much more money per hour than the swimming instructor for the tadpole class at the municipal pool.

The U.S. Department of Labor reports that the median earnings for sports coaches and instructors were $26,950 in 2006. The lowest 10 percent earned less than $13,990, while the highest 10 percent earned more than $58,890. Sports instructors and coaches who worked at colleges and universities earned a mean annual salary of $44,200 in 2006, while those employed by elementary and secondary schools earned $27,550.

Much of the work is part time, and part-time employees generally do not receive paid vacations, sick days, or health insurance. Instructors who teach group classes for beginners through park districts or at city recreation centers can expect to earn around $6 per hour. An hour-long individual lesson through a golf course or tennis club averages $75. Many times, coaches for children's teams work as volunteers.

Many sports instructors work in camps teaching swimming, archery, sailing and other activities. These instructors generally earn between $1,000 and $2,500, plus room and board, for a summer session.

Full-time fitness instructors at gyms or health clubs earned salaries that ranged from less than $14,880 to $56,750 or more per year in 2006, with a median salary of $25,910, according to the U.S. Department of Labor. Instructors with many years of experience and a college degree have the highest earning potential.

Most coaches who work at the high school level or below also teach within the school district. Besides their teaching salary and coaching fee—either a flat rate or a percentage of their annual salary—school coaches receive a benefits package that includes paid vacations and health insurance.

Head college football coaches at NCAA Division I schools earned an average of $950,000 a year in 2006, according to *USA Today*. A few top football coaches earn more than $2 million annually. Some top coaches in men's Division I basketball earn salaries of $1 million or more, according to *USA Today*. Women's basketball coaches at the college level typically earn lower salaries than their colleagues who coach men's sports—although top coaches earn salaries that are on par with coaches of men's basketball teams.

Coaches for professional teams often earn between $200,000 and $3 million a year. Some top coaches can earn more than $5 million annually. Many popular coaches augment their salaries with fees obtained from personal appearances and endorsements.

WORK ENVIRONMENT

An instructor or coach may work indoors, in a gym or health club, or outdoors, perhaps at a swimming pool. Much of the work is part time. Full-time sports instructors generally work between 35 and 40 hours per week. During the season when their teams compete, coaches can work 16 hours each day, five or six days each week.

It is not unusual for coaches or instructors to work evenings or weekends. Instructors work then because that is when their adult students are available for instruction. Coaches work nights and weekends because those are the times their teams compete.

One significant drawback to this job is the lack of job security. A club may hire a new instructor on very little notice, or may cancel a scheduled class for lack of interest. Athletic teams routinely fire coaches after losing seasons.

Sports instructors and coaches should enjoy working with a wide variety of people. They should be able to communicate clearly and possess good leadership skills to effectively teach complex skills. They can take pride in the knowledge that they have helped their students or their players reach new heights of achievement and training.

OUTLOOK

Americans' interest in health, physical fitness, and body image continues to send people to gyms and playing fields. This fitness boom has created strong employment opportunities for many people in sports-related occupations.

Health clubs, community centers, parks and recreational facilities, and private business now employ sports instructors who teach everything from tennis and golf to scuba diving.

According to the U.S. Department of Labor, these careers will grow faster than the average for all occupations through 2016. Job opportunities will be best in high schools and in amateur athletic leagues. Health clubs, adult education programs, and private industry will require competent, dedicated instructors. Those with the most training, education, and experience will have the best chance for employment.

The creation of new professional leagues, as well as the expansion of current leagues, will open some new employment opportunities for professional coaches, but competition for these jobs will be very intense. There will also be openings as other coaches retire, or are terminated. However, there is very little job security in coaching, unless a coach can consistently produce a winning team.

FOR MORE INFORMATION

For certification information, trade journals, job listings, and a list of graduate schools, visit the AAHPERD's Web site.

American Alliance for Health, Physical Education, Recreation and Dance (AAHPERD)
1900 Association Drive
Reston, VA 20191-1598
Tel: 800-213-7193
http://www.aahperd.org

For information on membership and baseball coaching education, coaching Web links, and job listings, visit the ABCA's Web site.

American Baseball Coaches Association (ABCA)
108 South University Avenue, Suite 3
Mount Pleasant, MI 48858-2327
Tel: 989-775-3300
Email: abca@abca.org
http://www.abca.org

For information on football coaching careers, contact

American Football Coaches Association
100 Legends Lane
Waco, TX 76706-1243
Tel: 254-754-9900
Email: info@afca.com
http://www.afca.com

For informational on hockey coaching, contact

American Hockey Coaches Association
7 Concord Street
Gloucester, MA 01930-2300
Tel: 781-245-4177
http://www.ahcahockey.com

For information on careers in sports and physical education, contact

National Association for Sport and Physical Education
1900 Association Drive
Reston, VA 20191-1598
Tel: 800-213-7193
Email: naspe@aahperd.org
http://www.aahperd.org/naspe

For information on basketball coaching, contact

National Association of Basketball Coaches
1111 Main Street, Suite 1000
Kansas City, MO 64105-2136
Tel: 816-878-6222
http://nabc.ocsn.com

For information on high school coaching opportunities, contact

National High School Athletic Coaches Association
PO Box 10065
Fargo, ND 58106-0065
Email: office@hscoaches.org
http://www.hscoaches.org

For information on the coaching of soccer, contact

National Soccer Coaches Association of America
800 Ann Avenue

Kansas City, KS 66101-3003
Tel: 800-458-0678
http://www.nscaa.com

For information on women's basketball coaching, contact

Women's Basketball Coaches Association
4646 Lawrenceville Highway
Lilburn, GA 30047-3620
Tel: 770-279-8027
Email: wbca@wbca.org
http://www.wbca.org

 SURGEONS

OVERVIEW

Surgeons are physicians who make diagnoses and provide preoperative, operative, and postoperative care in surgery affecting almost any part of the body. These doctors also work with trauma victims and the critically ill. Approximately 52,000 surgeons are employed in the United States.

THE JOB

The work of a surgeon will vary according to his or her work environment and specialty. For example, a general surgeon who specializes in trauma care would most likely work in a large, urban hospital where he or she would spend a great deal of time in the operating room performing emergency surgical procedures at a moment's notice. On the other hand, a general surgeon who specializes in hernia repair would probably have a more predictable work schedule and would spend much of his or her time in an ambulatory (also called outpatient) surgery center.

The surgeon is responsible for the diagnosis of the patient, for performing operations, and for providing patients with postoperative surgical care and treatment. In emergency room situations, the patient typically comes with an injury or severe pain. If the patient needs surgery, the on-duty general surgeon will schedule the surgery. Depending on the urgency of the case, surgery may be scheduled for the following day, or the patient will be operated on immediately.

A surgeon sees such cases as gunshot, stabbing, and accident victims. Other cases that often involve emergency surgery include appendectomies and removal of kidney stones. When certain problems, such as a kidney stone or inflamed appendix, are diagnosed at an early stage, the surgeon can perform nonemergency surgery.

There are several specialties of surgery and four areas of subspecialization of general surgery. For these areas, the surgeon can receive further education and training leading to certification. A few of these specializations include *neurosurgery* (care for disorders of the nervous system), *plastic and reconstructive surgery* (care for defects of the skin and underlying musculoskeletal structure), *orthopaedic surgery* (care for musculoskeletal disorders that are present at birth or develop later), and thoracic surgery (care for diseases and conditions of the chest). The subspecializations for general surgery are *general vascular surgery, pediatric surgery, hand surgery,* and *surgical critical care.*

REQUIREMENTS
High School

Training to become a surgeon or physician is among the most rigorous of any profession, but the pay is also among the highest. To begin preparing for the demands of college, medical school, and an internship and residency in a hospital, be sure to take as many science and mathematics courses as possible. English, communication, and psychology classes will help prepare you for the large amount of reporting and interacting with patients and staff that surgeons do on a daily basis.

Postsecondary Training

Many students who want to become a physician or surgeon enroll in premedical programs at a college or university. Premedical students take classes in biology, organic and inorganic chemistry, physics, mathematics, English, and the humanities. Some students who major in other disciplines go on to pursue a medical degree, but they generally have to complete additional course work in math and science. All students must take the standardized Medical College Admission Test (MCAT) and then apply to medical schools to pursue the M.D. degree. Note than medical school admissions are fiercely competitive, so developing strong study habits, attaining good grades, and pursuing extracurricular activities are all important characteristics for a medical school applicant to have.

Physicians wishing to pursue general surgery must complete a five-year residency in surgery according to the requirements set down by the Accreditation Council for Graduate Medical Education.

Throughout the surgery residency, residents are supervised at all levels of training by assisting on and then performing basic operations, such as the removal of an appendix. As the residency years continue, residents

---

SCHOOL SUBJECTS
Biology, Chemistry, Health

PERSONAL SKILLS
Helping/Teaching, Technical/Scientific

MINIMUM EDUCATION LEVEL
Medical Degree

CERTIFICATION OR LICENSING
Required by All States

WORK ENVIRONMENT
Primarily Indoors, Primarily Multiple Locations

---

gain responsibility through teaching and supervisory duties. Eventually the residents are allowed to perform complex operations independently.

Subspecialties require from one to three years of additional training.

Certification and Licensing

The American Board of Surgery administers board certification in surgery. The board certifies surgeons in the following fields: surgery (general surgery), vascular surgery, pediatric surgery, surgical critical care, surgery of the hand, and hospice and palliative medicine. While certification is a voluntary procedure, it is highly recommended. Most hospitals will not grant privileges to a surgeon without board certification. HMOs and other insurance groups will not make referrals or payments to a surgeon without board certification. Also, insurance companies are not likely to insure a surgeon for malpractice if he or she is not board certified.

To be eligible to apply for certification in surgery, a candidate must have successfully completed medical school and the requisite residency in surgery. Once a candidate's application has been approved, the candidate may take the written examination. After passing the written exam, the candidate may then take the oral exam.

Certification in surgery is valid for 10 years. To obtain recertification, surgeons must apply to the American Board of Surgery with documentation of their continuing medical education activities and of the operations and procedures they have performed since being certified, and submit to a review by their peers. They must also pass a written exam.

Certification is available in a number of surgical specialties, including plastic surgery, colon and rectal surgery, neurological surgery, orthopaedic surgery, and thoracic surgery. The American Board of Medical Specialties and the American Medical Association (AMA) recognizes 24 specialty boards that certify physicians and surgeons.

All physicians and surgeons must be licensed by the state in which they work.

Other Requirements

To be a successful surgeon, you should be able to think quickly and act decisively in stressful situations, enjoy helping and working with people, have strong organizational skills, be able to give clear instructions, have good hand-eye coordination, and be able to listen and communicate well.

EXPLORING

If you are interested in becoming a surgeon, pay special attention to the work involved in your science laboratory courses. Obviously, working on a living human being is a much weightier prospect than dissecting a lab sample, but what you learn about basic handling and cleaning of tools, making incisions, and identifying and properly referring to the body's structures will prove invaluable in your future career. Also ask your science teacher or guidance counselor to try to get a surgeon to speak to your biology class, so that he or she can help you understand more of what the job involves.

EMPLOYERS

There are about 52,000 surgeons employed in the United States. Almost half of all licensed physicians and surgeons in the United States work in private solo or group practices. Another 18 percent work for hospitals, and others work for federal and state government offices, educational services, and outpatient care facilities.

STARTING OUT

Many new physicians and surgeons choose to join existing practices instead of attempting to start their own. Establishing a new practice is costly, and it may take time to build a patient base. In a clinic, group practice, or partnership, physicians share the costs for medical equipment and staff salaries, and of establishing a wider patient base.

Surgeons who hope to join an existing practice may find leads through their medical school or residency. During these experiences, they work with many members of the medical community, some of whom may be able to recommend them to appropriate practices.

Another approach would be to check the various medical professional journals, which often run ads for physician positions. Aspiring physicians can also hire a medical placement agency to assist them in the job search.

Physicians who hope to work for a managed care organization or government sponsored clinic should contact the source directly for information on position availability and application procedures.

ADVANCEMENT

Surgeons typically advance by expanding their skills and knowledge, increasing the number of patients they treat, and by increasing their income. They may become fellows in a professional specialty or serve on the board of a medical association. Others achieve recognition by conducting research in new surgical procedures and treatments and publishing their findings in medical journals.

EARNINGS

According to the U.S. Department of Labor, surgeons with over a year of experience earned mean salaries of $184,150 in 2006. Even the lowest paid 10 percent of surgeons earned incomes of more than $116,850. Incomes may vary by specialty. According to Physician Search, a physician recruitment firm, surgeons earned the following average salaries by specialty in 2008: cardiovascular, $558,719; neuro, $438,426; vascular, $359,339; orthopedic, $357,224; plastic, $306,047; colon/rectal, $291,199; urology, $285,356; and oral & maxillofacial; $208,340. Other factors influencing individual incomes include the type and size of practice, the hours worked per week, the geographic location, and the reputation a surgeon has among both patients and fellow professionals.

Benefits for surgeons include vacation and sick time, health, and sometimes dental, insurance, and pension or 401 (k) plans.

WORK ENVIRONMENT

Surgeons work in sterile operating rooms that are well equipped, well lighted, and well ventilated. They meet patients and conduct all regular business in clean, well-lit offices. There are usually several nurses, a laboratory technician, one or more secretaries, a bookkeeper, and a receptionist available to assist the surgeon.

General practitioners usually see patients by appointments that are scheduled according to individual requirements. They may reserve all mornings for hospital visits and minor surgery. They may see patients in the office only on certain days of the week. General practitioners may also visit patients in nursing homes, hospices, and home-care settings.

More than 33 percent of surgeons worked 60 or more hours a week in 2006, according to the U.S. Department of Labor.

OUTLOOK

The wide-ranging skills and knowledge of the surgeon will always be in demand, whether or not the surgeon has a subspecialty. According to the Occupational Outlook Handbook, physician jobs, including surgeons, are expected to grow faster than the average for all careers through 2016. Many industry experts are now predicting a shortage of general surgeons in the next decade as more students enter nonsurgical specialties, such as anesthesiology and radiology, which require less intensive training. Because of the growing and aging population, more surgeons will be required to meet medical needs.

FOR MORE INFORMATION

For information on certification in medical specialties, contact

American Board of Medical Specialties
1007 Church Street, Suite 404
Evanston, IL 60201-5913
Tel: 847-491-9091
http://www.abms.org

For information on certification for plastic surgeons, contact

American Board of Plastic Surgery
Seven Penn Center, Suite 400
1635 Market Street
Philadelphia, PA 19103-2204
Tel: 215-587-9322
Email: info@abplsurg.org
http://www.abplsurg.org

For information on certification, contact

American Board of Surgery
1617 John F. Kennedy Boulevard, Suite 860
Philadelphia, PA 19103-1847
Tel: 215-568-4000
http://www.absurgery.org

For information on women in surgical careers, contact

Association of Women Surgeons
5204 Fairmont Avenue, Suite 208
Downers Grove, IL 60515-5058

Tel: 630-655-0392
Email: info@womensurgeons.org
http://www.womensurgeons.org

For information on surgical specialties, contact the following organizations:

American Academy of Orthopaedic Surgeons
6300 North River Road
Rosemont, IL 60018-4262
Tel: 847-823-7186
http://www.aaos.org

American Association of Neurological Surgeons
5550 Meadowbrook Drive
Rolling Meadows, IL 60008-3845
Tel: 888-566-2267
Email: info@aans.org
http://www.aabs.org

American Society for Aesthetic Plastic Surgery
11081 Winners Circle
Los Alamitos, CA 90720-2813
Tel: 888-272-7711
http://www.surgery.org

Society of Thoracic Surgeons
633 North Saint Clair Street, Suite 2320
Chicago, IL 60611-3658
Tel: 312-202-5800
Email: sts@sts.org
http://www.sts.org

□ SURGICAL TECHNOLOGISTS

OVERVIEW

Surgical technologists, also called *surgical technicians* or *operating room technicians*, are members of the surgical team who work in the operating room with surgeons, nurses, anesthesiologists, and other personnel before, during, and after surgery. They ensure a safe and sterile environment. To prepare a patient for surgery, they may wash, shave, and disinfect the area where the incision will be made. They arrange the equipment, instruments, and supplies in the operating room according to the preference of the surgeons and nurses. During the operation, they adjust lights and other equipment as needed. They

SCHOOL SUBJECTS
Biology, Health

PERSONAL SKILLS
Helping/Teaching, Technical/Scientific

MINIMUM EDUCATION LEVEL
Some Postsecondary Training

CERTIFICATION OR LICENSING
Recommended

WORK ENVIRONMENT
Primarily Indoors, Primarily One Location

count sponges, needles, and instruments used during the operation, hand instruments and supplies to the surgeon, and hold retractors and cut sutures as directed. They maintain specified supplies of fluids (for example, saline, plasma, blood, and glucose), and may assist in administering these fluids. Following the operation, they may clean and restock the operating room and wash and sterilize the used equipment using germicides, autoclaves, and sterilizers, although in most larger hospitals these tasks are done by other central service personnel. There are approximately 86,000 surgical technologists employed in the United States.

THE JOB

Surgical technologists are health professionals who work in the surgical suite with surgeons, anesthesiologists, registered nurses, and other surgical personnel delivering surgical patient care.

In general, the work responsibilities of surgical technologists may be divided into three phases: preoperative (before surgery), intraoperative (during surgery), and postoperative (after surgery). Surgical technologists may work as the *scrub person, circulator,* or *surgical first assistant.*

In the preoperative phase, surgical technologists prepare the operating room by selecting and opening sterile supplies such as drapes, sutures, sponges, electrosurgical devices, suction tubing, and surgical instruments. They assemble, adjust, and check nonsterile equipment to ensure that it is in proper working order. Surgical technologists also operate sterilizers, lights, suction machines, electrosurgical units, and diagnostic equipment.

When patients arrive in the surgical suite, surgical technologists may assist in preparing them for surgery by providing physical and emotional support, checking charts, and observing vital signs. They properly position the patient on the operating table, assist in connecting and applying surgical equipment and monitoring devices, and prepare the incision site by cleansing the skin with an antiseptic solution.

During surgery, surgical technologists have primary responsibility for maintaining the sterile field. They constantly watch that all members of the team adhere to aseptic techniques so the patient does not develop a postoperative infection. As the scrub person, they most often function as the sterile member of the surgical team who passes instruments, sutures, and sponges during surgery. After "scrubbing," which involves the thorough cleansing of the hands and forearms, they put on a sterile gown and gloves and prepare the sterile instruments and supplies that will be needed. After other members of the sterile team have scrubbed, they assist them with gowning and gloving and applying sterile drapes around the operative site.

Surgical technologists must anticipate the needs of surgeons during the procedure, passing instruments and providing sterile items in an efficient manner. Checking, mixing, and dispensing appropriate fluids and drugs in the sterile field are other common tasks. They share with the *circulator* the responsibility for accounting for sponges, needles, and instruments before, during, and after surgery. They may hold retractors or instruments, sponge or suction the operative site, or cut suture material as directed by the surgeon. They connect drains and tubing and receive and prepare specimens for subsequent pathologic analysis.

Surgical technologists most often function as the scrub person, but may function in the nonsterile role of circulator. The circulator does not wear a sterile gown and gloves, but is available to assist the surgical team. As a circulator, the surgical technologist obtains additional supplies or equipment, assists the anesthesiologist, keeps a written account of the surgical procedure, and assists the scrub person.

Surgical first assistants, who are technologists with additional education or training, provide aid in retracting tissue, controlling bleeding, and other technical functions that help surgeons during the procedure.

After surgery, surgical technologists are responsible for preparing and applying dressings, including plaster or synthetic casting materials, and for preparing the operating room for the next patient. They may provide staffing in postoperative recovery rooms where patients' responses are carefully monitored in the critical phases following general anesthesia.

Some of these responsibilities vary, depending on the size of the hospital and department in which the surgical technologist works; they also vary based on geographic location and health care needs of the local community.

REQUIREMENTS
High School

During your high school years, you should take courses that develop your basic skills in mathematics, science, and English. You also should take all available courses in health and biology.

Postsecondary Training

Surgical technology education is available through postsecondary programs offered by community and junior colleges, vocational and technical schools, the military, universities, and structured hospital programs in surgical technology. A high school diploma is required for entry into any of these programs.

More than 400 of these programs are accredited by the Commission on Accreditation of Allied Health Education Programs (CAAHEP) or the Accrediting Bureau of Health Education Schools. The accredited programs vary from nine to 12 months for a diploma or certificate, to two years for an associate's degree. You can expect to take courses in medical terminology, communications, anatomy, physiology, microbiology, pharmacology, medical ethics, and legal responsibilities. You gain a thorough knowledge of patient preparation and care, surgical procedures, surgical instruments and equipment, and principles of asepsis (how to prevent infection). In addition to classroom learning, you receive intensive supervised clinical experience in local hospitals, which is an important component of your education.

Certification or Licensing

Increasing numbers of hospitals are requiring certification as a condition of employment. Surgical technologists may earn a professional credential by passing a nationally administered certifying examination. To take the examination, you must be currently or previously certified or be a graduate of a CAAHEP-accredited program. The National Board of Surgical Technology and Surgical Assisting (NBSTSA) is the certifying agency for the profession. Those who pass the exam and fulfill education and experience requirements are granted the designation of certified surgical technologist (CST). To renew the four-year certificate, the CST must earn continuing education credits or retake the certifying examination. The NBSTSA also offers an advanced credential for surgical first assistants; this exam awards the designation of CST certified first assistant (CST/CFA). Another certification for surgical technologists can be obtained from the National Center for Competency Testing. To take the certification exam, candidates must either complete an accredited training program, attend a two-year hospital on-the-job training program, or have seven years of experience in the field. Upon passing the exam, surgical technologists obtain the designation of tech in surgery-certified, TS-C (NCCT). This certification must be renewed every five years either through reexamination or continuing education.

Other Requirements

Surgical technologists must possess an educational background in the medical sciences, a strong sense of responsibility, a concern for order, and an ability to integrate a number of tasks at the same time. You need good manual dexterity to handle awkward surgical instruments with speed and agility. In addition, you need physical stamina to stand through long surgical procedures.

EXPLORING

It is difficult to gain any direct experience on a part-time basis in surgical technology. The first opportunities for direct experience generally come in the clinical and laboratory phases of your educational programs. However, interested students can explore some aspects of this career in several ways. You or your teachers can arrange a visit to a hospital, clinic, or other surgical setting in order to learn about the work. You also can visit a school with a CAAHEP-accredited program. During such a visit, you can discuss career plans with an admissions counselor. In addition, volunteering at a local hospital or nursing home can give you insight into the health care environment and help you evaluate your aptitude to work in such a setting.

EMPLOYERS

Approximately 86,000 surgical technologists are employed in the United States. Most surgical technologists are employed in hospital operating and delivery rooms, clinics, and surgical centers. They also work in offices of physicians or dentists who perform outpatient surgery, hospital emergency departments, outpatient care centers, and central supply departments. Surgical technologists may also be employed directly by surgeons as private scrubs or as surgical first assistants.

STARTING OUT

Graduates of surgical technology programs are often offered jobs in the same hospital in which they received their clinical training. Programs usually cooperate closely with hospitals in the area, which are usually eager to employ technologists educated in local programs. Available positions are also advertised in newspaper want ads.

ADVANCEMENT

With increased experience, surgical technologists can serve in management roles in surgical services departments and may work as central service managers, surgery schedulers, and materials managers. The role of surgical first assistant on the surgical team requires additional training and experience and is considered an advanced role.

Surgical technologists must function well in a number of diverse areas. Their competency with multiple skills is demonstrated by their employment in organ and tissue procurement/preservation, cardiac catheterization laboratories, medical sales and research, and medical-legal auditing for insurance companies. A number are instructors and directors of surgical technology programs.

EARNINGS

Salaries vary greatly in different institutions and localities. According to the U.S. Department of Labor , the average salary for surgical technologists was $36,080 in 2006, and ranged from less than $25,490 to $51,140 or more a year (excluding overtime). The Department of Labor reports the following mean salaries for surgical technologists by specialty in 2006: offices of physicians, $39,340; outpatient care centers, $38,560; general medical and surgical hospitals, $36,900; and offices of dentists, $35,070. Some technologists with experience earn much more. Most surgical technologists are required to be periodically on call—available to work on short notice in cases of emergency—and can earn overtime from such work. Graduates of educational programs usually receive salaries higher than technologists without formal education. In general, technologists working on the East Coast and West Coast earn more than surgical technologists in other parts of the country. Surgical first assistants and private scrubs employed directly by surgeons tend to earn more than surgical technologists employed by hospitals.

Benefits for full-time workers include vacation and sick time, health, and sometimes dental, insurance, and pension or 401 (k) plans.

WORK ENVIRONMENT

Surgical technologists naturally spend most of their time in the operating room. Operating rooms are cool, well lighted, orderly, and extremely clean. Technologists are often required to be on their feet for long intervals, during which their attention must be closely focused on the operation.

Members of the surgical team, including surgical technologists, wear sterile gowns, gloves, caps, masks, and eye protection. This surgical attire is meant not only to protect the patient from infection but also to protect the surgical team from any infection or bloodborne diseases that the patient may have. Surgery is usually performed during the day; however, hospitals, clinics, and other facilities require 24-hour-a-day coverage. Most surgical technologists work regular 40-hour weeks, although many are required to be periodically on call.

Surgical technologists must be able to work under great pressure in stressful situations. The need for surgery is often a matter of life and death, and one can never assume that procedures will go as planned. If operations do not go well, nerves may fray and tempers flare. Technologists must understand that this is the result of stressful conditions and should not take this anger personally.

In addition, surgical technologists should have a strong desire to help others. Surgery is performed on people, not machines. Patients literally entrust their lives to the surgical team, and they rely on them to treat them in a dignified and professional manner. Individuals with these characteristics find surgical technology a rewarding career in which they can make an important contribution to the health and well-being of their community.

OUTLOOK

According to the U.S. Department of Labor, the field of surgical technology is projected to experience rapid job growth through 2016. Population growth, longevity, and improvement in medical and surgical procedures have all contributed to a growing demand for surgical services and hence for surgical technologists. As long as the rate at which people undergo surgery continues to increase, there will continue to be a need for this profession. Also, as surgical methods become increasingly complex, more surgical technologists will likely be needed. Surgical technologists who are certified will have the best employment opportunities.

An increasing number of surgical procedures are being performed in the offices of physicians and ambulatory surgical centers, requiring the skills of surgical technologists. As a result, employment for technologists in these non-hospital settings should be especially strong.

FOR MORE INFORMATION

For information on education programs and certification, contact the following organizations:

Association of Surgical Technologists
6 West Dry Creek Circle
Littleton, CO 80120- 8031
Tel: 303-694-9130
http://www.ast.org

National Board of Surgical Technology and Surgical Assisting
6 West Dry Creek Circle, Suite 100
Littleton, CO 80120-8031
Tel: 800-707-0057
Email: mail@nbstsa.org
http://www.lcc-st.org

National Center for Competency Testing
7007 College Boulevard, Suite 705
Overland Park, KS 66211-2440
Tel: 800-875-4404
http://www.ncctinc.com

☐ SURVEYING AND MAPPING TECHNICIANS

OVERVIEW

Surveying and mapping technicians help determine, describe, and record geographic areas or features. They are usually the leading assistant to the *professional surveyor, civil engineer,* and *mapmaker* (See "Surveyors"). They operate modern surveying and mapping instruments and may participate in other operations. Technicians must have a basic knowledge of the current practices and legal implications of surveys to establish and record property size, shape, topography, and boundaries. They often supervise other assistants during routine surveying conducted within the bounds established by a professional surveyor. There are approximately 76,000 surveying and mapping technicians working in the United States.

THE JOB

As essential assistants to civil engineers, surveyors, and mapmakers, surveying and mapping technicians are usually the first to be involved in any job that requires precise plotting. This includes highways, airports, housing developments, mines, dams, bridges, and buildings of all kinds.

The surveying and mapping technician is a key worker in field parties and major surveying projects and is often assigned the position of chief instrument worker under the surveyor's supervision. Technicians use a variety of surveying instruments, including the theodolite, transit, level, and other electronic equipment, to measure distances or locate a position. Technicians may be *rod workers,* using level rods or range poles to make elevation and distance measurements. They may also be *chain workers,* measuring shorter distances using a surveying chain or a metal tape. During the survey, it is important to accurately record all readings and keep orderly field notes to check for accuracy.

Surveying and mapping technicians may specialize if they join a firm that focuses on one or more particular types of surveying. In a firm that specializes in land surveying, technicians are highly skilled in technical measuring and tasks related to establishing township, property, and other tract-of-land boundary lines. They help the professional surveyor with maps, notes, and title deeds. They help survey the land, check the accuracy of

SCHOOL SUBJECTS
Geography, Mathematics

PERSONAL SKILLS
Following Instructions, Technical/Scientific

MINIMUM EDUCATION LEVEL
Some Postsecondary Training

CERTIFICATION OR LICENSING
Voluntary

WORK ENVIRONMENT
Primarily Indoors, Primarily Multiple Locations

existing records, and prepare legal documents such as deeds and leases.

Similarly, technicians who work for highway, pipeline, railway, or power line surveying firms help to establish grades, lines, and other points of reference for construction projects. This survey information provides the exact locations for engineering design and construction work.

Technicians who work for geodetic surveyors help take measurements of large masses of land, sea, or space. These measurements must take into account the curvature of Earth and its geophysical characteristics. Their findings set major points of reference for smaller land surveys, determining national boundaries, and preparing maps.

Technicians may also specialize in hydrographic surveying, measuring harbors, rivers, and other bodies of water. These surveys are needed to design navigation systems, prepare nautical maps and charts, establish property boundaries, and plan for breakwaters, levees, dams, locks, piers, and bridges.

Mining surveying technicians are usually on the geological staffs of either mining companies or exploration companies. In recent years, costly new surveying instruments have changed the way they do their jobs. Using highly technical machinery, technicians can map underground geology, take samples, locate diamond drill holes, log drill cores, and map geological data derived from boreholes. They also map data on mine plans and diagrams and help the geologist determine ore reserves. In the search for new mines, technicians operate delicate instruments to obtain data on variations in Earth's magnetic field, its conductivity, and gravity. They use their data to map the boundaries of areas for potential further exploration.

Surveying and mapping technicians may find topographical surveys to be interesting and challenging work. These surveys determine the contours of the land and indicate such features as mountains, lakes, rivers, forests, roads, farms, buildings, and other distinguishable landmarks. In topographical surveying, technicians help take aerial or land photographs with photogrammetric equipment installed in an airplane or ground station that can take pictures of large areas. This method is widely used to measure farmland planted with certain crops and to verify crop average allotments under government production planning quotas.

A large number of survey technicians are employed in construction work. Technicians are needed from start to finish on any job. They check the construction of a structure for size, height, depth, level, and form specifications. They also use measurements to locate the critical construction points as specified by design plans, such as corners of buildings, foundation points, center points for columns, walls, and other features, floor or ceiling levels, and other features that require precise measurements and location.

Technological advances such as the Global Positioning System (GPS) and Geographic Information Systems (GIS) have revolutionized surveying and mapping work. Using these systems, surveying teams can track points on the Earth with radio signals transmitted from satellites and store this information in computer databases.

REQUIREMENTS
High School

If you are interested in becoming a surveying and mapping technician, take mathematics courses, such as algebra, geometry, and trigonometry, as well as mechanical drawing in high school. Physics, chemistry, and biology are other valuable classes that will help you gain laboratory experience. Reading, writing, and comprehension skills as well as knowledge of computers are also vital in surveying and mapping, so English and computer science courses are also highly recommended.

Postsecondary Training

Though not required to enter the field, graduates of accredited postsecondary training programs for surveying, photogrammetry, and mapping are in the best position to become surveying and mapping technicians. Postsecondary training is available from institutional programs and correspondence schools. These demanding technical programs generally last two years with a possible field study in the summer. First-year courses include English, composition, drafting, applied mathematics, surveying and measurements, construction materials and methods, applied physics, statistics, and computer applications. Second-year courses cover subjects such as technical physics, advanced surveying, photogrammetry and mapping, soils and foundations, technical reporting, legal issues, and transportation and environmental engineering. Contact the American Congress on Surveying and Mapping (ACSM) for a list of accredited programs (see the end of this article for contact information).

With additional experience and study, technicians can specialize in geodesy, topography, hydrography, or photogrammetry. Many graduates of two-year programs later pursue a bachelor's degree in surveying, engineering, or geomatics.

Certification or Licensing

Unlike professional land surveyors, there are no certification or licensing requirements for becoming a surveying and mapping technician. However, technicians who seek government employment must pass a civil service examination.

Many employers prefer certified technicians for promotions into higher positions with more responsibility. The National Society of Professional Surveyors offers the voluntary certified survey technician designation at four levels. With each level, the technician must have more experience and pass progressively challenging examinations. If the technician hopes one day to work as a surveyor, he or she must be specially certified to work in his or her state. The American Society for Photogrammetry and Remote Sensing also offers voluntary certification programs for technicians.

Other Requirements

To be a successful surveying and mapping technician, you must be patient, orderly, systematic, accurate, and objective in your work. You must be willing to work cooperatively and have the ability to think and plan ahead. Because of the increasing technical nature of their work, you must have computer skills to be able to use highly complex equipment such as GPS and GIS technology.

EXPLORING

One of the best opportunities for experience is to work part time or during your summer vacation for a construction firm or a company involved in survey work. Even if the job does not involve direct contact with survey crews, you may be able to observe their work and converse with them to discover more about their daily activities. Another possibility is to work for a government agency overseeing land use. The Bureau of Land Management, for example, has employment opportunities for students who qualify, as well as many volunteer positions. The Forest Service also offers temporary positions for students.

EMPLOYERS

There are approximately 76,000 surveying and mapping technicians working in the United States. About 70 percent of technicians find work with engineering or architectural service firms. The federal government also employs a number of technicians to work for the U.S. Geological Survey, the Bureau of Land Management, the National Oceanic and Atmospheric Administration, the National Geospatial-Intelligence Agency, and the Forest Service. State and local governments also hire surveying and mapping technicians to work for highway departments and urban planning agencies. Construction firms and oil, gas, and mining companies also hire technicians.

STARTING OUT

If you plan on entering surveying straight from high school, you may first work as an apprentice. Through on-the-job training and some classroom work, apprentices build up their skills and knowledge of the trade to eventually become surveying and mapping technicians.

If you plan to attend a technical institute or four-year college, visit your school's career services office for help in arranging examinations or interviews. Employers of surveying technicians often send recruiters to schools before graduation and arrange to employ promising graduates. Some community or technical colleges have work-study programs that provide cooperative part-time or summer work for pay. Employers involved with these programs often hire students full time after graduation.

Finally, many cities have employment agencies that specialize in placing technical workers in positions in surveying, mapping, construction, mining, and related fields. Check your local newspaper, telephone book, or surf the Web to see if your town offers these services.

ADVANCEMENT

Possibilities for advancement are linked to levels of formal education and experience. As technicians gain experience and technical knowledge, they can advance to positions of greater responsibility and eventually work as chief surveyor. To advance into this position, technicians will most likely need a two- or four-year degree in surveying and many years of experience. Also, all 50 states require surveyors to be licensed, requiring varying amounts of experience, education, and examinations.

Regardless of the level of advancement, all surveying and mapping technicians must continue studying to keep up with the technological developments in their field. Technological advances in computers, lasers, and microcomputers will continue to change job requirements. Studying to keep up with changes combined with progressive experience gained on the job will increase the technician's opportunity for advancement.

EARNINGS

According to the U.S. Department of Labor, the 2006 median hourly salary for all surveying and mapping technicians, regardless of the industry, was $15.55 (amounting to $32,340 for full-time work). The lowest paid 10 percent earned less than $9.62 ($20,020 for full-time work), and the highest paid 10 percent earned more than $25.63 an hour (or $53,310 annually for full-time work). Technicians working for the public sector in federal, state, and local governments generally earn more per hour than those working in the private sector for engineering and architectural services. In 2006, surveying and mapping technicians working for the federal government made a mean salary of $44,610 per year.

Benefits include paid vacation, health, disability, life insurance, and retirement or pension plans.

WORK ENVIRONMENT

Surveying and mapping technicians usually work about 40 hours a week except when overtime is necessary. The peak work period for many kinds of surveying work is during the summer months when weather conditions are most favorable. However, surveying crews are exposed to all types of weather conditions.

Some survey projects involve certain hazards depending upon the region and the climate as well as local plant and animal life. Field survey crews may encounter snakes and poison ivy. They are subject to heat exhaustion, sunburn, and frostbite. Some projects, particularly those being conducted near construction projects or busy highways, impose dangers of injury from cars and flying debris. Unless survey technicians are employed for office assignments, their work location changes from survey to survey. Some assignments may require technicians to be away from home for varying periods of time.

While on the job, technicians who supervise other workers must take special care to observe good safety practices. Construction and mining workplaces usually require hard hats, special clothing, and protective shoes.

OUTLOOK

Employment for surveying and mapping technicians is expected to grow faster than the average for all occupations through 2016, according to the U.S. Department of Labor. New technologies—such as GPS, GIS, and remote sensing—have increased the accuracy and productivity of professionals in the field, but may reduce employment growth slightly in the short term.

One factor that may increase the demand for surveying services, and therefore surveying technicians, is growth in urban and suburban areas. New streets, homes, shopping centers, schools, and gas and water lines will require property and boundary line surveys. Other factors are the continuing state and federal highway improvement programs

and the increasing number of urban redevelopment programs. The expansion of industrial and business firms and the relocation of some firms to large undeveloped areas are also expected to create a need for surveying services.

The need to replace workers who have either retired or transferred to other occupations will also provide opportunities. In general, technicians with more education and skill training will have more job options.

FOR MORE INFORMATION

For more information on accredited surveying programs, contact

Accreditation Board for Engineering and Technology
111 Market Place, Suite 1050
Baltimore, MD 21202-4012
Tel: 410-347-7700
http://www.abet.org

For information on careers, scholarships, and educational programs, contact

American Congress on Surveying and Mapping
6 Montgomery Village Avenue, Suite 403
Gaithersburg, MD 20879-3546
Tel: 240-632-9716
Email: info@acsm.net
http://www.acsm.net

For information on certification, contact

American Society for Photogrammetry and Remote Sensing
5410 Grosvenor Lane, Suite 210
Bethesda, MD 20814-2160
Tel: 301-493-0290
Email: asprs@asprs.org
http://www.asprs.org

For information about the Bureau of Land Management and its responsibilities, visit its Web site.

Bureau of Land Management
Office of Public Affairs
1849 C Street, Room 406-LS
Washington, DC 20240-0001
Tel: 202-452-5125
http://www.blm.gov

For information on certification, contact

National Society of Professional Surveyors
6 Montgomery Village Avenue, Suite 403
Gaithersburg, MD 20879-3557
Tel: 240-632-9716
http://www.nspsmo.org

For more information on Geographic Information Systems (GIS), visit the following Web site:

GIS.com
http://www.gis.com

□ SURVEYORS

SCHOOL SUBJECTS
Geography, Mathematics

PERSONAL SKILLS
Communication/Ideas, Technical/Scientific

MINIMUM EDUCATION LEVEL
Some Postsecondary Training

CERTIFICATION OR LICENSING
Required

WORK ENVIRONMENT
Primarily Indoors, Primarily Multiple Locations

OVERVIEW

Surveyors mark exact measurements and locations of elevations, points, lines, and contours on or near the earth's surface. They measure distances between points to determine property boundaries and to provide data for mapmaking, construction projects, and other engineering purposes. There are approximately 60,000 surveyors employed in the United States.

THE JOB

On proposed construction projects, such as highways, airstrips, and housing developments, it is the surveyor's responsibility to make necessary measurements through an accurate and detailed survey of the area. The surveyor usually works with a field party consisting of several people. Instrument assistants, called *surveying and mapping technicians*, handle a variety of surveying instruments including the theodolite, transit, level, surveyor's chain, rod, and other electronic equipment. (See "Surveying and Mapping Technicians"). In the course of the survey, it is important that all readings be recorded accurately and field notes maintained so that the survey can be checked for accuracy.

Surveyors may specialize in one or more particular types of surveying.

Land surveyors establish township, property, and other tract-of-land boundary lines. Using maps, notes, or actual land title deeds, they survey the land, checking for the accuracy of existing records. This information is used to prepare legal documents such as deeds and leases. *Land surveying managers* coordinate the work of surveyors, their parties, and legal, engineering, architectural, and other staff involved in a project. In addition, these managers develop policy, prepare budgets, certify work upon completion, and handle numerous other administrative duties.

Highway surveyors establish grades, lines, and other points of reference for highway construction projects. This survey information is essential to the work of the numerous engineers and the construction crews who build the new highway.

Geodetic surveyors measure large masses of land, sea, and space that must take into account the curvature of Earth and its geophysical characteristics. Their work is helpful in establishing points of reference for smaller land surveys, determining national boundaries, and preparing maps. Geodetic computers calculate latitude, longitude, angles, areas, and other information needed for mapmaking. They work from field notes made by an engineering survey party and also use reference tables and a calculating machine or computer.

Marine surveyors measure harbors, rivers, and other bodies of water. They determine the depth of the water through measuring sound waves in relation to nearby land masses. Their work is essential for planning and constructing navigation projects, such as breakwaters, dams, piers, marinas, and bridges, and for preparing nautical charts and maps.

Mine surveyors make surface and underground surveys, preparing maps of mines and mining operations. Such maps are helpful in examining underground passages within the levels of a mine and assessing the volume and location of raw material available.

Geophysical prospecting surveyors locate and mark sites considered likely to contain petroleum deposits. *Oil-well directional surveyors* use sonic, electronic, and nuclear measuring instruments to gauge the presence and amount of oil- and gas-bearing reservoirs. *Pipeline surveyors* determine rights-of-way for oil construction projects, providing information essential to the preparation for and laying of the lines.

Photogrammetric engineers determine the contour of an area to show elevations and depressions and indicate such features as mountains, lakes, rivers, forests, roads, farms, buildings, and other landmarks. Aerial, land, and water photographs are taken with special equipment able to capture images of very large areas. From these pictures, accurate measurements of the terrain and surface features can be made. These surveys are helpful in construction projects and in the preparation of topographical maps. Photogrammetry is particularly helpful in charting areas that are inaccessible or difficult to travel.

Forensic surveyors serve as expert witnesses in legal proceedings that involve industrial, automobile, or other types of accidents. They gather, analyze, and map data that is used as evidence at a trial, hearing, or lawsuit. These professionals must have extensive experience in the field and be strong communicators in order to explain technical information to people who do not have a background in surveying.

REQUIREMENTS
High School

Does this work interest you? If so, you should prepare for it by taking plenty of math and science courses in high school. Take algebra, geometry, and trigonometry to become comfortable making different calculations. Earth science, chemistry, and physics classes should also be helpful. Geography will help you learn about different locations, their characteristics, and cartography. Benefits from taking mechanical drawing and other drafting classes include an increased ability to visualize abstractions, exposure to detailed work, and an understanding of perspectives. Taking computer science classes will prepare you for working with technical surveying equipment.

Postsecondary Training

Depending on state requirements, you will need some postsecondary education. The quickest route is by earning a bachelor's degree in surveying or engineering combined with on-the-job training. Other entry options include obtaining more job experience combined with a one- to three-year program in surveying and surveying technology offered by community colleges, technical institutes, and vocational schools.

Certification or Licensing

The American Congress on Surveying and Mapping (ACSM) has partnered with the Federal Emergency Management Agency to create a certification program for floodplain surveyors. Contact the ACSM for details on the program.

All 50 states require that surveyors making property and boundary surveys be licensed or registered. The requirements for licensure vary, but most require a degree in surveying or a related field, a certain number of years of experience, and passing of examinations in land surveying (typically a written examination given by the National Council of Examiners for Engineering and Surveying). Generally, the higher the degree obtained, the less experience required. Those with bachelor's degrees may need only two to four years of on-the-job experience, while those with a lesser degree may need up to 12 years of prior experience to obtain a license. Information on specific requirements can be obtained by contacting the licnsure department of the state in which you plan to work. If you are seeking employment in the federal government, you must take a civil service examination and meet the educational, experience, and other specified requirements for the position.

Other Requirements

The ability to work with numbers and perform mathematical computations accurately and quickly is very important. Other helpful qualities are the ability to visualize and understand objects in two and three dimensions (spatial relationships) and the ability to discriminate between and compare shapes, sizes, lines, shadings, and other forms (form perception).

Surveyors walk a great deal and carry equipment over all types of terrain so endurance and coordination are important physical assets. In addition, surveyors direct and supervise the work of their team, so you should be good at working with other people and demonstrate leadership abilities.

EXPLORING

While you are in high school, begin to familiarize yourself with terms, projects, and tools used in this profession by reading books and magazines on the topic. One magazine that is available online is Professional Surveyor Magazine at http://www.profsurv.com. One of the best opportunities for experience is a summer job with a construction outfit or company that requires survey work. Even if the job does not involve direct contact with survey crews, it will offer an opportunity to observe surveyors and talk with them about their work. Additionally, you should visit http://www.surveyingcareer.com for more information on career opportunities in the field.

Some colleges have work-study programs that offer on-the-job experience. These opportunities, like summer or part-time jobs, provide helpful contacts in the field that may lead to future full-time employment. If your college does not offer a work-study program and you can't find a paying summer job, consider volunteering at an appropriate government agency. The U.S. Geological Survey and the Bureau of Land Management usually offer volunteer opportunities in select areas.

EMPLOYERS

Approximately 60,000 surveyors are employed in the United States. According to the U.S. Department of Labor, almost 70 percent of surveying workers in the United States are employed in engineering, architectural, and surveying firms. Local, state, and federal agencies (mainly the U.S. Geological Survey, the Bureau of Land Management, the National Geodetic Survey, the National Geospatial Intelligence Agency, and the Army Corps of Engineers) are the next largest employers of surveying workers, and the majority of the remaining surveyors work for construction firms, oil and gas extraction companies, and public utilities. Only a small number of surveyors are self-employed.

STARTING OUT

Apprentices with a high school education can enter the field as equipment operators or surveying assistants. Those who have postsecondary education can enter the field more easily, beginning as surveying and mapping technicians.

College graduates can learn about job openings through their schools' career services offices or through potential employers that may visit their campus. Many cities have employment agencies that specialize in seeking out workers for positions in surveying and related fields. Check your local newspaper or telephone book or surf the Web to see if such recruiting firms exist in your area.

ADVANCEMENT

With experience, workers advance through the leadership ranks within a surveying team. Workers begin as assistants and then can move into positions such as senior technician, party chief, and, finally, licensed surveyor. Because surveying work is closely related to other fields, surveyors can move into electrical, mechanical, or chemical engineering or specialize in drafting.

EARNINGS

In 2006, surveyors earned a median annual salary of $48,290. According to the U.S. Department of Labor, the middle 50 percent earned between $35,720 and $63,990 a year. The lowest paid 10 percent earned less than $26,690, and the highest paid 10 percent earned more than $79,910 a year. In general, the federal government paid the highest wages to its surveyors, $72,180 a year in 2006.

Most positions with the federal, state, and local governments and with private firms provide life and medical insurance, pension, vacation, and holiday benefits.

WORK ENVIRONMENT

Surveyors work 40-hour weeks except when overtime is necessary to meet a project deadline. The peak work period is during the summer months when weather conditions are most favorable. However, it is not uncommon for the surveyor to be exposed to adverse weather conditions.

Some survey projects may involve hazardous conditions, depending on the region and climate as well as the plant and animal life. Survey crews may encounter snakes, poison ivy, and other hazardous plant and animal life, and may suffer heat exhaustion, sunburn, and frostbite while in the field. Survey projects, particularly those near construction projects or busy highways, may impose dangers of injury from heavy traffic, flying objects, and other accidental hazards. Unless the surveyor is employed only for office assignments, the work location most likely will change from survey to survey. Some assignments may require the surveyor to be away from home for periods of time.

OUTLOOK

The U.S. Department of Labor predicts that employment of surveyors will grow much faster than the average for all occupations through 2016 as a result of the widespread use of technology, such as the Global Positioning System and geographic information systems, and the increasing demand for detailed geographic information. The outlook will be best for surveyors who have college degrees, advanced field experience, and strong technical and computer skills.

Growth in urban and suburban areas (with the need for new streets, homes, shopping centers, schools, gas and water lines) will provide employment opportunities. State and federal highway improvement programs and local urban redevelopment programs also will provide jobs for surveyors. The expansion of industrial and business firms and the relocation of some firms to large undeveloped tracts will also create job openings. However, construction projects are closely tied to the state of the economy, so employment may fluctuate from year to year.

FOR MORE INFORMATION

For more information on accredited surveying programs, contact

Accreditation Board for Engineering and Technology
111 Market Place, Suite 1050
Baltimore, MD 21202-4012
Tel: 410-347-7700
http://www.abet.org

For information on certification and state affiliates and colleges and universities that offer land surveying programs, contact

American Congress on Surveying and Mapping
6 Montgomery Village Avenue, Suite 403
Gaithersburg, MD 20879-3546
Tel: 240-632-9716
Email: info@acsm.net
http://www.acsm.net

For information on awards and recommended books to read, contact

American Association for Geodetic Surveying
6 Montgomery Village Avenue, Suite 403
Gaithersburg, MD 20879-3546
Tel: 240-632-9716
Email: aagsmo@acsm.net
http://www.aagsmo.org

For information on photogrammetry and careers in the field, contact

American Society for Photogrammetry and Remote Sensing
5410 Grosvenor Lane, Suite 210
Bethesda, MD 20814-2160
Tel: 301-493-0290
Email: asprs@asprs.org
http://www.asprs.org

For information on certification, contact

National Society of Professional Surveyors
6 Montgomery Village Avenue, Suite 403
Gaithersburg, MD 20879-3557
Tel: 240-632-9716
http://www.nspsmo.org

For information on volunteer and employment opportunities with the federal government, contact

Bureau of Land Management
Office of Public Affairs
1849 C Street, Room 406-LS
Washington, DC 20240-0001
Tel: 202-452-5125
http://www.blm.gov

U.S. Geological Survey
12201 Sunrise Valley Drive
Reston, VA 20192-0002
Tel: 888-275-8747
http://www.usgs.gov

For more information on Geographic Information Systems (GIS), visit the following Web site:

GIS.com
http://www.gis.com

For comprehensive information on careers in surveying, visit

Measuring the World Around Us: A High-Tech Career In Professional Surveying
http://www.surveyingcareer.com

TECHNICAL WRITERS

OVERVIEW

Technical writers, sometimes called *technical communicators*, express technical and scientific ideas in easy-to-understand language. There are approximately 49,000 technical writers employed in the United States.

THE JOB

Technical writers prepare a wide variety of documents and materials. They work closely with *technical editors*, who revise written text to correct any errors and make it read smoothly and clearly. The most common types of documents they produce are manuals, technical reports, specifications, and proposals. Some technical writers also write scripts for videos and audiovisual presentations and text for multimedia programs. Technical writers prepare manuals that give instructions and detailed information on how to install, assemble, use, service, or repair a product or equipment. They may write manuals as simple as a two-page leaflet that gives instructions on how to assemble a bicycle or as complex as a 500-page document that tells service technicians how to repair machinery, medical equipment, or a climate-control system. One of the most common types of manuals is the computer software manual, which informs users on how to load software on their computers, explains how to use the program, and gives information on different features.

Technical writers also prepare technical reports on a multitude of subjects. These reports include documents that give the results of research and laboratory tests and documents that describe the progress of a project. They also write sales proposals, product specifications, quality standards, journal articles, in-house style manuals, and newsletters.

The work of a technical writer begins when he or she is assigned to prepare a document. The writer meets with members of an account or technical team to learn the requirements for the document, the intended purpose or objectives, and the audience. During the planning stage, the writer learns when the document needs to be completed, approximately how long it should be, whether artwork or illustrations are to be included, who the other team members are, and any other production or printing requirements. A schedule is created that defines the different stages of development and determines when the writer needs to have certain parts of the document ready.

The next step in document development is the research, or information gathering, phase. During this stage, technical writers gather all the available information about the product (for example, a new personal digital assistant that is being developed by a cell phone company), read and review it, and determine what other information is needed. They may research the topic by reading technical publications, but in most cases they will need to gather information directly from the people working on the product. Writers meet with and interview people who are sources of information, such as scientists, engineers, software developers, computer programmers, managers, and project managers. They ask questions, listen, and take notes or record interviews. They gather any available notes, drawings, or diagrams that may be useful.

After writers gather all the necessary information, they sort it out and organize it. They plan how they are going to present the information and prepare an outline for the document. They may decide how the document will look and prepare the design, format, and layout of the pages. In some cases, this may be done by an editor rather than the writer. If illustrations, diagrams, or photographs are going to be included, the writer (or an editor) makes arrangements for an illustrator, photographer, or art researcher to produce or obtain them.

Then, the writer starts writing and prepares a rough draft of the document. If the document is very large, a writer may prepare it in segments. Once the rough draft is completed, it is submitted to a designated person or group for technical review. Copies of the draft are distributed to managers, engineers, or other experts who

SCHOOL SUBJECTS
Business, English

PERSONAL SKILLS
Communication/Ideas, Technical/Scientific

MINIMUM EDUCATION LEVEL
Bachelor's Degree

CERTIFICATION OR LICENSING
None Available

WORK ENVIRONMENT
Primarily Indoors, Primarily One Location

can easily determine if any technical information is inaccurate or missing. These reviewers read the document and suggest changes.

The rough draft is also given to technical editors for review of a variety of factors. The editors check that the material is organized well, that each section flows with the section before and after it, and that the language is appropriate for the intended audience (scientists, engineers, a company's CEO or board of directors, etc.). They also check for correct use of grammar, spelling, and punctuation. They ensure that names of parts or objects are consistent throughout the document and that references are accurate. They also check the labeling of graphs and captions for accuracy. Technical editors use special symbols, called proofreader's marks, to indicate the types of changes needed.

The editor and reviewers return their copies of the document to the technical writer. The writer incorporates the appropriate suggestions and revisions and prepares the final draft. The final draft is once again submitted to a designated reviewer or team of reviewers. In some cases, the technical reviewer may do a quick check to make sure that the requested changes were made. In other cases, the technical reviewer may examine the document in depth to ensure technical accuracy and correctness. A walkthrough, or test of the document, may be done for certain types of documents. For example, a walkthrough may be done for a document that explains how to install or activate a product. A tester installs or activates the product by following the instructions given in the document. The tester makes a note of all sections that are unclear or inaccurate, and the document is returned to the writer for any necessary revisions.

Once the final draft has been approved, the document is submitted to the technical editor, who makes a comprehensive check of the document.

The editor returns the document to either the *writer* or a *word processor*, who makes any necessary corrections. This copy is then checked by a *proofreader*. The proofreader compares the final copy against the editor's marked-up copy and makes sure that all changes were made. The document is then prepared for printing. In some cases, the writer is responsible for preparing camera-ready copy or electronic files for printing purposes, and in other cases, a print production coordinator prepares all material to submit to a printer.

Some technical writers specialize in a specific type of material. *Technical marketing writers* create promotional and marketing materials for technological products. They may write the copy for an advertisement for a technical product or they may write press releases about the product. They also write sales literature, product flyers, Web pages, and multimedia presentations.

Other technical writers prepare scripts for videos and films about technical subjects. These writers, called *scriptwriters*, need to have an understanding of film and video production techniques.

Some technical writers prepare articles for scientific, medical, computer, or engineering trade journals. These articles may report the results of research conducted by scientists or engineers or report on technological advances in a particular field. Some technical writers also develop textbooks. They may receive articles written by engineers or scientists and edit and revise them to make them more suitable for the intended audience.

Technical writers may create documents for a variety of media. Electronic media, such as compact discs and online services, are increasingly being used in place of books and paper documents. Technical writers may create materials that are accessed through bulletin board systems and the Internet or create computer-based resources, such as help menus on computer programs. They also create interactive, multimedia documents that are distributed on compact discs on other media. Some of these media require knowledge of special computer programs that allow material to be hyperlinked, or electronically cross-referenced.

REQUIREMENTS
High School

In high school, you should take composition, grammar, literature, creative writing, journalism, social studies, math, statistics, engineering, computer science, and as many science classes as possible. Business courses are also useful as they explain the organizational structure of companies and how they operate.

Postsecondary Training

Most employers prefer to hire technical writers who have a bachelor's or advanced degree. Technical writers typically need to have a strong foundation in engineering, computers, or science. Many technical writers graduate with a degree in engineering or science and take classes in technical writing.

Many different types of college programs are available that prepare people to become technical writers. A growing number of colleges are offering degrees in technical writing. Schools without a technical writing program may offer degrees in journalism or English. Programs are offered through English, communications, and journalism departments. Classes vary based on the type of program. In general, classes for technical writers include a core curriculum in writing and classes in algebra, statistics, logic, science, engineering, and computer programming languages.

Many technical writers earn a master's degree. In these programs, they study technical writing in depth and may specialize in a certain area, such as scriptwriting, instructional design, or multimedia applications. In addition, many nondegree writing programs are offered to technical writers to hone their skills. Offered as extension courses or continuing education courses, these programs include courses on indexing, editing medical journals, writing for trade journals, and other related subjects.

Technical writers are often asked to present samples of their work. College students should build a portfolio during their college years in which they collect their best samples from work that they may have done for a literary magazine, newsletter, or yearbook.

Technical writers should be willing to pursue learning throughout their careers. As technology changes, they may need to take classes to update their knowledge. Changes in electronic printing and computer technology will also change the way technical writers do their jobs, and writers may need to take courses to learn new skills or new technologies.

Other Requirements

Technical writers need to have good communications skills, science and technical aptitudes, and the ability to think analytically. Technical writers need to be able to work as part of a team and collaborate with others on a project. They need to be highly self-motivated, well organized, and able to work under pressure.

EXPLORING

If you enjoy writing and are considering a career in technical writing, you should make writing a daily activity. Writing is a skill that develops over time and through practice. You can keep journals, join writing clubs, and practice different types of writing, such as scriptwriting and informative reports. Sharing writing with others and asking them to critique it is especially helpful. Comments from readers on what they enjoyed about a piece of writing or difficulty they had in understanding certain sections provides valuable feedback that helps to improve your writing style.

Reading a variety of materials is also helpful. Reading exposes you to both good and bad writing styles and techniques, and helps you to identify why one approach works better than another.

You may also gain experience by working on a literary magazine, student newspaper, or yearbook (or starting one of your own if one is not available). Both writing and editing articles and managing production give you the opportunity to learn new skills and to see what is involved in preparing documents and other materials.

Students may also be able to get internships, cooperative education assignments, or summer or part-time jobs as proofreaders or editorial assistants that may include writing responsibilities.

EMPLOYERS

There are approximately 49,000 technical writers currently employed in the United States. Employment may be found in many different types of places, such as in the fields of aerospace, computers, engineering, pharmaceuticals, and research and development, or with the nuclear industry, medical publishers, government agencies or contractors, and colleges and universities. The aerospace, engineering, medical, and computer industries hire significant numbers of technical writers. The federal government, particularly the Departments of Defense and Agriculture, the National Aeronautics and Space Administration, and the Nuclear Regulatory Commission, also hires many writers with technical knowledge.

STARTING OUT

Many technical writers start their careers as scientists, engineers, technicians, or research assistants and move into writing after several years of experience in those positions. Technical writers with a bachelor's degree in a technical subject such as engineering or computer science may be able to find work as a technical writer immediately upon graduating from college, but many employers prefer to hire writers with some work experience.

If you plan to work for the federal government, you need to pass an examination. Information about examinations and job openings is available at federal employment centers.

You may learn about job openings through your college's career services office and want ads in newspapers and professional magazines. You may also research companies that hire technical writers and apply directly to them. Many libraries provide useful job resource guides and directories that provide information about companies that hire in specific areas.

ADVANCEMENT

As technical writers gain experience, they move into more challenging and responsible positions. At first, they may work on simple documents or are assigned to work on sections of a document. As they demonstrate their proficiency and skills, they are given more complex assignments and are responsible for more activities.

Technical writers with several years of experience may move into project management positions. As project managers, they are responsible for the entire document development and production processes. They schedule and budget resources and assign writers, editors, illustrators, and other workers to a project. They monitor the schedule, supervise workers, and ensure that costs remain in budget.

Technical writers who show good project management skills, leadership abilities, and good interpersonal skills may become supervisors or managers. Technical writers can move into senior writer positions. These positions involve increased responsibilities and may include supervising other workers. Others writers may choose to become editors.

Many technical writers seek to develop and perfect their skills rather than move into management or supervisory positions. As they gain a reputation for their quality of work, they may be able to select choice assignments. They may learn new skills as a means of being able to work in new areas. For example, a technical writer may learn a new desktop program in order to become more proficient in designing. Or, a technical writer may learn a hypermedia or hypertext computer program in order to be able to create a multimedia program. Technical writers who broaden their skill base and capabilities can move to higher-paying positions within their own company or at another company. They also may work as freelancers or set up their own communications companies.

EARNINGS

Median annual earnings for salaried technical writers were $58,050 in 2006, according to the U.S. Department of Labor. Salaries ranged from less than $35,520 to more than $91,720.

Most companies offer benefits that include paid holidays and vacations, medical insurance, and 401(k) plans. They may also offer profit sharing, pension plans, and tuition assistance programs.

WORK ENVIRONMENT

Technical writers usually work in an office environment, with well-lit and quiet surroundings. They may have their own offices or share work space with other writers and editors. Most writers have computers. They may be able to utilize the services of support staff who can word-process revisions, run off copies, fax material, and perform other administrative functions or they may have to perform all of these tasks themselves.

Some technical writers work out of home offices and use computer modems and networks to send and receive materials electronically. They may go into the office only on occasion for meetings and gathering information. Freelancers and contract workers may work at a company's premises or at home.

Although the standard workweek is 40 hours, many technical writers frequently work 50 or 60 hours a week. Job interruptions, meetings, and conferences can prevent writers from having long periods of time to write. Therefore, many writers work after hours or bring work home. Writers frequently work in the evening or on weekends in order to meet a deadline.

In many companies there is pressure to produce documents as quickly as possible. Technical writers may feel at times that they are compromising the quality of their work due to the need to conform to time and budget constraints. In some companies, technical writers may have increased workloads due to company reorganizations or downsizing. They may need to do the work that was formerly done by more than one person. Technical writers also are increasingly assuming roles and responsibilities formerly performed by other people and this can increase work pressures and stress.

Despite these pressures, most technical writers gain immense satisfaction from their work and the roles that they perform in producing technical communications.

OUTLOOK

The writing field is generally very competitive—no matter the industry. Each year, there are more people trying to enter this field than there are available openings. The field of technical writing, though, offers more opportunities than other areas of writing, such as book publishing or journalism. Employment opportunities for technical writers are expected to grow faster than the average for all occupations through 2016, according to the U.S. Department of Labor. Demand is growing for technical writers who can produce well-written computer manuals. In addition to the computer industry, the pharmaceutical industry is showing an increased need for technical writers. Rapid growth in the high technology, electronics industries, and the Internet will create a continuing demand for people to write users' guides, instruction manuals, and training materials. Technical writers will be needed to produce copy that describes developments and discoveries in law, science, and technology for a more general audience.

Writers may find positions that include duties in addition to writing. A growing trend is for companies to use writers to run a department, supervise other writers, and manage freelance writers and outside contractors. In addition, many writers are acquiring responsibilities that include desktop publishing and print production coordination.

The demand for technical writers is significantly affected by the economy. During recessionary times, technical writers are often among the first to be laid off. Many companies today are continuing to downsize or reduce their number of employees and are reluctant to keep writers on staff. Such companies prefer to hire writers on a temporary contractual basis, using them only as long as it takes to complete an assigned document. Technical writers who work on a temporary or freelance basis need to market their services and continually look for new assignments. They also do not have the security or benefits offered by full-time employment.

FOR MORE INFORMATION

For information on writing and editing careers in the field of communications, contact

National Association of Science Writers
PO Box 890
Hedgesville, WV 25427-0890
Tel: 304-754-5077
http://www.nasw.org

For information on careers, contact
Society for Technical Communication
901 North Stuart Street, Suite 904
Arlington, VA 22203-1822
Tel: 703-522-4114
    http://www.stc.org

TOUR GUIDES

OVERVIEW

Tour guides plan and oversee travel arrangements and accommodations for groups of tourists. They assist travelers with questions or problems, and they may provide travelers with itineraries of their proposed travel route and plans. Tour guides research their destinations thoroughly so that they can handle any unforeseen situation that may occur. There are approximately 40,000 tour and travel guides employed in the United States.

THE JOB

Acting as knowledgeable companions and chaperons, tour guides escort groups of tourists to different cities and countries. Their job is to make sure that the passengers in a group tour enjoy an interesting and safe trip. To do this, they have to know a great deal about their travel destination and about the interests, knowledge, and expectations of the people on the tour.

One basic responsibility of tour guides is handling all the details of a trip prior to departure. They may schedule airline flights, bus trips, or train trips as well as book cruises, houseboats, or car rentals. They also research area hotels and other lodging for the group and make reservations in advance. If anyone in the group has unique requirements, such as a specialized diet or a need for wheelchair accessibility, the tour guide will work to meet these requests.

Tour guides plan itineraries and daily activities, keeping in mind the interests of the group. For example, a group of music lovers visiting Vienna, Austria, may wish to see the many sites of musical history there as well as attend a performance by that city's orchestra. In addition to sightseeing tours, guides may make arrangements in advance for special exhibits, dining experiences, and side trips. Alternate outings are sometimes planned in case of inclement weather conditions.

The second major responsibility of tour guides is, of course, the tour itself. Here, they must make sure all aspects of transportation, lodging, and recreation meet the planned itinerary. They must see to it that travelers' baggage and personal belongings are loaded and handled properly. If the tour includes meals and trips to local establishments, the guide must make sure that each passenger is on time for the various arrivals and departures.

Tour guides provide the people in their groups with interesting information on the locale and alert them

---

SCHOOL SUBJECTS
Foreign Language, History, Speech

PERSONAL SKILLS
Communication/Ideas, Leadership/Management

MINIMUM EDUCATION LEVEL
Some Postsecondary Training

CERTIFICATION OR LICENSING
Recommended

WORK ENVIRONMENT
Indoors and Outdoors, Primarily Multiple Locations

---

to special sights. Tour guides become familiar with the history and significance of places through research and previous visits and endeavor to make the visit as entertaining and informative as possible. They may speak the native language or hire an interpreter in order to get along well with the local people. They are also familiar with local customs so their group will not offend anyone unknowingly. They see that the group stays together so that members do not miss their transportation arrangements or get lost. Guides may also arrange free time for travelers to pursue their individual interests, although time frames and common meeting points for regrouping are established in advance.

Even with thorough preparation, unexpected occurrences can arise on any trip and threaten to ruin everyone's good time. Tour guides must be resourceful to handle these surprises, such as when points of interest are closed or accommodations turn out to be unacceptable. They must be familiar with an area's resources so that they can help in emergencies such as passenger illness or lost personal items. Tour guides often intercede on their travelers' behalf when any questions or problems arise regarding currency, restaurants, customs, or necessary identification.

REQUIREMENTS
High School

Although as a tour guide you will not necessarily need a college education, you should at least have a high school diploma. Courses such as speech, communications, art, sociology, anthropology, political science, and literature often prove beneficial. Some tour guides study foreign languages and cultures as well as geography, history, and architecture.

Postsecondary Training

Some cities have professional schools that offer curricula in the travel industry. Such training may take nine to 12 months and offer job placement services. Some two- and four-year colleges offer tour guide training that lasts six to eight weeks. Community colleges may offer programs in tour escort training. Programs such as these often may be taken on a part-time basis. Classes may include history, world geography, psychology, human relations, and communication courses. Sometimes students go on field trips themselves to gain experience. Some travel agencies and tour companies offer their own training so that their tour guides may receive instruction that complements the tour packages the company offers.

Certification or Licensing

The National Tour Association offers the voluntary certified tour professional designation to candidates who meet education, employment, and service requirements; complete coursework in three core areas (Leadership, Management, and Administration; Marketing and Sales; and Financial); and complete a learning portfolio.

Other Requirements

To be a tour guide, you should be an outgoing, friendly, and confident person. You must be aware of the typical travelers' needs and the kinds of questions and concerns travelers might have. As a tour guide, you should be comfortable being in charge of large groups of people and have good time-management skills. You also need to be resourceful and be able to adapt to different environments. Tour guides need to be fun-loving and know how to make others feel at ease in unfamiliar surroundings. Tour guides should enjoy working with people as much as they enjoy traveling.

EXPLORING

One way to become more familiar with the responsibilities of this job is to accompany local tours. Many cities have their own historical societies and museums that offer tours as well as opportunities to volunteer. To appreciate what is involved with speaking in front of groups and the kind of research that may be necessary for leading tours, you can prepare speeches or presentations for class or local community groups. You may also find it helpful to read publications such as *Courier* (http://www.ntaonline.com), the National Tour Association's monthly travel magazine.

EMPLOYERS

The major employers of tour guides are, naturally, tour companies. Many tour guides work on a freelance basis, while others may own their own tour businesses. Approximately 40,000 tour and travel guides are employed in the United States.

STARTING OUT

If you are interested in a career as a tour guide, you may begin as a guide for a museum or state park. This would be a good introduction to handling groups of people, giving lectures on points of interest or exhibits and developing confidence and leadership qualities. Zoos, theme parks, historical sites, or local walking tours often need volunteers or part-time employees to work in their information centers, offer visitors directions, and answer a variety of inquiries. When openings occur, it is common for part-time workers to move into full-time positions.

Travel agencies, tour bus companies, and park districts often need additional help during the summer months when the travel season is in full swing. Societies and organizations for architecture and natural history, as well as other cultural groups, often train and employ guides. If you are interested in working as a tour guide for one of these types of groups, you should submit your application directly to the directors of personnel or managing directors.

ADVANCEMENT

Tour guides gain experience by handling more complicated trips. Some workers may advance through specialization, such as tours to specific countries or to multiple destinations. Some tour guides choose to open their own travel agencies or work for wholesale tour companies, selling trip packages to individuals or retail tour companies.

Some tour guides become *travel writers* and report on exotic destinations for magazines and newspapers. Other guides may decide to work in the corporate world and plan travel arrangements for company executives. With the further development of the global economy, many different jobs have become available for people who know foreign languages and cultures.

EARNINGS

Tour guides may find that they have peak and slack periods of the year that correspond to vacation and travel seasons. Many tour guides, however, work eight months of the year. Salaries for tour guides ranged from less than $13,680 to $34,630 or more in 2006, according to the U.S. Department of Labor. The median salary for tour guides was $20,420. According to the National Tour Association's 2000 *Wage and Benefits Survey,* approximately 20 percent of NTA tour operator president/owner/partners earned more than $100,000 annually.

Guides receive their meals and accommodations free while conducting a tour, in addition to a daily stipend to cover their personal expenses. Salaries and benefits vary, depending on the tour operators that employ guides and the location in which they are employed.

Tour guides often receive paid vacations as part of their fringe benefits package; some may also receive sick pay and health insurance. Some companies may offer profit sharing and bonuses. Guides often receive discounts from hotels, airlines, and transportation companies in appreciation for repeat business.

WORK ENVIRONMENT

The key word in the tour guide profession is variety. Most tour guides work in offices while they make travel arrangements and handle general business, but once on the road, they experience a wide range of accommodations, conditions, and situations. Tours to distant cities involve maneuvering through busy and confusing airports. Side trips may involve bus rides, train transfers, or private car rentals, all with varying degrees of comfort and reliability. Package trips that encompass seeing a number of foreign countries may require the guide to speak a different language in each city.

The constant feeling of being on the go and the responsibility of leading a large group of people can sometimes be stressful. Unexpected events and uncooperative people have the capacity to ruin part of a trip for everyone involved, including the guide. However, the thrill of travel, discovery, and meeting new people can be so rewarding that all the negatives can be forgotten (or eliminated by preplanning on the next trip).

OUTLOOK

Because of the many different travel opportunities for business, recreation, and education, there will be a steady need for tour guides through 2016, with employment in the field expected to grow faster than the average for all occupations, according to the U.S. Department of Labor. Tours designed for special interests, such as to ecologically significant areas and wilderness destinations, continue to grow in popularity. Although certain seasons are more popular for travel than others, well-trained tour guides can keep busy all year long.

Another area of tourism that is on the upswing is inbound tourism. Many foreign travelers view the United States as a dream destination, with tourist spots such as New York, Disney World, and our national park system drawing millions of foreign visitors each year. Job opportunities in inbound tourism will likely be more plentiful than those guiding Americans in foreign locations. The best opportunities in inbound tourism are in large cities with international airports and in areas with a large amount of tourist traffic. Opportunities will also be better for those guides who speak foreign languages.

Aspiring tour guides should keep in mind that this field is highly competitive. Tour guide jobs, because of the obvious benefits, are highly sought after, and the beginning job seeker may find it difficult to break into the business. It is important to remember that the travel and tourism industry is affected by the overall economy. When the economy is depressed, people have less money to spend and, therefore, they travel less. Recent terrorist attacks have also adversely affected the travel and tourism industry. If the public perceives that travel is risky, they will travel less and, as a result, tour guides may see reduced employment opportunities.

FOR MORE INFORMATION

For information on the travel industry and the related career of travel agent, contact

American Society of Travel Agents
1101 King Street, Suite 200
Alexandria, VA 22314-2944
Tel: 703-739-2782
Email: askasta@astahq.com
http://www.astanet.com

For information on internships, scholarships, the certified tour professional designation, and a list of colleges and universities that offer tourism-related programs, contact

National Tour Association
546 East Main Street
Lexington, KY 40508-2342
Tel: 800-682-8886
Email: questions@ntastaff.com
http://www.ntaonline.com

For information on the travel industry, contact

Travel Industry Association
1100 New York Avenue, NW, Suite 450
Washington, DC 20005-3934
Tel: 202-408-8422
Email: feedback@tia.org
http://www.tia.org

TRUCK DRIVERS

OVERVIEW

Truck drivers generally are distinguished by the distance they travel. *Over-the-road drivers*, also known as *long-distance drivers* or *tractor-trailer drivers*, haul freight over long distances in large trucks and tractor-trailer rigs that are usually diesel-powered. Depending on the specific operation, over-the-road drivers also load and unload the shipments and make minor repairs to vehicles. *Short-haul drivers* or *pickup and delivery drivers* operate trucks that transport materials, merchandise, and equipment within a limited area, usually a single city or metropolitan area. There are approximately 3.4 million truck drivers employed in the United States.

THE JOB

Truckers drive trucks of all sizes, from small straight trucks and vans to tanker trucks and tractors with multiple trailers. The average tractor-trailer rig is no more than 102 inches wide, excluding the mirrors, 13 feet and six inches tall, and just under 70 feet in length. The engines in these vehicles range from 250 to 600 horsepower.

Over-the-road drivers operate tractor-trailers and other large trucks that are often diesel-powered. These drivers generally haul goods and materials over long distances and frequently drive at night. Whereas many other truck drivers spend a considerable portion of their time loading and unloading materials, over-the-road drivers spend most of their working time driving.

SCHOOL SUBJECTS
Business, Technical/Shop

PERSONAL SKILLS
Following Instructions, Mechanical/Manipulative

MINIMUM EDUCATION LEVEL
Apprenticeship

CERTIFICATION OR LICENSING
Required

WORK ENVIRONMENT
Primarily Outdoors, Primarily Multiple Locations

At the terminal or warehouse where they receive their load, drivers get ready for long-distance runs by checking over the vehicle to make sure all the equipment and systems are functioning and that the truck is loaded properly and has the necessary fuel, oil, and safety equipment.

Some over-the-road drivers travel the same routes repeatedly and on a regular schedule. Other companies require drivers to do unscheduled runs and work when dispatchers call with an available job. Some long-distance runs are short enough that drivers can get to the destination, remove the load from the trailer, replace it with another load, and return home all in one day. Many runs, however, take up to a week or longer, with various stops. Some companies assign two drivers to long runs, so that one can sleep while the other drives. This method ensures that the trip will take the shortest amount of time possible.

In addition to driving their trucks long distances, over-the-road drivers have other duties. They must inspect their vehicles before and after trips, prepare reports on accidents, and keep daily logs. They may load and unload some shipments or hire workers to help with these tasks at the destination. Drivers of long-distance moving vans, for example, do more loading and unloading work than most other long-haul drivers. Drivers of vehicle-transport trailer trucks move new automobiles or trucks from manufacturers to dealers and also have additional duties. At plants where the vehicles are made, transport drivers drive new vehicles onto the ramps of transport trailers. They secure the vehicles in place with chains and clamps to prevent them from swaying and rolling. After driving to the destination, the drivers remove the vehicles from the trailers.

Over-the-road drivers must develop a number of skills that differ from the skills needed for operating smaller trucks. Because trailer trucks vary in length and number of wheels, skilled operators of one type of trailer may need to undergo a short training period if they switch to a new type of trailer. Over-the-road drivers must be able to maneuver and judge the position of their trucks and must be able to back their huge trailers into precise positions.

Local truck drivers generally operate the smaller trucks and transport a variety of products. They may travel regular routes or routes that change as needed. Local drivers include delivery workers who supply fresh produce to grocery stores and drivers who deliver gasoline in tank trucks to gas stations. Other local truck drivers, such as those who keep stores stocked with baked goods, may sell their employers' products as well as deliver them to customers along a route. These drivers are known as *route drivers* or *route-sales drivers*.

Often local truck drivers receive their assignments and delivery forms from dispatchers at the company terminal each day. Some drivers load goods or materials on their trucks, but in many situations dockworkers have already loaded the trucks in such a way that the unloading can be accomplished along the route with maximum convenience and efficiency.

Local drivers must be skilled at maneuvering their vehicles through the worst driving conditions, including bad weather and traffic-congested areas. The ability to pull into tight parking spaces, negotiate narrow passageways, and back up to loading docks is essential.

Some drivers have *helpers* who travel with them and assist in unloading at delivery sites, especially if the loads are heavy or bulky or when there are many deliveries scheduled. Drivers of some heavy trucks, such as dump trucks and oil tank trucks, operate mechanical levers, pedals, and other devices that assist with loading and unloading cargo. Drivers of moving vans generally have a crew of helpers to aid in loading and unloading customers' household goods and office equipment.

Once a local driver reaches his or her destination, he or she sometimes obtains a signature acknowledging that the delivery has been made and may collect a payment from the customer. Some drivers serve as intermediaries between the company and its customers by responding to customer complaints and requests.

Each day, local drivers have to make sure that their deliveries have been made correctly. At the end of the day, they turn in their records and the money they collected. Local drivers may also be responsible for doing routine maintenance on their trucks to keep them in good working condition. Otherwise, any mechanical problems are reported to the maintenance department for repair.

REQUIREMENTS
High School

High school students interested in working as truck drivers should take courses in driver training and automobile mechanics. In addition, some bookkeeping, mathematics, and business courses will teach methods that help in keeping accurate records of customer transactions.

Postsecondary Training

Drivers must know and meet the standards set by both state and federal governments for the particular work they do and the type of vehicle they drive. In some companies, new employees can informally learn the skills appropriate for the kind of driving they do from experienced drivers. They may ride with and watch other employees of the company, or they may take a few hours of their own time to learn from an experienced driver. For jobs driving some kinds of trucks, companies require new employees to attend classes that range from a few days to several weeks.

One of the best ways to prepare for a job driving large trucks is to take a tractor-trailer driver training course. Programs vary in the amount of actual driving experience they provide. Programs that are certified by the Professional Truck Driver Institute meet established guidelines for training and generally provide good preparation for drivers. Another way to determine whether programs are adequate is to check with local companies that hire drivers and ask for their recommendations. Completing a certified training program helps potential truck drivers learn specific skills, but it does not guarantee a job. Vehicles and the freight inside trucks can represent a large investment to companies that employ truck drivers. Therefore, they seek to hire responsible and reliable drivers in order to protect their investment. For this reason, many employers set various requirements of their own that exceed state and federal standards.

Certification or Licensing

Truck drivers must meet federal requirements and any requirements established by the state where they are based. All drivers must obtain a state commercial driver's license. Truck drivers involved in interstate commerce must meet requirements of the U.S. Department of Transportation. They must be at least 21 years old and pass a physical examination that requires good vision and hearing, normal blood pressure, and normal use of arms and legs (unless the applicant qualifies for a waiver). Drivers must then pass physicals every two years and meet other requirements, including a minimum of 20/40 vision in each eye and no diagnosis of insulin-dependent diabetes or epilepsy.

Other Requirements

Many drivers work with little supervision, so they need to have a mature, responsible attitude toward their job. In jobs where drivers deal directly with company customers, it is especially important for the drivers to be pleasant, courteous, and able to communicate well with people. Helping a customer with a complaint can mean the difference between losing and keeping a client.

EXPLORING

High school students interested in becoming truck drivers may be able to gain experience by working as drivers' helpers during summer vacations or in part-time delivery jobs. Many people get useful experience in driving vehicles while serving in the armed forces. It may also be helpful to talk with employers of local or over-the-road truck drivers or with the drivers themselves.

The Internet provides a forum for prospective truck drivers to explore their career options. Two online magazines—*Overdrive* (http://www.etrucker.com) and *Land Line Magazine* (http://www.landlinemag.com)—provide a look at issues in the trucking industry and a list of answers to frequently asked questions for people interested in trucking careers.

EMPLOYERS

Approximately 3.4 million truck drivers are employed in the United States. About a third of all drivers work for for-hire carriers, and another third work for private carriers. Approximately 9 percent are self-employed.

Over-the-road and local drivers may be employed by either private carriers or for-hire carriers. Food store chains and manufacturing plants that transport their own goods are examples of private carriers. There are two kinds of for-hire carriers: trucking companies serving the general public (common carriers) and trucking firms transporting goods under contract to certain companies (contract carriers).

Drivers who work independently are known as *owner-operators*. They own their own vehicles and often do their own maintenance and repair work. They must find customers who need goods transported, perhaps through personal references or by advertising their services. For example, many drivers find contract jobs through "Internet truck stops," where drivers can advertise their services and companies can post locations of loads they need transported. Some independent drivers establish long-term contracts with just one or two clients, such as trucking companies.

STARTING OUT

Prospective over-the-road drivers can gain commercial driving experience as local truck drivers and then attend a tractor trailer–driver training program. Driving an intercity bus or dump truck is also suitable experience for aspiring over-the-road truck drivers. Many newly hired long-distance drivers start by filling in for regular drivers or helping out when extra trips are necessary. They are assigned regular work when a job opens up.

Many truck drivers hold other jobs before they become truck drivers. Some local drivers start as *drivers' helpers*, loading and unloading trucks and gradually taking over some driving duties. When a better driving position opens up, helpers who have shown they are reliable and responsible may be promoted. Members of the armed forces who have gained appropriate experience may get driving jobs when they are discharged.

Job seekers may apply directly to firms that use drivers. Listings of specific job openings are often posted at local offices of the state employment service and in the classified ads in newspapers. Many jobs, however, are not posted. Looking in the yellow pages under trucking and moving and storage can provide names of specific companies to solicit. Also, large manufacturers and retailing companies sometimes have their own fleets. Many telephone calls and letters may be required, but they can lead to a potential employer. Personal visits, when appropriate, sometimes get the best results.

ADVANCEMENT

Some over-the-road drivers who stay with their employers advance by becoming safety supervisors, driver supervisors, or dispatchers. Many over-the-road drivers look forward to going into business for themselves by acquiring their own tractor-trailer rigs. This step requires a significant initial investment and a continuing good income to cover expenses. Like many other small business owners, independent drivers sometimes have a hard time financially. Those who are their own mechanics and have formal business training are in the best position to do well.

Local truck drivers can advance by learning to drive specialized kinds of trucks or by acquiring better schedules or other job conditions. Some may move into positions as dispatchers and, with sufficient experience, they eventually become supervisors or terminal managers. Other local drivers decide to become over-the-road drivers to receive higher wages.

EARNINGS

Wages of truck drivers vary according to their employer, size of the truck they drive, product being hauled, geographical region, and other factors. Drivers who are employed by for-hire carriers have higher earnings than those who work independently or for private carriers.

Pay rates for over-the-road truck drivers are often figured using a cents-per-mile rate. Most companies pay between 20 and 30 cents per mile, but large companies are advertising higher rates to attract good drivers. Drivers employed by J.B. Hunt Transport Services, the nation's largest publicly held trucking company, can earn up to 42 cents a mile and earn up to $1,000 a week.

Tractor-trailer drivers usually have the highest earnings; average hourly pay generally increases with the size of the truck. Drivers in the South have lower earnings than those in the Northeast and West. The U.S. Department of Labor reports that median hourly earnings of heavy truck and tractor-trailer drivers were $16.48 in 2006. Wages ranged from less than $10.80 to more than $25.39 an hour (from $22,460 to $52,820 a year for full-time work). Median hourly earnings of light or delivery services truck drivers were $11.92, and wages ranged from less than $7.47 to more than $1.23 an hour ($15,540 to $44,160 a year). Median hourly earnings of driver/sales workers, including commission, were $9.99, and wages ranged from less than $6.19 to more than $20.30 an hour ($12,880 to $42,230 a year).

In addition to their wages, the majority of truck drivers receive benefits, many of which are determined by agreements between their unions and company management. The benefits may include health insurance coverage, pension plans, paid vacation days, and work uniforms.

WORK ENVIRONMENT

Although there is work for truck drivers in even the smallest towns, most jobs are located in and around larger metropolitan areas.

Even with modern improvements in cab design, driving trucks is often a tiring job. Many local drivers work 50 or more hours per week. Some drivers, such as those who bring food to grocery stores, often work at night or very early in the morning. Drivers who must load and unload their trucks may do a lot of lifting, stooping, and bending.

It is common for over-the-road truck drivers to work at least 50 hours a week. However, federal regulations require that drivers cannot be on duty for more than 60 hours in any seven-day period. Furthermore, after drivers have driven for 10 hours, they must be off duty for at least eight hours before they can drive again. Drivers often work the maximum allowed time to complete long runs in as little time as possible. In fact, most drivers drive 10 to 12 hours per day and make sure they have proper rest periods. A driver usually covers between 550 and 650 miles daily. The sustained driving, particularly at night, can be fatiguing, boring, and sometimes very stressful, as when traffic or weather conditions are bad.

Local drivers may operate on schedules that easily allow a social and family life, but long-distance drivers often find that difficult. They may spend a considerable amount of time away from their homes and families, including weekends and holidays. After they try it, many people find they do not want this way of life. On the other hand, some people love the lifestyle of the over-the-road driver. Many families are able to find ways to work around the schedule of a truck-driving spouse. In some cases, the two people assigned to a long-distance run are a husband and wife team.

OUTLOOK

The employment of truck drivers is expected to increase about as fast as the average for all occupations through 2016, according to the U.S. Department of Labor, because of continually increasing amounts of consumer goods that need to be transported quickly and safely. Employment of driver/sales workers will grow more slowly than the average as companies move more sales positions into central offices.

The need for trucking services is directly linked to the growth of the nation's economy. During economic downturns, when the pace of business slows, some drivers may receive fewer assignments and thus have lower earnings, or they may be laid off. Drivers employed in some vital industries, such as food distribution, are less affected by an economic recession. On the other hand, people who own and operate their own trucks usually suffer the most (especially when fuel costs are high).

A large number of driver jobs become available each year. Most openings develop when experienced drivers transfer to other fields or leave the workforce entirely. There is a considerable amount of turnover in the field. In fact, the U.S. Department of Labor predicts that 258,000 new jobs will become available through 2016. Beginners are able to get many of these jobs. Competition is expected to remain strong for the more desirable jobs, such as those with large companies or the easiest routes.

FOR MORE INFORMATION

For further information and literature about a career as a truck driver, contact the following organizations:

American Trucking Associations
950 North Glebe Road, Suite 210
Arlington, VA 22203-4181
Tel: 703-838-1700
http://www.trucking.org

Professional Truck Driver Institute
555 East Braddock Road
Alexandria, VA 22314-2182
Tel: 703-647-7015
http://www.ptdi.org

For career information, visit the following Web site:
GetTrucking.com
http://www.gettrucking.com

VETERINARIANS

OVERVIEW

The *veterinarian*, or *doctor of veterinary medicine*, diagnoses and controls animal diseases, treats sick and injured animals medically and surgically, prevents transmission of animal diseases, and advises owners on proper care of pets and livestock. Veterinarians are dedicated to the protection of the health and welfare of all animals and to society as a whole. There are about 62,000 veterinarians in the United States.

THE JOB

Veterinarians ensure a safe food supply by maintaining the health of food animals. They also protect the public from residues of herbicides, pesticides, and antibiotics in food. Veterinarians may be involved in wildlife preservation and conservation and use their knowledge to increase food production through genetics, animal feed production, and preventive medicine.

In North America, about 70 percent of veterinarians are employees of established veterinary practices. Although some veterinarians treat all kinds of animals, more than half limit their practice to companion animals such as dogs, cats, and birds. A smaller number of veterinarians work mainly with horses, cattle, pigs, sheep, goats, and poultry. Today, a veterinarian may treat llamas, catfish, or ostriches as well. Others are employed by wildlife management groups, zoos, aquariums, ranches, feed lots, fish farms, and animal shelters.

Veterinarians in private practice diagnose and treat animal health problems. During yearly checkups, the veterinarian records the animal's temperature and weight; inspects its mouth, eyes, and ears; inspects the skin or coat for any signs of abnormalities; observes any peculiarities in the animal's behavior; and discusses the animals eating, sleeping, and exercise habits at length with the owner. The veterinarian will also check the animal's vaccination records and administer inoculations for rabies, distemper, and other diseases if necessary. If the veterinarian or owner notes any special concerns, or if the animal is taken to the veterinarian for a specific procedure, such as spaying or neutering, dental cleaning, or setting broken bones, the animal may stay at the veterinarian's office for one or several days for surgery, observation, or extended treatments. If a sick or wounded animal is beyond medical help, the veterinarian may, with the consent of the owner, have to euthanize the animal.

During office visits and surgery, veterinarians use traditional medical instruments, such as stethoscopes, thermometers, and surgical instruments, and standard tests, such as X rays and diagnostic medical sonography, to evaluate the animal's health. Veterinarians may also prescribe drugs for the animal, which the owner purchases at the veterinarian's office.

Some veterinarians work in public and corporate sectors. Many are employed by city, county, state, provincial, or federal government agencies that investigate, test for, and control diseases in companion animals, livestock, and poultry that affect both animal and human health. Veterinarians also play an important public health role. For example, veterinarians played an important part in conquering diseases such as malaria and yellow fever.

Pharmaceutical and biomedical research firms hire veterinarians to develop, test, and supervise the production of drugs, chemicals, and biological products such as antibiotics and vaccines that are designed for human and animal use. Some veterinarians are employed in management, technical sales and services, and marketing in agribusiness, pet food companies, and pharmaceutical companies. Still other veterinarians are engaged in research and teaching at veterinary medical schools, working with racetracks or animal-related enterprises, or working within the military, public health corps, and space agencies.

The U.S. Department of Agriculture has opportunities for veterinarians in the food safety inspection service and the animal and plant health inspection service, notably in the areas of food hygiene and safety, animal welfare, animal disease control, and research. Agencies in the U.S. Department of Agriculture utilize veterinarians in positions related to research on diseases transmissible from animals to human beings and on the acceptance and use of drugs for treatment or prevention of diseases. Veterinarians also are employed by the Environmental Protection Agency to deal with public health and environmental risks to the human population.

Veterinarians are often assisted by veterinary technicians, who may conduct basic tests, record an animal's medical history for the veterinarian's review, and assist the veterinarian in surgical procedures .

REQUIREMENTS
High School

For the high school student who is interested in admission to a school of veterinary medicine, a college preparatory course is a wise choice. A strong emphasis on science classes such as biology, chemistry, and anatomy is highly recommended.

Postsecondary Training

The doctor of veterinary medicine (D.V.M.) degree requires a minimum of four years of study at an accredited college of veterinary medicine. Although many of these colleges do not require a bachelor's degree for admission, most require applicants to have completed 45–90 hours of undergraduate study. It is possible to obtain preveterinary training at a junior college, but since admission to colleges of veterinary medicine is an extremely competitive process, most students receive degrees from four-year colleges before applying. In addition to academic instruction, veterinary education includes clinical experience in diagnosing disease and treating animals, performing surgery, and performing laboratory work in anatomy, biochemistry, and other scientific and medical subjects.

There are 28 colleges of veterinary medicine in the United States that are accredited by the Council of Veterinary Medicine of the American Veterinary Medical Association. Each college of veterinary medicine has its own preveterinary requirements, which typically include basic language arts, social sciences, humanities, mathematics, chemistry, and biological and physical sciences. Veterinarians in private clinical practice become specialists in surgery, anesthesiology, dentistry, internal medicine, ophthalmology, or radiology. Many veterinarians also pursue advanced degrees in the basic sciences, such as anatomy, microbiology, and physiology.

Applicants to schools of veterinary medicine usually must have grades of "B" or better, especially in the sciences. Applicants must take the Veterinary Aptitude Test, Veterinary College Admission Test, Medical College Admission Test, or the Graduate Record Examination. Only about one-third of applicants to schools of veterinary medicine are admitted, due to small class sizes and limited facilities. Most colleges give preference to candidates with animal- or veterinary-related experience. Colleges usually give preference to in-state applicants because most colleges of veterinary medicine are state-supported. There are regional agreements in which states without veterinary schools send students to designated regional schools.

Certification or Licensing

Veterinarians who seek specialty board certification in one of 20 specialty fields must complete a two- to five-year residency program and pass an additional exami-

---

SCHOOL SUBJECTS
Biology, Chemistry

PERSONAL SKILLS
Helping/Teaching, Technical/Scientific

MINIMUM EDUCATION LEVEL
Medical Degree

CERTIFICATION OR LICENSING
Required

WORK ENVIRONMENT
Primarily Indoors, Primarily One Location

---

nation. Some veterinarians combine their degree in veterinary medicine with a degree in business or law.

All states and the District of Columbia require that veterinarians be licensed to practice private clinical medicine. To obtain a license, applicants must have a D.V.M. degree from an accredited or approved college of veterinary medicine. They must also pass one or more national examinations and an examination in the state in which they plan to practice.

Few states issue licenses to veterinarians already licensed by another state. Thus, if a veterinarian moves from one state to another, he or she will probably have to go through the licensing process again. Approximately half of the states require veterinarians to attend continuing education courses in order to maintain their licenses. Veterinarians may be employed by a government agency (such as the U.S. Department of Agriculture) or at some academic institution without having a state license.

Other Requirements

Individuals who are interested in veterinary medicine should have an inquiring mind and keen powers of observation. Aptitude and interest in the biological sciences are important. Veterinarians need a lifelong interest in scientific learning as well as a liking and understanding of animals. Veterinarians should be able to meet, talk, and work well with a variety of people. An ability to communicate with the animal owner is as important in a veterinarian as diagnostic skills.

Veterinarians use state-of-the-art medical equipment, such as electron microscopes, laser surgery, radiation therapy, and ultrasound, to diagnose animal diseases and to treat sick or injured animals. Although manual dexterity and physical stamina are often required, especially for farm vets, important roles in veterinary medicine can be adapted for those with disabilities.

Interaction with animal owners is a very important part of being a veterinarian. The discussions between vet and owner are critical to the veterinarian's diagnosis, so he or she must be able to communicate effectively and get along with a wide variety of personalities. Veterinarians may have to euthanize (that is, humanely kill) an animal that is very sick or severely injured and cannot get well. When a beloved pet dies, the veterinarian must deal with the owner's grief and loss.

EXPLORING

High school students interested in becoming veterinarians may find part-time or volunteer work on farms, in small-animal clinics, or in pet shops, animal shelters, or research laboratories. Participation in extracurricular activities such as 4-H are good ways to learn about the care of animals. Such experience is important because, as already noted, many schools of veterinary medicine have established experience with animals as a criterion for admission to their programs.

EMPLOYERS

Approximately 62,000 veterinarians are employed in the United States. Veterinarians may be employed by schools and universities, wildlife management groups, zoos, aquariums, ranches, feed lots, fish farms, pet food or pharmaceutical companies, and the government (mainly in the U.S. Departments of Agriculture, Health and Human Services, and Homeland Security). The vast majority, however, are employed by veterinary clinical practices or hospitals. Many successful veterinarians in private practice are self-employed and may even employ other veterinarians. An increase in the demand for veterinarians is anticipated, particularly for those who specialize in areas related to public health issues such as food safety and disease control. Cities and large metropolitan areas will probably provide the bulk of new jobs for these specialists, while jobs for veterinarians who specialize in large animals will be focused in remote, rural areas.

STARTING OUT

The only way to become a veterinarian is through the prescribed degree program, and vet schools are set up to assist their graduates in finding employment. Veterinarians who wish to enter private clinical practice must have a license to practice in their particular state before opening an office. Licenses are obtained by passing the state's examination.

ADVANCEMENT

New graduate veterinarians may enter private clinical practice, usually as employees in an established practice, or become employees of the U.S. government as meat and poultry inspectors, disease control workers, and commissioned officers in the U.S. Public Health Service or the military. New graduates may also enter internships and residencies at veterinary colleges and large private and public veterinary practices or become employed by industrial firms.

The veterinarian who is employed by a government agency may advance in grade and salary after accumulating time and experience on the job. For the veterinarian in private clinical practice, advancement usually consists of an expanding practice and the higher income that will result from it or becoming an owner of several practices.

Those who teach or do research may obtain a doctorate and move from the rank of instructor to that of full professor, or they may advance to an administrative position.

EARNINGS

The U.S. Department of Labor reports that median annual earnings of veterinarians were $71,990 in 2006. Salaries ranged from less than $43,530 to more than $133,150. The mean annual salary for veterinarians working for the federal government was $72,120 in 2006.

According to a survey by the American Veterinary Medical Association, the average starting salary for veterinary medical college graduates who worked exclusively with small animals was $61,322 in 2007. Those who worked exclusively with large animals earned an average of $56,659. Equine veterinarians earned an average of $39,864 to start.

Benefits include paid vacation, health, disability, life insurance, and retirement or pension plans. Self-employed veterinarians must provide their own benefits.

WORK ENVIRONMENT

Veterinarians usually treat companion and food animals in hospitals and clinics. Those in large animal practice also work out of well-equipped trucks or cars and may drive considerable distances to farms and ranches. They may work outdoors in all kinds of weather. The chief risk for veterinarians is injury by animals; however, modern tranquilizers and technology have made it much easier to work on all types of animals.

Most veterinarians work long hours, often 50 or more hours a week. Although those in private clinical practice may work nights and weekends, the increased number of emergency clinics has reduced the amount of time private practitioners have to be on call. Large animal practitioners tend to work more irregular hours than those in small animal practice, industry, or government. Veterinarians who are just starting a practice tend to work longer hours.

OUTLOOK

Employment of veterinarians is expected to grow much faster than the average for all careers through 2016. The number of pets (especially cats) is expected to increase because of rising incomes and an increase in the number of people aged 34 to 59, among whom pet ownership has historically been the highest. Many single adults and senior citizens have come to appreciate animal ownership. Pet owners also may be willing to pay for more elective and intensive care than in the past. In addition, emphasis on scientific methods of breeding and raising livestock, poultry, and fish and continued support for public health and disease control programs will contribute to the demand for veterinarians. The number of jobs stemming from the need to replace workers will be equal to new job growth.

The outlook is good for veterinarians with specialty training. Demand for specialists in toxicology, laboratory animal medicine, and pathology is expected to increase. Most jobs for specialists will be in metropolitan areas. Prospects for veterinarians who concentrate on environmental and public health issues, aquaculture, and food animal practice appear to be excellent because of perceived increased need in these areas. Positions in small animal specialties will be competitive. Opportunities in farm animal specialties will be better, since most such positions are located in remote, rural areas.

Despite the availability of additional jobs, competition among veterinarians is likely to be stiff. First-year enrollments in veterinary schools have increased slightly, and the number of students in graduate-degree and board-certification programs has risen dramatically.

FOR MORE INFORMATION

For career information, contact
Academy of Rural Veterinarians
PO Box 430
Burwell, NE 68823-0430
http://www.ruralvets.com

For more information on careers, schools, and resources, contact
American Veterinary Medical Association
1931 North Meacham Road, Suite 100
Schaumburg, IL 60173-4360

Tel: 847-925-8070
Email: avmainfo@avma.org
http://www.avma.org

For information on veterinary opportunities in the federal government, contact
Animal and Plant Health Inspection Service
1400 Independence Avenue, SW
Washington, DC 20250-0002
Email: APHIS.Web@aphis.usda.gov
http://www.aphis.usda.gov

For information educational programs, contact
Association of American Veterinary Medical Colleges
1101 Vermont Avenue, NW, Suite 301
Washington, DC 20005-3539
Tel: 202-371-9195
http://www.aavmc.org

For information on veterinary careers in Canada, contact
Canadian Veterinary Medical Association
339 Booth Street
Ottawa, ON K1R 7K1 Canada
Tel: 613-236-1162
Email: admin@cvma-acmv.org
http://www.canadianveterinarians.net

VETERINARY TECHNICIANS

OVERVIEW

Veterinary technicians provide support and assistance to veterinarians (See "Veterinarians"). They work in a variety of environments, including zoos, animal hospitals, clinics, private practices, kennels, and laboratories. Their work may involve large or small animals or both. Although most veterinary technicians work with domestic animals, some professional settings may require treating exotic or endangered species. There are approximately 71,000 veterinary technicians employed in the United States.

THE JOB

Many pet owners depend on veterinarians to maintain the health and well-being of their pets. Veterinary clinics and private practices are the primary settings for animal care. In assisting veterinarians, veterinary technicians

SCHOOL SUBJECTS
Biology, Chemistry

PERSONAL SKILLS
Helping/Teaching, Technical/Scientific

MINIMUM EDUCATION LEVEL
Associate's Degree

CERTIFICATION OR LICENSING
Required by Certain States

WORK ENVIRONMENT
Primarily Indoors, Primarily One Location

play an integral role in the care of animals within this particular environment.

A veterinary technician is the person who performs much of the laboratory testing procedures commonly associated with veterinary care. In fact, approximately 50 percent of a veterinary technician's duties involve laboratory testing. Laboratory assignments usually include taking and developing X rays, performing parasitology tests, and examining various samples taken from the animal's body, such as blood and stool. A veterinary technician may also assist the veterinarian with necropsies in an effort to determine the cause of an animal's death.

In a clinic or private practice, a veterinary technician assists the veterinarian with surgical procedures. This generally entails preparing the animal for surgery by shaving the incision area and applying a topical antibacterial agent. Surgical anesthesia is administered and controlled by the veterinary technician. Throughout the surgical process, the technician tracks the surgical instruments and monitors the animal's vital signs. If an animal is very ill and has no chance for survival, or an overcrowded animal shelter is unable to find a home for a donated or stray animal, the veterinary technician may be required to assist in euthanizing it.

During routine examinations and checkups, veterinary technicians will help restrain the animals. They may perform ear cleaning and nail clipping procedures as part of regular animal care. Outside the examination and surgery rooms, veterinary technicians perform additional duties. In most settings, they record, replenish, and maintain pharmaceutical equipment and other supplies.

Veterinary technicians also may work in a zoo. Here, job duties, such as laboratory testing, are quite similar, but practices are more specialized. Unlike in private practice, the *zoo veterinary technician* is not required to explain treatment to pet owners; however, he or she may have to discuss an animal's treatment or progress with zoo veterinarians, zoo curators, and other zoo professionals. A zoo veterinary technician's work also may differ from private practice in that it may be necessary for the technician to observe the animal in its habitat, which could require working outdoors. Additionally, zoo veterinary technicians usually work with exotic or endangered species. This is a very competitive and highly desired area of practice in the veterinary technician field. There are only a few zoos in each state; thus, a limited number of job opportunities exist within these zoos. To break into this area of practice, veterinary technicians must be among the best in the field.

Veterinary technicians also work in research. Most research opportunities for veterinary technicians are in academic environments with veterinary medicine or medical science programs. Again, laboratory testing may account for many of the duties; however, the veterinary technicians participate in very important animal research projects from start to finish.

Technicians are also needed in rural areas. Farmers require veterinary services for the care of farm animals such as pigs, cows, horses, dogs, cats, sheep, mules, and chickens. It is often essential for the veterinarian and technician to drive to the farmer's residence because animals are usually treated on-site.

Another area in which veterinary technicians work is that of animal training, such as at an obedience school or with show business animals being trained for the circus or movies. Veterinary technicians may also be employed in information systems technology, where information on animals is compiled and provided to the public via the Internet.

No matter what the setting, a veterinary technician must be an effective communicator and proficient in basic computer applications. In clinical or private practice, it is usually the veterinary technician who conveys and explains treatment and subsequent animal care to the animal's owner. In research and laboratory work, the veterinary technician must record and discuss results among colleagues. In most practical veterinary settings, the veterinary technician must record various information on a computer.

REQUIREMENTS
High School

Veterinary technicians must have a high school diploma. High school students who excel at math and science have a strong foundation on which to build. Those who have had pets or who simply love animals and would like to work with them also fit the profile of a veterinary technician.

Postsecondary Training

The main requirement is the completion of a two- to four-year college-based accredited program. Upon graduation, the student receives an associate's or bachelor's degree. Currently, there are 131 accredited programs in the United States. A few states do their own accrediting, using the American Veterinary Medical Association (AVMA) and associated programs as benchmarks.

Most accredited programs offer thorough course work and preparatory learning opportunities to the aspiring veterinary technician. Typical courses include mathematics, chemistry, humanities, biological science, communications, microbiology, liberal arts, ethics/jurisprudence, and basic computers.

Once the students complete this framework, they move on to more specialized courses. Students take advanced classes in animal nutrition, animal care and management, species/breed identification, veterinary anatomy/physiology, medical terminology, radiography and other clinical procedure courses, animal husbandry, parasitology, laboratory animal care, and large/small animal nursing.

Veterinary technicians must be prepared to assist in surgical procedures. In consideration of this, accredited programs offer surgical nursing courses. In these courses, a student learns to identify and use surgical instruments, administer anesthesia, and monitor animals during and after surgery.

In addition to classroom study, accredited programs offer practical courses. Hands-on education and training are commonly achieved through a clinical practicum, or internship, where the student has the opportunity to work in a clinical veterinary setting. During this period, a student is continuously evaluated by the participating veterinarian and encouraged to apply the knowledge and skills learned.

Certification or Licensing

Although the AVMA determines the majority of the national codes for veterinary technicians, state codes and laws vary. Most states offer registration or certification, and the majority of these states require graduation from an AVMA-accredited program as a prerequisite for taking the National Veterinary Technician Examination or a similar state or local examination. Most colleges and universities assist graduates with registra-

tion and certification arrangements. To keep abreast of new technology and applications in the field, practicing veterinary technicians may be required to complete a determined number of annual continuing education courses. The American Association for Laboratory Animal Science offers certification to veterinary technicians who are interested in working in research settings. The American Association of Equine Veterinary Technicians also offers certification to technicians who specialize in caring for horses.

Other Requirements

As a veterinarian technician, you should be able to meet, talk, and work well with a variety of people. An ability to communicate with the animal owner is as important as diagnostic skills.

In clinical or private practice, it is usually the veterinary technician who conveys and explains treatment and subsequent animal care to the animal's owner. Technicians may have to help euthanize (that is, humanely kill) an animal that is very sick or severely injured and cannot get well. As a result, they must be emotionally stable and help pet owners deal with their grief and loss.

EXPLORING

High school students can acquire exposure to the veterinary field by working with animals in related settings. For example, a high school student may be able to work as a part-time animal attendant or receptionist in a private veterinary practice. Paid or volunteer positions may be available at kennels, animal shelters, and training schools. However, direct work with animals in a zoo is unlikely for high school students.

EMPLOYERS

Approximately 71,000 veterinary technicians are employed in the United States. Veterinary technicians are employed by veterinary clinics, animal hospitals, zoos, schools, universities, and animal training programs. In rural areas, farmers hire veterinary technicians as well as veterinarians. Jobs for veterinary technicians in zoos are relatively few, since there are only a certain number of zoos across the country. Those veterinary technicians with an interest in research should seek positions at schools with academic programs for medical science or veterinary medicine. The majority of veterinary technicians find employment in animal hospitals or private veterinary practices, which exist all over the country. However, there are more job opportunities for veterinary technicians in more densely populated areas.

STARTING OUT

Veterinary technicians who complete an accredited program and become certified or registered by the state in which they plan to practice are often able to receive assistance in finding a job through their college's career services offices. Students who have completed internships may receive job offers from the place where they interned.

Veterinary technician graduates may also learn of clinic openings through classified ads in newspapers. Opportunities in zoos and research facilities are usually listed in specific industry periodicals.

ADVANCEMENT

Where a career as a veterinary technician leads is entirely up to the individual. Opportunities are unlimited. With continued education, veterinary technicians can move into allied fields such as veterinary medicine, nursing, medical technology, radiology, and pharmacology. By completing two more years of college and receiving a bachelor's degree, a veterinary technician can become a veterinary technologist. Advanced degrees can open the doors to a variety of specialized fields.

EARNINGS

Earnings are generally low for veterinary technicians in private practices and clinics, but pay scales are steadily climbing due to the increasing demand. Better-paying jobs are in zoos and in research. Those fields of practice are very competitive (especially zoos) and only a small percentage of highly qualified veterinary technicians are employed in them.

Most veterinary technicians are employed in private or clinical practice and research. The U.S. Department of Labor reports that the median annual salary for veterinary technicians and technologists was $26,780 in 2006. The lowest paid 10 percent made less than $18,280 annually, and the highest paid 10 percent made more than $38,850 annually. Earnings vary depending on practice setting, geographic location, level of education, and years of experience. Benefits vary and depend on each employer's policies.

WORK ENVIRONMENT

Veterinary technicians generally work 40-hour weeks, which may include a few long weekdays and alternated or rotated Saturdays. Hours may fluctuate, as veterinary technicians may need to have their schedules adjusted to accommodate emergency work.

A veterinary technician must be prepared for emergencies. In field or farm work, they often have to overcome weather conditions while treating the animal. Injured animals can be very dangerous, and veterinary technicians have to exercise extreme caution when caring for them. A veterinary technician also handles animals that are diseased or infested with parasites. Some of these conditions, such as ringworm, are contagious, so the veterinary technician must understand how these conditions are transferred to humans and take precautions to prevent the spread of diseases.

People who become veterinary technicians care about animals. For this reason, maintaining an animal's well-being or helping to cure an ill animal is very rewarding work. In private practice, technicians get to know the animals they care for. This provides the opportunity to actually see the animals' progress. In other areas, such as zoo work, veterinary technicians work with very interesting, sometimes endangered, species. This work can be challenging and rewarding in the sense that they are helping to save a species and continuing efforts to educate people about these animals. Veterinary technicians who work in research gain satisfaction from knowing their work contributes to promoting both animal and human health.

OUTLOOK

Employment for veterinary technicians will grow much faster than the average for all occupations through 2016, according to the U.S. Department of Labor. Veterinary medicine is a field that is not adversely affected by the economy, so it does offer stability. The public's love for pets coupled with higher disposable incomes will encourage continued demand for workers in this occupation. There should be strong opportunities for veterinary technicians in biomedical facilities, humane societies, animal control facilities, diagnostic laboratories, wildlife facilities, drug or food manufacturing companies, and food safety inspection facilities. Competitions for jobs in aquariums and zoos is expected to be very strong as a result of low turnover, the attractiveness of these positions, and slow growth in the construction of new facilities.

FOR MORE INFORMATION

For more information on careers, schools, and resources, contact the following organizations:

Academy of Veterinary Emergency and Critical Care Technicians
6335 Camp Bullis Road, Suite 12
San Antonio, TX 78257-9721
Tel: 210-826-1488
http://www.avecct.org

American Association for Laboratory Animal Science
9190 Crestwyn Hills Drive
Memphis, TN 38125-8538
Tel: 901-754-8620
http://www.aalas.org

American Association of Equine Veterinary Technicians
http://www.aaevt.com

American Veterinary Medical Association
1931 North Meacham Road, Suite 100
Schaumburg, IL 60173-4360
Tel: 847-925-8070
Email: avmainfo@avma.org
http://www.avma.org

Association of Zoo Veterinary Technicians
c/o Roger Williams Park Zoo
1000 Elmwood Avenue
Providence, RI 02907-3655
http://www.azvt.org

National Association of Veterinary Technicians in America
50 South Pickett Street, Suite 110
Alexandria, VA 22304-7206
Tel: 703-740-8737
Email: info@navta.net
http://www.navta.net

For information on veterinary careers in Canada, contact
Canadian Veterinary Medical Association
339 Booth Street
Ottawa, ON K1R 7K1 Canada
Tel: 613-236-1162
Email: admin@cvma-acmv.org
http://www.canadianveterinarians.net

INDEX